THE CAULDRON OF ARIANTAS

Black Sea Studies

1

Danish National Research Foundation's
Centre for Black Sea Studies

THE CAULDRON OF ARIANTAS

Studies presented to A.N. Ščeglov
on the occasion of his 70th birthday

Edited by
Pia Guldager Bilde, Jakob Munk Højte
and Vladimir F. Stolba

AARHUS UNIVERSITY PRESS

THE CAULDRON OF ARIANTAS

Studies presented to A.N. Ščeglov
on the occasion of his 70th birthday

Copyright: Aarhus University Press 2003

Cover design by Pia Guldager Bilde and Jakob Munk Højte
Scythian cauldron, bronze, 375-325 BC, h. 47 cm.
From Raskopana Mogila, the Lower Dnieper region,
D.I. Evarnickij's excavation, 1897.
The State Hermitage Museum, inv. no. Dn 1897 1/14.
(By courtesy of the State Hermitage Museum)

Layout by Jakob Munk Højte

Printed in Denmark by Narayana Press

ISBN 87 7934 085 7

The publication of this volume has been made possible by generous grants from
The Danish National Research Foundation, The New Carlsberg Foundation, and
The Aarhus University Research Foundation.

Danish National Research Foundation's
Centre for Black Sea Studies
Building 328
University of Aarhus
DK-8000 Århus C
www.pontos.dk

Contents

Preface

This publication celebrates the 70th birthday of Alexander Nikolaevič Ščeglov, senior researcher at the Institute for the History of Material Culture of the Russian Academy of Sciences, St Petersburg.

A.N. Ščeglov is truly one of the pioneers in the investigation of the archaeology and history of ancient Crimea, as well as a widely recognized authority in the studies of northern Black Sea antiquities. Before the methods of remote sensing surveys and aerial photography became widely used in landscape archaeology, he carried out large-scale investigations in the territory of Western Tauris employing these methods. These achievements facilitated a detailed study and mapping of the undisturbed areas of the ancient landscape. This has shed light on the character of an ancient Greek city-state on the northern littoral of the Black Sea, the interrelations between the ancient city and its rural territory, and also the system of the land use, including details such as the identification of the crops cultivated on a particular land plot by the ancient Greek settlers.

A pupil of Pavel Nikolaevič Schulz, A.N. Ščeglov began his archaeological career at an early age. In spite of a wide range of scientific interests stretching from the Taman' Peninsula to the Carpathian foothills, Western Crimea and especially the Tarchankut Peninsula always remained the particular object of his love and attention. His dissertation *Severo-Zapadnyj Krym v antičnuju epochu* (*The North-Western Crimea in Antiquity*) defended in 1971 and published seven years later as well as the monograph *Polis i Chora* (*Polis and Chora* 1976; French edition in 1992) are handbooks for everyone involved in the history of this region.

The Tarchankut expedition established by Ščeglov in 1959 explored a number of sites of the remote chora of Tauric Chersonesos. Panskoe I ranks among the most prominent of them. To this site, which became the field school of numerous Classical archaeologists of several generations, Alexander Nikolaevič devoted more than 30 years of his life.

Collaboration between the Institute for the History of Material Culture of the Russian Academy of Sciences, St Petersburg and the Institute of Classical Archaeology at the University of Aarhus initiated by Lise Hannestad goes back to 1992. From 2002 this was further extended to the Danish National Research Foundation's Centre for Black Sea Studies. This collaboration includes a joint project of the publication of the results of the excavations of Panskoe I, a unique and exceptionally well-preserved Greek settlement. The first volume of the publication series appeared in November 2002 (L. Hannestad, V.F. Stolba & A.N. Ščeglov (eds.), *Panskoye* I. Vol. 1. *The Monumental Building U6*. Aarhus 2002).

Being one of the oldest professors of the St Petersburg State University Alexander Nikolaevič has trained a veritable Pleiad of pupils. All of them went through his seminars on "Greek and Barbarian Interrelations", which he conducted for several decades. They often brought together students of different years and they were always a source of inspiration. More than once Alexander Nikolaevič came to Denmark as a visiting professor, and gave lectures at the University of Aarhus.

One of the articles by A.N. Ščeglov addresses the well-known legend in Herodotos concerning the bronze cauldron of the Scythian King Ariantas (Herodotos 4.81; see A.N. Ščeglov & K. K. Marčenko, K Gerodotu, IV, 81 [To Herodotus, IV, 81], *ArcheologijaKiev* 3, 1989, 117-121). According to the story, the colossal vessel was cast from a vast number of arrowheads, one brought by every Scythian, by the order of the king, who wanted to know how numerous the Scythians were. The "Cauldron of Ariantas" we present here to Alexander Nikolaevič is also the result of a common effort. It unites his friends, colleagues and pupils from different institutions of Ukraine, France, Great Britain, Russia and Denmark, who celebrate his anniversary with their scientific contributions.

The edition is prepared under the auspices of the Danish National Research Foundation's Centre for Black Sea Studies with assistance from the Institute for the History of Material Culture of the Russian Academy of Sciences, St Petersburg.

The editors wish to express their sincerest thanks to all the authors for their readiness to take part in this publication. We are particularly grateful to Alexej V. Gilevič, who translated most of the articles of the Russian and Ukrainian contributors into English, as well as to Neil Stanford and Stacey Cozart, who undertook the linguistic revision. We are much indebted to Lev M. Vseviov (IHMC RAS) for compiling the bibliography of Alexander Nikolaevič, to Evgenija V. Bobrovskaja (IHMC RAS) for her practical help in the process of preparing the book, as well as to Andrej Ju. Alexeev, who provided the beautiful image of the bronze cauldron from the Raskopana Mogila (The State Hermitage Museum, inv. no. Dn 1897 1/14) for the frontispiece. Finally, the editors want to express their heartfelt gratitude to the following foundations, without whom this publication would not have been realised: The Danish National Research Foundation, The New Carlsberg Foundation, and The Aarhus University Research Foundation.

A few practical remarks

Abbreviations in general follow *The Oxford Classical Dictionary*, 3rd edition, 1996, whereas abbreviations of periodicals are in accordance with Archäologische Bibliographie. In transliterating Greek names and toponyms we have tried to avoid Latinising forms. For reasons of legibility, absolute consistency could not be achieved and a few commonly used English forms like Cyprus and Plutarch have been retained. Transliteration of Russian follows mostly the system with diacritical signs employed in *Panskoye* I, rather than the phonetic transliteration commonly employed in English publications.

Pia Guldager Bilde
Jakob Munk Højte
Vladimir F. Stolba

Bibliography of
Alexander Nikolaevič Ščeglov

1960

1. Ob izučenii toponimiki Kryma, *ZOAO* 1 (34), 340-342 [On studying toponymics of the Crimea].
2. Svetil'nik s izobraženiem Gerakla, *SChM* 1, 21-24 [A lamp with a representation of Herakles].
3. Skul'pturnye izobraženija Asklepija, *SChM* 1, 9-16 [Sculptural representations of Asklepios].
4. Terrakotovaja statuetka komičeskogo aktera iz Glubokoj Pristani, *SovA* 1, 257-260 [Une statuette de terre cuite représentant un acteur comique de Gloubokaia Pristagne].

1961

5. K istorii drevnego vinogradarstva v Krymu, *Vinogradarstvo i sadovodstvo Kryma* 12, 40-42 [On the history of ancient viticulture].
6. Polevye raboty Chersonesskogo muzeja v Severo-Zapadnom Krymu v 1959-1960 gg., *Tezisy dokladov o raskopkach Chersonesa Tavričeskogo na antičnoj Sekcii sessii Otdelenija Istoričeskich Nauk AN SSSR i Plenume IA AN SSSR, posvjaščennoj rezul'tatam polevych archeologičeskich issledovanij v 1960 g.* Sevastopol', 3-6 [Field investigations of the Chersonesean Museum in the north-western Crimea].
7. Razvedki 1959 g. na zapadnom poberež'e Kryma, *SChM* 2, 70-80 [Surveys of 1959 on the west coast of Crimea].
8. Svetil'nik s klejmom XPYCOY, *SChM* 2, 45-51 [Lamps with the stamp XPYCOY].

1962

9. *Chersones Tavričeskij: Gosudarstvennyj istoriko-archeologičeskij muzej.* Kiev [Tauric Chersonesos: State Historical and Archaeological Museum].
10. *Chersones Tavričeskij: Putevoditel' po muzeju i raskopkam.* Simferopol' (in collaboration with I.A. Antonova, V.V. Borisova, A.M. Gilevič & S.F. Strželeckij) [Tauric Chersonesos: A Guidebook to the museum and excavated areas].

1963

11. Novye pamjatniki drevnego vinogradarstva v Krymu, *Vinodelie i vinogradarstvo SSSR* 7, 36-37 (in collaboration with V.M. Malikov) [New evidence of the ancient viticulture in the Crimea].

12. Raskopki gorodišča Tarpanči v 1960 g., *SChM* 3, 67-75 [Excavation at the settlement-site of Tarpanchi in 1960].

1964

13. *Podvigi Gerakla: Po pamjatnikam Chersonesa Tavričeskogo.* Leningrad [The labours of Herakles: visiting sites of Tauric Chersonesos].
14. O naselenii Severo-Zapadnogo Kryma v antičnuju epochu i ego vza-imootnošenijach s Chersonesom i Skifskim gosudarstvom, *Konferencija po izučeniju problem antičnosti. Tezisy dokladov.* Moskva, 135 [On the population of the north-western Crimea in the Greek period and its interrelations with Chersonesos and the Scythian state].
15. Pjat' chersonesskich nadgrobij s izobraženiem umeršich, *SovA* 2, 213-218 [Cinq épitaphes avec image de morts de Chersonèse].

1965

16. Zametki po drevnej geografii i topografii Sarmatii i Tavridy: 1. O-v Berezan' (k stat'e V.V. Lapina); 2. O mestopoloženii Dandaki, *VDI* 2, 107-113 [Notes on the ancient geography and topography of Sarmatia and Taurida].
17. O kul'te Asklepija v Chersonese Tavričeskom: (po numizmatičeskim i archeologičeskim dannym), *Dacia* 9, 373-382 (in collaboration with K.V. Golenko) [On the cult of Asklepios in Tauric Chersonesos (on the basis of numismatic and archaeological evidence)].
18. O promysle ryby u beregov Tarchankuta v antičnuju epochu, *Rybnoe chozjajstvo* 3, 21-23 (in collaboration with V.D. Burdak) [On the fishery near the shores of Tarkhankut in antiquity].
19. Opyt elektrorazvedki metodom simmetričnogo profilirovanija na ellinističeskoj sel'skoj usad'be v okruge Kalos Limena, *Materialy sessii, posvjaščennoj itogam archeologičeskich issledovanij 1964 g. v SSSR.* Baku, 122-123 (in collaboration with K.K. Šilik) [Experiments on resistivity surveys based on symmetrical profiles at a Hellenistic farmhouse in the vicinity of Kalos Limen].
20. Tarchankutskaja ekspedicija v 1962-1963 gg., *KSIA* 103, 140-147 [The Tarkhankut Expedition in 1962-1963].
21. Chersonesskoe ukreplenie na gorodišče Beljaus, *SovA* 2, 246-255 (in collaboration with O.D. Daševskaja) [Les fortifications de Chersonèse au gorodichtché de Beliaus].
22. Chora Chersonesa Tavričeskogo v IV-II vv. do n.e. (po materialam raskopok 1959-1964 g.), *Materialy sessii, posvjaščennoj itogam archeologičeskich i etnografičeskich issledovanij 1964 g. v SSSR. Tezisy dokladov.* Baku, 121 [The chora of Tauric Chersonesos in the 4th-2nd centuries BC (on the basis of the evidence from excavations of 1959-1964)].

1966

23. Issledovanie sel'skoj okrugi Kalos Limena, *Tezisy dokladov na plenume Instituta archeologii AN SSSR 1966 g. Sekcija antičnoj archeologii*. Moskva, 38-40 [Investigations of the rural surroundings of Kalos Limen].

24. K voprosu o gladiatorskich bojach v Chersonese Tavričeskom, *Eirene* 5, 99-105 [On the problem of gladiatorial plays in Tauric Chersonesos].

25. O naselenii Severo-Zapadnogo Kryma v antičnuju epochu, *VDI* 4, 146-157 [The population of northwestern Crimea in antiquity].

26. O tempe rosta, vozrastnom sostave stad i migracijach nekotorych morskich ryb v antičnuju epochu, *Ekologo-morfologičeskie issledovanija nektonnych životnych*. Kiev, 117-120 (in collaboration with V.D. Burdak) [On the growth rate and age composition of fish shoals and migrations of sea fish in antiquity].

1967

27. Dva votivnych rel'efa iz Ol'vii (K voprosu o svjazjach meždu Ol'viej i Frakiej), *ZOAO* 2, 255-259 [Two votive reliefs from Olbia (to the question of the links between Olbia and Thracia)].

28. Issledovanie sel'skoj okrugi Kalos Limena, *SovA* 3, 234-256 [L'exploration des environs ruraux de Kalos Limen].

29. Raskopki v Severo-Zapadnom Krymu, *AO* 1966, 210-212 [Excavations in the north-western Crimea].

1968

30. Issledovanija v Severo-Zapadnom Krymu, *AO* 1967, 213-214 [Investigations in the north-western Crimea].

31. Kolebanija urovnja Černogo morja v istoričeskoe vremja po dannym archeologo-geomorfologičeskich issledovanij v Jugo-Zapadnom Krymu, *IAN. Ser. geogr.* 2, 49-58 (in collaboration with N.S. Blagovolin) [Variations of the level of the Black Sea during the historical period on the basis of archaeological and geomorphological studies in the southwestern Crimea].

32. Osnovnye etapy istorii Zapadnogo Kryma v antičnuju epochu, *Antičnaja istorija i kul'tura Sredizemnomor'ja i Pričernomor'ja*. Leningrad, 332-342 [The main stages of the history of the western Crimea in antiquity].

33. Chersonesskie antropomorfnye stely s vreznymi izobraženijami, *Archeologija* 21, 214-221 [Chersonesean anthropomorphic stelae with carved representations].

1969

34. *Chersones Tavričeskij: Putevoditel' po muzeju i raskopkam*. Simferopol' (in collaboration with S.F. Strželeckij & L.G. Kolesnikova) [Tauric Chersonesos: A Guidebook to the museum and excavated areas].

35. Konservacionno-restavracionnye raboty v Chersonese Tavričeskom v 1962-1965 godach, *SNMSOPK* 4, 40-45 [Conservation and restoration works in Tauric Chersonesos in 1962-1965].

36. Novyj metod opredelenija veličiny ryb po ee češue i nekotorye dannye o promysle kefali v Severo-Zapadnom Krymu v I v. do n.e., *KSIA* 119, 128-130 [A new method of determination of size of fishes by their scales and some information on the fishing of grey mullet in the north-western Crimea in the 1st century BC].

37. Ochrannye raskopki i začistki na Geraklejskom poluostrove, *AO* 1968, 290-291 [Rescue excavations on the Herakleian Peninsula].

38. Primenenie archeologo-geomorfologičeskogo metoda dlja analiza sovremennych deformacij zemnoj poverchnosti i kolebanij urovnja morja, *Problemy sovremennych dviženij zemnoj kory: 3-j Meždunarodnyj simpozium*. Moskva, 447-454. (in collaboration with N.S. Blagovolin) [Application of archaeologo-geomorphological method to analysis of modern deformations of the Earth's surface and variations of the sea level].

39. Frakijskie posvjatitel'nye rel'efy iz Chersonesa Tavričeskogo, *MatIsslA* 150, 135-177 [Thracian dedicatory reliefs from Tauric Chersonesos].

40. Antičnaja bašnja na gorodišče Beljaus, *KSIA* 116, 85-92 (in collaboration with O.D. Daševskaja) [An ancient tower at the town-site of Belyaus].

1970

41. Poselenija Severo-Zapadnogo Kryma v antičnuju epochu, *KSIA* 124, 19-24 [Settlements in the north-western Crimea of the ancient period].

42. Rannesrednevekovye poselenija na Tarchankutskom poluostrove Kryma, *SovA* 1, 254-261 [Early medieval settlements on the Tarkhankut Peninsula in the Crimea].

43. Raskopki na territorii chory Chersonesa, *AO* 1969, 257-258 [Excavations in the territory of the chora of Chersonesos].

44. Terrakota iz ellinističeskoj sel'skoj usad'by v okruge Prekrasnoj Gavani (u buchty Vetrenoj), *SAI* G1-11, 66 [A terracotta from a Hellenistic farmhouse in the vicinity of Prekrasnaya Gavan' (near the Bay of Vetrenaya)].

45. Terrakotovaja statuetka iz poselenija Glubokaja Pristan', *SAI* G1-11, 56 [A terracotta figurine from the settlement of Glubokaya Pristan'].

46. Rev.: Bašnja Zenona: Issledovanija 1960-1961 gg. (*SChM* 4), Simferopol', 1969, *VDI* 3, 172-187 [Review of: The Tower of Zeno: Investigations of 1960-1961 (in *SChM* 4].

1971

47. Severo-Zapadnyj Krym v antičnuju epochu, *Thesis for a Candidate's degree, LOIA AN SSSR*. Leningrad [The north-western Crimea in antiquity].

48. Issledovanija bliz Jarylgačskoj buchty v Severo-Zapadnom Krymu, *AO* 1970, 251-251 (in collaboration with I.I. Saverkina & V.V. Glazunov) [Investigations near the Bay of Yarylgach in the north-western Crimea].
49. Tri pozdneellinističeskie tetradrachmy iz Severo-Zapadnogo Kryma, *VDI* 1, 41-47 (in collaboration with K.V. Golenko) [Three late Hellenistic tetradrachms from northwestern Crimea].

1972

50. *Chersones Tavričeskij: Putevoditel' po muzeju i raskopkam*, 2nd rev. ed. Simferopol' (in collaboration with S.F. Strželeckij & L.G. Kolesnikova) [Tauric Chersonesos: A Guidebook to the museum and excavated areas].
51. Voprosy antičnoj archeologii v izdanijach Char'kovskogo universiteta, *SovA* 1, 298-300 [Problems of the archaeology of the Greek and Roman period in publications of the Kharkov University].
52. Zametki po drevnej geografii i topografii Sarmatii i Tavridy. 3. K Polyb., IV, 41, *VDI* 2, 126-134 [The ancient geography and topography of Sarmatia and Tauris (To Polyb., IV, 41)].
53. Izučenie chory Chersonesa Tavričeskogo, *Kratkie tezisy dokladov k plenumu, posvjaščenomu itogam archeologičeskich issledovanij 1971 g*. Leningrad, 16-18 [Studies of the chora of Tauric Chersonesos].
54. K topografii drevnich gorodov Geraklejskogo poluostrova, *Tezisy dokladov 15-j naučnoj konferencii IA URSR*. Odesa, 248-252 [To the topography of ancient towns on the Herakleian Peninsula].
55. Kurgan-kenotaf bliz Jarylgačskoj buchty, *KSIA* 130, 70-82 [A cenotaph-kurgan near the Bay of Yarylgach].
56. Predvaritel'naja charakteristika poselenija i nekropolja Panskoe-1, *Tezisy dokladov na sekcijach, posvjaščennych itogam polevych archeologičeskich issledovanij 1971 g*. Moskva, 374-376 [A preliminary characterisation of the settlement and necropolis of Panskoe I].
57. Tarchankutskaja ekspedicija, *AO* 1971, 342-343 (in collaboration with N.L. Podol'skij, A.M. Gilevič & V.I. Kac) [The Tarkhankut Expedition].
58. Rev.: Morskie podvodnye issledovanija (Moskva, 1969), *SovA* 4, 279-281 [Review of: Marine underwater investigations, Moskva, 1969].

1973

59. Iz istorii keramičeskogo proizvodstva v poselenijach Severo-Zapadnogo Kryma, *KSIA* 133, 10-16 [From the history of ceramic production at the settlements of the north-western Crimea].
60. Issledovanija na chore Chersonesa, *AO* 1972, 353-354 (in collaboration with N.S. Blagovolin, A.M. Gilevič, V.V. Glazunov, V.I. Kac & N.L. Podol'skij) [Investigations in the chora of Chersonesos].
61. O strukture naselenija chory Chersonesa i Bospora v IV-II vv. do n.e., *Kratkie tezisy dokladov k naučnoj konferencii "Antičnye goroda Severnogo Pričernomor'ja i varvarskij mir"*. Leningrad, 36-37 [On the structure of the population of the chorai of Chersonesos and Bosporos in the 4th-2nd centuries BC].

62. Raboty Tarchankutskoj ekspedicii v 1972 g., *Tezisy dokladov sessii, po-svjaščennoj itogam polevych archeologičeskich issledovanij 1972 g. v SSSR*. Taškent 253-254 [Activities of the Tarkhankut Expedition in 1972].

63. Chersones i Nižnij Don v IV-III vv., *Archeologičeskie raskopki na Donu*. Rostov-na-Donu, 26-30 [Chersonesos and the Lower Don in the 4th-3rd centuries BC].

1974

64. Agrarnaja struktura Chersonesa Tavričeskogo v IV-II vv. do n.e., *XIII Congress intern. du Comite "Eirene": Resumes des communications*. Dubrovnic, 1974, 78 [The agrarian structure of Tauric Chersonesos in the 4th-2nd centuries BC].

65. Gerakl otdychajuščij, *Chersones Tavričeskij: Remeslo i kul'tura*. Kiev, 44-55 [The resting Herakles].

66. Issledovanija Tarchankutskoj ekspedicii, *AO* 1973, 365-366 (in collaboration with V.V. Glazunov, V.I. Kac & N.L. Podol'skij) [Investigations of the Tarkhankut Expedition].

67. O vnutrennej torgovle Chersonesa Tavričeskogo v IV-III vv. do n.e., *KSIA* 138, 44-50 [On the local trade of Tauric Chersonesos in the 4th-3rd centuries BC].

68. Ellinističeskie sel'skie poselenija (k metodike archeologičeskogo izučenija), *Rekonstrukcija drevnich obščestvennych otnošenij po archeologičeskim materialam žilišč i poselenij. Kratkie tezisy dokladov*. Leningrad, 38-40 [Hellenistic rural settlements (to the methods of archaeological investigation)].

1975

69. *Chersones Tavričeskij: Putevoditel'*. Simferopol' (in collaboration with S.F. Strželeckij & L.G. Kolesnikova) [Tauric Chersonesos: A Guidebook].

70. Izučenie poselenija i nekropolja Panskoe I na chore Chersonesa, *AO* 1974, 375-376 (in collaboration with A.M. Gilevič, V.V. Glazunov, V.I. Kac & E.Ja. Rogov) [Studies of the settlement and necropolis of Panskoe I in the chora of Chersonesos].

71. Itogi raskopok na poselenii i nekropole Panskoe I, *Novejšie otkrytija sovetskich archeologov: Tezisy dokladov*. Čast' 2. Kiev, 81-83 [The results of excavations at the settlement of Panskoe I].

72. Nekropol' u Pesočnoj buchty bliz Chersonesa, *KSIA* 143, 109-116 [A necropolis at the Bay of Pesochnaya near Chersonesos].

73. "Staryj" Chersones Strabona, *150 let Odesskomu archeologičeskomu muzeju AN USSR: Tezisy dokladov jubilejnoj konferencii*. Kiev, 135-136 [The "Old" Chersonesos of Strabo].

74. Rev.: Vani. T. 1. Archeologičeskie raskopki 1947-1969 (Tbilisi, 1972), *VDI* 2, 143-147, [Review of: Vani, Vol. 1. Archaeological excavations of 1947-1969 (Tbilisi, 1972)].

1976

75. *Polis i chora (Archeologičeskie pamjatniki Kryma)*. Simferopol' [Polis and chora].

76. Gerakl i ego atributy. Votivnye rel'efy zapadnopontijskogo i frakijskogo tipa. Nadgrobija rimskich soldat. Nadgrobija bosporskogo tipa, *Antičnaja skul'ptura: Catalogue*. Kiev, 29-36; 43-44; 120-129 [Herakles and his attributes. Votive reliefs of the West-Pontic and Thracian type. Gravestones of Roman soldiers. Gravestones of the Bosporan type].

77. Žiloj dom ellinističeskogo Kalos Limena (Opyt rekonstrukcii), *Chudožestvennaja kul'tura i archeologija antičnogo mira*. Moskva, 232-238 [A house in Hellenistic Kalos Limen (an essay of reconstruction)].

78. Raboty na Tarchankutskom poluostrove, *AO* 1975, 409-410 (in collaboration with T.V. Balt, M.Ju. Vachtina, G.N. Vnučkov, V.I. Kac & E.Ja. Rogov) [Investigations on the Tarkhankut Peninsula].

79. Sistema "polis-chora" i kontaktnye zony v Pričernomor'e, *Tezisy dokladov 14-j Meždunarodnoj konferencii antičnikov socialističeskich stran*. Erevan, 523-525 [The system "polis-chora" and contact zones in the Black Sea region].

1977

80. Zemel'nyj nadel u mysa Ojrat, *Istorija i kul'tura antičnogo mira*. Moskva, 210-215 [A land plot near Cape Oirat].

81. Kompleksnye metody issledovanija v archeologii, *Priroda* 4, 78-81 [Interdisciplinary methods of investigation in archaeology].

82. Nekotorye problemy grečeskoj kolonizacii, *Simpozium po problemam grečeskoj kolonizacii i strukture ranneantičnych gosudarstv Severnogo i Vostočnogo Pričernomor'ja*. Tbilisi, 80-103 (in collaboration with I.B. Brašinskij) [Some problems of the Greek colonisation].

83. Primenenie kvantovogo magnitometra v issledovanii archeologičeskich pamjatnikov, *Geomagnitnoe priborostroenie*. Moskva, 77-85 (in collaboration with V.V. Glazunov, A.P. Naumov & I.S. Chasiev) [Application of quantum magnetometer to studies of archaeological sites].

84. Problema grečeskoj kolonizacii, *Simpozium po problemam grečeskoj kolonizacii i strukture ranneantičnych gosudarstv Severnogo i Vostočnogo Pričernomor'ja*. Tbilisi, 8-9 (in collaboration with I.B. Brašinskij) [The problem of the Greek colonisation].

85. Tat'jana Nikolaevna Knipovič (1896-1975. Nekrolog), *SovA* 1, 322 [Tat'jana Nikolaevna Knipovič (1896-1975. Obituary)].

1978

86. *Severo-Zapadnyj Krym v antičnuju epochu*. Leningrad [The north-western Crimea in the antiquity].

87. Issledovanie chory Chersonesa v 1975-1977 gg., *AIU* 1976-1977, 83 [Investigation of the chora of Chersonesos in 1975-1977].

88. Tarchankutskaja ekspedicija, *AO* 1977, 405-406 (in collaboration with G.A. Vnučkov, V.I. Kac, A.P. Naumov & E.Ja. Rogov) [The Tarkhankut Expedition].

89. Tarchankutskaja ekspedicija v 1969-1975 gg., *KSIA* 156, 61-68 [The Tarkhankut Expedition in 1969-1975].

1979

90. Nekotorye problemy grečeskoj kolonizacii, *Problemy grečeskoj kolonizacii Severnogo i Vostočnogo Pričernomor'ja: Materialy 1-go Vsesojuznogo simpoziuma*. Tbilisi, 29-46 (in collaboration with I.B. Brašinskij) [Some problems of the Greek colonisation].

91. Tavry i grečeskie kolonii v Tavrike, *Materialy 2-go Vsesojuznogo simpoziuma po drevnej istorii Pričernomor'ja*. Tbilisi, 90-94, [Taurians and Greek colonies in Tauris].

92. Rev.: A.M. Chazanov, *Social'naja istorija skifov: Osnovnye problemy razvitija drevnich kočevnikov Evrazijskich stepej* (Moskva, 1976), *VDI* 1, 189-195 (in collaboration with I.B. Brašinskij & K.K. Marčenko) [Review of: A.M. Chazanov, *The social history of the Scythians: The main problems of the development of ancient nomads of Eurasian steppes* (Moskva, 1976)].

1980

93. Archeologija iznutri (O novych metodach v polevoj archeologii), *Znanie – sila* 4, 30-33 [Archaeology from inside (About new methods in the field archaeology)].

94. Kompleksnye issledovanija v Severo-Zapadnom Krymu, *AO* 1979, 354-355 [Interdisciplinary investigations in the western Crimea].

95. Novye materialy k izučeniju prostranstvennoj organizacii ranneellinističeskogo Chersonesa, *Problemy antičnoj istorii i klassičeskoj filologii. Tezisy dokladov Vsesojuznoj naučnoj konferencii*. Char'kov, 73. [New evidence for studies of the spatial organisation of the early Hellenistic Chersonesos].

96. Primenenie kompleksa estestvennych i točnych metodov v polevoj archeologii, *AIU* 1978-1979, 19-20. [Application of a complex of natural and precise methods to the field archaeology].

97. Utilisation de la photographie aérienne dans l'étude du cadastre de Chersonésos Taurique (IVe-IIe s. av. n.è.), *DialHistAnc* 6, 59-63.

1981

98. Gorodišče Rud' – Metonij Ptolemeja?, *VDI* 4, 121-137 (in collaboration with M.A. Romanovskaja & F.V. Šelov-Kovedjaev) [The town of Rud', the site of Ptolemy's Maitonion?].

99. Tavry i grečeskie kolonii v Tavrike, *Demografičeskaja situacija v Pričernomor'e v period Velikoj grečeskoj kolonizacii*. Tbilisi, 204-218 [The Tauroi and Greek colonies in Tauris].

100. Tarchankutskaja ekspedicija, *AO* 1980, 326-327 [The Tarkhankut Expedition].

1982

101. O greko-varvarskich vzaimodejstvijach na periferii ellinističeskogo mira, *Materialy 3-go Vsesojuznogo simpoziuma po drevnej istorii Pričernomor'ja*. Tbilisi, 107-109 [On Graeco-Barbarian interactions at the periphery of the Hellenistic world].

102. Ob opredelenii vysoty postroek po razvalam syrcovych sten, *KSIA* 172, 50-57 [On determination of the height of buildings by the debris of mud-brick walls].

1983

103. Pozdneskifskoe gosudarstvo v Krymu (K tipologii ellinizma), *Drevnie kul'tury Evrazii i antičnaja civilizacija: Tezisy dokladov naučnoj konferencii*. Leningrad, 31-33 [The Late-Scythian state in the Crimea (To the typology of the Hellenismus)].

104. Raboty na chore Chersonesa, *AO* 1981, 336 [Investigations in the chora of Chersonesos].

105. Razvedki i raskopki antičnych sel'skich poselenij i agrarnych sistem: Instrukcija, *Metodika polevych archeologičeskich issledovanij*. Moskva, 12-30 [Surveys and excavations of ancient rural settlements and agrarian systems: Instructions].

106. Tarchankutskaja ekspedicija v 1981-1982 gg., *Novye ekspedicionnye issledovanija archeologov Leningrada*. Leningrad, 17-18 [The Tarkhankut Expedition in 1981-1982].

1984

107. Archeologo-geofizičeskie issledovanija izvestnjakovych sooruženij dogrečeskogo i antičnogo periodov v Severnom Pričernomor'e, *Kompleksnye metody v izučenii istorii s drevnejšich vremen do našich dnej*. Moskva, 95-97 (in collaboration with T.N. Smekalova, A.V. Mel'nikov, A.A. Maslennikov & A.G. Zaginajlo) [Archaeological-geophysical investigations of limestone structures of pre-Greek and Greek periods in the northern Black Sea area].

108. Grečeskie i mestnye tradicii v architekturno-planirovočnom oblike i stroitel'stve pozdneskifskich poselenij, *2-j Vsesojuznyj simpozium po problemam ellinističeskoj kul'tury na Vostoke. Tezisy dokladov*. Erevan, 81 [Greek and local traditions in the architectural appearance, ground plans and buildings of Late-Scythian settlements].

109. Chersonesskoe gosudarstvo i Charaks: Istočniki i istorija voprosa, in: G.A. Košelenko, I.T. Kruglikova & V.S. Dolgorukov (eds.), *Antičnye gosudarstva Severnogo Pričernomor'ja*. Moskva, 45-49 [The Chersonesean state and Charax: The sources and history of the problem].

110. Chora Chersonesa. Okruga goroda na Geraklejskom poluostrove. "Staryj" Chersones i ego okruga. Kerkinitida. Prekrasnaja gavan' (Kalos Limen i ee okruga). Ostal'nye poselenija na chore Chersonesa, in: G.A. Košelenko, I.T. Kruglikova & V.S. Dolgorukov (eds.), *Antičnye gosudarstva Severnogo Pričernomor'ja*. Moskva, 53-56 [The chora of Chersonesos. The surroundings of the city on the Herakleian Peninsula.

The "Old" Chersonesos and its surroundings. Kerkinitis. Prekrasnaja Gavan' (Kalos Limen) and its surroundings].

111. O pervičnom opisanii archeologičeskogo materiala, in: I.B. Brašinskij (ed.), *Metody issledovanija antičnoj torgovli na primere Severnogo Pričernomor'ja*. Leningrad, 242-245 [On the primary description of archaeological materials].

112. Ot redaktora: I.B. Brašinskij. (1928-1982), in: I.B. Brašinskij (ed.), *Metody issledovanija antičnoj torgovli na primere Severnogo Pričernomor'ja*. Leningrad, 3-10 [Editorial notes to: I.B. Brašinskij (1928-1982)].

113. Pamjati Pavla Nikolaeviča Šul'ca: (1900-1983) [Nekrolog], *SovA* 3, 285-287 [In memory of Pavel Schultz (1900-1983). Obituary].

114. Raskopki i razvedki v Severo-Zapadnom Krymu, *AO* 1982, 345-346 [Excavations and surveys in the north-western Crimea].

1985

115. 25 let rabot Tarchankutskoj ekspedicii: itogi i perspektivy, *KSIA* 182, 3-76 [Twenty five years of works of the Tarkhankut Expedition: the results and prospects].

116. O greko-varvarskich vzaimodejstvijach na periferii ellinističeskogo mira, *Pričernomor'e v epochu ellinizma*. Tbilisi, 185-198 [Concerning the Graeco-barbarian interrelations in the periphery of the Hellenistic world].

117. Ol'vija i Chersones: novye materialy i aspekty problemy, *Problemy issledovanija Ol'vii. Tezisy dokladov*. Parutino, 84-86, [Olbia and Chersonesos: the new evidence and aspects of the problem].

118. Osnovnye metodičeskie principy izučenija poselenij na zemledel'českoj territorii antičnych gosudarstv Severnogo Pričernomor'ja, *Problemy issledovanija Ol'vii. Tezisy dokladov*. Parutino, 39-40 (in collaboration with S.D. Kryžickij) [The basic methodological principles of investigation of settlements in the agricultural territory of ancient states in the northern Black Sea region].

119. Pogrebenija v podbojnych mogilach v Nižnem Podnestrov'e i Severo-Zapadnom Krymu, *Problemy issledovanija Ol'vii. Tezisy dokladov*. Parutino, 86-88 (in collaboration with E.Ja. Rogov) [Burials in catacomb graves in the Lower Dniester region and north-western Crimea].

120. Raboty Tarchankutskoj ekspedicii, *AO* 1983, 376-377 [Activities of the Tarkhankut Expedition].

1986

121. Process i charakter territorial'noj ekspansii Chersonesa v IV v. do n.e., *Antičnaja graždanskaja obščina*. Leningrad, 152-176 [The process and character of the territorial expansion of Chersonesos in the 4th century BC].

122. Raboty v Černomorskom rajone Kryma, *AO* 1984, 333-334 [The works in the Chernomorsky Region of the Crimea].

123. Les amphores timbrées d'Amastris, *BCH. Suppl.* 13, 365-373.

1987

124. Izučenie antičnych pamjatnikov na Tarchankute, *AO* 1985, 440-441 [Studies of ancient sites in Tarkhankut].

125. Istočniki severočernomorskoj torgovli chlebom v IV v. do n.e., *Tezisy dokladov X Vsesojuznoj avtorsko-čitatel'skoj konferencii VDI*, 175-176 [The sources of the North Black Sea grain trade in the 4th century BC].

126. Konferencija "Problemy antičnoj i skifo-sarmatskoj archeologii", posvjaščennaja pamjati P.N. Šul'ca, *VDI* 2, 229-234 (in collaboration with V.A. Gorončarovskij) [La Conférence "Les problèmes de l'archéologie antique et scytho-sarmate" á la mémoire de P.N. Schulz].

127. Raboty Tarchankutskoj ekspedicii (1983-1986 gg.), *Zadači sovetskoj archeologii v svete rešenij XXVII s'ezda KPSS. Tezisy dokladov Vsesojuznoj konferencii*. Moskva, 293-294 [Activities of the Tarkhankut Expedition (1983-1986)].

128. Un établissement rural en Crimée: Panskoje I: (Fouilles de 1969-1985), *DialHistAnc* 13, 239-273.

1988

129. Bol'šoj Kastel' i svjatilišče II v. do n.e. v uročišče Džangul', *Problemy antičnoj kul'tury. Tezisy dokladov naučnoj konferencii* 3, 273-275 [Bol'šoj Kastel' and a sanctuary of the 2nd century BC in the *uročišče* of Džangul'].

130. Raskopki v Severo-Zapadnom Krymu, *AO* 1986, 353-354 [Excavations in the north-western Crimea].

131. Tavry v VII – pervoj polovine IV vv. do n.e. i greko-tavrskie vzaimootnošenija, *Mestnye etno-političeskie ob'edinenija Pričernomor'ja v VII-IV vv. do n.e.* Tbilisi, 53-81, [Taurians in the 7th – first half of the 4th centuries BC and Graeco-Taurian interrelations].

132. Chersones kak primer dorijskogo periferijnogo polisa, *Problemy issledovanija antičnogo i srednevekovogo Chersonesa 1888-1988 gg. Tezisy dokladov*. Sevastopol', 132-133. [Chersonesos as an example of a Doric peripheral polis].

1989

133. Agrarnyj Chersones, *Problemy istorii i archeologii drevnego naselenija Ukrainskoj SSR. Tezisy dokladov*. Kiev, 266-267 [The agrarian Chersonesos].

134. Gde nachodilsja kurgan Kara-Merkit (Ak-Mečetskij)?, *Skifija i Bospor: Archeologičeskie materialy k konferencii pamjati M.I. Rostovceva*. Novočerkassk, 95-97 [Where was the kurgan of Kara-Merkit (Ak-Mečetskij) situated?].

135. Ešče raz o pričine denežnogo krizisa III do n.e. v antičnych centrach Severnogo Pričernomor'ja, *Drevnee Pričernomor'e. Tezisy dokladov*. Odessa, 56-58 [Once more on the cause of the monetary crisis of the 3rd century BC in Greek centres of the northern Black Sea region].

136. Zemel'nyj fond Chersonesa vo vtoroj polovine IV – načale III vv. do n.e., *Problemy issledovanij antičnych gorodov. Tezisy dokladov.* Moskva, 129-131 [The land resources of Chersonesos in the second half of the 4th – beginning of the 3rd century BC].

137. Zemledelie na poselenii Panskoe I (Severo-Zapadnyj Krym) v IV – načale III v. do n.e., *Flora i rastitel'nost'.* Kišinev, 50-69 (in collaboration with N.N. Kuz'minova, Z.V. Januševič & E.S. Čavčavadze) [Agriculture at the settlement of Panskoe I (north-western Crimea)].

138. Izučenie sistem rasselenija v drevnosti s pomošč'ju materialov aerofotos'emki, *Novoe v metodike archeologičeskich rabot na novostrojkach.* Moskva, 37-39 [Studies of systems of settling in antiquity by means of aerial photographs].

139. K Gerodotu, IV, 81, *ArcheologijaKiev* 3, 117-121 (in collaboration with K.K. Marčenko) [To Herodotos, IV, 81].

140. Pozdneskifskoe gosudarstvo v Krymu: k tipologii ellinizma, *Drevnij Vostok i antičnaja civilizacija.* Leningrad, 29-40 [The Late-Scythian state in the Crimea: to the typology of the Hellenismus].

141. "Carskij" kurgan IV v. do n.e. v Zapadnom Krymu?, *Problemy skifo-sarmatskoj archeologii Severnogo Pričernomor'ja.* Čast' 1. Zaporož'e, 57-59 (in collaboration with V.I. Kac) [A "Royal" kurgan of the 4th century BC in the western Crimea?].

142. The Amastrian stamped pottery, *ArcheologiaWarsz* 40, 15-28 (in collaboration with V.I. Kac & V.I. Pavlenkov).

1990

143. O vremeni i obstojatel'stvach vozniknovenija Kalos Limena, *Problemy archeologii Severnogo Pričernomor'ja. Tezisy dokladov.* Cherson, 59-60 [On the date and circumstances of the foundation of Kalos Limen].

144. Obrazovanie territorial'nogo Chersonesskogo gosudarstva, *Ellinizm: ekonomika, politika, kul'tura.* Moskva, 310-37 (in collaboration with Ju.G. Vinogradov) [The formation of the territorial Chersonesean state].

145. Severopontijskaja torgovlja chlebom vo vtoroj polovine VII-V vv. do n.e.: pis'mennye istočniki i archeologija, *Pričernomor'e VII-V vv. do n.e.: pis'mennye istočniki i archeologija.* Tbilisi, 99-121 [North-Pontic grain trade in the second half of the 7th-5th century BC: the written evidence and archaeology].

146. Le commerce du blé dans le Pont septentrional (seconde moitié du VIIème-Vème siècle), *Le Pont-Euxin vu par les Grecs. Sources écrites et archéologie. Symposium de Vani (Colchide), septembre-octobre 1987.* Besançon 1990, 141-159.

1991

147. K osobennostjam dorijskoj kolonizacii Italii i Sicilii, *Drevnie kul'tury i archeologičeskie izyskanija. Materialy k plenumu IIMK 1991 g.* St Peterburg, 63-66 [On the peculiarities of the Doric colonisation in Italy and Sicily].

148. Nachodka monety Istrii v Severo-Zapadnom Krymu, *Drevnee Pričerno-*

mor'e. Tezisy dokladov 2-ch čtenij pamjati P.O. Karyškovskogo. Odessa, 22-23 (in collaboration with A.M. Gilevič & V.F. Stolba) [A find of a coin of Istria in the north-western Crimea].

149. O zernovom potenciale antičnych gosudarstv Severnogo Pričernomor'ja, *ArcheologijaKiev* 1, 46-56 (in collaboration with S.D. Kryžickij) [On the grain potential of the northern Black Sea region in antiquity].

150. A fourth-century BC Royal kurgan in the Crimea, *Metropolitan Museum journal* 26, 97-122 (in collaboration with V.I. Kac).

1992

151. *Polis et chora: Cité et territoire dans le Pont-Euxin*. Paris.

152. Optiko-petrografičeskoe issledovanie pričernomorskich klejmenych amfor IV-II vv. do n.e., *Grečeskie amfory: Problemy razvitija remesla i torgovli v antičnom mire*. Saratov, 32-50 (in collaboration with N.B. Selivanova) [Etude optique-pétrographique des amphores timbrées des IV-III siècles av. n.è. sur les territoires du Nord de la mer Noire].

153. Otvergnutaja recenzija, *Voprosy istorii estestvoznanija i techniki* 4, 146-150 [A rejected review].

154. Otvergnutaja recenzija (L.S. Klejn, *Archeologičeskie istočniki*. St Peterburg, 1995), 291-301 (in collaboration with G.P. Grigor'ev, P.M. Doluchanov & G.S. Lebedev) [A rejected review].

1993

155. K izučeniju mechanizma transljacij kul'tur v severočernomorskom areale rasselenija grekov, *Dinamika kul'turnych tradicij*. St Peterburg, 28-29 [On the studies of the mechanism of translations of cultures in the northern Black Sea area of the Greek settling].

156. Osnovnye strukturnye elementy antičnoj meževoj sistemy na Majačnom poluostrove (Jugo-Zapadnyj Krym), *Istorija i archeologija Jugo-Zapadnogo Kryma*. Simferopol', 10-38 [The main structural elements of the ancient land-division system on the Mayachny Peninsula (South-western Crimea)].

157. Pervye archeologičeskie karty Geraklejskogo poluostrova (k istorii archeologičeskoj topografii), *Problemy istorii otečestvennoj archeologii*. St Peterburg, 51-53 [The first archaeological maps of the Herakleian Peninsula (to the history of archaeological topography)].

1994

158. Gerakl v statuarnoj skul'pture Chersonesa, *Problemy archeologii* 3, 136-148 [Sculptural representations of Herakles from Chersonesos].

159. K izučeniju kul'turnych transljacij i vzaimodejstvij v Pričernomorskom regione rasselenija grekov, *Kul'turnye transljacii i istoričeskij process*. St Peterburg, 93-98. [To the studies of cultural translations and interactions in the Black Sea region].

160. Kompleksnye issledovanija: archeologo-geofizičeskij eksperiment na antičnom poselenii Panskoe I v Krymu (1970-1980), *Materialy konferencii*

po primeneniju metodov estestvennych nauk v archeologii, posvjaščennoj pa-mjati B.A. Kolčina. Tezisy dokladov. St Peterburg, 27-28 [Interdisciplinary investigations: an archaeologo-geophysical experiment at the ancient Greek settlement of Panskoe I in the Crimea (1970-1980)].

161. Monetnye nachodki na Majačnom poluostrove v Jugo-Zapadnom Krymu, *Tezisy dokladov Vserossijskoj numizmatičeskoj konferencii.* St Peterburg, 42-43 [Coin finds on the Lighthouse Point in the south-west-ern Crimea].

162. Raskopki na poselenii Panskoe I, *KM* 1, 149 (in collaboration with V.F. Stolba) [Excavations at the settlement of Panskoe I].

163. "Staryj" Chersones Strabona: Ukreplenie na perešejke Majačnogo polu-ostrova (topografija i fortifikacija), *Problemy istorii i archeologii Kryma.* Simferopol', 8-42 [The "Old" Chersonesos of Strabo].

1995

164. Krepostnye steny "starogo" Chersonesa, *Fortifikacija v drevnosti i sred-nevekov'e.* St Peterburg, 44-49 [Defensive walls of the "Old" Chersonesos].

165. O vremeni vozniknovenija "starogo" Chersonesa Strabona, *Antičnoe obščestvo: problemy istorii i kul'tury.* St Peterburg, 46-49 [On the time of the foundation of the "Old" Chersonesos].

166. Raboty Rossijsko-Datskoj Tarchankutskoj ekspedicii v Krymu, *AO* 1994, 335-336 (in collaboration with L. Hannestad & V.F. Stolba) [Activities of the Russian-Danish Tarkhankut Expedition in the Crimea].

167. Raskopki poselenija Panskoe I v Krymu, *Izučenie kul'turnych vzaimo-dejstvij i novye archeologičeskie otkrytija.* St Peterburg, 50-53 (in collabora-tion with V.F. Stolba & L. Hannestad) [Excavations of the settlement of Panskoe I in the Crimea].

168. Rossijsko-datskie raskopki na poselenii i nekropole Panskoe I (Severo-Zapadnyj Krym), *Archeologičeskie vesti* 4, 288-290 (in collaboration with L. Hannestad, H. Hastrup, S.V. Kašaev, L.B. Kirčo, V.F. Stolba & I. Sørensen) [Russian-Danish excavations of a settlement and cemetery at Panskoye I, north-western Crimea].

169. Chersonesec Batill, *Intellektual'naja elita antičnogo mira.* St Peterburg, 58-63 [Bathyllos of Chersonesos].

1996

170. Iz istorii izučenija antičnogo kul'turnogo landšafta v Krymu (konec XVIII-pervaja polovina XX vv.), *Tradicii rossijskoj archeologii.* St Peterburg, 27-32 (in collaboration with I.V. Tunkina) [From the history of the studies of the ancient cultural landscape in the Crimea].

171. Pervaja nachodka monety-strelki v Jugo-Zapadnom Krymu i ee zname-nie dlja ponimanija teksta Strabo, VI, 4, 2, *Tezisy dokladov 4-j Vserossijskoj numizmatičeskoj konferencii.* Moskva, 7-8 [The first find of an arrowhead coin in the south-western Crimea and its significance for the interpre-tation of Strabo, VI, 4.2].

172. Chersonesec Batill, syn Nikagora, *Hyperboreus* 2.2, 100-124 (in collaboration with A.M. Gilevič) [Bathyllos of Chersonesos].

173. Chersonesskij landšaft, *Greki na Černom more: Meždunarodnyj archeologičeskij simpozium*. Saloniki, (without pagination) [The Chersonesean landscape].

174. E.R. Štern v Rossii (neskol'ko popravok i zametok k tezisam A. Chojslera), *Tradicii rossijskoj archeologii*. St Peterburg, 56-57 [E.R. Stern in Russia, a few corrections and notes to the thesis of A. Heusler].

1997

175. Antičnaja archeologija Pričernomor'ja, *Programma bazovych kursov po archeologii*. St Peterburg, 55-63 [Classic archaeology in the Black Sea area].

176. Archeologija antičnogo mira, *Programma bazovych kursov po archeologii*, 44-55 [Archaeology of the Greek and Roman world].

177. Issledovanija Tarchankutskoj ekspedicii, *AO* 1994, 275-276 [Investigations of the Tarkhankut Expedition].

178. Materialy k numizmatičeskoj karte Severo-Zapadnogo Kryma, *Tezisy dokladov 5-j Vserossijskoj numizmatičeskoj konferencii*. Moskva, 21-22 (in collaboration with A.M. Gilevič) [Materials for a numismatic map of the north-western Crimea].

179. Neizvestnyj plan Chersonesskogo gorodišča, *Pamjatniki stariny. Koncepcii. Otkrytija. Versii* II. St Peterburg, 392-396 [An unknown plan of the town-site of Chersonesos].

180. "Staryj" Chersones Strabona. Ukreplenie na perešejke Majačnogo poluostrova: III. Sledy archaičeskogo poselenija na veršine Kazač'ej buchty, *Bachčisarajskij istoriko-archeologičeskij sbornik* 1, 42-54 [The "Old" Chersonesos of Strabo. A fortress on the isthmus of the Mayachny Peninsula: III. Traces of an archaic settlement at the end of the Kazachya Bay].

1998

181. Ešče raz o pozdneskifskoj kul'ture v Krymu (K probleme proischoždenija), *Problemy archeologii* 4, 141-153 [Once more on the Late-Scythian culture in the Crimea (To the problem of the origins)].

182. Zolotaja i serebrjanye monety IV-II vv. do n.e. iz slučajnych nachodok v Chersonese i ego okruge, *Tezisy dokladov 6-j Vserossijskoj numizmatičeskoj konferencii*. St Peterburg, 20-22 [Gold and silver coins of the 4th-2nd centuries BC among the chance finds from Chersonesos and its vicinity].

183. "Plavajuščie goroda" v del'te Dona, *Poselenija: sreda, kul'tura, socium*. St Peterburg, 16-19 [The "floating towns" in the delta of the Don River].

184. Problema kul'turnogo sloja v vizantijskoj archeologii, *VV* 55.2, 178-183. (in collaboration with A.I. Romančuk) [The problem of the cultural layer in the Byzantine archaeology].

185. Final kizil-kobinskoj kul'tury i pozdnjaja istorija tavrov, *Skify. Chazary. Slavjane. Drevnjaja Rus'*. St Peterburg, 66-70 [The final stage of the Kizil-Koba culture and the late history of the Taurians].

186. Chersonesskij kul'turnyj landšaft na Geraklejskom poluostrove: princip prostranstvennoj organizacii sel'skoj territorii periferii grečeskogo polisa, *Poselenija: sreda, kul'tura, socium*. St Peterburg, 125-132 [The Chersonesean cultural landscape on the Herakleian Peninsula: the principle of the spatial organisation of the rural territory at the periphery of a Greek polis].

1999

187. K izučeniju kanalizacionnych ustrojstv v domostroitel'stve Nimfeja IV v. do n.e., *Bosporskij gorod Nimfej*. St Peterburg, 91-94 [To the studies of drainage facilities in the house building of Nymphaion of the 4th century BC].

2000

188. Grečeskie domašnie svjatilišča (Po materialam raskopok na territorii Chersonesskogo gosudarstva), *Svjatilišča*. St Peterburg, 74-77 [Greek domestic sanctuaries (On the basis of excavations in the territory of the Chersonesean state)].

189. O vremeni pojavlenija kul'ta Sabazija na severnych beregach Ponta: sostojanie izučennosti, istočniki, interpretacija, rekonstrukcija, *Svjatilišča*. St Peterburg, 67-73 [On the time of the appearance of the cult of Sabazios on the northern littoral of Pontos: the state of studies, sources, interpretation, reconstruction].

2001

190. K izučeniju kul'ta Sabazija v Chersonese: Sostojanie izučennosti, istočniki, interpretacija, rekonstrukcija, *Chersones Tavričeskij: u istokov mirovych religij*. Sevastopol', 52-61 [On the studies of the cult of Sabazios in Chersonesos: the state of studies, sources, interpretation, reconstruction].

191. "Staryj" Chersones Strabona. Ukreplenie na perešejke Majačnogo poluostrova: IV. Tranšeja 1967 g. v veršine Kazač'ej buchty, *Bachčisarajskij istoriko-archeologičeskij sbornik* 2, 53-77 [The "Old" Chersonesos of Strabo. A fortress on the isthmus of the Mayachny Peninsula: IV. The trench of 1967 at the end of the Kazachya Bay].

2002

192. Antičnoe zemledelie, *Programmy special'nych kursov po archeologii*. St Peterburg, 61-67 [Ancient agriculture].

193. Preface, in: L. Hannestad, V.F. Stolba & A.N. Ščeglov (eds.), *Panskoye I.* Vol. 1. *The Monumental Building U6*. Aarhus, 9-10 (in collaboration with L. Hannestad & V.F. Stolba).

194. Introduction, in: Hannestad, Stolba & Ščeglov (eds.), 11-25.

195. Monumental Building U6, in: Hannestad, Stolba & Ščeglov (eds.), 29-98.

196. Tiles and Ceramic Containers, in: Hannestad, Stolba & Ščeglov (eds.), 101-126 (in collaboration with V.I. Kac, S.Ju. Monachov & V.F. Stolba).

197. Cult Sculpture, Altars, Sacred Vessels, Votives, in: Hannestad, Stolba & Ščeglov (eds.), 213-227.
198. Conclusion, in: Hannestad, Stolba & Ščeglov (eds.), 280-282 (in collaboration with L. Hannestad & V.F. Stolba).
199. Archaeological, Palaeogeographic, and Geomorphological Researches in the Lake Sasyk (Panskoye) Region, in: Hannestad, Stolba & Ščeglov (eds.), 285-302 (in collaboration with N.S. Blagovolin).
200. Petrographic Analyses of Stamped Amphorae, in: Hannestad, Stolba & Ščeglov (eds.), 303-316 (in collaboration with N.B. Selivanova).
201. Palaeoethnobotanical Material, in: Hannestad, Stolba & Ščeglov (eds.), 327-331 (in collaboration with Z.V. Januševič).

List of abbreviations

AO	*Archeologičeskie otkrytija.*
AIU	*Archeologičeskie issledovanija na Ukraine.*
BCH	*Bulletin de correspondance hellénique.*
DialHistAnc	*Dialogues d'histoire ancienne.*
IA	Institut archeologii AN URSR, Kiev.
IAN	*Izvestija Akademii nauk SSSR.*
KM	*Krymskij muzej.*
KSIA	*Kratkie soobščenija Instituta Archeologii AN SSSR.*
LOIA	Leningradskoe otdelenie Instituta archeologii SSSR, Leningrad.
MatIsslA	*Materialy i issledovanija po archeologii SSSR.*
SovA	*Sovetskaja archeologija.*
SAI	*Archeologija SSSR: Svod archeologičeskich istočnikov.*
SNMSOPK	*Soobščenija Naučno-metodičeskogo Soveta po ochrane pamjatnikov kul'tury Ministerstva kul'tury SSSR.*
SChM	*Soobščenija Chersonesskogo muzeja.*
VDI	*Vestnik drevnej istorii.*
VV	*Vizantijskij vremennik.*
ZOAO	*Zapiski Odesskogo Archeologičeskogo obščestva.*

Towards Determining the Chief Function of the Settlement of Borysthenes

Jaroslav V. Domanskij & Konstantin K. Marčenko

The site of Borysthenes, the earliest Greek settlement in the northern Black Sea area, is located on the island of Berezan' situated at the mouth of the estuaries of the Dnieper and Bug rivers. The large-scale historical and archaeological research currently being carried out there has already yielded a number of significant discoveries. Of particular importance is some additional evidence recently obtained on the date of the origin of this colony, its outward appearance, culture, and historical development, as well as its relations with the barbarians of the hinterland.[1] Yet the most important result of the excavations of recent years is the discovery of the sacred precinct at the settlement – the *temenos* with the remains of the Temple of Aphrodite from the second half of the 6th and beginning of the 5th century BC.[2] It is possible that this fact may tip the balance, at least for now, in favour of the hypothesis about the *polis* status of Borysthenes.

Nevertheless, it must be acknowledged that the very important question about the causes of and motivation behind the appearance of the first group of colonists in this remote region of the Greek *oikoumene* – i.e. the question about the basic function of early Borysthenes – has remained extremely controversial. In this respect, almost the entire conceivable spectrum of ideas and concepts co-exists comfortably in modern historiography. The question is, indeed, difficult to answer, not only with respect to Borysthenes itself but also to many other Greek settlements in the northern Black Sea area, and although there seem to be answers for the period of the mature and fully developed existence of the Greek cities, the problem becomes extremely complicated when focussing on the period of the formation and initial development of these cities. However, this problem constitutes a key issue, since it involves the elucidation of the essence of Greek colonisation, its goals and its directions.

Despite its importance, the problem of the earliest existence of Greek settlements on the coasts of the northern Pontos is still far from being resolved: a range of possible answers have been put forward. Formerly, it was believed that at the beginning of its existence the Berezan' settlement was a fishing station providing its metropolis with salted fish. However, this supposition was difficult to prove. Indeed, neither finds of fish bones nor weights of stone or other materials from fishing nets may be considered as evidence of such specialisation.

What also proved to be tenacious was the so-called "agrarian" theory, which gave preference to farming as the key economic activity of Borysthenes. But again, the interpretation of the archaeological arguments in favour of this view is somewhat doubtful. True, a number of pits dug in the bedrock, which possibly served for storing grain have been found, but aside from the fact that they may have been used for other purposes as well, including the storage of the grain always kept for home consumption, does not necessarily imply its export.

Finally, mention should be made of the hypothesis about the trade function of the settlement, which has been put forward several times, especially with regard to the mediating role of Borysthenes in the trade relations between Greece and the northern Black Sea region. It may be true that Berezan' functioned as such at some point in time, but not for the entire period of its existence. The cultural layers of the settlement abound in imported pottery, hence the conclusion that this pottery was redistributed from this site to the other northern Black Sea lands. But in fact, very few items of imported fine ware dated to the initial period of the life of Borysthenes have been found. Moreover, the pottery found may not necessarily have been intended for further sale. It is possible, however, that trade actually played a certain role in the existence of Borysthenes.

While some researchers consistently defend the view that there existed a crucial interest among the first settlers from Ionia in the development of their own agricultural production,[3] others with no less enthusiasm point out the necessity of taking into account the colonists' preoccupations with – and aspirations concerning – trade and raw-materials.[4]

We should mention that the current "stalemate" over this problem may, indeed, only be resolved by the appearance of some new historical and archaeological evidence. The hypotheses and concepts, though logical in themselves, are based in each case on some extremely limited and often rather incorrect or dubious information.

Of note in this context are the results of the recent excavations by the Berezan' (Nižnebugskaja) Archaeological Expedition of the State Hermitage Museum. In 1998-2000 the principal efforts of this expedition were directed towards the investigation of one of the earliest occupied areas in ancient Berezan', situated on the eastern (coastal) edge of the settlement (excavation area "Osnovnoj"). Here in what was the most ancient built-up area at the settlement which included 17 relatively primitive "earthen" structures and 47 pits for various purposes, it was possible to uncover what are clearly the remains of two copper-smelting workshops (Building Complexes nos. 6 and 13) dated to the end of the 7th and the first half of the 6th century BC – i.e. to precisely the period of the appearance and formation of the colony.

Fig. 1. Building Complex no. 6 in the excavation area "Osnovnoj". View from west.

Fig. 2. Building Complex no. 6 in the excavation area "Osnovnoj". View from north.

The first of them, Building Complex no. 6, consists of the remains of a relatively large house of dug-out type of quadrangular plan, oriented N-S along its long axis, measuring 4.5-4.75 x 4.0 m, 1.1-1.2 m deep and with an area of about 19 m² (Fig. 1-2). The bedrock walls of this dug-out were even and upright, without any visible traces of destruction, suggesting that the pit was filled fairly quickly after its construction and all apparently on a single occasion.

The floor of this structure presented a layer of dark, severely scorched clay, up to 5 cm thick, and impregnated with numerous tiny pieces of copper and charcoal. Within the layer of the floor, the following parts of internal constructions were found: 14 small conical pits (from 12 to 30 cm in diameter and from 7 to 30 cm deep), which mostly seem to have been for the insertion of supporting posts. The relative arrangement of these pits and the walls of the dug out suggests that its roof was double-pitched. In the same floor layer, in the northern half of the complex, there were two "reservoirs" or "pools" of oval plan, bowl-shaped cross-section, and measuring: a) 2.0 x 1.5 m and 55 cm deep, and b) 1.3 x 1.2 m and 55 cm deep. The bedrock walls and bottoms of these "reservoirs" showed traces of intense burning. Within the limits of the larger "reservoir", near its western edge, were found the remains of the adobe hearth (measuring 85 x 85 cm and 2 cm thick) of a round oven. The remains of another similar hearth were found near the northern wall of the pit, which bore to almost its entire height obvious traces of long-term exposure to fire.

In addition to the material mentioned above, the presence of 6 rather small oval (from 0.25 to 1.0 m long, from 10 to 15 cm wide, and about 10 cm deep) grooves found in the floor in the north-western corner of the building complex is worthy of note. These grooves were probably related in some way to the metal manufacturing process. Also probably related to metal manufacturing was the large cylindrical pit measuring 1.35 m in diameter found in the north-eastern corner of the complex. During the field seasons of 1998-2000 part of this pit was excavated to a depth of 3.6 m.

To conclude the description of the remains of the internal constructions we must mention the presence of a small quantity of seemingly collapsed, undressed limestone blocks lying on the floor near the southern wall of the house. These stones possibly sank from the ancient ground level during the filling of the pit. It is noteworthy that the character of the fill differed significantly from the fills of other "earthen" structures in this area of the Berezan' settlement. Traceable down the entire depth of the pit and right down to its adobe floor, was a dark, mixed ash-and-clay layer rich in fine pieces of charcoal and hardened drops and small shapeless ingots of copper weighing up to 125 g.

The excavation of the fill yielded material dated between the end of the 7th and the second quarter of the 6th century BC without any finds from later periods. The items found included 1759 fragments of pottery (mostly walls of amphorae) and 344 animal bones. It should be noted that, in contrast to the amphorae, all other categories of wheel-made pottery constituted a rather small group (about 15% of the total). The most numerous of these were the painted East Ionic pottery including some fragments of high quality, in particular a *dinos* with a representation of grazing wild goats dated as early as the end of the 7th or the very beginning of the 6th century BC. The

Fig. 3. Building Complex no. 13 in the excavation area "Osnovnoj".

most notable items found within the limits of the dug-out and which may in some way have been connected with its main function are, however, the 272 hardened splashes and ingots of copper with a total weight of 2.5 kg, and 187 pieces of various parts of ovens including one severely scorched tubular nozzle.

An emission analysis of the ingots from this complex, carried out in the Laboratory of Chemical Technology, IHMC RAS (analyst A.N. Egor'kov), showed that the basic constituent is copper with the following additions: Sn-0.1%, Pb-0.8%, Zn-0%, Bi-0%, Sb-0.3%, As-1.8%, Ag-0.09%, Ni-0.02%, Fe-0.06%, and Mn-0%. According to these data, the metal of the ingots may be described as arsenical bronze, though certain features (the ratio As:Sb in particular) suggest that the presence of arsenic may have been determined by the natural character of the ore.

The second building complex (no. 13) was situated 12 metres to the west of no. 6 described above (Fig. 3). Unfortunately, only the eastern half of the complex was preserved, since the western section of the structure had been completely destroyed, to be replaced by several, stratigraphically later pit-houses (nos. 10, 14, and 16).

Judging by the preserved remains, this complex was a house of dug-out type of either oval or nearly quadrangular plan with rounded corners. The dimensions of the preserved area are: 3.5 x 2.3 m, depth 65 cm – an area of over 10.0 m^2. The bedrock walls of the dug-out are somewhat indistinct indicating that the pit had been filled over a relatively long period rather than all at once.

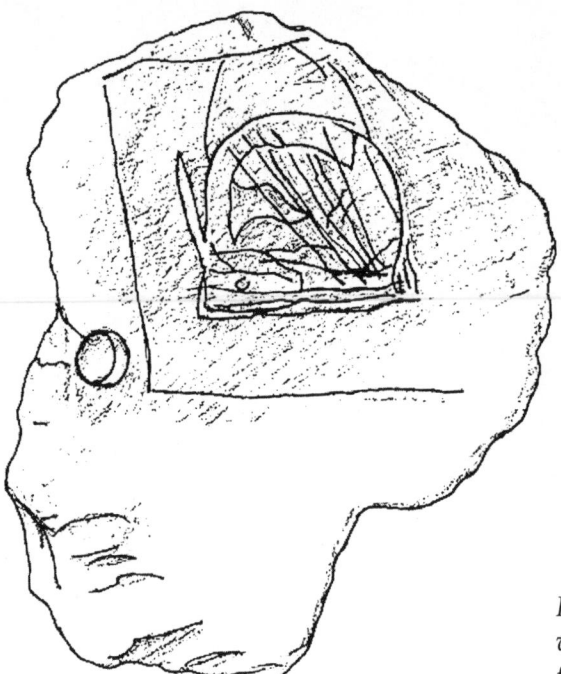

Fig. 4. Basalt net weight with representation of a ship from pit no. 47.

The floor consists of a layer of dark, severely burnt clay, up to 3 cm thick. On the floor it was possible to identify the following details of the inner constructions: 14 small rounded conical pits (from 20 to 35 cm in diameter and from 7 to 39 cm deep) for the insertion of the posts supporting the roof or some other internal construction. At present, however, we are not able to reconstruct reliably the type of roof of the complex. Also on the floor, in the north-eastern quarter of the house, were found two "pools" or "reservoirs" of oval plan and bowl-shaped vertical cross-section with the following dimensions: a) 1.35 x 1.0 m and 25 cm deep, and b) about 75 x 70 cm and 22 cm deep. The bedrock walls and bottoms of the "pools" were severely scorched.

Finally, near the eastern edge of the complex, in its central section, were found the remains of a vaulted adobe oven, with a diameter slightly over 80 cm, used over a long period of time. It is remarkable that the hearth of this oven consisted of a number of successively plastered clay layers with a total thickness of about 15 cm. In addition, fairly obvious traces of the hearth of another oven or an open fireplace measuring 95 x 73 cm were identified from a dense, nearly quadrangular accumulation of fired pieces of clay lying on the floor 50 cm from the southern edge of the house.

The excavation of the amorphous clay-and-ash fill of the dug-out yielded few but nevertheless fairly indicative items of the end of the 7th and first half of the 6th century BC (any significant finds dated to later periods being absent) including 876 fragments of pottery (mostly amphora walls) and 89 animal bones. In addition to the amphorae, the types of the wheel-made pottery included some fragments of East-Ionic *kylikes* of the late 7th century BC decorated with hatched rhomboids and a frieze with birds.

Especially noteworthy among the other substantial finds is an oval copper ingot weighing 3.5 kg, evidently intended for trade. The ingot was found on the floor of the complex, 5 cm to the west of the vaulted oven, which was close to the eastern edge of the structure.

The results of an emission analysis of this ingot, conducted by A.N. Egor'kov in the Laboratory of Archaeological Technology of IHMC, RAS, proved to be very similar to those of the metal from pit-house no. 6, namely: Cu-basis, Sn-0%, Pb-0.03%, Zn-0%, Bi-0%, Sb-0%, As-0.02%, Ni-0.04%, Co-0.03%, Fe-0.03%, and Mn-0.02%. The only difference is the nearly complete absence of arsenic in the composition of the metal, suggesting that in pit-house no. 13, the smelting of extremely pure copper was carried out. This fact, as well as the rather insignificant contents of all the other admixtures in the metal, may enable us to view the complexes under consideration as the remains of some highly specialised production process. This also seems to be suggested by the absence of any complete copper or bronze articles or half-finished products among the substantial finds.

It is also notable that the volumes of the metal production of the copper-smelting workshops of early Borysthenes seem to have considerably exceeded the needs of the inhabitants of the relatively small settlement of the earliest colony in the northern Black Sea region at the end of the 7th and the first half of the 6th century BC. Thus it is quite natural to suppose that the products of the first metal-workers from Berezan' may have been, at least partly, intended for export. The very low percentage of articles made from pure copper (about 4%) recorded throughout the territory of Scythia,[5] leads to the supposition that the main consumer of this metal was the mother city. In this sense, early Borysthenes can be compared to other ancient raw-material colonies in the Mediterranean area such as the settlement on Pithekoussai, al-Mina, Sukas, and Gela.[6] Finally, it is very remarkable that, judging from the presence of small admixtures of cobalt (0.03-0.05%) and nickel (0.02-0.04%) in all the investigated samples of Berezan' copper, the raw material may have been supplied from the south-western regions of the Black Sea littoral, i.e. from the area of the Carpathian-Danube basin.[7] We should also note that all the other observations made during the excavation of the copper-smelting workshops of early Borysthenes (in particular, the results of the analysis of the typological composition of the assemblage of handmade pottery and the major types of earthen constructions) seem to corroborate this conclusion.

Notes

1.	See, e.g., Vinogradov, Domanskij & Marčenko 1990, 121-139; Nazarov 1997a, 4-21; Solovyov 1999.
2.	Nazarov 1997b, 27-29.
3.	See, e.g., Košelenko & Kuznecov 1992, 10-12.
4.	See, e.g., Kopejkina 1979, 107-109; Marčenko 1980, 136; Vinogradov 1989, 53-57; Solovyov 1999, 129.
5.	Ol'govskij 2001, 94.
6.	See, e.g., Blavatskij, Košelenko & Kruglikova 1979, 12-13.
7.	See, e.g., Ol'govskij 1986, 90; Smekalova & Djukov 2001, 107.

Bibliography

Blavatskij, V.D., G.A. Košelenko & I.T. Kruglikova 1979. Polis i migracija grekov, in: *Problemy grečeskoj kolonizacii Severnogo i Vostočnogo Pričernomor'ja*. Tbilisi, 7-29.

Kopejkina, L.V. 1979. Osobennosti razvitija Berezanskogo poselenija v svjazi s chodom kolonizacii Nižnego Pobuž'ja, in: *Problemy grečeskoj kolonizacii Severnogo i Vostočnogo Pričernomor'ja*. Tbilisi, 106-113.

Košelenko, G.A. & V.D. Kuznecov 1992. Grečeskaja kolonizacija Bospora (v svjazi s nekotorymi obščimi problemami kolonizacii), in: *Očerki archeologii i istorii Bospora*. Moskva, 6-28.

Marčenko, K.K. 1980. Model' grečeskoj kolonizacii Nižnego Pobuž'ja, *VDI* 1, 131-143.

Nazarov, V.V. 1997a. Archäologische Untersuchungen auf Berezan', in: *Zur graeco-skytischen Kunst. Archäologisches Kolloquium Münster 24.-26. November 1995*. Münster, 4-21.

Nazarov, V.V. 1997b. Temenos Berezanskogo poselenija, in: *Materialy I-II Mikolajivs'koi kraeznavčoi konferencii "Istorija, etnografija, kul'tura. Novi doslidžennja"* 1. Mikolaiv, 27-29.

Ol'govskij, S.Ja. 1986. Metall litych monet Nižnego Pobuž'ja, in: *Ol'vija i ee okruga*. Kiev, 89-105.

Ol'govskij, S.Ja. 2001. Original'nye splavy cvetnych metallov v Severnom Pričernomor'e archaičeskogo vremeni, in: *Ol'vija ta antyčnyj svit*. Kyiv.

Smekalova, T.N. & Ju.L. Djukov 2001. *Monetnye splavy gosudarstv Pričernomor'ja. Bospor, Ol'vija, Tira*. St Peterburg.

Solovyov, S.L. 1999. *Ancient Berezan*. Leiden-Boston-Köln.

Vinogradov, Ju.G. 1989. *Političeskaja istorija Ol'vijskogo polisa VII-I vv. do n.e.* Moskva.

Vinogradov, I., I. Domanskij & K. Marčenko 1990. Sources écrites et archéologiques du Pont Nord-Ouest. Analyse comparative, in: *Le Pont-Euxin vu par les Grecs. Sources écrites et archéologie. Symposium de Vani (Colchide), septembre - octobre 1987*. Besançon, 121-139.

Archaic Buildings of Porthmion

Marina Ju. Vachtina

The identification of peculiarities in the layout of Greek cities and the investigation of their dwelling areas are among the most important and interesting objectives in the studies concerned with the archaeology of the Classical period in the Black Sea region. Of exceptional significance are the investigations of the most ancient structures in the various Greek settlements, which allow us to reconstruct the appearance they would have presented immediately after their construction, and the identification of the most important aspects of the development of ancient house-building. It is equally fascinating to uncover traces of various historical events as they are reflected in the archaeological evidence.

Like many other Classical archaeologists from St Petersburg, who have been fortunate enough to participate in the Tarkhankut Expedition of the Leningrad Division of the Archaeological Institute of the USSR Academy of Science (renamed the Institute of the History of Material Culture [IHMC] of the Russian Academy of Sciences, or IIMK RAN), I acquired much useful experience from this expedition, which further proved to be of great help in my own field studies. For many years this expedition carried out excavations at the settlement and necropolis of Panskoe I in the distant chora of Chersonesos. Alexander N. Ščeglov – one of the best field archaeologists in Russia – who directed the above-mentioned large-scale excavations, expended great efforts on sharing his vast knowledge with us students and postgraduates. Throughout the years, I have often gratefully recalled A.N. Ščeglov's "school" of archaeology.

My independent studies are connected with the excavations of the Greek city of Porthmion – one of the so-called "smaller" towns of the European Bosporos, and this paper is devoted to some of the results of this work.

Traditionally, Porthmion is identified with the remains of the ancient town situated north-east of the modern city of Kerch, on an elevated, rocky plateau near the shores of the Straits of Kerch (Fig. 1) on the outskirts of what is now the village of Žukovka.[1] Information about a settlement called Porthmion is provided by ancient authors (Ps.-Arr., *Peripl.P.Eux.* 69, 70, 117; Hdn., *Pr.Cath.* 3,1.289.36; Steph. Byz., s.v. Πορθμία καὶ Πορθμίον, who describe it as a kome on the European side of the Kimmerian Bosporos not far from Maiotis. That the name is derived from the Greek πορθμός (crossing) is fairly obvious and has never been questioned. Indeed, both written and

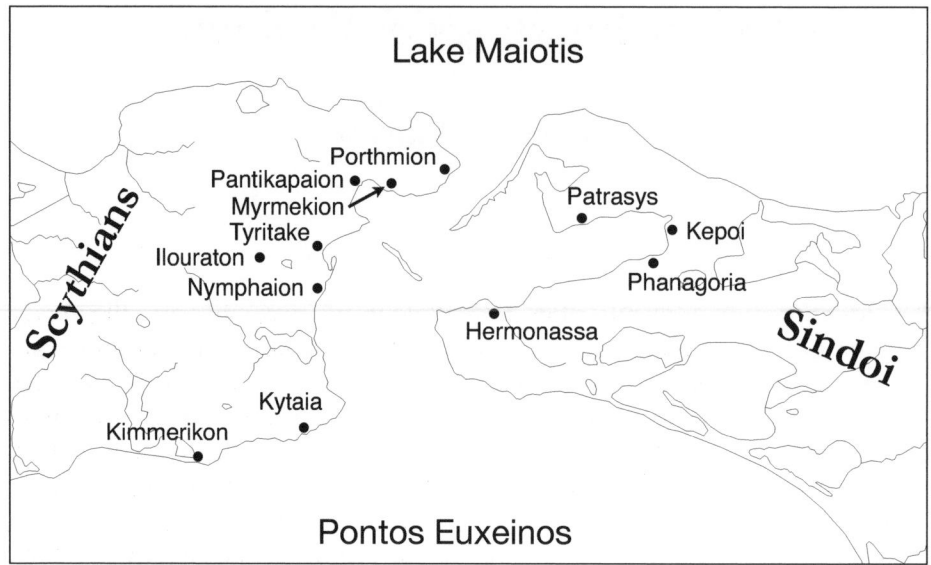

Fig. 1. The Kimmerian Bosporos.

archaeological sources suggest that one of the traditional routes across the Straits of Kerch linking the Kuban Region with the Crimea ran close to the city.[2]

As mentioned above, Porthmion was situated on a plateau. The dimensions of this plateau covering 0.7 ha actually determined the size of the Greek settlement. All the building remains were found within its limits. From 1953 to 1992, the excavations at this site were carried out by the Bosporan Archaeological Expedition of LOIA (now IHMC/IIMK) RAS. Quite a number of important discoveries are associated with the name of E.G. Kastanajan, who directed the excavations from 1986.[3] Under her guidance, the remains of Porthmion's fortifications of the Late Hellenistic period have been uncovered, the layout of the areas of habitation has been revealed, and various materials enabling us to form an idea of the economic activities of the settlers have been studied. As a result of this work, we know about the life of this small Bosporan fortress from the second half of the 3rd century to the middle of the 1st century BC. At present, Porthmion is the best studied Late Hellenistic fortified town within the territory of the European Bosporos.

However, a fortified Greek settlement existed there much earlier. The proximity to the traditional routes across the Kimmerian Bosporos, which gave certain economic advantages but at the same time presented a source of potential dangers, must have predetermined the fairly early appearance of Greek colonists here. At present, a considerable amount of evidence has been gathered concerning the initial stage of the occupation of Porthmion, suggesting that originally the town was designed and founded as a small fortress.

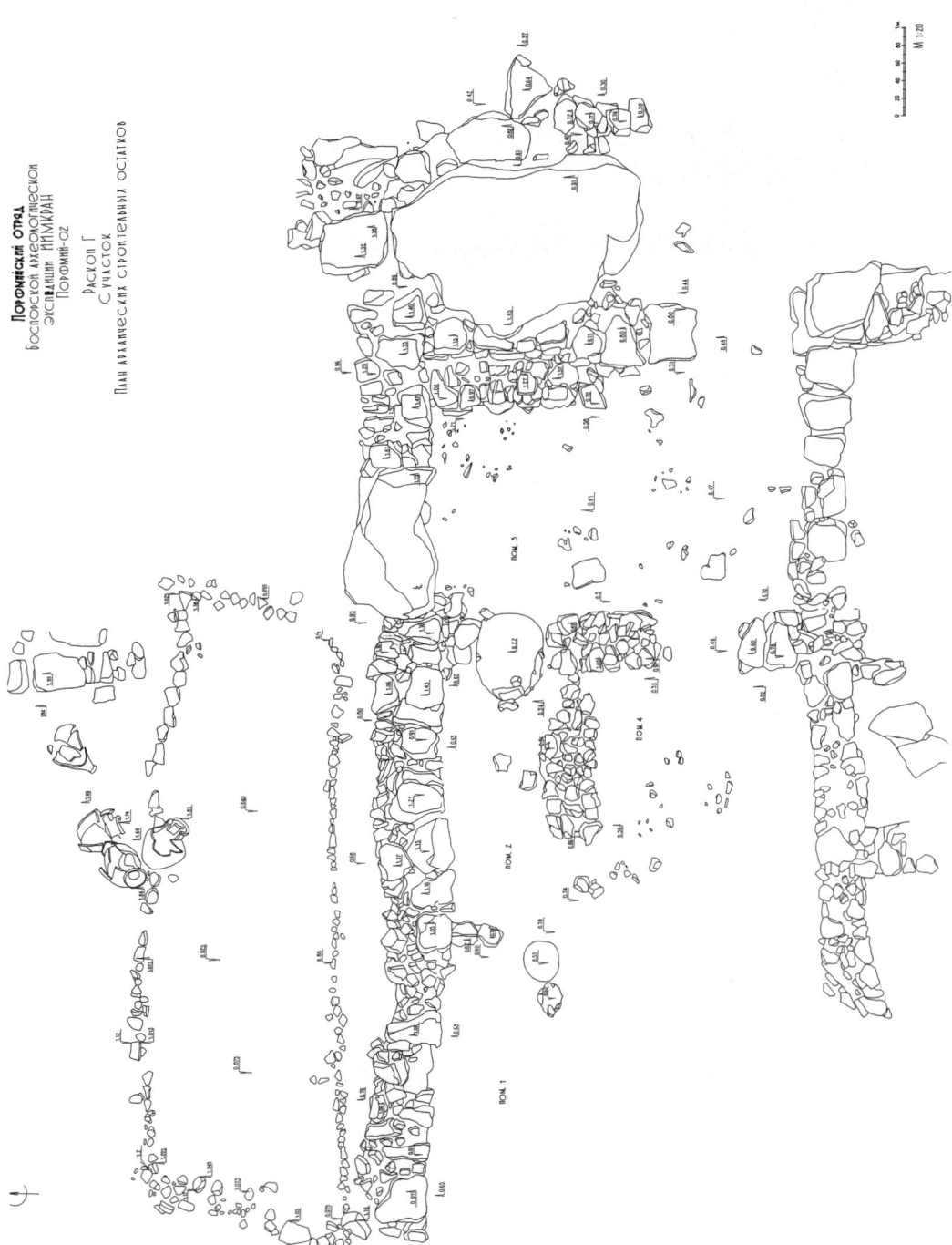

Fig. 2. Plan of the excavated dwelling complex.

Fig. 3. Fragment of the masonry of the socle of the eastern defensive wall. View from E.

The building remains dated to the second half of the 6th to the first third of the 5th century BC were uncovered in the eastern and south-eastern part of the site within an area of over 400 m². Here, traces of the Archaic fortifications were revealed. These are the oldest not only at this site, but also among the earliest discovered on the Kimmerian Bosporos and comparable in terms of their age and the construction technique only with the defensive walls of Myrmekion.[4]

Fig. 4. The "Bastion" in the south-eastern area of the defensive wall. View from NE.

Figs. 5-6. 5) Remains of the Archaic drainage system. View from N. 6) The bed of the drain.

In 1986, the foundation of the eastern Archaic defensive wall of Porthmion (Fig. 3) was discovered.[5] This wall was constructed on a NE-SW axis, along the natural slope of the plateau on which the town was situated. This is the place where the terrain slopes the least, thus presenting the most vulnerable spot during an attack. The foundation of the uncovered wall was constructed of a row of large limestone blocks (1-1.2 m long and 0.5-0.6 m wide). On the lower course of masonry, smaller stones were laid, the space between the latter being filled with small pieces of rubble. The maximum height of the preserved socle of the wall came to 1.2 m with a length of 12.8 m and a thickness of 1.0-1.1 m. Judging by the debris preserved, the upper part of the wall was constructed of mud-brick. Its southern end was built against the natural outcrop of rock, and here the structure formed a zigzag line in plan resembling a bastion (Fig. 4). On the inside of the wall, there was a drainage gutter (Figs. 5-6) by means of which the sewage was removed by the natural slope outside the confines of the town's area. The remains of this 0.4 m deep gutter are preserved to the length of 10 m. The mouth of the drain, through which the water flowed straight out beyond the outer face of the Archaic defensive wall, was discovered in the southern section of this wall. During the subsequent building period the drain ceased to function and its mouth was blocked with stones.

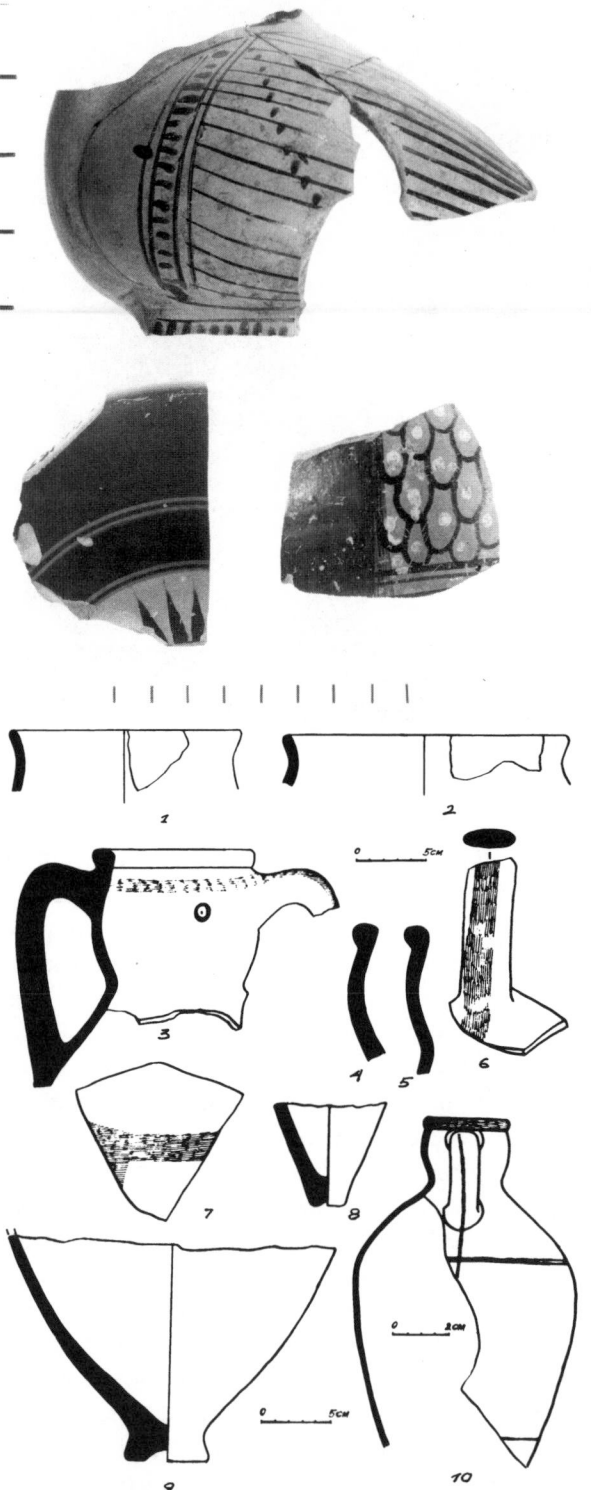

Figs. 7-8. 7) Top. Fragment of a figured bird-shaped vessel from the layer following the direction of the eastern Archaic defensive wall. 8) Left. Fragments of painted tableware of the second half of the 6th century BC from the layer following the direction of the Archaic defensive wall: 1) lid of an Attic black-figured lekanis; *2) wall of an amphora from Klazomenai with a "fish-scale" decoration.*

Fig. 9. Finds from the horizon of destruction following the direction of the eastern Archaic defensive wall: 1-2) fragments of handmade pottery; 3-10) fragments of Greek amphorae: 3-5, 10) from Chios; 6, 7, 9) from Klazomenai; 8) from an Aeolian centre.

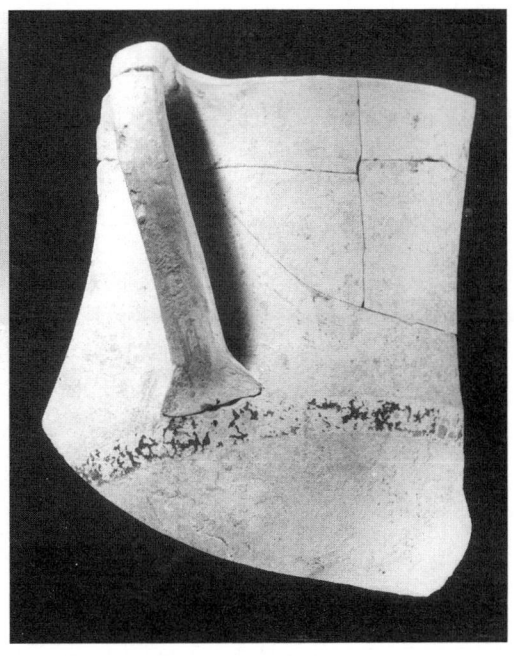

Figs. 10-11. 10) Above. Fragment of an Attic kylix *decorated with palmettes from the upper layer of the fill of the drainage. 11) Right. Fragment of a Chian beaker from the lower layer of the fill of the drainage.*

The southern line of the defences of Porthmion is much more poorly preserved although it is clearly identifiable across the entire excavated area (approximately 20 m long). In this section of the settlement, the fortifications follow the southern boundary of the plateau, which here has a steep incline. In the construction, huge natural blocks of limestone were used. These were sometimes slightly dressed with the interstices between them filled with small stones. In other places, masonry walls constructed of smaller stones continued the natural outcrops of limestone. A fragment of the town's early defensive wall also came to light during the excavation of a residential area of the Late Hellenistic period on the south-western side of the site. Here part of the Archaic wall was incorporated into a house of the late Hellenistic period. Apparently most of the early fortifications in the western part of Porthmion had been destroyed earlier.

The fortifications described above were related to the initial period of the city's existence. On the basis of the archaeological materials found on top of the line of the defensive walls (Figs. 7-9), and in the stones filling the drain (Figs. 10-11), these structures are datable to the second half of the 6th century BC. Towards the end of the 6th century BC, Porthmion must have suffered a catastrophe since traces of fire have been recorded over the entire area where Archaic remains have been uncovered. The calcined layer directly above the bedrock has a thickness of 3 cm, and the finds in it, including accumulations of crushed amphorae (Fig. 12), bore indications of a severe fire. Also recovered from this layer of destruction was a base fragment of an Attic

*Fig. 12. Fragmentary amphora from Klazomenai from the horizon of the fire fol-
lowing the direction of the eastern Archaic defensive wall.*

*Fig. 13. Fragment of the base of an Attic black-glazed bowl with a graffito of the
beginning of the 5th century BC.*

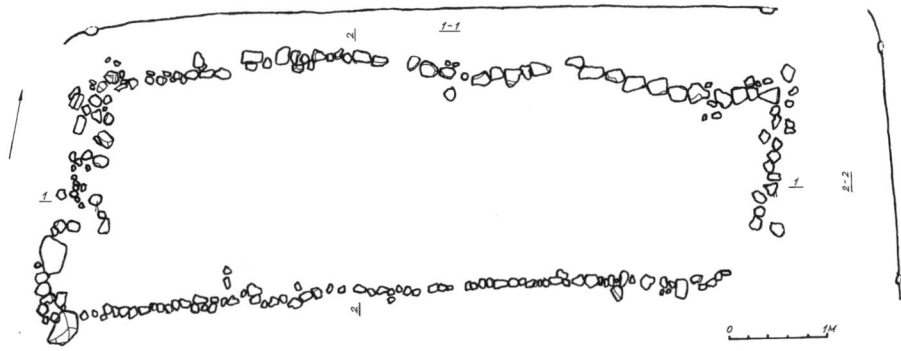

Fig. 14. Remains of the foundation of a dwelling complex of the second half of the 6th century BC within the context of a later building.

black-glazed bowl (Fig. 13) of the early fifth century BC with the graffito [- - -]Ξ ΠΑΡΘΕΝΩ[- - -].[6] In the area adjacent to the eastern defensive wall outside the town-site, small fragments of a human skull were found in the same stratigraphic horizon. The dwellings of the first colonists of Porthmion, who created the earliest defensive system at the settlement, have long remained undiscovered. All of the dwellings uncovered here so far were all dated later, to the late Archaic period. A fairly large plot built up with late Archaic houses was excavated in the eastern part of the settlement adjacent to the remains of the earliest defensive wall. Here, on the eastern slope of the rocky plateau, traces of a "terraced" building were uncovered. It is noteworthy however, that between the time of the erection of the earliest fortifications and that of the houses found close by there is a chronological gap, since the latter houses are dated not earlier than the end of the 6th or first third of the 5th century BC.

It would be natural to suppose, that the houses of the first colonists were so-called dug-outs as these are a local peculiarity of the Archaic Greek settlements in the northern Black Sea region.[7] Structures of such a type are known throughout the Bosporos,[8] for example in Pantikapaion[9] and in neighbouring Myrmekion.[10] However, all our attempts to identify dwellings of the dug-out type during the excavations in Porthmion have proved unsuccessful.

Meanwhile, continued excavation resulted recently in the discovery of the remains of a peculiar structure, built above ground and dated to the second half of the 6th century BC. In 2002, in the north-eastern part of the hill-fort, the remains of a room built in another technique and older than those previously known were uncovered. This find consists of the remains of a foundation cut into the bedrock of a building constructed of quite small

Fig. 15. Broken proto-Thasian amphorae related to the destruction of the dwelling complex.

pieces of limestone (the length of the largest not exceeding 20 cm) laid in one row. The width of the walls was determined by the size of these stones and came to 10-20 cm. This foundation made up a nearly rectangular room 6.9 x 2.2 m (northern wall: 6.72 m, southern: 7 m, eastern: 1.9 m, western: 2.4 m) oriented east-west (Fig. 14). Traces of adobe on the surface of the excavated area immediately suggested that once there were mud-brick walls constructed upon the lower stone foundation. The southern wall of the complex lies in close proximity (at the distance of 30-40 cm) to the northern wall of a large building of a later period, which was probably constructed according to the layout of the earlier structures. The period of occupation of the early complex under consideration can be dated to the second half of the 6th century BC. This date is particularly suggested by the remains of several so-called proto-Thasian amphorae found lying *in situ* on the calcined floor of the room (Figs. 15-17). Judging by the appearance of the finds, the building was destroyed in a fire which took place at the very end of the 6th century.

Thus the building remains uncovered in 2002 probably represent the ruins of the oldest habitation on the site contemporary with the Archaic defensive structures. Possibly the presence of the bedrock under a thin layer of soil made construction of dwellings of the dug-out type difficult. Therefore, the houses of the first colonists of Porthmion may from the very beginning have been built above ground with mud-brick walls on a foundation of small stones only slightly cutting into the bedrock. The ground plan

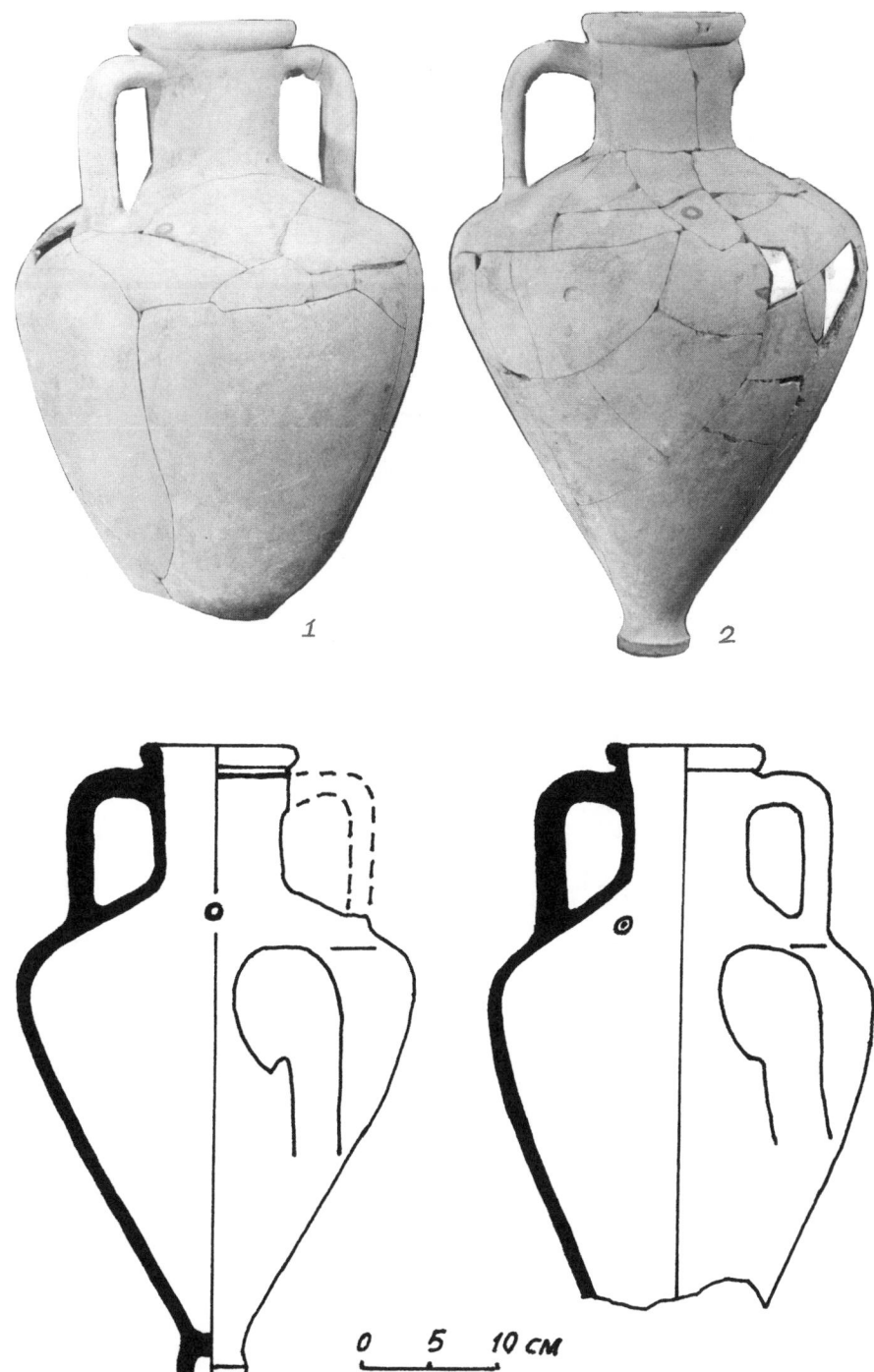

Figs. 16-17. Proto-Thasian amphorae from the destruction layer (drawings by S.Ju. Monachov).

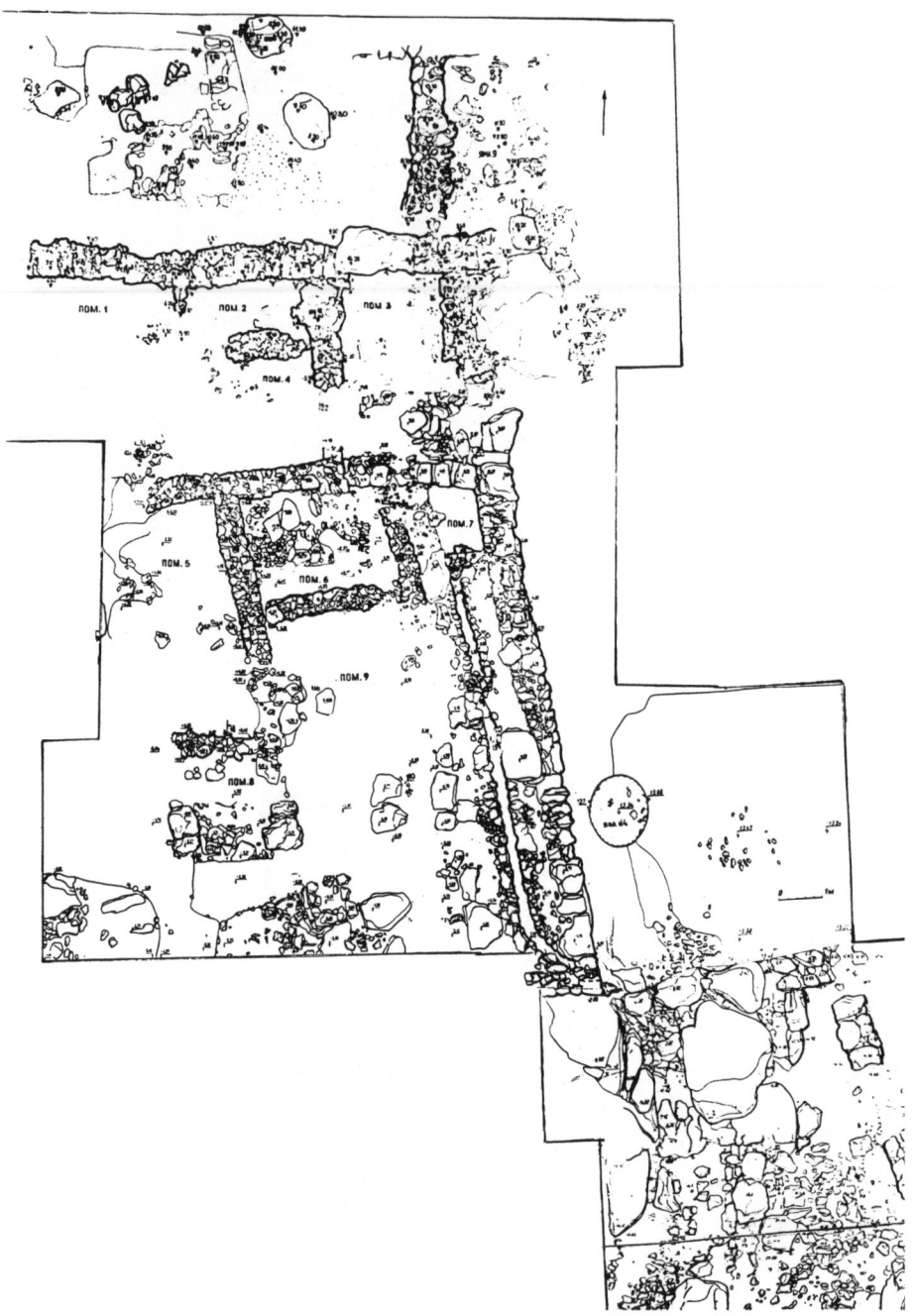

Fig. 18. Plan of the buildings of the late Archaic period to the west of the Archaic
defensive wall. The socle of the defensive wall and the remains of a large dwelling
complex (excavations of 1986-1988).

Fig. 19. Remains of the rooms of a large dwelling complex of the late Archaic period. View from S.

Fig. 20. Remains of the rooms of the large surface building complex of the late Archaic period (view from S). A room with a preserved fragment of stone pavement.

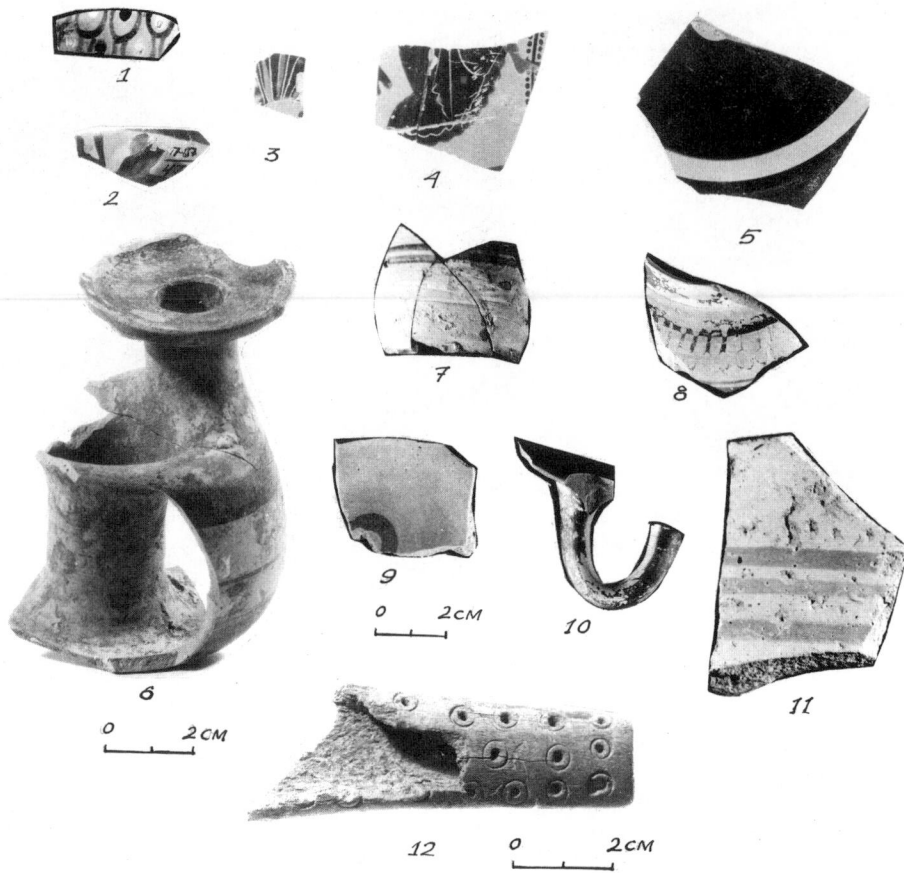

Fig. 21. Finds from the rooms: 1) fragment of the wall of an amphora from
Klazomenai with fish-scale decoration; 2-5) fragments of Attic black-figured vessels; 6-8, 11) fragments of East-Greek closed vessels; 9-10) fragments of Ionian
bowls; 12) fragment of a bone handle of a knife with circle decoration.

of the uncovered structure corresponded well with the eastern Archaic
defensive wall. We can probably expect to discover further remains of buildings of the same type.

This type of building is unique in the Bosporos during the Archaic period. Parallels may be found in Myrmekion situated not far from Porthmion.
According to information kindly offered by Ju.A. Vinogradov, who directed
the excavations there, fragments were found of single-rowed masonry constructed of fairly small stones that resemble the wall remains of the above-
mentioned complex in Porthmion. The structures in Myrmekion were likewise located in the immediate vicinity of the fragmentarily preserved
Archaic defensive wall.

After this complex of the second half of the 6th century BC had been destroyed by fire, a new phase of house-building began in Porthmion. New buildings constructed in the technique noted from other Bosporan settlements appeared. In the late 6th century BC, a large dwelling complex built above ground was added to the inner face of the eastern defensive wall (Fig. 18). This complex excavated within an area of 16 x 10 m consists of at least nine fairly small rooms. The foundations of the walls consisted of rows of small pieces of limestone with the interstices between the rows being filled with clay and gravel (Fig. 19). The upper parts of the walls were probably built of mud-brick. In some of the rooms, the masonry was preserved to a height of 50-70 cm. The floor of one room (no. 2) was paved with limestone slabs 50-60 cm in length and with fragments of pottery (Fig. 20). The finds in the rooms are dated to the last quarter of the 6th to the first third of the 5th century BC (Fig. 21). This building was constructed upon a calcined layer related to an earlier catastrophe at the site, and it was in turn covered over with a burnt layer indicating the occurrence of another, later, devastation. The fire which destroyed the complex can be dated to the end of the first third of the 5th century BC. Similar destruction layers have been recorded at many other settlements of the European Bosporos.

Conclusions

On the basis of the building remains uncovered in the large area on the eastern side of the hill-fort, we can distinguish two major stages in the development of Porthmion:

(1) From the very beginning of its existence the settlement was fortified. The defensive walls at the edges of the natural plateau occupied by the settlement were erected during the second half of the 6th century BC by the first Greek settlers, who used the natural slope in the construction of these walls.

The construction of the eastern defensive wall also included a drainage system by which the sewage flowed out from the confines of the settlement through a hole in the south-eastern section of the wall.

The closest parallel to the Archaic fortifications of Porthmion (both in terms of building technique and of the time of construction) is represented by the remains of the defensive walls discovered in Myrmekion. The fact that the earliest Greek fortifications reported in the European Bosporos are found at the sites closest to the traditional routes across the Kimmerian Bosporos can hardly be a coincidence.

The dwellings of the first Greek settlers in Porthmion were apparently not of the dug-out type, none of which have yet been discovered, but resembled rather the recently excavated complex in the north-eastern part of the hill-fort. Judging by the finds, this complex was contemporary with the fortifications uncovered nearby. This unusual type of complex of the second half of the 6th century BC should encourage a re-evaluation of the validity of the established concepts about the character of the dwellings on the northern coasts of the Black Sea. It is generally accepted that initially, the dwellings of the first Greek colonists in the northern Black Sea region were so-called dug-outs, while some time later the transition to dwellings built above ground took place. Such a development has been recorded from excavations at quite a number of settlements in the region. Nevertheless, it is quite possible that in future, a greater variety of dwellings of the Archaic period will be discovered. Furthermore, it cannot be ruled out either that a more careful examination of the earliest strata at the Greek settlements will reveal a variety of building types contemporary with the dug-outs.

The erection of the defensive walls in Porthmion was not a mere tribute to caution, but was rather dictated by the harsh realities of life. Towards the very end of the 6th century BC, the settlement was subject to a fairly large-scale catastrophe, during which the dwellings of the settlers were destroyed by fire. It is still impossible to reconstruct what causes lay behind the destruction of the settlement. We can note however, that a similar event took place at Myrmekion, where traces of fire dated to the same period have also been recorded.

(2) Immediately after the catastrophe mentioned above, Porthmion was quickly rebuilt. The foundations of various walls of the subsequent building period were constructed right on top of the burned layer. During this period, a large complex consisting of several rooms was built on terraces on the natural eastern slope of the plateau occupied by the town. These rooms were immediately adjacent to the eastern defensive wall.

In the first third of the 5th century BC this complex was in its turn also destroyed by fire, and this period is justly considered as one of destabilisation and upheaval both in Bosporos[11] and throughout the entire northern Black Sea region.[12] Hence, analogies to the fire in Porthmion can easily be found among the evidence from other Bosporan centres struggling to survive.[13]

Such are, in my opinion, the oldest buildings in Porthmion – the small Greek fortress founded not far from the narrowest part of the Straits of Kerch. Their construction and catastrophic destruction are excellent illustrations of the complicated situation that existed in the region of the Kimmerian Bosporos during the Archaic period. This situation was fairly precarious but it nevertheless allowed the foundation of a permanent settlement at Porthmion. Evidently, the site for the city was chosen for its natural advantages.

Life at the settlement finally ceased around the middle of the 1st century BC, when the fortress was abandoned never to be restored again. Having survived all the calamities of the preceding periods, the inhabitants of the city deserted it after the Mithridatic wars, during an epoch of prolonged crisis.

Notes

1.   Veselov 1952, 227-237; Šurgaja 1984, 69-71; Tsetskhladze 1997, 62.
2.   Vachtina, Vinogradov & Rogov 1980.
3.   Kastanajan 1970; 1971; 1972; 1975; 1983; Kastanajan & Vachtina 1987.
4.   Vinogradov 1999, fig. 3.1-2; Vachtina & Vinogradov 2001.
5.   The field photographing was carried out by S.V. Jabločkin.
6.   Tochtas'ev 1993.
7.   Vinogradov & Rogov 1997.
8.   Butjagin 2001, 36-41.
9.   Tolstikov 1992, 59-62.
10. Vinogradov 1991, 11-19.
11. Vinogradov 2002, 15-16.
12. Vinogradov & Marčenko 1991, 149-151; Alekseev 1992, 7, 118-119.
13. Tolstikov 2001, 45-48.

Bibliography

Alekseev, A.Ju. 1992. *Skifskaja chronika*. St Peterburg.

Butjagin, A.M. 2001. Zemljanočnoe stroitel'stvo na archaičeskom Bospore (genezis i razvitie), in: Zuev et al. (eds.), 36-41.

Kastanajan, E.G. & M.Ju. Vachtina 1987. Issledovanija Porfmija. Nekotorye itogi i perspektivy, in: V.P. Šilov (ed.) *Zadači sovetskoj archeologii v svete rešenij 27 s'ezda KPSS. Tezisy dokladov Vsesojuznoj konferencii (Suzdal', 1987 g.).* Moskva, 78-79.

Kastanajan, E.G. 1970. Terrakoty iz Porfmija, in: M.M. Kobylina (ed.), *Terrakoty Severnogo Pričernomor'ja (SAI G 1-11).* Moskva, 118-119.

Kastanajan, E.G. 1971. Raskopki Porfmija, in: *Archeologičeskie issledovanija na Ukraine* 3. Kiev, 187-191.

Kastanajan, E.G. 1972. Raskopki Porfmija v 1968 g., *KSIA* 130, 77-82.

Kastanajan, E.G. 1975. Itogi raskopok Porfmija ellinističeskoj epochi, in: *Novejšie otkrytija sovetskich archeologov* 2. Kiev, 103-104

Kastanajan, E.G. 1983. Porfmij, *Centre d'archéologie Mediterranéenne de l'Academie Polonaise des Sciences. Etudes et Travaux* 13, 162-168.

Kastanajan, E.G. 1987. Nadgrobnaja nadpis' iz Porfmija, *VDI* 2, 85-87.

Košelenko, G.A. et al. (eds.) 1984. *Antičnye gosudarstva Severnogo Pričerno-mor'ja.* Moskva.

Šurgaja, I.G. 1984. Porfmij, in: Košelenko et al. (eds.) 1984, 69-70.

Tochtas'ev, S.R. 1993. Posvjatitelnoe graffito iz Porfmija, in: *Drevnee Pričernomor'e. Kratkie soobščenija Odesskogo Archeologičeskogo obščestva.* Odessa, 74-75.

Tolstikov, V.P. 1992. Pantikapej – stolica Bospora. *Očerki archeologii i istorii Bospora.* Moskva.

Tolstikov, V.P. 2001. Archeologičeskie otkrytija na akropole Pantikapeja i problema bosporo-skifskich otnošenij v 6-5 vv. do n.e., in: *Bosporskij fenomen. Kolonizacija regiona. Stanovlenie polisov. Vozniknovenie gosudarst-va.* St Peterburg, 45-57.

Tsetskhladze, G.R. 1997. A Survey of the Major Urban Settlements in the Kimmerian Bosporos (with the Discussion of their Status as Poleis), in: Th.H. Nielsen (ed.), *Yet more studies in the Greek Polis.* Stuttgart 1997, 39-81.

Vachtina, M.Ju. & Ju.A. Vinogradov 2001. Ešče raz o rannej fortifikacii Bospora Kimmerijskogo, in: Zuev et al. (eds.) 2001, 41-45.

Vachtina, M.Ju., Vinogradov, Ju.A. & E.Ja. Rogov 1980. Ob odnom iz maršru-tov voennych pochodov i sezonnych migracij kočevych skifov, *VDI* 4, 155-161.

Veselov, V.V. 1952 Drevnie gorodišča v rajone Sipjagino (k voprosu o mestopoloženii Parfenija i Porfmija), *Archeologia i istorija Bospora* 1. Simferopol', 227-237.

Vinogradov, Ju.A. & E.Ja. Rogov 1997. Nekotorye osobennosti i zakonomer-nosti stanovlenija i razvitija grečeskich gosudarstv v Severnom Pričernomor'e, *Stratum + PAV.* St Peterburg-Kišinev, 66-72.

Vinogradov, Ju.A. & K.K. Marčenko 1991. Severnoe Pričernomor'je v skif-skuju epochu. Opyt periodizacii istorii, *SovA* 1, 145-155.

Vinogradov, Ju.A. 1991. Rannie kompleksy Mirmekija, in: *Voprosy istorii i archeologii Bospora.* Voronež-Belgorod, 12-19.

Vinogradov, Ju.A. 1999. Selected Findings from the Myrmekion Acropolis, *Centre d'archéologie Mediterranéenne de l'Academie Polonaise des Sciences. Etudes et Travaux* 18, 280-293.

Vinogradov, Ju.A. 2002. *Greki i varvary na Bospore Kimmerijskom v dorimskuju epochu. Avtoreferat dissertacii.* St Peterburg.

Zuev, V.Ju. et al. (eds.) 2001. *Bosporskij fenomen. Kolonizacija regiona. Stanovlenie polisov. Vozniknovenie gosudarstva.* St Peterburg.

Scythian and Spartan Analogies in Herodotos' Representation: Rites of Initiation and Kinship Groups

George Hinge

This article will focus on certain parallels between the descriptions of Scythians and Spartans in Herodotos. Even though there are fundamental differences between the two ethnic groups' ways of life (nomadism vs. sedentarianism), and they occupy divergent positions in relation to the writers themselves (Barbarian vs. Hellenic), they are both representatives of the other. They are situated more or less in the same position in the scheme of classical ethnography, and certain attitudes considered typical of unspoiled man are attributed indiscriminately to both. Furthermore, Dorian culture allegedly kept certain "primitive" (i.e., "tribal") features in its social organisation that may be related to similar elements in Scythian culture.

To some extent, the Spartans and the Scythians occupy parallel positions in the narrative of Herodotos, too. Both are attacked by the Persian army and both walk victorious off the battlefield. When Dareios demands "earth and water" from the Scythians, they send him enigmatic gifts, a bird, a mouse and a frog as some sort of riddle (Hdt. 4.131-132).[1] Faced with the same claim, the Spartans throw the envoys into a well, and tell them to take their "earth and water" from there (Hdt. 7.133). In fact, the Scythians offer an alliance to the Spartans against Dareios; unfortunately, King Kleomenes spends too much time with the Scythians, so he becomes accustomed to drinking unmixed wine and eventually loses his mind! (Hdt. 6.84).

Referring to the only wonder to see in Scythia, the colossal cauldron at Exampaios (the exact location of which is disputed) erected by the otherwise unknown King Ariantas,[2] Herodotos immediately compares it to another cauldron erected by the Spartan Pausanias at the very mouth of the Black Sea (Hdt. 4.81). In addition to the geographical symmetry, the two cauldrons being at opposite ends of the same sea, it also demonstrates the excesses of the king – Ariantes' excess being six times larger than that of Pausanias (who, it is true, was not truly a king). Yet another example of autocratic manners is the royal burials, which Herodotos depicts similarly in both cultures (Hdt. 4.71-75 and 6.58-60).[3]

However, the two cultures are normally not directly compared. Thus, in the case of the Spartan burials, Herodotos' explicit point of comparison is not the Scythians but rather the Asiatic barbarians such as the Egyptians and Persians (νόμος δὲ τοῖσι Λακεδαιμονίοισι κατὰ τῶν βασιλέων τοὺς θανάτους ἐστὶ ὡυτὸς καὶ τοῖσι βαρβάροισι τοῖσι ἐν τῇ Ἀσίῃ). On two occasions, Herodotos has the two cultures meet each other: Anacharsis says that the Lakedaimonians are the only Greeks who speak reasonably – an obvious pun on the Lakonian brachylogy; yet Herodotos himself doubts the authenticity of this apophthegm (Hdt. 4.77). The other occasion is, as we have seen, when the Scythian envoys cause the madness of King Kleomenes by teaching him their uninhibited drinking habits (Hdt. 6.84). One might consider this story, ascribed by Herodotos to the Scythians themselves, a parallel to the story about the Scythian King Skyles, who, in the eyes of the Scythians, goes mad consorting with the Olbians in Dionysiac rituals. Wine leads to the insanity and dethronement of the ruler in both cases.[4] On the other hand, these analogies are, after all, superficial and should not be pushed too far.

The Scythian myth of origin

More exciting is the fact that Spartan institutions and traditions may also elucidate Herodotos' Scythian version of the myth of origin (Hdt. 4.5-7). We hear about three brothers – Lipoxais, Arpoxais und Kolaxais – the sons of Targitaos, himself the son of Zeus and the river Borysthenes. One day, some golden objects fell from the sky: "a plough and a yoke, a battle-axe and a cup" (ἄροτρόν τε καὶ ζυγόν καὶ σάγαριν καὶ φιάλην). The older brothers could not touch the objects, but the youngest brother succeeded in grabbing the golden gifts and as a result was announced king of the Scythians. The oldest brother, Lipoxais, became the forefather of the Auchatai, the middle brother, Arpoxais, the forefather of the Katiaroi and the Traspies, and the youngest brother, Kolaxais, the forefather of the kings, which were called Paralatai. However, the territory was too large and was therefore divided into three parts, which Kolaxais distributed to his three sons.

Georges Dumézil, who had a keen interest in Scythian and Ossetic cultures, tried of course to analyse this myth according to his celebrated model of the three functions.[5] Even if one does not accept this model as a comprehensive key to all Indo-European ideology in the mother culture(s) and in the single cultures,[6] it is hard not to accept its presence in our case. Hence, he relates the golden cup to the first function of the priest, the golden battle-axe to the second function of the warrior, and, finally, the golden plough and the golden yoke, which are really one thing,[7] to the third function of the provider (similar gifts are presented by the Central Asiatic Scythians in Quintus Curtius 7.8.18-19 *jugum boum et aratrum, sagitta, hasta, patera*).

The names Auchatai, Katiaroi, Traspies and Paralatai do not appear again in Herodotos, and they are almost never mentioned in later ethnographical

literature.[8] There is thus good reason to doubt that they were living eth-
nonyms in the age of Herodotos. Nevertheless, Holzer identifies them with
the *Skythai geōrgoi* ("Farmer Scythians"), the *Skythai nomades* ("Nomad
Scythians"), and the *Skythai basilēioi* ("King Scythians") mentioned in the
geographical excursus (Hdt. 4.17-20).[9] They correspond perfectly to
Dumézil's tripartite scheme. However, as Dumézil has pointed out, the *genē*
of the myths cannot be geographically distinct groups since all tribes had of
course providers and warriors among them,[10] and the regional division is
moreover covered by the second triad represented by the sons of Kolaxais,
which would otherwise be superfluous. At the time of the Persian invasion,
Herodotos speaks about three Scythian realms under the kings Skopasis,
Idanthyrsos and Taxakis (Hdt. 4.120). Apparently, one of the kings, probably
the one who seized the largest realm, was considered the Great King of the
Scythians.[11] Nothing supports that these three kingdoms are identical with
the three economically different kinds of Scythians.

Grantovskij has suggested, also on the basis of Dumézil's system, that the
Katiaroi/Traspies, the Auchatai and the Paralatai were social classes with
qualities corresponding to the three functions – i.e., commoners, priests and
warriors respectively.[12] This is confirmed, he says, by Lucian, *Scythes* 1,
where it is said of Anacharsis that he does not belong to the royal family (τοῦ
βασιλείου γένου) or the ones who wear felt caps (τῶν πιλοφορικῶν), but to the
common people called eight-footed (οἱ ὀκτάποδες) because they possessed
only one carriage and two oxen. It may however be disputed whether the
felt cap is a sign of the priest, as it seems to be a common garment of the
Scythian warriors.[13] Dumézil argues that the Auchatai, the Katiaroi, the
Traspies and the Paralatai cannot be social classes, either, since the Scythians
did not have a specialised priest caste like the Indian Brahmans.[14] The transsexual diviners called *Enarees* (Hdt. 1.105.4, 4.67.2) or *Anarieis* (Hipp. *Aer.*
22.1) are not a separate class, but isolated gifted individuals. Instead,
Herodotos' *genē* are human types existing everywhere, an ideal model that
has nothing to do with real Scythian society. There was certainly a social
diversity in Scythian society, which could be and probably was conceived in
the framework of the tripartite structure.[15] The question is, however, if proper castes existed.

The scholarly literature has suggested quite different etymologies for the
names of the three brothers – *Arpoxais*, *Lipoxais* and *Kolaxais* – and the corresponding four groups: *Auchatai*, *Katiaroi*, *Traspies*, *Paralatai*. The first names
are obviously compounds with the Iranian noun *kšaya-* ("ruler"), but the first
parts of the words are less evident. The roles ascribed by different scholars
to these three ancestors and their descendants differ according to the etymology chosen. Of course, from a methodological point of view it is rather
problematic to suggest etymologies for words that do not have an established denotation, and even more problematic if these etymologies are

exploited as an argument for defining the denotation of the word in question. If one accepts the tripartite structure as a valid model in our case, the
range of denotations is of course limited to three – i.e., provider ~ warrior ~
priest. The key person is Kolaxais, as he becomes the ruler of the others and
eventually the ancestor of three Scythian royal dynasties, so it is necessary to
find an etymology in accordance with this particular role.

Dumézil argues that the Scythian kings belonged to the first function,
that of religion (not to the second one, as Grantovskij assumes). Thus,
Aristotle ascribes the effeminacy disease of the *Enarees* to the Scythian kings
(Arist. *Eth.Nic.* 7.8, 1150ᵇ). The name of the group to which the royal families
belonged, *Paralatai*, seems to be related to Iranian *Paraδāta*, which in the
Avesta is a constant epithet of Haošiiaŋha, the mythic founder of the Iranian
kingdom and the destroyer of demons and sorcerers, and hence, in
Dumézil's analysis, representative of the first function.[16] *Auchatai* is (in spite
of the unusual *g* ~ *ch* alternation) connected with Avestic *aogah-* "force" (i.e.,
"the strong ones"), and identified with the second function of the warrior.
Accordingly, the Katiaroi and the Traspies, both descendants of Lipoxais,
must represent the third function; Dumézil derives *Katiaroi* from **Gau-
čahrya-* ("with cow-meadows") or **Hu-čahrya-* ("with good meadows")
(Avest. *čaŋra-*), and *Traspies* is presumably connected with the Avestic horse
god *Drvāspā*.

Askold I. Ivantchik maintains in a recent article that Kolaxais and the
Paralatai represent the second function of the warrior, whereas Arpoxais and
the Auchatai represent the priests, and Lipoxais and the Katiaroi and
Traspies the providers.[17] This partition of the roles is supported by a more
adequate linguistic and mythological analysis of the names transmitted in
Herodotos: Ivantchik rejects the idea that Haošiiaŋha Paraδāta should be a
representative of the priest caste; in Avestic mythology he is described as the
prototypical warrior. *Auchatai* belongs to *vahu-* ("good"), a word regularly
connected with the function of the priest in the Iranian tradition. As for
Katiaroi and *Traspies*, Ivantchik accepts the etymologies of Dumézil.
Furthermore, the ancestors of the groups have names corresponding with
their assumed functions: *Kola-* = **hwarya-* ("sun") (Scythian **xola-* with the
regular development *ry* > *l*), *Arpo-* = **āpra* > **ārpa* ("water") (Ossetic *arf*) and
Lipo- = **ripa* ("mountain") (Greek *Rhipai*, Vedic [Rgveda 3.5.5] *Ripa*).[18] The
first equation is very convincing, as in the Avestic tradition, the ancestor of
the warriors is called *Hvar.čiθra-* / *Xuršēδčihr*, a compound with the very
same **hwarya-* ("sun"), as in Kolaxais. Thus the three groups are connected
to three different cosmic levels, just like the three families in the Ossetic Nart
Epic: at the bottom, the *Boratæ*, who were rich with cattle; in the middle, the
intelligent *Alægatæ*, and at the top, the brave and strong *Æxsærtægkatæ*.[19]

Initiation

The gold items, which symbolise the three functions, are in the hands of the Scythian kings and are displayed at a festival once a year (Hdt. 4.7). It is furthermore stated that "whoever sleeps with the gold in the open during the festival, will not, according to the Scythians, live through the year, and he is given all the land he is able to ride around himself in one day".

I suggest that the ritual described here is part of the initiation rites into the world of male adults – to be exact, the so-called *rite of marginality* or *liminality*, which is characterised by a perilous isolation outside of society itself and a suspension of ordinary societal values.[20] The rite of liminality is frequently described in death metaphors – indeed, the initiand is often thought of as dead himself. The ritual of spending the night with the religious objects may be a solemn staging (or circumscription?) of the youth's life in the bush.

This interpretation is not as farfetched as it may seem. It is no coincidence that in a passage describing Cretan institutions Ephoros introduces gifts almost identical to those playing a central role in the ritual described above, namely a warrior dress, an ox and a drinking cup, which are given to the young man by his lover during a festival celebrating the youth's admission into adulthood (FGrHist 70 F 149 ap. Strab. *Geogr.* 10.4.21 στολὴν πολεμικὴν καὶ βοῦν καὶ ποτήριον). As Bernhard Sergent points out, the three functions are present here, too: the war equipment represents the second function (= the battle-axe), the ox the third function (= the plough and yoke) and the cup the first function (= the phiale).[21] These gifts are presented to the youth at the festival celebrating his inclusion into the ranks of the adult men. In several respects Sparta's social structure, especially the education of children – the so-called *agōgē* – resembled that of Crete (the tradition reflects this idea in the myth about Lykurgos importing his Spartan laws from Crete). Even though we have no record of a similar ritual in the case of Sparta, Sergent suggests that the Hellenistic poet Lykophron provides testimony of the same gifts being given in Sparta, inasmuch as he states that on his return from Troy, Menelaos came through Iapyge, where he dedicated a shield, Helene's shoe and a crater to Athena Skylatria (*Alex.* 852-855 Ταμάσσιον κρατῆρα καὶ βοάγριον καὶ τὰς δάμαρτος ἀσκέρας εὐμαρίδας).[22] Iapyge lies in the vicinity of the Spartan colony of Taras, and Menelaos and Helene are themselves Spartan heroes. At any rate, the Dumézilian objects are in my opinion a symbol of the initiation into the clubs of adult men, and thus their presence in both Scythian myth and ritual is a key to the interpretation.

Later, in the Scythian logos (Hdt. 4.64-65), Herodotos writes that the young Scythian drinks the blood of the first man he slays. Every year there is a festival that only those men who have killed an enemy already are allowed to attend; we are told that it is very shameful for an adult not to have killed anyone yet (cf. also Arist. 7, 1324^b). This account resembles the Spartan *Krypteia*, i.e., the liminal phase of the boys' initiation, a year during which the youths had to live isolated from society itself in the *chora*, sleeping on the bare ground, stealing their food and killing innocent helots.[23] The festival in question is different from the one described at the beginning of book 4. The first one is in the hands of the local chieftains[24] (Hdt. 4.65 νομάρχης ἕκαστος ἐν τῷ ἑωυτοῦ νομῷ), whereas the latter is arranged by the kings (Hdt. 4.7 οἱ βασιλέες ἐς τὰ μάλιστα καὶ θυσίῃσι μεγάλῃσι ἱλασκόμενοι μετέρχονται ἀνὰ πᾶν ἔτος). I would suggest that the common festival marks the rite of marginality, whereas the local festival marks the rite of aggregation and is therefore only for those who have accomplished the liminal ordeal.

In Sparta, three festivals representing the rite of separation, the rite of liminality and the rite of aggregation, respectively, celebrate the boys' rite of passage.[25] The *Hyakinthia* mark the separation from community: the aetiological myth is the tragic death of Apollon's young favourite, Hyakinthos. The *Gymnopaidia* mark civilisation turned upside down, with naked dances in the summer heat and *sphairomachia*, a combination of football and boxing.[26] Finally, the inclusion into the *polis* is celebrated by the *Karneia*, which unlike the two first pan-Spartan festivals are celebrated separately in nine so-called tents, each with three *phratriai* (Ath. 4, 414[e-f]), most likely one from each *phyle*. Just as the Spartan initiation ruled admission into the community, or rather secret society, of male Spartiats, which was conceived, it seems, in terms of kinship (*phyle*) and expressed in common meals reserved (and obligatory) for adult male citizens,[27] so the Scythian initiation was obviously connected with the membership of the *genē* described in the myth of origin and celebrated once a year at a local drinking festival.

The Dorian myth of origin

Gregory Nagy has drawn the attention to the fact that the Dorian *phylai* fit perfectly into Dumézil's scheme of the three functions.[28] In the Dymanes he recognises the first function of the priest, in the Hylleis the second function of the warrior, and in the Pamphyloi the third function of the provider. The Dorian royal families are correspondingly derived from the eponymous hero Hyllos (cf. Hdt. 6.52, 7.204, 8.31). Furthermore, an inscription from Kos connects the Hylleis with Herakles' sanctuary, the Dymanes with the Anaxilea ("the sovereign's sanctuary") and the Pamphyloi with Demeter's sanctuary (*ICos* 140). It is interesting to note that the choral lyric of Alkman (Sparta, 7th century BC) mentions only the Dymanes of these three *phylai*.[29] Hence, the Dymanes may have had a special connection to the Spartan cult, which supports the idea that the *phyle* did in fact embody the first function. Alkman's famous Partheneion (fr. 1) seems to have been performed by Hylleis girls, one of whom is called Agido (literally, "from the (royal) House of Agis"), and the choir describes itself as cousins. However, this does not disturb the overall notion that the Dymanes played a special role in Spartan cult.[30]

Dorian myth	Scythian myth
1. Aigimios begets two sons: Dymas and Pamphylos, and adopts Hyllos	1. Targitaos begets three sons: Lipoxais, Arpoxais and Kolaxais
2. Hyllos, the adopted son, becomes king	2. Kolaxais, the youngest son, becomes king
3. Three *phylai* trace themselves back to Dymas, Pamphylos and Hyllos	3. Three *genē* trace themselves back to Lipoxais, Arpoxais and Kolaxais
4. Hyllos' grandchild begets three sons, each of whom receive one kingdom	4. Kolaxais begets three sons, each of whom receive one kingdom

Fig. 1. The Scythian and Spartan myths compared.

In this connection, it is interesting that the Dorian myth of origin[31] also corresponds in many respects with the Scythian myth in Herodotos (Fig. 1): Aigimios, the son of the eponymous forefather Doros, begot two sons, Dymas and Pamphylos, and adopted a third one, Hyllos; they are the ancestors of three *phylai*, just as the *genē* Auchatai, Katiaroi, Traspies and Paralatai originate from Targitaos' sons, Arpoxais, Lipoxais and Kolaxais. Furthermore, both in the Dorian and the Scythian version, the royal power was allotted to the youngest/adopted son. Finally, Hyllos' great-grandchild had three sons: they divided the kingdom among themselves and were the founders of the royal houses of Argos, Messene and Sparta. The genealogies of the Dorians and the Scythians match astonishingly well: in both we have two rows of three brothers, the first of which procreates a social division, whereas the second row leads to a regional division (Fig. 2-3).

The two discrepancies are easily accounted for: I. Hyllos is described as Herakles' biological son to legitimise the Dorian kings' claim to the Peloponnese ("the return of the Heraklids").[32] II. Two generations are inserted between Hyllos and the three kings to account for the traditional time span between the pre-Trojan era of Herakles and the Dorian immigration.

The Spartan *phylai* and the Scythian *genē* are envisaged within Dumézil's tripartite structure. However, this does not mean that all Pamphyloi or Katiaroi/Traspies were necessarily producers, that all Hylleis or Paralatai were warriors, or that all Dymanes or Auchatai were priests. All social roles were in principle present in all *phylai/genē*. Yet, the three *phylai/genē* were after all co-dependent, and they represent jointly the whole ideological spectrum. This being said, certain privileges tended to be allotted to certain *phylai/genē*. It is neither a regional nor an economical division, but a kinship division cutting across all distinctions.

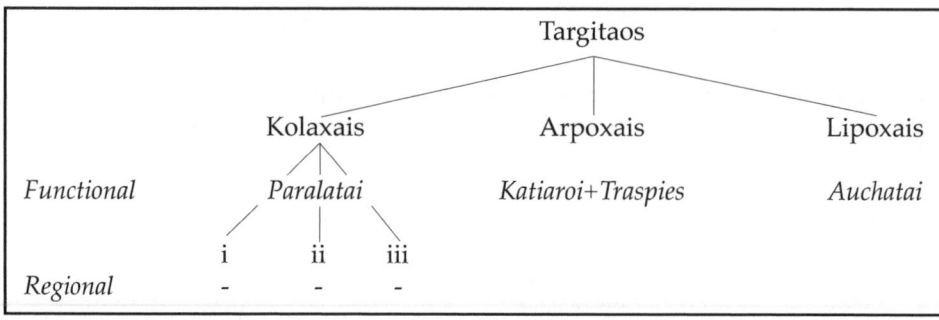

Fig. 2. Scythian genealogy.

The Dumézilian model has been criticised for the fact that the triad is a universal division. Given that man tends to divide the world into three, the tripartite structure is not necessarily of Indo-European origin. This objection touches only the naive version of Dumézilianism. Only the triad that organises the same three functions of the priest, the warrior and the provider in a closed and mutually co-dependent system can be called a real tripartite structure. The figure three is of course not sufficient in itself. Thus, the simple geographical division into three kingdoms is not a Dumézilian triad, as it occurs in virtually all human mythologies. Noah begets three sons, Shem, Ham and Japheth, who divide the earth among themselves – after all, *Genesis* is not a likely repository for Indo-European ideology. Thus, the fact that both the Scythians and the Dorians have settled in three kingdoms, and that this triad is projected by mythology back to three brothers, does not prove that the mythologies are interdependent. On the other hand, it cannot be accidental that this obviously common human geographical triad has been subjected to a Dumézilan tripartite structure in both mythologies.

Eduard Norden points to the extensively corresponding myths of origin of the Scythians and Germans in Herodotos and Tacitus, respectively.[33] In Tacitus, too, there is both a native version that speaks about an obscure progenitor and three brothers and a foreign version that departs from Herakles. In the Tacitean narrative, however, there is only one – geographical – triad of brothers: the ancestors of Ingaevones, Hermiones and Istaevones, the three tribal leagues. It is not my purpose here to decide whether Tacitus depends ultimately on Herodotos, perhaps through intermediary informants like Poseidonios. At any rate, Tacitus' myths have no Dumézilian features in them.

In the Iranian Pehlevi tradition (in *Ayātkār i Jāmāspīk*), Frētōn (Ferīdūn) has three sons who represent the three functions: Salm gets wealth, Tōz courage and Ēric law and religion. They are allotted three parts of the world too: Salm possesses Rome (= the Byzantine Empire), Tōz Central Asia and Ēric Iran and India.[34] The two levels, the functional and geographical divi-

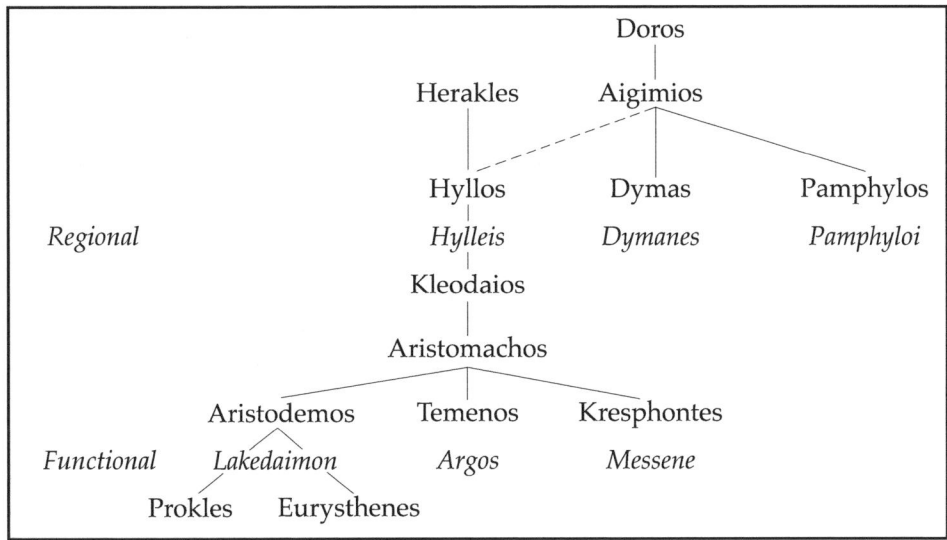

Fig. 3. Dorian genealogy.

sions, are combined, and the geographical division is not within the tribe, but embraces the whole world. In this respect, it is more similar (on a larger scale) to the Pontic Greek version of the myth of origin, according to which Herakles begot three sons, Agathyrsos, Gelonos and Skythes, the forefathers of the Agathyrsoi, the Gelones and the Scythians, respectively (Hdt. 4.10).

The wide range of parallels between the Scythian and the Dorian myths of origin does show that the explanatory strategy of source criticism is inadequate, and that we are not only dealing with a literary convention of the ethnography of the barbarians, but also in part with a common Indo-European heritage in all the described nations and in part with a basic ideology to which the ethnography of the Greeks and Romans ultimately adheres. The question is where the heritage stops and the ideology begins, which is of course difficult to determine, as the ideology has arisen on the basis of the heritage.

Ideology

Are the Scythian *genē* therefore some sort of *phylai* as well? In the chapter in question, rather than using the word *ethnos*, Herodotos uses the word genos, i.e., a stock and not a people. However, according to the etymology of the word *genos*, it designates any group that claims a common origin (*syngeneia*), and according to context it may mean family, *phyle* or people.[35] A social class, on the other hand, would hardly be called *genos*. The Scythian and Doric *phylai* may be a common inheritance, but the question is whether we are allowed to project the three functionally distinct *phylai* back to Indo-European times. However, Dénis Roussel argues in a rather influential book that the Doric *phylai* were not some old tribal relict surviving in the historical societies, but an innovation of the Classical *polis*.[36]

Thus, the possibility exists that the intimate correspondence between the Spartan and the Scythian institutions is due to the Greeks describing those customs. Herodotos and his Greek informants (we do not know if Herodotos had any opportunity to interview native Scythians,[37] but if he did, he certainly did it in Greek, and then the discourse remained Greek anyway) would necessarily express the Scythian culture within the framework of Greek ideology. So, they may have unconsciously interpolated both the embedded genealogy and the familiar *phyle/genos* system of the Greek *polis* into their description of Scythian society and mythology.

Within Greek culture itself, Sparta represented in the eyes of classical observers a more simple cultural level than Athens and Ionia (which were originally non-Greek according to Hdt. 1.56). Her cruel tribal customs and underdeveloped *polis* structure made her a natural scheme for the construction of the primitive other in Athenian and Ionic ideology.[38] Furthermore, the Spartan *agōgē* seemed to have adopted a nomadic stereotypy. The back-to-basics phase of Spartan initiation, *Krypteia*, conforms to the sedentary agriculturalists' stereotype of nomadic life. The Byzantine lexicographer Photios (s.v. συνέφηβος) states that the Eleans call the ephebes "Scythians", and it is well known that the Athenian guards, who were probably young citizens, were dressed as and called Scythians. After the *Krypteia*, the best of the young Spartan men were chosen for the corps of the Three Hundred, the so-called *Hippeis* (Hdt. 1.67.5, 8.124.3), which were elected by three *hippagretai* (Xen. *Lac.* 4.3), probably according to *phylai*. Thus, like the Scythian elite, the best of the Spartan youth consisted of horse warriors.

This ideology worked both ways. As a people the Scythians were themselves pictured as ephebes, too.[39] Just as the Spartan *agōgē* preserves certain "tribal" elements, which were conceived of as similar to the Scythian way of life, so Scythian society was in a sense depicted as a full-scale rite of liminality. The whole space of Scythia is described as marginal, and, accordingly, the inhabitants live a non-urbanised, non-settled, non-agricultural life in which ordinary values are turned upside down.

Herodotos' tale about the origin of the Sauromatians (Hdt. 4.110-116) is interesting in this context: The Greeks took some Amazons prisoner at Thermodon and sailed away with them. But the Amazons killed their new masters and landed on Kremnoi at the Sea of Azov, where they ran into a herd of grazing horses, on which they rode away. At first the Scythians thought they were young men, but gradually they realised the Amazons were women, and so they sent a group of young men out to them on the steppes. They lived the same life nearby each other, became accustomed to each other and eventually paired off. The Scythians proposed going home to their parents and property, but the Amazons did not think they would be able to live with the Scythian women, who were doing women's work at the carriages and did not hunt, so instead the men fetched their property, and they all left to live beyond the Tanais.

The Spartan women were notorious for their unrestricted life (which according to Aristotle (*Pol.* 2, 1269^b-1270^a), was the very cause of Sparta's final decline). Normally Herodotos does not speak much about Greek women – who lived secluded from the public – but the Spartan women are often described as strong and independent individuals in line with the eastern women – e.g., Eurysthenes' and Prokles' mother Argeia (6.52), the Spartan wives of the Minyans (4.145-146), Anaxandrides' wife (5.39-41), Kleomenes' daughter Gorgo (5.51, 7.205, 7.239) and Demaretos' mother (6.61-63, 6.67).[40] It is typical that Herodotos only speaks about intellectually and erotically independent women in connection with royal (or tyrant) houses. In other words, it is an unspoken premise in Herodotos (and a spoken one in Aristotle) that autocratic societies are also gynecocratic.

In reality, it is true that the Spartan women did not enjoy political independence, and their place was at the hearth just like the Athenian or, for that matter, the Scythian women. However, the *agōgē* of the young girls was characterised by a liberty that was unparalleled in classical Athens. In the girls' rites of passage there was of course a period of liminality, too, in which values were turned upside down, and the young girls dedicated themselves to athletics, public choirs and amorous liaisons.[41] This phase is connected with the cult of Artemis, whose sanctuaries are not infrequently located on the border of Lakonia: in Limnai (at the frontier with Messenia), Karyai (at the frontier with Arkadia) and Epidauros Limera (on the east coast). Herodotos' story about the young Scythian men's encounter with the Amazons has a lot in common with the mythology, which supports the rite of passage of the young Spartan girls (young men raping dancing girls), and the goddess protecting this rite of passage, Artemis, is the prototype of all Amazons.

According to Herodotos (Hdt. 4.8-10), the Pontic Greeks traced the Scythians back to Herakles, who, having come accidentally to the Black Sea region, met a sex-hungry monster, with whom he begot three sons: Agathyrsos, Gelonos and Skythes. The royal power was allotted to the youngest brother (once more), whereas the two older brothers had to leave the country. In Hartog's mind, the derivation of the Scythians from Herakles is rather problematic, because it suggests a congeniality of Greeks and Scythians that is in conflict with the otherness demanded by the narrative.[42] He takes refuge in the ambiguous nature of Herakles (he is wild and unrestrained) and considers it – paradoxically, I might add – hellenocentric to derive foreign races from a Greek ancestor. Yet, both the Pontic Greeks and Scythians accept this genealogy.[43]

Interestingly, in Herodotos, three nations (or their royal houses) are traced back to the hero Herakles: the Scythians, the Lydians (Hdt. 1.7) and the Dorians (Hdt. 6.52, 7.204, 7.31). Being the ideal representative of the function of the warrior, Herakles is of course a natural founder of the royal houses of the warlike Scythians and Spartans. Yet Herakles also moves in the liminal sphere. The twelve labours are an enlargement of the ordeals that the initiand goes through and they are located on the desolate margin of civilisation. The Pontic Greek version of the myth of origin explicitly takes one of Herakles' labours as its point of departure: the theft of the Geryonic oxen? Herakles follows a route on the edge of the world, along the river Okeanos, and he sleeps on the ground.

Herodotos states that the lineage of the Heraklids stemming from Herakles and a slave girl ruled Sardeis successively for twenty-two generations, or 550 years, until being overthrown by Kroisos' ancestor Gyges. There exists a tradition that also derives the Mermnads, to which Kroisos belongs, from Herakles – what is more, from his liaison with Queen Omphale (Apol. *Bibl.* 2.7.8). This is of course an attempt to make the Mermnad dynasty even more legitimate than its Heraklid predecessor (the tradition is therefore probably older than the fall of Kroisos). The significance of Herakles in the political discourse of Lydia is perhaps a mythical expression of the intimate contacts between Lydia and Sparta in the 7th century BC.[44] The Kimmerian presence on the Lydian scene in the 7th century is also rather puzzling in this context.[45]

Herodotos does not say what Herakles was doing in Lydia. After having stolen the Delphic tripod, Hermes sold him as a slave to the Lydian queen Omphale, who dressed him as a woman and kept him as her sex slave (Apol. *Bibl.* 2.6.3), just like the monster in the Pontic Greek myth. Cross-dressing, slavery and sexual abuse are commonplaces in the rite of liminality (so the transsexual *Enarees* are yet another example of Scythia's liminal character).[46] In all probability, Herodotos was familiar with this myth, as it is alluded to not only in *Trachinians* (248-253) by his friend Sophokles (staged c. 435 BC), but also in Aischylos' *Agamemnon* (1040-1041) from c. 458 BC.[47] The same tragedy tells the story about the end of Herakles' earthly life, when he instructs his son Hyllos – the ancestor of the Dorian royal houses! – to burn him on a pyre so as to make him an immortal god, the ultimate initiation, of which all previous labours and troubles are nothing but the preparatory liminal phase.

On the other hand, the two myths of origin are contrasted in Herodotos. The Pontic Greek version, which pictures a full-scale liminal Scythia dominated by the warrior function alone, is an expression of Greek ideology, whereas the Scythian version is more balanced, as rather than presenting liminality as a condition, it only presents it as a ritual, and it includes all three functions.

Tribal rites

The fact that Herodotos' description of Scythian culture fits into the scheme of Greek ideology does not rule out the fact that its basic lines are true, i.e., have a real existence in Scythian culture outside of Greek discourse. The Scythians were after all nomads (and the Sarmatian women were occasionally horse warriors).[48] Even if Herodotos and his informants are influenced by Greek ideology in their conception of Scythian myths and customs, I am convinced that they try to tell what they believe to be the truth.

Roussel is definitely on firm ground when criticising the tradition that sees in the phylai initially autonomous and ethnically heterogeneous tribes that immigrated together into southern Greece and eventually merged into one Doric nation. However, this does not mean that one has to exclude any reconstruction of a previous stage in which the three *phylai* had another function. In fairness, Roussel ought to explain why the Dorian *poleis* choose exactly those three *phylai* out of the blue. Roussel's followers argue that before the 8th century BC, there was no overall feeling of unity that would enable the establishment of identical institutions such as the *phylai*, and the small-scale Doric-speaking communities could support only rather primitive societal structures in their proto-home and even after migrating into the Peloponnese ca. 1100-1000 BC.[49] However, this does not rule out the possibility that they had a complex ideology of kinship relations (to appreciate the invalidity of that argument, one just has to consider the Australian Aboriginals, whose intricate kinship patterns rule all social interactions). As a matter of fact, the notion of a face-to-face society may in fact support the existence of kinship groups in earlier times already.

Peter Funke uses the concept of "segmentary society" to account for the development of the Dorian *phylai*.[50] A segmentary society is characterised by equality among its disparate units. Even though it lacks a central authority, it shows a high level of integration and solidarity, which is thought to warrant the independence of each unit. The Dark Ages were indeed segmentary, as is reflected in the innumerable kings and peoples mentioned in Homer's narrative. The concept of the *phyle* (or better its pre-*polis* predecessor) is a natural measure against the anarchy of a world without a centralised government. In Classical times, Sparta was of course a *polis*, but it is noteworthy that the city was not yet synoecised properly and had no city wall; it still consisted of five distinct villages (Thuc. 1.10). If we are allowed to believe the testimony of Plato (*Leg.* 6, 778ᵈ-779ᵃ) and the stylised apophthegms (Ps.-Plut. *Apophth. Lac.* 210ᵉ, 212ᵉ, 215ᵈ, 217ᵈ, 221ᵉ, 228ᵉ; *Gnomologium Vaticanum* 69), the Spartans considered it womanish to hide behind city walls. Apparently, they adhered to (and were described in the terms of) an ideology of nomadism.

It is intelligible that people organised themselves in co-dependent kinship groups in a period when the state structure was still rather weak. As Nagy points out, it is not the *phylai* themselves that are old tribes:[51] while in Classical times they were subdivisions of the *polis* that regulated the political rights and obligations of the citizen, in prehistoric times they were subdivisions of the tribe that ensured a stability between its individual members and legitimised rights to land and obligations for the common good of the tribe.

The Scythians may have been organised in pretty much the same way. After all, the concepts of kinship and descent generally play an important role in nomadic societies. As their peculiar economy is characterised by an inherent mobility and constant instability, rights to pasture and social and military obligations are distributed within the kinship system.[52] A popular word in this context is "clan", which, however, is not always defined particularly well. It is also occasionally used to designate the *genē* of Herodotos' myth of origin.[53] A "clan" may be defined as a group that claims descent from a common, usually mythical (and most likely fictitious) ancestor. The kinship groups are in other words natural substitutes for the organised and centralised state, and they become even more important when the society is expanding and migrating, which was the case for both the Scythians and the early Dorians.

The *phylai* are comparable to the political parties of modern society in the sense that they distribute the power of the individuals in the framework of ideology (whether it is tripartite or orientated along a left-right axis). In principle, they also transgress social and geographical borders. The essential difference is of course that modern political parties are not (or are not supposed to be) hereditary, but that is more a matter of different phrasing. The tribal concept of shared blood is without doubt a social construct (like the political programmes of modern parties). When new individuals or communities are admitted into the tribal society, a lineage is constructed (or re-constructed in the eyes of the constructers themselves), which attribute to them the appropriate position in the common order. The Greeks deriving the Scythians from Herakles is a beautiful example of this strategy.

The tripartite structure may be considered fundamentally incompatible with nomadic life, and the plough fallen from heaven may seem a bit out of place for a people whose existence depends on cattle.[54] Yet pastoral nomadism is in general intimately connected both economically and ideologically with neighbouring sedentary agriculturalists.[55] As a matter of fact, specialised nomadism seems to have arisen as a response to organised agriculture, and the two economies have contributed to the each other's gradual development. If we are to trust the testimony of the classical authors (Hdt. 4.17-20, Hippoc. *Aer.* 20.1), a minority of the Scythians did in fact practice agriculture – for instance, the tribes in the forest steppe zone. No matter what their original ethnic status, they were obviously considered part of the Scythian world in the 5th century BC, and the agricultural way of life also had a place in Scythian ideology, even if it was held in low esteem.

Conclusion

The *genē* of Herodotos' Scythian myth of origin are neither tribes nor castes – the two most popular suggestions made by the scholars – but rather kinship groups like the Dorian *phylai*, i.e., a subdivision of the people that traverses both the regional and social axes.[56] The adult male population forms undisclosed societies, confirmed, it is thought, by old ties of blood and conceived in terms of the tripartite ideology. Admission to them is ruled by a ritualised initiation cycle, including, as is the rule both in modern ethnographic parallels and in the Spartan *agōgē*, a period of liminality, during which the youth live a savage life in the bush and are expected to murder their first man. Herodotos describes two festivals that celebrate this phase of liminality and the subsequent inclusion into the ranks of the adult males, respectively.

The ritual and mythological analogies between Scythian and Spartan culture are not due to an interpolation of Greek categories into a Scythian context. To some extent, they are the result of the formulation of Scythian customs and beliefs in a Greek discourse. Being a Greek and writing in Greek for a Greek audience, Herodotos could not help Hellenising the people he described. Furthermore, the Scythians may very well have adopted elements of Greek discourse into their own ideology. The Greeks and the Scythians constructed their identities in direct response to each other. The role of Herakles is one example, and the tales of Anacharsis and Skyles illustrate the Scythian response (or rather the Greek conception of it) to their encounter with Greek civilisation, which eventually leads to the construction of a nomadic identity sharing certain elements with the Spartan culture that was the natural representative of "Old Greece" in the 5th century discourse. The convergent representations of the Spartan and Scythian myths and rites point to similar ideological constructions both externally, in relation to the average Greek observer, and internally, in the societal structure reflected by the ancient historians and the mythological traditions. The tribal stereotypy is a consequence of the Scythians and Spartans occupying similar roles as the typical, and topical, contrast to the normal urbanised settled life of the mainstream Greek, but at the same time, it is also a real parallelism originating in the Scythians' and Greeks' common heritage and in the Scythian nomads' and the prehistoric Dorians' comparable ways of life.

I have accepted the framework of Dumézil's tripartite structure for both the Scythian and the Spartan mythologies and rituals. I must however emphasise that this does not mean that we are necessarily dealing with a common heritage, in the sense that the Indo-European proto-culture had three *phylai*, the admission to which was organised in terms of the three functions. On the other hand, I do not adhere to the agnostic school, which prohibits any attempt to reconstruct an Indo-European ideology. The common origin of the Indo-European languages is an undeniable fact, and language is not only about vocabulary and grammar, but also about formulating the world. In the Indo-European grammar of thought, the tripartite structure was but a brick, which eventually led to analogous structures in similar daughter cultures. The Greeks and the Scythians have inherited and developed an analogous mythic-ideological grammar. The Scythian myths and rites in the *Histories* of Herodotos originate from Scythian sources, but the actual realisation of the single myth has been formulated on the basis of the syntax of Greek mythology.

Notes

1. Cf. West 1988.
2. The veracity of Herodotos, who apparently claims to have seen the cauldron with his own eyes (τοσόνδε μέντοι ἀπέφαινον ἐς ὄψιν, has been questioned; cf. Armayor 1978 (criticism Pritchett 1993, 132-138). I am not convinced by the attempt of West (2000) to discount Herodotos' claim with an alternative linguistic analysis.
3. Hartog 1991, 166-170.
4. Herodotos says that the Scythians despise the Bacchic cult (4.79.3 Σκύθαι δὲ τοῦ βακχεύειν πέρι ῞Ελλησι ὀνειδίζουσι). In Plato's *Laws*, Megillos claims that Spartan men did not engage in Bacchic rites either (*Leg.* 637[a-b]); cf. Parker 1988.
5. Dumézil 1978, 178-192. Cf. also Benveniste 1938.
6. Cf. the criticism of Schlerath 1995; 1996.
7. Benveniste (1938, 533) compares ἄροτρόν τε καὶ ζυγόν with the Avestic dvandva *aēša-yugō.sǎmi* "plough and yoke".
8. Auchatae, Cotieri are tribal names in Plin. *HN* 4.48, 6.22, 6.50; Colaxes and Auchus are personal names in Valerius Flaccus *Arg.* 6.48-64. It is however disputed whether those authors are independent of Herodotos, cf. Dumézil 1978, 184-188, and Ivantchik 1999.
9. Holzer 1989. He agrees with Abaev (1981) that *Skythai geōrgoi* stands for Scythian **gauwarga* (cowboy). However, it is unlikely that Herodotos heard about the Scythian tribes in Scythian and even less likely that a local, possibly bilingual informant would believe that **gauwarga* was identical to Greek *geōrgos* "agriculturalist", if the people in question were pastoral nomads.
10. As is clear from the geographical excursus, there were however both pastoralist and agriculturalist tribes; cf. Hinge, 2003. Yet both economies belong by definition to the third function.
11. Grakov 1971, 37-38 = 1978, 32-33; Chazanov 1975, 52, 191-199.
12. Grantovskij 1960.
13. Cf. Lebedynsky 2001, 83-84.
14. Dumézil 1978, 183-197; 1983, 90-96; cf. Chazanov 1975, 200-202 (quoted in Dumézil 1978, 199-202).
15. Raevskij (1977, 145-161) sees a reflection of such stratification in the burials at Scythian Neapolis.
16. He finds support for the first function in the fact that *Para-dāta-* (literally, "put ahead") corresponds formally to the Vedic *puróhita* ("priest") (Dumézil 1978, 189, no. 4 "exact équivalent"). However this is only a superficial parallel, since *puróhita* is most probably derived in Indo-Aryan itself from the verb *purodhā-* ("choose"), *puras* ("before") + *dhā* ("put"). Cf. Mayrhofer 1977, 67.
17. Ivantchik 1999.

18. Abaev 1958-1989, I 63, IV 247-248; Grantovskij 1960; Ivantchik 1999, 145-148. Dumézil (1978, 192) explains the first members of the names differently: Sanskrit *kula* ("wooden"), *árbha* ("little") (in the sense of "work", as in German *Arbeit* and Russian *rabota*) and Osset. *læppū* ("youngster"). However, these etymologies are unsatisfying both linguistically and semantically.

19. Dumézil 1986, 457-466; 1978, 204-211 (a response to the criticism in Smith & Sperber 1971, 559-586).

20. Gennep 1909; Turner 1964.

21. Sergent 1996, 26-39 (differently 395-396).

22. Sergent 1996, 26-39.

23. Pl. *Leg.* 1, 633[b-c] (+ Sch.), Plut. *Lyc.* 28. Cf. Jeanmaire 1913; 1939, 550-558; Brelich 1969, 155-157; Ducat 1999.

24. Apparently, the Scythian kingdoms were divided into *nomoi*; cf. Grakov 1971, 33-34 = 1978, 29-30; Chazanov 1975, 111-122; Lebedynsky 2001, 142-143. There seems to have been a larger division into *archēia* ("provinces") as well; cf. Hdt. 4.61.1. Rosén 1987, 385, has emended τῶν ἀρχα/ε/ηίων of the mss. to τὠρχαῖον, thus eliminating the *archēia* from the Scythian administration; however, ηι (ει) is *lectio difficilior*. An older conjecture (Stein, Hude) is τῶν ἀρχέων in the same meaning as τῶν ἀρχήιων.

25. Jeanmaire 1939, 524-540; Brelich 1961, 139-154; 1969, 113-228; Pettersson 1992.

26. Xen. *Lac.* 4.6, Paus. 3.14.6, Luc. *Anach.* 38, Sch. Pl. *Leg.* 1, 633[c], cf. Chrimes 1952, 131-133; Pettersson 1992, 46-47.

27. Singor 1999.

28. Nagy 1987.

29. Fr. 4.5.4, 10(b).8-9 and (in a papyrus commentary) 11, col. 1, fr. 5.

30. Cf. Calame 1977, I 272-276.

31. Cf. Hdt. 6.52, 7.204, 8.31; Pind. *Pyth.* 1.61-66; Apol. *Bibl.* 2.8.

32. Cf. Hall 1997, 56-65.

33. Norden 1920, 48-55.

34. Molé 1952.

35. Hall 1997, 34-40.

36. Roussel 1976.

37. On one occasion, Herodotos claims a Scythian source: Tymnes, the *epitropos* of King Ariapeithes (Hdt. 4.76.6).

38. Herodotos' description of Sparta relies to a great extent on local sources; cf. Tigerstedt 1965, I 81-107.

39. Hartog 1991, 71-72.

40. Millender 1999.

41. Cf. Calame 1977, passim.

42. Hartog 1991, 41-45.

43. Cf. Raevskij 1977, 161-171. King Ataias, who united Scythia in the 4th century BC, put Herakles on his coins. This hero also appears on the Olbian coin of Eminakos, who was perhaps the local representative of the Scythian king (cf. Vinogradov 1989, 93-94).

44. Cf. the traditional belief that the Spartan poet Alkman came from Sardeis; this was probably invented in the 4th century BC (perhaps by Aristotle) and is due to the many references to Lydian culture in his poetry. Alkman, fr. 1, v. 59 ἵππος ... Κολαξαῖος, fr. 90 ʽΡίπας and fr. 156 ʽΕσσηδόνας may demonstrate that the Lydian connection also included references to Scythian mythology (cf. Ivantchik 1999, 147). However, I find it rather hard to believe that Alkman and Herodotos interpreted Scythian *Xola-* as Κολα- independently (why not

**Χολα-?). Devereux (1965) suggests Aristeas' *Arimaspeia* as a common source. Herodotos relies on him explicitly in the 4th book (cf. 4.13-16) but in the traditional chronologies Alkman is somewhat older than Aristeas.

45. Cf. Hdt. 1.15 and Ivantchik 2001, 70-72.
46. On the *Enarees*, cf. Donat 1993.
47. Herodotos recounts that the woman with whom Herakles had his son was the slave of King Iardanos, the father of Queen Omphale (as we know from other sources). Apparently, Herodotos, Sophokles and Aischylos expect their readers to know the whole story already. The vase paintings have no clear representations of the myth before the 5th century BC; cf. *LIMC*, VII 45-53.
48. Rolle 1980; Davis-Kimball 1997.
49. Welwei 1979; 1988; Qviller 1981; Donlan 1989.
50. Funke 1993.
51. Nagy 1987, 246-247.
52. Chazanov 1984, 138-144; Barfield 1993, 147-149.
53. E.g., Minns 1913, 44.
54. Raevskij 1977, 29; Hartog 1991, 40.
55. Hinge 2003.
56. Chazanov (1975, 118-120) observes that Herodotos' text presents three different divisions: *genos* (genealogical), *ethnos* (ethnical) and *nomos* (regional).

Bibliography

Abaev, V.I. 1981. Gerodotovskie Skythai georgoi, *Voprosy jazykoznanija* 1981.2, 74-76.

Abaev, V.I. 1958-1989. *Istoriko-etimologičeskij slovar' osetinskogo jazyka*. Moskva-Leningrad.

Armayor, O.K. 1978. Did Herodotus ever go to the Black Sea?, *HarvStClPhil* 82, 45-62

Barfield, T.J. 1993. *The Nomadic Alternative*. Englewood Cliffs, NJ.

Benveniste, E. 1938. Traditions indo-iraniennes sur les classes sociales, *Journal Asiatique* 230, 529-549.

Brelich, A. 1961. *Guerre, agoni e culti nella Grecia arcaica*. Bonn.

Brelich, A. 1969. *Paides e parthenoi*, vol. 1. Roma.

Calame, C. 1977. *Chœurs des jeunes filles en Grèce archaïque*. Rome.

Chazanov, A.M. 1975. *Social'naja istorija skifov. Osnovnye problemy razvitija drevnich kočevnikov evrazijskich stepej*. Moskva.

Chrimes, K.M.T. 1952. *Ancient Sparta*. 2nd edition. Manchester.

Davis-Kimball, J. 1997. Warrior Women of the Eurasian Steppes, *Archaeology* 50.1, 44-48.

Devereux, G. 1965. The Kolaxaian Horse of Alkman's Partheneion, *ClQ* 15, 176-184.

Donat, M. 1993. *Skythische Schamanen? Die Nachrichten über Enarees-Anarieis bei Herodot und Hippokrates*. Schaffhausen.

Donlan, W. 1989. The pre-state community in Greece, *SymbOslo* 64, 5-29.

Ducat, J. 1999. Perspectives on Spartan Education in the Classical Period, in: Hodkinson & Powell (eds.) 1999, 43-66.

Dumézil, G. 1978. *Romans de Scythie et d'alentour*. Paris.

Dumézil, G. 1983. *La Courtisane et les seigneurs colorés*. Paris.

Dumézil, G. 1986. *Mythe et Épopée, I, L'idéologie des trois fonctions dans les épopées des peuples indo-européens*. 2nd edition. Paris.

Funke, P. 1993. Stamm und Polis, in: J. Bleicken (ed.), *Colloquium aus Anlaß des 80. Geburtstag von Alfred Heuß*. Kallmünz, 29-48.

Gennep, A. van. 1909. *Les rites de passages*. Paris.

Grakov, B.N. 1971. *Skify. Naučno-populjarnyj očerk*. Moskva.

Grakow, B.N. 1978. *Die Skythen*. Berlin.

Grantovskij, E.A. 1960. *Indo-iranskie kasty u skifov* (XXV meždunarodnyj kongress vostokovedov. Doklady delegacii SSSR). Moskva.

Hall, J.M. 1997. *Ethnic Identity in Greek Antiquity*. Cambridge.

Hartog, F. 1991. *Le miroir d'Hérodote. Essai sur la représentation de l'autre*. 2nd edition. Paris.

Hinge, G. 2003. Herodots skythiske nomader, in: T. Bekker-Nielsen & G. Hinge (eds.), *På randen af det ukendte*. Århus.

Hodkinson, S. & A. Powell (eds.) 1999. *Sparta: New Perspectives*. London.

Holzer, G. 1989. Namen skythischer und sarmatischer Stämme, *DenkschrWien* 125, 193-213.

Ivantchik, A.I. 1999. Une légende sur l'origine des Scythes (Hérodote IV, 5-7) et le problème des sources du Scythikos logos d'Hérodote, *REG* 112, 141-192.

Ivantchik, A.I. 2001. *Kimmerier und Skythen*. Moskau.

Jeanmaire, H. 1913. La cryptie lacédémonienne, *REG* 26, 121-150.

Jeanmaire, H. 1939. *Couroi et courètes. Essai sur l'éducation spartiate et sur les rites d'adolescence dans l'antiquité hellénique*. Lille.

Chazanov, A.M. 1984. *Nomads and the outside world*. Cambridge.

Lebedynsky, I. 2001. *Les Scythes. La civilisation des steppes (VIIe - IIIe siècles av. J.-C.)*. Paris.

Mayrhofer, M. 1977. *Iranisches Personennamenbuch, I.1, Die avestischen Namen*. Wien.

Millender, E. 1999. Athenian Ideology and the Empowered Spartan Woman, in: Hodkinson & Powell (eds.) 1999, 355-391.

Minns, E.H. 1913. *Scythian and Greeks*. Cambridge.

Molé, M. 1952. Le partage du monde dans la tradition iranienne, *Journal Asiatique* 240, 455-463.

Nagy, G. 1987. The Indo-European heritage of tribal organization, in: S.N. Skomal & E.C. Polomé (eds.), *Proto-Indo-European: The Archaeology of a Linguistic Problem*. Washington, DC, 245-266.

Norden, E. 1920. *Die germanische Urgeschichte in Tacitus Germania*. Leipzig-Berlin.

Parker, R. 1988. Demeter, Dionysus and the Spartan Pantheon, in: R. Hägg, N. Marinatos & G.C. Nordquist (eds.), *Early Greek Cult Practice*. Stockholm, 99-104.

Pettersson, M. 1992. *Cults of Apollo at Sparta*. Stockholm.

Pritchett, W.K. 1993. *The Liar School of Herodotus*. Amsterdam.

Qviller, B. 1981. The dynamics of the Homeric society, *SymbOslo* 56, 109-55.

Raevskij, D.S. 1977. *Očerki ideologii skifo-sakskich plemen*. Moskva.

Rolle, R. 1980. Oiorpata, in: T. Krüger & H.-G. Stephan (eds.), *Beiträge zur Archäologie Nordwestdeutschlands und Mitteleuropas*. Hildesheim, 275-294.

Rosén, H.B. 1987. *Herodoti Historiae*, vol. 1. Leipzig.

Roussel, D. 1976. *Tribu et cité*. Paris.

Schlerath, B. 1995. Georges Dumézil und die Rekonstruktion der indogermanischen Kultur 1, *Kratylos* 40, 1-48.

Schlerath, B. 1996. Georges Dumézil und die Rekonstruktion der indogermanischen Kultur 2, *Kratylos* 41, 1-67.

Sergent, B. 1996. *Homosexualité et initiation chez les peuples indo-européens*. Paris.

Singor, H.W. 1999. Admission to the syssitia in fifth-century Sparta, in: Hodkinson & Powell (eds.) 1999, 67-89.

Smith, P. & D. Sperber 1971. Mythologiques de Georges Dumézil, *Annales Économie Société Civilisations* 26, 559-586.

Tigerstedt, E.N. 1965. *The Legend of Sparta in Classical Antiquity*. Stockholm-Göteborg-Uppsala.

Turner, V.W. 1964. Betwixt and between, in: J. Helm (ed.), *Symposium on New Approaches to the Study of Religion*. Seattle-London, 4-20 [= The Forest of Symbols. New York 1967, 93-111].

Vinogradov, Ju.G. 1989. *Političeskaja istorija Ol'vijskogo polisa*. Moskva.

Welwei, K.-W. 1979, Die spartaniche Phylenordnung im Spiegel der großen Rhetra und des Tyrtaios, *Gymnasium* 86, 178-196.

Welwei, K.-W. 1988. Ursprünge genossenschaftlicher Organisationsformen in der archaischen Polis, *Saeculum* 39, 12-23.

West, S. 1988. The Scythian Ultimatum, *JHS* 108, 207-211.

West, S. 2000. Herodotus in the North? Reflections on a Colossal Cauldron (4.81), *ScrClIsr* 19, 15-34.

The Graeco-Scythian Slave-trade in the 6th and 5th Centuries BC

Nadežda A. Gavriljuk

After A.N. Ščeglov published his articles on the grain trade between the Scythians and the Greeks,[1] the myth in archaeology and ancient history that Greece had been supplied with grain from Scythia disappeared. However, the problem of identifying which goods were exchanged for those coming from Greece to Scythia in the 6th-4th centuries BC remained. Here I shall attempt to show that it was possibly slaves. It should be said at once that the questions of slave-holding in antiquity and of the character of slavery in Greece, in the Greek colonies and in Scythia, are not the subject of my investigation, though they will inevitably be touched upon. Instead I will deal with the slave-trade and its causes, directions and peculiarities. The number of monographs published in Russian which consider the issue in general, is limited to those by A. Vallon, V.D. Blavatskij and A.I. Dovatur.[2] Although the question is treated more or less seriously by all modern scholars within the field of ancient studies, for instance, Ju.G. Vinogradov and E.D. Frolov, and by the representatives of the "Kiev school" of ancient studies N.A. Lejpunskaja and S.D. Kryžickij,[3] the fact that slaves were traded from the north Pontic area to Greece is disputed by no one.

The first to take note of the problem of slavery among the Scythians was A.P. Smirnov.[4] Later, the issue was also considered by B.N. Grakov, in some of his early works.[5] In the opinion of A.M. Chazanov and D.B. Šelov, who examined the social structure of the nomads,[6] the Scythians, similarly to other early nomads, did not need a large number of slaves. The birth of the slave-holding ideology was first considered on the basis of archaeological evidence by V.A. Il'inskaja.[7] A.I. Terenožkin characterised the Scythian communities as "an early class society with certain slave-holding tendencies".[8]

In all these works, attention was primarily focused on the social aspects of the phenomenon, while the economic aspects of slavery were overlooked. Only T.D. Zlatkovskaja in her work devoted to the Thracians mentioned the role of barbarian slave-traders in the development of slavery.[9] By contrast, in western literature slavery and the slave-trade were considered mainly as an economic phenomenon rather than a social one.[10] However, western authors have not taken account of the evidence from the northern Black Sea region. Only recently a paper by D. Braund and G. Tsetskhladze about the export of

slaves from Kolchis appeared,[11] and slightly later an article was published
by T. Taylor, who made an attempt to compile all the written documents concerning slave-trade during the Greek and Roman periods and to compare
this information with archaeological evidence of the early Iron Age, including Scythian material.[12]

The slave-trade was one of the most important elements in the economies
of the various societies in the northern Black Sea region during the early Iron
Age, but this aspect has received insufficient study. The subject of this paper
is, therefore, to trace the formation and development of the slave-trade in the
northern Black Sea region in the 6th–5th centuries BC as one of the structural components of trade in general and to evaluate its export-import potential, as well as to determine the place of the slave-trade in the structure of the
trade which was once carried out along the route from the forest steppe,
through the steppe, to the Greek colonies in the northern Black Sea region.

In different communities of the early Iron Age, man's mechanical, i.e.
muscular, strength was widely used in many types of manufacture. The
demand for manpower was great and it was met mainly by the exploitation
of slaves. Thus there is every reason to consider slave-holding as the use of
a renewable energy resource, and to measure the economic potential of a
given ethno-cultural formation directly by the supply of this resource.

With such an approach, the manpower of slaves is considered as a source
of mechanical (muscular) energy along with other more usual kinds of energy: thermal energy, tractive power of animals, and, to a lesser extent, the
energies of wind and water. The number of slaves in the *ergasteria* ranged
from several dozens up to several hundreds in larger ones.[13] In quarries up
to several thousand men may have been employed simultaneously.
Manpower was also used to move Greek ships.

During the early Iron Age, the problem of sources of muscular power evidently assumed the highest importance for the success of the society. Means
for renewing that resource were therefore necessary for maintaining the
number of one's slaves, as those slaves aged, were mutilated, escaped, or
died. Moreover, the need for slaves grew due to the tendency to expand production volumes. Decrease or cessation of the supply of slaves was equivalent to an energy crisis in the ancient world.

As has been demonstrated by modern history, the roots of an energy crisis may be found far beyond the confines of one particular state. This
prompts the fairly paradoxical conclusion that in the early Iron Age a stable
(peaceful) situation could not but forebode a crisis in the given geopolitical
system or parts of it. Such a conclusion derives from the fact that wars and
raids were the main source for renewal of this basic energy resource.
Apparently, the inverse statement is also equally true: maintenance of a stable condition of a geopolitical system during the early Iron Age would have
demanded successful wars. At the same time, supplies of slaves to the slave

owners were most effectively provided via trade, i.e. a mechanism functioning at its best in conditions of regional peace. The most exhaustive exploitation of slaves for obtaining maximum profits from their labour also required
peaceful conditions.

Trade in slaves was one of the most important branches of the ancient
economy, providing its viability throughout almost an entire millennium.
During that period much of the slave-holding history of western civilisation
was to a greater or lesser extent connected with the northern Black Sea
region. For that reason, the territorial frame of this study is limited to that
geographical area. Here we find the interaction of the main ethno-cultural
formations of the early Iron Age: forest steppe and Scythia, Olbia and its
chora, the steppes of the Crimea, Bosporos, and Greece.

Usually, in traditional societies trade is analysed in terms of various
groups of goods: agricultural, craft, and raw material. It is unlikely that the
Greek colonists and their *metropoleis*, whose principal branches of economy
were agriculture and animal husbandry, would have been in desperate need
of food or finished goods from Scythia. It was also the case that the mineral
resources of the steppe zone of the northern Black Sea littoral were somewhat scarce and therefore hardly relied upon by the Greeks. On the other
hand, trade between Greeks and Scythians was undoubtedly of a large-scale
character, as indicated by the finds of large quantities of Greek products,
even in remote parts of Scythia. But since trade implies counter-goods of
equivalent value, we may suppose that the most important exports from
barbarian countries were energy resources in the form of slaves. Almost
every kind of product that was manufactured by Greek craftsmen was
exported to Scythia: highly sophisticated as well as plain tableware,
amphorae of wine, ceremonial weapons, bronze mirrors and various personal adornments.[14]

The need for slaves in the economy determined the market demand for
them. Greece was always, especially during the Archaic period, the main
consumer of slave labour.[15] In Greece slave labour was widely used in the
household, but far greater still was the number of slaves employed in manufacturing.

The practice of selling slaves from the Pontic countries, in particular from
Scythia, to Greece undoubtedly existed as early as the 6th century BC. This
is suggested by the names of slaves such as Kolchos and Skythas among the
painters of Attic pottery.[16] Without going into a detailed discussion of the
problem of Scythian policemen in Athens,[17] we can note that it seems unlikely that the Athenians would have armed a considerable contingent of slaves.
However, the presence of ethnic Scythians in Athens as early as the Archaic
period is beyond dispute.

In the 5th century BC, after the Persian War, Scythian slaves were imported into Attica in somewhat greater numbers.[18] In the inventory of the

belongings of a certain metic Kephisodoros, condemned in the case of the Hermokopids (414-413 BC), a Scythian is mentioned at a price of 144 drachms among a dozen slaves put up for sale.[19] Slaves were brought to the markets after military operations by Greek mercenaries, who usually sold their captives as slaves as attested by Xenophon's *Anabasis* (Xen., *Anab.* 7.3.48).

Later, Polybios and Strabon also wrote about the export of slaves from Scythia (Polyb. 4.38.4; Strab. 11.11.12). The former author noted the high quality of the slaves supplied from the region. His evidence is confirmed by a statement of Paulus Orosius about 20,000 Scythian boys and women enslaved as a result of the war between Philip II of Macedon and Ataias (Oros. 3.13.4). In contrast, Strabon included slaves in the number of nomadic trade goods, noting the mediatory role of the Scythian tribes, who thus acted as trade partners of Greeks trading in slaves.

The fact that even a metic could own a great number of slaves, as well as the widespread practice of enslaving civilians in the course of war, suggests that the demand for slaves in Greece was considerable in the 6th and 5th centuries BC and that a certain number of them were provided from the colonies in the northern Black Sea region.

It seems that the Greek colonists tried to avoid direct conflict with the Scythians but instead maintained a business-like relationship with the neighbouring nomads. The slaves were brought from Scythia to the Greek colonies mainly by means of trade. Here we should return to the controversy about the hypothesis of the grain trade. Ščeglov rightly noted that none of the literary sources mentioning the export of grain from the northern Black Sea state that the grain came from Scythia. Let me add that the Scythian kings, who supposedly wanted to "monopolise the grain trade" lived in the territories bordering the Greek colonies in Scythia, where, it should be remembered, no farming was practised during the period under consideration. Therefore, the knowledge of grain farming must have been learnt by the Scythian kings either from their forest-steppe neighbours or from the Greeks. The steppe-dwelling Scythians might even have imported grain from their northern neighbours. However, so far no studies of the agriculture in the forest-steppe zone have shown that grain was grown for export.[20] The possible imports from the forest-steppe must therefore be limited to the crops typically associated with nomads – barley and millet. We may suppose with a fair degree of probability that the export of grain from the forest steppe terminated in the steppe – with the traditional and undemanding consumers of these grain species.

Long-distance transportation of grain apparently presented considerable difficulties for nomadic societies. Thus, for instance, during the raids of the late Crimean nomads into the Dnieper region, grain has never been recorded among their loot.[21] If capturing grain was the purpose of the nomadic for-

Commodity	Price in drachms
Wine of high quality (1 l)	0.2-0.3
Wine of poor quality (1 l)	0.1
Grain (wheat) (1 medimnos)	6-9
Grain (barley) (1 medimnos)	3-5
Horse	1200
Slave (educated)	1200
Slave (average individual)	200
Slave (average individual)	300
Slave (average individual)	450
Slave (immature)	100
Slave (mine worker)	225
Slave (foreman)	350
Slave (workshop manager)	550
Slave (steward)	6000

Fig. 1. The value of different kinds of goods in Classical Greece according to written sources: wine (Jajlenko 1982, 236), grain (Vinogradov 1971, 67), horses (Dovatur 1980, 60) & slaves (Vallon 1941, 97; Dovatur 1980, 60).

ays, then they should have had to co-ordinate their raids with the harvest season when the grain-bins were full.

Let us compare the price of slaves with that of wheat – two kinds of Greek imports which have both been put forward as the most important. The cost of a slave from the northern Black Sea region in the late 5th century BC (144 drachms) was close to the price of 624 litres of wheat (144/12 x 52=624) from the same region. It should be noted that Ju.G. Vinogradov, on the basis of a recent epigraphic find, confirmed Blavatskij's assumption that the cost of wheat in Attica was 22.5-30% higher than in the markets of Berezan' and Phanagoria in the northern Black Sea region.[22] Hence we may suppose that any goods delivered from the Pontic colonies could have been sold with a retail margin of at least 20-30% (transportation expenses, cargo insurance, various dues etc.).

It is thus clear that it was more profitable to export slaves than to export wheat from Scythia (or perhaps rather barley or millet, as the palaeobotanical evidence indicates). Indeed, a feature of the grain trade is its seasonality. It was necessary first to cultivate the grain in a zone which did not offer optimal conditions for agriculture, then to harvest, transport, and preserve it during transit. By contrast, slaves could quite easily have been captured by the nomads in any season of the year and sold shortly after in the slave-market. For that reason the cost of growing grain in the northern Black Sea region was relatively high, while its price in the markets in Attica was relatively low. By contrast, the cost of capturing a barbarian slave was low, while the market price was fairly high as compared to other goods.

The profitability of slave-trade was certainly higher than that of the grain-trade in terms of the cost of transportation from the northern Black Sea area. On the evidence of the Athenian prices (Fig. 1), according to which 1 kg of grain cost 12/(52 x 0.63)=0.37 drachms (0.63 – the coefficient of conversion of dry measures to weight), while 1 kg of the live article cost 144/70=2.06

drachms (70 kg – the weight of an average individual), we can deduce that the trade in slaves must have been 2.06/0.37=5.7 times more profitable than the grain-trade. Moreover, the cost of transporting slaves was lower, in particular due to their smaller size (624 litres of wheat occupies almost ten times more room than a slave).

Among the Greek centres most prominent in the slave-trade was the island of Chios – one of the most prosperous in Greece according to Thucydides.[23] The wealth and power of Chios during the period under consideration suggests that the number of slaves traded must have been very high. It should also be noted that Chios was known for its excellent wine and therefore one of the largest wine exporters. A point of significance for our study is the fact that Chian amphorae number among the most frequent imports in the northern Black Sea region. Olbia and the settlement of Elizavetovskoe were undoubtedly transit points in the trade with the barbarian hinterland.[24] Therefore, we will consider the trade in these centres in detail.

Written evidence of the 6th and the first half of the 5th century BC from Olbia and its periphery (including the letter of Achillodoros from Berezan', the letter of an unknown author from Olbia written on the wall of an amphora in the Fikellura style, and the letter of Apatourios) have been compiled and analysed by Ju.G. Vinogradov, V.P. Jajlenko, and A.S. Rusjaeva.[25] The majority of the slaves in Olbia and at the settlements in its neighbourhood were barbarians. On the evidence of the letter of Achillodoros, a family of citizens with eight members had at their disposal five slaves.[26] It is true that these calculations are far from being indisputable, and the source itself does not indicate that slave-holding was common. Nothing indicates large-scale slave-holding in the Greek cities on the northern Black Sea littoral during the Archaic period.[27] This is especially true for the period from the 6th to the first quarter of the 5th century BC, when the use of slaves was limited to household production, while in agriculture and animal husbandry slaves were seldom employed.

Since the general demand for slaves in Olbia of the 6th and in first quarter of the 5th century BC was negligible, it is quite possible that the Olbiopolitans transferred most of the slaves from Scythian lands to the slave-market on Chios, receiving in exchange large quantities of wine and, of course, olive oil. Pottery from Chios is widely represented among the materials from Olbia "…beginning with the ware painted over a light coating of the end of the 7th to the first half of the 6th century BC and finishing with the plump-necked amphorae of the second quarter of the 5th century BC".[28]

The economy of the nomadic Scythian society did not require any great number of slaves, having a completely different basis to that of its more civilised neighbours. In the early Scythian period, defeated enemies were killed and scalped rather than enslaved, as witnessed by Herodotos, according to whom the Scythians had no purchased slaves at all (Hdt. 4.72). He also mentions the presence of domestic slaves only: usually these were blinded captives – milk-churners (Hdt. 4.2) or shepherds. Moreover, killing instead of capturing enemies was considered an act of exceptional valour by the early Scythians:

> "The Scythian soldier drinks the blood of the first man he over-throws in battle. Whatever number he slays, he cuts off all their heads, and carries them to his king; since he is thus entitled to a share of the booty, whereto he forfeits all claim if he does not produce a head" (Hdt. 4.64).

At the beginning of the Archaic period the Scythians did not impede the trade links between the forest steppe on the right bank of the Dnieper and the Greek colonies, Olbia in particular. This is suggested by the fact that in the middle of the 6th century BC the regular importation of wine to the right-bank steppe (via the southern Bug River) had already started; later it spread to the left-bank area (via the Dnieper) as well. Greek articles were conveyed by Greek merchants, who freely passed through the sparsely set-tled steppe territories.[29]

Considering the character in general of the slave-trade in the northern Black Sea region during the 6th and the first quarter of the 5th century BC, we may state that most of the barbarian slaves were intended for export.

That situation changed dramatically from around 475 BC. This period is defined as the primary period of Olbia's urbanisation characterised by a reduction of the *chora*, the boom in construction within the city and the rapid development of various manufactures.[30] As a consequence the use of slave labour expanded. In construction work in particular, the need for unskilled slave-labour increased and the majority of slaves who were being delivered from Scythia, must have been required by Olbia itself. The dynamic nature of the Scythian slave-trade afforded a quick respond to the rapid develop-ment of the Greek colonies.[31]

Owing to the fact that the need for slaves in steppe Scythia was negligi-ble, it was possible for it to become the main supplier of slaves to the devel-oping Greek *poleis*. Probably in the first half of the 5th century BC the Scythians felt the intensification of the demand for slaves by the colonists. The nomadic Scythians were unquestionably interested in maintaining peaceful relations with their southern neighbours because of the develop-ment of the slave-trade. An increase in the amount of Greek imports found in Scythian burials[32] is observable which may be interpreted as revenue from the slave-trade.

The question arises as to the sources of the captives. As I have demon-strated earlier, the sphere of economic interests of the Scythians included both the Greeks and the population of the forest steppe.[33] A feature of the forest steppe was the presence of numerous settlements with developed agricultural lands supporting a high density of fairly peace-loving people. It should be noted in this context that the penetration of different elements of the material culture of the forest steppe into the adjacent territories was minimal, being represented only by traces of a cultural diffusion rather than by results of any expansion. The peaceful character of the forest steppe population is unquestionable. Thus there have been discovered in the Kiev-Čerkassk region three town-sites, 25 settlement-sites, and about 200 burials from the 7th century BC; and 15 town-sites, 14 settlement-sites and only 97 burials from the 6th and 5th centuries BC. These data indicate that the region was fairly densely populated.[34] A considerable number of sites of settled population of the same period are also located in the territory on the left bank of the Dnieper, the settlement-site of Bel'skoe being the most significant and well-studied among them.

The town-sites are concentrated in the southern part of the right bank of the Dnieper forming a system of defence. The military threat to the forest steppe from the steppe Scythians took the form of raids of varying intensity, which were aimed not at the capture of territories but rather at the capture of cattle and people, and perhaps the establishment of military and political control by means of the establishment of a number of controlling bases. An incursion (lasting two weeks, of which plundering of the settlement took one to two days) might have been undertaken in any season of the year. In the course of one raid, according to later written sources, it was possible to seize from several hundreds to several tens of thousands of captives.[35] The cost of the captured slaves was determined by the expenses of escorting the slaves from north to south.[36] Slaves might have been sold at any time in Olbia or in Bosporos, from where some of them were possibly shipped off at once to Chios, Athens etc.

On the basis of what has been said above, we can conclude that in the middle of the 5th century BC the major constituent of the Graeco-Scythian trade (which was to become the basis of the growth in the wealth of steppe Scythia) was not the grain trade but rather the developing slave- trade that towards 400 BC had taken on a systematic character.

Several stages may be tentatively distinguished in the slave-trade and associated with the economic relations between Greeks and Scythians in the northern Black Sea area. During the first stage (from the 6th to the middle of the 5th century BC), there were on the one hand, in the forest steppe, some economically advanced regions with a peaceful population who had no special need for economic contacts with their southern neighbours; on the other hand in the South in the steppe and on the Pontic coast new immigrants were still settling – both Scythians and Greeks. The Scythian nomads, due to the nature of their economy, had no need of a great number of slaves. The Greeks had no need of slaves either. Hence, the slave-trade in the initial phase of the Archaic period (approximately the entire 6th century BC) was of a moderate character and its development was determined mostly by the need of slaves in Greece.

The situation in the slave-trade changed in the second stage starting around 475 BC. The urbanisation of Olbia lead to an increased need for slaves for construction and manufacturing. The nomads of steppe Scythia began to play a still more active role in the supply of slaves. Accordingly, the attitude of the nomads to their captives also changed: killing them ceased and they were used as trade objects instead. The steppe Scythians began to understand that the trade in slaves was more profitable than trade in other goods, including the grain-trade. The most probable source of slaves was the population of the forest steppe. In the 5th century BC the foundations were laid for an economic system based on slave-trade which generated wealth for steppe Scythia.

Notes

1. Ščeglov 1987, 99-122; Kryžickij & Ščeglov 1991, 54-67.
2. Vallon 1941; Blavatskij 1954, 31-56; Dovatur 1980.
3. Vinogradov 1983, 283; Frolov 1998, 135-152; Lejpuns'ka 1991, 76-87; Kryžickij & Otreško 1986, 3-17; Kryžickij, Bujskich, Burakov & Otreško 1989.
4. Smirnov 1935.
5. Grakov 1939, 231-312; 1950, 10-15.
6. Chazanov 1972; Šelov 1972.
7. Il'inskaja 1966.
8. Terenožkin 1977, 3-29.
9. Zlatkovskaja 1971.
10. Finley 1962 51-90; Patterson 1982; Arnold 1988 179-192; Cunliffe 1988.
11. Braund & Tsetskhladze 1989, 114-125.
12. Taylor 2001, 27-43.
13. Vallon 1941, 103; Dovatur 1980, 97.
14. Vachtina 1984, 9.
15. Lejpuns'ka 1991, 85.
16. Grakov 1939, 231-312.
17. D.P. Kallistov considered them to be slaves, see Kallistov 1949, 139.
18. Blavatskij 1954, 31-54.
19. Kljačko 1966, 114-127.
20. Kovpanenko & Januševič 1975, 147-151; Šramko 1987, 86; Paškevič 2001, 133-137.
21. Boplan 1990, 61; Krymskij 1996, 185.
22. Vinogradov 1971, 75.
23. Blavatskij 1954, 31-56; Kallistov, Nejhardt, Šifman & Šišova 1968; Dovatur 1980, 92.
24. Brašinskij 1980, 102-103.
25. Vinogradov 1971; 1983, 293; Jajlenko 1974, 138-140; 1975, 133-149; Rusjaeva 1987, 134-154.
26. Kryžickij 1989, 93.
27. Lejpuns'ka 1991, 85.
28. Kryžickij 1989, 80.
29. Vachtina 1984.
30. Kryžickij 1989, 14.

31. Gavriljuk 1995, 69.
32. Onajko 1970; Bandurovskij 2001, 76.
33. Gavriljuk 1996, 290.
34. Kovpanenko 1989, 135.
35. Boplan 1990, 61.
36. Boplan 1990, 60, 62.

Bibliography

Bandurovskij, O.V. 2001. Antyčni amfory z kurganiv skifskogo periodu livo-
        berežnoi lisostepovoi Ukrainy, *ArcheologiaKiev* 1, 68-79.
Blavatskij, V.D. 1954. Rabstvo i ego istočniki d antičnych gosudarstvach
        Severnogo Pričernomor'ja, *SovA* 20, 31-56.
Boplan, G. 1990. *Opys Ukrainy*. Kyiv.
Brašinskij, I.B. 1980. *Grečeskij keramičeskij import na Nižnem Donu v V – III vv.
        do n.e.* Leningrad.
Braund, D.C. & G.R. Tsetskladze 1989. The export of slaves from Colchis,
        ClQ 39, 114-125.
Chazanov, A.M. 1972. O charaktere rabovladenija u skifov, *VDI* 1, 23-28.
Cunliffe, B. 1988. *Greeks, Romans and Barbarians: Spheres of Interaction.*
        London.
Dovatur, A.I. 1980. *Rabstvo v Attike v VI-V vv. do n.e.* Leningrad.
Finley, M.I. 1962. The Black Sea and Danubian Regions and the Slave Trade
        in Antiquity, *Klio* 40, 51-90.
Frolov, E.D. 1998. Skify v Afinach, *VDI* 1, 135-152.
Gavriljuk, N.A. 1995. *Skotovodstvo Stepnoi Skifii*. Kiev.
Gavriljuk, N.A. 1996. Ekonomičeskij aspekt otnošenij kočevogo i osedlogo
        naselenija Severnogo Pričernomor'ja v VI - ser. V vv. do n.e., in: O.B.
        Suprunenko et al. (eds.), *Bil'ske gorodišče v konteksti vyvčennja pam'jatok
        rann'ogo zaliznogo viku Europy*. Poltava, 286-292.
Grakov, B.N. 1939. Materialy po istorii Skifii v grečeskich nadpisjach Balkan-
        skogo poluostrova i Maloi Azii, *VDI* 3, 231-312.
Grakov, B.N. 1950. Skifskij Gerakl, *Kratkie soobščenija instituta istorii materi-
        al'noj kul'tury* 34, 10-15.
Il'inskaja, V.A. 1966. Skifskie kurgany okolo Borispolja, *SovA* 3, 152-172.
Jajlenko, V.P. 1974. K datirovke i čteniju berezanskogo pis'ma Achillodora,
        VDI 1, 133-152.
Jajlenko, V.P. 1975. Voprosy interpretacii berezanskogo pis'ma Achillodora,
        VDI 3, 133-150.
Jajlenko, V.P. 1982. *Grečeskaja kolonizacija VII-III vv. do. n.e.* Moskva.
Kallistov, D.P. 1949. *Očerki po istorii Severnogo Pričernomor'ja antičnoj epochi.*
        Leningrad.
Kljačko, N.B. 1966. Stely germokopidov kak istočnik svedenij o rabach v V v.
        do n.e., *VDI* 3, 114-127.
Kallistov, D.P., A.A. Nejhardt, I.S. Šifman & I.A. Šišova 1968. *Rabstvo na peri-
        ferii antičnogo mira*. Leningrad.

Kovpanenko, G.T. & Z.V. Januševič 1975. Otpečatki zlakov na keramike Trachtemirovskogo gorodišča, in: A.I. Terenožkin (ed.), *Skifskij mir*. Kiev, 147-151.

Kovpanenko, G.T., S.S. Bessonova & S.A. Skoryj 1989. *Pamjatniki skifskoj epochi Dneprovskogo Lesostepnogo Pravoberež'ja*. Kiev.

Krymskij, A. 1996. *Istorija Turetčiny*. Kyiv-Lviv.

Kryžyc'kyj, S.D. & O.M. Ščeglov 1991. Pro zernovyj potencial antičnych deržav Pivničnogo Pryčornomor'ja, *ArcheologijaKiev* 1, 54-67.

Kryžickij, S.D. & V.M. Otreško 1986. K probleme formirovanija Ol'vijskogo polisa, in: *Ol'vija i ee okruga*. Kiev, 3-17.

Kryžickij, S.D., S.B. Bujskich, A.V. Burakov & V.M. Otreško 1989. *Sel'skaja okruga Ol'vii*. Kiev.

Lejpuns'ka, N.O. 1991. Stanovlennja antyčnogo sposoby vyrobnyctva u Nyžnjomu Pobuži (za archeologičnymy danymy), *ArcheologiaKiev* 3, 76-87.

Onajko, N.A. 1970. *Antičnyi import v Pridneprov'je i Pobuž'je v VII-V vv. do n.e.* Moskva.

Paškevič, G.A. 2001. Paleobotaničeskie issledovanija materialov Motroninskogo gorodišča, in: *Motroninskoe gorodišče skifskoj epochi*. Kiev-Krakov, 133-137.

Patterson, O. 1982. *Slavery and Social Death*. Cambridge.

Rusjaeva, A.S. 1987. Epigrafičeskie pamjatniki, in: S.D. Kryžickij (ed.), *Kultura naselenija Ol'vii i ee okrugi v archaičeskoe vremja*. Kiev, 134-154.

Smirov, A.P. 1935. Rabovladel'českij stroj u skifov-kočevnikov. Moskva.

Ščeglov, A.N. 1987. Severopontijskaja torgovlja chlebom vo vtoroj polovine VII-V vv. do n.e. in: O. Lordkipanidze (ed.), *Pričernomor'e v VII – V vv. do n.e.* Vani, 99-122.

Šelov, D.B. 1972. Social'noe razvitie skifskogo obščestva, *Voprosy istorii* 3, 63-78.

Šramko, B.A. 1987. *Bel'skoe gorodišče skifskoj epochi (gorod Gelon)*. Kiev.

Taylor, T. 2001. Believing the ancients: quantitative and qualitative dimensions of slavery and the slave trade in later prehistoric Eurasia, *World Archaeology* 33.1, 27-43.

Terenožkin, A.I. 1977. Obščestvennyj stroj skifov, in: *Skify i sarmaty*. Kiev, 3-29.

Vachtina, M.Ju. 1984. *Greko-varvarskie kontakty VII-VI vv. do n.e. po materialam stepnoj i lesostepnoj zon Severo-Zapadnogo Pričernomor'ja i Kryma*. Leningrad.

Vallon, A. 1941. *Istorija rabstva v antičnom mire*. Moskva.

Vinogradov, Ju.G. 1971. Drevnejšee grečeskoe pis'mo s ostrova Berezan', *VDI* 4, 74-100.

Vinogradov, Ju.G. 1983, Polis v Severnom Pričernomor'e, in: E.S. Golubcova (ed.), *Antičnaja Grecija*. Moskva, 366-420.

Zlatkovskaja, T.D. 1971. O charaktere rabstva vo Frakii VII-V vv. do n.e., *VDI* 1, 54-64.

An Istrian Dedication to Leto

Alexandru Avram

One of the fragments included in the corpus of Istrian inscriptions by D.M. Pippidi under the heading *Varia incerta* is a small piece of marble with beautiful engraved letters (*I. Histriae* 380). Nothing is known about the circumstances of this find. The editor noted that the fragment is broken on both the left and right sides and dated it to the 4th century BC. In his book-review of *I. Histriae*, L. Moretti suggested that this fragment could belong to a decree.[1] However, he failed to observe that, according to the description given by Pippidi, only the lateral sides of the stone were broken. This would mean that the text could not have had more than four lines; not enough for a decree!

The stone is, in fact, a base which could support a small bronze (?) statuette, so the attempt to restore the text must search for a dedication formula. Pippidi gave the following transcription:

- - - ΟΘΕΜ - - - - - - -
- - - ΤΟΓΕΝ - - - - -
- - - ΝΗΚΟΣ - - - - -
- - - ΛΗΤΟ - - - - -

A revised examination (August 2002) of the stone in the *lapidarium* of the Museum of Histria / Istros (inv. no. 238) revealed that the first letter (l. 1) is an *omega*, that in l. 2 before the *tau* there are the remains of the right foot of another *omega* and, particularly important, there is no trace of any letter before the *lambda* at the beginning of l. 4. The disposition of the letters indicates a good *stoichedon*. It is therefore certain that ΛΗΤΟ is the beginning of the last word, and insofar as the text seems to be a dedication, I assume that we have here the dative Λητο[ῖ].

Starting from this crucial point, the next step would be to identify the name of the dedicator. The combination of the letters revealed by l. 2 offers plenty of scope to develop it into a common Greek personal name, while the letters in l. 1 could permit other solutions. The key seems to be l. 3: it is hard to conceive of the group ΝΗΚΟΣ as being a part of one word (neither *ethnikon* nor anything else), and the sole remaining – but very attractive way of dividing it – is [- - -]ΝΗ ΚΟΣ[- - -]. I suggest [γυ]νὴ κόσ[μημα] and consequently the genitive [Πρ]ωτογέν[ους] for the name in l. 2, which both make a perfect *stoichedon*. An alternative possibility is to presuppose a formula such as [ἡ δεῖνα] | [Πϱ]ωτογέν[ους], | [γυ]γὴ Κοσ[- - -], i.e. "daughter of Protogenes and wife of Kos[- - -]", without any mention of the object of the dedication; however, although not obligatory, a δέ after [γυ]γή might be expected.[2]

The person who consecrated an ornament (κόσ[μημα])[3] to Leto was therefore a woman, the wife of Protogenes. Her name needs to be identified in l. 1, and the only possible solution would be to find a *compositum* of -θεμις.[4] Feminine names composed with -θεμις seem to be rather rare, and I have not found any name (masc. or fem.) ending in [- - -]ωθεμις.[5] However, [Σ]ωθεμ[ίς] seems to me acceptable as an onomastic composition.[6] This would also contribute to the symmetry of the text.

I suggest therefore the following restoration:

[Σ] Ω Θ Ε Μ [Ι Σ]
[Π Ρ] Ω Τ Ο Γ Ε Ν [Ο Υ Σ]
[Γ Υ] Ν Η Κ Ο Σ [Μ Η Μ Α]
Λ Η Τ Ο [Ι]

[Σ]ωθεμ[ὶς]
[Πϱ]ωτογέν[ους]
[γυ]γὴ κόσ[μημα]
Λητο[ῖ]

"Sothemis, wife of Protogenes, (dedicated) the ornament to Leto".

Pippidi dated the inscription to the 4th century BC. However, a date towards the end of 5th century seems to me more attractive. In fact, the genitive in l. 2 is restored, and an Ionic [Πϱ]ωτογέν[εος] (claimed by a higher dating) still remains possible.

This is the second document attesting the cult of Leto in Istros. The other inscription is that on a large base (now lost) for a statue of the goddess (end of the 5th century BC) edited by S. Lambrino[7] and republished by M.L. Lazzarini,[8] by Pippidi in *I. Histriae* 170 and finally by M. Alexandrescu Vianu[9]. All the editors restored:

[ὁ δεῖνα] Ἱ[ππο]λό[χο - - -]εμιος Λητοῖ
[ἀ]νέθηκ[ε]ν ἐπὶ Ἱπ[πολόχ]ο τõ Θεοδ[ότο]
ἱέ[ϱε]ω.

Lambrino and Pippidi connected not only the priest Hippolochos, son of Theodotos, but also the presumed Hippolochos (l. 1) to a well-known family of priests of Apollon Ietros. However, l. 1 remains a bold restoration of the patronymic, while in this case the next visible letters, [- -]εμιος – a clear Ionic genitive ending – cannot be explained. The drawing shows l. 1 at the place of the supposed I the lower part of an inexpressive *hasta* and then, after a space allowing the insertion of 3 or 4 letters, an oblique *hasta* which could belong to a triangular letter (Α, Δ, Λ) or to an M as well (see the form of the M in [- - -]ΕΜΙΟΣ) and a round letter, perhaps an Ο. The preserved genitive at the end of the line suggests [- - -θ]έμιος, i.e. another *compositum* of -θεμις as in our previous inscription. Initially, I thought of ['Απολ]λο[θ]έμιος but the *lacuna* before [- - - θ]εμιος indicates at least 3, if not 4 missing letters. I would therefore suggest, with due caution, Μο[λποθ]έμιος,[10] a good Apollonic name which occurs at Nymphaion.[11] The dedicator would be a son or (less convincingly) a daughter of this Molpothemis.

The coincidence that a woman possibly called Σωθεμίς and the son (or the daughter) of a man possibly called Μολπόθεμις – bearing anyway names which are *composita* of -θεμις – both gave dedications to Leto is less surprising if we remember a quite similar case in the family of the dedicators to Leto's son Apollon.[12] They bear in fact the same traditional names ('Ιππόλοχος, Θεόδοτος etc.). I suggest therefore, that the woman of *I. Histriae* 380 and the father of the dedicator of *I. Histriae* 170 belonged to the same family, and I suspect that they had close connections to the family of Apollon's priests.

"Letokult ist für Milet/Didyma also spätestens seit dem 6. Jh. v. Chr. anzunehmen, und es wäre zunächst durchaus denkbar, dass die Göttin schon früher gekommen ist. Leto gilt als kleinasiatische Göttin, die zusammen mit Apollon eingewandert ist".[13] A short time after these lines had been written, this assertion found confirmation through the Orphic tablets of bone found at Berezan' (last quarter of the 6th century BC), where Leto is mentioned in a "Didymaic" context: μέμνημαι Λητō(ς).[14] It should be noted that with the exception of Berezan' and Istros, the cult of Leto is not yet attested in other Milesian colonies.[15]

Although obviously less spectacular, the two inscriptions from Istros (*I. Histriae* 170 and now also 380) can therefore provide good evidence for the diffusion of the cult of Leto from Didyma to the Pontic colonies of Miletos.

Notes

1. Moretti 1983, 53: "riterrei tuttavia lacinie di decreti i nrr. 380, 381, 386, 398". More convincingly about the same inscription: Vinogradov & Karyškovskij 1984, 180-181.
2. For a dedication made by the wife of a citizen, see e.g. Lazzarini 1976, 185, no. 41 = *IG* I³, 894 (Athens, c. 430-420 BC) : [..... Π]ρέπιδο[ς γυνὲ] | [Χσυπετ]αιōνος [τει] | ['Αθεναί]αι ἀνέθ[εκεν].
3. This seems to me a plausible restoration, although the "ornament" (which could mean a number things) is not listed among the objects dedicated to gods by Lazzarini 1976. I do not know of any special study devoted to the term κόσμημα but I think I have found a convincingly restored context for its use in the decree Şahin 1994, l. II.35-36 (= *SEG* XLIV, 949), where the "ornaments" are juxtaposed with vases: ποτήρια ἢ κοσμ[ήματα ἀργυρᾶ ἢ χρυσᾶ]. For the architectural cognates κόσμος (French "ordre, frise"), κόσμησις or ἐπικόσμησις ("ornementation, embellissement"), see Hellmann 1992, 231-233.

4. "Ce type de noms en -θεμις est bien attesté par de nombreux composés variés": Robert 1967, 20, who refers to Bechtel 1917 and adds Λυσίθεμις (Βόμβος Λυσιθέμιδος from Assos: Robert 1966, 16-17, l. 9-10 of the decree, now also in *I. Ilion* 10, 77 BC).
5. I used especially Bechtel 1917, 200-201, and the *LGPN*.
6. See, as a close parallel, ’Ανθεμίς: *LGPN* I (Rhodos, Samos), II (Athens), III A (Lipara), III B (Larissa), with references.
7. Lambrino 1937, 352-362.
8. Lazzarini 1976, 202, no. 173.
9. Alexandrescu Vianu 2000, 87-88, no. 102 (and fig. 4, Lambrino's drawing). I prefer the earlier dating, mentioned above (Lambrino and Alexandrescu Vianu), to the 4th century admitted by Lazzarini and Pippidi.
10. Robert 1967, 20: "nom dont la première partie forme des noms surtout dans les pays ioniens ou influencés par l'Ionie, particulièrement à Milet où florissait l'institution des *molpoi*". Cf. Masson 1984, 52 = Masson 1992 II, 431: "les noms en Μολπο- sont également caractéristiques pour le domaine ionien, comme le montrent déjà les exemples de Bechtel 323-324".
11. Sokolova, Pavličenko & Kasparov 1999, 330: Μολποθέμιος τô ’Αλεξάνδρο. Cf. the references given by the authors to Μολπαγόρης and Μολπᾶς attested on the North coast of the Black Sea (to be found in *LGPN* IV, forthcoming).
12. The genealogy of this family suggested by Lambrino and Pippidi has been convincingly changed by Alexandrescu Vianu 1989, 1-5.
13. Ehrhardt 1988, 159 (with references to the cult of Leto in Didyma). See also Kahil 1992.
14. Rusjaeva 1986, 25-64 (= *SEG* XXXVI, 694) = Dubois 1996, 146-154 no. 93; cf. Ehrhardt 1987, 116-117; Rusjaeva 1992, 29-41.
15. Ehrhardt (1988, 160), prudently adds the theophoric name Λητόδωρος from the Milesian Gorgippia (*CIRB* 1179.25-26: [Λη?]τοδώρου, 3rd cent. AD) and the Teian Phanagoria (*CIRB* 976.4, AD 151) but he accepts himself that "beide Belege stammen allerdings erst aus der Kaiserzeit". The restoration of the name in the Gorgippian inscription is not absolutely certain. Consequently the name will be not registered in *LGPN* IV.

Bibliography

Alexandrescu Vianu, M. 1989. Notes de prosopographie histrienne: la famille d'Hippolochos, fils de Théodotos, in: *Mélanges Pierre Lévêque* III. *Anthropologie et société* (Annales littéraires de l'Université de Besançon 429). Besançon, 1-5.

Alexandrescu Vianu, M. 2000. *Histria IX. Les statues et les reliefs en pierre.* Bucarest–Paris.

Bechtel, F. 1917. *Die historischen Personennamen des Griechischen bis zur Kaiserzeit.* Halle.

Dubois, L. 1996. *Inscriptions grecques dialectales d'Olbia du Pont.* Genève.

Ehrhardt, N. 1987. Die politischen Beziehungen zwischen den griechischen Schwarzmeergründungen und ihren Mutterstädten. Ein Beitrag zur Bedeutung von Kolonialverhältnissen in Griechenland, in: *Rapports et communications. 9ᵉ Congrès international d'épigraphie grecque et latine.* Trinovi, 78-117.

Ehrhardt, N. 1988. *Milet und seine Kolonien. Vergleichende Untersuchung der kultischen und politischen Einrichtungen*[2]. Frankfurt am Main–Bern–New York–Paris.

Hellmann, M.-Chr. 1992. *Recherches sur le vocabulaire de l'architecture grecque, d'après les inscriptions de Délos*. Athènes–Paris.

Kahil, L. 1992. Léto, *LIMC* VI.1, 256-264.

Lambrino, S. 1937. La famille d'Apollon à Histria, *AEphem* 100, 352-362.

Lazzarini, M.L. 1976. Le formule delle dediche votive nella Grecia arcaica, *MemLinc*, ser. 8, 19.2, 47-354.

Masson, O. 1984. Quelques noms de magistrats monétaires grecs IV. Noms de monétaires à Abdère et Maronée, *RNum*, 6e sér., 26, 48-60.

Masson, O. 1992. *Onomastica Graeca selecta* I–II. Paris.

Moretti, L. 1983. Il Corpus delle iscrizioni di Histria e una dedica arcaica ad Afrodite, *RFil* 111, 52-57.

Robert, L. 1966. *Monnaies antiques en Troade*. Genève-Paris.

Robert, L. 1967. *Monnaies grecques. Types, légendes, magistrats monétaires et géographie*. Genève.

Rusjaeva, A.S. 1986. Milet-Didimy – Borisfen-Ol'vija. Problemy kolonizacii Nižnego Pobuž'ja, *VDI* 2, 25-64.

Rusjaeva, A.S. 1992. *Religija i kul'ty antičnoj Ol'vii*. Kiev.

Sokolova, O.Ju., N.A. Pavličenko & A.K. Kasparov 1999. Novye nachodki na territorii Nimfejskogo nekropolja, *Hyperboreus* 5.2, 326-339.

Şahin, S. 1994. Piratenüberfall auf Teos. Volksbeschluß über die Finanzierung der Erpressungsgelder, *EpigrAnat* 23, 1-36.

Vinogradov, Ju.G. & P.O. Karyškovskij 1984. Rev. of I. Histriae, *VDI* 3, 174-183.

Abbreviations

CIRB   V.V. Struve et al., *Corpus inscriptionum Regni Bosporani*. Moskva-Leningrad 1965.

I. Histriae   D.M. Pippidi, *Inscripţiile din Scythia Minor greceşti şi latine* 1. *Histria şi împrejurimile*. Bucureşti 1983.

I. Ilion   P. Frisch, *Die Inschriften von Ilion* (Inschriften griechischer Städte aus Kleinasien 3). Bonn 1975.

LGPN   P.M. Fraser & E. Matthews (eds.), *A Lexicon of Greek Personal Names*. Oxford. I (1987); II (1994); III A (1997); III B (2000); IV (forthcoming).

The Main Development of the Western Temenos of Olbia in the Pontos

Anna S. Rusjaeva

In the latter half of the 20th century, two large ritual precincts were discovered in Olbia – the Eastern and the Western .[1] In the former, sanctuaries of Apollon Delphinios, Zeus and a common Sanctuary of Zeus and Athena were excavated. Unearthed in the second *temenos* were sanctuaries of Apollon Ietros and Apollon Boreas (possibly worshipped simultaneously with Apollon Ietros), the Mother of the Gods, the Dioskouroi, Hermes, Aphrodite, Athena, and other deities not mentioned in the inscriptions.

The total area of the excavated part of these sacred precincts now exceeded 6500 m². Taking into account that these two zones were separated from each other by a very broad street (10-11 m wide), probably constructed between the two *temenoi* as early as the second half of the 6th century BC to accommodate religious festivals and processions, the total space used for various ritual activities must have been even greater.[2] That such a large area was allotted in the central part of the Upper Town for worshipping a number of different deities, distinguishes Olbia from other ancient cities situated around the Black Sea, in that the construction of sacred precincts of this character with such a large number of sanctuaries was uncommon.

The economic and cultural prospering of Olbia, the periodic crises, invasions by barbarians – in particular of that of the Getae under the leadership of Burebista – and other calamities, were reflected *inter alia* in various materials recovered from the city's sanctuaries – both in the urban ones and in the extra-urban ones, including those on the border. These all functioned contemporaneously with the *polis* itself and were closely related to the life of the city's community. But the most significant place in the ideology of the Olbiopolitans was occupied by the worship of the main deities – the original patrons and protectors of their state for almost 10 centuries.[3]

The various epigraphical and archaeological evidence from the Western Temenos studied by the author enables us to consider its development throughout the four major periods of the history of the ancient world in general, and of the Olbian *polis* in particular: (1) the Archaic period (the second quarter of the 6th – first decade of the 5th century BC), (2) the Classical period (the second decade of the 5th – second third of the 4th century BC), (3) the Hellenistic period (the last third of the 4th – the middle of the 1st centu-

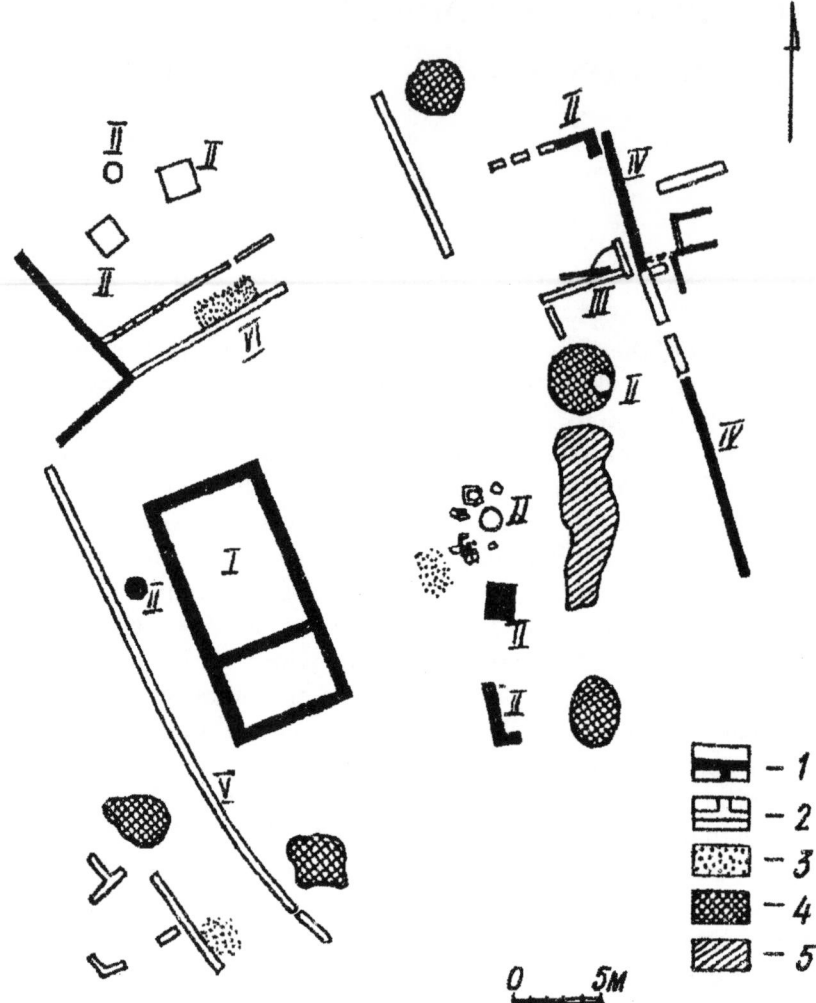

Fig. 1. Central part of the Western Temenos (after Kryžickij 1993 with corrections of A.S. Rusjaeva). 1) Stone masonry of the late Archaic period; 2) stone masonry of the Classical and Hellenistic periods; 3) pavements; 4) bothroi *of the 6th-5th century BC.*

ry BC), and (4) the Early Graeco-Roman period (the second half of the 1st century BC – 1st century AD). In each of these periods, certain local features and peculiarities are characteristic both in the building activities and in administrative and ritual activities, as well as in the diversity of the archaeological material, which is our main source for a comprehensive study of the development of the *temenos* in general and each particular sanctuary within its boundaries.

The Archaic period

For the beginning of the first stage (the late Archaic period), relatively few ritual activities have been recorded. They took the form of separate bonfires or single wooden altars for burning sacrificial offerings, and also included a very small number of votive gifts.[4] For these, in the 6th century some wooden tables and partitions were erected, as well as some primitive structures on posts on which traditionally were set *xoana*, statues and figurines of the worshipped deities. That such structures did indeed exist, is suggested by pits of various size found at the spots where the ancient surface is preserved intact.

No division between the separate sanctuaries of the early period has been discerned. Evidently, the first settlers, like all the Pontic Greeks of the Archaic period in general, still had no definite ideas about the necessity to demarcate the boundaries of individual sanctuaries. To all appearances, the sacred complexes were generally arranged arbitrarily, as was the case with many other early Greek sanctuaries. The possibility should not, however, be excluded that some structures and fences being made of wood have not, therefore, been preserved, and that trees, bushes and flowers may have been planted constituting additional features of the site.

Considering the excavated building remains and the fragments of pottery found (mostly East Greek of the second quarter of the 6th century BC), one should bear in mind that these were discovered within the oldest archaeological horizons with Greek material, which were later repeatedly subjected to modification and destruction during the building of later ritual structures of various types and periods, including numerous *bothroi*. Beneath many of the late structural remains still preserved *in situ*, the Archaic layers have never been excavated. As a result, we are entitled to presume that the first settlers organised their religious festivals and the related rituals observing the traditions brought from the *metropolis*.

At present, numerous early ceramic materials (mostly of the second quarter of the 6th century BC), similar to those found in the *temenos*, have already been recovered from excavations in Olbia itself, particularly in its south-eastern part.[5] Such materials from both sites confirm that the first religious rituals in honour of the main patron deities took place at the *temenos* at the time of the foundation of Olbia itself.[6] If this is so, then it was probably here that the Olbiapolitans kept the small bronze statue of the first patron Apollon Ietros in wearing a *kalathos* and holding a bow. Notwithstanding the periodic shifts in their political and religious ideas, sudden changes in the fate of their state, and various crises and disastrous barbarian incursions, they were able to preserve this, their most ancient idol for at least eight centuries, as is suggested by its representations on coins from the second half of the 2nd century AD.[7]

There can hardly be any doubt that as early as the 580s-550s BC, separate sanctuaries of Apollon Ietros – the chief god of the Milesian founders of many *poleis* in the Pontic region – were functioning within the Upper Town, as well as sanctuaries of the Mother of the Gods, also popular with all the Ionians, and Athena, whose cult was popular in Miletos and its territory during the period of colonisation. It is to precisely these deities that the oldest East Greek and Attic black-figured vessels with dedicatory graffiti in the Western Temenos were offered.[8] Although no dedications to Aphrodite Urania or the Dioskouroi have been found in the *temenos* from this period, it is probable that they were also worshipped here from the time of Olbia's foundation. The discovery of a Sanctuary of Aphrodite Urania dating to the 7th-5th century BC in Miletos,[9] and some very early evidence for her cult in Istria,[10] Borysthenes[11] and Olbia,[12] undoubtedly indicate that this goddess, along with other female deities, appeared as patroness of the Milesian-Pontic colonisation and of the family as the basic unit of the rising *poleis*. In the Western Temenos, there was a small sanctuary of this goddess. This was of the closed type with an altar and a stone fence and, judging by two graffiti found in it, it was called "ἄβατα 'Αφροδίτης – the *sancta sanctorum* of Aphrodite".[13]

The number of offerings that had previously been rising gradually, increased significantly in the third quarter of the 6th century – i.e. in the period when a new group of colonists had already come to the lower Bug region as a consequence of the Persian conquest of Ionia, which abruptly changed the entire situation in that region.[14] The social and political disturbances, very characteristic of many *poleis* during the period of colonisation, were probably the main reason why the Olbian *epoikoi* consulted the Didymean oracle. As a result, the *polis* not only received its name, but also, instead of the cult of Apollon Ietros, the cult of a new protector of the city– Apollon Delphinios (the aboriginal patron of Miletos) – was instituted.[15]

Contemporary with the introduction of this cult was a new type of currency – bronze coins in the shape of a dolphin, which for many years became was one of the main symbols of the Olbian *polis*.[16] Having rejected Apollon Ietros as the supreme god and his symbol, the arrowhead-coin,[17] Olbia thus to a certain extent segregated itself in its religious aspect from the other Milesian *apoikai*, in particular the western Pontic ones, which continued to consider Ietros their main protector. However, it is unlikely that the Olbiopolitans, especially the descendants of the aristocratic families of the first settlers, would have finally relinquished their participation in the sacral amphictyony, created by their ancestors under the aegis of this god. [18]

Thus the oldest evidence of the rites at the Western Temenos leads to three important conclusions:

(1) that the *apoikia* which later received the name of Olbia, or more exactly 'Ολβίη πόλις, probably arose in the second quarter of the 6th century BC;

(2) that Apollon Ietros, whose cult in particular was established in the early Milesian-Pontic *poleis*, was originally considered the city's main divine protector; and,

Fig. 2. Trenches remaining after the removal of stones from the foundation of the temple of Apollon Ietros. On the preserved parts of the adobe platforms are the structural remains of stone altars from the second half of the 1st century BC to 1st century AD (view from SW).

(3) that from the very beginning of the colonisation, an important role was also played by the cult of the Mother of the Gods.

Possibly, already in the earliest period of Olbia's history, a common temple was erected to these two deities. During the entire existence of this sacred precinct, they were worshipped (to a greater or lesser extent) at the same site, apparently as the original protectors of the first colonists. For the sacral protection in the new localities, in particular of those Greeks who penetrated the northern lands of the *oikoumene*, the cult of Apollon Boreas, only recorded in Olbia, was introduced. In the course of the excavations in the Western Temenos, three inscriptions dedicated to this god have been found: one on the neck of an amphora from Klazomenai dated to the middle or the third quarter of the 6th century BC, and two others on the fragments of Attic black-figured vessels of the last quarter of the same century.[19] In the first of these inscriptions, an offering of honey to Apollon Boreas, the dedicant, in the interpretation of Ju.G. Vinogradov, was a certain Anaperres, son of Anacharsis, probably to be identified with the well-known Graeco-Scythian sage Anacharsis.[20] It is quite likely that there was in Olbia a religious association of the elite propagating the significance of Apollon as the almighty

Fig. 3. General view of the Sanctuary of Apollon Ietros (left) and the Mother of the Gods (right). In the background, the sanctuary of an anonymous deity with a stepped altar and eschara *(view from S).*

god, as is suggested by the presence of the cult of Apollon Boreas – not to mention that of Apollon Ietros.[21]

The introduction of the cult of Apollon Delphinios and the foundation of his separate *temenos* on a new plot of land, though in the immediate vicinity of the old one discussed above, marked the beginning of a phase of intensive construction of cult buildings in all of the sanctuaries in the second half of the 6th century BC. In the north-western part of the *temenos*, in the third quarter of the 6th century, a small temple, the first in Olbia, was built of mud-bricks and wood with a small altar in front of its facade.[22]

The possibility cannot be ruled out that at the same time, in the course of the remodelling of the earlier sacred precinct, the latter or perhaps just one of the chief sanctuaries there were enclosed by a low wooden fence, the dedication of which is mentioned in a fragmentary graffito of this period.[23] It is common knowledge that a sacred fence, especially in the absence of any natural boundary, was traditionally an indispensable part of any Greek *temenos*.[24]

At the end of the 6th century BC, possibly even immediately after the destruction of the first temple, a new temple of Apollon Ietros was erected to the south of it on a well-levelled surface of soil for which many architectural decorations were produced in Miletos (Fig. 2).[25] According to the available evidence, this temple remained for 80 years a dominating feature not only of the sacred precinct but the entire city. It had been built much earlier than the mud-brick-and-wood temple of Apollon Delphinios in the Eastern Temenos, which did not possess such rich architectural décor.[26]

This difference in the two main cults of Apollon, one with the *epiklesis* of Ietros, and the other of Delphinios, may be explained by the prolonged social and ideological opposition between *apoikoi* and *epoikoi*. Judging by the evidence from the Olbian Archaic necropolis and the Western Temenos, in the second half of the 6th century BC many of the first settlers and their descendants were the richest persons in the *polis*. They possessed the best land in the area, and must have regarded themselves as the traditional patrimonial aristocracy.

It was undoubtedly at their expense that different temples, altars and some less important ritual buildings were erected in the Western Temenos; that various architectural decorations and sculptures (including some tomb monuments) were imported from the *metropolis* and other cities; that some general municipal improvements were carried out, and that the festivials and rituals common to the entire *polis* were organised. It was from their ranks that the priests and other religious officials must have been elected. In contrast, the *epoikoi* (who had escaped from Ionia after the Persian invasion and belonged to a lower social stratum) were probably not able to immediately build a temple to their original god Apollon Delphinios.

It was only after the lapse of some time and the corresponding change of generations, when the cult of Apollon Ietros in the *hypostasis* of the *archegetes* had begun to lose its former significance even among its traditional worshippers, that a temple was erected to Apollon Delphinios at the expense of the entire Olbian community, the citizens of which were no longer so highly differentiated in wealth – as may be judged by the mass burials of this period.[27] A fairly important role in the popularising of this cult and its increasing influence in public life was played by the union of the Molpoi in the name of which most of the dedications of this period were set up in the sanctuary of this god.[28]

In the second half of the 6th and beginning of the 5th century BC, throughout the entire area of the Western Temenos, the sanctuaries of many deities underwent various improvements.[29] The epigraphic evidence suggests that there was a certain chronological difference regarding the appearance of the first signed dedicatory offerings: those to Apollon Ietros are dated to the second quarter of the 6th century, those to the Mother of the Gods and Athena to the 560-550s, those to Apollon Boreas to the middle and the third quarter of the 6th century, those to the common Sanctuary of Aphrodite and Dionysos to the third quarter of the 6th century, and those to the Dioskouroi and Hermes to the last quarter of the same century.[30]

It is worth noting that the fragments bearing dedications (though rather rare), found in different *bothroi* on top of the ancient surface or trampled into

Fig. 4. Votive reliefs of the Mother of the Gods from the late Archaic period in the course of the excavation.

the soil, indicate that among the first settlers there were some well-educated citizens. An indication of a definite familiarity with the various myths is a dedication to Athena (the earliest in the northern Black Sea region) on a black-figured bowl of the second quarter of the 6th century with a representation of a seated Zeus and two standing Eileithyias with fillets in their hands, awaiting the birth of Athena from the god's head. The graffito is drawn over the heads of these figures, the initial letters of the name of Athena being arranged over the head of Zeus thus disclosing the meaning of the entire scene.[31] Dedications this early are fairly scarce even in different sanctuaries of the major centres of Greece to say nothing of the North Pontic ones. It was of no small importance that the leading families of the colonists were descendants of aristocratic and well-educated families originally from Miletos, where, as is well known, Greek philosophy had its cradle and the religious culture was highly developed as early as the first half of the 6th century.

The semi-dug-outs of the late Archaic period unearthed in the eastern part of the *temenos* and formerly regarded as the earliest dwellings of the colonists,[32] now seem rather to have been in some way related to this sacred area, although similar structures found in other areas of the city may, of course, have functioned as dwellings. Possibly, the builders of the first tem-

Fig. 5. Structural remains of the stone fences, altars, and a portico in the sanctuaries of Hermes and Aphrodite (view from N).

ple resided temporarily in some of the earliest semi-dug-outs within the *temenos*, while in others valuable offerings or building materials may have been stored. Corresponding to the period of the erection of the second temple are a number of semi-dug-outs ranged along the main longitudinal street. In some of these structures, various fragments of architectural elements of stone and terracotta, votives with different dedications, and numerous fragments of pottery from various manufacturing centres – Ionic bowls of different types in particular – were found.[33] Here, it seems, such pits served for burying the items of ritual furnishings and apparatus no longer in use.

Thus, in the course of the first stage, during the late Archaic period, the entire territory of the Western Temenos was divided into separate sanctuaries, the largest areas among them being occupied by the Sanctuary of Apollon Ietros and that of the Mother of the Gods located in close mutual proximity (Fig. 3). In the second half of the 6th century, when various temples and altars had already been built, the number of votives dedicated to different deities increased considerably, and various rituals with libations and animal sacrifices, including offerings not only of small livestock (mostly sheep and goats) but also of bulls, became much more frequent.[34]

Fig. 6. The remains of semi-dugout houses, bothroi *and stone one- and two-roomed buildings (view from SW).*

Of note among the votive gifts are the fragments of a variety of East Greek pottery, black-figured and red-figured vessels, including those produced by first-rate Athenian vase-painters, and apparently very expensive items of armour. A fragment of a bronze plate with a relief representation of two male figures, which was part of the decoration of an Argive shield, must be considered a unique find.[35] Especially amazing is the rich collection of Archaic architectural polychrome terracottas, which is so far unequalled both as regards sheer quantity and diversity in any other of the Pontic cities.[36] In the second half of the 6th century, two small votive steles for the Sanctuary of the Mother of the Gods were carved from local limestone but based on a Milesian model (Fig. 4).[37]

The Classical period

In its second phase, the Western Temenos gradually acquired its new appearance. The sanctuaries on its territory(?) were improved; in each of them stone altars were erected and some sanctuaries were encircled by low stone fences with entrances.[38] On all sides, the *temenos* was probably bordered by streets. The broad and well-made main street, situated between the two *temenoi*, served as a sacred road during various festivals and ritual processions. Different sport *agons* and ritual processions with torches took place

Fig. 7. Dedication of Andokides to Apollon on the bottom of an Attic black-glazed skyphos.

here, since it is unlikely that there was room for such activities in the dense-ly built-up city itself. Access to the small sanctuaries proper was possibly forbidden except to the priests and other officials of the cults, and also the builders of the sacred edifices. Indirectly, this is suggested by the stone enclosures for offerings, partially preserved near the fences of the sanctuary.

Throughout almost the entire 5th century, the Temple of Apollon Ietros, the decorations of which had already been produced in the late Archaic peri-od dominated in the *temenos*. In the other sanctuaries, only stone altars, mostly rectangular in form, were set up (Fig. 5).[39] After the temple had been constructed, the semi-dugouts described above ceased to exist, and over their fills various small one-roomed and two-roomed buildings were con-structed of stone and mud-brick. These structures undoubtedly belonged to the *temenos* and served as small storehouses for amphorae containing wine, oil and honey intended for libations and other ritual activities, and also for the storage of diverse cult equipment and votive gifts. They may also have been *thesauroi* or shops for selling votives. These were located mostly in the north-eastern part of the sacral area (Fig. 6).

Most of the votives found throughout the entire *temenos* belong to the period when the first Temple of Apollon Ietros was in use. It is to the period from the end of the 6th to the last quarter of the 5th century that the majori-ty of the fragments of amphorae, mainly imported from Chios and Thasos, are dated. Hence it is clear that the best Greek wines were purchased for the rituals. Many of the black-glazed *kylikes* and *skyphoi* bear different graffiti indicating that they belonged to the sanctuaries either of the Mother of the Gods or of the Dioskouroi.[40] It seems that these sanctuaries were thus sepa-

Fig. 8. The stock of a stone anchor and a stone block from an altar in the process of excavation (view from NE).

rated from those of the other deities, especially those located nearby, in particular the sanctuaries of Apollon Ietros, Aphrodite and Hermes, which were also very important in the 5th century BC.

Rituals involving libations and the sacrifice of animals including both smaller livestock and bulls and horses, and to a lesser extent wild animals, became much more frequent.[41] The majority of the *bothroi*, into which bones and disused ritual equipment of the 6th-5th were thrown, dated to the 5th century. It is worth noting in this context that predominant among all the categories of imported pottery of Classical period was the Attic ware of various types.

It should be mentioned that votives such as sculptures and terracotta figurines are extremely uncommon here. Only one stone inscription with a dedication to Apollon Ietros, the Lord of Istria, made by the Olbiopolitan Xanthos, has been found; this was engraved on the base, possibly that of a tripod or a small bronze statue.[42] The possibility cannot be excluded however that a *proxenos* from Keos also erected a statue of Apollon Ietros, of which part of the base with a dedicatory inscription dated to the second quarter of the 5th century is preserved.[43] Of special interest is a unique dedication from Andokides to Apollon, incised on the base of a black-glazed *skyphos* of the same period: in this dedication the four *epikleses* of that god (Delphinios,

Fig. 9. The western fence of the Sanctuary of Apollon Ietros. In the foreground, bothroi *and fragments of stone and adobe altars (view from SW).*

Ietros, Targelios and Lykeios) are mentioned together with the enumeration of all the months of the Olbian calendar, which correspond completely to the Milesian one (Fig. 7).[44] Also unique is a dedication to Aiginean Apollon on a black-glazed bowl of the first half of the 4th century, offered probably either by an inhabitant of the island of Aigina or by an Olbiopolitan, who had travelled there and had successfully returned under the aegis of the god.[45]

Thus during the 5th century many of the elements characteristic of the previous phase persisted. These included not only the functioning of the temple and altars with the architectural décor produced in the second half of the 6th century, but also the Archaic sculptures of the Mother of the Gods and the ritual application of various ceremonial black-figured vessels, the work of prominent Athenian vase painters, e.g. a *krater* of Lydos, and other extremely valuable vases with representations of different mythological characters; this pottery was undoubtedly handled very carefully by the temple servants and it was often repaired by means of lead clamps.

At the same time, certain completely new types of votive gifts were now offered, namely the stocks of imported stone anchors of the 5th century and rather carelessly manufactured local limestone anchors dedicated in the Sanctuary of the Dioskouroi (Fig. 8);[46] numerous votives in the form of spe-

Fig. 10. Structural remains of a stone temple without architectural order of the Classical period with layered substructure of the Hellenistic period inside (view from N).

cially dressed *ostraca* of various shapes and sizes, made from different parts of vessels and animal bones, and some primitive small altars set up as though each was some kind of enclosure. Only in this *temenos* were there found numerous unique votives made from Korinthian *kalypteroi* sawed into small pieces, some with graphic representations of a temple and an altar, and bearing characters indicating their dedicatory purpose.[47]

Of special note is the fact that in the sanctuaries of any gods, and particularly in the *bothroi*, a great number of dolphin-shaped coins of various types have been found, while the round coins were much more uncommon there. As mentioned above, the dolphin-shaped coins served as a particular symbol and votive in the cult of Apollon Delphinios. However, on the basis of the finds from the Western Temenos it is also clear that such coins were used as votives in the cults of other deities too. In the sanctuary of an anonymous deity, four cast coins of the third quarter of the 6th century with a representation of the head of Gorgone Medusa were put under a small limestone altar as a kind of votive.

During the late Classical period, all of the sanctuaries continued to exist, but the remains of the new structures built within them are more uncommon, suggesting that in the majority of cases this was restricted to the erection of a number of altars. The number of offerings also slightly decreased.

Fig. 11. Fragmentary marble statue of Apollon of the second half of the 4th century BC at the moment it was unearthed.

Predominant among the tableware was the Attic black-glazed pottery and, to a lesser extent, red-figured pottery of the corresponding vessel types; these rarely bore graffiti. Apparently the practise of "inventorying" the pottery belonging to different sanctuaries was abandoned.

The decrease in the ritual activities in the Western Temenos was probably related to the considerable changes in the public life of Olbia – the establishing of the democratic constitution and the spread of the worship of Apollon Delphinios and Zeus in the hypostases of Soter and Eleutherios. In general, both the town-planning and the burial rites, the material culture and the onomastic evidence, as well as different finds from excavations in the rural territory of Olbia, suggest that the main mass of the urban and rural population of the Olbian *polis* was fairly homogeneous in terms of its social composition.[48]

Beginning with the end of the 5th and, especially in the 4th century BC, the practise of issuing various laws and decrees in the name of the *demos* was intensified.[49] This was probably the period when the Olbiopolitans enjoyed more or less equal rights. The aristocratic stratum, the representatives of which had earlier made up various *thiasoi* (the Molpoi, Noumeniastai, and Backchistai), seems to have been dissolved. At least are none of these religious guilds ever mentioned in the inscriptions from Olbia thereafter.[50] Instead there arose a new religious union of the clan of the Euresibiadai.[51]

The Hellenistic period

The Hellenistic period in Olbia is characterised by two major processes: (1) the economic and cultural zenith in the last third of the 4th and first third of the 3rd century BC, and (2) a lingering crisis caused by repeatedly bad harvests and wars, relative subjugation by the kingdom of Skilouros, then joining for a brief period the Pontic Kingdom of Mithridates VI Eupator; finally there was the devastating invasion of the Getae under the leadership of Burebista about the middle of the 1st century BC.[52]

After Zopyrion's siege, when many rich foreigners had entered the civic community of Olbia, large-scale rebuilding was undertaken and the private house-building expanded, in some cases with the use of architectural orders, mosaic floors and wall-paintings.[53] The cultural appearance of the city was changed significantly due to the construction of new temples in the Eastern Temenos, *stoai*, a theatre, a *gymnasion*, a *dikasterion*, and other public buildings, as well as the construction of terraces and defensive walls with towers. The considerable renovation of the city was quite probably promoted by the resuscitation of the *isopolitia* with Miletos, owing to which the Milesians enjoyed full civic rights in Olbia, and the Olbiopolitans the same in Miletos.[54]

In contrast to all the aforementioned renovations in the city,[55] the changes recorded in the Western Temenos are not of such a spectacular character. On the site of the late Archaic temple of Apollon Ietros and the supposed Sanctuary of Aphrodite, relatively large clay platforms appeared. The old stone altars continued to function here, but new ones were also set up, including a fairly well preserved stepped altar and a low *eschara* made nearby, as well as a ritual complex with a monolithic cylindrical altar and numerous small, primitive, but peculiar altars in the form of enclosures.[56] The Sanctuary of Apollon was walled in from the west by a sacred fence, of which the outside was of adequate workmanship (Fig. 9). Directly to the south-west of this feature, inside a small temple to an anonymous deity, a thick platform was constructed of alternating layers of clay and ash, presumably to support a large stepped altar (Fig. 10).

In the eastern part of the *temenos* there were two deep cisterns for water. In order to drain the rain-water, a stone well and a drain was constructed near the main street, possibly joining the drainage system of the Eastern Temenos. The Western Temenos was flanked by two large stone structures at two of its corners (the north-eastern and south-eastern) – presumably the buildings of the Collegium of the Seven and of the Law-Court respectively, due to the construction of which the total area of the earlier sacred plot was reduced. Flanking the main street were a number of one-roomed and two-roomed stone buildings.

Among the offerings, tableware of Olbian manufacture and pottery imported from Athens predominatel. However, compared to the finds of pottery dated to the Classical period the amount decreased. In contrast to the

Fig. 12. Remains of a sacred fence of the 2nd to the first half of the 1st century BC (view from N).

previous period, the number of terracotta figurines of the Mother of the Gods increased significantly; also, various small marble statues appeared: Apollon, Hermes, Hermaphroditos, Aphrodite, and other deities unidentified because of their poor state of preservation (Fig. 11).[57] It is probable that in the last third of the 4th century, a bronze statue of Apollon Ietros created by the Athenian sculptor Stratonides and commissioned by a certain rich Olbiopolitan, Leokrates of the clan of the Eurisibiadai, was installed in the Western Temenos.[58] A peculiar result of the religious and philosophical development of the cult of Apollon in Olbia is represented by an apophthegm of the members of the aforementioned *thiasos* of the Boreikoi, according to which this god appears already devoid of any *epikleses* – in the *hypostasis* of an universal deity personifying the Sun, Earthly Welfare, Light and Life.[59]

Dedicatory inscriptions on vessels are extremely uncommon, and therefore it has remained unclear to what deities the altars of this period were dedicated, whether during various periods of rebuilding those places sacred to the worship of Apollon, the Mother of the Gods, the Dioskouroi, and Hermes were either displaced, or whether in their place altars to new deities (not worshipped earlier or poorly known) appeared. The cults of these new deities became popular during the Hellenistic period due to the expansion of economic and political contacts, the integration of foreigners into the civic community, new cultural and political links to various cities in Asia Minor, the territorial expansion of the Olbian *polis* and the increasingly intensive cultivation of grain.

Concerning the last factor, it is worthy of note that although no sanctuary of Demeter or Kore has been unearthed within the area under consideration, nevertheless the fragments of some terracottas of Olbian manufacture representing these goddesses and coins with the figure of Demeter have been found in different spots in the *temenos*, among them the large cistern. The latter, after its destruction, was used as a *bothros*, into which were thrown various ritual gifts and votives from the sanctuaries of the Mother of the Gods, of Hermes and of Aphrodite. Far more numerous fragments of terracotta representations of the same type have been found in the Eastern Temenos – in the fill of an enormous cistern, also transformed into a *bothros* in the second half of the 2nd century BC.[60] Various gifts with representations of Demeter in terracottas and on coins, which were offered in the sanctuaries of other deities were fairly widespread due to the fact that it was precisely in the 4th and first half of the 3rd century that this goddess was the most popular in the Olbian *polis* after the expansion of the city's *chora*.[61]

A.N. Ščeglov's investigations showed that during this period "in all Greek centres in the northern Black Sea region, an intensive development of their own agricultural base, the economic exploitation of their territories and the rapid increase of the rural population" all occurred, creating the opportunity to maintain a regular grain trade.[62] In respect to Olbia, his supposition is confirmed inter alia by the evidence on the cult of Demeter, in particular the numerous peculiar representations of this goddess wreathed in corn or with a separate ear of grain on coins of different issues.[63]

In the Late Hellenistic period, when a lingering economical crisis began to afflict Olbia and the city fell into a certain dependence first on the Scythian king Skilouros, and then on the Pontic Kingdom of Mithridates VI Eupator, the worship of different deities in the *temenos* continued, though it was not as clearly expressed as before. Apparently, some of the altars previously erected were still in their original settings, especially in the low area of the *temenos* adjoining the main longitudinal street, as well as on special elevations in its western part. However, in the late 2nd century BC or slightly later, no more refuse from cult practice was buried in the water cisterns, which, by this time were already half destroyed.

On the stepped altar, libations and certain rituals were performed involving the use of mouldmade pottery of the 2nd century BC (mostly produced in Asia Minor). Relatively numerous fragments of various bowls were found in the ash-deposit located directly to the west of this altar. During the period under consideration, the thickness of the cultural layer increased throughout the entire expanse of the *temenos*, evidently because the tidying up and burial of refuse in the pits became less frequent. In the 3rd century BC, in the peripheral areas of the *temenos*, one-roomed and two-roomed buildings with basements or semi-basements were constructed, and to the west and north of it, large dwelling houses were built on the layers, which partially occupied the area covered by the earlier *temenos*. In the early Hellenistic period, the area of the Eastern Temenos was also reduced due to the enlargement of the *agora* and construction of the *stoa*.[64]

Only in the south-eastern part of the Western Temenos have fragments survived of the structural remains of three late sacred fences, which once enclosed some new sanctuaries on the site of the earlier Sanctuary of the Dioskouroi (Fig. 12). These fences were carefully built from small pieces of rubble and fragments of tiles and amphorae held together with a clay-and-earth mortar, thus symbolising in their way the extremely poor conditions of the Olbiopolitans not long before the invasion of the Getae. It is not clear what the other cult structures inside the fences and near them would have looked like, since only single pieces of rubble, which probably once composed the inner fill of some rectangular altars, remained of these. The ritual equipment is represented by a small quantity of assorted local tableware, single examples of painted beakers from Asia Minor, and amphorae from Sinope, Kos, Knidos, Rhodos, Kolchis and other centres, as well as single examples of almost flat plates of brown clay decorated with polished stripes.

The early Roman period

During the last phase (the second half of the 1st century BC – the first half of the 1st century AD), the Olbiopolitans erected two small altars in the Western Temenos directly over the place, where the oldest Sanctuary of Apollon Ietros (Fig. 1) had previously been situated, and a rather small ritual complex of several primitive altars was built in the western part on the pavementof the Northern Street. It was during the first centuries of the new era that most of the surface structures, which had to varying degrees survived the incursions of the Getae, were dismantled and removed.

In the *temenos*, as well as throughout the entire area surrounding it, a number of human burials (mostly devoid of grave goods) appeared. In the cultural layer, numerous isolated human bones were found. These are probably the remains of the graves of those Olbiopolitans killed in the invasion, their resting places disturbed in the search for stone slabs or damaged by grave robbers, as is suggested by separate fragments of amphorae and red-glazed beakers from the first centuries AD found at a relatively considerable depth or in the areas of disturbed masonry.

Nevertheless, no traces of any building or economic activities during the period of the second flourishing of Olbia in the 2nd century BC have been recorded here. Although the Olbiopolitans had taken away from here almost

Anna S. Rusjaeva

all the stone slabs suitable for new buildings, they probably still remembered that this place had, for a long period been consecrated to the deities worshipped by their ancestors.

On the basis of what has been said above, it may be concluded that notwithstanding the yet unfinished excavation in the Western Temenos and the extremely poor state of preservation of its cultural layers caused by the numerous replannings and alterations during various phases of its existence and because of the dismantling of its structures during the first centuries of this era, the search for building materials in the recent periods, and archaeological explorations and excavations of the 19th and beginning of the 20th century, rich archaeological and epigraphical evidence has survived, enabling us to supplement considerably our knowledge about the religion, history, culture, architecture and trade of Olbia.

Notes

1. Karasev 1964, 27-130; Levi 1964, 131-174; Levi 1985, 65-88; Rusjaeva 1991, 123-138; Rusjaeva 1994, 80-102.
2. Karasev 1964, 27, 129; Levi 1985, 73; Rusjaeva 1999a, 75-76.
3. Rusjaeva 1992, 29-83.
4. Rusjaeva 1991, 124.
5. Cf. Rusjaeva 1986, fig. 3; Rusjaeva 1999a, fig. 1; Krapivina & Bujskich 2001, figs. 1-2.
6. Rusjaeva 1998, 164-165.
7. Cf. Pick 1898, 172-173; Zograf 1951, 143; Karyškovskij 1986, 31, fig. 2.5; Anochin 1989, no. 382; Rusjaeva 1986, 47-48; 1992, 37.
8. Rusjaeva 1986, 42, figs. 3.2-5, 4.2-10; 1992, 30-32, 90-92; Rusjaeva 1999a, 76-81, fig. 1.3; Dubois 1996, 108-109.
9. Gans 1991, 137-140; Senff 1992, 105-108.
10. Alexandrescu-Vianu 1997, 15-20.
11. Nazarov 2001, 154-165.
12. Rusjaeva 1992, 100-103.
13. Beleckij 1975, 101; Rusjaeva 1992, 102, figs. 31.3-4, 32; Dubois 1996, 120.
14. Vinogradov 1989, 74-80.
15. For details, see Rusjaeva 1986, 25-64; Vinogradov 1989, 78; Burkert 1990, 155-160.
16. Cf. Rusjaeva 1986, 55-56; Karyškovskij 1988, 38-40; Anochin 1989, 8-10.
17. Cf. Anochin 1986, 83-85; 1989, 5-10; Rusjaeva 1986, 47-49; Karyškovskij 1988, 30-34.
18. Rusjaeva 1992, 40-41.
19. For details, see Vinogradov & Rusjaeva 2001, 136-137.
20. Vinogradov & Rusjaeva 2001, 141.
21. Rusjaeva 1992, 18-20, 196-197; Dubois 1996, 155-156.
22. Rusjaeva 1991, 124-125, fig. 1; 2002, 12-14.
23. Rusjaeva 1994, 81.
24. Bergquist 1967, 5, 62 ff.
25. Rusjaeva 1988a, 33-51; 1988b, 166-174; Kryžickij 1998, 170-190 – with a graphic reconstruction.
26. Cf. Karasev 1964, 51-73; Kryžickij 1998, 170-190.

27. Cf. Kozub 1974; Skudnova 1988.
28. Karyškovskij 1984, 42-51; Rusjaeva 1992, 193-195.
29. Rusjaeva 1994, 85-96.
30. Vinogradov & Rusjaeva 1980, 23, fig. 5.1; Rusjaeva 1986, 42; 1992, 30-32, 87-88, 90-92; Vinogradov & Rusjaeva 1998, 163-164; Vinogradov & Rusjaeva 2001, 134-137.
31. Rusjaeva 1992, fig. 26.3.
32. For references, see Kryžickij 1993, 42.
33. For details, see Crygitsky & Roussjaeva 1980, 73-100; Rusjaeva & Sazonova 1986, 48-63.
34. Žuravl'ov & Markova, 1995, 70-79.
35. Rusjaeva & Nazarov 1995, 251-260.
36. Rusjaeva 1988a, 33-51; Kryžickij 1998, 188-190.
37. Cf. Naumann 1983, Taf. 16; Graeve 1986, Taf. 9.2; Rusjaeva 1992, 144-145; Rusjaeva 1994, fig. 7.
38. Rusjaeva 1991, 125-138; Rusjaeva 1994, 82-102.
39. Rusjaeva 1991, 131-132.
40. Rusjaeva 1992, 116-117, fig. 36, 144, fig. 46.
41. Žuravl'ov & Markova 1995, 70-77.
42. Rusjaeva & Vinogradov 2001, 229-234.
43. *IOSPE* I², 164; Vinogradov 1989, 111.
44. For details, see Vinogradov & Rusjaeva 1980, 24-64; Dubois 1996, 160-164 (with references).
45. Vinogradov & Rusjaeva 2001, 137-138.
46. Rusjaeva & Diatroptov 1993, 106-107.
47. Rusjaeva 1988b, 168, fig. 1.
48. For references, see Kozub 1974, 128-132; Kryžickij & Lejpunskaja 1999, 98 ff.; Rusjaeva 1999a, 411-431.
49. Vinogradov 1989, 139-140.
50. Vinogradov 1989, 149.
51. *NO* 71; Vinogradov 1989, 147-150.
52. Cf. Vinogradov 1989, 150 ff.; Saprykin 1996, 132 ff.; Kryžickij & Lejpunskaja 1999, 158 ff.
53. For details and references, see Levi 1985, 26-64; Kryžickij & Lejpunskaja 1999, 158-190.
54. *Milet* 3, 136; *Syll.*³, 286.
55. Karasev 1964, 30-31; Levi 1985, 71-72.
56. Rusjaeva 1991, figs. 3.9-10; Rusjaeva 1994, figs. 11-12.
57. Rusjaeva 1992, fig. 10.66; Rusjaeva 1994, figs. 8-9.
58. *NO* 65; Levi 1965, 86-95; Rusjaeva 1992, 36.
59. Rusjaeva 1992, 18-20; Dubois 1996, 155-156.
60. Levi 1964, 166-173.
61. Rusjaeva 1992, 85 (with references).
62. Ščeglov 1987, 175-176.
63. Gilevič 1972, 74-78; Karyškovskij 1988, 54-70; Anochin 1989, 32-38.
64. Levi 1985, 67-69.

Bibliography

Alexandrescu-Vianu, M. 1997. Aphrodites orientales dans le bassin du Pont-Euxin, *BCH* 121, 15-32.

Anochin, V.A. (ed.) 1980. *Issledovanija po antičnoj archeologii Severnogo Pričernomor'ja*. Kiev.

Anochin, V.A. 1986. Monety-strelki, in: Rusjaeva (ed.) 1986, 68-89.

Anochin, V.A. (ed.) 1986. *Antičnaja kul'tura Severnogo Pričernomor'ja v pervye veka n.e.* Kiev.

Anochin, V.A (ed.) 1988. *Antičnye drevnosti Severnogo Pričernomor'ja*. Kiev.

Anochin, V.A. 1989. *Monety antičnych gorodov Severo-Zapadnogo Pričernomor'ja*. Kiev.

Avram, A. & M. Babeş (eds.) 2000. *Civilisation grecque et cultures antiques périphériques*. Bucarest.

Beleckij, A.A. 1975. Grečeskie nadpisi Ol'vii iz raskopok 1950-1967 gg., chranjaščiesja v Kieve, in: Kryžickij (ed.) 1975, 92-117.

Bergquist, B. 1967. *The Archaic Greek Temenos. A Study of Structure and Function*. Lund.

Burkert, V. 1990. Apollon Didim i Ol'vija, *VDI* 2, 155-160.

Crygitsky, S.D. & A.S. Roussijaeva 1980. Les plus anciennes habitations d'Olbia, *DialHistAnc* 6, 73-100.

Dubois, L. 1996. *Inscriptions grecques dialectales d'Olbia du Pont*. Genève.

Dzis-Rajko, G.A. (ed.) 1984. *Severnoe Pričernomor'e*. Kiev.

Gajdukevič, V.F. (ed.) 1964. *Ol'vija. Temenos i agora*. Moskva-Leningrad.

Gans, U. 1991. Die Grabung auf dem Zeytintepe, *IstMitt* 41, 137-140.

Gilevič, A.M. 1972. Klad "assov" iz Olvii, *NumEpigr* 10, 74-78.

Graeve, V., von 1986. Über verschiedene Richtungen der milesischen Skulptur in archaischer Zeit, *IstMitt* 31, 81-94.

Karasev, A.N. 1964. Monumental'nye pamjatniki ol'vijskogo temenosa, in: Gajdukevič (ed.) 1964, 27-130.

Karyškovskij, P.O. 1984. Ol'vijskie mol'py, in: Dzis-Rajko (ed.) 1984, 42-51.

Karyškovskij, P.O. 1986. Monetnoe delo Ol'vii vo vtoroj polovine II v. n.e., in: Anochin (ed.) 1986, 25-36.

Kozub, Ju.I. 1974. *Nekropol' Ol'vii V-IV st. do n.e.* Kiev.

Krapivina, V.V. & A.V Bujskich 2001. Novye nachodki vostočnogrečeskoj keramiki iz Ol'vii, in: *Bosporskij fenomen: kolonizacija regiona, formirovanie polisov, obrazovanie gosudarstva* 2. St Peterburg, 21-29.

Kryžickij, S.D. (ed.) 1975. *Ol'vija*. Kiev.

Kryžickij, S.D. 1993. *Architektura antičnych gosudarstv Severnogo Pričernomor'ja*. Kiev.

Kryžickij, S.D. 1998. Chram Apollona Vrača na Zapadnom temenose Ol'vii, *VDI* 1, 170-190.

Kryžickij, S.D. & N.A. Lejpunskaja 1999. Nižnee Pobuž'e, in: Kryžickij et al. (eds.) 1999, 35-229.

Kryžickij, S.D., A.S. Rusjaeva, V.V. Krapivina, N.A. Lejpunskaja, M.V. Skržinskaja & V.A. Anochin 1999. *Ol'vija. Antičnoe gosudarstvo v Severnom Pričernomor'e*. Kiev.

Levi, E.I. 1964. Materialy ol'vijskogo temenosa, in: Gajdukevič (ed.) 1964, 131-174.

Levi, E.I. 1965. Ol'vijskaja nadpis' s posvjaščeniem Apollonu Vraču, *VDI* 2, 86-95.

Levi, E.I. 1985. *Ol'vija. Gorod epochi ellinizma*. Leningrad.

Lordkipanidzé, O. & P. Lévêque (eds.) 1999. *Religions du Pont-Euxin. Actes du VIIIe Symposium de Vani (Colchide) 1997*. Paris.

Naumann, F. 1983. *Die Ikonographie der Kybele in der phrygischen und der griechischen Kunst*. Tübingen.

Nazarov, V.V. 2001. Svjatilišče Afrodity v Borisfene, *VDI* 1, 155-165.

Pick, B. 1898. Thrakische Münzbilder, *JdI* 13, 132-174.

Rusjaeva, A.S. 1986. Milet-Didimy – Borisfen-Ol'vija. Problemy kolonizacii Nižnego Pobuž'ja, *VDI* 2, 25-64.

Rusjaeva, A.S. (ed.) 1986. *Ol'vija i ee okruga*. Kiev.

Rusjaeva, A.S. 1988a. Archaičeskaja architekturnaja terrakotta iz Ol'vii, in: Anochin (ed.) 1988, 33-51.

Rusjaeva, A.S. 1988b. Novye dannye o kul'te Apollona Vrača v Ol'vii, in: Anochin (ed.) 1988, 166-174.

Rusjaeva, A.S. 1991. Issledovanija Zapadnogo temenosa Ol'vii, *VDI* 4, 123-138.

Rusjaeva, A.S. 1992. *Religija i kul'ty antičnoj Ol'vii*. Kiev.

Rusyaeva, A.S. 1994. Investigations of the Western Temenos of Olbia, *Ancient Civilizations from Scythia to Siberia* 1.1, 80-102.

Rusjaeva, A.S. 1998. K voprosu ob osnovanii ionijcami Ol'vii, *VDI* 1, 160-170.

Rusjaeva, A.S. 1999a. Les temene d'Olbia à la lumière de son histoire au VI siècle av. n.è., in: Lordkipanidzé & Lévêque (eds.) 1999, 75-84.

Rusjaeva, A.S. 1999b. Naselenie Ol'vii, in: Kryžickij et al. 1999, 391-471.

Rusjaeva, A.S. 2001. Afrodita Uranija – patronessa miletsko-pontijskoj kolonizacii, in: *Bosporskij fenomen: kolonizacija regiona, formirovanie polisov, obrazovanie gosudarstva* 1. St Peterburg, 17-21.

Rusjaeva, A.S. 2002. K istorii izučenija pervonačal'nych granic temenosov i drevnejšich chramov v Ol'vii Pontijskoj, in: Toločko (ed.) 2002, 8-20.

Rusjaeva, A.S. & P.D. Diatroptov 1993. Dva kultovych kompleksa Zapadnogo temenosa Ol'vii, *Archeologični doslidžennja v Ukraini 1991 r*. Luck, 106-107.

Rusyaeva, A.S. & V.V. Nazarov 1995. A Shield Fragment from Olbia, *Ancient Civilizations from Scythia to Siberia* 2.3, 251-260.

Rusjaeva, A.S. & N.G. Sazonova 1986. Keramičnyj kompleks archaičnogo času iz Ol'vii, *ArcheologiaKiev* 55, 48-63.

Rusjaeva, A.S. & Ju.G. Vinogradov 2000. Apollon Ietros, Herrscher von Istros, in Olbia, in: Avram & Babeş (eds.) 2000, 229-234.

Saprykin, S.Ju. 1996. *Pontijskoe carstvo*. Moskva.

Senff, R. 1992. Die Grabung auf dem Zeytintepe, *IstMitt* 42, 105-108.

Skudnova, V.M. 1988. *Archaičeskij nekropol' Ol'vii*. Leningrad.

Ščeglov, A.N. 1987. Istočniki severopričernomorskoj torgovli chlebom v IV v. do n.e., *Tezisy Desjatoj avtorsko-čitatel'skoj konferencii "VDI"*. Moskva, 175-176.

Toločko, P.P. (ed.) 2002. *Severnoe Pričernomor'e v antičnoe vremja*. Kiev.

Vinogradov, Ju.G. 1989. *Političeskaja istorija Ol'vijskogo polisa VII-I vv. do n.e. Istoriko-epigrafičeskoe issledovanie*. Moskva.

Vinogradov, Ju.G. & A.S. Rusjaeva 1980. Kul't Apollona i kalendar' v Ol'vii, in: Anochin (ed.) 1980, 19-84.

Vinogradov, Ju.G. & A.S. Rusjaeva 1998. Phantasmomagica Olbiopolitana, *ZPE* 121, 153-164.

Vinogradov, Ju.G. & A.S. Rusjaeva 2001. Graffiti iz svjatilišča Apollona na Zapadnom temenose Ol'vii, in: Zolotarev (ed.) 2001, 134-142.

Zograf, A.N. 1951. *Antičnye monety* (MatIsslA, 16). Moskva-Leningrad.

Zolotarev, M.I. (ed.) 2001. *ΑΝΑΧΑΡΣΙΣ. Pamjati Ju.G. Vinogradova*. Sevastopol'.

Žuravl'ov, O.P. & A.V. Markova 1995. Osteologični materiali iz kultovich kompleksiv Ol'vii, *ArcheologiaKiev* 2, 70-79.

Abbreviations

Milet   *Milet. Ergebnisse der Ausgrabungen und Untersuchungen seit dem Jahre 1899*.
NO   *Nadpisi Ol'vii* (1917-1965). Leningrad 1968.
IOSPE   B. Latyschev, *Inscriptiones antiquae orae septentrionalis Ponti Euxini Graecae et Latinae*. Petropolis 1885-1916.
Syll.[3]   W. Dittenberger, *Sylloge inscriptionum Graecarum*, vols. I-IV. Leipzig 1915-1924 (3rd ed.).

Bronze Weights from Olbia

Valentina V. Krapivina

Weights from the northern Black Sea region became the subject of studies as early as the second half of the 19th century. Later, publication of weights was continued both in works devoted entirely to these objects and, in other publications, together with other finds from excavations. Nevertheless, the study of weights is still far from completion, as new finds constantly necessitate corrections of the prevailing assumptions.

The weights from Olbia are mostly rectangular, square, and occasionally oval or rounded, metal plates, some of which have a small vertical ridge round their edges. Some weights are of conical, trapezoid or spheroid shape with a flattened base. Some examples are carefully executed, while others are of rather careless workmanship.[1]

All of the previously published bronze weights from Olbia served as control weights. Noteworthy is the presence of a relief representation and an inscription on some of them (the names of the city and the *agoranomos*).[2] During recent years, new material has accumulated, which enables us to expand and refine our knowledge of the subject. First, I will describe all the bronze weights from Olbia known to me, both those previously published and the ones recently discovered.

Catalogue

1. Collection of the Institute of Archaeology of the National Academy of Sciences of Ukraine (IA NASU), Kiev.
Found on the shore of the *liman* (the river delta) in the northern part of Olbia, below the area NGS (the Lower City). Not cleaned; well preserved. The weight is rectangular, measuring 1.20 x 0.90-0.95 x 0.06 cm; weight 0.78 g. This specimen is of fairly careful workmanship, probably made from a bronze plate, and weighs roughly one obol.

2. Private collection (Fig. 1).
Cleaned; well preserved. Trapezoidal, measuring 0.7-0.8 x 0.8 x 0.05-0.15 cm; weight 0.85 g. On the obverse there is an image of a head in a helmet right – probably Athena; on the reverse a stylized representation of a dolphin. The head of Athena is fairly common as a countermark on the Olbian silver and copper coins from the 3rd-2nd century BC and typical on the coins of small-

er denominations with the abbreviation BΣE from the first quarter
of the 2nd century BC.[3] The
weight is close to 1/2 of the coins
of small denomination mentioned
above.

3. Former Collection of P.O. Buračkov, State Historical Museum,
Moscow?
On the obverse is the head of
Helios l., on the reverse two
foreparts of horses joined back to
back.[4] Countermarks bearing similar representations are typical on
Olbian coins from the 3rd century

Fig. 1. Weight no. 2. From a private collection.

BC.[5] The weight is 1.14 g being close to 1/4 of a drachm of the Euboic-Attic
system.

4. Collection of IA NASU, Kiev, inv. no. O-59/98.
Found in area E-6 in a layer dating from the 5th-3rd century BC Cleaned;
well preserved. The shape is square, measuring 1.7 x 1.7 x 0.2 cm. It is made
of an Olbian coin, a *"Borysthenes"*. The weight is 4.99 g, corresponding to a
drachm of the Euboic-Attic system; a lead weight from the Athenian Agora
of similar weight bears a sign denoting a drachm.[6]

5. Private collection (Fig. 2).
Cleaned and mostly well preserved. It is almost square, measuring 1.8 x 1.7
x 0.2 cm; weight 5.64 g. On the obverse is a rather unclear representation of
a human head *en face* (Demeter?); on the reverse is a dolphin l. and a low
frame.

   A photograph of a weight of similar shape and dimensions has been published among the plates of P.O. Karyškovskij,[7] but unfortunately its actual
weight is not specified. On the obverse of the last-mentioned is a representation of the head of Demeter in profile, l.[8] The image on the reverse is similar to that on our example: dolphin l. and a low frame. Karyškovskij linked
this weight to the local silver coins bearing a representation of Demeter from
the second half of the 4th century BC.[9]

   The weight of no. 5 corresponds to 1/2 of the silver coins with Demeter
of Subgroups 1-3 and to the weight of some individual coins of Subgroup 3.[10]
In contrast, this weight corresponds to 10 obols of the Chian-Rhodian system
(cf. no. 6 below).

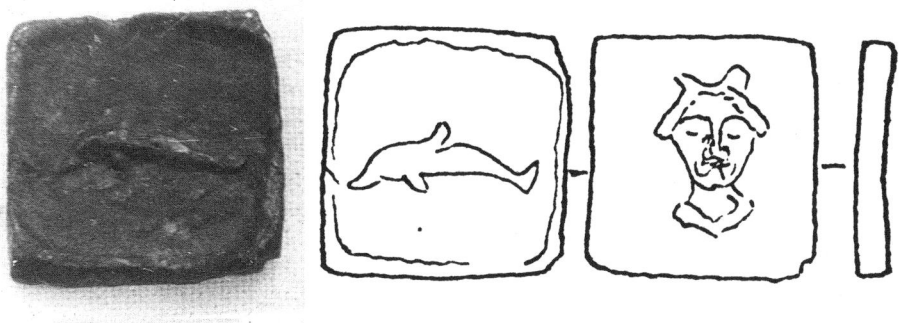

Fig. 2. Weight no. 5. From a private collection.

6. Collection of IA NASU, Kiev.
Found in the *liman* part of the Lower City of Olbia. Cleaned; well preserved. The shape is quadrangular, measuring 1.20 x 1.20 x 0.45 cm; weight 5.641 g. On the obverse there is a carved inscription consisting of two lines: ΔEK | OBO – i.e. ten obols; on the basis of the palaeography of the inscription, the weight is dated to the 4th or 3rd century BC. The weight seemingly corresponds to the Euboic-Attic system of standard 129.[11]

In my opinion, however, the identification of the weight system presented by V.I. Nazarčuk is erroneous. In contrast to the standard of 126, the weight standard of 129 was not recorded in the Athenian Agora.[12] If we proceed from the weight of a drachm being equal to 3.36 g, as has been deduced from the weight of no. 6, then it should be consistent with the Chian-Rhodian system according to which silver coins were struck in Olbia in the 3rd century BC.[13]

7. Collection of IA NASU, Kiev.
Stray find (Fig. 3). Not cleaned except for its obverse surface; well preserved. The item is of almost rectangular shape with slightly elongated lateral sides; dimensions: 1.40 x 1.10-1.20 x 0.45-0.55 cm; weight 8 g. On the obverse is an unclear representation of a rosette (?). The weight corresponds to two drachms of the Euboic-Attic system of standard 100.

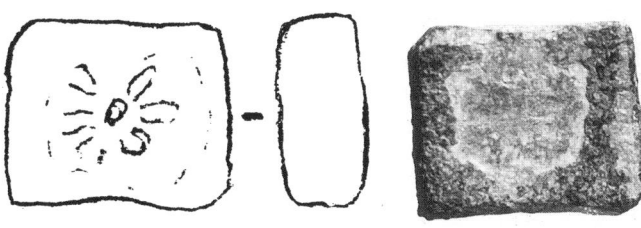

Fig. 3. Weight no. 7.

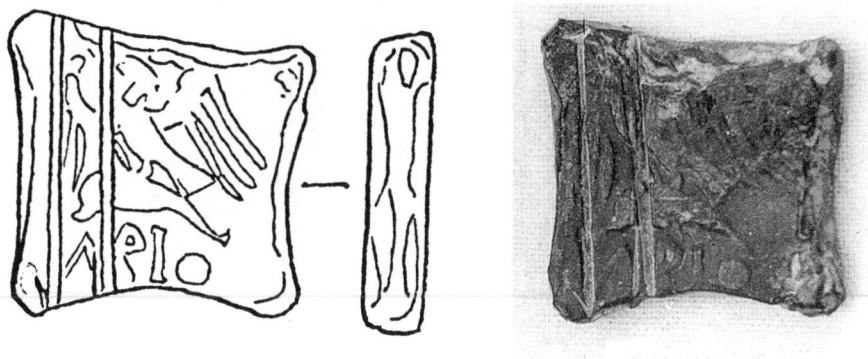

Fig. 4. Weight no. 11. From a private collection.

8. Former Collection of P.O. Buračkov, State Historical Museum, Moscow? Poor state of preservation. Weight 12.65 g. On the obverse there is the image of the head of Demeter in profile l. similar to the representations on the local silver coins; the reverse has a dolphin l. with the inscription ΑΡΙΣΤΟ above it and ΟΛΒΙΟ beneath.[14] The weight of the object, taking into account wear and tear, corresponds to 1/32 of the Euboic-Attic mina of standard 100.[15]

9. Originally collection of P. Mavrogordato,[16] now in the British Museum, inv. no. 1905, 1215.2.
Not cleaned; well preserved. Of rectangular shape, measuring 2.4 x 2.2 x 0.4 cm. Weight 16.91 g. The edges of the object are uneven, and probably for that reason it has not been cleaned, as this might cause loss in weight. On the obverse there is a rather small frame on three sides and a dolphin l. with the inscription ΟΛΒΙΟ above it and a three-line inscription beneath. The inscription is poorly imprinted; below and to the right of it, some burrs of metal are discernible; the scarcely legible text has been roughly reconstructed as ΟΕΥΚΑΙ(?) Ι ΟΥΣΚΑΕ Ι [...]ΑΝΑ[...] possibly representing three names. The weight corresponds to four drachms of the Euboic-Attic system of standard 100. Parallels have been recorded in the Athenian Agora[17] and at Olynthos.[18]

A photograph of an example of similar shape and dimensions has been published among the plates of P.O. Karyškovskij,[19] but unfortunately with its weight unspecified. On the obverse of this specimen is a representation of a bearded head in profile, l.; on the reverse is a representation similar to that on no. 9: a dolphin l. and a low frame, but without inscription. Karyškovskij thought this weight to be closely linked to the silver coins of the 4th century BC bearing the representation of Demeter.[20]

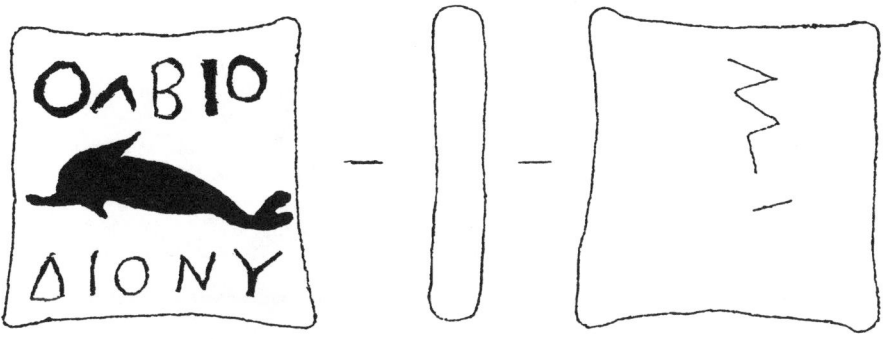

Fig. 5. Weight no. 13. Collection of the Institute of the History of Material Culture, Russian Academy of Sciences, St Petersburg.

10. Collection of IA NASU, Kiev, inv. no. O-59/124f.
Cleaned; well preserved. Rather careless workmanship. The item is almost circular, measuring 2.2-2.3 cm in diameter and 0.5 cm thick; weight 18.6 g. On the obverse, a circular depression 0.4 cm in diameter and up to 0.2 cm deep has been made. Marked at a distance of 0.20-0.25 cm from the edge of the weight is a circle 1.6-1.7 cm in diameter its line being 0.1 cm thick and up to 0.1 cm deep. The weight corresponds to four drachms of the Euboic-Attic system of standard 126.

11. Private collection (Fig. 4).
The weight has been cleaned; the state of preservation is rather poor. The shape is rectangular with slightly pronounced corners; dimensions: 2.5-2.8 x 2.1-2.6 x 0.5 cm; weight 31.04 g. On the right side of the obverse are two parallel incisions cut through a representation of an eagle on a dolphin – the emblem of Olbia. Below this the inscription OΛBIO is discernible; this image is similar to that on the reverse of silver coins with Demeter from the 4th century BC.[21] The weight of our specimen corresponds to eight drachms of the Euboic-Attic system of standard 100.

12. Archaeological Museum NASU, Odessa.
Not cleaned; excellent state of preservation. The shape is rectangular, measuring 3.8 x 3.6 x 0.4 cm; weight 45.17 g. On the obverse is a dolphin facing right with the inscription OΛBIO | KPITOBOY under it. The weight corresponds to 10 drachms of the Euboic-Attic system of standard 105.

In its dimensions and iconography it resembles a weight from the collection of the Kherson collector E.F. Mamaenko, which differs in its inscription OΛBIO | XAPINAY.[22] The weight of this specimen is unknown.

Fig. 6. Weight no. 14. Museum of Archaeology IA NASU, Kiev.

13. Collection of the Institute of the History of Material Culture, Russian Academy of Sciences, St Petersburg, inv. no. O-61/3634 (Fig. 5).
Cleaned; excellent state of preservation. The shape is rectangular with slightly pronounced corners, measuring 3.3-3.6 x 3.2-3.4 x 0.5 cm; weight 48.691 g. On the obverse is a dolphin, facing left; the inscriptions OΛBIO above it and ΔIONY beneath it are visible. On the reverse illegible signs have been incised. The weight was found in a room in area E-2; and it can be dated to the 3rd century BC.[23] The weight corresponds to 1/8 of the Euboic-Attic mina of standard 100.[24]

14. Museum of Archaeology IA NASU, Kiev (Fig. 6).
Not cleaned; excellent state of preservation. It is square with slightly pronounced corners; dimensions: 2.7-3.0 x 2.7-3.0 x 0.5 cm; weight 49.393 g. On the obverse is a dolphin l., represented in high relief with the inscriptions OΛBIO above it and AΠO beneath it. Drawn on the obverse is a monogram, which may read: TE. The weight corresponds to 1/8 of the Euboic-Attic mina of standard 100.[25]

15. Private collection (Fig. 7).
Cleaned; well preserved. The weight is rectangular, measuring 3.6 x 3.4 x 0.4 cm; weight 51.3 g. On the obverse a dolphin r. is schematically represented. Beneath it the inscription OΛBIO ǀ ΦIΛΩ is legible. Below the tail of the dolphin is a circular countermark 0.8-0.9 cm in diameter with a representation of a woman – possibly Demeter – *en face*. The weight corresponds to 1/8 of the Euboic-Attic mina of standard 100.

16. State Historical Museum, Moscow.
Weight 51.75 g. On the obverse is a dolphin r. with the inscription OΛBIO ǀ KPITOBOY beneath it; on the reverse there is the incision "φ".[26] As noted by

P.O. Karyškovskij, L.I. Čuistova erroneously identified the material of the object as lead.[27] The weight corresponds to 1/8 of the Euboic-Attic mina of standard 100.

17. Museum of Archaeology IA NASU, Kiev (Fig. 8).
Cleaned; well preserved. The weight is rectangular, measuring: 3.4 x 2.9-3.0 x 0.4-0.5 cm;

Fig. 7. Weight no. 15. From a private collection.

weight 52.52 g. On the obverse, represented in low relief, is a male head in profile l.; in front of it an arrowhead pointing downwards. Possibly Apollon is intended. Beneath his image is the inscription OΛBIO. Above the arrowhead is a circular countermark 1.0 cm in diameter, 0.05 cm deep, representing a flying butterfly. On the reverse, an incision: +I can be seen. The weight corresponds to 1/8 of the Euboic-Attic mina of standard 100.[28]

18. Originally in P. Mavrogordato's collection, now in the British Museum, inv. no. 1905, 1215.1.
Not cleaned; well preserved. Rectangular weight, measuring 3.4 x 2.9-3.0 x 0.4-0.5 cm; weight 52.65 g. On the obverse is a slightly blurred representation

Fig. 8. Weight no. 17. Museum of Archaeology IA NASU, Kiev.

Fig. 9-10. 9) Weight no. 19. Museum of Archaeology IA NASU, Kiev. 10) Weight no. 20. Museum of Archaeology IA NASU, Kiev.

of a male head l., probably Apollon,[29] and beneath it the inscription ΟΛΒΙΟ with the "Λ" almost indiscernible. In the upper part of the lateral surface are small depressions. This weight is quite similar to no. 17, with regard to dimensions and weight. The two weights were probably cast in the same mould.

19. Museum of Archaeology IA NASU, Kiev, inv. no. O-96/P-25/553 (Fig. 9). Cleaned; well preserved. Made of an Olbian *"aes"* with a Gorgoneion. Such *"aeses"* are dated to the third quarter of the 5th century BC.[30] Dimensions: 3.60 x 0.19-0.35 cm; weight 58 g. However, *"aeses"* of this type weigh an average of 113 g.[31] The weight is roughly equivalent to 1/8 of the Euboic-Attic mina of standard 105. Some examples of similar weights are reported from the Athenian Agora.[32]

20. Museum of Archaeology IA NASU, Kiev (Fig. 10).
Not cleaned; excellent state of preservation. The weight is rectangular with slightly pronounced corners, measuring 3.9-4.0 x 3.6-3.8 x 0.8 cm.; weight 101.895 g. On the obverse there is a fairly realistic representation of a dolphin facing l. with the inscriptions ΟΛΒΙΟ above and ΑΡΙϹΤΟ beneath it. Placed above the dolphin's tail is a circular countermark with a diameter of 0.9 cm and a depth of 0.10-0.25 cm, bearing the letters ΠΟ ("Ο" written inside "Π"). The weight corresponds to 1/4 of the Euboic-Attic mina of standard 100.[33]

21. Museum of Archaeology IA NASU, Kiev (Fig. 11).
Not cleaned; excellent state of preservation. Almost square weight, measuring 4.2-4.3 x 4.2 x 0.6 cm; weight 103.584 g. Represented on the obverse is a male head in profile with laurel wreath l. and an arrowhead pointing down-

Fig. 11-12. 11) Weight no. 21. Museum of Archaeology IA NASU, Kiev.
12) Weight no. 22. Museum of Archaeology IA NASU, Kiev.

wards in front of it. The head is evidently that of Apollon(?). Beneath it is the inscription OΛBIO. On the lateral side of the weight: ΓΗ. The weight corresponds to 1/4 of the Euboic-Attic mina of standard 100.[34]

In terms of its shape and dimensions this item is identical to that published in Karyškovskij's book,[35] but the weight of the latter is not specified. This piece has the inscription OΛBIO under a representation of the head of a deity (probably Demeter) in three quarters view. The iconography of Demeter is the closest counterpart to the facing goddess on an extremely rare Olbian silver coin dated by Karyškovskij to the third quarter of the 4th century BC[36] and by V.A. Anochin to 330-300 BC.[37]

22. Museum of Archaeology IA NASU, Kiev (Fig. 12).
Not cleaned; well preserved. The weight is rectangular with slightly pronounced corners, measuring 4.6-5.2 x 4.3-5.0 x 0.7 cm; weight 107.694 g. On the obverse, a dolphin r. is schematically represented, beneath it the inscription OΛBIO | KPITOBOY. The weight corresponds to 1/4 of the Euboic-Attic mina of standard 100.[38]

23. Museum of Archaeology IA NASU, Kiev, inv. no. O-57/017 (Fig. 13).
Cleaned; well preserved. The weight is rectangular, measuring 4.0-4.1 x 3.5-3.6 x 0.8 cm; weight 113.63 g. On the obverse, there is a dolphin facing right and beneath it the inscription OΛBIO | APIΣTO. Incised on the reverse: EY. This item was found in a room of the Western Trade Row in the Agora and is dated to the 3rd century BC.[39] The weight corresponds to 1/4 of the Euboic-Attic mina of standard 105.[40]

Fig. 13. Weight no. 23. Museum of Archaeology IA NASU, Kiev.

Conclusion

Out of the twenty-three Olbian bronze weights from the third quarter of the 4th to the first quarter of the 2nd century BC, two items are common weights (nos. 1 and 10), seven were intended for control weighing, but were not related to any *agoranomoi* (nos. 2-7 and 19), and 14 are control weights belonging to the *agoranomoi* (nos. 8, 9, 11-18, 20-23). The weight of the various examples varies from 0.78 g to 113.163 g, but the majority of them correspond in weight to either 1/4 or 1/8 of the Euboic-Attic mina of standard 100. Practically all of them have parallels in Athens or Olynthos. Moreover, the weight standard in Olbia was subject to the same changes as in Attica. This can be seen from the fact that from the 6th to the 2nd century BC the Euboic-Attic weight system was in use in Olbia.[41]

The control weights are represented mainly by small bronze specimens (nos. 2-7), which may have been parts of sets of weights used for weighing coins in the course of exchange. The iconography of the majority of these is connected closely with that of the local coins. They mostly correspond to the Euboic-Attic weight system. However, as early as 1911 A.L. Bertier-Delagard warned that small weights should not be considered since they may equally well have been part of a different weight system.[42] It is worth noting that the weight made from an *"aes"* (no. 19) appears to weigh half as much as the weight bearing the inscription ΟΛΒΙΟ | ΑΡΙΣΤΟ (no. 23), and corresponding to the Euboic-Attic weight system of standard 105.

The control weights of the board of *agoranomoi* are the most numerous and the most important for the history of Olbia.[43] These can be dated to a shorter time-span than the other bronze weights, possibly to the period between 350 and 200 BC. Their appearance must have been connected with the final stage of the transition from cast coins to struck ones. Therefore, in my opinion, the earliest is the weight with the inscription OΛBIO and a representation of Demeter in three quarter view.[44] This iconography continued the tradition of representing Demeter on cast "*aeses*" and they closely resemble the images of Demeter on the local silver coins. Logically the next in the line of development should be the one of the same size (no. 21) bearing the representation of Apollon, the protector of the *polis*, as well as its smaller fractions (nos. 17-18) also with Apollon. The object in front of the god's face is probably, an arrowhead – the attribute of Apollon, the archer – rather than a spearhead, as had been previously assumed.

The small weights with a representation of a deity's head on the obverse and a dolphin facing left on the reverse can be dated to within a short period,[45] as they are probably contemporary with the silver coins showing Demeter. The weight with an eagle on a dolphin and the inscription OΛBIO (no. 11) should also be dated to the same period.

The weight with a representation of Demeter on the obverse, and a dolphin on the reverse with the inscription APIΣTO above and OΛBIO beneath it (no. 8) exemplifies the transition between the type described above and the type with a representation of a dolphin, the city's name and the name of the *agoranomos*.

The representations of a dolphin are associated with Apollon Delphinios worshipped in Olbia, and these in fact continue the tradition of representing a deity on control weights. The earliest among these are, in my opinion, the carefully executed weights with a realistic representation of a dolphin facing left with the city's name above and the name of the *agoranomos* beneath it. These include, in particular, the examples with the names ΔIONY and APIC-TO (nos. 13 and 20), which have practically identical iconography. Also, they are multiples of the same unit – 1/8 and 1/4 of mina, respectively (48.691 g and 101.895 g). The weight with AΠO (no. 14; weight 49.393 g) is of inferior craftsmanship, but the positions of the inscription and the dolphin are practically identical to those on the previously mentioned examples.

The latter examples are followed chronologically by the weights with a schematic representation of a dolphin facing right and an inscription beneath it containing two lines giving the name of the city and the name of the *agoranomos* (nos. 12, 15-16, 22-23). These weights bear the following names: KPITOBOY (45.170 g, 51,75 g, and 107.694 g), APIΣTO (113.163 g), and XAPINAY. The weight with the name ΦIΛΩ closely resembles the style of these, although its shape is more regular and without any pronounced corners. The latest is probably the weight bearing three names (no. 9). V.V. Ruban, having analysed the stamps on measuring vessels from Olbia from the 4th-1st century BC, came to the convincing conclusion that originally they contained only a single name of the *agoranomos*. Three names appeared in stamps not earlier than the last third of the 3rd century BC.[46]

Various countermarks and scratched symbols are found only on control weights of the *agoranomoi*. These are probably connected with verification of weights under other *agoranomoi*. The countermark ΠΟ on a weight may be connected with the *agoranomos* Posideios, and the scratched EY is possibly related to the *agoranomos* Eumenos known from some stamps on Olbian measuring *oinochoai*.[47]

Notes

1. Buračkov 1884; Bertier-Delagard 1907; 1911; Čuistova 1962; Jarovaja 1962; Krapivina 1980; 1988; 1997.
2. Krapivina 1980, 84; 1997, 63.
3. Karyškovskij 2003, 62, 92.
4. Buračkov 1884, 59; Bertier-Delagard 1907, 4.
5. Karyškovskij 1988, 90-91.
6. Lang 1964, LW 60.
7. Karyškovskij 2003, pl. XI = C, CXV.
8. Similar to the representation on the weight described below under no. 8.
9. Karyškovskij 2003, 166, pl. XI = C; 1988, 60, 68.
10. Anochin 1989, 106.
11. Nazarčuk 2002, 78-79, fig. 1.
12. For details on the weight standards, Lang 1964, 3-20; Krapivina 1980, 85-89.
13. Karyškovskij 1988, 78.
14. Buračkov 1884, 65; Bertier-Delagard 1907, 6.
15. Krapivina 1980, 86.
16. I am extremely grateful to Dr. Susan Walker for her kind permission to examine the collection of finds from Olbia in the British Museum.
17. Lang 1964, BW 7. This weight bears a sign denoting its equivalence to four drachms.
18. Robinson 1941, 467.
19. Karyškovskij 2003, pl. XI = C, CXV.
20. Karyškovskij 2003, 166, pl. XI = C.
21. Karyškovskij 2003, 166, pl. XI = C.
22. Karyškovskij 2003, fig. 4.2.
23. Karasev & Levi 1965, 85, 87.
24. Krapivina 1980, 86.
25. Krapivina 1980, 86, 90.
26. Buračkov 1884, 41; Bertier-Delagard 1907, 1; Čuistova 1962, 65-66.
27. Karyškovskij 2003, 39, n. 91.
28. Krapivina 1980, 86, 90.
29. The mould, in which the weight was probably cast, had already been used before.
30. Karyškovskij 2003, 160.
31. Karyškovskij 2003, 58.
32. Lang 1964, 4-5.
33. Krapivina 1980, 86, 89-90.
34. Krapivina 1980, 86, 90.
35. Karyškovskij 2003, pl. CXV.
36. Karyškovskij 1988, 60.
37. Anochin 1989, 106, pl. X, 96.
38. Krapivina 1980, 86, 89.

39. Čuistova 1962.
40. Krapivina 1980, 86, 89.
41. Krapivina 1980, 85-89.
42. Bertier-Delagard 1911, 79-80.
43. Karyškovskij 1973, 98-101.
44. Karyškovskij 2003, pl. CXV.
45. Karyškovskij 2003, pl. XI = C, CXV.
46. Ruban 1982, 36.
47. Ruban 1982, 39; Diatroptov & Rusjaeva 1993, 107.

Bibliography

Anochin, V.A. 1989. *Monety antičnych gorodov Severo-Zapadnogo Pričernomor'ja*. Kiev.

Bertier-Delagard, A.L. 1907. *Popravki obščego kataloga monet P.O. Buračkova*. Moskva.

Bertier-Delagard, A.L. 1911. Otnositel'naja stoimost' monetnych metallov na Bospore i Borisfene v polovine IV v. do r. Ch., *Numizmatičeskij sbornik 1*, Moskva, 1-100.

Buračkov, P.O. 1884. *Obščij katalog monet, prinadležaščich ellinskim kolonijam, suščestvovavšim v drevnosti na severnom beregu Černogo morja, v predelach nynešnej Južnoj Rossii*. Odessa.

Čuistova, L.I. 1962. Antičnye i srednevekovye vesovye sistemy, imevšie choždenie v Severnom Pričernomor'e, *Archeologija i istorija Bospora 2*. Simferopol', 7-235.

Diatroptov, P.D. & A.S Rusjaeva 1993. Dva kul'tovych kompleksa Zapadnogo temenosa v Ol'vii, *Archeologični doslidženn'ja v Ukraini 1991 roku*. Luck, 106-107.

Jarovaja, E.F. 1962. O nekotorych girjach Pantikapeja i Ol'vii, *Materialy po archeologii Severnogo Pričernomor'ja 4*. Odessa, 243-246.

Karasev, A.N. & E.I. Levi 1965. Raboty Ol'vijskoj ekspedicii LOIA v 1960-1962 gg., *KSIA 103*, 80-93.

Karyškovskij, P.O. 1973. Pro deržavnij ustrij Ol'vii, *Ukrainskij istoričnij žurnal 2*. Kiev, 98-101.

Karyškovskij, P.O. 1988. *Monety Ol'vii*. Kiev.

Karyškovskij, P.O. 2003. *Monetnoe delo i denežnoe obraščenie Ol'vii (6 v. do n.e. – 4 v. n.e.)*. Odessa.

Krapivina, V.V. 1980. Vesovye giri Ol'vii, in: V.A. Anochin, S.N. Bibikov & A.S. Rusjaeva (eds.), *Issledovanija po antičnoj archeologii Severnogo Pričernomor'ja*. Kiev 1980, 83-98.

Krapivina, V.V. 1988. Neopublikovannye giri iz raskopok Ol'vii, *Antičnye drevnosti Severnogo Pričernomor'ja*. Kiev, 88-194.

Krapivina, V.V. 1997. Antičnye vesovye giri Ol'vii i Chersonesa, *Chersones v antičnom mire. Istoriko-archeologičeskij aspekt. Tezisy dokladov meždunarodnoj naučnoj konferencii*. Sevastopol', 63-65.

Lang, M. 1964. *Weights and Measures* (Athenian Agora, 10). Princeton.

Nazarčuk, V.I. 2002. "Desjat' obolov" iz Ol'vii, in: *Severnoe Pričernomor'e v antičnoe vremja. Sbornik naučnych trudov. K 70-letiju S.D. Kryžickogo.* Kiev, 78-79.

Robinson, D. 1941. *Metal and Minor Miscellaneous Finds* (Excavations at Olynthus, 10). Baltimore-London.

Ruban, V.V. 1982. Magistratura agoranomov v Ol'vii, *ArcheologijaKiev* 39, 30-40.

The Chersonesean Chora
in Light of the New Investigations in the
Herakleian Peninsula (1991-2003)

Galina M. Nikolaenko

Alexander Nikolaevič Ščeglov has always taken the problem of the preservation of archaeological sites very seriously. As early as the 1960s, when
work was carried out in the Chersonesos Museum with the aim of documenting the area's many different sites, Ščeglov, at the head of a small surveying detachment travelled around the entire neighbourhood of
Chersonesos with binoculars, a camera and a surveyor's rod, identifying
new archaeological sites. Alexander Nikolaevič has always considered rescue excavations a high priority. In the autumn of 1968, during a bout of cold
November rain, he and his two assistants excavated a burial vault from the
early Medieval period on the western shore of the Omega Bay (Sevastopol),
where new development of one of the city's beaches was in progress. This
event has predetermined all my subsequent work in Chersonesos. I have
had to visit the *chora* of Chersonesos on the Herakleian Peninsula fairly
often, helping Alexander Nikolaevič with the recording of the ancient land-
division, which at that time was excellently discernible on the surface. After
he left for Leningrad, it seemed to me quite natural to continue these studies in the *chora*, particularly because since that time intensive construction
work has started there.

So far the Herakleian Expedition has investigated a considerable expanse
of the territory of the *chora*, but this paper is devoted to that part of it where,
owing to Alexander Nikolaevič, my archaeological training began, namely
the western shore of the Omega Bay, which now belongs to the Archaeological
Park (Fig. 1, areas 3-4 and 5).

The territory of the Archaeological Park comprises several areas abound-
ing in remains of ancient land division, which are better preserved than any-
where else (Fig. 2). The system of transport and division roads; the demarcation of plots for vine-growing; peculiar agrotechnical structures used for
growing vines on rocky soils; farmhouses, fortified with powerful towers,
which defended large winemaking complexes – all of this was accomplished
by the civic community of Tauric Chersonesos as early as the 4th century BC.
Today, by means of aerial photographs, surface surveys and excavations, it
has all been brought to light and documented.

Area 2) Farmhouse on the landplot 86 near the Victory Park

Area 3) On the point between Kruglaya Bay and Kamyshovaya Bay

Area 4) Farmhouse on the landplot 6 near P. Korchagin Street

Area 5) Farmhouse on the landplot 9 near P. Korchagin Street

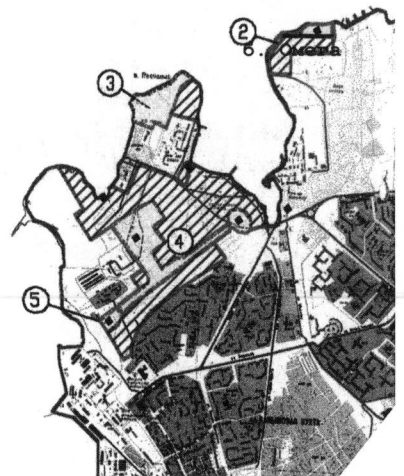

	Archaeological monuments on the territory belonging to the Preserve of the Tauric Chersonesos.
	Protected area with archaeological monuments
◆ ◆	Farmhouses of the 4th century B.C.

Fig. 1. General map with the location of archaeological sites on the western shore of the Omega Bay with indication of the areas belonging to the Preserve of Tauric Chersonesos.

The land constituting this part of the Park is bounded on the north-east by the western shore of Omega Bay, on the north-west by the steep rocky seashore, on the west by the right shore of Kamyševaja Bay, and on the south by the transverse road II. Within this territory, the following land plots of the ancient *chora* are situated: 1; 2; 2a; 3; 4; 5; 6; 7; 7a; 8; 9; 10; 11; 12, covering a total area of about 400 hectares (Fig. 3).

The north-western coastal region of the chora was one of its important elements. Here the outer harbours of Chersonesos were situated and, along-side their shores, various settlements and fortified farmhouses were located.

The geographical and climatic conditions of this region – thick topsoil formed of red earth and the presence of sources of fresh water on the slopes of the *balkas* (gullies) – were favourable for successful farming and fishing. These circumstances encouraged the Greeks to occupy the region and its territory was thickly covered with vineyards.

Amidst the vineyards there were farmhouses protected by defensive towers. One of the rural houses was discovered on a shoal in the middle of the bay, probably the farmhouse of the ancient Land Plot no. 13. Now it is indiscernible on the surface, but until the end of the 19th century, before which the sea level was lower than it is today, the shoal looked like an island.

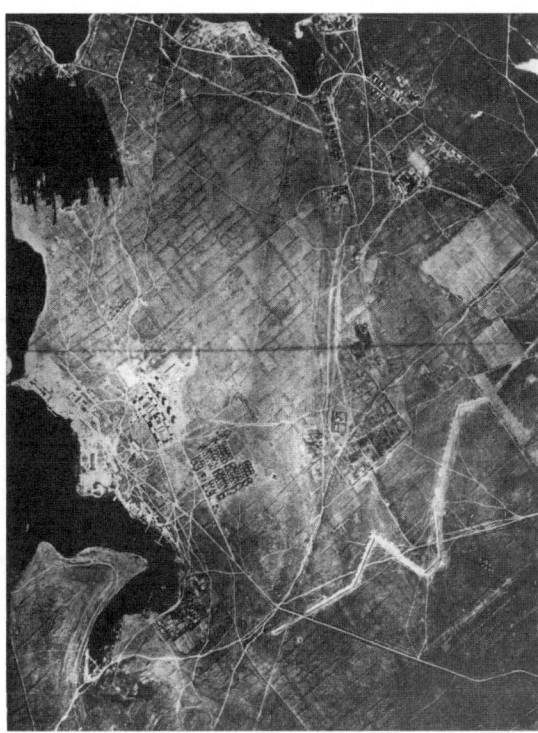

Fig. 2. Aerial photograph of the region.

The Academician P.S. Pallas wrote that "the gulf, which is justly called the *Kruglaja* (i.e. round, now called *Omega*) Bay, is less than one *verst* (= 3500 ft) wide and long, and not deeper than six *sazhens* (one *sazhen* = 2.13 m). In its centre there is a small islet surrounded by shallow water, and on the shores of the bay there are two salt lakes – one directly opposite the obtuse end of the bay, separated from the bay by a narrow dam, the other – on the western side of the bay and separated from it by a broader bridge of land. The distance to Kruglaja Bay from Streleckaja Bay is less than one *verst*, while from the next, Kazackaja Bay it is much greater; the capes separating Kruglaja Bay from the two neighbouring bays are not high".[1]

A.N. Ščeglov, who carried out investigations on the shores of this bay, came to the following conclusion: "Near the coasts of the entire Herakleian Peninsula at the time when the land plots were being demarcated, the sea level was 3-4 m lower than it is today. Throughout the entire Graeco-Roman period and perhaps part of the Medieval period as well, Kruglaja Bay did not exist within its present-day boundaries, but was a small open gulf of similar dimensions to the bays of Martynova, Pesočnaja and the unnamed one situated between Kruglaja and Kamyševaja Bays … The modern ingression of the sea probably started not earlier than the 10th-12th centuries AD … Finds of various pottery on the bottom must evidently be linked to the existence of a rural house, which was occupied for a long time: possibly from

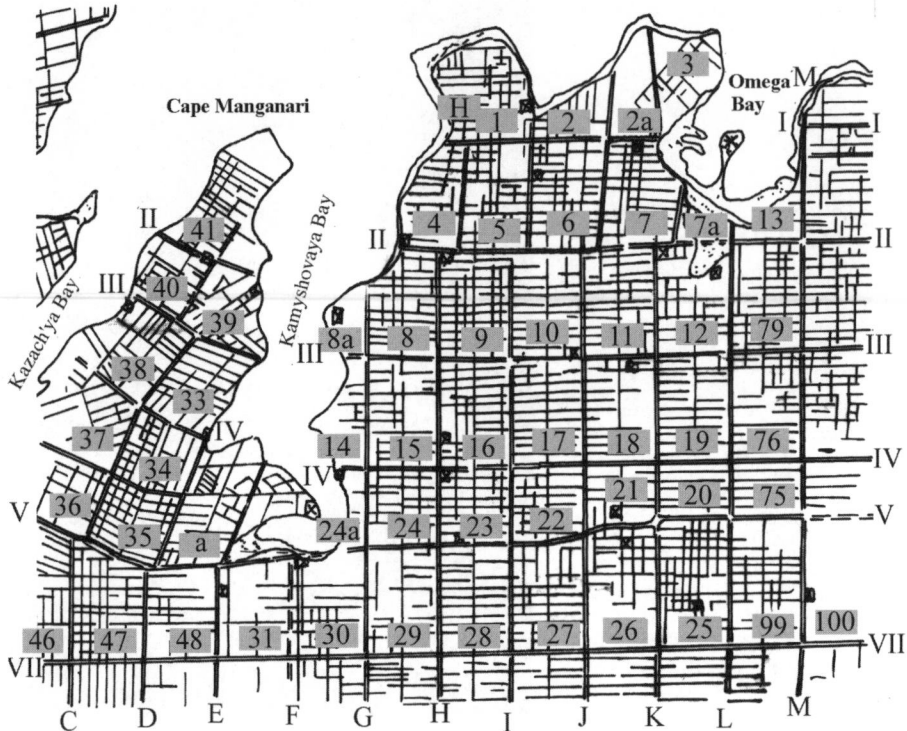

Fig. 3. Schematic representation of the ancient land-division.

the middle or the end of the 4th century BC until the 10th to 12th century AD. The contours of the bottom of the bay, although probably slightly transformed through the ages, indicate that the place where the farmhouse might have been located is in the southern part of the bay with the lowest water".[2]

Presented below is a description of the ancient land plots investigated by the Herakleian Expedition from 1976-2001.

Land Plot 2a

This plot is situated on the cape isthmus between the western shore of Omega Bay and the shore of a small gulf in the north-west. It is shaped like an elongated triangle. This area was marked off by myself from the area of Plot 2. On an aerial photograph taken in the 1960s, a transverse road separating these two plots is discernible. The preserved length of the road is 200 m. The length of the fence on the side of Plot 3 is about 600 m. The width of the land plot under consideration is 320-330 m to the south-east, and about 200 m to the north-west. During the Hellenistic period it was divided into a number of separate land plots, which were further divided into fields of the standard size of 52.5 x 52.5 m, i.e. 2.25 *plethra* (= 0.275 hectares).

In the eastern corner of the plot, on the shore of Omega Bay there was a farmhouse. According to S.F. Strželeckij, the house occupied a patch of ground c. 40 x 40 m. The surface finds are represented by fragments of tiles and various pottery of the Graeco-Roman period, predominant among which are fragments of amphorae and tableware of the first centuries AD. In addition, a number of fragments of stamped tiles, *kalypteroi*, amphorae, jugs and other ware of the 9th to 11th century AD have been found.[3]

Plot 3

This land-plot is situated on the western cape of Omega Bay. The surface of the cape is fairly even, except for its south-eastern part, which slopes gently down to the shore of the bay. It is covered with red soils rich in marl and is exposed to northerly and north-westerly winds. The rocky northern part of the plot has been eroded by the sea.

In antiquity, the plot was probably of a size close to the standard (630 x 420 m). At the south-west end, the stone fence flanking the road and separating this plot from Land Plot 2a, is discernible. The preserved length of this road is about 600 m. The plot was divided into fields measuring 52.5 x 52.5 m, i.e. 2.25 *plethra*. The height of the fences around the fields is now between 1.0 and 1.5 m; evidently, these fences were considerably higher in antiquity and sheltered the plants effectively from the cold northerly and north-westerly winds blowing from the sea. In the fields the low stone walls of the vineyard are still visible. The walls are oriented according to the predominant wind direction. This was done to prevent the cold wind from staying too long and forming eddies in the vineyard, which would have chilled the vines. By contrast, the warm wind blowing along the rows of vines would disperse the pollen.

Visual examination of the plot revealed that its northern part had been restructured probably during the Roman period. Restructuring of the plots is a fairly common phenomenon, but here it is of a unique character since in this instance we can see evidence of Greek surveying based on the Greek foot of 0.350 m, through the superimposed Roman planning of the 1st or 2nd century AD which was based on the standard Roman foot 0.297 m and on a different spatial orientation. This fact indicates both that the system of measurement was subjected to regulation, i.e. its reduction to a common unit – the Roman foot of 0.297 m – throughout the entire territory of the Roman Empire, and that the climate in this particular region had changed, especially as regards the direction of the prevailing winds and the humidity.

As established by S.F. Strželeckij, the farmhouse was situated on the low coast of Omega Bay, at a distance of 90 m from the southern corner of the plot. The farmhouse occupied a patch of ground 35 x 35 m. In its southern part there was a tower whose base measured 7 x 7 m built of large limestone blocks.

The surface finds of the Hellenistic period were represented by fragments of tiles and amphorae of Thasian, Rhodian, and Chersonesean manufacture, as well as fragments of various other pottery. A few fragments of tiles and tableware are dated to the first centuries AD. The surface finds also include the rim of a jug from the 9th to 11th century AD.[4]

Plot 5

This plot is situated at the high point between the right shore of Kamyševaja Bay and a small *balka* situated southwards from the western gulf of Omega Bay. The surface of the plot is even, covered in places by a fairly thick topsoil, and exposed to north-easterly winds.

The plot is shaped like a parallelogram measuring 630 x 420 m. In the middle of the 4th century BC land-surveyors divided it into six areas, each of 36 *plethra* (4.4 hectares) as individual land-lots for Chersonesean citizens. The lots were divided into fields measuring 52.5 x 52.5 m, i.e. 2.25 *plethra* and 52.5 x 105 m (4.5 *plethra* = 0.55 hectares). These fields were planted with vines. It is an astonishing fact that, since the time of the first land-division, the fields have not been subject to any alteration, and consequently they are a unique museum of the agrotechnical knowledge of the 4th century BC. The fences of the fields are fairly well preserved, some of them reaching a height of 1.0-1.2 m. Some of the fields are filled with stone walls of the vineyard.

In 1991 the Herakleian Expedition of the National Preserve of Chersonesos excavated the eastern corner of the plot and several sections of the roads adjacent to it, the land-dividing road leading to the farmhouse of the neighbouring lot and a transport road running from the western shore of Streletskaja Bay to the eastern shore of Kamyševaja Bay. The remains of the rubble masonry of the walls of a small building were excavated. Found in the lower layers of the fill, inside the uncovered building remains, were fragments of Sinopean tiles, one with a stamp from the late 360s BC (attribution by V.I. Kac), and a few fragments of black-glazed vessels including a plate with stamped decoration.

This open structure had not been occupied for long: all the finds date to the 4th century BC. This fact enables us to suppose that simultaneously with the beginning of the land-surveying in the middle of the 4th century BC, after the road was built, a small building was constructed not far from it as accommodation for those who surveyed the lots and built the plantation walls in the vineyards.

The transport road led to the commercial port in Kamyševaja Bay. When danger threatened from the land side, they were able to use this road to reach the ships and bring with them their most valuable possessions. In 1944 a jug with 740 Chersonesean coins from 330-230 BC was found by chance in a trench dating from World War II located near this road.

Plot 6

A plot situated in the bed, and on the western slope of a small, rather gentle *balka* ranging from the south-west towards Omega Bay. It is exposed to north-easterly winds. The topsoil on the slope is fairly thin, but in the bed of the *balka* it can reach a depth of 1 m.

The plot resembles a parallelogram measuring 630 x 420 m. It is divided into six individual land-lots with an area of 36 *plethra* (4.4 hectares) each. Most of the lots are divided into fields measuring 52.5 x 52.5 m, i.e. 2.25 *plethra*, and less commonly 52.5 x 105 m (4.5 plethra) and 105 x 105 m (9 plethra). The major part of each field is covered with the planting walls of the vineyard.

In the southern corner of land-lot no. 1, near the south-western transverse road, there was a farmhouse. It was Γ-shaped and measured 55 x 35 m according to S.F. Strželeckij. In the course of the clearing of the area carried out by the Herakleian Expedition in 1992-1992 (detachment headed by V. Eremenko) it was possible to identify a number of small rooms constructed of rubble adjacent to the wall of the farmhouse. These served simultaneously as the fence of the field covered with planting walls to the south-east of the house.

In the centre of the farmhouse there was a courtyard, on the south-western side of which two adjacent rooms were uncovered. In the floors of the rooms there were pits with 21 Sinopean *pithoi* of the 350s-340s BC. The ceramic finds from the farmhouse are mostly fragments of tiles, amphorae, *pithoi* and tableware from different centres of the second half of the 4th and the 3rd century BC. Individual fragments of black-glazed ware are dated to the last quarter of the 3rd and the beginning of the 2nd century BC. The finds also included several handles of stamped Chersonesean amphorae dated 315-272 BC. Most of the stamps belong to the period 315-300 BC.

In the course of the excavation of the field adjoining the south-eastern wall of the farmhouse, it was revealed that the planting walls here were built of large pieces of detrital limestone laid upon the bedrock. The thickness of the walls came to 1.2-1.5 m, and the height to 50-70 cm. The areas between the walls were covered with red soil. The planting walls adjoined the south-eastern fence of the land-lot which was constructed from rubble of moderate size. The thickness of the fence was 3.0-3.2 m and was preserved to a height of 70-80 cm.

Here were found fragments of rims and toes of Chersonesean and Sinopean amphorae of the last quarter of the 4th to the beginning of the 3rd century BC and fragments of black-glazed vessels of the 3rd century BC. All the finds from the farmhouse and its immediate surroundings indicate the practice of intensive vine-growing and commercial wine-making in the second half of the 4th and 3rd centuries BC.

In the 1st century BC production of wine intended for trade decreased sharply. The world market was dominated by the demand for the cereals, salt and fish which fed the enormous Roman army occupying the Greek East.

Chersonesos was not overlooked by the Romans. In the city itself, a Roman garrison was established, and the bays of Streleckaja, Kamyševaja and Kazač'ja, became a Roman naval base. The Roman legions brought no devastation with them, but the life of the Chersoneseans changed irrevocably. The vineyards no longer covered the Herakleian Peninsula with a continuous green carpet as before. In many places on the slopes and in the beds of the *balkas*, the planting walls were demolished and the vineyards were transformed into fields for growing cereals.

Some of the vineyards were stubbed up and their row-spacing adjusted for burials. The Herakleian Expedition investigated a small area of the vineyard in the northern part of the plot under consideration. Here, between the stone walls which were spaced at intervals of 2 m, a number of graves were found cut into the bedrock and covered with slabs. The objects uncovered in the course of clearing the graves are dated to the 2nd century AD. In one of the graves, a copper Chersonesean coin issued in 161-180 AD was found (detachment headed by O. Šarov, excavation of 1991).

Plot 7

This plot is situated on the south-western shore of Omega Bay and occupies the bed and slopes of the small *balka* running into the bay to the west. The bed of the *balka* is boggy, especially at its mouth. The topsoil (red earth, rich in marl) is fairly thick in the *balka* itself, and between 30 and 40 cm deep on its slopes. The surface of the plot is exposed to north-easterly winds. It forms a parallelogram in plan measuring 630 x 415 m. The northern part of the plot bounding the shore of the bay has eroded. The plot was divided into six land-lots with an area of 36 *plethra* each. The lots were demarcated into fields measuring 52.5 x 52.5 m (2.25 *plethra*), 52.5 x 105 m (4.5 *plethra*), and 105 x 105 m (9 *plethra*). In the major part of the fields, stone planting walls of the vineyard are discernible.

What is probably the earliest part of the plantation has been revealed near the eastern corner of the plot. Here, the walls are built from rather small pieces of rubble and are spaced at an interval of 2.3 m (excavation by V. Eremenko, 1992).

In some areas of the plot, the planting walls are constructed from fairly large pieces of rubble and the intervals between them are smaller than usual – on the average 1.0 m as compared with the usual 2.0 m (excavation by O. Šarov, 1992).

On the plot, two farmhouses have been registered. Farmhouse 1 was located near the north-western transverse road, 100 m from the western corner of the plot. The gateway of the farmhouse gave access to the road. The building was of rectangular plan measuring 35 x 25 m. It had two pyramidal towers. Large blocks from one of the towers measuring 10 x 8 m, are discernible on the surface.

The surface finds are datable to the Greek and Roman periods, mostly fragments of tiles and amphorae from the Hellenistic period, as well as fragments of amphorae and tableware from the first centuries AD. Of interest among the finds is a fragment of the hand of a terracotta figurine of Kybele from the 2nd century BC (dated by A. Ševčenko).

In the course of the rescue excavations of 2002, a drain covered over by limestone slabs was found near the northern wall of the tower. One of the slabs proved to be a relief from the 2nd-3rd centuries AD with a representation of a standing Dionysos (identi-

Fig. 4. Relief representing Dionysos from the farmhouse on Land Plot 7.

fied by A. Ševčenko; Fig. 4). Similar reliefs are often found during excavations in the northern and western Black Sea area. The majority of researchers are of the opinion that these are imitations of Thracian votive reliefs.

Farmhouse 2 was situated near the north-eastern transverse road, on the shore of the bay. It occupied a fairly large area measuring c. 80 x 50 m. On the northern side of the building was a tower adjacent to the road whose base measured 8 x 8 m. The surface finds and the cultural layer exposed in robber trenches indicate that the farmhouse was destroyed in a fire at the end of the Roman period.[5]

During his examination of the sites in the winter of 1967, A.N. Ščeglov unearthed the masonry of a submerged ring-shaped structure, about 5 m in diameter with walls 45-50 cm in thickness. In his opinion, this structure was erected in the western corner of the farmhouse.[6]

Plot 7a

This plot occupied the bottom of what is now Omega Bay. All that has survived is the south-western part of the plot and its southern corner. The plot resembles an elongated triangle: the longitudinal sides were 630 m long and of the transverse ones the south-eastern was 300 m long and the north-western 200 m. According to the reconstruction of the plot, its northern corner coincides with the islet in the centre of the bay where the remains of buildings from the Graeco-Roman and Medieval periods have been found. In 1967, within the territory of the plot, not far from Farmhouse 2 on Plot 7,

A.N. Ščeglov discovered and excavated a burial vault of the early Medieval period in which 37 skeletons were found, including those of five children. Of the 13 skulls preserved, five were artificially deformed.[7]

Plot 9

This plot is situated 200 m north-east of the right shore of Kamyševaja Bay. The surface of the plot is of consistent height except for its south-western part, which slopes gently towards the shore of the bay. The topsoil is red earth rich in crumbled marl reaching in some areas a considerable depth (0.60-0.70 m). The plot is exposed to southerly and westerly winds. The plot is rectangular measuring 630 x 420 m and divided into six land-lots of 36 *plethra* each, within which fields are demarcated, most of which measure 52.5 x 52.5 m, i.e. 2.25 *plethra*, the others 52.5 x 105 m (4.5 *plethra*). Almost the entire territory of the plot is built up with stone planting walls of the vineyard.

During the excavation of 1974, planting walls and pits for planting vines were revealed in the northern part of the plot. In the opinion of I.T. Kruglikova, these walls were built during the restructuring of the Roman period as demarcations.[8]

In 1991, the Herakleian Expedition excavated part of the Hellenistic vineyard adjacent to the north-western fence of the plot and the northern side of the farmhouse (detachment headed by Kalašnikov). The vineyard had not been visible on the surface before excavations. The excavations revealed stone planting walls 1 m thick and up to 50 cm high, spaced at the intervals of 2 m from each other. Between the walls and the fence which surrounded the plot a pathway 1.2 m wide was reserved. It is possible that the upper courses of the planting walls were demolished and covered with soil during the Roman period. In this way, the vineyard was transformed into a field for growing cereals.

In the western corner of the plot there are remains of a farmhouse built in the last quarter of the 4th century BC. Its dimensions are 35 x 30 m. The centre of the complex was a large courtyard around the periphery of which the rooms of the house were situated. In one of the rooms there was a winery. At the western corner, a tower, additionally protected by a pyramidal anti-ramming belt, was erected. The farmhouse was rebuilt in the 1st century AD. It was probably during this period or slightly later that a wall was raised around the tower blocking the access to the farmhouse from the road.

During the excavation, abundant ceramic material was found, among which fragments of Sinopean *pithoi* and amphorae predominated. A number of local Chersonesean amphorae have also been found. Judging by their stamps they were brought to the farmhouse during the period from 325 till 272 BC. The majority of the stamps are dated to 285-272 BC. At the same time, no stamps dated to 300-285 BC have been found. However, numerous fragments of red-slipped vessels have been encountered, as well as several fragments of early-Medieval amphorae. Noteworthy among the other finds were a vine-dresser's knife, a small stone altar, and another limestone altar with a representation of a cross-like human figure resembling a crucifix.[9]

Plot 11

This plot is located in the upper reaches of Omega Bay, on the south-eastern slope of the hill situated between the *uročišče* (a tract of isolated wood, often situated within a *balka*) of Omega to the south-east and the nameless *balka* to the north-west. It is exposed to north-easterly, north-westerly and southern winds. Most of the plot is occupied by stone planting walls of the vineyard.

In 1978, the Herakleian Expedition carried out an excavation of the vineyard, in which planting walls and holes cut in the rock for planting vines were uncovered. The farmhouse was located near the transport road running between Streletskaja and Kamyševaja Bays. Here, fragments of ceramics from the Hellenistic and late Roman periods were collected on the surface, and excavations initiated this season confirm its location.

Plot 12

Plot 12 is situated in the upper reaches of Omega Bay and at the mouth of the *uročišče* of Omega. The western and south-western parts of the plot constitute a raised slope facing the bay by its gently sloping rocky terraces. The northern part of the plot is submerged under the waters of the bay. The south-eastern part is situated on a rather low right slope of the *uročišče* of Omega. In the elevated areas, the topsoil consists of red earth. The plot is exposed to north-easterly winds.

The plot is rectangular measuring 630 x 420 m. It is divided into six land-lots 36 *plethra* each and demarcated into fields measuring 52.5 x 52.5 m (2.25 *plethra*) and 52.5 x 105 m (4.5 *plethra*). In the north-western and south-western parts of the plot, planting walls of the vineyard are visible on the surface.

In the plot, two farmhouses have been recorded. Farmhouse 1 is situated in the western corner of the plot. It is discernible on the surface as a blurred hill measuring approximately 35 x 35 m. The surface finds are datable to the Hellenistic period. To the south-east of the farmhouse there is a large mound of stone resembling a kurgan. Beneath it, a stone ring-shaped foundation of a small structure – a *yurt* (nomad's tent) with a rectangular fence was found. No dateable material has been revealed, but on the basis of analogies we may tentatively date it to the early Medieval period.

During the excavations of the planting and supporting walls within this plot, two burials with grave goods from the 2nd to 3rd century AD were uncovered (detachment of V. Eremenko, excavations of 1991-92).

Farmhouse 2 was located in the northern part of the plot on the right shore (in the upper reaches of the modern bay). The northern half of the farmhouse is submerged. According to S.F. Strželeckij's description, the dimensions of the farmhouse were at least 40 x 40 m. The house had a tower with a pyramidal anti-ramming belt constructed of huge stone blocks showing no traces of dressing. In the southern corner of the tower there was a pit, which revealed three horizontal courses of blocks.[10] Found on the surface were fragments of tiles, *pithoi*, amphorae, and various other ware dated to the last quarter of the 4th century BC to the 4th or 5th century AD.

Plot 13

This plot is situated on the eastern shore of Omega Bay. The greater part of it is submerged. The area preserved is about 12 hectares. It was divided into land-lots of 36 *plethra* and demarcated into fields measuring 52.5 x 52.5 m (2.25 *plethra*). It is presently covered with grass and in some places by juniper or Christ's thorn. It is exposed to north-westerly winds.

According to the reconstructed plan, the western corner of the plot coincides with the islet in the centre of the bay, where building remains and surface finds of the Graeco-Roman and early Medieval periods have been discovered. Most probably, in antiquity the island was connected to the mainland at the point where the roads crossed which separated the plots. On one of the plots there was a farmhouse.

Near the north-eastern fence of the plot, 120 m from the seashore, there was once a farmhouse. Now it is a low hill measuring 15 x 7-8 m and up to 1.5-1.7 m high. On the surface, only one room of rectangular plan measuring 5 x 3.5 m is discernible.

The surface finds are mostly wall fragments of Chersonesean and Sinopean amphorae of the Hellenistic period which offer little in terms of dating.

The ancient land plots adjoin the causeway that once connected the two navigable bays, Streleckaja and Kamyševaja, across Omega Bay, which in antiquity was passable although boggy.

On the basis of the results of underwater investigations it was established that there were harbour constructions situated on the western shore of Streleckaja Bay in antiquity (today ships dock here to take on fuel). Similar structures also existed on the eastern shore of Kamyševaja Bay, where today ships are moored in exactly the same place as the ancient anchorage.

By this road, agricultural produce and wine, provisionally stored in coastal farmhouses, were transported to the ships. To date, this road is excellently preserved in the section which lies between the Kamyševaja and Omega Bays. The width of the entire road reached 5-5.5 m, and the width of the part paved with slabs of detrial limestone measured 3 m. Along the carriage-way, footpaths slightly raised above the road-bed were constructed. This remarkable feature of the 4th century BC remained in use until the early Medieval period.

Conclusion

The ancient land plots of the region under examination presented a single entity: here the ideal notions of the Greeks, expressed by Platon and Aristoteles, about the spatial organisation of the territory of the *chora* owned by a democratic community were given a practical form.

The land plots demarcated by Chersonesean land-surveyors in the 4th century BC were in use throughout the entire Graeco-Roman period. On the three plots (nos. 7, 12, and 13) situated contiguous to the shore of the bay, two farmhouses have been registered. These were built in the Hellenistic period and were occupied until the 4th or 5th century AD.

In all the farmhouses of the Greek period, numerous restructurings of Roman times have been identified, which are probably connected with transformation of their functions and perhaps also with changes in the size of the individual properties. On the same sites traces of restructuring of the fields and the appearance of cemeteries within the territory of the Hellenistic vineyards in the first centuries AD, as well as obliteration of the most of the demarcation during the Medieval period, have also been revealed.

Notes

1. Pallas 1881, 94.
2. Ščeglov 1967 (Archives of the National Preserve of the Tauric Chersonesos, file 865, sheet 12).
3. Strželeckij 1961, 163.
4. Strželeckij 1961, 163.
5. Strželeckij 1961, 164.
6. Ščeglov 1967 (Archives of the National Preserve of the Tauric Chersonesos, file 865, sheet 9 ff.).
7. Ščeglov 1969, 290-291.
8. Kruglikova 1975, 302-303.
9. Kruglikova 1983, 43-44. For a detailed description of the farmhouse, see Saprykin 1994, 13-28.
10. Strželeckij 1961, 165.

Bibliography

Kruglikova, I.T. 1975. Chersonesskaja ekspedicija, *Archeologičeskie Otkrytija 1974 g*. Moskva, 302-303.

Kruglikova, I.T. 1983. Chersonesskaja usad'ba na nadele no. 10, *KSIA* 174, 43-51.

Nikolaenko, G.M. 1999. *Chora Chersonesa Tavričeskogo*. Part I. Sevastopol'.

Nikolaenko, G.M. 2001. *Chora Chersonesa Tavričeskogo*. Part II. Sevastopol'.

Pallas, P.S. 1881. Putešestvie po Krymu akademika Pallasa v 1793-1794 godach, *ZOOID* 12, 62-208.

Saprykin, S.Ju. 1994. *Ancient farms and land-plots on the khora of Khersonesos Taurike (Research in the Herakleian peninsula 1974-1990)*. Amsterdam.

Strželeckij, S.F. 1961. *Klery Chersonesa Tavričeskogo* (ChSbor, 6). Simferopol'.
Ščeglov, A.N. 1969. Ochrannye raskopki i začistki na Geraklejskom polu-ostrove, *Archeologičeskie Otkrytija 1968 g*. Moskva, 290-291.

Abbreviations

ZOOID   *Zapiski Odesskogo obščestva istorii i drevnostej.*
ChSbor   *Chersonesskij sbornik.*

The Chersonesean Farmhouse on Land-plot no. 49 on the Lighthouse Point

Sergej Ju. Saprykin

In 1990, the archaeological mission of the Institute of Archaeology of the Academy of Sciences of the USSR together with the Museum and National Preserve of Tauric Chersonesos conducted excavations of a farmhouse on land-plot no. 49, which belonged to the adjacent *chora* of Tauric Chersonesos on the Majak peninsula. This land-plot, adjoining land-plots nos. 50 and 57, has an area of around 19 ha. It is situated on a cape between Kazak Bay and Solenaja Bay, occupying the western slope of a ravine going down to Kazak Bay (Fig. 1.1-2).[1] The southern part of the plot functioned during the Hellenistic period as a vineyard with cultivation belts 2.3 m wide and plantation walls 1.2 m wide. On the southern slope of the cape, plantation walls form terraces up to 0.3 m high. Here the small farm is situated close to the sea-shore (Fig. 2). The adjacent terrace wall served as the farm's western outer wall.[2] Excavations have uncovered a courtyard and several rooms, which were rebuilt in the course of the farm's existence. Unfortunately, it remains incompletely excavated in the northern sector, so we cannot exclude the possibility that further rooms may have been situated beyond a trench which cuts off this part of the farmhouse (Fig. 3). Still, we can say with confidence that we are dealing with three building phases of the farm belonging to the late Classical and Hellenistic periods. Isolated finds of Roman pottery – for example the rim of a red-glazed cup from the 1st century AD (Fig. 4.4) – do not suffice to demonstrate that the farm continued in operation. The lack of Roman building activity seems conclusive in showing that during the first centuries AD, the land-plot probably only contained temporary buildings, as is usual for the *kleroi* of Tauric Chersonesos, including those on Lighthouse (or Majak) Point.

The first building phase

The dating of the first building phase is still provisional. During this phase the farmhouse only occupied the northern part of the later complex and consisted only of rooms 1, 2, 4 and 6. Unit 2 must have functioned as a court-yard enclosed by the other rooms (Figs. 3, 5). The farmhouse covered an area of 10.5 x 9 m, and it seems highly probable that wall 12, supporting the ter-race, was at that time smaller or perhaps did not exist at all. Thus the farm-

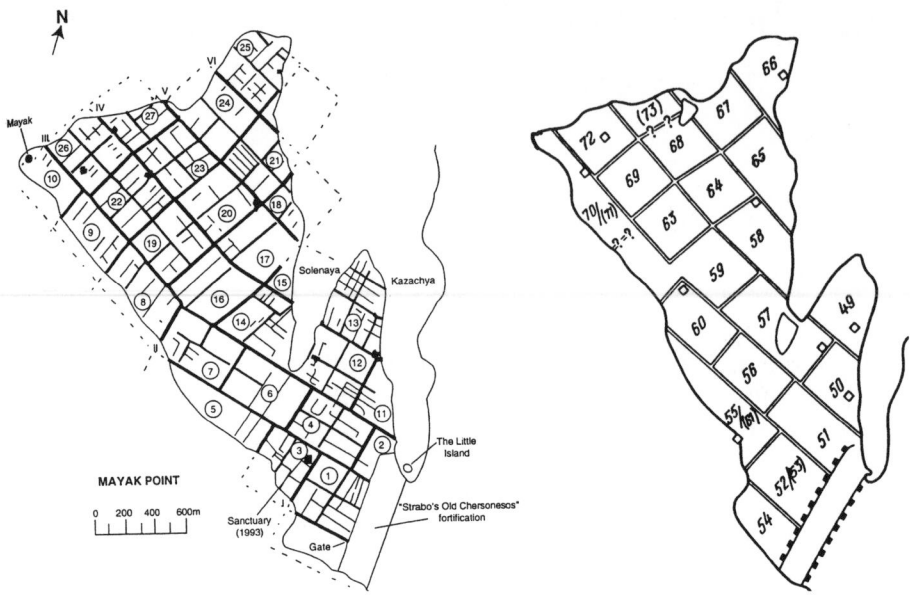

Fig. 1. Two maps of the Lighthouse Point by G.M. Nikolaenko and E.N. Žerebcov.

house of the first building phase was nearly square in plan and was without any fortifications. All rooms had exits to the courtyard and the main entrance leading directly to the courtyard was initially on its western side. Here part of the pavement of a road (Fig. 3, marked A), was discovered which was dismantled when the supporting wall 12 was enlarged and turned into a plantation wall.

The chronological framework of the first building phase is still uncertain, as we only managed to reach the floor level of the last phase of the farm's existence. Material providing an absolute date of its construction and its abandonment is absent. The architecture of the building seems to be of the usual type without a tower as fortification. The configuration of the buildings around the courtyard recalls the farm on land-plot no. 9 in the *chora* of Chersonesos on the Herakleian peninsula during its first construction phase,[3] and also the plans of unfortified rural houses in Attica, such as the Dema House or the Vari House.[4] Features have also been found which it shares with a rural house known as Baklan'ja Skala on the *chora* of the European side of the Kimmerian Bosporos dated to the first half of the 3rd century BC[5] and with urban houses of the 4th-3rd century BC in Kalos Limen and to a lesser extent with the farm by Vetrenaja Bay in its *chora*.[6] However, there are no direct parallels. The closest analogy seems to be the rural estates nos. 3-4 on the Lighthouse Point, excavated by N.M. Pečenkin. He argues that they appeared at the same time as the farmhouse on land-

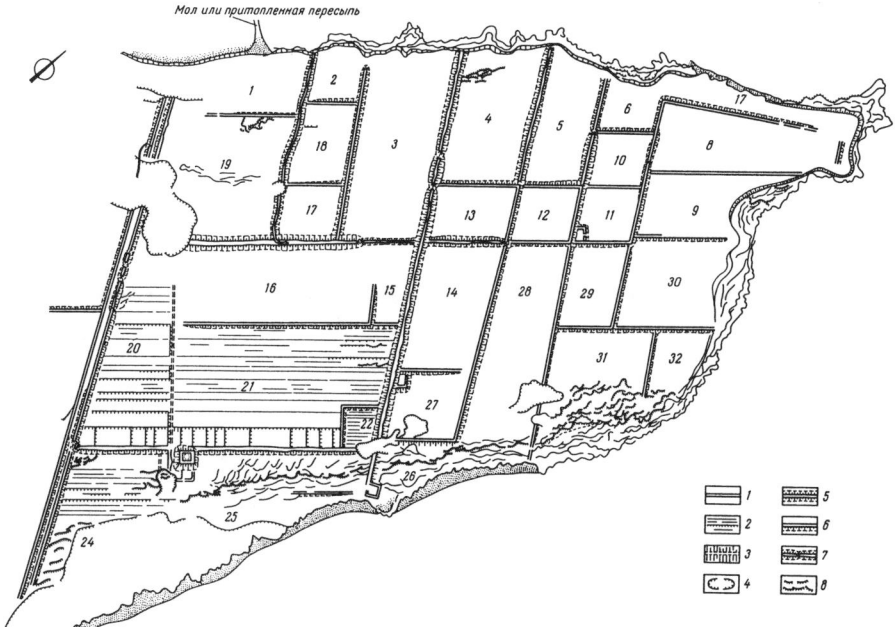

Fig. 2. Plan of land-plot no. 49 by E.N. Žerebcov.

plot no. 49.[7] In as far as the farms on the Lighthouse Point appeared between the second quarter and the middle of the 4th century BC,[8] it is quite possible that the farmhouse on land-plot no. 49 may also have been built at that time.

The second building phase

During the second building phase the farmhouse was greatly enlarged. Area 2 completely changed its functions and stopped being a courtyard, as the transverse wall 11 between the walls 7 and 14 created a narrow corridor about 1 m wide, probably intended as a storeroom (Fig. 6, no. 5). The entrance to this room was made between walls 7 and 12, where the masonry was removed (Figs. 3, 6, 7). Wall 12, a supporting terrace and the outer western extent of the farmhouse, was enlarged and reached 2.30-2.35 m in width, having been built as two parallel masonry faces with an inner core filled with small stones. A section of its masonry is placed so that it is in direct contact with the ground, testifying to its later erection. Room 2 was divided by wall 13 into two parts and now had two entrances, one of which (0.85-0.90 m wide) led into room 1. This was blocked during the last building phase. The other was used as an exit to the courtyard. The main entrance to the farmhouse during the first building phase had been blocked while wall 12 was enlarged and a new one was made several metres to the south,

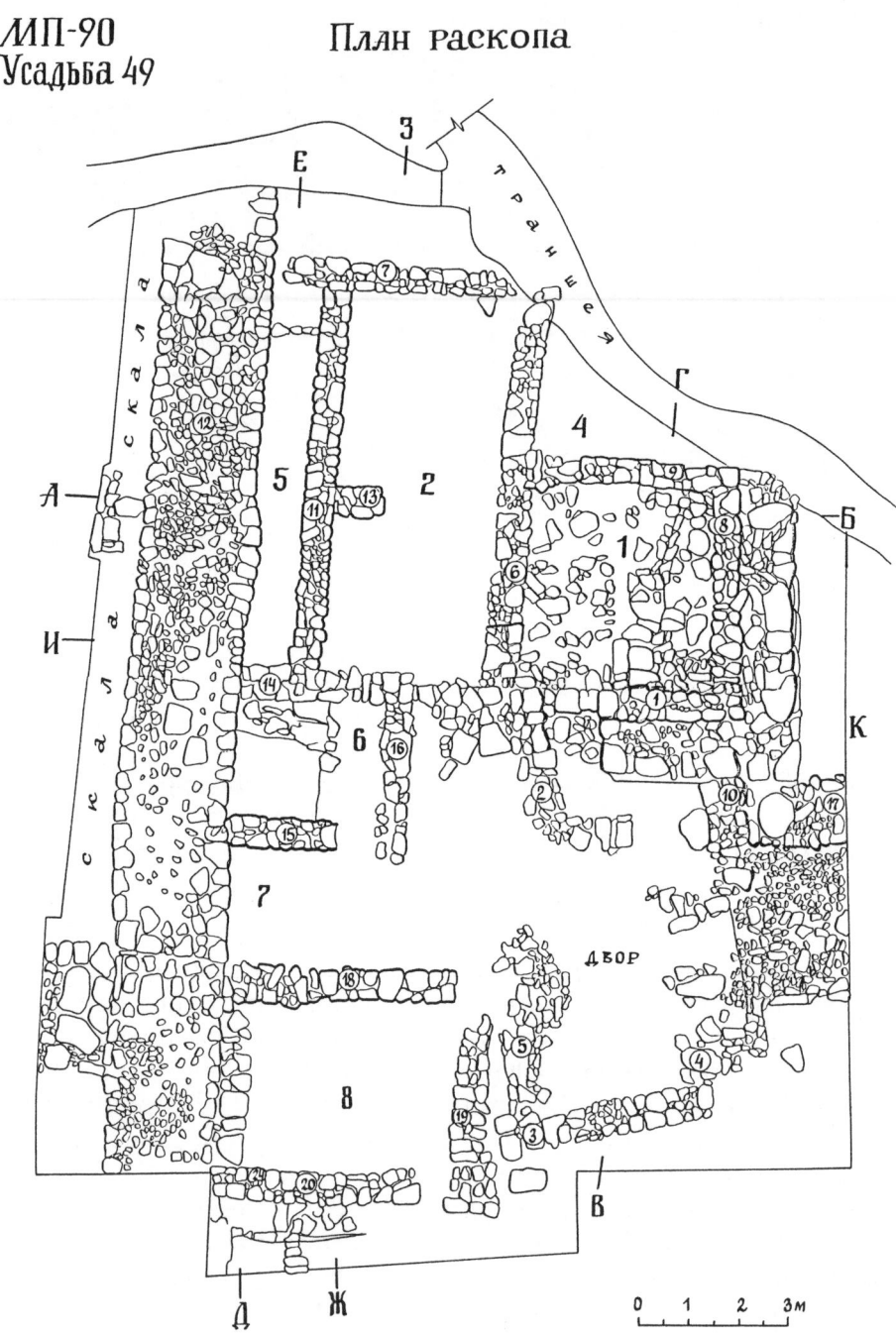

Fig. 3. Overview plan of the farmhouse on land-plot no. 49.

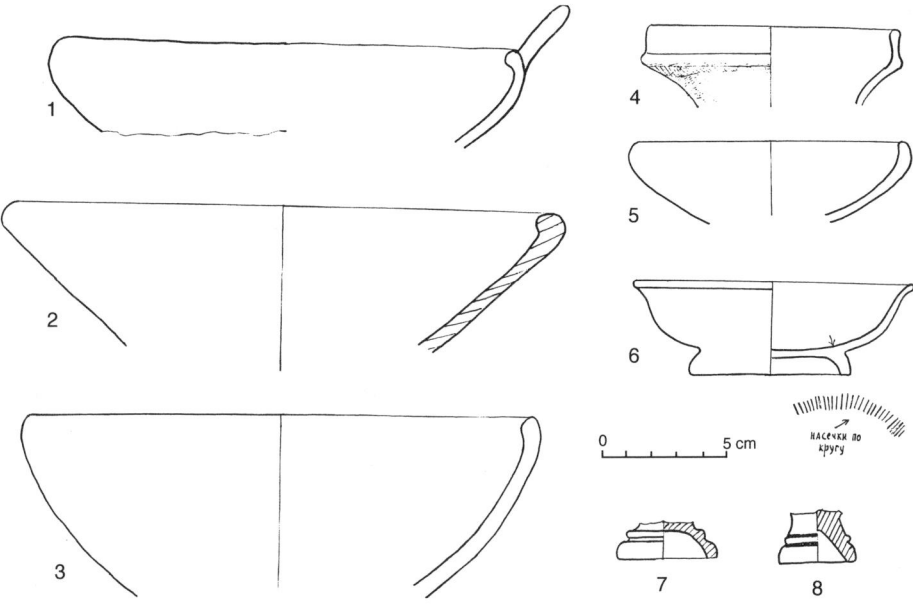

Fig. 4. Common ware fragments from Farmhouse no. 49.

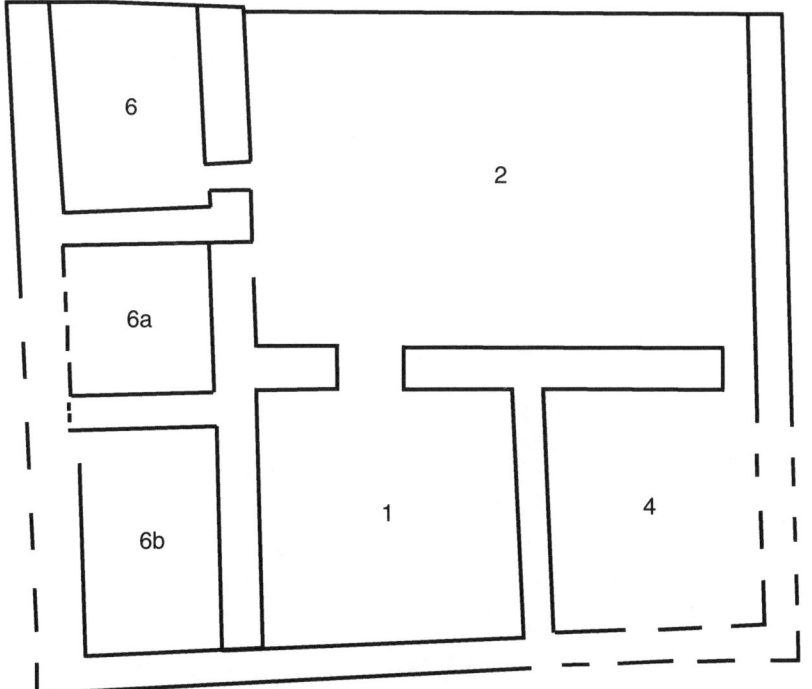

Fig. 5. Farmhouse no. 49. Plan of the first building phase.

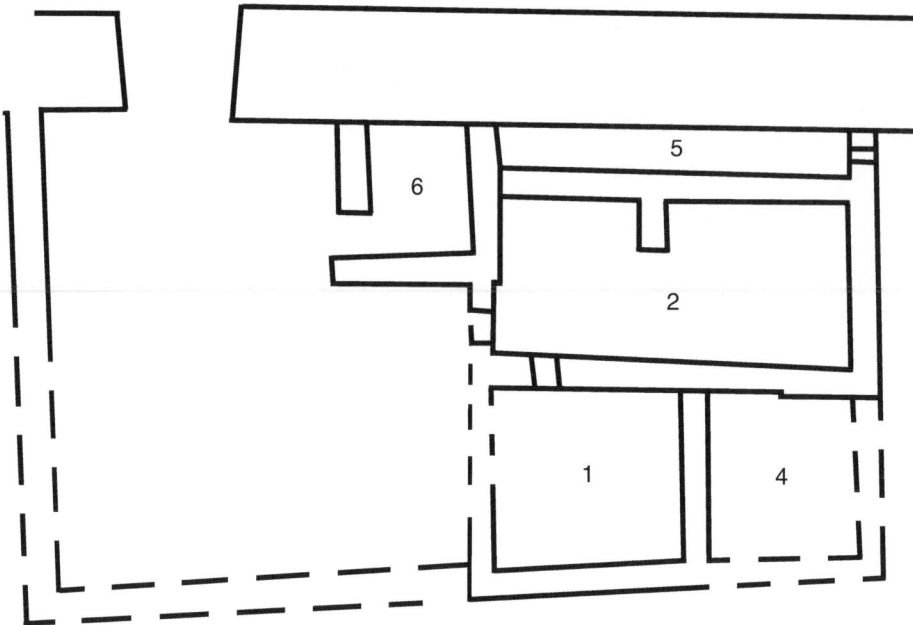

Fig. 6. Farmhouse no. 49. Plan of the second building phase.

Fig. 7. Room 5 in Farmhouse no. 49.

Fig. 8. Bronze coin of Tauric Chersonesos from Farmhouse no. 49.

where a road came up to wall 12 from the west. It was constructed of large and middle-sized stones and led directly to the courtyard through a 2.30-2.35 m wide opening in wall 12. The rooms around the previous courtyard, adjacent to the south to walls 1-14 and initially the farmhouse's outer wall, were dismantled and the entrance in wall 14 was filled in. The entrance to room 6 was now from the courtyard. Only the rooms nos. 1, 4, 6 were retained, while wall 20 was turned into the southern outer border of the whole farm. The new enlarged farmhouse, 17 x 9.30 m in size, remained unfortified, although its productive functions increased, as confirmed by the large size of its courtyard and of unit 2 (Fig. 6, no. 2).

The date of the second building phase is fixed by amphorae stamps and a coin – a *dichalkon* of Chersonesos with, on the obverse, Parthenos striking down a hind with a spear l. and on the reverse, a butting bull l. standing on club, below bow and quiver, EYΔPOMOY (Fig. 8)[9] – dated to 300-290 BC or 305-300 BC, the latter date being more likely.[10] In the courtyard an amphora handle was found with a stamp of Chersonesos, dated by the name of MAT[PIO]Σ A[ΣΤΥΝΟΜΟΥ] to 315-300 BC according to V.I. Kac's classification (group IB).[11]

From a trench, dug by soldiers in recent times, comes another Chersonesean amphora stamp (Fig. 9), put on the handle during the magistracy of [HPO]NIKOY [AΣΤΥ]NO[MOY] between 325-315 BC according to Kac's classification (group IA).[12] The amphora bases from Sinope, Herakleia Pontike, and Chersonesos are dated to the last quarter of the 4th to the first third of the 3rd century BC (Fig. 10.1-7) and are synchronous to pottery assemblages from sites from the second half of the 4th to the early 3rd century BC such as Panskoe I/U7 in north-western Taurica,[13] Western General'skoje, Pustynnyj Bereg, Košara in east Taurica on the Azov coast,[14] Elizavetovskoe on the Lower Don[15] and others. The base of a black-glazed

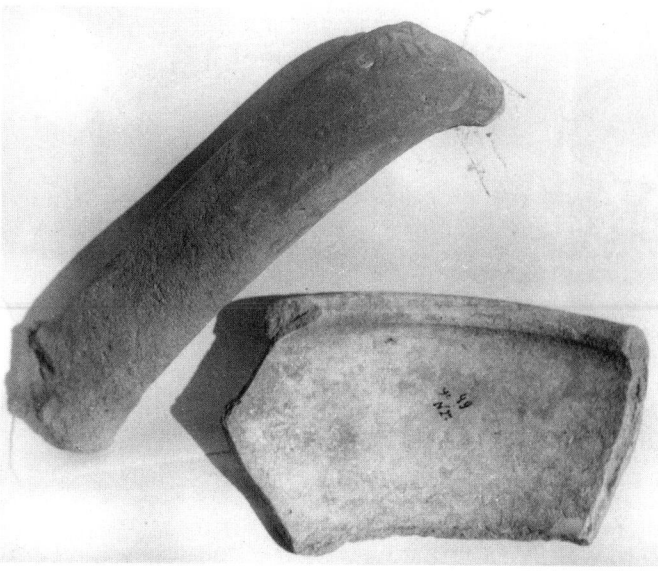

Fig. 9. Amphora handle with a Chersonesean stamp and the rim of a basin.

kantharos with extended shaft (Fig. 4.7) corresponds completely to those of the second half of the 4th to the first half of the 3rd century BC from the farm Pustynnyj Bereg I.[16] Another (Fig. 4.8) corresponds to *kantharoi* with ribbed body and dark glaze with metallic sheen from a cistern in the Central Temenos from the 3rd century BC[17] in Olbia as well as Olbia's Hellenistic layers.[18] Consequently, the second building phase can be dated to the last quarter of the 4th to the first third of the 3rd century BC, coinciding with the rebuilding of the neighboring farmhouse on land-plot no. 57 and building activity at other farmhouses of the Herakleian peninsula. This was the period when the Chersonesean *chora* was flourishing.

The third building phase

The third building phase is characterized by re-building, although the size of the farmhouse did not change (Figs. 3, 11). The entrance to the courtyard in wall 2 was filled in and a new one with gates led in from the side of the bay. In the place where the gates of the second building phase had been situated, there now appeared a new room, 8, which was surrounded by walls 18, 19, 20-24 and 12a – the latter serving as an additional supporting terrace wall for wall 12, where the previous gateway had been walled up. As a result a new additional room 7 was created 2 x 2 m in size, which was surrounded by walls 15 and 18 and linked by a passage to room 6, which was still in use. In the corner of room 7, an ash layer with a large quantity of Chersonesean and Herakleian amphorae fragments along with sherds of Chersonesean common ware were discovered. Underneath on the bedrock were found fragments of black-glazed *kantharoi* and plates. By wall 12 in room 6 remains of a hearth were preserved. It was constructed of roof-tile fragments, placed

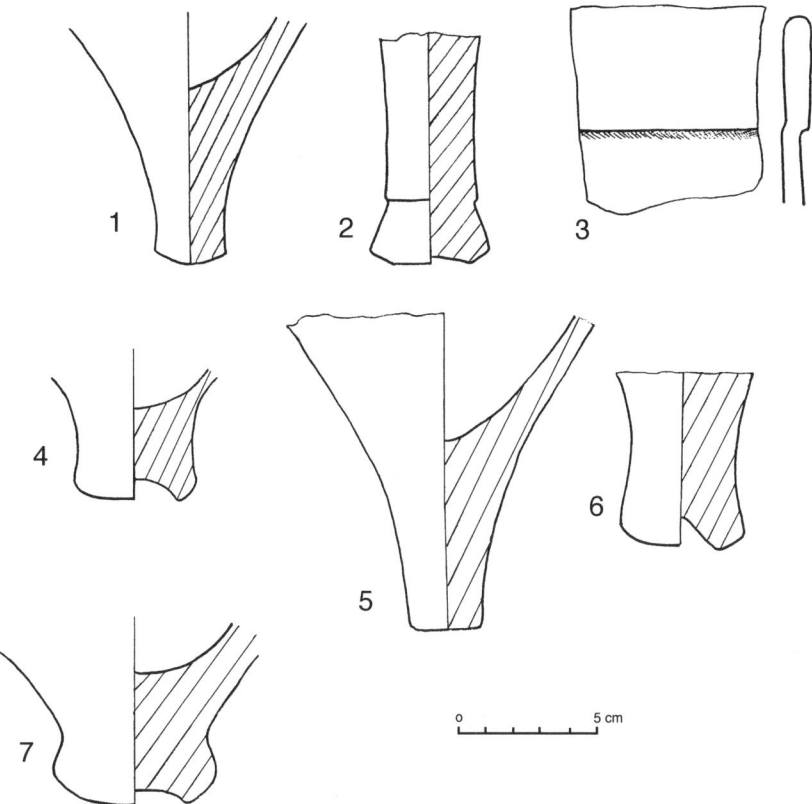

Fig. 10. Amphorae bases from Farmhouse no. 49.

vertically on the edge and laid horizontally in the bottom. On top and on the outside it was covered with clay. The base of the hearth was assembled from roof-tiles and the lower part of stone press (*tarapan*). The preserved height is 0.20 m and it is 0.50 m in width (Fig. 12). Some ash and coal still remained inside, and an ash layer can be traced over the entire floor showing the room's domestic character.

Room 8, formed by walls 18, 19, 20 and 4.15 x 3 m in size, initially had its entrance cut through wall 19 at the point of its junction with wall 3. This was later filled in and a new entrance was made in wall 20 to allow passage directly to the plot. Wall 3, now the outer edge of the farmhouse, is in direct contact with the blocked entrance in wall 19. Along with the remains of wall 4, it stopped at the farm's gates. The parallel walls 4 and 17 enclosed the driveway to the courtyard and small crushed limestone fragments were used to pave both the courtyard and the road.

Room 1, whose function had remained unchanged from the early period of the farm's existence, was now fortified with an anti-ramming belt triangular in section around walls 1 and 8. Its construction can be dated by a

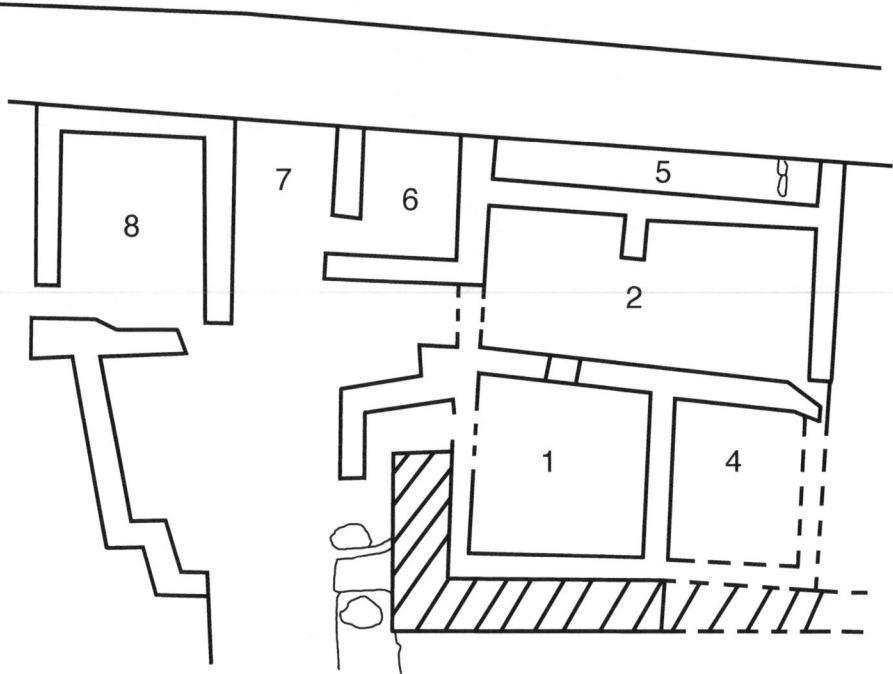

Fig. 11. Farmhouse no. 49. Plan of the third building phase.

Sinopean amphora stamp with the name of the *astynomos* Posis, son of Astios (Fig. 13). According to N.F. Fedoseev's latest classification, it belongs to the period 240-220 BC, although he previously dated it to 263-251 BC.[19] As the stamp was discovered on the outer side of wall 8 by its base, it gives an accurate date of the construction of the belt. The entrance to this room from the courtyard side was in wall 1 and was approached through a passage formed by wall 2 and an anti-ramming belt built against the wall.

Room 2 still consisted of two parts 3.15 x 3.72 m and 3.25 x 3.15 m in size. It had two passages – one in wall 6, 0.85-0.90 m wide leading to the neighboring room 1 (later filled in), and another – 1.35 m wide leading out to the courtyard. The room is oriented precisely along the line of the walls from north-east to south-west. As the excavations only reached the floor level of the third building phase, the function of the room cannot be determined with certainty. It was presumably a storeroom, although the possibility cannot be excluded that from the beginning until the end of the second building phase it was used as a vinery. Room 5 remained in use. It looks like a corridor divided by a barrier in the northern sector. The use of the room is rather difficult to establish. It was probably also a kind of storeroom for amphorae, various goods and agricultural equipment (Fig. 7).

Fig. 12. Hearth in room 6 of Farmhouse no. 49.

Fig. 13. Sinopean amphora handle with stamp.

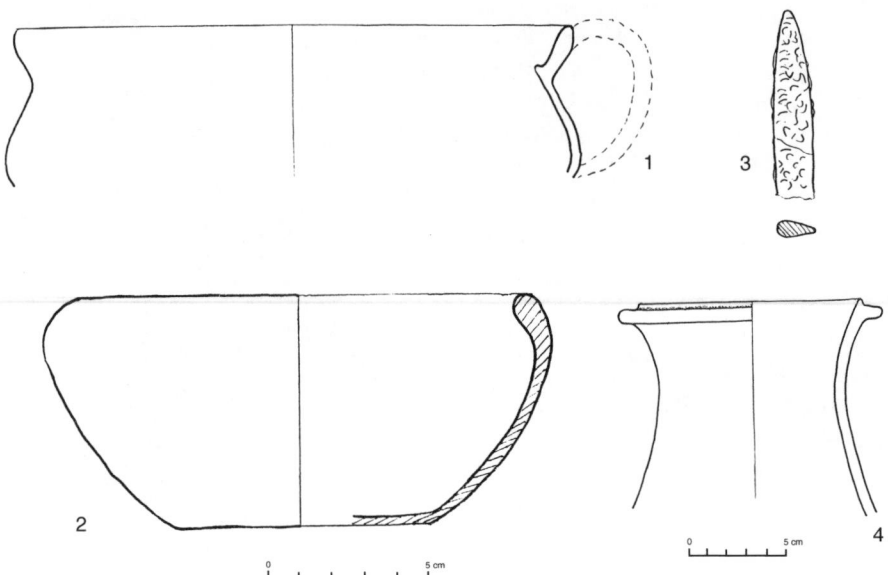

Fig. 14. Fragments of common ware from Farmhouse no. 49.

Fig. 15. Black-glazed bowl from Farmhouse no. 49.

The third building phase is dated by the Sinopean amphora stamp mentioned above and is confirmed by the anti-ramming belt. The lack of Rhodian and Hellenistic relief ceramics, i.e. Megarian bowls from Asia Minor, common to layers of the 2nd century BC, suggests that the farm was abandoned by its inhabitants in the late 3rd or early 2nd century BC. Traces of fire or evidence of serious destruction through military action are absent.

Fig. 16. Anti-ramming belt on Farmhouse no. 49.

Most of the finds are fragments of black-glazed and common ware – plates, basins, cups, fish-plates, and salt-cellars (Figs. 4.1-6, 14.1-2, 15). The assemblage is rather similar to that found on the land-plot no. 57, which differs the farms of the Majak peninsula from the other land-plots of the Herakleian peninsula. The same is true for establishing the chronological division between the second and the third building phases. The results of the excavations on the *chora* of Chersonesos have revealed that for nearly half a century around the middle of the third century BC, the rural estates of the Herakleian peninsula practically stopped functioning, only to be revived in the last quarter of the century.[20] Changes in the architecture and in the planning of the farmhouse in the third building phase, particularly the rebuilding in the south-eastern corner of its courtyard, the removal of the gates on the opposite side and the curvature of the main line of the farm's outer fence indicate a short, temporary break in the inhabitants' activity. Its revival in the third building phase began in the third quarter of the 3rd century BC at which time the farmhouse was strengthened by anti-ramming belt (Fig. 16).

The latter allows us to agree with those scholars, who date the appearance of anti-ramming belts to the mid-second half of the 3rd century BC in the wake of the growing danger of barbarian attacks. The belts around towers on various sites in north-western Crimea may have been built slightly earlier than those serving as protection for the towers or around entire farm-

Fig. 17. Small limestone slab for casting and a lead ring, cast on this slab.

houses on the Herakleian peninsula, as the distant *chora* of Tauric Chersonesos in the western Taurica was the first to suffer from the attacks of the Scythians and probably also of the Sarmatians.[21]

The construction of anti-ramming belts took place throughout the whole *chora* of Chersonesos. That is why they appeared in some places at the turn of the 3rd-2nd century BC.[22] The proposed date of the beginning of the third building phase is also supported by the fact that the neighboring farmhouse on land-plot no. 57 had no additional fortifications when it was abandoned by its inhabitants around the middle to the third quarter of the 3rd century BC owing to the Scythian or Sarmatian threat.[23] This implies that the third building phase can be limited to the second half of the 3rd to the early 2nd century BC. At the same time we would agree with E.Ja. Turovskij's and V.I. Kac's idea that the decline of activity on the farms of the Herakleian peninsula set in not later than 190s-180s BC.[24] However, at this time it only happened on the Majak peninsula, while on the Herakleian peninsula the farms continued to exist until the second half or even until the last quarter of the 2nd century BC.[25] The anti-ramming belt constructed in the third quarter of

Fig. 18. Ceramic weights and a whetstone from Farmhouse no. 49.

the 3rd century BC on a farm, which was only functioning for 50 to 70 years, compels us to revise the view that anti-ramming belts appear only in the 2nd century BC because they are absent on farms which ceased to exist in the first quarter of the 2nd century BC, as they have been found on farms, which were active until the middle of the century.[26] The third building phase of the farmhouse on land-plot no. 49 testifies that some of the unfortified farmhouses on the Lighthouse Point, for example those on land-plots nos. 55[27] and 57,[28] ceased to exist as early as the first half to the middle of the 3rd century BC and were not revived at all, while others were reconstructed after a short break and continued to exist until the beginning of the following century.

Fig. 19. Stone shots from Farmhouse no. 49.

Fig. 20. Limestone slab for casting small-size shots from Farmhouse no. 49.

The economy and mode of life on Farm no. 49 are known only from the archaeological material. Gardening and wine-making certainly took place, and its residents also practiced domestic crafts. This is confirmed by the find of a bilateral casting mould, which looks like a limestone slab with cut off oval recesses for casting rings and a special hollow for making spear- or arrow-heads. The rings cut into the slab were intended for casting lead rings, two of which have been found in room 6 (Fig. 17), as well as flag plaques with three semi-circular projections. Lead rings and plaques cast in lateral or bilateral forms, were used as sinkers for fishing nets.[29] Similar weights in terracotta were also found (Fig. 18). This is strong evidence that the inhabitants fished. If this was the case, they may have sent fish to the city, as they did with their agricultural produce. The archaeological material also included bronze and iron nails, a whetstone (Fig. 18), a flint arrow-head, three small stone round-shots (Fig. 19) and a piece of limestone slab with curved holes for making small lead half-balls or shots (Fig. 20) along with a sharp-pointed knife of iron with a single cutting edge (Fig. 14.3). Among the finds one should also mention two fragments of a grey-ware lamp with closed *discus*.

The material from the farm shows that the activities of its residents included gardening, wine-making, crafts and possibly military service necessitated by the increased threat of barbarian attacks in the second half of the 3rd century BC. At the same time nothing testifies to any kind of sacred or temple lands on the Majak peninsula, as the rural complexes studied there correspond directly to the well-known farms and land-division system on the *polis* land, known on the Herakleian peninsula and in other parts of the Greek world. The inventory of finds is rather poor, which is characteristic of the farms in the *chora* of Chersonesos.

Notes

1.   Saprykin 1994a, 9; Nikolaenko 2001, 179; Nikolaenko 2001a, 34.
2.   Žerebcov 1985, 39-40.
3.   Saprykin 1994a, 16, fig. 5.
4.   Pečirka 1973, 129, figs. 2.1, 3.1; Nowicka 1975, 110, fig. 10.
5.   Maslennikov 1998, 62, fig. 29.
6.   Ščeglov 1978, 79, fig. 38.
7.   Strželeckij 1961, fig. 10; Pečirka 1973, fig. 2.2-3.
8.   Nikolaenko 2001, 189.
9.   Anochin 1977, no. 17.
10. On the dating of this coin-type based on the stratigraphical observations at the site of Panskoe I/U6, see now Stolba 1989, 63, 67; Gilevič 2002, 248, 249. Cf. Turovskij 1997, 56, nos. 77-81.
11. Kac 1994, 51, 103, no. 74.
12. Kac 1994, 50, 98, no. 57.
13. Monachov 1999, figs. 217.1, 218.5, 218, 8. See also Hannestad, Stolba & Ščeglov 2002, pl. 45. 7-8.
14. Maslennikov 1998, figs. 41-43, 51-52.
15. Monachov 1999, pl. 209, 1.
16. Maslennikov 1998, 75, fig. 43.6.
17. Levi 1985, 82, fig. 72.
18. Levi 1964, 246, fig. 7.1-2.
19. Fedoseev 1994, 188-190. For the most recent chronology of the Sinopean amphora-stamps, see Fedoseev 1999, 34.
20. Zolotarev & Turovskij 1990, 81.
21. Golencov 1995, 51; Turovskij 1995, 54, 55; Saprykin 1997, 206.
22. Ščeglov 1978, 74 ff.; Daševskaja 1969, 89; Zolotarev & Turovskij 1990, 84.
23. Saprykin 1994a, 60; 1994b, 134.
24. Kac 1994, 73; Turovskij 1998, 226.
25. Zolotarev & Turovskij 1990, 81; Saprykin 1994a, 20.
26. Kruglikova 1986, 170-173.
27. Nikolaenko 1997, 76, 77.
28. Saprykin 1994b, 134-136.
29. Kulikov 1998, 188, figs. 9-10.

Bibliography

Anochin, V.A. 1977. *Monetnoe delo Chersonesa.* Kiev.

Daševskaja, O.D. 1969. Antičnaja bašnja na gorodišče Beljaus, *KSIA* 116, 85-93.

Fedoseev, N.F. 1994. Chronologija sinopskich magistratskich klejm, in: Toščev (ed.) 1994, 188-190.

Fedoseev, N.F. 1999. Classification des timbres astynomiques de Sinope, in: Y. Garlan (ed.), *Production et commerce des amphores anciennes en Mer Noire. Colloque international organise à Istanbul, 25-28 mai 1994.* Aix-en-Provence, 27-48.

Gajdukevič, V.F. (ed.) 1964. *Ol'vija. Temenos i agora*. Moskva-Leningrad.

Gilevič, A.M. 2002. Coins, in: Hannestad, Stolba & Ščeglov (eds.) 2002, 245-251.

Golencov, A.S. 1995. Fortifikacii gorodišča Kul'čuk, in: Masson (ed.) 1995, 50-52.

Hannestad, L., Stolba, V.F. & A.N. Ščeglov (eds.) 2002. *Panskoye I*. Vol. 1. *The Monumental Building U6*. Aarhus.

Kac, V.I. 1994. *Keramičeskie klejma Chersonesa Tavričeskogo*. Saratov.

Košelenko, G.A. (ed.) 1986. *Problemy antichnoj kul'tury*. Moskva.

Kruglikova, I.T. 1986. Bašni na sel'skochozjastvennych usad'bach Geraklejskogo poluostrova, in: Košelenko (ed.) 1986, 168-175.

Kulikov, A.V. 1998. Materialy k izučeniju drevnich morskich promyslov, *Drevnosti Bospora* 1, 186-201.

Levi, E.I. 1964. Keramičeskij kompleks III-II vv. do n.e. iz raskopok ol'vijskoj agory, in: Gajdukevič (ed.) 1964, 225-281.

Levi, E.I. 1985. *Ol'vija. Gorod epochi ellinizma*. Leningrad.

Maslennikov, A.A. 1998. *Ellinskaja chora na kraju ojkumeny. Sel'skaja territorija evropejskogo Bospora v antičnuju epochu*. Moskva.

Masson, V.M. (ed.) 1995. *Fortifikacija v drevnosti i srednevekov'e*. St Peterburg.

Monachov, S.Ju. 1999. *Grečeskie amfory v Pričernomor'e*. Saratov.

Nikolaenko, G.M 1997. Issledovanija na Majačnom poluostrove. 1993-1995, *ChSbor* 8, 75-88.

Nikolaenko, G.M. 2001. The Adjacent Chora of Tauric Chersonesus in the 4th Century BC, in: Tsetskhladze (ed.) 2001, 177-205.

Nowicka, M. 1975. *Les maisons à tour dans le monde grec*. Warszawa.

Pečirka, J. 1973. Homestead Farms in Classical and Hellenistic Hellas, in: Vernant (ed.) 1973, 113-147.

Saprykin, S.Ju. 1994a. *Ancient Farms and Land-Plots on the Khora of Khersonesos Taurike. Research in the Herakleian Peninsula 1974-1990*. Amsterdam.

Saprykin, S.Ju. 1994b. O vnutrennej kolonizacii Chersonesa Tavričeskogo, *VDI* 3, 126-143.

Saprykin, S.Ju. 1997. *Heracleia Pontica and Tauric Chersonesus before Roman Domination*. Amsterdam.

Stolba, V.F. 1989. Novoe posvjaščenie iz Severo-Zapadnogo Kryma i aspekty kul'ta Gerakla v Chersonesskom gosudarstve, *VDI* 4, 55-70.

Strželeckij, S.F. 1961. *Klery Chersonesa Tavričeskogo*. Simferopol'.

Ščeglov, A.N. 1978. *Severo-Zapadnyj Krym v antičnuju epochu*. Leningrad.

Toščev, G. (ed.) 1994. Problemy skifo-sarmatskoj archeologii Severnogo Prichernomor'ja. II. Zaporož'e.

Tsetskhladze, G.R. (ed.) 2001. *North Pontic Archaeology. Recent Discoveries and Studies*. Leiden-Boston-Köln.

Turovskij, E.Ja. 1995. O charaktere fortifikacij sel'skich usadeb Chersonesa na Geraklejskom poluostrove, in: Masson 1995, 54-55.

Turovskij, E.Ja. 1997. *Monety nezavisimogo Chersonesa IV – II vv. do n.e.* Sevastopol'.

Turovskij, E.Ja. 1998. Monety iz raskopok ellinističeskich usadeb Chersonesa na Geraklejskom poluostrove, *ChSbor* 9, 225-228.

Vernant, J.-P. (ed.) 1973. *Problèmes de la terre en Grèce ancienne*. Paris.

Vinogradov, Ju.G. (ed.) 1990. *Drevnee Pričernomor'e*. Odessa.

Žerebcov, E.N. 1985. Materialy k periodizacii antičnych pamjatnikov Majačnogo poluostrova, *KSIA* 182, 38-44.

Zolotarev, M.I. & E.Ja. Turovskij 1990. K istorii antičnych sel'skich usadeb Chersonesa na Geraklejskom poluostrove, in: Vinogradov (ed.) 1990, 71-89.

Wandering Images: From Taurian (and Chersonesean) Parthenos to (Artemis) Tauropolos and (Artemis) Persike

Pia Guldager Bilde

This paper contains more questions than answers. It was occasioned by my attempts to explain why and more importantly how the notion of the Taurian goddess turned up in the writings of Ovid and Strabon concerning the Sanctuary of Diana Nemorensis in Italy.[1] During this work it became clear that there must have existed a relationship between the epithet *elaphochthonos*, "deer-killing", for the pre-Greek, Taurian goddess by the name of Parthenos mentioned by Euripides in his play *Iphigenia in Tauris* (1115) and the repeated depiction of a deer-killing female deity on the coins of Chersonesos. It also became evident that not only was the epithet *elaphochthonos* extremely rare, but so too were the depictions. The coincidence could thus hardly be fortuitous. The question is therefore whether there might be a relationship between the wandering image of the Taurian goddess known from literary sources and the sparse diffusion of the iconography of a deer-killing female deity.

From Taurian Parthenos to Tauropolos

As is well known, the notion of the Taurian goddess expressed through the wanderings of her image became a literary topos of long-standing popularity in antiquity, providing the chief example of a god demanding human sacrifice, and it was used as a convenient cultural marker to set up a demarcation between the civilized and the barbarian world.[2] The first preserved description of the Taurian goddess was created in the third quarter of the 5th century BC by Herodotos. The well-known passage in 4.103 reads:

> "Among these, the Tauri have the following customs: all ship-wrecked men, and any Greeks whom they capture in their sea-raids, they sacrifice to the Virgin goddess as I will describe: after the first rites of sacrifice, they strike the victim on the head with a club; according to some, they then place the head on a pole and throw the body off the cliff on which their temple stands; others agree as to the head, but say that the body is buried, not

thrown off the cliff. The Tauri themselves say that this deity to whom they sacrifice is Agamemnon's daughter Iphigenia" (translation: A.D. Godley).

A few years later, Euripides turned to the same subject in his play *Iphigenia in Tauris* (*IT*), written in 412 BC or slightly earlier. Whether he drew on Herodotos' description of the Taurian goddess Parthenos created a few decennia earlier or whether they had a common source is not of importance here. But as Herodotos also Euripides vividly described the deity and the human sacrifice demanded by her.

It was foremost Euripides' image of how Iphigenia administred the sinister cult of a Taurian goddess on the southern shore of the Crimea that had a considerable impact on later Greek and Roman culture.[3] Throughout the play the goddess is called Artemis, but also in one instance *Anassa Parthenos* (1230), and the deity's epithet, *elaphochthonos*, is also provided (1115). Euripides operated within a particular *Athenian* discourse, as his play was the aithiological explanation for a symbolical human sacrifice in the Sanctuary of Artemis Tauropolos at Halai Araphnides through the exegesis of her epithet, Tauropolos.[4] This aithiology cemented the fundamental misunderstanding that Tauropolos meant "worshipped by the Taurians",[5] a misunderstanding that is important when trying to establish where, when and how the perception of the spread of the Taurian cult beyond the Black Sea region has been understood by ancient (and modern) authors.

The wanderings of the image of the Taurian goddess

With Euripides' *IT* and the transfer of the image from the Taurian sanctuary to Attica, the cult statue became a wandering image, primarily appearing in the eastern Mediterranean (Fig. 1).[6] Pausanias 3.16.7-8 is particularly illuminating as to the existence of rivalling myths in various cities. According to him, especially Sparta and Athens had competing versions of the myth. Pausanias professed himself to be inclined to believe the Spartans in their claim to possess the Taurian image in the Sanctuary of Artemis Orthia (3.17.7). Apart from informing us that the "Cappadocians in the Euxine" and the "Lydians venerating Artemis Anaitis" also claimed to have the image, he furthermore refers to the Athenians' complicated version – which even differs from that of Euripides: that the image was taken by Iphigenia to Brauron,[7] whence it was removed as booty by the Persians to sojourn in Susa until it was donated by Seleukos to Laodikeia in Syria (3.16.8).[8] We shall return below to a possible identification of the Kappadocian and Lydian localities hinted at by Pausanias.

Strabon provides us with a different set of localities mentioning the image of the Taurian goddess. According to him, Orestes and Iphigenia established her cult not only at Halai Araphnides (9.1.22), but also at two

Fig. 1 Distribution map of sites where according to ancient literary sources the image of the Taurian goddess was taken.

Cilician localities in the Tauros Mountains(!), Komana (12.2.3)[9] and Hieropolis-Kastabala (12.2.7). Also the Sanctuary of Diana Nemorensis near Lake Nemi in Central Italy could, following Strabon, boast of the Taurian image (5.3.12).[10] According to Cassius Dio, even Komana Pontike had a filial of the cult (36.11.1-2).[11] Earlier versions of the myth, moreover, linked the image to Phokaia,[12] and also to Rhodos.[13]

Starting with Euripides, the reason for claiming to house the Taurian image was in many cases to explain local rites with (symbolical) human sacrifices. This is mentioned in particular in the case of Halai (cutting a man in the throat with a sword)[14], Phokaia (a man burnt as a holocaust offering),[15] Sparta, Sanctuary of Artemis Orthia (flogging of male youths),[16] Lake Nemi (duel until death between the priest, Rex Nemorensis, and his challenger),[17] and it is reconstructed for other localities.[18]

Tauropolos in other sources

It was frequently with the Euripidean epithet "Tauropolos" that the image of the Taurian goddess traveled throughout the ancient world. Besides from Euripides, a goddess of the same name was also known from other literary and epigraphical sources.[19] The earliest attestation of her cult comes from Attica and the above-mentioned sanctuary at Halai – and Euripides is, to my knowledge, the oldest known literary source for it.[20] Apart from Halai, Tauropolos was known above all as the primary goddess of Amphipolis, especially favoured by the Macedonian kings.[21] She was also venerated in many localities in Asia Minor,[22] in particular in Karia.[23] The connection between the various Tauropoloi remains to be studied. It is doubtlessly necessary to discriminate between localities where we have epigraphical evidence, the majority of which are documented in the 4th through 2nd centuries BC (Fig. 2), and localities mentioned exclusively in literary sources (Fig. 1), predominantly Roman, as we may potentially be dealing with two separate phenomena: on the one hand, (i) an actual cult of a "bull-handling" female deity (*Tauro-pólos*) originating in Attica (Halai or Brauron) and (perhaps) spreading with the Macedonians through Amphipolis to the Hellenized East as far as Ikaros in the Arabic Gulf, and on the other hand, (ii) a female deity "worshipped by the Taurians" (*Tauró-polos*) and based on the false ethymology created by Euripides and spread throughout the ancient world especially through Strabon's writings[24] as a literary topos, in particular as aithiological explanations of the above-mentioned local bloody rites.[25] These two deities did not necessarily share anything but their name. At Brauron[26] and Amphipolis,[27] Tauropolos was with certainty depicted as a bull-handler riding side-saddle on a bull, frequently with a torch in her hand. Moreover, with the evident exception of Halai, in none of the localities claiming to possess the Taurian image do we also find inscriptions mentioning the veneration of Tauropolos.

Elaphochthonos and representations of a deer-killing goddess

As mentioned above, Tauropolos was also elaphochthonos. In general, the extreme rarity of the term "deer-killer" in ancient literature[28] is matched by the almost complete lack of depictions of a female deer-killer as well. Some of the depictions have been collected in the *Lexicon Iconographicum Mythologiae Classicae* by L. Kahil in her 1984-article on Artemis; more can be added. An early example is a marble relief from Attica in Kassel from the late 5th century BC showing a female standing with raised spear beside a deer already hit by another spear.[29] However, the main iconographical type features a female forcing the deer down with her knee in its back, aiming at it with a torch – as in a *pelike* ascribed to the Herakles Painter in British Museum E 432[30] and a *kalyx krater* ascribed to the LC Group in Paris, Musee du Louvre, CA4516,[31] with a sword or knife – as in a terracotta mould from Syrakousai,[32] or with a spear (see below).[33] The representations mentioned above date to the late 5th and 4th century BC and they make up the almost complete repertoire of the iconographical type of a deer-killing deity. There are a few later depictions to which we shall return below.

Related depictions are found on two other monuments of the 4th century BC: a beautiful handle attachment from a bronze *hydria* in the Metropolitan Museum, where a winged female deity is forcing down a deer,[34] and a fragmentary relief *lekythos* found at Lamptrai in Attica.[35] In respect to both depictions, we are uncertain which deity is represented and of the intent of subduing the deer. A series of later Imperial coins minted in Ephesos showing Artemis wrestling (not killing) a fallen stag or forcing it down by the antlers is also vaguely related.[36] But since none of these depictions show with certainty the killing of the deer, they should at the outset be excluded from the investigation, inasmuch as the semantics of the scene with the shift in ritual acting from subduing to actual killing must be considered decisive.

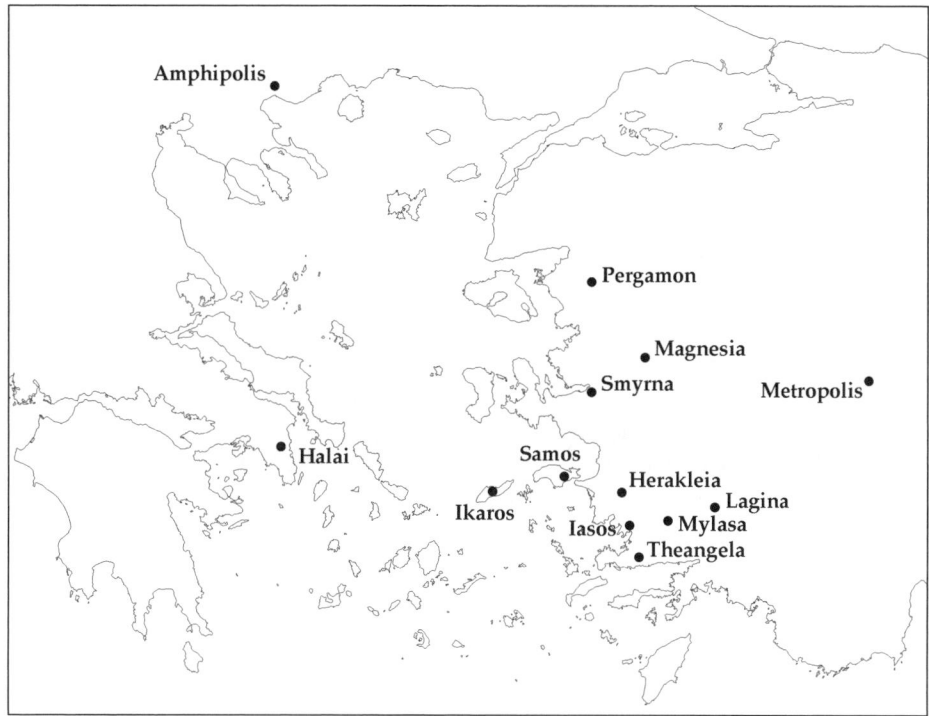

Fig. 2 Distribution map of sites where according to inscriptions (and literary sources) Tauropolos was venerated. One further site, Ikaros in the Persian Gulf, is not included on the map.

Parthenos as elaphochthonos

The only locality where a deer-killing goddess was depicted in profusion and through almost eight centuries was Taurian Chersonesos. In the late 4th century BC, a coin type was created that shows the city goddess Parthenos kneeling with her right knee on the back of a deer, forcing it down and at the same time thrusting a spear into its neck with her right hand (Fig. 3).[37] This type continued basically unaltered with short intervals until the latest ancient issues of the city in the mid-3rd century AD. It has been suggested by A.N. Zograf that this coin type depicted a well-known Chersonesean statue.[38]

The scientific discussion of the relationship between the pre-Greek, Taurian goddess and the later main goddess of the Chersonesean state, Parthenos,[39] and both deities' relation (or lack thereof) with Artemis has been long and shall not be repeated here.[40] As expressions of state cult institutions, Chersonesean coins are the most reliable sources of Parthenos's iconography,[41] and from these we can easily deduce why Euripides interpreted Parthenos in Greek terms as Artemis, since her iconography, at least

Fig. 3 Chersonesos. Head of Parthenos/Deer-killing Parthenos. Silver, 5.8 g. Late 4th century BC. Previously in W. Niggler's collection. After a cast (V.F. Stolba).

from the 4th century BC, coincided with that of the Greek goddess. Concidering the extreme rarity of the epithet and of depictions referring to a deer-killing goddess, the connection between the Taurian goddess called *elaphochthonos* by Euripides and the Chersonesean Parthenos portrayed repeatedly as a deer-killer on the city's coins supports the hypothesis that the Chersoneseans incorporated the local, powerful goddess of the recently conquered land of the Taurians into their own city pantheon (Fig. 4). However, it is unknown whether deer-killing was a particular element in the cult of the Taurian deity, which then inspired Euripides, or rather whether it was a trait that the Chersoneseans took up precisely *because* it was described by Euripides as part of an older (local) cult. On the one hand, the deer figured prominently as one of the main symbolic animals in the local, Scythian animal-style, wherefore it would be natural for the main, local deity to curb precisely that animal. But as the Chersonesean coins featuring the deer-killing goddess are no older than the late 4th century BC, the latter interpretation is certainly a possibility too.

The same scene is repeated on a handsome but fragmentary marble relief also found in Chersonesos in 1911, probably dating to the late Classical or Hellenistic period and now in the archaeological museum of Sevastopol.[42]

Late Hellenistic statues of a deer-killing goddess

Though still rare (with the exception of Chersonesos), in the late Hellenistic and Roman period, the frequency of representations of a deer-killing goddess increased slightly. In Delos, the main meeting place of the *oikoumene* in

Fig. 4 Chersonesos. Head of Parthenos/Deer-killing Parthenos. Silver, 2.62 g. Early 2nd century BC. The National Preserve "Taurian Chersonesos". After a cast (V.F. Stolba).

the late Hellenistic period, two statues of a deer-killing goddess have been found, both dating to the years around 100 BC. The best-preserved one was unearthed in the *Quartiere du theàtre*, House III S (Fig. 5),[43] and the second one, sadly fragmented, in the sanctuary complexes on Mount Kynthos.[44] The presence of a deer-killing Artemis(?) in the island of Delos may be due to the fact that this is one of Artemis' main cult localities, and that this rare depiction is just an expression of the island's extraordinary richness in representations. However, it cannot be completely excluded that the statues could be representations of the Chersonesean Parthenos, or, as we shall see below, of Tauropolos. No inscriptions were found in House III, so we are not informed of its inhabitants. It is even possible, as suggested by Chamonard,[45] that the find spot was not the statue's original place of erection. However, the second fragment came with certainty from the public space.

Chersonesos and its citizens were prominently present on Delos. As we can glean from inscriptions found in the island, they provided the temples with rich offerings and they instituted a festival, called the Chersonesia, of which we, unfortunately, do not possess much information.[46]

In Rome, one or perhaps two representations presumeably of the same statue group and the same date have been found. In one group only the collapsed deer and the sandalled right foot of its female attacker are preserved. This group made of Parian marble was found on the Esquiline Hill in via del Principe Umberto, where the Horti Tauriani belonging to Statilius Taurus(!) were situated.[47] These *horti* went into the Imperial domain under Claudius,

Fig. 5 Delos, Quartiere du theàtre, House III S, courtyard. H. with base 1.44 m.
C. 100 BC. In Delos Museum. After M. Kreeb, Untersuchungen zur figürlichen
Ausstattung delischer Privathäuser. Chicago 1988, frontispice.

and later Nero donated them to his favourite *liberti*, Pallas and Epaphroditus
(hence the subsequent name of the *horti*).[48]

One further representation can probably be identified in an otherwise
poorly known and little discussed beautiful statue segment in the Toledo
Museum of Art in Ohio, again in Parian marble and definitely of late
Hellenistic date (Fig. 6).[49] It derives from the Roman art market in the begin-
ning of the 20th century, and it may have come from the Sanctuary near Lake
Nemi, though this cannot be proved.[50]

Fig. 6 Bought in Rome, from Nemi? C. 100 BC. The Toledo Museum of Art in Ohio, inv. 1937.5. Photo courtesy of the Museum.

Late Hellenistic and Roman coins with a deer-killing goddess

Apart from Chersonesos, a few more localities in the eastern Mediterranean also depicted a deer-killing goddess on their coins. None of them are earlier than the late Hellenistic period, and, accordingly, contemporary with or slightly later than the marble sculptures just mentioned.

Hierakome, later called *Hierokaisareia* (Lydia)
(a)   Obv. Bearded head with Persian cap turned right
         Rev. Deer-killing female in short dress turned right. Monogram
         IEP (Fig. 7).[51]
         Date: (early) 1st century BC?[52]
(b)   Obv. Bust of Artemis with bow and quiver on her back turned right.
         Rev. Deer-killing female in short dress turned right. Inscription
         ΗΙΕΡΟΚΑΙΣΑΡΕΟΝ.[53]

Whereas type (b) is firmly ascribed to Hierokaisareia due to its reverse
inscription, type (a) has been attributed to various localities with names
starting with the syllable "Hier-".[54] Only one additional coin type provides
us with the same monogram, namely, coins with a bust of Artemis on the
obverse, occasionally inscribed with the name of Persike and with the
forepart of a kneeling stag and the monogram on the reverse.[55] The male
head in a Persian cap of type (a) is reminiscent of the representations on the
anonymous Pontic obols dating to the time of Mithridates VI.[56] However, in
contrast to the clean-shaven youth on the Pontic obols, the coin from
Hierakome-Hierokaisareia represents a male with a beard. In both cases,
however, the male with the Persian cap may allude to the cult's Persian
priesthood. Thus, with some probability, the coin from Hierakome-
Hierokaisareia can also be dated to the time of Mithridates VI.

Stratonikeia (Karia)
         Obv.: Head of Zeus Panamaros turned right.
         Rev.: Deer-killing female in short dress turned right.
         Date: 2nd-1st century BC or Roman?[57]

Sebastopolis (Karia)[58]
(a)   Obv.: Head of Marcus Aurelius turned right.
         Rev.: Deer-killing female in short dress turned right.
         Date: Marcus Aurelius as Caesar, AD 139-161.[59]
(b)   Obv.: Bust of the personified Senate turned left.
         Rev.: Deer-killing female in short dress turned right.
         Date: Roman.[60]

The coins mentioned are all extremely rare and exist in limited numbers
only, so to make any definite interpretations based on them may seem haz-
ardous. We have no external identification of the deity shown on the coins
of the two Karian cities of Stratonikeia and Sebastopolis. Only the inscriptions on the coins from Hierakome-Hierokaisareia offer an identification of
the deer-killing goddess, namely, as the Persian Artemis, Artemis or Thea
Persike.
     Inscriptions also reveal that Persike was worshipped in Hierakome-
Hierokaisareia,[61] where a Persian or Persianized cult prevailed, as vividly

Fig. 7 Hierakome-Hierokaisareia (Lydia). Bearded head with Persian cap/Deer-killing deity. Bronze, 5.97 g. (Early) 1st century BC? SNG Copenhagen (Lydia), 1947, no. 172. Photo courtesy of the Museum (Helle Horsnæs).

described by Pausanias. The cult featured a *magus* and Oriental fire magic inside a temple (5.27.5). That the priest put on a *tiara* during the rites was also mentioned by Pausanias, and it is therefore tempting to accept Imhoof-Blumer's identification of the above-mentioned male with a Persian cap on the obverse of the coin type (a) of Hierakome as that of a Persian priest.[62]

In connection with identifying the deer-killing goddess on the coins of Hierakome-Hierokaisareia as (Artemis) Persike, the aforementioned passage by Pausanias concerning the rivalling myths of possession of the Taurian image, should be briefly mentioned:

> "And yet, right down to the present day, the fame of the Tauric goddess has remained so high that the Cappadocians dwelling on the Euxine claim that the image is among them, a like claim being made by those Lydians also who have a sanctuary of Artemis Anaeitis" (3.16.8. Translation: G.P. Gould (ed.)).

With Artemis Anaitis and Artemis Persike the same deity is intended, a Persianized hypostasis of Artemis.[63] It is, therefore, tempting to suggest that Hierakome-Hierakaisareia, the main sanctuary of Persike, is to be identified with the Lydian locality housing the image of the Taurian goddess, since the first mentioned locality must refer to Komana Pontike. If this is the case, even though this does not explain why this deity was suddenty conceived of as Persian,[64] we have valuable evidence of a locality not only claiming to house the image of the Taurian goddess, but also having the visual representation of her as a deer-killer on its coins.

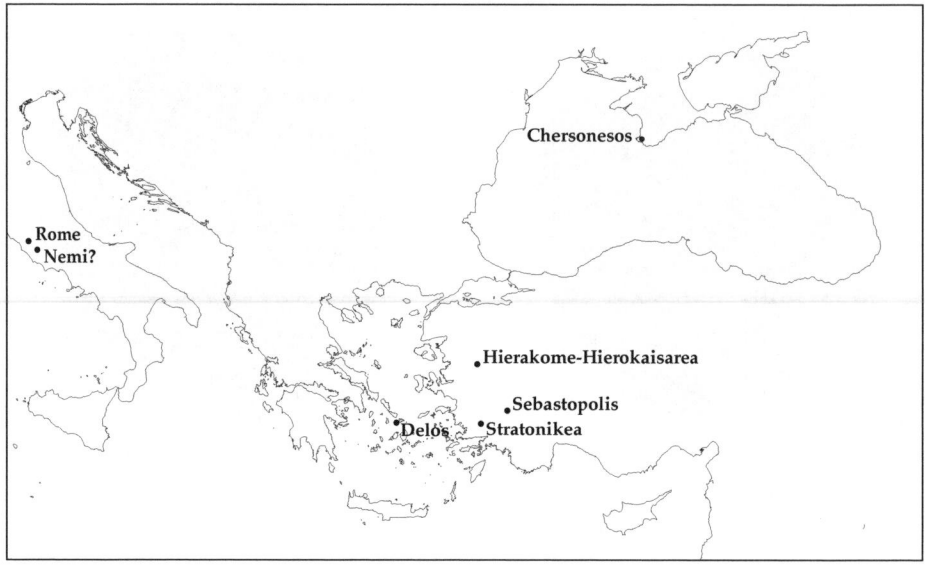

Fig. 8 Distribution map of sites with Hellenistic and Roman representation of a female deer-killing deity.

Mithridates VI and Tauropolos?

Obviously, the Taurian cult statue, if it ever existed, could not have been physically present at all the localities claiming to possess it. When depicted as imagined in its Taurian temple, it was shown as an under life-sized Archaic statue.[65] This was the normal way of depicting venerable age in antiquity after the Archaic period. However, although plenty of Archaïsing sculptures have been preserved from antiquity, to my knowledge not in one single instance was such a sculpture ever employed as a cult statue.[66] It was, therefore, not an option to "reproduce" an imaginary Archaic statue for a cult statue in the late Hellenistic and Roman periods. Due to the general rarity of representations of a deer-killing goddess, I propose considering the significence of Chersonesean depictions in several media thereof. The very eccentricity of its iconography, which shows acts of killing, could have been decisive for the choice of iconography apart from the Crimean origin of both myth and image. Accordingly, it is likely that in the late Hellenistic and Roman period, the iconograpy of the wandering image of the Taurian goddess, the Tauró-polos in the Euripidean sense, may have been understood in terms of the deer-killing deity known from Tauric Chersonesos and from Chersonesean representations.

The approximate contemporaneity of the four preserved marble statues of a deer-killing goddess all dating to the years around 100 BC may suggest the reign of Mithridates VI as the most likely period for the creation of this iconography of the wandering image of the Taurian goddess (Fig. 8).[67] In all probability, the years of the Mithridatic Wars were also the time when Tauropolos was first recognised in the Sanctuary of Diana near Lake Nemi.[68] The iconography may even have been created in the Persian milieu of the Pontic Kingdom. One of the localities possessing the Taurian image, Komana Pontike, was a significant religious site in that kingdom.[69] Unfortunately, the sources for its cult are scarce, so we have no means to evaluate the city's role in the spreading of the cult to, for instance, Cilician Komana. However, if the cult's secondary Persian elements were introduced during Mithridates VI's reign it would be in keeping with Mithridatic religious policy.

Notes

1. Ov. *Met*. 14.331; Strab. 5.3.12. The considerations were first given as a paper at the St Petersburg conference *Bosporskij Fenomen* II, November 2002; see Guldager Bilde, forthcoming.
2. Graf 1979; Rives 1995.
3. E.g., Graf 1979; Kahil 1984; Kahil 1990; Rives 1995; Koukouli-Chrysanthaki 1997.
4. Probably to be identified with modern Loutsa in Attica. Here there was a temple dedicated to (Artemis) Tauropolos, which is also known from inscriptions. Kotzias 1925; 1926, 168-177; Stauropoullos 1932, 30-32; Papadimitriou 1956, 87-89; Papadimitriou 1957, 45-47; Knell 1983, 39-43; inscriptions: see also *SEG* XXXIV, 103.
5. With the explanation that Tauró-polos meant "worshipped by the Taurians", Euripides suggested that the root -*polos* is passive. According to similar word constructions, the root must be active, so that *tauro-pólos* signifies a person handling or taming bulls in an actual context – e.g., agricultural – or in a symbolic context – e.g. in cult or ritual. I am greatful to G. Hinge for providing me with the reading of the word Tauropolos. Oppermann (1934, 35) reached the same conclusion with different arguments.
6. E.g., Oppermann 1934; Graf 1979.
7. Brauron was mentioned already in Euripides' version of the myth: Iphigenia was destined to go there from Halai to become the priestess in the Brauronian sanctuary (1463-1464).
8. Susa, the Achaemenid capital, came in the possession of Alexander the Great after the battle at Gaugamela. Seleukos must be one of the Seleucid kings, but Pausanias does not note which one he is. As Laodikeia was founded by Seleukos I Nikator (305/4-281 BC), Pausanias was probably referring to him.
9. Also mentioned in Cass. Dio 36.11.1-2.
10. Guldager Bilde, forthcoming. Lake Nemi is the only place in the West where it is certain that the image ended up. It was also thought to have been brought to Rhegion as Artemis Phakelitis; see Schmidt 1937, 1609; or to Tyndaris; see Graf 1979, no. 4 with references, but the sources are late and inconclusive.
11. Olshausen 1990, 1870-1871.
12. Pythokles, a 4th century BC author, quoted by Clemens of Alexandria, *Protr*. 3.42.22 (Marcovich).
13. Apollodoros 6.27 (Frazer p. 277).

14. Eur. *IT* 1459-1460.
15. Clem. Al. *Protr.* 3.42.22 (Marcovich).
16. Paus. 3.16.7.
17. Strab. 5.3.12.
18. Graf 1979. This may even have been the case concerning Laodikeia, where at some point a virgin was sacrificed annually to Athena (Porph. *Abst.* 2.56). We do not know whether this goddess was Tauropolos; however, from the city's coins it can be seen that the iconography of the goddess mixes elements of Athena (shield), Artemis (stags) and probably the local Astarte (battle ax); see Imhoof-Blumer & Gardner 1887, 56-58, pl. N.XI-XII.
19. The only general study of Tauropolos is Hans Oppermann's short article in *RE* from 1934 (33-38). Tauropolos has not yet been included in *LIMC* with a separate article. She is mentioned briefly in the article by Kahil on Artemis (Kahil 1984). Since the appearance of Oppermann 1934, especially the inscriptions have become much more numerous. This makes an updated study of Tauropolos a *desideratum*.
20. Further attestations from mainland Greece: Lokris (*IG* IX, 1², 716); Attica (*IG* II², 1604, *IG* II², 1611 face A front col. b and c (three times), *IG* II², 1605 face A front, *IG* II², 1612 face A front col. A); Dion (*SEG* XXXVIII, 603); Epidauros (*IG* IV, 1², 496 = *IAEpid.* 201); Sparta (Paus. 3.16.7). Ikaros in the Persian Gulf (Strab. 16.3.2; Dionys. *Per.* 610).
21. *SEG* XXVII, 245; *SEG* XXVIII, 534 and 536; *SEG* XXXI, 614-615; *SEG* XXXIII, 499; Liv. 44.44.4; Diod. 18.4.5; Lorber 1990, 12-13.
22. Komana (Strab. 12.2.3); Hieropolis-Kastabala (Strab. 12.2.7); Ikaros near Samos (*SEG* XLII, 779; Strab. 14.1.19); Ilion (*IGSK* 3, 118, 123); Magnesia ad Sipyllum (*CIG* 3137 = *OGI* 229, 60); Metropolis (*MAMA* 4, 122); Mylasa (*Mylasa* 427; *IGSK* 34.1, 404; *CIG* 2699 = *Mylasa* 261); Pergamon (*I. Pergamon* I, 13.24 = *OGI* 266.24 and 52); Phokaia (Clem. Al. *Protr.* 3.42.6, p. 32, 6 Stäh.); Rhodos (Apollod. 6.27 Frazer p. 277); Samos (*I. Samos* 330.5); Smyrna (*IGSK* 24.1, 573).
23. Herakleia by Latmos (*SEG* XLVI, 1563); Iasos (*Iasos* 83 = *IGSK* 28.1, 2; *Iasos* 95; *Iasos* 96 = *IGSK* 28.1, 3); Lagina (*Lagina* 189); Mylasa (*IGSK* 34.1, 404); Theangela (*Theangela* 8).
24. Halai, Lake Nemi, Kastabala, Komana, Ikaros in the Arabic Gulf, the island of Ikaros near Samos.
25. It is only for Halai, Amphipolis and Ikaros near Samos that we possess evidence both in the form of inscriptions *and* literary sources. The varied and abundant sources at Halai and Amphipolis underline the key position of these two localities in her cult.
26. Terracotta reliefs, c. 500 BC; see Kahil 1984, 674, nos. 700-701.
27. Kahil 1984, 674, no. 703. This was the dominating reverse type of civic bronze coins between Augustus and Commodus (Lorber 1990, 13); cf. *SNG American Numismatic Society* 7 (Macedonia I), 1987, nos. 150-154, 195 and numerous coins in-between. The identification is ascertained by frequent inscriptions on the coins labelling her Tauropolos.
28. Guldager Bilde, forthcoming.
29. Bieber 1915, 36 no. 75, pl. 32; Kahil 1984, no. 397.
30. Kahil 1984, no. 396.
31. Beazley 1963, 1457.12; Carpenter et al. 1989, 380.
32. Borbein 1968, pl. 9.1-2; Kahil 1984, no. 397a. See also below.
33. The origin of the type is briefly discussed in Guldager Bilde, forthcoming.
34. Richter 1937, 532-538, fig. 4; Kahil 1984, no. 403a.
35. Themelis 1975, 275-291, pls. 6-8. It should be noted that the figure subduing the

deer on the *lekythos* is dressed in long trousers, which sets the scene in a "barbarian" milieu. On the group of Attic relief vases, see Zervoudaki 1968.

36. Commodus (*ANS* inv. 1944.100.46111), Septimius Severus (*ANS* inv. 1944.100.46112), Caracalla (*ANS* inv. 1944.100.46120, 1944.100.46121), Geta (*SNG Deutschland* (v. Aulock, Ionien), 1968, no. 7874), Severus Alexander (*ANS* inv. 1944.100.46147, 1956.28.211; *SNG Deutschland* (v. Aulock, Ionien), 1968, no. 7880); Gallienus (*ANS* inv. 1944.100.46185). The same representation is found on a coin of Valerian minted at Hadrianoi in Mysia: v. Fritze 1913, 544, pl. IX.10; *SNG Deutschland* (v. Aulock, Mysien), 1957, no. 1144.

37. Stolba 1989, 62-63. The date is now further confirmed by the stratigraphy of Panskoe I, U6, see Gilevič 2002, 248-249.

38. Zograf 1922.

39. An essential text on the Chersonesean Parthenos is E. Diehl's article from 1949 in *RE* and the recent monograph Rusjaeva & Rusjaeva 1999. Parthenos is also briefly mentioned in Koukouli-Chrysanthaki 1997. It should be noted that we have absolutely no evidence that the Chersonesean deity was ever worshipped locally under the name of Tauropolos.

40. Diehl 1949, 1965-1967 with earlier literature. A good overview of especially Sovjet and Russian scholarship on this issue can be found in Rusjaeva & Rusjaeva 1999, 4-9; see also Braund, forthcoming.

41. Anokhin 1980; Stolba 1996.

42. Inv. 22226, see Ivanova et al. 1976, no. 94, fig. 55. The relief has been interpreted mistakenly as Mithras killing the Bull, and has, accordingly, been dated (probably wrongly, but I have not had the opportunity to see the relief) to the Roman period. The person kneeling on the back of the animal, far too slender to represent a bull, has bare legs and is not wearing trousers, which Mithras always does. There can, therefore, hardly be any doubt that Parthenos as *elaphochthonos* is intended.

43. *Exploration archéologique à Délos* VIII. Paris 1922, 222, fig. 98; Kahil 1984, no. 402.

44. *Exploration archéologique à Délos* XI. Paris 1928, 127, fig. 28; Kahil 1984, no. 403.

45. *Exploration archéologique à Délos* VIII. Paris 1922, 222.

46. *I. Délos* 1-2.328, 353, 354, 399, 439, 442, 461, 465; see also Grakov 1939, 262. According to Ps.-Scymnos, Delos may even have taken part in the founding of Chersonesos (828).

47. Capitol, Palazzo dei Conservatori, inv. 320: Stuart Jones 1926, 95-96, pl. 34.12; Mustili 1939, 136, pl. 85.

48. Royo 1999, 197.

49. Inv. 1937.5. I am very grateful to curator S. Knudsen of the Toledo Museum of Art in Ohio, for providing me not only with information about and photos of the statue, but also for allowing me to publish the picture, Fig. 6. See Ridgway 2000, pl. 69a-b; 241; 260 n. 31, pl. 69a-b, with earlier references; Knudsen, Craine & Tykot 2002, 231-239, esp. p. 234, fig. 3.

50. This is tentatively argued in Guldager Bilde, forthcoming.

51. *SNG Copenhagen* (Lydia), 1947, no. 172; Imhoof-Blumer 1883, 354, no. 23a, pl. H.7; Imhoof-Blumer 1897, 6-7, pl. I.3; Imhoof-Blumer 1901-1902, 447.

52. Imhoof-Blumer (1897, 6) suggests a date in the 1st century BC or (1897, 10-11) in the period of "Augustus or earlier".

53. Imhoof-Blumer 1897, 13, pl. I.9; Catalogue of Greek Coins in the British Museum (Lydia), 1901, 102, no. 3.

54. Imhoof-Blumer 1883, 354; Imhoof-Blumer 1901-1902, 447. The issue was finally settled by Imhoof-Blumer himself (1897, 5-11). However, much confusion still exists in the scientific literature; see Robert 1964, 47-51, which discusses this further.

55. Imhoof-Blumer 1883, 353-354, no. 23; Imhoof-Blumer 1887, 5-6, pl. 1.2 (with the inscription PERSIKE); Imhoof-Blumer 1901-1902, 447 (with the correct attribution). *SNG Copenhagen* (Lydia), 1947, no. 170-171; *SNG Deutschland* (v. Aulock, Lydien), 1963, no. 2951 (with the inscription PERSIKE). An anonymous single bronze coin with the head of Apollo carries the same monogram. It has been ascribed to Hierakome too (Imhoof-Blumer 1897, 11).
56. Golenko 1969, 130-154. I am much obliged to V.F. Stolba and J.M. Højte for alerting me to this fact.
57. *Catalogue of Greek Coins in the British Museum Catalogue (Caria and Islands)*, 1897, pl. 24.3; *SNG Deutschland* (v. Aulock, Karien), 1962, no. 2659 (date between 167 BC and Augustus); *ANS* inv. 1944.100.48067 (Roman); Kahil 1984, no. 401.
58. Robert & Robert 1954, 313-336, esp. p. 333, the present name is from the Augustan period; the pre-Augustan name is unknown; 330, 332 (coins with deer-killing Artemis).
59. *SNG Deutschland* (v. Aulock, Karien), 1962, no. 2651.
60. Robert 1970, 359-360, pl. XXVII.19.
61. *TAM* V, 1244-1245 and 1396. The find spot of 1396 is uncertain but is probably in a village near Hierakome; see Welles 1966, 2, 273-276. The inscription is dated to the late Hellenistic period, 138 BC or later. See also Tac., *Ann.* 3.62.1 (Diana Persica).
62. Imhoof-Blumer 1897, 10-11; Imhoof-Blumer 1901-1902, 447.
63. Brosius (1998) thoroughly discusses the relationship between the Persian Artemises and the actual Persian Anahita, concluding that Anahita is not a Hellenized Persian goddess, but rather that the Persian Artemises signal the Persianization of a Greek deity.
64. The existence of a variant tradition of the transmission myth involving a certain Persian aspect has already been mentioned above (Paus. 3.16.7-8). At Hieropolis-Kastabala, according to Strabon (12.2.7), the Taurian goddess was venerated as the Perasian Artemis, and the author explains that the Kastabala "Tauropolos was called "Perasian" because she was brought "from the other side"". The epithet Perasian is only known from this passage (and repeated in Steph. Byz., s.v. *Castabala*) and from a single inscription found in the city, where it was used as a theophoric name (Robert 1964, 51). The apparent similarity between Perasian and Persian has (mis)led many researchers to view the cult in Kastabala as *Persian* (Robert 1964, 47-51). Yet, however tempting it may be to assume that Strabon's need to explain the meaning of the word originated from information he misunderstood, Perasian and Persian cannot be equated linguistically, as I have been kindly informed by G. Hinge.
65. E.g. Kahil 1990, 714-715, nos. 19, 22.
66. Ridgway 1975, 445-461; Zagdoun 1989; Fullerton 1990.
67. Not only Chersonesos was active in Delos, but also to a considerable extent Mithridates VI, of whom portraits were erected on the island and to whom a monument was dedicated by the priest Helianax in 102/1 BC with portraits of Mithridates' *philoi*; see Bruneau & Ducat 1983, 69, 77, 222-223, no. 94 with references.
68. Guldager Bilde, forthcoming.
69. Saprykin 1996, 248-266.

Bibliography

Anokhin, V.A. 1980. *The Coinage of Chersonesos* (BAR, 69). Oxford.

Beazley, J.D. 1963. *Attic Red-Figure Vase-Painters²*. Oxford.

Bieber, M. 1915. *Die antiken Skulpturen und Bronzen in Cassel*. Marburg.

Borbein, A.H. 1968. *Campanareliefs. Typologische und stilkritische Unter-suchungen* (RM Ergänzungsheft, 14).

Braund, D. (forthcoming). Parthenos and the Nymphs at Crimean Chersonesus: colonial appropriation and native integration, to be printed in the conference volume: *Cités grecques, sociétés indigènes et empires mondiaux dans la region nord-pontique: origins et développement d'une koiné politique, économique et culturelle (VIIe s. a.C. – IIIe s. p.C.)*. Bordeaux.

Brosius, M. 1998. Artemis Persike and Artemis Anaitis, in: M. brosius & A. Kuhrt (eds.), *Achemenid History* 11. *Essays in Memory of David M. Lewis*. Leiden, 227-238.

Bruneau, Ph. & J. Ducat 1983. *Guide de Délos³*. Paris.

Carpenter, Th. et al. 1989. *Beazley Addenda²*. Oxford.

Diehl, E. 1949. Parthenos (2), *RE* 18.4, 1957-1967.

Fullerton, M.D. 1990. *The Archaistic Style in Roman Statuary*. Leiden.

Gilevič, A.M. 2002. Coins, in: L. Hannestad, V.F. Stolba & A.N. Ščeglov (eds.), *Panskoye* I. Vol. I. *The Monumental Building U6*. Aarhus, 245-251.

Golenko, K.V. 1969. Pontijskaja anonimnaja med', *VDI* 1, 130-154

Graf, F. 1979. Das Götterbild aus dem Taurerland, *Antike Welt* 10.4, 33-41.

Grakov, B.N. 1939. Materialy po istorii Skifii v grečeskich nadpisjach Balkanskogo poluostrova i Maloj Azii, *VDI* 3, 72-312.

Guldager Bilde, P. (forthcoming). What was Scythian about the Scythian Diana at Nemi?, *Archeologičeskie vesti*.

Imhoof-Blumer, F. 1897. *Lydische Stadtmünzen*. Genf-Leipzig.

Imhoof-Blumer, F. 1883. *Monnaies grecques*. Paris-Leipzig.

Imhoof-Blumer, F. 1901-1902. *Kleinasiatische Münzen* I-II. Wien.

Imhoof-Blumer, F. & P. Gardner 1887. *A Numismatic Commentary on Pausanias*. London.

Ivanova, A.P. et al. 1976. *Antičnaja skul'ptura Chersonesa*. Kiev.

Kahil, L. 1984. Artemis, *LIMC* II. Zürich-München, 618-753.

Kahil, L. 1990. Iphigeneia, *LIMC* V. Zürich-München, 706-729.

Knell, H. 1983. Der Tempel der Artemis Tauropolos in Lutsa, *AA* 1983, 39-43.

Knudsen, S.E., C. Craine & R.H. Tykot 2002. Analysis of classical marble sculptures in the Toledo Museum of Art, in: J.J. Herrmann Jr., N. Herz & R. Newman (eds.), *ASMOSIA 5: Interdisciplinary Studies on Ancient Stone*. London, 231-239.

Kotzias, N. 1925-1926. Démotikon pséphisma Halon ton Raphnidon, *ArchEph* 168-177.

Koukouli-Chrysanthaki, H. 1997. Parthenos, *LIMC* VIII. Zürich-Düsseldorf, 944-948.

Krauskopf, I. 1990. Iphigeneia in Etruria, *LIMC* V. Zürich-München, 729-734.

Lorber, C.C. 1990. *Amphipolis. The Civic Coinage in Silver and Gold*. Los Angeles.

Mustili, D. 1939. *Il Museo Mussolini*. Roma.

Olshausen, E. 1990. Götter, Heroen und ihre Kulte in Pontos, *ANRW* II.18.3, 1865-1906.

Oppermann, H. 1934. Tauropolos, *RE* 2.5, 34-38.

Papadimitriou, J. 1956. Anaskaphai en Brauróni, *Praktika*, 87-89.

Papadimitriou, J. 1957. Anaskaphai en Brauróni, *Praktika*, 45-47.

Richter, G.M.A. 1937. A Greek Bronze Hydria in the Metropolitan Museum, *AJA* 41, 532-538.

Ridgway, B.S. 1975. *The Archaic Style in Greek Sculpture*. Chicago.

Ridgway, B.S. 2000. *Hellenistic Sculpture* II: *the Styles of 200-100 B.C.* Madison.

Rives, J. 1995. Human sacrifice among pagans and Christians, *JRS* 85, 65-85.

Robert, L. 1964. *La déesse de Hiérapolis Castabala (Cilicie)*. Paris.

Robert, L. & J. Robert 1954. *La Carie. Histoire et géographie historique* II. *Le plateau de Tabai et ses environs*. Paris.

Royo, M. 1999. *Domus Imperatoriae. Topographie, formation et imaginaire des palais impériaux du Palatin*. Rome.

Rusjaeva, A. & M. Rusjaeva 1999. *Verchovnaja boginja antičnoj Tavriki*. Kiev.

Saprykin, S.Ju. 1996. *Pontijskoe carstvo*. Moskva.

Schmidt, J. 1937. Phakelitis, *RE* 19, 1609.

Schwertheim, E. 1987. *Die Inschriften von Hadrianoi und Hadrianeia, IGSK* 33. Bonn.

Stauropoullos, Ph. 1932. Timétikon pséphisma Halon ton Araphnidon, *ArchEph Archaiologika chronika*, 30-32.

Stuart Jones, H. 1926. *A Catalogue of the Ancient Sculptures Preserved in the Municipa Collections of Rome. The Sculptures of the Palazzo dei Conservatori*. Oxford.

Stolba, V.F. 1989. Novoe posvjaščenie iz Severo-Zapadnogo Kyma i aspekty kul'ta Gerakla v Chersonesskom gosudarstve, *VDI* 4, 55-70.

Stolba, V.F. 1996. La couronne de la déesse Parthénos: Ápropos d'un aspect du monnayage de Chersonèse au IV-IIe siècle av. J.C., *Bulletin de l'Association des amis du Cabinet des médailles, Lausanne* 9, 11-20.

Themelis, P. 1975. Epitymbia apo tis Lamptres, *AAA* 8, 275-291.

v. Fritze, H. 1913. *Die antiken Münzen Mysiens* I. Berlin.

Welles, C.B. 1966. *Royal Correspondance of the Hellenistic Period*. Roma.

Zagdoun, M.A. 1989. *La sculpture archaïsante dans l'art hellénistique et dans l'art romain du haut-empire*. Paris.

Zervoudaki, E.A. 1968. Attische polychrome Reliefkeramik des späten 5. und des 4. Jahrhunderts v. Chr., *AM* 83, 1-88.

Zograf, A.N. 1922. Statuarnye izobraženija Devy v Chersonese po dannym numizmatiki, *Izvestija Rossijskoj Akademii Istorii Material'noj Kul'tury* 2, 337-360.

Abbreviations

ANS	*The American Numismatic Society.*
IGSK	*Inschriften griechischer Städte aus Kleinasien.* Bonn 1972-.
LIMC	*Lexicon Iconographicum Mythologiae Classicae.*

Interpretation of a Group of Archaeological Sites in the Vicinity of Tauric Chersonesos

Vitalij M. Zubar' & Evelina A. Kravčenko

The study of the characteristics of the initial period of Greek settlement on the Herakleian peninsula represents one of the principal aims concerned directly with some peculiarities in the earliest history of the Chersonesean polis. These studies were commenced by S.F. Strželeckij,[1] with whom A.N. Ščeglov has been working for many years. It was Ščeglov who initiated the further and more detailed study of various sites of the pre-Greek settlement on the Herakleian peninsula, and formulated and successfully solved an entire complex of problems related to this subject. From his pen have come a number of fundamental works devoted to the character of the Graeco-barbarian contacts, and the analysis of these provided the basis for building a model of the stage-by-stage Greek occupation of agricultural lands in the neighbourhood of Chersonesos. A chronology of this process was proposed, and well-founded conclusions were drawn as to the specific features of the relations between Doric Greeks and the bearers of the Kizil-Koba archaeological culture – who were the Taurians of the written sources – during the period of the foundation and the earliest stages of the existence of Chersonesos.[2] It may be said without exaggeration that the results achieved by A.N. Ščeglov in this field represent a massive contribution to our science in the second half of the 20th century, and he may now state, with full justification: *feci quod potui, faciant meliora potentes.*

However, archaeological science is never static. The conclusions, which seem to have been already well-established, are actually in constant need of correction or refinement on the basis of a more thorough examination of the various sources, first and foremost, the archaeological evidence, which is of principal value in studies of Graeco-barbarian contacts in western Taurica. The treatment of this evidence is somewhat complicated and involves certain difficulties. Its interpretation sometimes entails a degree of ambiguity. Moreover, archaeological evidence, unfortunately, has its limits, which are highly undesirable to overstep when reconstructing historical events. Therefore, a scrupulous analysis of the archaeological materials is the first and perhaps the most important stage of a historical and archaeological investigation. This fact has been brilliantly demonstrated in the works of Ščeglov and his followers.[3]

Moreover, the archaeological evidence used as a basis for scientific hypotheses and historical reconstructions does not always answer to the present-day methodological requirements. Occasionally rather careless and superficial archaeological investigations and subsequent analysis have led to various unfortunate mistakes. That is why the most concentrated attention must be paid to such facts, and such conclusions must be corrected as early as possible. It is time to look around, to examine what has been done and how, and to lay down a plan for future work, in the course of which, we are certain, A.N. Ščeglov will achieve many new results and discoveries.

The collection of papers of the 1st All-Union Symposium on the Ancient History of the Black Sea Region in Tskhaltubo in 1977 devoted to different problems of the Greek colonisation on the northern and eastern coasts of the Black Sea contains *inter alia* O.Ja. Savelja's article about Greco-barbarian relations in south-western Crimea in the 6th-4th century BC. With reference to the results of his excavations in the neighbourhood of Chersonesos, Savelja wrote:

> "It is of note also that the settlements [i.e. those of the barbarian population – *V.Z & E.K*] of the 4th and 3rd century BC were not situated nearer than 1-1.5 km from the boundary of that part of the Herakleian peninsula which was regularly divided into farm plots. In other words, the topographical belt of the settlements is distinctly linked to the system of farm plots, the arrangement of the settlements suggesting a obligatory element in the selection of their location, though also certain ecological principles in the location of these settlements are consistent with those peculiar to Kizil-Koba and late Scythian sites in south-western Crimea. It seems that the settlements of the 4th-3rd century BC around the Herakleian peninsula were part of the structure of the agrarian territory of Chersonesos in south-western Crimea, along with the territory divided into plots and various categories of the unsettled lands of the city's community which lay between the system of plots and the belt of settlements. The composition of the evidence obtained from excavations and archaeological surveys suggests that ethnically the population of these settlements was fairly heterogeneous. Most probably this population may be considered as dependent and half-dependent. A similar model of the inclusion of the indigenous population into the economical and social structures of a polis was peculiar particularly to the mother country of Chersonesos, Herakleia Pontike".[4]

This undoubtedly interesting conclusion was immediately accepted by the overwhelming majority of scholars and was included as an incontestable fact in many general and more specialized works on the archaeology and history of the Classical period in the northern Black Sea area.[5] Based on this thesis and following D. Pippidi, one of the present authors has assumed that a form of dependence, similar to that of the helot system, existed in Chersonesos in the 4th and 3rd centuries BC.[6]

However, after the publication of Savelja's article, the fact remained overlooked that to confirm this obviously very important statement he neglected to refer to any detailed examination of the archaeological evidence or to its full-scale publications; rather he proceeds from his own suppositions and some preliminary communication on the excavations in which the chain of the Kizil-Koba sites near the Sapun-Gora mountain received only a brief mention.[7] This fact has induced us to examine the reports about the excavations mentioned above, which are now kept in the archives of the National Preserve "Tauric Chersonesos" and in the Institute of Archaeology, the National Ukrainian Academy of Sciences, in a belated attempt to verify what was actually the basis for the conclusion which unfortunately with only rare exceptions[8] has been considered an axiom for many years.

The gathering of artefacts and the undertaking of archaeological excavations in the locality near Sapun-Gora were initiated by L.N. Solov'ev as far back as the beginning of the 20th century. The evidence obtained, however, was published by S.F. Strželeckij much later.[9] Half a century further on, it became possible for the Preserve of Chersonesos to resume regular archaeological investigations in the vicinity of Sapun-Gora directed by O.Ja. Savelja. During the period 1973-1974, the gathering of surface materials and preliminary trenching were undertaken. This made it possible to map about 30 sites in this region with finds of artefacts, trace several ancient rural houses on the eastern slope of Sapun-Gora, and to conjecture the existence of a number of settlements near the village of Oktjabr'skoe and in the *uročišče* (isolated wood) of Kavkaz.[10] Since the territory adjoining the Sapun-Gora was devastated during World War II, no investigations of the stratigraphy of its cultural layers were conducted, and thus the dating of the archaeological materials from them was of a very general nature. Nevertheless, this fact has not prevented Savelja from presuming the existence of about 19 settlements and two cemeteries within the confines of this relatively small area. Fourteen of those sites were interpreted as belonging to the Kizil-Koba culture and were dated on the basis of the surface finds to the 4th and 3rd centuries BC.[11] In addition "clearing of the walls and bottom of one isolated bomb-crater of the war period has been carried out in order to obtain some materials for dating the site and preliminary information on its stratigraphy".[12] During the excavations of 1974, a number of fairly small areas at the settlements situated near the village of Oktjabr'skoe and in the *uročišče* of Kavkaz were investigated.[13] The reports of 1973-1974 contain neither any description of the technique in which the excavations were conducted nor their sequence, and the illustrative material appended to them is very scanty.

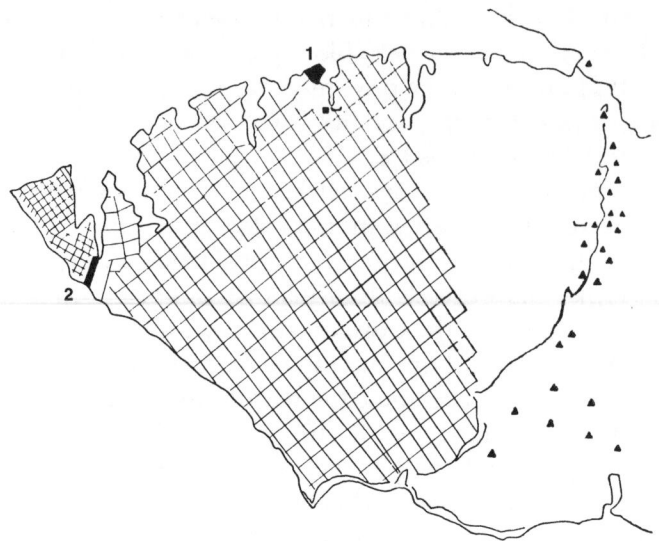

Fig. 1. Map of archaeological sites in the eastern reaches of the Herakleian peninsula according to A.N Ščeglov (1981, 215).

In 1978 and 1979, the excavations in the region of Sapun-Gora were resumed at a settlement of the Kizil-Koba culture near the village of Oktjabr'skoe. Discovered in the course of the excavation were a wine-pressing platform cut in the rock with a *tarapan* (pressing stone), as well as several stone socles of different periods and two later burials. In addition, a few household pits were cleared, and a fragment of a wall was excavated in the southern part of the settlement. Outside the settlement, a cremation burial was discovered.[14]

In 1986 the excavations near Oktjabr'skoe were continued. This season saw the unearthing of the remains of a winery,[15] several rooms which belonged to the settlement of the barbarian population, and a Greek stone structure.[16] In 1987, investigations were conducted in the *uročišče* of Taš-Kulle on Sapun-Gora.[17] During these surveys and excavations no signs of any barbarian settlement were found, but the remains of various Greek structures – towers and buildings – were discovered. In 1989, archaeological studies of the region of Sapun-Gora were conducted on the territory of the "Energetik" gardening co-operative society. No structural remains were discovered during this excavation. The clearing of a few household pits of different periods, however, enabled the excavators to posit the existence of a settlement, which was given the name "Energetik".[18]

Thus, on the basis of the evidence from O.Ja. Savelja's reports, it seems reasonable to discuss only the following settlements and burials of the Kizil-Koba culture recorded and investigated in the region of Sapun-Gora:

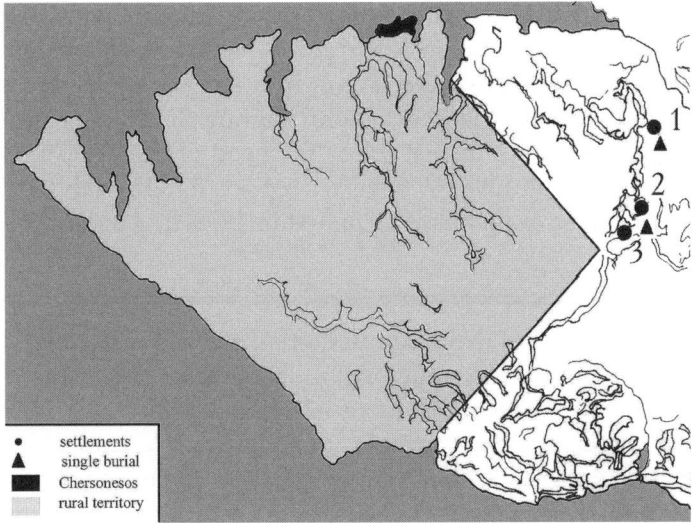

Fig. 2. Map of archaeological sites in the eastern reaches of the Herakleian peninsula.
1. Oktjabr'skoe
2. Kavkaz
3. "Energetik"

● settlements
▲ single burial
■ Chersonesos
  rural territory

Oktjabr'skoe

A settlement of the Kizil-Koba culture near the village of Oktjabr'skoe, on the eastern slope of Sapun-Gora (the settlement of Oktjabr'skoe) (Fig. 2, no. 1).

The surface materials include handmade black-burnished pottery with incised decoration, isolated finds of unburnished pottery decorated with separated cylinder-made indentations, and abundant Greek pottery of the Hellenistic period. Scattered along the slope, the remains of ancient fortifications, a winery, a presumed farmhouse and the remains of a wall dated to the late antique period were traced. Also uncovered were the remains of a trapezoid stone building containing in its fill various artefacts including handmade pottery, which suggested that this structure might have belonged to the Kizil-Koba settlement.[19] Predominant in the fill were fragments of Greek pottery of the 4th and 3rd century BC, which supplied a date for the building. Fragments of pottery bearing combed decoration also were encountered in these layers. Related to the barbarian settlement were, in addition, three semi-dugout dwellings, the fill of which contained ashes, fragments of burnished and comb-decorated unburnished handmade vessels as well as Greek pottery. In these houses of the dug-out type, the remains of fireplaces were uncovered; the clayey plaster of the aboveground parts of these structures showed the effects of extreme heat, which, along with other archaeological evidence, suggested that the settlement was destroyed by fire. At a distance of 200 m south of the site, a test trench was dug in which a cremation burial in an amphora and other artefacts including fragments of *kantharoi*, a Chersonesean amphora, a handmade burnished bowl and a vessel with combed ornamentation were discovered. Within the limits of the settlement, two burials – one of an adult and another of an adolescent – were discovered dug into the ancient layers. The skeletons were found lying on their backs with slightly flexed legs and oriented with their heads to the south-east. Near the head of the adolescent was a handmade salt-cellar.[20] From O.Ja. Savelja's reports it follows that the burials mentioned above were excavated twice: first in 1978, and again in 1986.[21]

Kavkaz

Several areas of the accumulation of surface materials – the eastern slope of Sapun-Gora and a settlement in the *uročišče* of Kavkaz (Fig. 2, no. 2).

Among the surface materials found in the area framed by Sapun-Gora and in the east by the heights of Fedjuchiny Vysoty, were fragments of handmade vessels of the Kizil-Koba type including several black-burnished examples, as well as flint artefacts and fragmentary amphorae of the early Hellenistic period (4th-3rd century BC), but the particular types of the latter are not specified in the report. On the eastern slope of Sapun-Gora, the structural remains of a number of Greek rural houses were recorded.[22]

The results of test trenching in the *uročišče* of Kavkaz led to conjecture about the existence of two buildings of the 4th or 3rd century BC. However, no detailed description of their remains was presented. In the report, a cemetery of the 4th-3rd century BC is also mentioned, but again without any detailed information. In addition, a number of household pits of different periods were uncovered on the site. The aggregate of the finds mentioned above suggested the possibility of a settlement here (the settlement of Kavkaz). In the fill of the household pits, fragments of Greek pottery of the 4th century BC were encountered. Generally, the finds from the *uročišče* of Kavkaz are similar in terms of their types to the surface materials collected near the House-building Factory on the eastern slope of Sapun-Gora.[23]

In the *uročišče* of Taš-Kulle, on the south-eastern slope of Sapun-Gora, at the boundary between the Herakleian peninsula and the Balaklava Valley, the remains of a tower and some structure related to it were traced on the flat spur of a terrace. A few fragments of late Scythian and Saltovo pottery were also found. The peculiarities of the masonry of the tower and the adjoining structure, as well as the ceramic evidence from their fills, supply a date of the 4th and 3rd centuries BC. In Savelja's report it is noted that these structures were destroyed in a fire.[24]

Energetik

A settlement of the Kizil-Koba culture on the ridge of Sapun-Gora, on the territory of the gardening co-operative society "Energetik" (Fig. 2, no. 3). Recorded here were several household pits, the infills of which contained

Greek pottery dated to the Classical and Hellenistic periods, fragments of handmade pottery both slightly burnished and unburnished and decorated with combed ornamentation in the form of three parallel lines, and examples of handmade pottery of the so-called Scythian type with finger indentations round the rim dated on the basis of the accompanying Greek wheel-made pottery to the 4th century BC. In addition, there were found fragments of flint, bones of dogs and a bronze finger-ring in the form of a coiled snake, along with several scorched stones from some fireplace structure. The report also mentions the remains of two rooms dated to the 4th-3rd century BC and found by test trenching on the eastern slope of Sapun-Gora. However, no further description is presented. O.Ja. Savelja considers the sites of Kavkaz and Energetik as a single settlement with a total area of 10-12 hectares dated to the 4th and 3rd centuries BC.[25]

On the basis of the available evidence we can posit the existence of only three barbarian settlements on Mt. Sapun-Gora and its environs, the finds from which undoubtedly need further analysis to date these sites more exactly. The surveys described above have not enabled us to form any idea about the archaeological situation in this locality, since the finds they yielded were only of an isolated character, dated to differing periods and recorded in no definite stratigraphical contexts, thus indicating only the presence of some barbarian population in the vicinity of Sapun-Gora without fixing any narrow chronological frames. Also the cemeteries recorded by Savelja are represented only by isolated burials.

The situation, as suggested by closer examination of the reports and field documentation, seems to be as follows. On the ridge and eastern slope of Sapun-Gora, only three settlements were situated, rather than an entire chain of them. These three settlements appeared not earlier than the 4th century BC and were deserted not later than the middle of the 4th century BC. Typologically, the pottery from these sites constitutes a single assemblage, which indicates their synchronous occupation and shows their similarity to other similar sites of the Kizil-Koba culture which have been recorded to the east of the Herakleian peninsula.[26] Apparently, Oktjabr'skoe was the only settlement which continued to exist in the middle of the 4th century BC. Its lowest layers containing Greek structures are datable to the last quarter of the 4th century BC, and cannot be linked to the Kizil-Koba population.[27]

It needs to be stressed that practically all of the excavated settlements on the eastern border of the Herakleian peninsula were destroyed in fires, the traces of which[28] were covered later by the structural remains of Greek farmhouses, wineries and other complexes in the Hellenistic period. However, there is no reason to connect these fires with any barbarian population. The surface materials which gave the basis to the conjecture about the existence of a chain of settlements located along the ridge, on the eastern slope and around the Sapun-Gora, mostly derive from re-deposited layers formed due to soil erosion and acts of war in the 19th and 20th centuries. This material may not indicate much more than the presence of some temporary Kizil-Koba settlements.

The cemeteries O.Ja. Savelja described in his publications and reports,[29] actually never existed. On the basis of the evidence available to us, we can only identify isolated burials dug into the earlier layers, for example the cremation in a Herakleian amphora of the 4th century BC [30], and a few inhumations with the skeletons lying on their backs with slightly flexed legs.[31] The latter burials are, however, on the basis of the data available impossible to attribute to the Kizil-Koba population in the vicinity of Chersonesos. On the contrary, the pits of these graves were sunk into Hellenistic layers, and thus suggest a later appearance.

Thus the conclusions about the presence of numerous barbarian settlements on the borders of the Chersonesean *chora* on the Herakleian peninsula in the 4th and 3rd century BC are unfounded. Furthermore there is no evidence to suggest that their inhabitants were bound as dependants to cultivate the agricultural lots of the Chersoneseans. On the contrary, the sources described above show quite clearly that by the middle of the 4th century BC, when the total division of the most of the Herakleian peninsula had been completed,[32] the Kizil-Koba, or Taurian, population had been driven out (probably by force) beyond the limits of the peninsula, of which fact *inter alia* the fires mentioned above are an indication. This theory is perfectly consistent with the increase in the number of settlements east of the Herakleian peninsula, beyond the Chernaya River. The finds from these settlements present numerous examples of the handmade black-burnished pottery decorated with incised triangles and combed ornamentation, typical of the Kizil-Koba culture, as well as handmade unburnished ware decorated with an appliquéd flange. On the basis of the Greek imports usually accompanying these types of pottery, they are dated to the 5th to 4th century BC and 4th to 3rd century BC respectively.[33] The defensive wall and towers were probably built not later than the turn of the 4th and 3rd century BC, on the site of the previously existing settlements of the Kizil-Koba culture on the ridge of Sapun-Gora.[34] The remains of these could still be seen by travellers who visited this area at the end of the 18th and first half of the 19th centuries.[35] The possibility cannot be ruled out that these defensive systems were raised by Agasikles who was in charge of the defence of the possessions of the Chersoneseans on the Herakleian peninsula which was constantly threatened by the barbarian population inhabiting the area to the east of the territory divided into land plots (*IOSPE* I², 343; Strab. 7.4.7).[36]

Notes

1.   Strželeckij 1954; 1959, 66-67.
2.   Ščeglov 1976, 76; 1978, 119, 124; 1981, 172-173; 1986, 162-163; 1988, 8-25; Vinogradov & Ščeglov 1990, 312-314, 320 etc.
3.   See, e.g., Hannestad, Stolba & Ščeglov (eds.) 2002.
4.   Savelja 1979c, 173.
5.   See, e.g., Ščeglov 1981, 172-173; 1984, 54; 1986, 162; Vinogradov & Ščeglov 1990, 312, with a map; Saprykin 1986, 66; Nikolaenko 1999, 72; Zubar', Lin'ova & Son 1999, 113; Pal'ceva 1999, 204, n. 293; Nikolaenko 2001.
6.   Zubar' 1993, 70.
7.   Savelja 1974, 338; 1975, 101-102; cf. Nikolaenko & Savelja 1975, 331-332.
8.   Rogov 1999, 121; cf. Pal'ceva 1999, 202.
9.   Strželeckij 1954, 82-85.
10. Savelja 1977, 4-11.
11. Savelja 1974, 337-338; 1977, 4-13.
12. Savelja 1977, 11.
13. Savelja 1977, 14-21.
14. Savelja 1979a, 398; 1979b, 23-25.
15. Savelja 1986, 9.
16. Savelja 1986, 12-13, 19.
17. Savelja 1987, 5.
18. Savelja 1990, 13.
19. Savelja 1986, 19.
20. Savelja 1974, 337-338; 1977; 1979a, 398; 1979b, 42; 1986, 9-19.
21. Savelja 1979a, 398; 1979b, 24; 1986, 10.
22. Savelja 1977, pl. 2.
23. Savelja 1977, 17-25.
24. Strželeckij 1954, 82-85; Savelja 1977, nos. 12-14, 22; 1987, 5-8; Nikolaenko 1999, 23.
25. Savelja 1974, nos. 19-20, 22; 1990, 13; Nikolaenko 1999, 23.
26. Savelja 1977, nos. 1-5, 8; Senatorov 1998, 12.
27. Savelja 1986, 19.
28. Savelja 1986, 9-19; 1987, 5-8.
29. Savelja 1974, 338; 1979a, 398; 1979b, 24; 1986, 10.
30. Savelja 1974, 338.
31. Savelja 1979a, 398; 1979b, 24; 1986, 10.
32. Nikolaenko 1999, 41.
33. The results of the analysis of the archaeological evidence are now under preparation and will soon be published.
34. Nikolaenko 1985, 282; Zubar' 1993, 18; 2002, 205-206; Marčenko 1996, 193-194; cf. Nikolaenko 1999, 72-73.
35. For further details, see Danilenko 1993, 237.
36. The activities of Agasikles, son of Ktesias, who was in charge of strengthening the defences of the Chersonesean *chora* on the Herakleian peninsula, will be discussed in a special paper currently being prepared for publication.

Bibliography

Baran, V.D. (ed.) 1975. *Novejšie otkrytija sovetskich archeologov. Tezisy dokladov.* Kiev.

Danilenko, V.N. 1993. Chersones i tavry Geraklejskogo poluostrova, *MAIET* 3, 233-239.

Frolov, E.D. (ed.) 1986. *Antičnaja graždanskaja obščina. Problemy social'no-političeskogo razvitija i ideologii.* Leningrad.

Golubcova, E.S. (ed.) 1990. *Ellinizm: ekonomika, politika, kul'tura.* Moskva.

Hannestad, L., V.F. Stolba & A.N. Ščeglov (eds.) 2002. *Panskoye I.* Vol. 1. *The Monumental Building U6.* Aarhus.

Košelenko G.A. et al. (eds.) 1984. *Antičnye gosudarstva Severnogo Pričernomor'ja. Archeologija SSSR.* Moskva.

Lordkipanidze O. (ed.) 1979. *Problemy grečeskoj kolonizacii Severnogo i Vostočnogo Pričernomor'ja.* Tbilisi.

Lordkipanidze O. (ed.) 1981. *Demografičeskaja situacija v Pričernomor'e v period Velikoj grečeskoj kolonizacii.* Tbilisi.

Londkiparidze, O. (ed.) 1985. *Pričernomor'e v epochu ellinizma.* Tbilisi.

Londkiparidze, O. (ed.) 1988. *Mestnye ekonomičeskie ob'edinenija Pričernomor'ja v 7-4 vv. do n.e.* Tbilisi.

Marčenko, L.V. 1996. Zaščita chory, *ChSbor* 7, 193-197.

Nikolaenko, G.M. & O.Ja. Savelja 1975. Raboty na Geraklejskom poluostrove, *AO 1974 g.,* 331-332.

Nikolaenko, G.M. 1985. Organizacija chory Chersonesa Tavričeskogo na Geraklejskom poluostrove, in: Londkiparidze (ed.) 1985, 277-285.

Nikolaenko, G.M. 1999. *Chora Chersonesa Tavričeskogo. Zemel'nyj kadastr 4-3 vv. do n.e.* 1. Sevastopol'.

Nikolaenko, G.M. 2001. *Chora Chersonesa Tavričeskogo. Zemel'nyj kadastr 4-3 vv. do n.e.* 2. Sevastopol'.

Pal'ceva, L.A. 1999. *Iz istorii archaičeskoj Grecii: Megary i megarskie kolonii.* St Peterburg.

Rogov, E.Ja. 1999. Nekotorye problemy stanovlenija i razvitija Chersonesskogo gosudarstva, *Stratum plus* 3, 116 -144.

Savelja, O.Ja. 1974. Raskopki i razvedki v okrestnostjach Sevastopolja, *AO 1973 g.,* 337-338.

Savelja, O.Ja. 1975. K probleme vzaimootnošenij Chersonesa Tavričeskogo s varvarami Jugo-Zapadnogo Kryma v 5-3 vv. do n.e., in: Baran (ed.) 1975, vol. 2, 100-102.

Savelja, O.Ja. 1977. *Otčet ob archeologičeskich razvedkach i raskopkach na territorii goroda Sevastopolja v 1974 g.,* Scientific Archives of the Institute of Archaeology of the National Ukrainian Academy of Sciences, f. 1977, d. 1974/129, 7985.

Savelja, O.Ja. 1979a. Raskopki i razvedki u Sapun-gory, *AO 1978 g.,* 398.

Savelja, O.Ja. 1979b. *Raskopki i razvedki u Sapun-gory,* Scientific Archives of the National Preserve of "Tauric Chersonesos", f. 1979, d. 2042, 23-25.

Savelja, O.Ja. 1979c. O greko-varvarskich vzaimootnošenijach v Jugo-Zapadnom Krymu v 6-4 vv. do n.e., in: Lordkipanidze, O. (ed.) 1979, 173.

Savelja, O.Ja. 1986. *Otčet o polevych issledovanijach Sevastopol'skoj ochranno-novostroečnoj archeologičeskoj ekspedicii Chersonesskogo goszapovednika v* zonach novostroek g. *Sevastopolja v 1986 g.*, Scientific Archives of the National Preserve of "Tauric Chersonesos", f. 1986, d. 2697.

Savelja, O.Ja. 1987. *Raskopki poselenija v uročišče Taš-Kulle na Sapun-gore*, Scientific Archives of the National Preserve of "Tauric Chersonesos", 1987, d. 2766, 5-9.

Savelja, O.Ja. 1990. *Otčet Sevastopol'skoj archeologičeskoj ekspedicii o polevych issledovanijach v g. Sevastopole v 1989 g.*, Scientific Archives of the National Preserve of "Tauric Chersonesos", f. 1990, d. 2912.

Saprykin, S.Ju. 1986. *Gerakleja Pontijskaja i Chersones Tavričeskij.* Moskva.

Senatorov, S.N. 1998. Poselenie pozdnego etapa kizil-kobinskoj kul'tury Karan'–2, *ChSbor* 9, 8-16.

Smirnov, A.P. (ed.) 1959. *Problemy istorii Severnogo Pričernomor'ja v antičnuju epochu.* Moskva.

Strželeckij, S.F. 1954. *Očerki istorii Geraklejskogo poluostrova i ego okrugi v epochu bronzy i rannego železa (seredina 2 tys. – 5 v. do n. e.)*, Scientific Archives of the National Preserve of "Tauric Chersonesos", f. 1954, d. 1343.

Strželeckij, S.F. 1959. Osnovnye etapy ekonomičeskogo razvitija i periodizacija istorii Chersonesa Tavričeskogo v antičnuju epochu, in: Smirnov (ed.) 1959, 63-85.

Ščeglov, A.N. 1976. *Polis i chora.* Simferopol'.

Ščeglov, A.N. 1978. *Severo-Zapadnyj Krym v antičnuju epochu.* Leningrad.

Ščeglov, A.N. 1981. Tavry i grečeskie kolonii v Tavrike, in: Lordkipanidze (ed.) 1981, 204-218.

Ščeglov, A.N. 1984. Chora Chersonesa, in: Košelenko et al. (eds.) 1984, 53-55.

Ščeglov, A.N. 1986. Process i charakter territorial'noj ekspansii Chersonesa v 4 v. do n.e., in: Frolov (ed.) 1986, 152-176.

Ščeglov, A.N. 1988. Tavry v 7 – pervoj polovine 4 v. do n.e. i greko-varvarskie vzaimootnošenija, in: Lordkipanidze (ed.) 1988, 8-25.

Vinogradov, Ju.G. & A.N. Ščeglov 1990. Obrazovanie territorial'nogo Chersonesskogo gosudarstva, in: Golubcova (ed.) 1990, 310-371.

Zubar', V.M. 1993. *Chersones Tavričeskij v antičnuju epochu (ekonomika i social'nye otnošenija).* Kiev.

Zubar', V.M., E. Lin'ova & N. Son 1999. *Antyčnyj svit Pivničnogo Pryčornomor'ja.* Kyiv.

Zubar', V.M. 2002. Nekotorye voprosy istorii tavrov i Chersonesa v konce 2 – načale 1 v. do n.e., *Starožytnosti stepovogo Pryčornomor'ja i Krymu* 10, 196-215.

Abbreviations

AO	Archeologičeskie otkrytija, Moskva.
ChSbor	Chersonesskij sbornik, Sevastopol'.
MAIET	Materialy po archeologii, istorii i etnografii Tavrii, Simferopol'.

The Bosporan Kings and Classical Athens: Imagined Breaches in a Cordial Relationship (Aisch. 3.171-172; [Dem.] 34.36)

David Braund

Our knowledge of the relationship between the Athenian democratic state and the rulers of the Bosporos depends on very different kinds of evidence. At one extreme we have inscribed decrees: their contents provide unimpeachable data about the relationship, though neither singly nor collectively can they offer much more than a series of momentary insights. Moreover, even if we had every decree passed on the relationship (and we may be sure enough that we do not), the formal outcomes which these decrees present tell us very little about the broader social, economic and political context which caused them.

By contrast, at the other extreme we have the orators, especially Aischines and Demosthenes. There can hardly be more slippery sources of information. That fact is well-known as a general principle: it is well understood, by and large, that the orators distort, deliberately misrepresent and deploy every trick they have at their disposal to win the argument. Limitations to their artful deception are provided only by the general plausibility of their statements in the minds of their audiences at the time of delivery: what they say need not be simply true, but it must appear plausible. And, the orators offer the modern historian excellent insight into what was deemed plausible at the time of speaking. Accordingly, their speeches (the work of orators of a standard beyond basic competence) may be taken to offer what an audience was expected to want to hear, to respond to with warmth, belief and even pleasure. But they may well not (though they may) describe events, persons and relationships in a way that would satisfy modern standards of historical truth. After all, these are not histories, but speeches in direct contest with each other, often with major matters at stake (and usually we only have one side of the argument). It is worth insisting on this simple point because, however much it may be understood as a general phenomenon, that understanding has not always been brought to bear on the particular relationship between Athens and the Bosporos.

Any interpretation of Athens' dealings with the Bosporan rulers requires the reconciliation of these extremely different kinds of evidence. That can only be a very delicate procedure, especially in view of the enormous gaps in our evidence of any sort. All the more so when we bear in mind (as we must) that democratic Athens created and maintained its relations with the Bosporos and other states and rulers through public debate. Open discussion and argument was characteristic of all aspects of Athenian public life: such was typical of democracy and recognised as such by the many ancient critics of the system (e.g. Hdt. 3.80-82). Accordingly, the internal political struggles and rivalries of the Athenians were readily caught up with and expressed in the foreign relations of the Athenian democracy as a whole. So much is obvious enough, for example, in the hostility between Demosthenes and Aischines, which we find played out in the context of the Athenian state's complex dealings with Philip II of Macedon. It would be naïve to expect that it was otherwise in Athens' dealings with other powers about whom we know less, including the rulers of the Bosporos. Rather, it is to be expected that the Athenian democracy's relations with the Bosporan rulers were caught up not only in the conflict between Aischines and Demosthenes, but also in the plurality of other rivalries which formed the sinews of the democracy at work.

In view of all that, there is in fact a remarkable consistency in the direct statements in our sources of all types about the political relationship between the Athenian democratic state and the rulers of the Bosporos. Our sources offer a consistent picture of friendship and cooperation which may seem all the more surprising when traced across more than a century from the early years of the Spartokids down to the time of Alexander and indeed well beyond. Since those years involved changing circumstances, not least changes of ruler in the Bosporos, it is easy enough to understand why some modern scholars have tried to find dissonances in the extended harmony. By making subtle inferences from our very different sources, scholars have claimed to find at least two periods of disharmony, indeed even outright hostility, between Athens and the Bosporos. In what follows I shall review the evidence and attempt to demonstrate that it does not permit such inferences. Remarkable as it is, the political relationship between the Athenian democracy and the rulers of the Bosporos does indeed seem to have remained harmonious, as far as we can form any judgment at all.

Gylon and the "tyrants" of the Bosporos

The case of Gylon has been taken to show an early breach between Athens and the Bosporans. For Aischines claims that Gylon had betrayed the city of Nymphaion to Athens' enemies and had subsequently been granted the town of Kepoi ("Gardens") by the rulers of the Bosporos:

> "There was a certain Gylon of Kerameis. He, having betrayed to
> the enemy Nymphaion in the Black Sea (a place which the city

then held), became an exile from the city to escape impeach-
ment, and was condemned to death.[1] He reached the Bosporos
where he received as a gift from the tyrants so-called Gardens.
And he married a woman who was wealthy, for sure, and
brought him much gold, but who was a Scythian by blood.
From her he had two daughters, whom he sent here with substantial wealth... Demosthenes of Paiania took to wife the second of these, ignoring the laws of the city; it was she that bore
you this busybody and informer. So by inheritance from his
grandfather he would be an enemy of the people (for you condemned his forbears to death), while by inheritance from his
mother he would be a Scythian, a barbarian playing the Greek
in his speech. Therefore, with regard to his misconduct he is not
a native of the city" (Aisch. 3.171-172. Author's translation)

This kind of vitriol is typical enough of the orators. And it is entirely in place
among the insults and denunciations traded back and forth between
Aischines and Demosthenes. That is enough to warn us that caution is needed: Aischines' whole interest in the story of Gylon is that it can be used to
discredit Demosthenes. What, then, can be made of the story?

First, we should observe the chronology. Aischines delivered his speech
in 330 BC. The date of Gylon's activities cannot be fixed with any precision,
but is usually and reasonably located in the closing stages of the
Peloponnesian War. In other words, more than 70 years had elapsed between
Gylon's alleged treachery and Aischines' speech. That is important because
it means that Aischines could be confident that his audience would have no
direct knowledge of events at Nymphaion. He knew that he could make allegations which might be believed. Gylon had died by the later 380s, so that
few in 330 would have much memory of him at all.[2]

Secondly, Athenian law. Condemnation to death would be appropriate
enough for treason, which no doubt leads Aischines to claim that Gylon was
so condemned. It also helps his further claim to the effect that Demosthenes
hated the Athenian people. However, the disputes after Gylon's death have
not a word to say about any such condemnation. Rather, Gylon seems to
have been fined, and not necessarily for events at Nymphaion: the issue after
his death was whether or not he had paid the fine, which he seems in fact to
have done.[3] A fine sits less well with a major act of treachery, though it cannot be ruled out *a priori*.[4] Meanwhile, the good marriages made by Gylon's
daughters (named Kleoboule and Philia) surely establish beyond much
doubt that any crime he had committed had left no great stain on his family. Both daughters married men of considerable social standing at Athens
within a couple of decades of the supposed treason: while Kleoboule married Demosthenes' father, Philia married the prominent Demochares.[5] There

can have been no question-mark against their Athenian citizenship. Gylon's marriage had presumably taken place by 403/2 BC when the Athenian law on citizenship was re-asserted after the upheavals of the Peloponnesian War and its aftermath.[6] After all Gylon had many choices: he did not need to find husbands for his daughters at Athens. That he did so is a further indication of Aischines' misrepresentation: Gylon retained and valued his links with Athens and may well have returned there in person, if only to arrange his daughters' marriages. But Aischines could be sure enough that his audience in 330 would have known little or nothing of all these details.

We do not know the identity of the "Scythian" lady whom Gylon married: she was hardly a nomad, as Aischines alleges elsewhere (2.78; cf. 180). Most probably she was a member of the Bosporan elite, even the ruling Spartokid dynasty, for such a wife would have been appropriate to the master of Kepoi. As such she would more usually have been considered a Greek. There is no reason to query Aischines' claim that she was wealthy, but Gylon would have had enough opportunity to amass wealth for himself anyway at Kepoi. Presumably Aischines depicts her as a Scythian because he can thereby direct at Demosthenes all the negative stereotypes that might be evoked by such ethnicity, in particular bloodthirstiness, stupidity and idiosyncratic (at best) oratory. Typically enough the vitriol of the orator plays also with the humour more familiar on the comic stage: Aischines' attack involves mockery as well as insult. Both in the courts and on the comic stage it was quite usual to offer (and receive) insults and allegations about matters of citizenship and ethnic identity, however preposterous they might be.[7] To that extent, in suggesting that Demosthenes was really a Scythian, Aischines is indulging in an accepted ploy of rhetoric and abuse. At the same time, latent also in his rhetoric is an auxiliary explanation for Demosthenes' hostility to Philip, which Aischines may mean also to insinuate. For earlier in the speech he had noted Philip's expedition against the Scythians (3.128-129, stressing bribery): small wonder, Aischines may imply, that the Scythian Demosthenes did not like him.

Thirdly, Nymphaion and the Bosporos. Nymphaion lies only some 15 km from Pantikapaion, the key city of the Crimean part of Bosporos. Its good harbour was a notable feature. We are told by a fragment of Krateros's *Decrees* (quoted by Harpokration) that it paid tribute of one talent to Athens.[8] How the Bosporan rulers viewed this arrangement is simply beyond our knowledge. It is easy enough to suppose that they resented Athenian interference in their own area. Yet it is as easy to suppose that they welcomed a friendly force which could support and perhaps even extend their dominions over their many neighbours.[9] The appointment of Gylon at Kepoi might (though it need not) be interpreted as an indication of such an attitude. After all, scholars have often observed that the emergence in c. 437 BC of the Spartokids is more-or-less contemporary with Perikles' expedition into the

Black Sea, which left an Athenian presence at Sinope and perhaps Amisos. The coincidence has encouraged the thought that Perikles may have played some part in the creation of the Spartokid kingdom. However, that intriguing and suggestive coincidence has recently been disturbed by the publication of an Athenian casualty-list, which seems to show Athenian losses around Sinope in the later 430s. It has been taken, therefore, to offer a date for Perikles' expedition a few years after the emergence of the Spartokids in c. 437. But the new list cannot do that much. No doubt the process of Athenian settlement at Sinope took some time and the process may have entailed significant resistance and Athenian casualties. Accordingly, the casualty-list can do no more than suggest a *terminus ante quem* for Perikles' expedition.[10]

Further, it has often been thought that Gylon was in command of an Athenian garrison there, though even Aischines does not say that. In fact Aischines has nothing to say about Gylon's official position at the time of his alleged treason at Nymphaion; it is even possible that he did not have one. But what did Gylon actually do? The crucial observation is that even Aischines does not say that Gylon betrayed Nymphaion to the Bosporans, though he has often been taken to do so.[11] In fact, he suggests quite the opposite. We should not be surprised that he does not clarify the matter, for it was of no particular concern to him and his argument: the treason itself was enough, while the precise identity of the enemy did not much matter. Indeed, if the treason is itself Aischines' exaggeration (or even, to take an extreme position which cannot be wholly excluded, his invention), the orator may well have found it difficult to identify the enemy to whom Gylon betrayed Nymphaion. In any event, it was not the Bosporans, for then Aischines would have said so, and perhaps made some further remark about Kepoi and perhaps the "Scythian" wife as Gylon's reward for his treachery. He does not. On the contrary, he first speaks of "the enemy" and then shifts to talking of the Bosporans, with no sign that they are the enemy of whom he was speaking. He could not suppose that his audience would identify the two, even if the Bosporans had been the enemy in question: his expression is against it, while, as we have seen, the chronology is against much memory of these events in Athens of the 330s. Indeed, it is symptomatic that he mentions the Bosporans as "the tyrants": that was a possible usage at Athens when speaking of the rulers of Bosporos in 330, but it was hardly appropriate to the Bosporan regime of the late fifth century BC, where Satyros seems to have presided alone.[12]

Where in all this can one find a breach in the friendship between Athens and the Bosporos? They are not "the enemy", who (if they are a reality) are best understood as anti-Athenian forces within Nymphaion itself, though it is likely enough that the Spartan harmost at Byzantion, Klearchos, probed into the Black Sea too. However, if we wish to press details in Aischines' account (and we have seen how risky that must be), we might still take the Bosporan reception of fugitive Gylon as sufficient sign of a breach. However, that is hardly persuasive either. Even if we go so far as to accept Aischines' details, it remains to consider the context of all this: the closing years of the Peloponnesian War, as far as we can tell.

These were difficult and unstable years, especially under the Thirty at Athens. We know that Satyros took in Athenians at this time. The young aristocrat of Lysias 16, one Mantitheos, actually rebutted the suggestion of his complicity in the deeds of the Thirty by claiming to have spent these years at the court of Satyros (Lys. 16.4). The fact that he did so, shortly after the event establishes beyond reasonable doubt that not only was such a refuge acceptable in the minds of a contemporary Athenian audience, but Satyros was no enemy of the Athenian democracy in these years. If he had been, Mantitheos' defence would have been immediately self-defeating. No doubt Satyros had some difficulty in keeping up with the swiftly changing situation at Athens through defeat and violent oligarchy and back by force of arms to democracy. However, it is absolutely clear that once democracy was restored at Athens the Athenians looked upon Satyros without rancour and with active goodwill. Accordingly, the speaker of Isokrates' *Trapezitikos* of the 390s, after many indications of the cooperation of Athens and Satyros, concludes his case by urging the Athenians to remember all that Satyros has done for them in the past. Of course, he has in mind especially favours in grain-export, but the conclusion would be so clumsy as to be hardly thinkable if Satyros had been Athens' enemy only a few years earlier.

In this way the broadly contemporary evidence of Lysias and Isocrates amply confirms the case against any suggestion of a breach between the Bosporans and the Athenian democracy in the late fifth century BC. After all, even Aischines had not claimed that there was one, as we have seen. As for Gylon's alleged treason, the fact that neither Aischines nor, as far as we know, Demosthenes' other detractors choose elsewhere to harp on it must surely encourage us to think that this particular line of attack was not even very successful in 330. All the more so when we find those detractors casting other aspersions on Demosthenes' relationship with the Bosporans.[13] Finally, it is surely telling against the veracity of Aischines' claims that even Plutarch voices his doubt about them and seems to have known them only from the speech of Aischines itself (Plut. *Dem.* 4).

Pairisades, Lampis and grain-privileges for Athens

The very fact that Athenian orators like Aischines and Deinarchos can be critical of Demosthenes' relations with the Bosporans has been taken to suggest a breach between the Athenian state and the rulers of the Bosporos.[14] However, we should remember that the Athenian democracy was typified by disputes and contestation: it would be remarkable if there were no critical statements about the Bosporans, or about any of Athens' other friends and allies. Yet the fact is that in the works of Aischines and even Deinarchos we find scant criticism of the Bosporans: these orators' primary target is Demosthenes, through whom the Bosporans come into play only a little. It is true that in an attack upon Demosthenes Deinarchos calls the rulers of the Bosporos "tyrants", but not in a speech directed at them. Moreover, in contexts of this kind the term "tyrants" need not be critical: it was more likely to be neutral or even positive.[15] Deinarchos' specific claim – that they send grain to Demosthenes – is about as harsh as his critique of the Bosporans gets: by the standards of Athenian oratory that hardly counts as criticism at all. It seems safer to argue that the rather delicate treatment of the Bosporans by Demosthenes' enemies suggests that the Athenian state remained on good terms with them. That Demosthenes' enemies did not wish to alienate the Bosporans is illustrated well enough by Androtion's sponsorship of honours for them. Demosthenes' enemies and rivals might well wish to supplant or challenge his particular links with the Bosporans, founded not least in his family ties, but there was not much to be gained from attacking the Bosporans themselves.[16]

However, it is a speech in the Demosthenic corpus which has given rise to the notion of a breach in cordial relations between Athens and the Bosporos in the fourth century BC, namely a passage in the *Against Phormio*:

> "So if, gentlemen of the jury, it were only me that Lampis despised it would be nothing remarkable. But, as it is, he has done much worse than him (sc. Phormion) to you all. For when Pairisades made a proclamation in Bosporos that anyone taking grain to Athens, to the Attic emporion, would not pay tax on its export, Lampis, who was visiting the Bosporos, took on a load of grain for export and paid no tax by giving the name of Athens. When he had filled a large vessel with grain he carried it to Acanthos and there unloaded it…" ([Dem.] 34.36. Author's translation).

The argument for a breach rests on the interpretation of Pairisades' proclamation. The speech can be dated on internal evidence to summer 327.[17] Since Pairisades attained sole rule in 344 or thereabouts, his proclamation at the time of Lampis' visit to the Bosporos shortly before the court-case of 327 is taken to show the absence of special privileges for grain-export to Athens in the first decade and more of his reign. Pairisades, it is argued, had chosen not to renew the privileges which Athens had enjoyed under his predecessors. That is the essence of the argument for a breach in cordial relations between Athens and the Bosporos.

However, although impressive at first sight, the argument is hardly strong. First, there is the general problem that we cannot press the details of a lawcourt-speech like the *Against Phormio*. The fact that the prosecutor claims that events took a certain course in the Bosporos does not make it so, or so in precisely the way which the speaker leads us to think. In this case we should be especially on our guard because the speaker is using the proclamation to suggest that Lampis' behaviour is a slight not only against him but against the Athenian state itself. Moreover, there is an alternative interpretation which deserves serious attention. It has been observed that Pairisades was engaged in a war with the Scythians which, according to the speaker of the *Against Phormio*, had affected the Bosporan market to the extent that Phormion could not sell his imported wares (34.8). Here again, we need not believe him. However, if we do give him any credence on the point, it is not impossible to think that Pairisades' difficulties had caused some hiatus in his favours for Athens. We need not be surprised if, as the speaker claims, Phormion did not anticipate market-disruption until he reached the Bosporos (34.8), or indeed that goods could still be found to export, including grain (34.36).[18]

Moreover, there is a refinement to that explanation which needs to be considered before we go so far as to infer a breach between Athens and the Bosporans. We must begin by observing that the speaker does not say that Pairisades proclaimed tax-exemption for the first time in his reign when Lampis was in Bosporos, but only that he made a proclamation (or better had a proclamation made) that there was an exemption. What kind of proclamation? There is every reason to take this proclamation as a regular event, for that was one way in which the exemption could be kept a current matter of general knowledge.[19] That was all the more important in view of the fact that the exporters might well be new to the Bosporos and its regulations. Even with civic honours the regular proclamation of a one-off decision was usual enough. For example in Hellenistic Chersonesos the award of a crown to an honoured citizen was proclaimed each year: this too, like the proclamation of Pairisades, is termed a *kerugma*, a proclamation.[20]

However, the speaker talks of the *making* of a proclamation, which is paralleled in monarchical contexts of various kinds – both in the literary tradition and in epigraphy.[21] His choice of expression better suits the issuing of a decision than the announcement of an established regulation. Once again our interpretation comes to depend on the precise and literal truth of the speaker's claim. We cannot be sure. However, we may proceed, at least provisionally, by taking the speaker's words to be a precise enough presentation of what happened, because his audience may well have included men who would have known about established practices in the Bosporos. Even if Pairisades really did make a proclamation of a new decision, as the speaker's language suggests, there is still no strong case for inferring a previous breach between him and Athens. For it is much easier to suppose that he (and perhaps previous rulers of the Bosporos) made a fresh proclamation each year, having taken thought for the available harvest, the military situation, Athens' and Athenians' conduct and much else besides. What we hear from inscriptions and the orators about Bosporan favours for Athens tends to suggest that Athens regularly benefited from such proclamations, but there is nothing in our sources to indicate that there was only one such proclamation per reign, as some scholars seem to have assumed.

If the proclamation is seen as a regular event in the Bosporos (for example, an annual one) and if the statements of Deinarchos and Aischines are understood to be as restrained as they indeed are, we can dispense with the revisionist view that "Pairisades' policies, far from being beneficial to Athens, were for many years actually detrimental to her interests".[22] There is no sign of that in *Against Phormio* or any of our other evidence. And once that step has been taken, there are no grounds for further hypotheses, for example, about the date at which Demosthenes had Pairisades' statue erected at Athens, which could as well be before 327 as after it. If, as is entirely possible, the statue was erected before 327, the limited significance of the proclamation (beyond the story of Phormion and Lampis) would be all the more apparent, for a statue seems unlikely if indeed Pairisades was at odds with Athens.[23]

As we have seen, there is no reason to suppose that Pairisades was ever at odds with Athens, rather as there is also no sign of breach between Athens and Satyros decades earlier. Inevitably perhaps the conclusion is negative. However, it also has a positive side, for we may be confident enough in the remarkable continuity of good relations between the Athenian state and the rulers of the Bosporos, for all the *lacunae* in our knowledge. Further, we have also acquired a methodological case-study: we should be slow to insist on the literal truth of the details of the claims made by orators in debate. Finally, those who choose to press hard the language of *Against Phormio* 36 can and probably should infer that Pairisades, and probably other Bosporan rulers too, made a proclamation every year, usually but not inevitably to the benefit of those shipping grain to Athens. That this proclamation was a regular (presumably annual) event offers some further encouragement to the contemporary tendency among scholars to move away from once-popular notions of a bustling, vital and uninterrupted flow of grain from the Bosporos to Athens.[24] However, while the export of Bosporan grain to Athens may have always been a matter of uncertainty (despite the overblown claims of Demosthenes, in particular), there is no sign of a political rift between classical Athens and the Bosporos, under Satyros I, Pairisades I or others.

Notes

1. As Hansen (1975, 84) implies, the full Greek text here is not always printed in modern editions, thanks to the predilections of its various editors. Here I trans-

late Blass' Teubner edition, which refrains from editorial intervention at this point.

2. Gylon is referred to as dead in Dem. 28, occasioned by the famous property disputes in the aftermath of the death of Gylon's son-in-law, the father of Demosthenes the orator.

3. Dem. 28.1-4. We may cautiously infer that he had paid the fine from the fact that Demosthenes won the dispute of which Dem. 28 forms part. Demosthenes accepts that Gylon had once had an outstanding fine.

4. We are not told that the fine (as opposed to the alleged condemnation) was connected with events at Nymphaion. The notion that condemnation was commuted to a fine has found favour (e.g. Davies 1971, 121), but we need a plausible reason why that should have been done. Hansen (1975, 84) contends that the fine related to events after 403 BC; the evidence is thin.

5. Badian (2000, 13-14) suspects that these prominent Athenians were attracted by the wealth of their brides, but that hardly affects the basic point: the daughters of a traitor, even wealthy, were an unlikely match for two such men. The name Philia is inferred from *IG* II², 6737a, cf. Davies 1971, 141-142 on her and the rest of Demochares' family.

6. Marriage by 403/2 fits well enough with what we may infer about the age of Gylon's daughters, see Davies 1971, 121.

7. On comedy in the law-courts, see Hall 1995; cf., on law and the courts on the comic stage, Carey 2000. On allegations about citizenship and ethnicity, see MacDowell 1993.

8. Cf. also its possible mention in a fragment of the quota-lists, which has been put in doubt, perhaps irresponsibly.

9. Gajdukevič (1971, 191) tends to the latter view.

10. Burstein (1993, 82) seizes upon the inscription as evidence to show that Perikles' expedition had no part in the emergence of the Spartokids, after Clairmont 1979. On continuing issues there, cf. Thuc. 4.75; Justin 16.3.10.

11. As by an ancient scholiast on the passage, properly castigated by Žhebelev 1953, 189-190; among recent examples, see Burstein 1993, esp. 82, while rightly observing how little we know about the earliest dealings between Athens and the Spartokids. A less than critical approach to Aischines' claims can still be taken: e.g. Skržinskaja 1998, 172-173.

12. For the usage, compare Deinarchos 1.43. Satyros is spoken of quite differently in Lysias 16 and Isokrates 17, though uncertainty about his regime must also be acknowledged: e.g. Werner 1955; Tuplin 1982.

13. Cf. Deinarchos 1.15 on his "Scythian" blood and 1.43 on his receipt of grain from the Bosporan tyrants of his own day: Gylon's supposed treason is conspicuously absent. Plut. *Dem.* 4 shows that Theopompos did not have much to say about it all.

14. Burstein 1978, esp. 430.

15. Worthington (1992, 206) considers the term "tyrants" here to be insulting, citing Burstein's arguments. But see, for the opposite view, Kallet 1998, 52-53 and the literature she cites.

16. *IG* II², 653; Davies (1971, 514) notes also the role of Polyeuktos, inheriting his father's link with Androtion. On Athenians' competition for Bosporan favours, see Košelenko 2002 and the Russian literature he cites.

17. Isager & Hansen 1975, 169.

18. *Pace* Burstein (1978, 431, esp. n. 16), where he also supposes that Pairisades was at Pantikapaion, which is beyond our evidence: certainly he did not need to be there for a proclamation to be made there in his name.

19. Brashinsky (1971, 120-121) sees the proclamation as Pairisades' confirmation, but he seems not to envisage a regular announcement.
20. *IOSPE* I², 353, in Doric as *karugma*, of course. The term seems not to occur at all in Bosporan epigraphy. Burstein's objection, that Lampis sought the privilege only after the proclamation, is not cogent, for not only does it press very hard the details of the speech, but it also assumes that Lampis must have known the arrangement in the Bosporus before (Burstein 1978, 431, n. 13).
21. For a royal proclamation, e.g. *Syll.*³, 741, line 20; cf. [Arist.] *Oec.* 1349b, 1351b. In fourth century BC oratory, compare especially Hyperides, *Dem.* 34 (sadly fragmentary).
22. Burstein 1978, 433. *Pace* Burstein, the rate of imports of Athenian goods is hardly traceable archaeologically without significant reservations, but is in any event irrelevant. As [Dem.] 34 and 35 both seem to show, ships might trade to the Bosporos from Athens in goods from elsewhere, e.g. the wine of Chalkidike. See further, Kuznecov 2000.
23. Burstein (1978, 433) tries to group events around what he takes to be the key proclamation of 327 BC, but without sufficient reason. For example, even his attempt to place the erection of the statue between 330 and 324 rests on inferences from the rhetorical choices of Aischines and Deinarchos. As he fairly states, the date is not attested: we cannot proceed beyond that.
24. Kuznecov 2000 offers a valuable and critical review of the scholarly literature.

Bibliography

Badian, E. 2000. The road to prominence, in: I. Worthington (ed.), *Demosthenes, statesman and orator*. London, 9-44.

Brashinsky, I.B. 1971. Epigraphical evidence on Athens's relations with the North Pontic Greek states, in: *Acta of the fifth international congress of Greek and Latin epigraphy, Cambridge 1967*. Oxford, 119-124.

Burstein, S.M. 1978. IG II² 653, Demosthenes and Athenian relatons with Bosporus in the fourth century BC, *Historia* 27, 428-436.

Burstein, S.M. 1993. The origin of the Athenian privileges at Bosporus: a reconsideration, *American History Bulletin* 7, 81-83.

Carey, C. 2000. Comic law, *Annali dell' Università di Ferrara* n.s.1, 65-85.

Clairmont, C.W. 1979. New light on some public Athenian documents of the 5th and 4th century, *ZPE* 36, 123-126.

Davies, J.K. 1971. *Athenian propertied families*. Oxford.

Gajdukevič, V.F. 1971 (revd. German edn.). *Das Bosporanische Reich*. Berlin.

Hall, E. 1995. Lawcourt dramas, *BICS* 40, 39-58.

Hansen, M.H. 1975. *Eisangelia*. Odense.

Isager, S. & M.H. Hansen 1975. *Aspects of Athenian society in the fourth century BC*. Odense.

Kallet, L. 1998. Accounting for culture in fifth century Athens, in: D. Boedeker & K. Raaflaub (eds.), *Democracy, empire and the arts in fifth century Athens*. Cambridge, Mass., 43-58.

Košelenko, G.A. 2002. Ešče odin predstavitel' Bosporskogo lobbi v Afinach?, *Drevnosti Bospora* 5, 133-138.

Kuznecov, V.D. 2000. Afiny i Bospor: chlebnaja torgovlja, *RossA* 1, 107-119.

MacDowell, D.M. 1993. Foreign birth and Athenian citizenship, in: A. Sommerstein et al. (eds.), *Tragedy, comedy and the polis*. Bari, 359-371.

Skržinskaja, M.V. 1998. *Skifija glazami ellinov*. St Peterburg.

Tuplin, C. 1982. Satyros and Athens: IG II² 212 and Isokrates 17.5, *ZPE* 49, 121-128.

Werner, R. 1955. Die Dynastie der Spartokiden, *Historia* 4, 412-444.

Worthington, I 1992. *A historical commentary on Dinarchus*. Ann Arbor.

Žebelev, S.A. 1953. *Severnoe Pričernomor'e*. Moskva-Leningrad.

Abbreviations

IOSPE   B. Latyschev, *Inscriptiones antiquae orae septentrionalis Ponti Euxini Graecae et Latinae*. Petropolis 1885-1916.

Syll.³   W. Dittenberger, *Sylloge inscriptionum Graecarum*, vols. I-IV. Leipzig 1915-1924 (3rd ed.).

Bosporos and Chersonesos in the 4th-2nd Centuries BC

Evgenij A. Molev

The political relations between the two leading states in Taurica – Bosporos and Chersonesos – have for long attracted the attention of scholars. However, the conclusions reached about the nature of the relations during various historical periods differ widely due to the almost complete lack of evidence from the literary sources. This paper will consider once again the character of the political contacts between Bosporos and Chersonesos during the Hellenistic period, beginning from the moment when "Crimea was in fact divided"[1] between these two states until they both became subjects to the Kingdom of Pontos.

Only one written document contains direct evidence about the political contacts between Bosporos and Chersonesos during this period – namely the Chersonesean decree in honour of Syriskos of the 3rd century BC (*IOSPE* I², 344). Nevertheless, indirect information can be obtained from epigraphy, numismatics and material from archaeological excavations. On the basis of this, a number of researchers have come to the conclusion that the first contact concerned the struggle for Theodosia where they opposed each other. In favour of this view, the following arguments have been put forward:

1) Theodosia, Phanagoria, and Chersonesos borrowing the coin types of Herakleia suggests that some sort of alliance existed between these cities.[2]

2) Theodosia issuing coins with Chersonesean types at the Chersonesean mint, may indicate open participation of Chersonesos in the war against Bosporos.[3] This hypothesis, put forward by M.I. Zolotarev, has been supported by S.Ju. Saprykin and Ju.G. Vinogradov.[4]

3) The majority of Herakleian imports in Bosporos belong to the second half of the 4th century BC, i.e. only after the war between Herakleia and Bosporos had ended.[5]

4) The possibility that Bosporos attempted to advance further to the west towards Chersonesos after the capture of Theodosia.

Evgenij A. Molev

Town	Number of stamps	400-370 BC	370-300 BC
Pantikapaion	357	86	264
Myrmekion	73	18	52
Nymphaion	39	9	27
Phanagoria	60	19	40
Bosporos total	529	132	383
Theodosia	74	19	55
Chersonesos	235	109	12

Fig. 1. Herakleian amphora stamps found in the northern Black Sea region. Based on IOSPE *III and Saprykin 1986, 90-91.*

It should be noted that the final argument lacks support in the sources. All the subsequent (and indeed previous) activities of the Spartokids strongly suggest that their main political interests were linked to the East – the territory of Sindike. It was here that Satyros I commenced his aggressive moves against Phanagoria and the Sindikos Limen at the end of the 5th century BC, and if we accept the similarity of the coin types of the two cities being the result of an alliance, it was precisely as a response to this aggression that Theodosia and Herakleia must have proceeded against Bosporos. Hence, the advance of Bosporos against Theodosia was not necessarily considered a hostile act in Chersonesos.

Mints borrowing coin types of other cities can be evidence of a political union, but should not be considered conclusive if unsupported by other evidence. Economic ties may have been of greater importance. Similarity of coin types and denominations offered the possibility of a stable and long-term exchange of goods that, in turn, could indeed lead to political agreements. Nevertheless the economy was always the primary factor. And the economic ties between Herakleia and Theodosia, Phanagoria and Chersonesos were undoubtedly strong, if we judge by the evidence of ceramic containers. With Pantikapaion, the ties seem to have been stronger still. A study of the data from the corpus of ceramic stamps in *IOSPE* III and the information on the Herakleian stamps from the Museum of Chersonesos, re-examined by Saprykin,[6] demonstrates this (Fig. 1).

Thus, between 400-370 BC (i.e. the period of the wars for Theodosia) the export from Herakleia to Pantikapaion alone considerably exceeded that to Theodosia, and even exceeded the export to Chersonesos. If one takes into account the archaeological evidence from excavations in all of the Bosporan cities, the total exports of Herakleia to the cities of Bosporos clearly exceeded that to Chersonesos. In Kytaia for example, the peak in the import of

Herakleian stamped amphorae falls in the period 386-376 BC, when the level was nine times the average for the entire period of stamping (according to V.I. Kac's calculations). Even more telling is the predominance of Herakleian stamps of the first third of the 4th century BC at the settlement of Elizavetovskoe.[7] The passage of Herakleian merchant ships through the Kimmerian Bosporos could hardly have proceeded unchecked by the Bosporan state if the protection of its economic interests were threatened.

Considering this evidence, the supposed anti-Bosporan alliance whose existence has been deduced from the similarity of the coin types and the corresponding economic interests of the allies, does not seem to be well founded. The possibility that such an alliance existed, is furthermore contradicted by the gravestones of a Chersonesean (*CIRB* 173, 195) and a Theodosian (*CIRB* 231) citizen found in the necropolis of Pantikapaion, as well as by the gravestone of a Herakleiot found in the necropolis of Nymphaion (*CIRB* 923). All these are dated to the first half of the 4th century BC, i.e. to the period when these cities supposedly were at war with Bosporos. In my opinion, it seems more probable that each of the participants of the war pursued their own political objectives. Herakleia, for one, came to the assistance of Theodosia not by virtue of an alliance, but rather at its request, due to the increasing threats from the Bosporan and Athenian alliance precisely when Herakleia itself was making approaches to Persia.[8]

The possibility that Chersonesos likewise took part in the war is more difficult to assess. The issue of a series of Theodosian coins at the Chersonesean mint seems to be a weighty argument in favour of Chersonesos supporting its *metropolis*. However, if one takes into account the relatively late establishment of the mint at Chersonesos (about 390-380 BC[9]), when Theodosia had already issued four series of coins,[10] the argument becomes less convincing. Moreover, the series of Theodosian coins found in Chersonesos dated 390-380 BC also contradicts the notion, since it reveals the existence of close economic ties between Theodosia and Chersonesos during this period.[11]

Thus no evidence – even indirect – available to us indicates the open participation of Chersonesos in the struggle for Theodosia, apart perhaps from the assumption that Chersonesos being closely connected with its *metropolis* may have taken part in the war. But if so, Chersonesos, in my opinion, probably acted merely as an operational base for the activities of the Herakleian fleet against Bosporos.

As mentioned above, the political contacts between Chersonesos and Bosporos in the 3rd century BC are hinted at by the Chersonesean decree in honour of Syriskos. According to this text, Chersonesos for some time maintained friendly relations with "the cities and kings" (lines 17-19). Since the preamble of the decree (line 5) specifically mentions the Bosporan kings, we must assume that the friendly relations included them as well. Use of the plural suggests that several representatives of the Spartokid dynasty were concerned; possibly all the kings from Eumelos to Spartokos III,[12] or perhaps only Pairisades II and Satyros III. The last named is known from a graffito on a fresco from Nymphaion.[13] Such facts as the dating of the decree to the second half of the 3rd century BC and the high esteem in which the efforts of Syriskos were held by his fellow-citizens implies only Pairisades II and Satyros III. Such esteem undoubtedly proves that to Chersonesos the friend-ly relations mentioned in the decree were important precisely in the period of its issue. In addition, the policy of Eumelos on the shores of the Euxine, which was aimed at uniting all the cities and tribes of the region under his power, seems unlikely to have been favouring a rapprochement between Chersonesos and Bosporos. Chersonesos at this time reached the peak of its economic power, and its potential for grain exports, according to some cal-culations,[14] became comparable to that of Bosporos. It is unlikely, therefore, that Chersonesos by mere chance should have been left unmentioned among the cities to which the benefits of Eumelos were extended.

The situation was quite different in the second half of the 3rd century BC. By the 270s BC, the settlements situated in the Chersonesean *chora* had already ceased to exist due to barbarian attacks.[15] The main adversaries of Chersonesos were the Scythians. Since the Scythians and Bosporos were allied,[16] it is not surprising that Chersonesos tried to approach the latter. The decree in honour of Syriskos shows that friendly relations were established. However, it remains unclear, what precisely was concealed behind the for-mula of the decree. Probably Bosporos managed, by way of diplomacy, to convince their allies to suspend the attacks on Chersonesos, but they were not able to solve the problem permanently.

As a result, the Chersoneseans appealed for help from the adversaries of Bosporos – the Sarmatians. This we are told by the Greek writer Polyainos in his narrative about the Sarmatian Queen Amage (*Strat.* 8.56). The story is of such legendary character that researchers have been at a loss even to agree upon its date. Most probably though, the events described by Polyainos belong to a period not later than the end of the 3rd century BC. According to his account, the Chersoneseans appealed to the Sarmatian Queen Amage who "was famed throughout the whole of Scythia" with the request to accept them as one of her allies. The only trustworthy element in this story is possibly the Chersonesean request for help from the Sarmatians and the help offered by the latter. During the following century Chersonesos was unable to find such protection, and its position became still more precarious. Hence, its relations with Bosporos changed correspondingly.

The available sources for the political contacts between Bosporos and Chersonesos at the end of the 3rd century and in 2nd century BC contain scarcely any information of value. We may gain a glimpse of the character of their relations from the agreement of 179 BC between the Pontic king,

Pharnakos, and his adversaries (Polyb. 25.2.1-14). As is well known, two representatives from the northern Black Sea region are mentioned in the treaty: Chersonesos and the Sarmatian King Gatalos. The inclusion of Chersonesos into the treaty is easily explicable. The city already had a separate treaty of friendship and mutual assistance with Pharnakos, apparently concluded about 180 BC, i.e. during the war between Pharnakos and Eumenes.[17] Some years ago K.M. Kolobova quite rightly posited that it was the Chersoneseans who were the initiators of this treaty.[18] This fact would suggest that the *polis*, which not long before had set its hopes upon the aid of Bosporos to protect its independence, could no longer expect such aid. The fact that Chersonesos appealed for help to Pontos indicates that the Chersoneseans were well acquainted with the political situation in Asia Minor. Pharnakos was then at the peak of his success. This was known in Bosporos as well, but Pairisades III was not on friendly terms with Pontos since from the beginning of the 3rd century BC Bosporos had maintained fairly strong economic ties with Sinope which had now been captured by the Pontic king. Moreover, the main adversary of Sinope in the Black Sea trade – Herakleia – also proved to be in the camp of the supporters of the Pontic king and was included in the treaty referred to by Polybios. All this suggests that the relations between Bosporos and Chersonesos were becoming cooler during that period.

Their relations were also affected by the position of King Gatalos. His kingdom was most probably situated in the northern Caucasus and consisted of a Maeoto-Sarmatian union.[19] Since the second half of the 3rd century BC, the relations between Bosporos and this union were becoming more and more strained. In the opinion of most scholars, King Gatalos was included in the Treaty of Pharnakos as a party friendly to Pontos.[20] Since there is no evidence that he took part on the side of Pontos in the war in Asia Minor, we may suppose that his task was to contain the potential opponent, Bosporos, which was closer to Gatalos' own possessions. They had reacted against the capture of Sinope by the King of Pontos. The relations between Bosporos and Pontos may have been inimical even without that cause. In any case, the alliance between Chersonesos and Pontos and possibly with King Gatalos, made the former *polis* a potential adversary of Bosporos that relied on the support of the Scythians. From this point and until their subjugation by Mithridates Eupator, Chersonesos and Bosporos maintained neutral relations at best, and limited themselves mainly to unofficial trade contacts. The participation of Chersonesos in the suppression of the revolt of Saumakos may suggest an even worse situation.

Thus, in the 3rd and 2nd centuries BC the relations between Bosporos and Chersonesos varied from inimical to friendly and *vice versa*. This was to a great extent caused by the changes in the ethno-political situation in the region, the difference between the political systems of either state and the directions of their economic development.

Notes

1.   Domanskij & Frolov 1995, 86.
2.   Minns 1913, 559; Maksimova 1956, 164; Saprykin 1986, 74-82.
3.   Zolotarev 1984, 89-92.
4.   Saprykin 1986, 79; Vinogradov 1995, 19.
5.   Saprykin 1986, 83-89.
6.   Saprykin 1986, 90-91.
7.   Brašinskij 1980, 39-41; 1984, 150-152; Garlan 1982, 4.
8.   Burstein 1976, 43-59; Šelov-Kovedjaev 1984, 118; Zavojkin 2000, 265.
9.   Anochin 1977, 18-20; Turovskij 1997, 12-13.
10. Anochin 1986, 15-19.
11. Kovalenko 1999, 122.
12. Turovskij 1995, 153.
13. On this fresco, see Grač 1984, 81-88; 1987, 87-96.
14. Vinogradov & Ščeglov 1990, 332.
15. Ščeglov 1978, 128; Puzdrovskij 1995, 142.
16. Vinogradov 1987, 85; Molev 1994, 36.
17. Molev 1995, 17-18.
18. Kolobova 1949, 31.
19. Polin 1992, 92-94; Marčenko 1996, 124-126; Molev 1998, 37-39.
20. Lomouri 1979, 54; Pal'ceva 1979, 75; Saprykin 1979, 56.

Bibliography

Anochin, V.A. 1977. *Monetnoe delo Chersonesa (IV v. do n.e. – XII v. n.e.)*. Kiev.

Anochin, V.A. 1986. *Monetnoe delo Bospora*. Kiev.

Brašinskij, J.B. 1980. *Grečeskij keramičeskij import na Nižnem Donu v V – III vv. do n.e.* Leningrad.

Brašinskij, J.B. 1984. *Metody issledovanija antičnoj torgovli*. Leningrad.

Burstein, S.M. 1976. *Outpost of Hellenism. The Emergence of Heraclea on the Black Sea*. Berkeley-Los Angeles-London.

Domanskij, Ja.V. & E.D. Frolov 1995. Osnovnye etapy razvitija mežpolisnych otnošenij v Pričernomor'e v dorimskuju epochu (VIII – I vv. do n.e.), in: *Antičnye polisy i mestnoe naselenie Pričernomor'ja*. Sevastopol', 78-99.

Garlan, Y. 1982. Elisavetovskoe, un emporion grec sur le Bas-Don, *DialHistAnc* 8, 145-152.

Golubcova, E.S. (ed.) 1990. *Ellinism: ekonomika, politika, kul'tura*. Moskva.

Grač, N.L. 1984. Otkrytie novogo istoričeskogo istočnika v Nimfee, *VDI* 1, 81-88.

Grač, N.L. 1987. Ein neu entdecktes Fresko aus hellenistischer Zeit in Nymphaion bei Kertsch, *Skythika. Kolloquium, München 7.9.1985* (AbhMünchen, 98). München, 87-96.

Kolobova, K.S. 1949. Farnak I Pontijskij, *VDI* 3, 27-35.

Kovalenko, S.A. 1999. O monetnom dele Chersonesa Tavričeskogo v pozd-neklassičeskuju epochu, *NumEpigr* 16, 108-131.

Lomouri, N.Ju. 1979. *K istorii Pontijskogo Carstva*. Tbilisi.

Maksimova, M.I. 1956. *Antičnye goroda jugo-vostočnogo Pričernomor'ja*. Moskva.

Marčenko, I.I. 1996. *Siraki Kubani*. Krasnodar.

Minns, E. 1913. *Scythians and Greeks*. Cambridge.

Molev, E.A. 1994. *Bospor v period ellinizma*. Nižnij Novgorod.

Molev, E.A. 1995. *Vlastitel' Ponta*. Nižnij Novgorod.

Molev, E.A. 1998. K voprosu o mestopoloženii carstva Gatala. *Problemy istorii i tvorčeskoe nasledie professsora N.P. Sokolova*. Nižnij Novgorod, 37-39.

Pal'ceva, L.A. 1979. Chersones i pontijskie cari, in: *Antičnyj polis*. Leningrad, 71-81.

Polin, S.V. 1992. *Ot Skifii k Sarmatii*. Kiev.

Puzdrovskij, A.E. 1995. O skifo-chersonesskich konfliktach v III – II vv. do n.e., in: *Antičnye polisy i mestnoe naselenie Pričernomor'ja*. Sevastopol', 142-146.

Saprykin S.Ju. 1979. Gerakleja, Chersones i Farnak I Pontijskij, *VDI* 3, 43-59.

Saprykin, S.Ju. 1986. *Gerakleja Pontijskaja i Chersones Tavričeskij*. Moskva.

Sčeglov, A.N. 1978. *Severo-Zapadnyj Krym v antičnuju epochu*. Leningrad.

Šelov-Kovedjaev, F.V. 1984. Istorija Bospora v VI – IV vv. do n.e. in: *Drevnejšie gosudarstva na territorii SSSR, 1984 g*. Moskva, 5-187.

Turovskij, E.Ja. 1995. K voprosu o vnešnej politike grečeskich gosudarstv Pričernomor'ja v IV-III vv. do n.e., in: *Antičnye polisy i mestnoe naselenie Pričernomor'ja*. Sevastopol', 150-157.

Turovskij, E.Ja. 1997. *Monety nezavisimogo Chersonesa IV-II vv. do n.e.* Sevastopol'.

Vinogradov Ju.G. 1987. Votivnaja nadpis' dočeri carja Skilura iz Pantikapeja i problemy istorii Skifii i Bospora vo II v. do n.e., *VDI* 1, 55-87.

Vinogradov, Ju.G. & A.N. Sčeglov 1990. Obrazovanie territorial'nogo Chersonesskogo gosudarstva, in: Golubcova (ed.) 1990, 310-371.

Vinogradov, Ju.G. 1995. Pont Evksinskij kak politiko-ekonomičeskoe i kul'turnoe edinstvo i epigrafika, in: *Antičnye polisy i mestnoe naselenie Pričernomor'ja*. Sevastopol', 5-56.

Zavojkin, A.A. 2000. Afiny - Bospor - Gerakleja Pontijskaja. in: O.L. Gabelko & V.D. Žigunin (eds.) *Mežgosudarstvennye otnošenija i diplomatija v antičnosti*. Kazan', 249-268.

Žolotarev, M.I. 1984. Dva tipa redkich monet Feodosii IV v. do n.e., *VDI* 1, 89-92.

Abbriviations

CIRB   V.V. Struve et al., *Corpus inscriptionum Regni Bosporani*. Moskva-Leningrad 1965.

IOSPE   B. Latyschev, *Inscriptiones antiquae orae septentrionalis Ponti Euxini Graecae et Latinae*. Petropolis 1885-1916.

Two Waves of Sarmatian Migrations in the Black Sea Steppes during the Pre-Roman Period

Jurij A. Vinogradov

In the late 1960s, A.N. Ščeglov proposed a new periodization of the history of the north-western Crimea during Classical and Hellenistic times, and drew the important conclusion that the Sarmatians moved into the northern Black Sea region as early as the end of the 4th century BC.[1] A few years later, D.A. Mačinskij on the basis of his analysis of the literary sources came to the conclusion that the Sarmatians had become the dominant power throughout the lands between the Don and Dnieper rivers as early as 310 BC.[2]

This discussion about the dating of the Sarmatian advance into the northern Black Sea area has continued into our own times, and a fairly large volume of evidence has been accumulated. Claiming no final solution to the problem, I would like nevertheless to make an attempt at putting forward a hypothesis about the fluctuating character (most probably involving two extensive waves of migrations) of the history of the Sarmatians during the period from the end of the 4th to the 2nd century BC in the steppe regions contiguous with the northern coasts of the Black Sea.

The studies of the early history of the Sarmatians are complicated by the lack of any consistent information in the works of the various ancient authors on the ethno-political history of the region in question during the period from the downfall of Greater Scythia up to the reign of Mithridates VI Eupator. For two centuries, the northern Black Sea region fell outside the scope of the ancient historians and geographers.[3] A highly significant point is, to my opinion, that the famous historian Polybios regarded as "fairy tales" all the stories of his contemporaries about these lands (Polyb. 3.38.2-3), and Strabon relates that this world was discovered for Greece only by Mithridates and his generals (Strab. 1.2.1). I believe that the latter statement is very important in many respects, in particular for dating the ethno-political map of the northern Black Sea area drawn for us by that ancient geographer, but this will be discussed below.

Among the various written traditions about the appearance of the Sarmatians in the northern Black Sea region, that of Diodoros Siculos seems to be of considerable importance. He states (Diod. 2.43.7) that the

Sauromatians (i.e. Sarmatians) "devastated a considerable part of Scythia and, exterminating all the conquered to a man, reduced most of the country to a desert". The opponents of the theory of an early date for the Sarmatian invasion of the northern Black Sea area regard this passage as semi-legendary, and insist that there is no absolutely reliable evidence in the written sources for the presence of the Sarmatians in this region until the 2nd century BC.[4] However, such evidence does exist. Ju.G. Vinogradov in his analysis of the well-known Chersonesean decree *IOSPE* I², 343 pointed out that l. 15 of this inscription deals precisely with Sarmatians who were preparing their invasion of the West. Ju.G. Vinogradov was inclined to date the decree to the first quarter of the 3rd century BC, although he did not rule out a wider chronological limit even to the middle of the 3rd century BC.[5] On the basis of the evidence from this inscription, it may be concluded that the Sarmatians attacked the northern Black Sea area at this time and possibly not for the first time.[6] It is probably with these raids that the aforementioned statement of Diodoros about the devastation of Scythia should be connected (Diod. 2.43.7).

Scythia was practically reduced to a wilderness then – the steppe areas of the northern Black Sea region were abandoned for a long time, and are almost completely devoid of archaeological sites dated to before the 2nd century BC. One must acknowledge, however, that notwithstanding their victorious raids, the Sarmatians did not occupy these lands in the 3rd century BC, since the encampments of these nomads are distributed throughout the regions of the Don and Kuban rivers during this period.[7]

But then, who were the nomadic tribes who actually made the westward advance? From the text of the decree *IOSPE* I², 343 it follows that they were the Sarmatians. However in this case it is of the greatest importance to know whether this term should be used collectively to designate the Iranian-speaking nomads of the post-Scythian epoch in general as it came to be used in the later ancient tradition and in modern science, or are we dealing with the name of only one nomadic tribe, or, rather, a group of tribes that advanced westwards and took a very active part in the events related to the break-up of Greater Scythia. The supposition that this was a group of tribes seems to be the most probable,[8] since we know that distinguished amidst the Sarmatian communities were certain "Royal" Sarmatians (Strab. 7.3.17; App. *Mithr.* 69). In the opinion of T. Sulimirski,[9] the latter played an important role in the devastation of Scythia, and for that reason they took the place of the former "Royal" Scythians in the system of the intertribal links in the region (Hdt. 4.20).

In the decree in honour of Protogenes (*IOSPE* I², 32), which possibly dates from the 220s-210s BC[10] we learn about the tribe of the Saioi, whom many researchers identify as the "Royal" Sarmatians.[11] Quite possibly, the Saioi were based in encampments situated along the Don from where it was fairly easy to raid various cities of the northern Black Sea area including Olbia, and even further to the west.[12]

In other words, it is possible that this specific group of tribes, or the first wave of Sarmatian migrations to the west, should be called the Sarmatians proper, while this appellation was only transferred to the other groups later. Notwithstanding the scarcity of information available to us, there are reasons to suppose that the first wave of the Sarmatian migrations included the Sirakoi, who fairly early moved into the Kuban region and in 310/9 BC took part in the internal struggle between the sons of the Bosporan King Pairisades I. Various sinuosities of that struggle are marvellously recounted by Diodoros (Diod. 20.22-24). As far back as 1895 it was suggested that it was actually the Sirakoi who were the allies of Eumelos (one of the pretenders to the throne) and who are called the "Thracians" in the text.[13] The Sarmatian tribe of the Sirakoi certainly may have had considerable armed forces at their disposal.[14] Strabon states that in the times of Pharnakes, the Sirakoi could, if necessary, immediately put 20,000 horsemen in the field (Strab. 11.5.8). No wonder that the hypothesis mentioned above finds many supporters.[15]

The description of the Sirakoi left by Strabon in the context of the Bosporan history after Mithridates (Strab. 11.5.8) leads some researchers to think that this tribe appeared in the Kuban region fairly late, perhaps in the second third of the 2nd century BC.[16] However, this suggestion seems highly unlikely.

In this context, the chronological aspect of the ethno-political situation described by Strabon is of prime importance. The problem with the sources he used, in particular the sources for book VII dealing with the northern Black Sea area, is highly complicated.[17] First of all, one should consider carefully the aforementioned statement by Strabon that the lands between Tyras and the Caucasus were discovered only by Mithridates Eupator and his generals (Strab. 1.2.1). Also revealing is Strabon's opinion that among all other authors the most trustworthy are the historians of the Mithridatic Wars (Strab. 11.2.14).

Hence, the opinion of those scholars who believe that Strabon's description concerns the last decade of the 2nd century BC[18], the very end of the 2nd century BC[19], or the late 2nd – early 1st century BC is that his account seems to be credible.[20]

Probably, the settling of the different tribes as presented by Strabon had in the main taken place by the end of the 2nd century BC, although the account was perhaps subjected to certain changes later, since Strabon may have been supplementing and correcting it right up till his death.[21] However, it is unlikely that those corrections would have been of critical importance.

The acknowledgement of this fact is, in my opinion, of considerable significance for the reconstruction of the history of Sarmatian migrations in the steppes of the northern Black Sea area. The point is that the peculiarities of the economic system, which according to Strabon (11.2.1) were characteristic of the Sirakoi and certain other tribes, are quite untypical for any nomads who had appeared there not long before: some of them moved together with their herds while others were arable farmers, which was typical of those peoples who had entered the period of crisis of the nomadic economy.[22]

Of great importance in this context is the periodization of the historical cycles of the development of nomadic communities in the northern Black Sea area proposed by S.A. Pletneva on the basis of the ideas suggested by S.I. Rudenko.[23] Pletneva distinguishes the following three major stages:

The first period – the period of the invasion when the nomads having advanced from the East were conquering their "new motherland" and wandered without observing definite routes and having no fixed areas of summer and winter pasture. This period, which lasted approximately 50 years in the history of the nomads, has yielded almost no archaeological record. It is strange that in Strabon's description none of the nomadic peoples fit such a description.

The second stage, is characterized by the nomads having already established stable routes of migration, areas of the summer and winter pastures, and tribal cemeteries. In the *Geography* of Strabon, we find at this stage the Roxolanoi who used to winter on the pastures near the Sea of Azov and move to the north to spend the summers (Strab. 7.3.17). The ancient geographer designates as nomads most of the other tribes from the northern Black Sea region (Strab. 7.3.17), whom J. Harmatta, with nothing to support this view, considers semi-nomads.[24]

The third stage is that of a crisis when some of the impoverished nomads had to settle and adopt agriculture, while other richer families continued their nomadic movements. This stage constitutes a relatively long time-span (certainly more than one century) in the history of the nomads following their invasion of the northern Black Sea area. It is noteworthy that the Scythians started practising agriculture only in the 4th century BC.[25]

Thus, if by the end of the 2nd century BC the Sirakoi, as they were recorded by Strabon, had already entered the crisis of the nomadic economy then they must have appeared in the Kuban region not later than the 3rd century BC – most probably at the end of the 4th century BC. It is curious though, that the same may be supposed about the Aorsoi who lived to the north of the Sirakoi, occupying the vast steppe areas stretching from the River Don to the Caspian Sea. Their life and economy described by Strabon were very similar to that of the Sirakoi – the Aorsoi also practised nomadic stock-rearing along with arable farming (Strab. 11.2.1). In other words, they cannot be considered as newcomers in the region though this fact is rarely acknowledged in archaeological literature.[26] Most scholars assume that the Aorsoi advanced westwards relatively late.[27] It is interesting that Strabon always

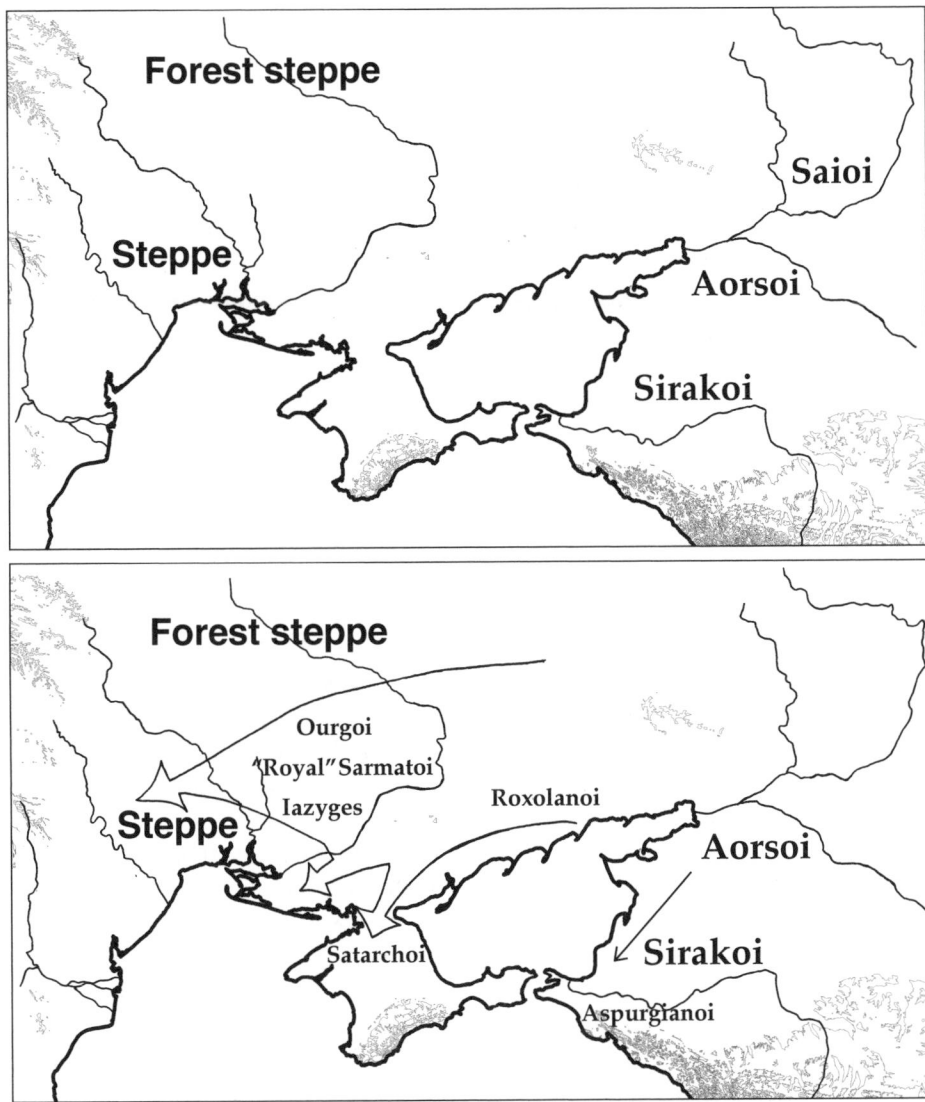

Fig. 1-2. *The two waves of Sarmatian migrations. The first (top) in the end of the 4th century BC. The second (bottom) in the middle of the 2nd century BC.*

mentions the Sirakoi and Aorsoi together, and in general there are reasons to suppose that these "permanent enemies" in the words of V.B. Vinogradov,[28] appeared in this region simultaneously.

It is known that the Aorsoi held a special position in the regional system of those international trade links reaching as far as India and Babylon. According to Strabon, the so-called "Upper" Aorsoi actively participated in this trade (Strab. 11.5.8). It hardly makes any sense to discuss here whether the "Upper" Aorsoi were occupied exclusively with escorting different caravans,[29] as was highly typical of nomads,[30] or whether their role in trade was of a more significant nature.[31] It should be stressed, however, that the formation of this trade route could scarcely have been an instantaneous event.

Here we will attempt to answer the question as to when this trade route may have appeared – or rather what archaeological evidence may indicate when it was functioning. Obviously, in the first place such evidence includes coin finds: eastern coins found in the northern Black Sea area and from various Greek states situated on the northern coasts of the Black Sea deposited in the East. Such finds may indicate that the trade caravans indeed covered long distances in the early centuries of our era. But we have grounds to discuss even earlier periods, too.

In my opinion, it is evident that the "Upper" Aorsoi actually brought caravans to the Greek cities which were closest to the areas of migration, i.e. the cities of the Bosporan Kingdom. Hence it is important to know when Bosporan coins first appeared in the East. It should be mentioned at once that the early finds in that area are extremely rare, but then so are the later ones.

Thus a coin of Phanagoria from 250-200 BC was found in Chorasmia.[32] A hoard of Bosporan coins was found even further to the east (*IGCH* 1821). For some unknown reason this hoard has been almost disregarded by scholars, although the authenticity of the find seems to be fairly indisputable.[33] This hoard consisted of 16 Bosporan coins of which 15 were from Pantikapaion and one from Phanagoria. The latest examples date from the 2nd century BC.

A significant point is that the earliest eastern coins, in particular Parthian and Graeco-Bactrian ones, found in the northern Black Sea region are dated to the 2nd century BC.[34] All the coin finds mentioned above suggest, in my opinion, that the formation of the system of international trade in which different cities of Bosporos and, in one way or the another, the nomadic societies of the region were involved, began in the second half of the 3rd or first half of the 2nd century BC. There are reasons to believe that this was a period when the northern Black Sea region enjoyed a degree of stability between the two waves of Sarmatian incursions.[35]

That relatively trouble-free epoch ended, apparently, about the middle of the 2nd century BC with the invasion of new nomadic tribes. This second wave of the Sarmatian migration now reached the Dnieper. According to Strabon's text, this wave can be linked with the Roxolanoi, Iazyges, and possibly the Ourgoi. Probably it also involved the "Royal" Sarmatians, who as mentioned above may have been living in the steppes of the Don region and who were recorded by Strabon as occupying the right bank of the Dnieper. Another group who must have been related to this wave were the Satarchoi. Pliny relates that these crossed the Don (Plin. *HN* 6.22), and one inscription mentions their presence in the Crimea in the second half of the 2nd century

BC (*IOSPE* I², 672). Ju.M. Desjatčikov linked the appearance of the Satarchoi with the nomads from Central Asia, who were settling widely throughout the West and overwhelmed the Graeco-Bactrian kingdom.[36]

At this point, the Aorsoi and the Sirakoi were probably not displaced from their territories, although D.A. Mačinskij, on the basis of some relatively late sources (Plin. *HN* 4.80; Ptol. 3.5.7-10), suggested that the Aorsoi (or better perhaps, some of them) were carried along with the movement toward the West.[37] Serious changes in the position of these two tribes seem to have been caused by the appearance of the Aspurgianoi in the Asiatic part of Bosporos (Strab. 11.2.11). Their advance here is usually dated to the last quarter of the 2nd century BC[38], and later the Aspurgianoi assumed a very important role in the events of Bosporan history.[39]

The acute crisis, which affected various Greek cities in the northern Black Sea region as a result of such significant changes in the world of the neighbouring barbarians and the general destabilisation of the situation in this region, finally compelled the Greeks to look to the Pontic king Mithridates VI for rescue.

Notes

1. Ščeglov 1968, 336-337, map 3.
2. Mačinskij 1971, 46, 51.
3. See Rostowzew 1931, 105 ff.; Mačinskij 1974, 122-123; Olbrycht 2001a, 426-427; Polin 1992, 88.
4. Polin 1992, 94; Stolba 1993, 59-61; Simonenko 1994, 279; Skripkin 1994, 103.
5. Vinogradov 1997a, 111.
6. Vinogradov 1997a, 122.
7. Marčenko 1996, 72; Polin & Simonenko 1997, 92; Simonenko & Lobaj 1991, 78; Vinogradov 1997a, 123, n. 96; Vinogradov 1999, 57-58, 76.
8. Olbrycht 2001a, 442.
9. Sulimirski 1970, 102.
10. Vinogradov 1997a, 106; 1997b, 88-90.
11. *CIG* II p. 103-105; Karyškovskij 1971, 44; Karyškovskij & Klejman 1985, 67-68; Mačinskij 1971, 47; Smirnov 1984, 119; Vinogradov 1997a, 106; 1997b, 88, n. 98; cf., however, Harmatta 1950, 40-41; 1970, 11.
12. Simonenko & Lobaj 1991, 78; Polin & Simonenko 1997, 92.
13. See Tomaschek 1895, 845; Kissling 1910, 759.
14. See Vinogradov 1965, 108.
15. See Žebelev 1953, 177; Desjatčikov 1977, 46; Marčenko 1988, 113-114; Rostovtzeff 1922, 145; 1930, 577; Sulimirski 1970, 95, 103.
16. Harmatta 1950, 28; 1970, 34; Olbrycht 2001a, 446, 448.
17. Rostowzew 1931, 92, 126 ff.; Gracianskaja 1988, 34 ff.
18. Harmatta 1950, 6-7, 17; 1970, 14.
19. Sulimirski 1970, 102; Bosi 1994, 113.
20. Mačinskij 1974, 126.
21. Gracianskaja 1988, 33.
22. Chazanov 1984, 83, 198-202.
23. See Rudenko 1961, 3-4; Pletneva 1967, 180 ff.; 1982, 13 ff., 36 ff., 77 ff.

24. Harmatta 1994, 566.
25. Gavriljuk 1999, 155, 163-164, 168.
26. Vinogradov 1963, 148; Smirnov 1984, 118.
27. Blavatskaja 1959, 151-152; Harmatta 1950, 28; 1970, 34; Sulimirski 1970, 116; Vinogradov 1997b, 540; Olbrycht 2001b, 540.
28. Vinogradov 1963, 161.
29. Vinogradov 1994, 161, n. 64.
30. Chazanov 1984, 209, 211.
31. Olbrycht 2001a, 438 ff.; 2001b, 106 ff.
32. Vajnberg 1977, 176 ff., no. 6.
33. Olbrycht 2001b, 118.
34. Mielczarek 1989, 91, nos. 94, 96, 153.
35. Marčenko 1996; Vinogradov 1999.
36. Desjatčikov 1973, 143.
37. Mačinskij 1974, 131.
38. Molev 1994, 55.
39. Gajdukevič 1971, 328 ff., 337 ff., 362, 471.

Bibliography

Blavatskaja, T.V. 1959. *Očerki političeskoj istorii Bospora v V-IV vv. do n.e.* Moskva.

Bosi, F. 1994. The Nomads of Eurasia in Strabo, in: Genito (ed.) 1994, 109-122.

Chazanov, A.M. 1984. *Nomads and the Outside World.* Cambridge.

Desjatčikov, Ju.M. 1973. Satarchi, *VDI* 1, 131-144.

Desjatčikov, Ju.M. 1977. Arifarn, car' sirakov, in: Kobylina (ed.) 1977, 45-48.

Gajdukevič, V.F. (ed.) 1968. *Antičnaja istorija i kul'tura Sredizemnomor'ja i Pričernomor'ja.* Leningrad.

Gajdukevič, V.F. 1971. *Das Bosporanische Reich.* Berlin.

Gavriljuk, N.A. 1999. *Istorija ekonomiki Stepnoj Skifii VI-III vv. do n.e.* Kiev.

Genito, B. (ed.) 1994. *The Archaeology of the Steppes. Methods and Strategies.* Napoli.

Gracianskaja, L.I. 1988. "Geografija" Strabona. Problemy istočnikovedenija, *Drevnejšie gosudarstva na territorii SSSR* 1988, 6-175.

Harmatta, J. 1950. *Studies on the History of the Sarmatians.* Budapest.

Harmatta, J. 1970. *Studies in the History and Language of the Sarmatians.* Szeged.

Karyškovskij, P.O. 1971. Istrija i ee sosedi na rubeže III-II vv. do n.e., *VDI* 2, 36-56.

Karyškovskij, P.O. & I.B. Klejman 1985. *Drevnij gorod Tira.* Kiev.

Kobylina, M.M. (ed.) 1977. *Istorija i kul'tura antičnogo mira.* Moskva.

Mačinskij, D.A. 1971. O vremeni pervogo aktivnogo vystuplenija sarmatov v Podneprov'e po svidetel'stvam antičnych pis'mennych istočnikov, *ASbor* 13, 30-54.

Mačinskij, D.A. 1974. Nekotorye problemy etnogeografii vostočnoevropejskich stepei vo II v. do n.e. – I v. n.e., *ASbor* 16, 122-132.

Marčenko, I.I. 1996. *Siraki Kubani.* Krasnodar.

Marčenko, K.K. 1996. Tretij period stabilizacii v Severnom Pričernomor'e antičnoj epochi, *RosA* 2, 70-80.

Mielczarek, M. 1989. *Ancient Greek Coins Found in Central, Eastern and Northern Europe*. Wroclaw-Warszawa-Kraków-Gdańsk-Lódź.

Olbrycht, M.J. 2001a. Die Aorser, die Oberen Aorsen und die Siraker bei Strabon. Zur Geschichte und Eigenart der Völker in nordostpontischen und nordkaukasischen Raum im 2.-1. Jh. v.Chr., *Klio* 83, 425-449.

Olbrycht, M.J. 2001b. Der Fernhandel in Ostsarmatien und in den benachbarten Gebieten. Zweite Hälfe des 2. Jhs. – 1. Jh. v. Chr., *Laverna* 12, 86-122.

Pletneva, S.A. 1967. *Ot kočevij k gorodam* (MatIsslA, 142). Moskva.

Pletneva, S.A. 1982. *Kočevniki srednevekov'ja. Poiski istoričeskich zakonomernostej*. Moskva.

Polin, S.V. 1992. *Ot Skifii k Sarmatii*. Kiev.

Polin, S.V. & A.V. Simonenko 1997. Skifija i sarmaty, *Donskie drevnosti* 5, 87-98.

Rostovtzeff, M. 1922. *Iranians and Greeks in South Russia*. Oxford.

Rostovtzeff, M. 1930. The Bosporan Kingdom, *CAH* 8, 561-589.

Rostowzew, M. 1931. *Skythien und der Bosporus*. Berlin.

Rudenko, S.I. 1961. K voprosu o formach skotovodčeskogo chozjajstva i o kočevnikach, *Geografičeskoe obščestvo SSSR. Materialy po otdeleniju etnografii* 1, 2-13.

Simonenko, A.V. 1994. The problem of the Sarmatian penetration in the North Pontic area according to archaeological data, *Il Mar Nero* 1, 99-136.

Simonenko, A.V. & B.I. Lobaj 1991. *Sarmaty Severo-Zapadnogo Pričernomor'ja v I v. do n.e.* Kiev.

Skripkin, A. 1994. The Sarmatian Phenomenon, in: Genito (ed.) 1994, 279-285.

Smirnov, K.F. 1984. *Sarmaty i utverždenie ich političeskogo gospodstva v Skifii*. Moskva.

Stolba, V.F. 1993. Demografičeskaja situacija v Krymu v 5-2 vv. do n.e. (po dannym pis'mennych istočnikov), *Peterburgskij archeologičeskij vestnik* 6, 56-61.

Ščeglov, A.N. 1968. Osnovnye etapy istorii Zapadnogo Kryma v antičnuju epochu, in: Gajdukevič (ed.) 1968, 332-342.

Ščukin, M.B. 1994. *Na rubeže er*. St Peterburg.

Tomaschek, 1895. Aripharnes, *RE* 2, col. 845.

Vajnberg, B.I. 1977. *Monetnoe delo Chorezma*. Moskva.

Vinogradov, Ju.A. 1999. Severnoe Pričernomor'e posle padenija Velikoj Skifii, *Hyperboreus* 5,1, 56-82.

Vinogradov, Ju.G. 1994. Očerk voenno-političeskoj istorii sarmatov v I v. n.e., *VDI* 2, 151-170.

Jurij A. Vinogradov

Vinogradov, Ju.G. 1997a. Chersonesskij dekret "O nesenii Dionisa" IOSPE I²
    343 i vtorženie sarmatov v Skifiju, *VDI* 3, 104-124.
Vinogradov, Ju.G. 1997b. *Pontische Studien. Kleine Schriften zur Geschichte und
    Epigraphik des Schwarzmeerraumes.* Mainz.
Vinogradov, V.B. 1963. *Sarmaty Severo-Vostočnogo Kavkaza.* Groznyj.
Vinogradov, V.B. 1965. Sirakskij sojuz plemen na Severnom Kavkaze, *SovA* 1,
    108-121.
Žebelev, S.A. 1953. *Severnoe Pričernomor'e.* Moskva-Leningrad.

Abbreviations

IGCH   M. Thompson, Mørkholm, O. & C. Kraay (eds.), *An Inventory
                of Greek Coin Hoards.* New York 1973.
IOSPE   B. Latyschev, *Inscriptiones antiquae orae septentrionalis Ponti
                Euxini Graecae et Latinae.* Petropolis 1885-1916.

On the Problem of the Reliability of Reconstructions of Greek Architecture in the Northern Black Sea Region

Sergej D. Kryžickij

The reconstruction of the original appearance of the excavated remains of any architectural structure belongs to the concluding stage of its studies. However, while researchers seek to adduce as much evidence as is within their power when trying to determine the date of a structure, studying the finds accompanying it or when proposing a historical interpretation, this is seldom the case with regard to the reconstruction of the structure.

In general, excavators limit themselves to the reconstruction of the ground plan of the structures uncovered. Unfortunately, these efforts are frequently deficient in any solid basis. They make no attempts to elucidate and do not attempt to clarify its spatial and three-dimensional parameters. Meanwhile, in many cases the correct reconstruction of the ground plan, especially that of dwellings, is possible only through analysis of the spatial design of the building.

Thus the complex argumentation for a particular reconstruction is mostly either totally lacking or is not correctly set out. Similarly, there seem to be no attempts to evaluate the proposed reconstruction more or less objectively or to compare different possible variants.

This situation is characteristic not only of the northern Black Sea area but also for the entire Mediterranean. Thus, according to V.V. Voronov, for instance, who examined 428 reconstructions of various ancient structures "... only 36, or 8%, of them have preserved all the major elements of the three-dimensional and spatial composition. As fas as the publication of the Classical architecture in Greece is concerned, only 195 examples (43%) are presented completely".[1] In other words, we can only be confident about eight percent of the buildings published. In the remaining 92% the reliability of the reconstruction is unknown.

I have several times emphasized the necessity of developing common approaches concerning the evaluation of architectural reconstructions.[2] However, no attempts have till now been made to remedy the situation. My proposal for a method for evaluating reliability can give an idea of the reliability of a particular reconstruction, without repeatedly going into detail.

In Russian scholarship the scientific approach[3] to the reconstructions of the architectural remains found in the northern Black Sea region goes back to the beginning of the twentieth century, when B.V. Farmakovskij and the architect P.P. Pokryškin proposed the first reconstruction of a dwelling house discovered during excavations in 1902-1903 in Olbia.[4] Their research founded the so-called academic school as one of the three approaches in work concerned with the reconstruction of the Graeco-Roman architecture. Based heavily on the descriptions and recommendations left by ancient authors, in particular by Vitruvius, this method also made extensive use of analogies. Such reconstructions were devoid of any analysis of the archaeological contexts as regards the construction elements of the particular building, their dating and interrelations. Now this trend may be defined as the reconstruction of the building facades on the basis of their architectural details, parallels and the accounts given by ancient authors. In the second half of the last century this school was represented by I.N. Sobolev,[5] V.D. Blavatskij,[6] L.E. Kovalevskaja,[7] B.N. Fedorov,[8] E.A. Savostina,[9] A.V. Bujskich,[10] O.G. Svitaševa,[11] and, most thoroughly, by I.R. Pičikjan.[12]

Of course, the reconstructions carried out within the frame of the direction mentioned above, suffer from a number of essential drawbacks. Mostly, these include the impossibility of achieving a reliable restoration not only of the ground plan but also of the type,[13] or even the category of the structure under investigation and its horizontal dimensions. There is also the absence of any fixation of the positioning within the site or reliable dating. The last-mentioned was usually an estimate based on stylistic peculiarities rather than any stratigraphical evidence. Moreover there is, with rare exceptions, no certainty that architectural elements uncovered actually belong to a particular type of building. This makes, the reconstruction of a pediment facade, for example, problematic since the architectural elements may have belonged to some unpedimented structures – *stoai, peristyles*, etc. Even if there are grounds to suppose that a certain detail belonged to a colonnade which really had a fronton, it does not necessarily mean that this pedimental portico was part of a temple. Neither is it possible to establish whether a presumed temple had a stereobate or a podium on the basis of columns or the entablature. Moreover, the possibility that certain deviations from the typical Greek schemes occured on account of the remoteness from the Mediterranean World is not taken into consideration. One can refer to the representations of five-columned temples on coins, pendants and on a gravestone found in the northern Black Sea area.[14]

Nevertheless, the method of reconstruction based on architectural details, even in the case of an unreliable attribution of the entire building, provides an opportunity to form a fairly trustworthy idea of the height of a particular portico up to the cornice crowning it (except for the tympanon of the gable and stereobate or podium). The reliability of the attribution of the building type and the restoration of its ground plan usually does not exceed here the probability of any alternative variant, and mostly it is significantly less than 0.5 (if 1 denotes the utmost reliability). All of this limits the applicability of reconstruction based on the architectural details found *in situ* to the restoration of the architectural order and to such fairly typical buildings as temples or *stoai*.

Around the middle of the 20th century, two other trends in architectural reconstruction appeared. These are the archaeologico-architectural and the theoretical approaches.[15]

The archaeologico-architectural approach implies the elaboration of a well-grounded archaeological basis for the architectural reconstruction, namely: proving the existence of the ties (in those cases where such ties are not obvious) between particular building elements found *in situ*; establishing its outer limits, internal divisions and the existence of functional links between particular rooms; an analysis of the stratigraphy in order to identify the building periods and fix the absolute dates of the object; and, finally, substantiating the supposition that particular architectural details had belonged to the specific object under reconstruction. In all other respects, the three-dimensional reconstruction of buildings with architectural orders is carried out according to the method of the academic school. In structures devoid of an order, heights are determined on the basis of parallels, recommendations of ancient authors and the indirect evidence available.[16]

The archaeologico-architectural reconstructions offer a considerably higher reliability in determining the building-type, the ground plan and the volume, than the reliability of the reconstructed height, in particular, of the order. The application of this method is indispensable in reconstructions of non-standard buildings and dwellings. Hence, it is evident that a combined use of the first two methods is the most effective.

The most successful application of the archaeologico-architectural method in combination with the academic one is found in works of A.N. Karasev,[17] S.D. Kryžickij,[18] V.P. Tolstikov,[19] A.N. Ščeglov,[20] N.I. Sokol'skij, A.A. Voronov and Ja.M. Paromov.[21]

All the above explains the importance of the third, theoretical, approach, which is concerned with various problems of reconstruction methodology, in particular, with the problem of the evaluation of reliability. The absence of a common method of evaluation[22] makes comparative analysis of the different variants of reconstructions impossible. This is of crucial importance where extremely poorly preserved buildings are concerned or when reconstruction is based only on architectural details not found *in situ*. Such a situation is often encountered in the northern Black Sea area where the state of preservation of the buildings is so poor that it can lead to erroneous ideas about their original appearance.

Although the works representing the theoretical school are few, certain results have nevertheless been achieved in the development of a general theoretical approach.[23] Reconstruction of the facades of temples[24] and the reconstruction techniques used on dwelling houses has improved, and the estimation of reliability coefficients of reconstructions of private and temple architecture is more solidly based.[25]

The evaluation of the degree of reliability of a reconstruction presents a number of difficulties. These are concerned mainly with the impossibility of establishing common criteria for all categories of buildings. Indeed, the criteria should take into account whether the building is a temple or a dwelling. Thus, for a temple with columns in antis just four elements are sufficient to identify its plan (location of the four walls – the outer walls and the wall separating the *naos* from the *pronaos*), while for a dwelling house the necessary number of elements is at least twice as large (in addition to the external walls, the limits of the courtyard must be identified). Nevertheless, a numerical estimation of the reliability of a reconstruction is possible in both cases. Such a numerical criterion may be expressed either in percentages (with absolute reliability of the reconstruction expressed as 100%) or in coefficients (absolute reliability expressed as 1).

To distinguish the major elements which determine the main spatial parameters of the buildings under reconstruction, and to evaluate the relative significance of these elements presents considerable difficulties. This is true above all with regard to buildings without architectural order.

Establishing the dependence of the general estimate of the reconstruction reliability upon the series of particular estimates: reconstructions of the plan, volumes, facade, order etc. also creates a problem. Certainly, the ideal case is one where it is possible to evaluate a reconstruction of the entire building, but such opportunities rarely exist. Therefore, in many cases we must limit ourselves to estimations of the reliability of reconstructions of particular features such as – plans, facades, orders, etc.

In the development of the evaluation method, at least in the preliminary stages of this work, a subjective approach is inevitable. However, it is also evident that evaluating a number of similar buildings on the basis of some general positions (even with some subjective but constant inaccurances) we may achieve more or less comparable results. The propagation of the method proposed below will enable us to increase the objectivity of evaluation without resorting to formalised multilevel statistical calculations, the final result of which, in any case, is predetermined by the program, i.e. by that which is actually of the highest complication in our case.

As mentioned above, I developed a method some time ago to calculate the coefficients of reconstruction reliability pertaining to dwelling houses found in the northern Black Sea area.[26] According to this technique the factor of the degree of reconstruction reliability (K_r) comprises the coefficient of the reliability of reconstruction of the volume (K_v) with the correction to the coefficient of the reliability of the ground plan reconstruction (K_p). Later, an

enhanced variant of this evaluation technique offering the possibility of esti-
mating the reliability of reconstruction not only of dwelling houses but also
of temples and architectural order was proposed.[27]

The factor determining the reconstruction of the ground plan of a house
devoid of architectural order is the position of the major elements of its layout: the sides of the courtyard and the external walls of the house. Of secondary importance for the reconstruction of the volume of a house is information about the number of rooms, their demarcation, interrelation of the
particular rooms and the location of the entrance to the house. The major elements (*a*), in the ideal cases, are estimated to 0.1 (there are eight of them
according to the number of the sides of the house and the inner courtyard),
the secondary elements (*b*) each are estimated to 0.05 each.[28]

Establishing the number of the storeys, the height of the rooms or the
height of the order, and the degree of the inclinations of the roof is decisive
in the reconstruction of the volume of a building. The value of the first element (*a*) is assumed to be 0.4, those of the two secondary (*b*) are set at 0.2
each. The elements of minor importance such as the construction of the walls
and the ceilings, doorways and window openings, and the type of the roof
together make a sum of 0.2.

Since in the reconstruction of volume, it is mainly the determination of
the heights of the rooms and the number and direction of the inclinations of
the roofs that depends directly on the reliability of the restoration of the
plan, it is reasonable to express the relation of K_p and K_v exactly through
these two elements multiplying by K_p each of the elements (*b*) of the coefficient K_v. The values of the elements which compose the coefficients K_p and
K_v hold good if the reliability of their reconstruction is 100 percent, the correction factors K being introduced in those cases where complete reliability
is unattainable.

For dwelling houses, I proposed the following scale of the correction factors K: K=1.0 in the case of a direct confirmation on the site; K=0.9 – reconstruction on the basis of proportional or modular ratios determined fairly
reliably (e.g. the determination of the height of a column by its lower diameter); K=0.8 – reconstruction based on two hypothetical suggestions;[29] K=0.7
– reconstruction based on one hypothetical suggestion; K=0.6 – reconstruction based on direct analogies; K=0.5 – in the case of different alternatives;
K=0.3 – the use of arbitrary assumptions based on general rules; K =0.0 –
when any basis whatsoever is lacking. Hence the resulting general formula
is: K_r=0.4 x K + (0.2 x K + 0.2 x K) x K_p+0.2 x K, where K_r is the reliability
index of the entire reconstruction; K – correction factors; K_p – the reliability
index of the reconstruction of the plan.

Naturally, in the reconstruction of some other category of structures, in
particular a temple, both the system of the structural elements considered
and their values should be changed.

In order to simplify the evaluation of the reliability indexes of reconstruction of temple buildings, it is expedient to differentiate such reconstructions segregating the following coefficients: K_T – the reliability index of the identification of the type; K_P – the reliability index of the establishing of the plan; K_F – the reliability index of restoring the facade; K_O – the reliability index of the identification of the order. Each of these coefficients is equal to the sum of the corresponding main elements:

K_T (for rectangular temples): the number of the porticos – 0.7; the type of the main portico (in antis or prostyle type) – 0.3;

K_T (for circular temples): the number of the porticos – 0.5; the presence of the cella walls – 0.5;

K_P (for rectangular temples): naos (dimensions – 0.1; the location of the entrance – 0.1) – 0.2; pronaos (the number of columns alongside the main facade – 0.4; the deepness of the pronaos or portico – 0.4) – 0.8;

K_P (for circular temples): naos (dimensions – 0.1; the location of the entrance – 0.1) – 0.2; the external colonnade (the number of the columns – 0.2; the depth of the portico – 0.2) – 0.4; the internal colonnade (the number of the columns – 0.2; the depth of the colonnade – 0.2) – 0.4. If only one colonnade is present then the doubled values for its constituents are taken.

K_F the presence of a fronton – 0.1; the type of the order – 0.2; the number of columns – 0.1; height of the columns – 0.2; the height of the entablature – 0.2; the intercolumniation – 0,2 (for the early centuries AD, the height of the entablature or the type of the foundation – stereobate or podium – 0.1 each);

K_O the type of the order – 0.2; the height of the columns – 0.3 (height of the bases – 0.1, height of the shaft – 0.1, and height of the capital – 0.1); height of the entablature – 0.3 (height of the architrave – 0.1, height of the frieze – 0.1, and height of the cornice – 0.1); the diameter of the column – 0.2.

In special cases, for instance for a tholos, it is reasonable to introduce, in addition, the coefficient of the degree of reliability of the reconstruction of the volume (K_{vr}) consisting of the sum of the main elements (up to 1) each corrected by means of a corresponding correction factor. Since the reliability of the reconstruction of volumes depends on the reliability of reconstruction of the plan of the building, the former may be corrected by multiplying it by the reliability indices of the restoration of the ground plan, thus yielding the total reliability index of the reconstruction: $Kr = K_{vr} \times K_P$.

For the correction of the main elements mentioned above, I recommend the use of the following correction factors:

-absolute reliability (completely preserved) – 1.0.
-reconstruction based on reliably established proportional or modular ratios

(for instance, determination of the height of columns by their lower diameter) – 0.8.

-reconstruction based on certain other hypothetical suppositions – 0.7;

-one alternative (two equivalent possibilites for different variants of the reconstruction, any third alternative being virtually impossible) – 0.5;

-reconstruction based successively on two hypothetical suppositions – 0.4;

-the same, but with three or more suppositions – 0.3; 0.25, and so on;

-when any basis whatsoever is lacking – 0.0.

As mentioned above, the "values" of the elements of any structure and their correction factors are introduced by me rather arbitrarily on the basis of their presumed importance in the reconstructions of an order, facade, ground plan or determining their type.

Presented below (Fig. 1) as an example of the application of the proposed method of the estimation of the reliability of reconstructions are the results of approximate calculations for a number of order-possessing structures from the northern Black Sea region.[30]

Fig. 1 demonstrates that the weak spot of most of the reconstructions of buildings with architectural order is the determination of their type and plan.. Of the twenty reconstructions, only seven have a degree of reliability of the determination of the type over 0.5, and only eight (virtually the same reconstructions) exceed 0.5 in their reliability index for the reconstruction of the plan. In other words, all the other structures, except for the Temple of Aphrodite from the early Christian era in Chersonesos, might actually not be the temples at all. The majority of the more or less reliable reconstructions (an index exceeding 0.5) are those of the order (12 examples), the second place being held by reconstructions of facades (9 examples). Eight of the reconstructions under consideration exceed 2.0 in the sum of the four coefficients (out of a maximum of 4.0). Except for one, all these eight cases have an index of the reliability of determination of the type over 0.5, and thus we have only eight sufficiently reliable reconstructions.

As mentioned above, the unavoidable subjectivity in the determination of the importance of different elements, i.e. the "constant error", is of no special significance for the comparative evaluation of a series of reconstructions of one and the same type of building. Of course, later, in the course of the utilisation of the proposed technique, more accurate estimations will possibly be accepted both for the "values" of the structural elements and their correction factors, and for the composition of sets depending on the category of the building under reconstruction, e.g. a semi-dugout house, an ordinary dwelling house, a temple, a burial complex or a theatre.

In this paper the problem of the estimation of the reliability of reconstruction is considered using as its examples architectural constructions found in Greek centres in the northern Black Sea area. However, the proposed method may be applied both to other types of the buildings as well as to other chronological periods.

Reconstructed buildings with an architectural order	Index of the type, K_T	Index of the plan, K_P	Index of the facade, K_F	Index of the order, K_O	SK
Buildings with architectural orders of the 6th-2nd century BC					
Temple of Aphrodite on Berezan Island (Kryžickij 2001)	0.91	0.80	0.72	0.50	2.93
Temple of Apollon Ietros in Olbia (Kryžickij 1998, 190)	0.79	0.78	0.70	0.44	2.71
Temple of Apollon Delphinios of the 5th century BC in Olbia (Karasev 1964, 49 ff.)	0.50	0.53	0.46	0.42	1.91
A similar temple but dated to the Hellenistic period (Karasev 1964, 41 ff.; cf. Kryžickij 1993, 114-115)	0.32	0.00	0.00	0.00	0.32
Temple of Zeus in Olbia (Karasev 1964, 113 ff.)	0.85	0.85	0.30	0.30	2.30
Temple (?) on Mount Mayskaya near Phanagoria (Marčenko 1963, 86 ff.)	0.91	0.80	>0.50	?	2.21
Temple of Aphrodite in Kepoi (Sokol'skij 1964, 101 ff.)	0.50	0.55	>0.50	?	1.55
The Taman' Tholos (Sokol'skij 1976, 55 ff.)	0.82	0.78	0.50	0.80	2.90
Doric temple (?) in Gorgippia (Savostina 1980, fig. 5a)	0.26	0.00	0.65	0.76	1.67
Ionic temple (?) in Gorgippia (Savostina 1980, fig. 5b)	0.00	0.00	0.36	0.61	0.97
Temple of Apollon in Pantikapaion (Blavatskij 1957, 32-33; Pičikjan 1984, 156 ff.)	0.70	0.36	0.81	0.90	2.77
Doric temple(?) in Pantikapaion, 5th century BC (Pičikjan 1984, 174-175)	0.00	0.00	0.00	0.67	0.67
Doric temple of the 4th century BC in Pantikapaion (Tolstikov 1992, 83-87; Svitaševa 1999)	0.80-0.90	0.80-0.90	0.80-0.90	0.80-0.90	3.20-3.60
Temple(?) at Myrmekion (Kovalevskaya 1958; Pičikjan 1984, 191 ff.)	0.30	0.00	0.69	0.79	1.78
Temple of the Ionic order in Chersonesos (Pičikjan 1984, 207 f.)	0.36	0.00	0.81	0.94	2.11
Temple of Aphrodite in Chersonesos (Zolotarev & Bujskih 1994)	>0.30	0.00	>0.30	<0.70	1.30
Buildings with architectural orders of the 1st-3rd century AD					
Temple of Aphrodite in Chersonesos (Pičikjan 1984, 248 ff.)	0.00	0.00	0.68	0.93	1.61
Temple with masks of Silvanus in Pantikapaion (Pičikjan 1984, 231 ff.)	0.25	0.00	0.51	0.82	1.58
Temple (?) of Aspourgos (Blavatskij 1957, 68 ff.; Pičikjan 1984, 229-30)[31]	0.00	0.00	0.30	0.82	1.12
Temple (?) of the Corinthian order in Gorgippia (Pičikjan 1984, 245-246)	>0.30	0.00	0.71	0.42	1.43

Fig. 1. Reconstruction reliability coefficients for buildings with architectural order in the northern Black Sea region.

Notes

1. Voronov 1978, 8.
2. Kryžickij 1971a; 1993, 25-31; 2000b, 3-5; Kryžickij & Bujskich 1996, 20-23.
3. By scientific approach, I mean propositions based on archaeological evidence, analogies, theoretical calculations, etc. Unfortunately, even nowadays many excavators do not present such arguments.
4. Farmakovskij 1906. For further details on the history of reconstruction, see Kryžickij & Bujskich 1996.
5. Sobolev 1953.
6. Blavatskij 1957, 29-34.
7. Kovalevskaja 1958.
8. Fedorov 1975; 1985.
9. Savostina 1980.
10. Zolotarev & Bujskich 1994.
11. Svitaševa 1999.
12. Pičikjan 1984.
13. Perhaps the only exception in this respect is the reconstruction of the Doric temple of the 4th century BC in Pantikapaion carried out by O.G. Svitaševa (1999). This reconstruction was conducted without an analysis of the archaeological context, on the basis of the practically completely preserved foundation of the structure, and it was concerned only with the restoration of the order.
14. Kryžickij 2000a.
15. Theoretically, a reconstruction on the basis of graphical representation of the building or a literary description is possible. However, the degree of the reliability of such a reconstruction is extremely low, especially in the latter case.
16. Thus, e.g., the height of a tiled roof may be determined on the basis of the transversal gable *kalipteroi* (they yield the inclination of the roof) and the size of the roofed span.
17. Karasev 1964.
18. Kryžickij 1971b; 1982; 1993; 1998; 2001; Kryžickij & Lejpunskaja 1988.
19. Tolstikov 1989; 1992.
20. Chtcheglov 1992; Hannestad, Stolba & Ščeglov 2002.
21. Sokol'skij 1976; Voronov 1975.
22. It should be stressed that the estimates of the reliability of the reconstruction of any structure calculated according to different methods may yield results, which contradict each other. The examples of this are numerous: the temple of Zeus in Akragas, the tomb of King Mausolos in Halikarnassos, the house from the excavations of 1902-1903 near the Zeus Kurgan in Olbia, etc.
23. Voronov 1978.
24. Pičikjan 1984, 257-264.
25. Kryžickij 1971a; 1971b, 88-96; 1993, 25-31; 2000b.
26. Kryžickij 1971a.
27. Kryžickij 1993, 29-31.
28. In case a dwelling house has an architectural order, then the set of the main elements must include the degree of reliability of the determination of the number of porticos and their outer limits. In this case, $a=0.08$. If K_p is estimated for the plan only, without any further calculation of K_r, then it is reasonable to equalise the main and secondary elements: $a = b = 0.08$ for each of the elements in a non-order house, and $a = b = 0.07$ – for houses with order.
29. It is implied here that no direct evidence is at variance with these two hypotheses.

30. Kryžickij 1993, 132-142, 191-195; 1998; 2001.
31. A careful examination of the architrave, on the basis of which the reconstruction of the Temple of Aspourgos was proposed, showed that this architectural detail can not have belonged to a portico with an odd number of columns (Kryžickij 2000a). Therefore the reliability indexes of the reconstruction of the temple of Aspourgos calculated by me earlier (Kryžickij 1993, 194) has proven incorrect.

Bibliography

Blavatskij, V.D. 1957. Stroitel'noe delo Pantikapeja po dannym raskopok 1945-1949 i 1952-1953 gg., *MatIsslA* 56, 5-95.

Chtcheglov, A. 1992. *Polis et chora. Cité et territoire dans le Pont-Euxin*. Paris.

Fedorov, B.N. 1975. O kompozicii i rekonstrukcii žilogo doma IV-III vv. do n. e. v VII kvartale Chersonesa, *Problemy razvitija zarubežnogo iskusstva* 5, 18-25.

Fedorov, B.N. 1985. K voprosu o rekonstrukcii Severo-Vostožnoj ploščadi Chersonesa Tavričeskogo, *KSIA* 182, 8-11.

Gajdukevič, V.F. (ed.) 1964. *Ol'vija. Temenos i agora*. Kiev.

Hannestad, L., V.F. Stolba & A.N. Ščeglov (eds.) 2002. *Panskoye I*, Vol. 1. *The Monumental Building U6*. Aarhus.

Karasev, A.N. 1964. Monumental'nye pamjatniki ol'vijskogo temenosa, in: Gajdukevič (ed.) 1964, 27-130.

Kovalevskaja, L.E. 1958. Iz istorii architektury Mirmekija (Opyt rekonstrukcii doričeskogo ordera po architekturnym fragmentam), *MatIsslA* 85, 317-329.

Kruglikova, I.T. (ed.) 1980. *Gorgippija. Materialy Anapskoj archeologičeskoj ekspedicii* 1. Krasnodar.

Kryžickij, S.D. 1971a. Dejaki pytannja metodyky rekonstrukcii žytlovych budynkiv Pivničnogo Pryčornomorja antyčnoi epochi, *ArcheologijaKiev* 1, 56-68.

Kryžickij, S.D. 1971b. *Žilye ansambli drevnej Ol'vii. IV-II vv. do n. e.* Kiev.

Kryžickij, S.D. 1982. *Žilye doma antičnych gorodov Severnogo Pričernomor'ja (VI v. do n.e. – IV v. n.e.)*. Kiev.

Kryžickij, S.D. 1993. *Architektura antičnych gosudarstv Severnogo Pričernomor'ja*. Kiev.

Kryžickij, S.D. 1998. Chram Apollona Vrača na Zapadnom temenose Ol'vii (Opyt rekonstrukcii), *VDI* 1, 170-190.

Kryžickij, S.D. 2000a. K probleme stroitel'stva v Severnom Pričernomor'e chramov s nečetnym količestvom kolonn po glavnomu fasadu, *VDI* 1, 144-152.

Kryžickij, S.D. 2000b. Osnovnye principy metodiki opredelenija stepeni dostovernosti rekonstrukcii architekturnych sooruženij antičnoj epochi v Severnom Pričernomor'je, in: *Archeologija i drevnjaja architektura Levoberežnoj Ukrainy i smežnych territorij*. Doneck, 3-5.

Kryžickij, S.D. 2001. Chram Afrodity na Berezani. Rekonstrukcija, *VDI* 1, 165-175.

Kryžickij, S.D. & A.V. Bujskich 1996. Do istorii rekonstrukcij ordernych sporud antyčnych deržav Pivničnogo Pryčornomor'ja, *Architekturna spadščyna Ukrainy* 3, 9-24.

Kryžickij, S.D. & N.A. Lejpunskaja 1988. Kompleks Zapadnych vorot Ol'vii, *Antičnye drevnosti Severnogo Pričernomor'ja*. Kiev, 10-32.

Marčenko, I.D. 1963. Nekotorye itogi raskopok na Majskoj gore, *KSIA* 95, 86-90.

Pičikjan, I.R. 1984. *Malaja Azija – Severnoe Pričernomor'e. Antičnye tradicii i vlijanija*. Moskva.

Savostina, E.A. 1980. Ob architekturnych fragmentach iz Gorgippii, in Kruglikova (ed.) 1980, 51-73.

Sobolev, I.N. 1953. O rekonstrukcii ol'vijskogo žilogo doma II v. do n.e., otkrytogo B.V. Farmakovskim v 1902-1903 gg., *VDI* 1, 188-192.

Sokol'skij N.I. 1964. Svjatilišče Afrodity v Kepach, *SovA* 4, 101-118.

Sokol'skij N.I. 1976. *Tamanskij tolos i rezidencija Chrisaliska*. Moskva.

Svitaševa, O.G. 1999. Doričeskij chram v antach IV v. do r.Ch. iz Pantikapeja (variant rekonstrukcii), *Archeologija i istorija Bospora* 3, 121-132.

Tolstikov, V.P. 1989. Fantalivs'kyj ukriplenyj rajon v istorii Bospors'kogo carstva, *ArcheologijaKiev* 1, 52-65.

Tolstikov, V.P. 1992. Pantikapej – stolica Bospora, in: *Očerki archeologii i istorii Bospora*. Moskva, 45-99.

Voronov, A.A. 1975. Antičnoe obščestvennoe zdanie III-II vv. do n.e. v Kerč'. Problemy rekonstrukcii, *Architektura SSSR* 3, 51-55.

Voronov, A.A. 1978. *Voprosy teorii rekonstrukcii pamjatnikov architektury (na materiale drevnegrečeskich ordernych sooruženij). Avtoreferat dissertacii na soiskanie učenoj stepeni kandidata architektury*. Moskva.

Zolotarev, M.I. & A.V. Bujskich 1994. Temenos antičnogo Chersonesa: Opyt architekturnoj rekonstrukcii, *VDI* 3, 78-101.

Crucible or Damper?

Pierre Dupont

Some years ago, in a paper devoted to new evidence regarding bronze casting on the acropolis of ancient Pantikapaion, Michail Treister again picked
up the old detailed reconstruction drawing of a metallurgical workshop
found during the 1937 excavation season in Olympia,[1] and compared it with
the smelting furnace and the casting pit for a mould of a statue found there,
intended for the lost wax technique.[2]

   This reconstruction (Fig. 1) by Kurt Kluge owes a great deal to the very
realistic scenes of metallurgical workshops depicted on Attic black- and red-
figure vases,[3] first and foremost on the famous "Foundry Cup" in the Berlin
Museum, attributed to the Foundry Painter and dated c. 490 BC.[4] In spite of
numerous adverse critical comments,[5] it is still used as a reference model
(Fig. 2).

   The foremost problem to solve concerns the identification of the curious
vessel set on top of the furnace, at first interpreted as a "preheating crucible
for alloy components". Theoretically, the separate preheating at lower temperature of the secondary components of bronze alloy would be somewhat
illogical, because mixing tin – and possibly lead too[6] – directly with the
charge of copper ingots lowers the melting point and the smelting is made
easier.[7] However, many authors consider that bronze was obtained by simultaneous smelting of copper and tin ores, rather than by smelting ingots of
these two metals together,[8] although Theophilos recommends the mixing
with tin only after the melting of copper.[9] Thus, Greek bronze-makers may
well have put a container for smelting tin temporarily on top of their furnaces, presumably at the end of the smelting process of copper, either to heat
it separately before mixing it with the smelted copper,[10] or for brazing.[11]
Conversely, one can exclude the hypothesis of a crucible intended for the
direct smelting of bronze ingots either for casting[12] or soldering,[13] which
would have required a temperature impossible to obtain at the upper level
of the charge hole. However, as Oddy and Swadling already noticed,[14] the
weight of such a crucible when filled with molten metal would be too heavy
for easy handling. Even a wax content of a much lower density, intended for
lost wax castings, as suggested by the same authors,[15] would have been very
unlikely. Considering that the temperature at the mouth of the furnace must
have been between 300 and 500°C, this material would probably have vapor-
ized rapidly, even in a double boiler. As for the last possible liquid content

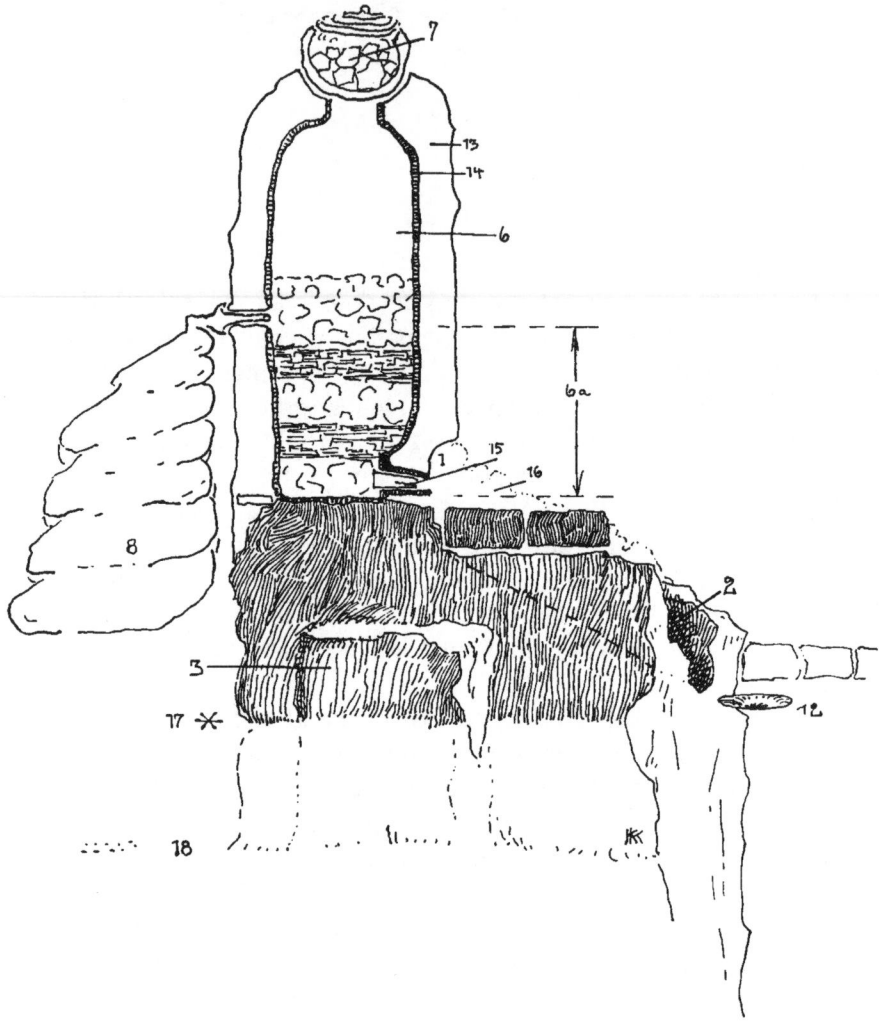

Fig. 1. Bronze-smelting furnace at Olympia as reconstructed by Kluge (JdI 52, 1937).

proposed, namely water, used as humidifier within the (usually open air!) workshop,[16] its evaporation would have been even faster!

It is a pity that none of these large-sized vessels have survived in situ: both the bronze cauldron discovered in a foundry context within the Samian Heraion,[17] and the one from beneath the so-called Pheidias-workshop at Olympia[18] may well have been used for several different purposes and not solely as crucibles. As mentioned above, their existence is attested only in figured scenes on Greek vases. In addition to the Foundry Cup, it occurs on other pots as well,[19] most of the time crowning in an upright position the charge hole of the furnace, but sometimes at a slight angle. As on the Berlin

Fig. 2. Representation of a bronze-making workshop. Foundry Cup. Berlin Museum.

pot, we are faced with the same type of bulging container, the design of which is related to the shape of Greek cooking-pots.

At this stage, it is worth noting that in all representations, without exception,[20] this vessel is covered with an odd stepped pyramidal lid, fitted on top with a ring- or knob-grip. Two questions arise concerning the purpose and the manufacture of this lid: 1) In what cases or for what type of contents was such a device needed? 2) Are we dealing with a regular lid? If the vessel is really a container, two purposes are conceivable: either as a crucible for smelting copper, bronze alloy or tin and possibly lead, or as a kind of cauldron intended for pickle for brazing. Except in the event of a caustic pickler agent to be heated gently and carefully, it seems, at first sight, that there is basically no obvious necessity to cover the container with a lid, a *fortiori* with a special lid. Still, one must bear in mind that such metals as tin or lead are miscible with copper only in a reduced state, and for that reason, a lid would have been required to avoid oxidization inside the crucible.

Nevertheless, Attic vase-painters seem to have deliberately rendered a stacking of separate circular elements of decreasing diameter and supposedly fitting into each other, rather like the concentric rings on old-fashioned kitchen-stoves. If such was the case, it would recall the somewhat enigmatic circular implements, flat and slightly slanting in section, and of various diameters, obviously with the same clay properties as the kitchen-wares found on several sites, for example at Akragas,[21] Kamarina,[22] and Miletos.[23] These have been interpreted as stacking-devices to separate pots inside the firing-chamber of the potter's kilns (Fig. 3).

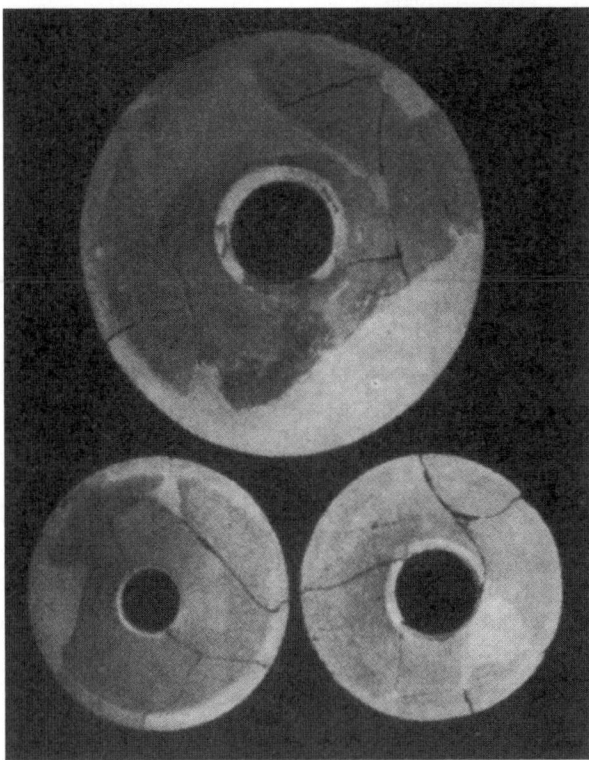

*Fig. 3. "Valvole di for-
nace" from Agrigento
(after E. de Miro,
MonAnt 46, 1963).*

As a matter of fact, authors have mainly focused their attention on the content of the vessel, without actually noticing that when fitted into the upper charge hole of the furnace-shaft, the rounded "vessel" would have shut off, quite hermetically, the draught of the furnace,[24] and for that reason cannot have stood there permanently. The bellows operated by an attendant blew fresh air into the lower part of the shaft, but to maintain a normal draught for obtaining the required smelting temperature, a vent-hole is required at the top of the furnace[25] without a stopper.[26] Inversely, too much draught would induce overheating and prevent the forming of a reducing atmosphere, especially during the conversion of copper sulphide Cu_2S into copper. For that reason, our modern blast furnaces are fitted at the mouth with some kind of damper, not only intended for draught regulation but also as a valve flap to regulate gas pressure within the shaft of the furnace (the so- called "cup and cone" exhaust valve). Therefore, the "vessel" on top of the furnace might well correspond to a gas regulation system, consisting of a bottomless fireproof vessel of kitchenware type, the rounded walls of which allowed close fitting into the charge hole and which could, to a cer- tain extent, be swivelled round, according to the direction of wind. In order to regulate airflow and inner gas pressure, the mouth of this vessel may have been lidded by a set of concentric rings, removable when required. Unlike

Oddy and Swaddling, the present author cannot see any reason why the fact that such a device was inserted rather than being an integral part of the body of the furnace would render such an interpretation invalid. At the same time, this accessory could also have played the role of a charge-hopper, the lower part of which being perhaps funnel-shaped and not rounded.[27] Even the less hard burnt upper section of the furnace was subjected to acute weathering and thus a removable edge piece would have been required.

To sum up, the purpose of the "vessel" now seems restricted to two possibilities: a crucible for secondary components (tin, lead) of the bronze alloy, or an adjustable damper intended for draught control inside the shaft of the furnace. In the first case, one cannot exclude the possibility that, at determined stages of the smelting process (viz. each time a reducing atmosphere was required),[28] it was possible to insert a lidded (sieve?-) crucible into the top of the furnace, intended for heating secondary components of the bronze alloy with low melting point, viz. tin or lead. In the second case, there seem to be good reasons, when excavating ancient Greek metallurgical workshops, for keeping a watchful eye on the possible occurrence of a significant number of clay discs, calibrated to regulate the updraught in the case of a damper. Most important would be to determine the exact shape of the bottom of the vessel, for which evidence is still completely lacking. This would clarify our understanding of Greek bronze-making immensely.[29]

Notes

1. Treister 1984, 150-151, fig. 3-4.
2. Kluge 1927, 13, fig. 5; Hampe & Jantzen 1937, 28-41.
3. Listed by J. Ziomecki 1975, 98-102, 154, no. 29, fig. 19, 148, no. 8, fig. 23, 155, no. 36, fig. 25; Oddy & Swaddling 1985, 43-52.
4. *CVA Deutschland* 21, pl. 72-73; Villanueva-Puig 1992, 78 (good colour illustration).
5. See recently, Vidale & Prisco 1997, esp. 110-112.
6. On the practice of adding a significant amount of lead (12.5%) in the bronzes used for statues, see Plin. *HN* 34.95, 34.97.
7. The melting temperature of a bronze alloy containing 20% stain is lowered by c. 180°C.
8. Grébénart 1988, 19. However, one cannot see how it was possible to estimate the right proportions of copper and tin ores for obtaining the type of bronze alloy needed for each purpose.
9. Theophilos, *Schedula diversarum artium* 85. But just after mixing, the temperature of the new alloy is still too close to that of the molten copper, involving a risk of solidifying too soon during the pour (Craddock 1977, 113).
10. Possibly in using some sieve-crucible pierced with one or several holes in the bottom, from which molten tin would have dripped down into the molten copper at the bottom of the shaft, as reconstructed by Kluge (1985, fig. 5).
11. The vessel may also have contained some pickling agent for surface cleaning of bronze parts before brazing.

12. Hauser 1932, 81-86.
13. Mattush 1996, 18; Heilmeyer 1993, 13-28. Ancient Greek founders actually joined the different parts of their castings by soldering them with added bronze alloy and not by brazing them with tin.
14. Oddy & Swadling 1985, 48.
15. Oddy & Swadling 1985, 48-49.
16. Vidale & Prisco 1997, 112.
17. Schmidt 1972, 77.
18. Mallwitz & Schiering 1964, 43-45.
19. Especially on the black-figured *oinochoe* British Museum B 507 (c. 510-500 BC) (Jenkins 1986, 65, fig. 85) and on the red-figured cup Ashmolean Museum 518 (by the Antiphon Painter, c. 480) (*CVA Oxford* 1, pl. 2.8; Villanueva-Puig 1992, 80).
20. The only unlidded example illustrated by Schwandner, Zimmer & Zwicker 1983, 69, fig. 8f (=black-figured *lekythos*, Providence, Museum of the Rhode Island School of Design, inv. 25.109), obviously corresponds to a simple cauldron for providing public baths with hot water.
21. De Miro 1963, 156, fig. 71-72 ("valvole di fornace"). Diameters ranging from 3.3 to 29.7 cm.
22. Di Stefano 2001, 32, fig. 2 ("coperchi").
23. Recent excavations at Miletos have produced quite a number of such rings, seemingly still unpublished. For this piece of information, I am indebted to Dr. P. Hommel.
24. No other vent hole is visible in the upper part of the furnace, and on the Berlin Foundry Cup the vase-painter even rendered hot fumes emanating from under the vessel.
25. Pliny twice points out the importance of the flaming up – "in ipso fornacium ore, qua flammae eructantur" (34.101) and of the emission of copper particles "ac repente vehementiore flatu exspuitur aeris palea quaedam. Solum, quo excipiatur, stratum esse debet marilla" (34.130).
26. However, Dioskorides (5.84) reports the insert of some wire-netting to collect the *cadmea*.
27. Kluge 1927, 13, fig. 5.
28. Stopping operating the bellows meant that the resultant atmosphere was not reducing enough.
29. I am much indebted to André Cochet, Michel Fournier and Maurice Picon for kind information and advice. The illustrations have been processed by Yves Montmessin.

Bibliography

Craddock, P.T. 1977. The composition of the copper alloys used by the Greek, Etruscan and Roman Civilizations, Pt. 2: The Archaic, Classical and Hellenistic Greeks, *JASc* 4, 103-123.

De Miro, E. 1963. Agrigento: scavi nell'area a sud del tempio di Giove, *MonAnt* 46, 81-198.

Di Stefano, G. 2001. La "Fattoria delle Api" sull'Irminio, *Sicilia Archeologica* 36, fasc. 99.

Grébénart, D. 1988. *Les origines de la métallurgie en Afrique occidentale*. Paris.

Hampe, R. & U. Jantzen 1937. Bericht über die Ausgrabungen in Olympia. Herbst 1936 - Frühjahr 1937, *JdI Suppl.* 52, 28-41.

Hauser, F. 1932. Schale in den Königlichen Museen zu Berlin. Ergiesserei, in: A. Furtwängler, F. Hauser & K. Reichhold, *Griechische Vasenmalerei* III. München, 81-86.

Heilmeyer, W.-D. 1993. Progresso tecnico nella fusione dei bronzi di età classica?, in: E. Formigli (ed.), *Antiche officine del bronzo. Materiali, strumenti, tecniche. Atti del seminario di studi ed esperimenti, Murlo 26 - 31 luglio 1991*. Siena, 13-28.

Jenkins, I. 1986. *Greek and Roman Life*. London.

Kluge, K. 1927. *Die antike Erzgestaltung und ihre technischen Grundlagen. Die antiken Grossbronzen*, vol. 1. Berlin-Leipzig.

Mallwitz, A. & W. Schiering 1964. *Die Werkstatt des Pheidias in Olympia* (Olympische Forschungen, 5). Berlin.

Mattush, C.C. 1996. *The Art and Craft of Greek and Roman Statuary*. London.

Oddy, W.A. & J. Swaddling 1985. Illustrations of Metalworking Furnaces on Greek Vases, in: P.T. Craddock & M.J. Hughes (eds.), *Furnaces and Smelting Technology in Antiquity* (British Museum Occasional Paper, 48). London, 43-52.

Schmidt, G. 1972. Heraion von Samos: eine Brychon-Weihung und ihre Fundlage, *AM* 87, 165-185.

Schwandner, E.L., G. Zimmer & U. Zwicker 1983. Zum Problem der Öfen griechischer Bronzegiesser, *AA* 1983, 57-80.

Treister, M. 1984. New data on artistic metalwork in Bosporus, *VDI* 1, 146-160.

Vidale, M. & G. Prisco 1997. Ripensando la Coppa del Pittore della Fonderia: dalle techniche antiche al contesto sociale di produzione, *AnnAStorAnt* 4, 105-136.

Villanueva-Puig, M.-C. 1992. *Images de la vie quotidienne en Grèce dans l'antiquité*. Paris.

Ziomecki, J. 1975. *Les représentations d'artisans sur les vases attiques*. Wrocdaw.

Amphorae from Unidentified Centres in the Northern Aegean

(the so-called "proto-Thasian" series according to I.B. Zeest)

Sergej Ju. Monachov

Some time ago, V. Grace and I.B. Zeest distinguished the series of "Samian" and "proto-Thasian" amphorae, which in fact have nothing to do with either Samos or Thasos, as recently established by P. Dupont on the basis of a comparative analysis of the clays.[1] The two series are related by a certain morphological uniformity – the ovoid shape of the body, the cylindrical neck with a massive out-turned rim, and especially the characteristic shape of the profiled toe with a chamfered base, which reminds one slightly of the toes of the Thasian amphorae of the 4th century BC. Long ago it was also noted, that the fabric and the shape of the amphorae vary significantly, suggesting that they come from several different manufacturing centres rather than from a single one.[2] V.V. Ruban, though, attributed all or nearly all amphorae with a "profiled" toe (proto-Thasian) of the 6th and first half of the 5th century BC to Milesian workshops.[3]

These amphorae are fairly common at sites in the Black Sea area, but they are practically absent from southern Ionia. This circumstance suggests a North-Aegean provenance for some of the series of amphorae, the more so since evidence has recently appeared which indicates that some of them were possibly produced on Thasos[4] and in Abdera, the colony of Teos on the coast of Thrace.[5] This hypothesis of P. Dupont seems quite justifiable.[6]

Out of the entire collection of amphorae with a "profiled toe" ("proto-Thasian" according to I.B. Zeest), two series, judging by the outward appearance, must be considered as the earliest.

The first series

The first (pithoid) series is represented by an amphora in the Odessa Museum kept among a number of undocumented Olbian finds (Fig. 1.1)[7] and by a similar amphora with a relief stamp in the form of the letter "E" on its handle in the museum in Nicosia.[8] The rather low neck passes smoothly into a slightly sloping shoulder and a broad, almost spherical body. The massive rim is semi-cylindrical in shape; the foot is low and broad – c. 7 cm in diameter. The fabric of the Olbian example is red and dense, containing no special tempers. There are no reliable grounds on which the aforementioned vessels can be dated, but the neck of a similar amphora was found in Well no. 5 on Berezan' (Fig. 1.2),[9] suggesting that the entire series may be dated to the middle or third quarter of the 6th century BC. Vessels which should be considered as a later continuation of the same series are two amphorae from the complex of the Athenian Well Q 12:3,[10] which is dated to the end of the 6th to the beginning of the 5th century BC. These examples have a slightly shorter neck, while the toe is taller and has a smaller diameter (Fig. 1.3).

The second series

This series is distinguished by its tall neck of cylindrical or funnel-like shape which is quite distinct from the shoulder and has an out-turned rim, 2-2.5 cm high; the body is slightly more elongated than that of the first series. The peculiarities of the morphology of the second series are well demonstrated by the two amphorae from the Olbian necropolis. One was found in Grave no. 38/1909 excavated by B.V. Farmakovskij (Fig. 1.4),[11] the second was uncovered in Burial M1 in 1989 (Fig. 1.5).[12] The difference in fabric of these two morphologically identical examples is clearly discernible: in the first case the red clay contains sparse white inclusions, while in the second it is very rich in finely dispersed mica. In addition, two other amphorae from the Athenian Well Q 12:3,[13] one jar from the necropolis of Nymphaion,[14] as well as two amphorae from the Nesebur and Burgas museums,[15] which are distinguished from those described above by the larger body diameter (Fig. 1.6), can possibly be attributed to the second series. The basis for a reliable dating is provided only by the first of the Olbian examples. In the grave excavated in 1909, a black-glazed *kylix* of the third quarter of the 6th century BC was found. However, the Athenian finds suggest that such containers may have been manufactured until at least the turn of the 6th and 5th century BC.

Thus the amphorae of the first two series appeared about the middle of the 6th century BC and were manufactured throughout the entire second half of that century.[16] In the last quarter of the 6th century, however, the tendency became prevalent to elongate the proportions, shorten the foot and separate more distinctly the neck from the shoulder, as the materials from Athenian Well Q 12:3 indicate. The first series of amphorae, i.e. those characterised by the smooth profile of the boundary between the neck and the shoulder, was still manufactured with slight modifications even at the beginning of the 5th century BC.[17]

However in general, most of the proto-Thasian amphorae from the end of the 6th century and the beginning of the 5th century BC are distinguishable by their more slender proportions, the body being almost conical, the toe as a rule of a small diameter (4.5-6.5 cm), and the rim semi-cylindrical in

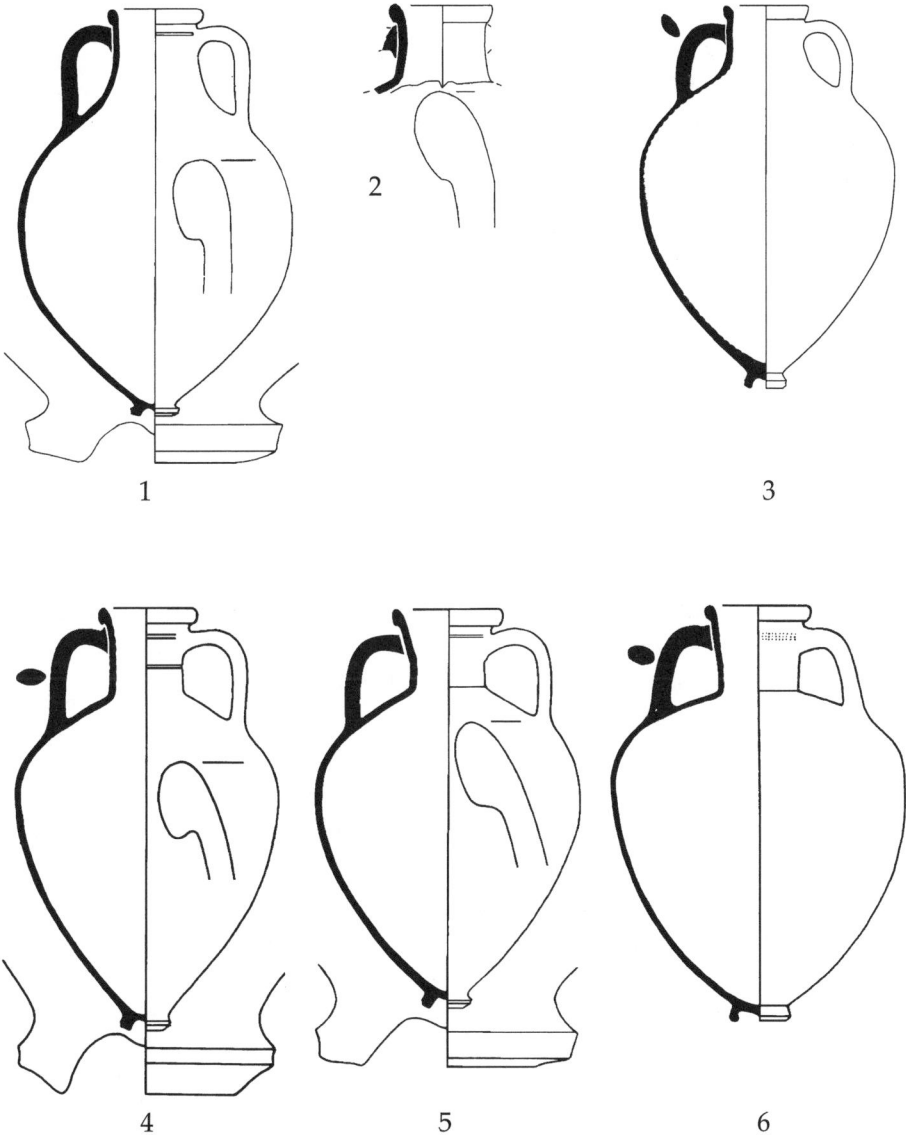

Fig. 1. Amphorae with "profiled" toe of series I (nos. 1-3) and II (nos. 4-6) from 1) the Odessa Museum; 2) the Berezan' well no. 5; 3) the Athenian well Q12:3 (after Roberts 1986, no. 441); 4) the Olbian grave 38/1909; 5) the Olbian grave M 1/1989; 6) the Nesebur Museum (after M. Lazarov).

shape, sometimes fairly massive. The lower part of the neck is almost always rendered distinct from the shoulder. On the basis of particular morphological features it is possible among the rather numerous examples of this type to identify yet a third and fourth series, which are likely to comprise containers from more than just two production centres.

The third series

The containers of this series has a height of about 50 cm and is distinguished from the later jars by a funnel-shaped neck ending in the out-turned rim and by a conical shape of the body combined with the rather smoothly sloping shoulder. Attributed to this series may be an amphora from the village of Rigi (Fig. 2.1),[18] two amphorae from the Berezan' Well no. 4 (Fig. 2.2), and some jars from the Chersonesos Museum (Fig. 2.3),[19] the excavation of 1967 at the Berezan' necropolis (Fig. 2.4),[20] and a number of others.[21] Of special interest among this series are the stamped examples, among which I am aware of two amphorae from the excavations of 1975 and 1988 at the Olbian necropolis (Figs. 2.5-6),[22] one from the settlement near the village of Staraja Bogdanovka (Fig. 3.1),[23] and another from Hermonassa (Fig. 3.2).[24] In all these cases, the relief stamps are positioned on the handles: the first three vessels bear the stamp in the form of the letter "E", and the last – "Σ" within an oval frame. The stamps with the letter "E" are recorded on many finds both from the Black Sea area[25] and from the Aegean region,[26] including the already mentioned intact amphora of the first series in the Nicosia Museum. A date between the end of the 6th – beginning of the 5th century is suggested by the vessels from the Berezan' Well no. 4, but the stamp "E" is also recorded on the earlier amphora of the first series from Nicosia.

The fourth series

In contrast to the third, the fourth series of "proto-Thasian" amphorae is characterised by a shorter neck of cylindrical rather than funnel-like shape. On the neck and shoulder of these amphorae, dipinti marks in black or red paint in the form of the letter "Θ" are fairly common. The majority of these amphorae come from accidental finds or rather broadly dated complexes. Useful examples include the vessels from the excavations of the town-site (Figs. 3.4-5)[27] and necropolis of Olbia (Fig. 4.2-3),[28] the Berezan' settlement and necropolis (Figs. 3.3, 6),[29] and from Porthmion (Fig. 4.4).[30] There are numerous undocumented finds in different museum collections, in particular, in the Odessa Museum (Fig. 4.1).[31] In addition, mention should be made of the complex from the burial excavated in Myrmekion in 1938,[32] among others.[33] In those cases where accompanying finds, in particular the fine ware, supply dating criteria, these amphorae belong to the first third of the 5th century BC.

The fifth series

The amphorae of the fifth series with a profiled toe is more varied than the preceding ones. Its main distinguishing feature is the conical shape of the body and fairly distinct separation between the neck and the shoulder. To this series may be assigned vessels from Berezan' (Fig. 4.5) and the settle-

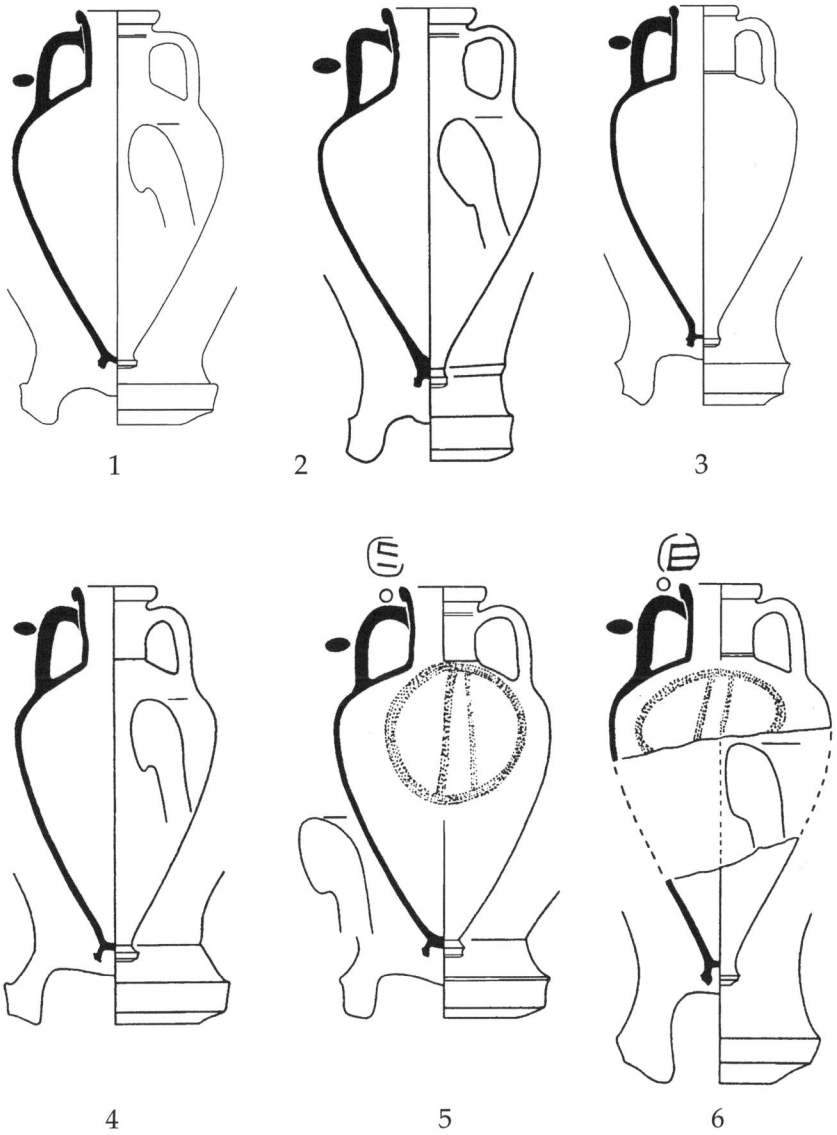

Fig. 2. Amphorae with the "profiled" toe of series III from: 1) tumulus near the village of Rigi; 2) the Berezan' well no. 4; 3) Chersonesos (no. 3156); 4) necropolis of Berezan' (SHM, B.67.50); 5) necropolis of Olbia, 1975; 6) necropolis of Olbia, 1988.

ment of Stanislav in the *chora* of Olbia (Fig. 4.6),[34] as well as a number of undocumented finds kept in the Odessa Museum (Fig. 4.7).[35] Similar characteristics are exhibited by an amphora from the Kavala Museum which has been identified as a product of Abdera.[36] Also closely morphologically related are some amphorae from Burial 12 near the *khutor* (farmstead) of Rassvet

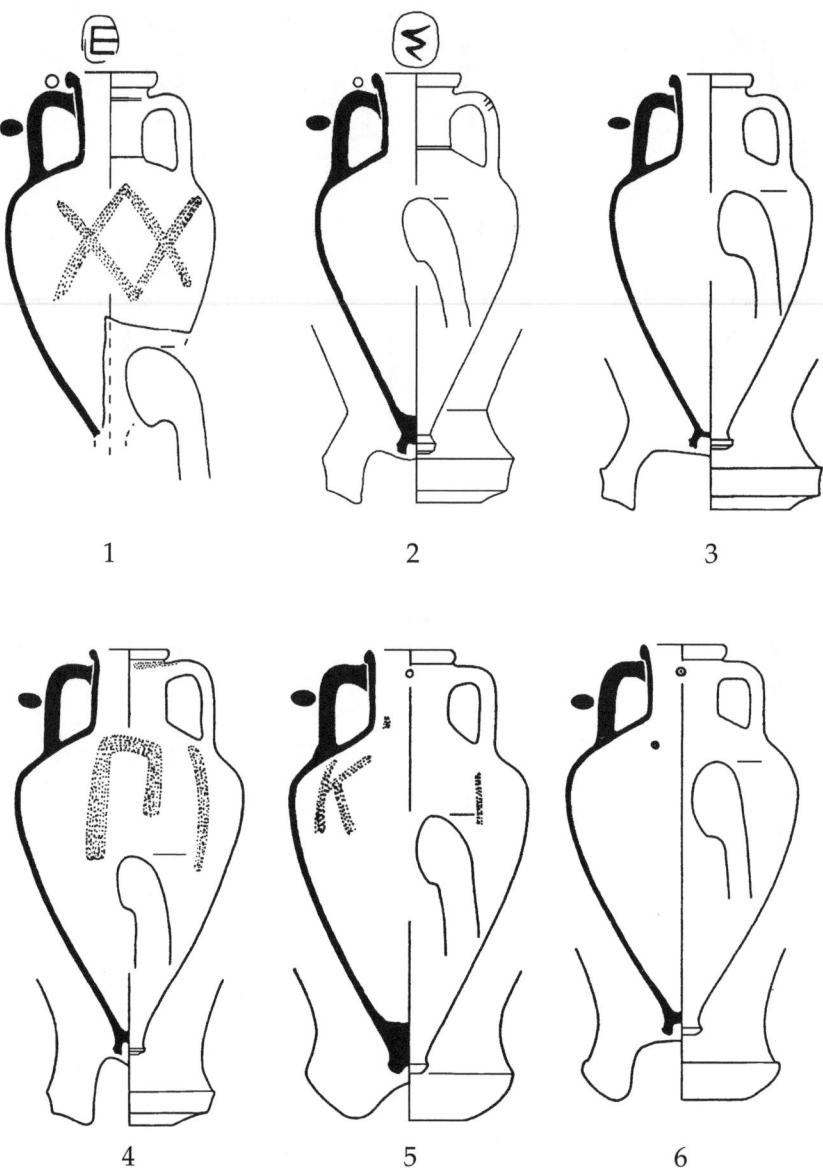

Fig. 3. Amphorae with "profiled" toe of series III (nos. 1-2) and IV (nos. 3-6) from: 1) Staraja Bogdanovka; 2) Hermonassa, 1984; 3) necropolis of Berezan' (SHM, B.67.21); 4-5) the town-site of Olbia; 6) necropolis of Berezan' (SHM, B.67.174).

(Fig. 5.1),[37] Kurgan 16 at the Pereščepino cemetery near the settlement-site of Bel'skoe,[38] the *khutor* of Suvorovo-Čerkesskij (Fig. 5.2),[39] and the burial excavated in 1913 near the village of Tamanskaja (Fig. 5.3);[40] all the latter

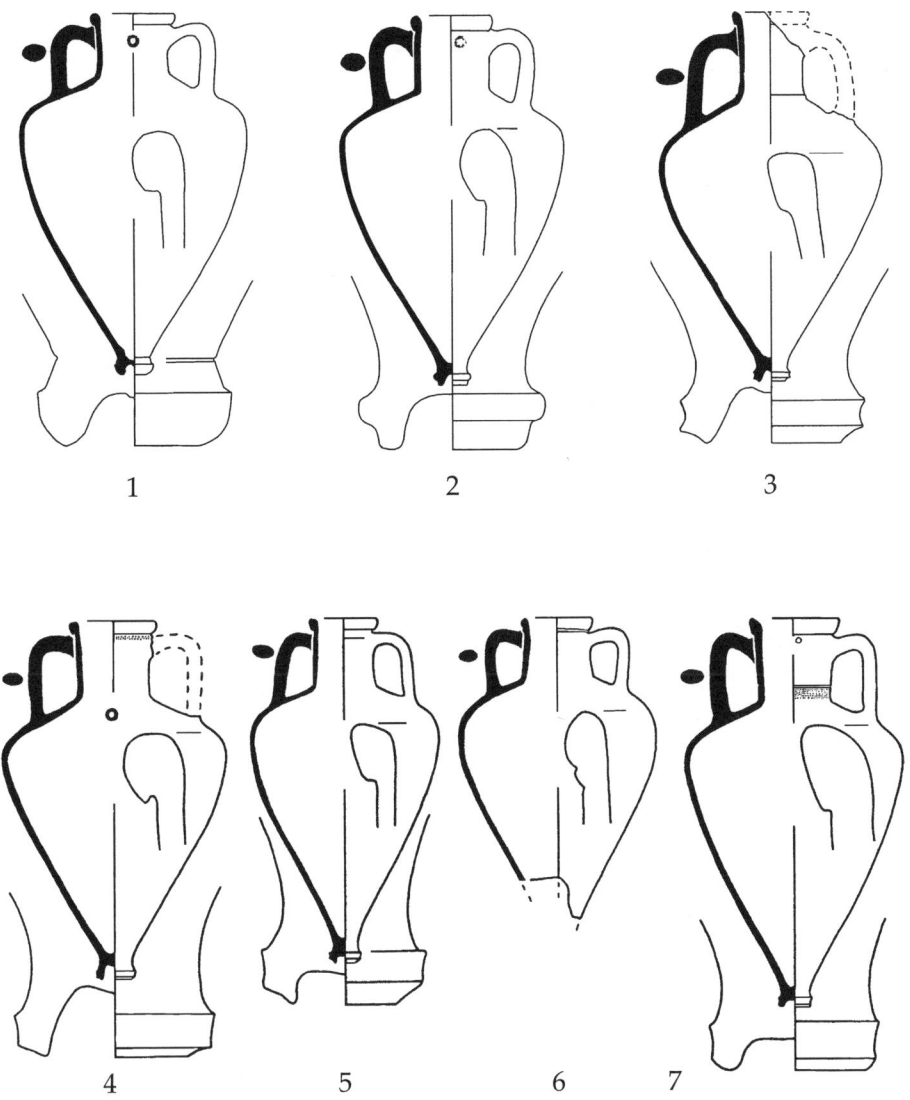

Fig. 4. Amphorae with "profiled" toe of series IV (nos. 1-4) and V (nos. 5-7) from: 1) the Odessa Museum (OAM, no. 250300); 2) necropolis of Olbia (grave 7/1992); 3) necropolis of Olbia, 1994; 4) Porthmion, 1988; 5) excavations in Berezan' (SHM, B.84.402); 6) the settlement of Stanislav; 7) the Odessa Museum (OAM, no. 25033).

examples, though, are distinguished by still more slender proportions, in particular the absolutely conical body, tall neck, and rather short rim and toe. This series is dated to the first half of the 5th century BC. In a pit at the settlement of Stanislav, along with the aforementioned amphora, beaker-shaped feet of Lesbian amphorae of the specified period were found; the

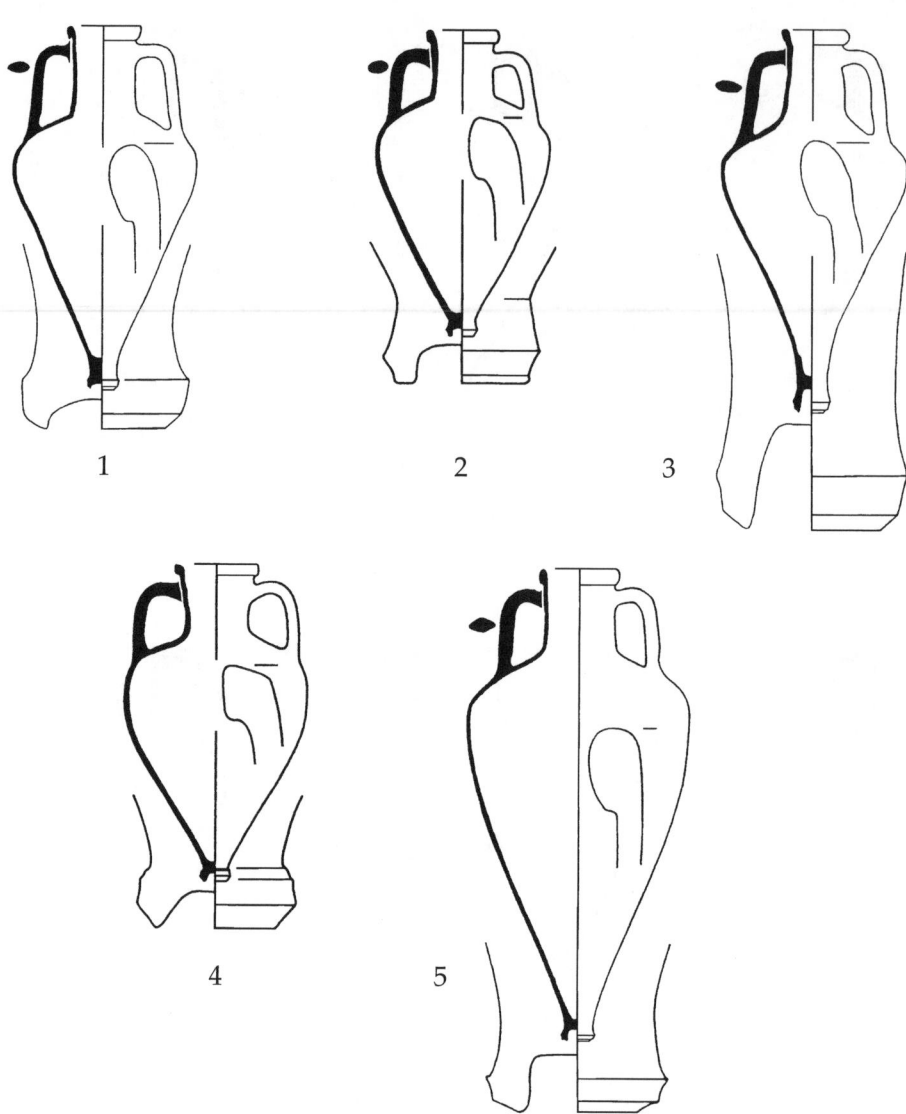

Fig. 5. Amphorae with the "profiled" toe of series V (nos. 1-3) and "isolated" (nos. 4-5) from: 1) the khutor *of Rassvet; 2) the* khutor *of Suvorovo-Čerkesskij; 3) Taman'; 4) the Simferopol Museum; 5) excavations in Olbia, 1981.*

amphora from Kavala is dated to the second quarter of the 5th century BC on the basis of the coins bearing representations of similar amphorae.

Among the amphorae with profiled toe there are several examples, which do not match any of the series mentioned above, and therefore must be classed as individual examples. Thus, one undocumented amphora from

Findspot/Present location	Dimensions, mm						Capacity	Stamps	Plate
	H	H.	H₁	H₃	D	d			
1	*2*	*3*	*4*	*5*	*6*	*7*	*8*	*9*	*10*
Series I									
OAM, 48660	532	518	285	110	361	98	25,00		1.1
Berezan', well 5				90					1.2
Athens, Roberts, no. 441	518				338				1.3
Athens, Roberts, no. 440	524				359				
Athens, Roberts, no. 412	560				376				
Athens, Roberts, no. 413	546				385				
Series II									
SHM, Ol.1909.110 P.38/1909	550	535	245	110	344	100			1.4
APO, M 1/1989	526	508	255	105	346	120			1.5
Nesebur, no. 411 according to Lazarov	540	520	220	110	390	107			1.6
Series III									
Tumulus near the village of Rigi	475	462	205	92	285	85			2.1
Berezan', well 4	503	464	200	105	300	88	12,00		2.2
Berezan', well 4		500	195	95	300	85	13,50		
NTPCh no. 3156	453	438	165	91	254	70	8,73*		2.3
SHM, B.67.50	496	473	190	98	274	84	10,14*		2.4
APO, necropolis 1975, findl. O-75/472	490	465	195	100	296	86		E	2.5
APO, necropolis 1988			195	100	307	86		E	2.6
APO, 77/4715, St. Bogdanovka-2		490	225	115	285	90		E	3.1
Hermonassa, 1984	495	455	200	100	275	100		Σ	3.2
FM, tumulus 9 near the v. Krylovtsy	465	450	170	100	272	74			
Series IV									
SHM, B.67.21	496	476	185	100	278	80	10,96*		3.3
APO, O-87/1203	544	513	200	100	314	87			3.4
APO, O-89/996	568	500	210	100	324	90			3.5
SHM, V.67.174	520	490	200	88	315	90	15,00*		3.6
OAM, no. 25030		463	160	80	308	88	13,70		4.1
APO, O-92/75, necropolis, grave 7	490	462	175	95	302	80			4.2
APO, O-94/157A	490	460	210	112	304	78			4.3
IHMC, Porthmion, 1988	472	438	180	92	304	90	12,44*		4.4
IHMC, Porthmion, 1988		500	195	98	295	90	11,40*		
APO, O-72/8611		450	180	90	300	80			
Series V									
SHM, B.84.402	456	424	165	88	256	70	7,16*		4.5
IHMC, Stanislav, pit 7/1988			166	78	268	75	8,53*		4.6
OAM, no. 25033	515	487	190	105	300	86	12,00		4.7
AAM, no.10169, khutor Rassvet	488	444	190	120	257	74	7,00*		5.1
AAM, no. 10096, khutor Suvorovo-Cherkassky	412	380	160	86	235	69	5,90		5.2
KM, no. 6629/59, Taman' 1913	504	460	188	110	259	70	6,91*		5.3
Pereshchepino burial ground, tumulus 16	465				270				
Kavala Museum, no. A3908	440				260				
Isolated									
SMRS, no no.	416	390	180	90	244	90	7,15		5.4
IHMC, Olbia, 1981, no. 543		603	210	110	307	83	17,80		5.5

Fig. 6. The metric characteristics of the North Aegean amphorae (the so-called "proto-Thasian" series of I.B. Zeest). The capacities are measured with water or grain; those marked with an asterisk (*) are calculated on the basis of drawings made in scale 1:1.

the Simferopol Museum has a very short, broad body with a plump shoulder (Fig. 5.4).[41] By contrast, the amphora from the pit of 1981 in Olbia has an elongated body of almost conical shape (Fig. 5.5).[42] This latter vessel is dated roughly to the middle of the 5th century BC on the basis of the necks of the late plump-necked Chian amphorae found in the same context.

To sum up the review of this extremely varied group of amphorae with profiled toe, we are drawn to the conclusion that we are dealing with containers from a number of manufacturing centres, probably from the Thracian coast of the Aegean where wine-making was intensively developed from the Archaic period onwards.[43] The apt comparison of some amphorae from the fifth series with the coin series of Abdera of the second quarter of the 5th century BC is noteworthy in this context.[44] The fact that such vessels were manufactured in different centres of this region is suggested by their extremely varied clays. The prevailing clays are red with admixtures of mica, but fabrics with inclusions of limestone and even pyroxenes have also been recorded. The evolution of the shape of these containers has been traced throughout approximately one century – from the middle of the 6th to the middle of the 5th century BC. During that period, the body of the amphorae gradually became more elongated, having changed from pithoid or ovoid to conical. The toe developed from low, broad shapes towards relatively tall and slender ones, first with a distinct separation at the place of transition to the body, which was later replaced by a rather smooth curve. At the same time, a great number of diverse variants of such toes have been recorded, especially for the last three to four decades of the manufacture of these containers. The rim likewise displays great variation. It is normally of out-turned, semi-cylindrical shape, but some examples with a flat chamfer both on the inner and on the outer surface have been encountered.

The capacities are also very diverse, varying from 23-25 l for the amphorae of the first series to 6-7 l for the amphorae of the fifth series. The general tendency towards smaller dimensions is quite obvious (Fig. 6). However, no reconstruction of the metric characteristics is possible, at least until we are able to attribute the amphorae to the different manufacturing centres.

Notes

1. Cook & Dupont 1998, 178-186, fig. 23.10-12; Dupont 1999, 153-157, pls. 5-7.
2. Lejpunskaja 1981, 23.
3. Ruban 1991.
4. Koukouli-Chrisanthaki 1979, pl. 142.
5. Peristeri-Otatzi 1986, 496, fig. 13.
6. Dupont 1999, 153.
7. OAM, inv. no. 48660 on display. This may be the amphora that was published by Dupont (1999, 156, pl. 5.5).
8. Nicolaou 1986, 531, fig. 15.

9. Monachov 1999, 48, pl. 6.2.
10. Monachov 1999, 62, pls. 10-13, nos. 440-441.
11. SHM, inv. no. Ol. 1909.110. Evidently, it is this amphora that was regarded as Samian by I.B. Brašinskij (Brašinskij 1967, 24; 1984, 101, pls. II.5 and XII.3). The context can be dated quite precisely on the basis of a black-figured *kylix* from the third quarter of the 6th century BC, see Skudnova 1988, 47.
12. APO, find list O-89/26, unpublished.
13. Monachov 1999, 62, pls. 10-13, amphorae nos. 412 and 413. According to Roberts (1986, 65) these are Samian.
14. Grač 1999, 43, fig. 7. GE, inv. no. NNF.74.55. This amphora was found out of context (Object A34).
15. Lazarov 1973, 17-18, pls. VI-VII, nos. 65, 72.
16. A similar conclusion had been drawn earlier, see Johnston 1981, 42, no. 48, pl. 29; Johnston 1981; 1990, 60-62, nos. 105-106, fig. 7.
17. Monachov 1999, 62.
18. Kurgan no. 1 near v. Rigi in the Poltava Region, excavations of 1983. Once kept in the Institute of Archaeology of the National Academy of Sciences of Ukraine, it was handed over in 1933 to the regional museum.
19. Monachov & Abrosimov 1993, 120, pl. 1.1.
20. From excavations at the Berezan' necropolis: SHM, inv. no. B.67.50.
21. E.g. the amphora from Kurgan 9 near v. Krylovcy of the Pervomajskij Region in the Crimea. See Solomonik 1993, 110, no. 31, fig. 5.
22. APO, find list O-75/472 and APO, find list O-88/58.
23. APO, find list St. B.-2/77/4715.
24. PMFA, find list TMGS-84, pit 2.
25. *IOSPE* III, 187-194. Predominantly in Olbia, but also in Pantikapaion and Porthmion, see Gajdukevič (ed.) 1964, fig. 3.2.
26. Johnston 1990, 51, fig. 10, no. 122.
27. APO, find list O-87, AGD/1203; find list O-89, NGS/996.
28. APO, find list O-92/75. Burial no. 7 (1991). Together with this amphora a black-glazed Attic *kylix* of the beginning of the 5th century BC was found, see Papanova 1993, 36, fig. 15; APO, find list Ol-94.nekr.-157A.
29. SHM, inv. no. B. 67.21. Grave 9; SHM, inv. no. B. 67.174. Area I.
30. Excavations of 1988. Two amphorae kept in IHMC, St Petersburg.
31. OAM, inv. no. 25030.
32. The burial is dated not later than 470 BC by a black-figured *lekythos* of the Chaimon's group, see Monachov 1999, 103, pl. 31.
33. One such amphora was found in Tyritake (Gajdukevič 1952, 85, no. 25, fig. 104.3). Another was found at a necropolis on the Taman Peninsula (Paromov & Sudarev 2000, 203, fig. 4).
34. Berezan': SHM B.84.402; Stanislav: pit no. 7 (1988) containing material of the end of the 6th to the beginning of the 5th century BC, kept in IHMC.
35. OAM, inv. no. 25033.
36. Peristeri-Otatzi 1986, 496, fig. 13.
37. Burial no. 12 excavated in 1969 near the *khutor* of Rassvet: The Anapa Archaeological Museum, inv. no. 10169.
38. Known to me only from the publication: Murzin, Rolle, Hern, Machortych & Belozor 1998, 34, fig. 30.
39. The Anapa Archaeological Museum, inv. no. AM-10096.
40. The Krasnodar Museum, inv. no. 6629/59.
41. The Simferopol Museum, no inv. no.

42.   Kept in IHMC, find list O-81/543. Excavations of V.I. Pruglo-Denisova.
43.   Salviat 1986, 145-146; Salviat 1990, 457-476.
44.   Peristeri-Otatzi 1986, 496, fig. 13.

Bibliography

Brašinskij, I.B. 1967. Novye dannye o torgovle Ol'vii s Samosom, *KSIA* 109, 22-26.

Brašinskij, I.B. 1984. *Metody issledovanija antičnoj torgovli*. Leningrad.

Cook, R.M. & P. Dupont 1998. *East Greek Pottery*. London-New York.

Dupont, P. 1999. La circulation amphorique en mer Noire à l'époque archaïque. Spécificités et problèmes, in: Y. Garlan (ed.), *Production et commerce des amphores anciennes en Mer Noire*. Aix-en-Provence, 143-161.

Empereur, J.-Y. & Y. Garlan (eds.) 1986. Recherches sur les amphores grecques (BCH Suppl. 13). Paris.

Gajdukevič, V.F. 1952. Raskopki Tiritaki v 1935–1940 gg., *MatIsslA* 25, 15-134.

Gajdukevič, V.F. (ed.) 1964. *Ol'vija. Temenos i agora*. Moskva-Leningrad.

Grač, N.L. 1999. *Nekropol' Nimfeja*. St Peterburg.

Johnston, A.W. 1981. Imported Greek Storage Amphorae, in: *Excavations at Kition 4, The Non-Cypriote Pottery*. Nicosia, 37-44.

Johnston, A.W. 1990. Aegina. Aphaia-Tempel 13. The Storage Amphorae, *AA* 1990, 37-64.

Koukouli-Chrisanthaki, Ch. 1979. Thasos, *ADelt* 34 B2, 322-300.

Lazarov, M. 1973. Antični amfori (VI-I pr. n.e.) ot Bolgarskoto Černomorie, *IzvVarna* 9, 3-52.

Lejpunskaja, N.A. 1981. *Keramičeskaja tara iz Ol'vii*. Kiev.

Monachov, S.Ju. 1999. *Grečeskie amfory v Pričernomor'e: kompleksy keramičeskoj tary VII–II vv. do n. e*. Saratov.

Monachov, S.Ju. & E.N. Abrosimov 1993. Novoe o starych materialach iz chersonesskogo nekropolja, *Antičnyj mir i archeologija* 9, 118-159.

Murzin, V.Ju., R. Rolle, W. Hern, S.V. Machortych & V.P. Belozor 1998. *Issledovanija sovmestnoj ukrainsko-nemeckoj archeologičeskoj ekspedicii v 1998 g*. Kiev.

Nicolaou, I. & J.-Y. Empereur 1986. Amphores rhodiennes du musee de Nicosie, in: Empereur & Garlan (eds.) 1986, 513-533.

Papanova, V.A. 1993. *Nekropol' Ol'vii*. Berdjansk.

Paromov, Ja.M. & N.I Sudarev 2000. Novye pogrebenija iz raskopok nekropolja u pos. Peresyp' ("Tiramba"), *Drevnosti Bospora* 3, Moskva, 201-220.

Peristeri-Otatzi, C. 1986. Amphores et timbres amphoriques d'Abdere, in: Empereur & Garlan (eds.) 1986, 491-496.

Roberts, S.R. 1986. The Stoa gutter well. A late archaic deposit in the Athenian Agora, *Hesperia* 55, 1-72.

Ruban, V.V. 1991. Opyt klassifikacii tak nazyvaemych miletskich amfor iz Nižnego Pobuž'ja, *SovA* 2, 182-195.

Salviat, F. 1986. Le vin de Thasos. Amphores, vin et sources écrites, in: Empereur & Garlan (eds.) 1986, 145-196.

Salviat, F. 1990. Vignes et vins anciens de Maronée à Mendé, in: Ch. Koukouli-Chrisanthaki & O. Picard (eds.), *Mnimi D. Lazaridi. Polis kai chora stin archaia Makedonia kai Thraki*. Thessaloniki, 457-476.

Skudnova, V.M. 1988. *Archaičeskij nekropol' Ol'vii*. Leningrad.

Solomonik, E.I. 1993. Napysy na kryms'kych amforach peršych stolit' našoj ery, *ArcheologijaKiev* 2, 102-116.

Abbreviations

AAM	The Anapa Archaeological Museum.
APO	The Archaeological Preserve "Olbia", Parutino.
FM	The Feodosia Museum.
IHMC	The Institute of the History of Material Culture RAS, St Petersburg.
IOSPE	B. Latyschev, *Inscriptiones antiquae orae septentrionalis Ponti Euxini Graecae et Latinae*. Petropolis 1885-1916.
KM	The Kuban Museum, Krasnodar.
NPTCh	National Preserve "Taurian Chersonesos", Sevastopol.
OAM	The Odessa Archaeological Museum.
PMFA	The Pushkin Museum of Fine Arts, Moscow.
SHM	The State Hermitage Museum, St Petersburg.
SMRS	The Simferopol Museum of Regional Studies.

A New Chronology for the Ceramic Stamps of Herakleia Pontike

Vladimir I. Kac

Among the ceramic stamps from excavations of various Greek sites on the Pontic littoral, the most numerous are those from Herakleia, Sinope and Chersonesos – the three Black Sea centres in which extensive and systematic stamping of ceramic containers and roof tiles was practised during the late Classical and Hellenistic periods.

At present we have at our disposal fairly well founded chronological sequences for stamps of Sinope[1] and Chersonesos,[2] which enable us to carry out an effective analysis of their distribution both as regards location and date. But the possibilities for conducting similar studies on imprints from Herakleia are rather limited since the method of chronological classification available at present is flawed by significant imperfections. The objective of the development of the exhaustive scheme of Herakleian stamping is fairly urgent also due to the fact that for the majority of Black Sea sites it is the Herakleian stamps which are the main – and not infrequently the only – evidence of date. Therefore, during S.Ju. Monachov's work on the monograph dedicated to the analysis of assemblages of ceramic containers from the northern Black Sea region,[3] it was deemed necessary for a group of archaeologists from the Department of Greek and Roman Archaeology of the Saratov University to thoroughly analyse the chronological schemes for Herakleian stamping, which existed at the beginning of the 1990s.

The amphorae with englyphic stamps, usually found on the necks, were ascribed to Herakleia Pontike by B.N. Grakov as early as 1920s.[4] The attribution proposed by him, although based only on certain indirect arguments, was consistent with the evidence of the literary tradition and lapidary inscriptions and was therefore accepted by practically all researchers dealing with the history and archaeology of the Black Sea littoral. More surprising were the theses of P. Balabanov who attempted to prove that the place of production of the amphorae with englyphic stamps was Apollonia Pontike.[5] The main argument in favour of this rather eccentric hypothesis was an analysis of a large collection of stamps amounting to over 1300 specimens, which was found during the excavation of a Thracian sanctuary situated 30 km from Apollonia, near the village of Debelt. About 95% of this collection was composed of englyphic stamps. Balabanov believed that this high concentration of stamps suggested direct contacts between the inhabitants of Debelt and the centre where the amphorae were produced. The Greek city of Apollonia, being the closest to the sanctuary, was an obvious candidate.

Thus Balabanov paid tribute to a fairly widespread conception that in the wine-producing centres the majority of the manufactured ceramic containers were used on the site. Were that the case, a high concentration of stamps of a certain type at one site or another may indeed indicate local production. However, we have no grounds to substantiate this argument. Thus, most of the Thasian stamps of the early style, for example, have not been found on the island itself but elsewhere.[6] The density of their distribution on Thasos is in fact several times lower than that which has been recorded in the centres to which Thasian wine was exported.[7]

Let us present another recent example. During the excavation at the settlement of Novopokrovka 1, situated 20 km from Feodosia (ancient Theodosia), an unusually high concentration of stamps for a rural settlement was recorded.[8] As at Debelt, over 90% of these stamps were englyphic. Following Balabanov's logic, one would suppose that amphorae with these stamps were produced in Theodosia. However, a more plausible explanation for the concentration of englyphic stamps near Theodosia, and in addition one further argument in favour of their Herakleian provenance, is supplied by written sources telling us about a special relationship between these two *poleis*.

Apparently realising the implausibility of his own hypothesis, P. Balabanov produced additional arguments to confirm it. The weightiest of these is the assertion that there are "exact parallels as regards both the names and the manufacturing technique between the stamps on amphorae and roof tiles of the local production ... the stamps on the tiles from Apollonia are englyphic".[9] In fact, these parallels are not surprising, since here we are most probably dealing with imported Herakleian tiles and not with ones produced locally.

Balabanov's statement that "the chronology and dynamics of the manufacture of amphorae with englyphic stamps agrees well with the information about the general economic development of Apollonia" is also without validity. In this context we may recall an article written by Balabanov some twenty years ago[10] when he still shared the "orthodox" conception of a Herakleian provenance for the englyphic stamps. He also believed at that time that the chronology of the amphora stamps corresponded well with known historical events not of Apollonia, but of Herakleia. Thus this attempt to revise Grakov's attribution of the englyphic stamps cannot be considered successful. Furthermore, there are no grounds to regard Apollonia as the centre of production of ceramic containers. It is indicative that during the fairly comprehensive excavations at Apollonia itself and in the territories adjoining it, no traces of any extensive ceramic manufacture have been recorded. Meanwhile, judging by the number of fabricants' names recorded on the englyphic stamps of the magistrates, there must have been, in some years, at least 20-30 workshops functioning simultaneously.

It is true that none of the Herakleian *ergasteria*, neither of the late Classical nor of the early Hellenistic period, have yet been discovered. However, the city has been very poorly investigated archaeologically, and the remains of a workshop manufacturing light-clay amphorae of the Roman period were found not long ago in the vicinity of the city.[11] This raises hopes of future discoveries of earlier ceramic workshops.

Besides the attribution of these stamps, B.N. Grakov was also responsible for developing their first chronological classification. However, this has subsequently been refined first by Grakov himself[12] and later by two generations of experts in ceramic epigraphy.[13] Notwithstanding the advances achieved by the efforts of many researchers, no complete and exhaustive sequence of Herakleian stamping had been created by the beginning of the 1990s.[14] The scholar who came closest to the solution of the problem was I.B. Brašinskij who in his two last papers presented the most elaborate classification of Herakleian stamps.

Following tradition, the chronological classification was preceded by a typological analysis of the imprints. All the stamps were divided into seven typological groups:[15]

Group 1: stamps containing a single name, either that of the magistrate or the workshop-owner.

Group 2 (early): stamps with two names, of which one is presented in highly abbreviated form.

Group 2 (late): stamps with two names written in full.

Group 3 (early): stamps with a single name preceded by the preposition ЕПI.

Group 3 (late): stamps with two names of which one is preceded by an eponymous preposition (ЕПI).

Group 4: stamps with a single name (probably that of the fabricant) differing from the 1st group by a number of palaeographic, grammatical and orthographic peculiarities.

Group 5 (early): imprints containing the abbreviation of a single name.

Group 5 (late): stamps with NI or a similar abbreviation.

Group 6: figured stamps.

Group 7: anepigraphic imprints.

This typological classification, though at present the most advanced one, suffers from a number of drawbacks. Firstly, any clear definition of typological signs is absent. The majority of the typological groups listed above are distinguished according to the substance of their legend, but for *Group 6* (figured stamps) the typological sign is the form of the imprint; meanwhile, various figured stamps have been employed practically throughout the entire period of stamping, and by the composition of their legend they differ in no way from the imprints which Brašinskij himself assigned to other typological groups. The figured stamps thus represent no special type being rather variants of other types. Also we must consider the stamps of groups 1 and 4 as two variants of one and the same type containing only the names of the fabricants.

Having considered the correlation between the types of Herakleian amphorae, their capacity and the types of their stamps, Brašinskij divided the Herakleian stamps into three major chronological periods:

Period A: the first and the beginning of the second quarter of the 4th century BC comprising the stamps of typological groups 1, 2 early, 5 early, and 6.

Period B: the second and the beginning of the last quarter of the 4th century BC comprising the stamps of groups 2 late, 3 late, and possibly some of the stamps of group 7 (the other imprints of group 7 probably belonging to period A).

Period C: the end of the 4th to the first quarter of the 3rd century BC comprising the stamps of groups 4 late and 5 late.

Unfortunately, this chronological classification cannot be said to be optimal. Having quite justifiably rejected the previous concept of a rigid sequence in the change of different types of stamps, Brašinskij did not succeed in achieving a detailed chronology either. The first period (*period A*) proved to be fairly varied in its composition, and it would be quite reasonable to subdivide it into a series of successive stages. Undoubtedly, the stamps of the long second period (*period B*) must also be subdivided into separate chronological stages. Moreover, no lists of names of fabricants and magistrates related to each of the periods were presented.[16] Such was the point of departure from which the Saratov research team commenced its work on developing a new chronological classification.

A successful solution to the problems pertaining to classification depends directly on the volume of the initial material and on those principles, which are incorporated into the basis of its systematisation and analysis. Therefore, first of all we built and maintained a database of stamps. In the course of these studies we have adjusted the information included in Volume III of *IOSPE* and this has enabled us to correct readings of many damaged stamps reconstructed by the compilers. In addition, most of the Herakleian stamps found after Volume III had been compiled were studied, and in the course of these studies the following particulars have been observed: between 10 and 15% of the stamps from each collection were represented by unknown dies. In the legends of these, a considerable number of previously unrecorded combinations of names and new names of fabricants and magistrates were encountered. This laborious work resulted in the compilation of the first version of a catalogue of Herakleian stamps containing information on more than 1200 dies. This information made possible a much more extensive application of the data in a synchronous analysis of the stamps. Moreover, practically all of the presently known ceramic assemblages containing series of Herakleian stamps have been considered.

About two hundred different stamps have been identified and grouped according to the content of the legends into three typological groups:

Group 1: stamps containing a single name

Group 2: stamps with two or three names

Group 3: anepigraphic stamps

Analysis of the stamps of group 1 enabled a subdivision into five variants:

Variant A: monograms

Variant B: isolated letters

Variant C: names abbreviated to two or three letters

Variant D: names written in full or in a slightly abbreviated form

Variant E: stamps containing a single name preceded by the preposition EΠI

Although the stamps of this group were in use throughout the entire period of stamping, the stratigraphical, morphological, synchronistic and palaeographic analyses showed that most of them belong either to the initial or to the final phases of stamping. Apart from some dies of variant D and all of the dies of variant E, which undoubtedly contain the names of early eponyms, all the other stamps of typological *Group 1* are the stamps of the fabricants.

Analysis of the stamps of *Group 2* enabled a subdivision into three variants:

Variant A: stamps composed of two names in complete or abbreviated form

Variant B: stamps containing two names one of which is preceded by an eponymous preposition (EΠI)

Variant C: stamps containing three names frequently in an abbreviated or, less frequently, complete form.[17]

A preliminary study of the correlation of stamps of particular types with securely dated ceramic material from complexes confirmed, as already observed, that contemporary stamps prove to be typologically heterogeneous. Thus, some stamps of *Group 1* belonging to the same type, and not infrequently even to the same variant, were encountered among the ceramic complexes from both the beginning of the 4th century BC and the beginning of the third century. Asynchronous are also a few anepigraphic stamps of the typological *Group 3*. The assumption about the long period of coexistence of different variants of stamps of the typological *Group* 2 was also confirmed. At the same time it proved possible to establish a certain logic in the development of the legends of Herakleian stamps, that in turn enabled us to identify three successive periods of stamping of varying length (Fig. 1).

The majority of the stamps of the first period are represented by one-, two- or three-line stamps of typological Group 1 containing single names executed by means of rectangular, less frequently of figured (leaf-like) dies. Representations rarely accompany the names. Very few of the stamps of this period contain names in highly abbreviated form. I.B. Brašinskij and B.A. Vasilenko suggested that these contain the names of both fabricants and magistrates. However, a collation of these names and the presence of a number of complexes comprising only stamps of typological Group 118 testify that during that early period stamping had a non-public character but was conducted exclusively by the fabricants. The list of workshop-owners of the Early Fabricants' Group (EFG) contains at present about 50 names. Moreover, the workshops of 19 of these "fabricants" were active only within the EFG, while the others were active also under the magistrates of MG I (cf. appendix).

Magistrates

The longest period is the second – the *Magistrates' Period*. At present, the list of Herakleian officials who controlled the manufacture of amphorae already includes 90 names. For 40 of the eponyms, parallel employment of dies of differing variants of typological *Group 2* has been recorded. The practice of using an eponymous preposition with the name of a magistrate was finally established during the last three decades of this period. Therefore, the grouping of the magistrates within this lengthy period was carried out by means of the synchronistic method taking into account the set of the combinations of the names of magistrates and manufacturers. In order to verify the results obtained, an analysis of numerous complexes containing magisterial stamps was carried out.

As a result, all of the Herakleian magistrates known up till now have been preliminarily subdivided into five successive chronological groups.

In the first *Magistrates' Group* (MG I) 13 officials were included (cf. the appendix). The stamps of the earliest of them (Aristokles and Orthesilas)

Period	Group	Chronological limits (BC)	Number of fabricants or magistrates	Total number of dies	% of figured dies	% of dies with ΕΠΙ	% of dies with emblem
I	EFG	415-400	49	130	5	0	15
II	MG I	390s	13	114	0	7	0
	MG II	end of 390s-middle of 370s	19	347	7	55	8
	MG III	end of 370s-middle of 350s	17	268	17	66	42
	MG IV	middle of 350s-beginning of 330s	21	213	18	17	54
	MG V	330s-310s	22	52	0	98	0
III	LFG	end of the 4th to c. 275	32	82	7	0	3

Fig. 1. A new typology and chronology of Herakleian stamping.

usually contain the names in the complete or slightly abbreviated form. An eponymous preposition before the name is fairly uncommon. In the stamps of the subsequent officials of this group, these were practically absent. At this stage, two-line stamps containing two names each, of which one was written in a highly abbreviated form were widely employed. Vasilenko was of the opinion that the latter names belonged to the fabricants,[19] but this assumption has not been confirmed: the names abbreviated to two, occasionally three letters, are characteristic of most of the eponyms included in MG I.

The majority of the presently known dies of this group bear a combination of the names of a magistrate and a fabricant. However at the initial stage of the eponymous stamping, the traditions of the preceding *Fabricants' Group* still continued. The practice became fairly widespread of accompanying a magisterial stamp (variants D and E of typological *Group 1*) with a separate fabricant's stamp not infrequently of the same die as the isolated imprints of the EFG. The shape of the stamps varies: while rectangular stamps predominate, there are nevertheless a few figured ones (round and cross-shaped). Emblems were used during this period mostly in some fabricant's stamps, which accompany the stamps of magistrates.

The magistrates of this group are subdivided into two subgroups. *Subgroup A* comprises in addition to Aristokles and Orthesilas, three other magistrates, the names of which are highly abbreviated: ᾽Ια(...), Λυ(...), Πα(...).

A characteristic feature of this subgroup is a relatively large number of dies recorded for each magistrate (from 10 to 23).

Subgroup B now includes eight magistrates, the names of which are highly abbreviated and during whose office only a few (not more than five) workshops were active. It may seem that during this period, a considerable recession in the production of ceramic containers occurred in Herakleia. However, it was apparently not that serious. Since the practice of magisterial stamping had still not been completely established, the possibility cannot be ruled out that the annual control over the ceramic production was exercised not by one official, as was later the case, but rather by a board of magistrates. Indirectly, this is suggested by a stamp found in Kytaia,[20] in the three-line legend of which the magistrate's name Φι(...) is followed by one more name Ἡρ(...) known in other stamps also as the name of an eponym. This assumption would explain the numerous cases where the narrowly dated burial complexes contain both the amphorae stamped by early magistrates [Ἴα(...), Λυ(...), Πα(...)] and jars marked by the eponyms of *Subgroup B* of MG II [Μολοσσός, Αἰθέρ(...), Ἀρίστων, Ἀλκέτας, Στύφων].[21] During the time span between the activities of these two series of magistrates, at least 15 other officials must have been working, but the total length of this period seems to be considerably less than a decade and a half.

A characteristic trait of the stamps of the officials who controlled the ceramic production in Herakleia throughout the subsequent half a century (MG II-MG IV) is the use of the same magistrates' names both with and without an eponymous preposition.

In the *Magistrates' Group II* (MG II) 19 officials are enumerated. While in the legends of the earliest of these, the newly reappeared eponymous preposition is rather uncommon, by the end of this group it is already present on half of the stamps. Practically all of the magistrates from this group have stamps on which their names like those of the officials of *Subgroup B* of MG I are written in a strongly abbreviated form. However, the slightly abbreviated names are predominant, and gradually the complete form of the names becomes prevalent. Half of the magistrates are represented both by rectangular and figured stamps (round, triangular, or rhomboid). Stamp devices are relatively uncommon.

As a working hypothesis, we may divide the magistrates of this group into two subgroups of unequal number. *Subgroup A* is constituted by the first six magistrates during whose office the recession in the ceramic manufacture observed in the precedent decade was being gradually overcome: while at the beginning of the period, there were one or two workshops active, down to the end of the subgroup the number of such workshops increased to six or seven. An eponymous preposition appears only on solitary stamps.

The following stage, which is linked to the 13 magistrates of *Subgroup B*, constitutes the period of the highest amphora production in Herakleia. Each series of a particular magistrate is represented by 15 to 50 dies. This facilitates the application of synchronous analysis to determine the sequence of the magistrates. An exception is the eponym Λαίσας known from one die only. However, the finds of the amphorae stamped with his name in burial contexts containing jars marked by eponyms of the end of MG II[22] compels us to include also this magistrate in the group under consideration. In the majority of the stamps of *Subgroup B,* the name of the official is introduced with a preposition ΕΠΙ. Emblems are found in single examples.

Attributed to the *Magistrates' Group III* (MG III) were 17 eponyms (cf. appendix). In two thirds of the dies of this group the name of the official is preceded by ΕΠΙ. The use of figured stamps becomes more widespread. For some officials they amount to 20-40%, and in the case of Karakydes even to 100%. In the majority of the series, emblems are fairly uncommon, although on the stamps of five official emblems, (apparently eponymous) devices occur repeatedly (a grape for Karakydes, Skythas and Philinos; a crescent for Dionysios II; a club for Andronikos). The volume of the production decreased slightly under these magistrates, but it still remained fairly high, although there was considerable fluctuation throughout the entire period. The number of known dies for individual magistrates varies from four to 40.

Preliminarily, seven officials have been grouped in *Subgroup A.* The first six of these were placed fairly reliably within this subgroup on the basis of the accompanying fabricants' names and their amphorae having been found together in the same narrowly dated burial complexes. The last magistrate Κρυπτ(...) is known only from one die where he appears together with the fabricant Euarchos, whose activities came to the end under the magistrates of the beginning of *Group III.*

The sequence of the magistrates of *Subgroup B* has also been reliably identified because the majority of them are represented by a considerable number of dies. Exceptions are two eponyms: Ἔχεμος and Κέραυνος. The first is known on three dies and the second on only one. However, due to the fact that the first of them is linked through one of the dies with the fabricant Eukleion and the second with Sosibios, whose workshops were active only during MG III, these two magistrates can also be included quite reliably into the group under consideration.

In addition, a new element appeared in the practice of Herakleian stamping at this stage, which continues on the stamps of the subsequent group MG IV: in almost half of the eponyms we encounter solitary stamps containing only the name of the magistrate. Judging by two known intact amphorae, these magistrates' stamps, in contrast to similar imprints of eponyms of MG I, were not always accompanied by separate fabricants' stamps.[23]

Magistrates' Group IV (MG IV) includes 21 officials (see appendix). Here, a much more limited use of the preposition ΕΠΙ is characteristic: it is present only on 17% of the dies. It is indicative that this percentage is considerably higher on stamps of the later magistrates from this group. The employment of figured stamps also became a rather uncommon phenomenon, while more than half of the stamps had an emblem.

The sequence of the four earliest magistrates from this group (*Subgroup A*) can be reliably identified. During the office of these magistrates, as well as under the six eponyms of the next subgroup (*Subgroup B*), from 10 to 20 workshops were active. Exceptional is Apollonios I on whose stamps the names of only four fabricants have as yet been recorded. These four, though, include Euphraios whose workshop was active only under the magistrates of the end of *Group III* and the beginning of *Group IV*.

Another 11 officials are included in *Subgroup C*. They are known only from single imprints in which their names are recorded in combination with the names of fabricants typical for group MG IV. Probably, only some of them belonged to the final stage of MG IV, while the others may have been synchronous with the eponyms of *Subgroup B*. Of special interest are the two latest magistrates Arkesas and Nikokles, who are known as yet only from tile stamps.

Finally, 22 eponyms are attributed to the last *Magistrates' Group V* (MG V) (see appendix). In practically all the stamps of these magistrates, the names are preceded by the preposition ΕΠΙ. All of the stamps are rectangular and devoid of any emblems. The majority of the officials from this group are known from a limited number of stamps executed with one or two dies. The sequence of the nine magistrates from *Subgroup A* is relatively reliable. Since the remaining 13 eponyms are known only from single stamps, their names are only listed alphabetically among *Subgroup B*.

The Late Fabricants' Group (LFG)

After magisterial stamping had ceased, ceramic containers still continued to be marked for some time (*Period III*) with stamps containing a single name sometimes in slightly abbreviated form (typological variant 1D). In some instances they are highly abbreviated to one or two letters only (typological variants 1A and 1B). Also from the same period are some of the anepigraphic stamps of the typological *Group 3*. At present, no one questions that in all these cases we are dealing with the stamps of the workshop-owners. These *ergasteriarchoi* constitute therefore the *Late Fabricants' Group* (LFG). This group was first distinguished and isolated by I.B. Brašinskij, who noted peculiar letter patterns characteristic of the later stages of the script development (lunar sigma and some elements of cursive writing). The stamps are mostly of the rectangular shape although a few figured examples have also been recorded. Brašinskij pointed out that the presence of a frame surrounding the inscription is characteristic of this group.[24] However, the conclusion is far from indisputable, since some framed stamps undoubtedly dating to an earlier period are known. Also of note are some other traits peculiar to the last stage of Herakleian stamping: the increased number of relief imprints uncommon during the previous periods as well as the habit of stamping the amphora handles. At present, it is possible to identify about 30 names of fabricants of LFG (see appendix).

Along with the development of a comprehensive relative chronology of Herakleian stamps, we have attempted to determine the absolute dates of the chronological periods and subgroups more precisely. The primary method employed in establishing an absolute chronology was an analysis of complexes where Herakleian amphorae have been found together with stamped jars from other centres, particularly those of Sinope and Thasos, with more developed chronologies.

All scholars now agree that the stamping of ceramic containers in Herakleia started at the turn of the 5th to the 4th century BC. As proof of this date, numerous finds of stamps of the earliest Herakleian magistrates together with the earliest emblem-free stamps of Thasos can be cited.[25]

Perhaps the most informative complex of this kind is the Olbian storage-cellar of 1947. Here, a fairly representative assemblage consisting of 49 stamped Herakleian and eight Thasian amphorae has been recorded.[26] Most of the Herakleian amphorae bear manufacturers' stamps of the EFG. However, almost twenty of the latest jars prepared by the first magistrates of the MG I Aristokles and Orthesilas. The Thasian jars are marked with the earliest emblem-free stamps of chronological *Group 1* datable to the beginning of the 390s BC. Thus we have good reasons to ascribe the earliest magisterial stamps of Herakleia to the very beginning of the 4th century BC.

The above dating can be verified by an analysis of the amphora material from the *dromos* of the stone vault at Kurgan no. 8 of the "Five Brothers" barrow-group in the necropolis of Elizavetovskoe. Here, nine stamped amphorae of Herakleia bearing the names of four different magistrates along with five morphologically uniform Sinopean jars were unearthed, of which one has a stamp of the *astynomos* Chabrias.

The dating of this complex is disputed. I.B. Brašinskij who was the first to publish it, supposed that the Sinopean amphorae were the latest material here and that the mention of the *astynomos* Chabrias who was magistrate around 325 BC should date the erection of the kurgan.[27] A different date for the complex was proposed by B.A. Vasilenko, who applied his own chronology for the Herakleian stamps to the ones found here and assigned the deposit to the beginning of the second quarter of the 4th century.[28] Brašinskij did not agree with this proposal, although he admitted that his original dating was too narrow and that it could be expanded to cover the entire third quarter of the century.[29]

Curiously, both of the proposed dates proved to be justifiable, as shown by the recent re-examination of the assemblage by S.Ju. Monachov. In fact, the Herakleian amphorae from Kurgan no. 8 represent a rather long time span, and they can reasonably be divided into two chronological blocks: five vessels of type II were produced under the magistrates Andronikos and Lysitheos of MG III, while four jars of the late variety of type III bearing the stamps of the magistrates Archippos and Peisistratos belong to the beginning of MG V.[30] The time span between these two blocks amounts to about 30 years.

The question arises therefore, which of these two blocks the Sinopean *astynomos* Chabrias should be linked to? Referring to N.F. Fedoseev's article, then in print, Monachov dated the activities of Chabrias to 345-340 BC and supposed that his amphora should be contemporary with the jars of Lysitheos. However, when the article he was referring to was published, it proved to date Chabrias to the end of 350s.[31] Moreover, from the moment of the appearance of Fedoseev's chronology of Sinopean stamping,[32] his absolute chronology was criticised, and the suggestion was made to lower his dates by 15-20 years.[33] Thus in the most recent chronological system developed by N. Conovici, Chabrias is assigned to the very beginning of the chronological *Group II* and dated to the end of the 330s.[34]

The acceptance of this date would settle the issue. The Sinopean amphorae from Kurgan no. 8 are contemporary not with the earlier but with the later group of Herakleian amphorae bearing the stamps of Archippos and Peisistratos. They consequently have to be dated to the end of the 330s as well. Taking into account that about 70 officials of MG I-MG IV preceded these two magistrates of MG V, the date of the beginning of magisterial stamping in Herakleia must be the turn of the 5th to the 4th century BC.

However, as stated above, the first magisterial stamps in Herakleia are preceded by a period of stamping with fabricants' names. Defining its length would set up the initial date of the stamping of ceramic containers. The answer to this question was obtained by studying the most representative collections of early Herakleian stamps from the excavations in Chersonesos and Kerkinitis.

Under consideration were all of the stamps of the EFG and the stamps of the five first magistrates of MG I (*Subgroup A*) found there. In Chersonesos 337 stamps of the EFG and 121 stamps of the first stage of the magisterial stamping were registered (the ratio being 2.8:1). A similar picture is provided by the stamps from Kerkinitis: 228 and 90 stamps respectively (the ratio being 2.5:1). As it seems unlikely that the density of the distribution of stamps throughout the first period (EFG) differed significantly from that of the first five magistrates of *Subgroup A* of MG I, it is quite reasonable to suppose that the stamps of the EFG must have been in use respectively 2.5-3 times longer, i.e. during a period of at least 12-15 years. We then arrive at 415-410 BC, which in my opinion, is the most likely date for the beginning of stamping amphorae in Herakleia.

Incidentally, such a date is quite consistent with the economical and political history of Herakleia during the last quarter of the 5th century BC.

The *polis* had by then become one of the largest producers of marketable wine. Naturally, the Herakleians could hardly overlook the markets of the various cities in the northern Black Sea area, and it is in the last quarter of the 5th century BC that great opportunities for the commercial penetration of that region were opened due to the reduction of the trade and political activities of the Athenians during the course of the Peloponnesian War.[35] One can hardly consider as accidental the closeness in time of such important events in the life of Herakleia as the successful repulse of the siege by the Athenian fleet, the establishment of the colony of Tauric Chersonesos in 422/421,[36] and the mass exportation of Herakleian wine to the northern Black Sea region. The appearance of the practice of amphora stamping in Herakleia during precisely this period thus seems quite natural.

The turn of the 5th to the 4th century became the starting point for the establishing of the absolute chronological limits of particular magisterial groups (Fig. 1), which were estimated according to the number of the eponyms represented in each of the groups. Since by now we know of 91 magistrates who controlled the ceramic production in Herakleia, the terminal date for magisterial stamping must be assigned to the end of the 4th century BC. Some time ago, P. Balabanov attempted to link the abolition of the institution of eponyms and the shift to the fabricants' stamps of the LFG with the general weakening of the central power in the course of the internal struggle unleashed after the death of the tyrant Dionysios in 305 BC.[37] It still remains unclear whether there was such a link, but there is no doubt that the two phenomena were fairly close in time.

On the other hand, the hypothesis of Balabanov about the cessation of the amphora stamping immediately after Herakleia was seized by the troops of Lysimachos in 285 BC can hardly be accepted. Some archaeologically complete amphorae with the stamps of the LFG which are far from being the latest were found lying on the floor of the buildings in the Area U7 at the settlement of Panskoe I which perished in the 270s BC.[38] The very latest stamps of the group are well represented among the materials from the settlement of Elizavetovskoe, which was deserted in the late 260s. Thus, the cessation of stamping ceramic containers in Herakleia should be dated between 275 and 265 BC.

What has been presented here is only the first version of the chronological classification of the stamps of Herakleia. Most of the names of the fabricants of EFG and LFG have been identified, and 91 eponyms have been divided into five magisterial groups. At the same time, we have not yet been able to verify a number of single amphora stamps containing magisterial names mentioned in some publications and reports. These have not been included in our list. Undoubtedly, most of these names result from incorrect reading of damaged stamps. The possibility cannot, however, be ruled out, that some of them will supplement our list of the magistrates, thus permitting the completion of the stamping scheme of Herakleia Pontike.

Notes

1. Fedoseev 1994; 1999; Conovici 1997; 1998.
2. Kac 1994.
3. Monachov 1999.
4. Grakov 1926.
5. Balabanov 2001.
6. Garlan 1999, 1.
7. Kac 1996, 52.
8. Gavrilov & Fedoseev 2002, 49-50.
9. Balabanov 2001, 21.
10. Balabanov 1985.
11. Arsen'eva, Kassab Tezgor & Naumenko 1997.
12. Grakov 1955, 15 ff.
13. Brašinskij 1965; 1980; 1984; Vasilenko 1970; 1974; Balabanov 1985; Pavličenko 1992.
14. Cf. Pavličenko 1999, 13-21.
15. Brašinskij 1980, 38-41.
16. Later, in the appendix to N. Pavličenko's paper (1999, 18-19) a list of Herakleian magistrates was presented which contained 69 names. However, this list is not complete and the magistrates are not divided into chronological groups.
17. At present, only a few stamps of this variant are known. The third name is probably the patronymic of the workshop-owners, although one cannot rule out the possibility that in one case we are dealing with two strongly abbreviated names of magistrates (cf. note 20).
18. Monachov 1999, 160-248.
19. Vasilenko 1974, 6.
20. Stamp: ΗΡΑΚΙΛΕΔΑΦΙΙΗΡ: Kytaia 1982. Inventory no. A 1/5.
21. Burial 72 (1862) in Kerch, Kurgans no. 1 near the village of Pribugskoe and 4x and 4s near the village of Petuchovka (Monachov 1999, 258-260, 272-274, 276-277).
22. The barrows situated near the village of Krasnoflotovskoe and in the Sivash area (Monachov 1999, 303, 311).
23. Monachov 1999, pls. 113.3, 115.2.
24. Brašinskij 1965, 26.
25. Monachov 1999, 193-238.
26. Vinogradov 1972, 47; Brašinskij 1965 22-24; Monachov 1999, 194-201.
27. Brašinskij 1961, 178-186.
28. Vasilenko 1970, 17; 1971, 247.
29. Brašinskij 1980, 43.
30. Monachov 1999, 358-362.
31. Fedoseev 1999, 41.
32. Fedoseev 1992; 1994, 189-190.
33. Turovskij 1997, 219; Conovici 1997, 153.
34. Conovici 1998, 26, 51.
35. Frolov 1974, 128; Saprykin 1981, 176; Kac 1990, 105.
36. Tjumenev 1938.
37. Balabanov 1985, 18.
38. Monachov 1999, 517-519.

Appendix

Early Fabricants Group (EFG): the late 5th to early 4th century BC

Fabricants engaged within the EFG only	*Fabricants active within the EFG and the MG I*	
1. Ἀγάθων I	20. Ἀργεῖος	39. Λάκων
2. Αἰάκης	21. Ἀρίστιππος	40. Μόσχος
3. Ἀρίσταρχος	22. Ἀρίστων	41. Νόσσος
4. Γῆρυς	23. Ἀρχέλας	42. Ὄνασος
5. Ἐργασίων	24. Ἀρχέστρατος	43. Πυρονίδας
6. Ἑρμαγόρας	25. Δαμάτριος	44. Σατυρίων
7. Ἑρμᾶντος	26. Δᾶος	45. Σιλανός
8. Εὐῶπις	27. Διοκλῆς	46. Σωτήρ
9. Εὐφράνωρ	28. Διονύσιος	47. Τιμόλυκος
10. Κώκημος	29. Εὔαρχος	48. Χίων
11. Μέχων	30. Εὐκλείων	49. Ὠφελίων
12. Μίκκος	31. Εὐπάμων	
13. Νικασίων	32. Εὐρύδαμος	
14. Ῥαμφίας	33. Ἡραίων	
15. Σάμυος	34. Ἡρακλείδας	
16. Σύρος	35. Θεογένης	
17. Τιμάσανδρος	36. Θεόξενος	
18. Φώκριτος	37. Καλλίας	
19. Χαρέσιος	38. Κρομνίτης	

Eponyms of MG I: 390s BC

Subgroup A		*Subgroup B*
1. Ὀρθεσίλας	6. Θε(...)	11. Λευ(...)
2. Ἀριστοκλῆς	7. Κόας	12. Τυ(...)
3. Ἴα(...)	8. Νικ(...)	13. Φι(...)
4. Πα(...)	9. Ἡρ(...)	
5. Λυ(...)	10. Εὐκ(...)	

Eponyms of MG II: the end of the 390s to the middle of the 370s BC

Subgroup A		*Subgroup B*
1. Βόταχος	7. Διονύσιος I	14. Εὐγειτίων
2. Ἀθανόδωρ(...)	8. Μολοσσός	15. Ὧρος
3. Μένιππος	9. Αἰθέρ(...)	16. Κερκῖνος
4. Σωσίος	10. Ἀρίστων	17. Κῦρος
5. Κρωμνι(...)	11. Ἀλκέτας	18. Παυσανίας
6. Εὐπιτίων	12. Στύφων	19. Λαίσας
	13. Δεινόμαχος	

Eponyms of MG III: the end of the 370s to the middle of the 350s BC

Subgroup A   *Subgroup B*

1. Λύκων	8. Καλλίας	15. Ἔχεμος
2. Διονύσιος II	9. Ἀνδρόνικος	16. Εὔξενος
3. Ἀγνόδαμος	10. Λυσίθεος	17. Κέραυνος
4. Καρακύδης	11. Εὐφρόνιος	
5. Σκύθας	12. Φιλῖνος	
6. Μᾶτρις	13. Μνασίμαχος	
7. Κρυπτ(...)	14. Σάτυρος	

Eponyms of MG IV: the middle of
the 350s to the beginning of the 330s BC

Subgroup A   *Subgroup B*   *Subgroup C*

1. Ἀμφίτας	5. Ἀπολλώνιος	11. Ἀγάθων
2. Βάκχος	6. Μενοίτιος	12. Ἔλυρος
3. Ἡρακλείδας	7. Δαμάτριος	13. Θεώνικος
4. Ἀγασίλλος	8. Σπίνταρος	14. Μαρονίδης
	9. Εὐρυφῶν	15. Μελάνοππος
	10. Φιλόξενος	16. Σιλανός
		17. Σῖμος
		18. ?Στρός (Ἴστρος?)
		19. Φυλεύς
		20. Ἀρκέσας
		21. Νικοκλῆς

Eponyms of MG V: the 330s to the 310s BC

Subgroup A   *Subgroup B*

1. Ἄνταγος	10. Γέρος	19. Λεύκιππος
2. Ἀμφίκρατος	11. Δημήτριος	20. Πίνδαρος
3. Λεόφαντος	12. Δημοκράτης	21. Πυθοκλη(...)
4. Ἄρχιππος	13. Θέμιστ(...)	22. Φώκριτος
5. Πεισίστρατος	14. Θεόκυρος	
6. Ἀπολλώνιος	15. Θεόπροπος	
7. Κρόνιος	16. Θεύδορος	
8. Ἰφικράτης	17. Κλισ(...)	
9. Ματρόδωρος	18. Ληώδας	

Late Fabricants Group (LFG): the end of the 4th
to the first quarter of the 3rd century BC

1. Ἀριστοκράτης
2. Ἄψογος
3. Βάκχιος
4. Βατίων
5. Γλαῦκος
6. Γόργιος
7. Δαμόξενος
8. Διοκλῆς I
9. Διονύσιος II
10. Δοῦλος
11. Εἰρηναῖος

12. Ἐπικράτης
13. Ἐράτων
14. Ἔτυμος
15. Ἡρακλέδας
16. Ἡράκλειτος
17. Ἡρακλέων
18. Ἡρόδωρος
19. Κερκῖνος
20. Μεημ(...)
21. Μένης
22. Μένιππος

23. Μηνητος
24. Νι(...)
25. Νικόστρατος
26. Πασιάδας
27. Πομ(...)
28. Πυθιον(...)
29. Σωκράτης
30. Σωτήρ II
31. Τι(...)
32. Φιλίσκος I
33. Φιλότιμος

Bibliography

Arsen'eva, T., D. Kassab Tezgor & S. Naumenko 1997. Un depotoir d'atelier d'amphores a pate clare. Commerce entre Heraclee du Pont et Tanais a l'epoque Romaine, *Anatolia Antiqua*. V, 187-198.

Balabanov, P. 1985. Analiz i datirovanie amfornych pečatej Geraklei Pontiki, *Tracia Pontica* 2, 12-23.

Balabanov, P. 2001. Englifičeskie pečati na amforach: novaja postanovka problemy, *Ol'vija ta antičnij svit*. Odessa, 20-21.

Brašinskij, I.B. 1961. Amfory iz raskopok Elizavetovskogo mogil'nika v 1959 godu, *SovA* 3, 178-186.

Brašinskij, I.B. 1965. Keramičeskie klejma Geraklei Pontijskoj, *NumEpigr* 5, 10-27.

Brašinskij, I.B. 1980. *Grečeskij keramičeskij import na Nižnem Donu v V-III vv. do n.e.* Leningrad.

Brašinskij, I.B, 1984. Voprosy chronologii keramičeskich klejm i tipologičeskogo razvitija amfor Geraklei Pontijskoj, *NumEpigr* 14, 3-22.

Conovici, N. 1997. Problèmes de la chronologie des timbres sinopéens, *Pontica* 30, 117-154.

Conovici, N. 1998. *Histria VIII. Les timbres amphoriques* 2. *Sinope*. Bucarest-Paris.

Fedoseev, N.F. 1992. Itogi i perspektivy izučenija sinopskich keramičeskich klejm, in: *Grečeskie amfory*. Saratov, 147-163.

Fedoseev, N.F. 1994. Chronologija sinopskich magistratskich klejm, in: *Problemy skifo-sarmatskoj archeologii Severnogo Prichernomor'ja. Tezisy dokladov konferencii*. Zaporož'e, 188-190.

Fedoseev, N.F. 1999. Classification des timbres astynomiques de Sinope, in: Garlan (ed.) 1999, 27-48.

Frolov E.D. 1974. Tiranija v Geraklee Pontijskoj, *Antičnyj mir i archeologija* 2, 117-139.

Garlan, Y. 1999. *Les timbres amphoriques de Thasos* I. *Timbres Protothasiens et Thasiens Anciens*. Paris.

Garlan, Y. (ed.) 1999. *Production et commerce des amphores anciennes en Mer Noire*. Aix-en-Provence.

Gavrilov, A.V. & N.F. Fedoseev 2002. Amfornye klejma iz antičnych pamjatnikov okrugi Feodosii, in: *Bospor Kimmerijskij, Pont i varvarskij mir v period antičnosti i srednevekov'ja*. Kerch, 44-59.

Grakov, B.N. 1926. Englifičeskie klejma na gorlach nekotorych ellinističeskich ostrodonnych amfor, *Trudy Gosudarstvennogo Istoričeskogo Muzeja* 1, 165-206.

Grakov, B.N. 1939. Gerakleja Pontijskaja. Klejma na gorlach amfor, na kalipterach i keramidach, IOSPE III. Archives of the Institute of Archaeology RAS, R-2, no. 2179.

Kac, V.I. 1990. Emporij Chersones, *Antičnyj mir i archeologija* 7, 97-111.

Kac, V.I. 1994. *Keramičeskie klejma Chersonesa Tavričeskogo*. Saratov.

Kac, V.I. 1996. Pričiny perechoda ot "rannich" k "pozdnim" ottiskam v praktike fasosskogo klejmenija, in: *Drevnee Pričernomor'e. III čtenija pamjati professora P.O. Karyškovskogo*. Odessa, 51-53.

Monachov, S.Ju. 1999. *Grečeskie amfory v Pričernomor'e. Kompleksy keramičeskoj tary VII-II vv. do n.e*. Saratov.

Pavličenko, N.A. 1992. K voprosu o vremeni bytovanija predloga ЕΠΙ v geraklejskich klejmach, in: *Grečeskie amfory*. Saratov, 138-147.

Pavličenko, N. 1999. Les timbres amphoriques d'Héraclée du Pont: bilan et perspectives de recherché, in: Garlan (ed.) 1999, 13-19.

Saprykin, S.J. 1979. Ekonomičeskie osnovy kolonizacionnoj dejatel'nosti Geraklei Pontijskoj, *Problemy grečeskoj kolonizacii Severnogo i Vostočnogo Pričernomor'ja*. Tbilisi. 177-178.

Turovskij, E.Ja. 1997. K voprosu ob absoljutnych datach sinopskich klejm, in: *Nikonij i antichnyj mir Severnogo Pričernomor'ja*. Odessa, 217-220.

Tjumenev, A.I. 1938. Chersonesskie etjudy, 1. K voprosu o vremeni i obstojatel'stvach vozniknovenija Chersonesa, *VDI* 2, 245-275.

Vasilenko, B.A. 1970. Zametki o geraklejskich klejmach, *SovA* 3, 217-224.

Vasilenko, B.A. 1971. K voprosu o datirovke sinopskich klejm, *SovA* 3, 245-250.

Vasilenko, B.A. 1974. O charaktere klejmenija geraklejskich amfor v pervoj polovine IV v. do n.e., *NumEpigr* 11, 3-38.

Vinogradov, Ju.G. 1972. Keramičeskie klejma ostrova Fasos, *NumEpigr* 10, 3-63.

Some Reflections on the Amphora Stamps with the Name of Amastris

Vladimir F. Stolba

As long ago as 1917, the amphora stamps bearing the legend ΑΜΑΣΤΡΙΟΣ became known after E.M. Pridik's publication of the Hermitage collection.[1] It took, however, almost three quarters of a century to bring together the isolated evidence about the old finds[2] and the newly discovered stamps, as well as to systematize them and supply them with corresponding historical comments. In this work particular merit is due to A.N. Ščeglov, who first considered the problem of their chronology based on highly diverse evidence, including an analysis of the archaeological contexts of the finds.

Since the appearance of Ščeglov's paper in the supplement to *Bulletin de Correspondance Hellénique*[3] and his later article written jointly with V.I. Kac and V.I. Pavlenkov,[4] no significant addition to these materials has been recorded. At present, we know of nineteen stamps from excavations in Kallatis,[5] Olbia, Pantikapaion, Gorgippia, the settlement of Elizavetovskoe in the delta of the Don River,[6] and from the territory of the Chersonesean *polis* in western Crimea. Surprisingly, to my knowledge, such stamps have not been reported from outside the limits of the northern and western littorals of the Black Sea.

Three almost completely preserved vessels from excavations in the *chora* of Chersonesos in north-western Crimea provide an idea of the shapes of the amphorae marked by these stamps, indicating not only the hands of different potters, but also their adherence to differing traditions of manufacture. The first of these jars was found in building U6 at the settlement of Panskoe I and presents an individual type (type 1), the shape of which, according to Kac, Pavlenkov and Ščeglov, resembles the amphorae of Sinope. The two others (types 2 and 3) undoubtedly imitate some vessels of Herakleia. Both of these varieties are characterised by a distinctive rounded rim with a two-stepped faceting underneath.

Besides varying palaeographical features, the legends of the stamps are not especially diverse. Despite I.B. Zeest's belief that ΑΜΑΣΤΡΙΟΣ must be understood as the name of a city founded by Amastris,[7] A.N. Ščeglov recognised it as the name of the queen herself.[8] Correspondingly, the only possible candidate for this amphora production seems to be the city of Amastris, founded by the widow of Dionysios of Herakleia by the synoecism of the four coastal settlements of Tieion, Sesamos, Kromna and Kytoros. To explain the remarkable combination of technological and morphological features, Ščeglov supposed that Kytoros, which according to Strabon (12.3.10) had previously been an *emporion* of Sinope, could also have supplied (along with Herakleia) the newly created *polis* with skilled potters.[9]

In contrast to the proposed attribution, which seems to have won general acceptance, the question of the chronology of this group of amphorae became a matter of dispute. Presupposing that amphorae could be stamped with the name of Amastris only during her lifetime, these jars were dated to the period from 300 to 284 BC,[10] when the queen fell victim to her own sons.[11] This seemed to correspond to the archaeological contexts of the finds, in particular the presumed dating of the monumental building U6 at the Panskoe I settlement to 300 to the 270s BC.

However, as early as 1991, I.T. Kruglikova and S.Ju. Saprykin proposed a later date in their publication of a newly found stamp from the country house on land plot no. 57 near Chersonesos.[12] Based on the fact that Amastris' name appears exclusively with the title ΒΑΣΙΛΙΣΣΗ on the coins struck in the newly founded *polis* during her lifetime, these authors assign all the stamps to the period after her death. Taking into account the morphologically similar Herakleian amphorae of the same fabric, they would not have started later than 281 BC, when the city became independent of Herakleia for a short while. In the opinion of the authors, the Sinopean shapes of the amphorae in question must have been characteristic already of the next period of the city's history, their production having been continued until the city became a part of the Pontic Kingdom at the end of the 260s or beginning of the 250s. They found the time span of fifteen years proposed by Ščeglov to be too short to explain the aforementioned peculiarities of the morphology of the amphorae and the typology of the stamps, which will also be discussed at greater length below.

In this case the following question arises: How should the legend of the stamps be understood? This appears to be the most vulnerable point in the argumentation of Kruglikova and Saprykin, who are led to the conclusion that the image of Amastris must have been considered as some kind of symbol of the city. In their view, the legend reflected in the stamp was "the name of the city as a symbol of the deified ruler who, in the capacity of an honorary magistrate, certified by her power the high quality of the products and the public standard of the containers".[13]

The above-mentioned circumstances induce us to scrutinise once again the available evidence which may be decisive in establishing the chronology and attribution of this group of pottery.

Shape of the jars

Type 1 (Fig. 1.1, 4). Kac, Pavlenkov and Ščeglov consider the amphorae of Sinope as the most probable source of inspiration for the general shape, size

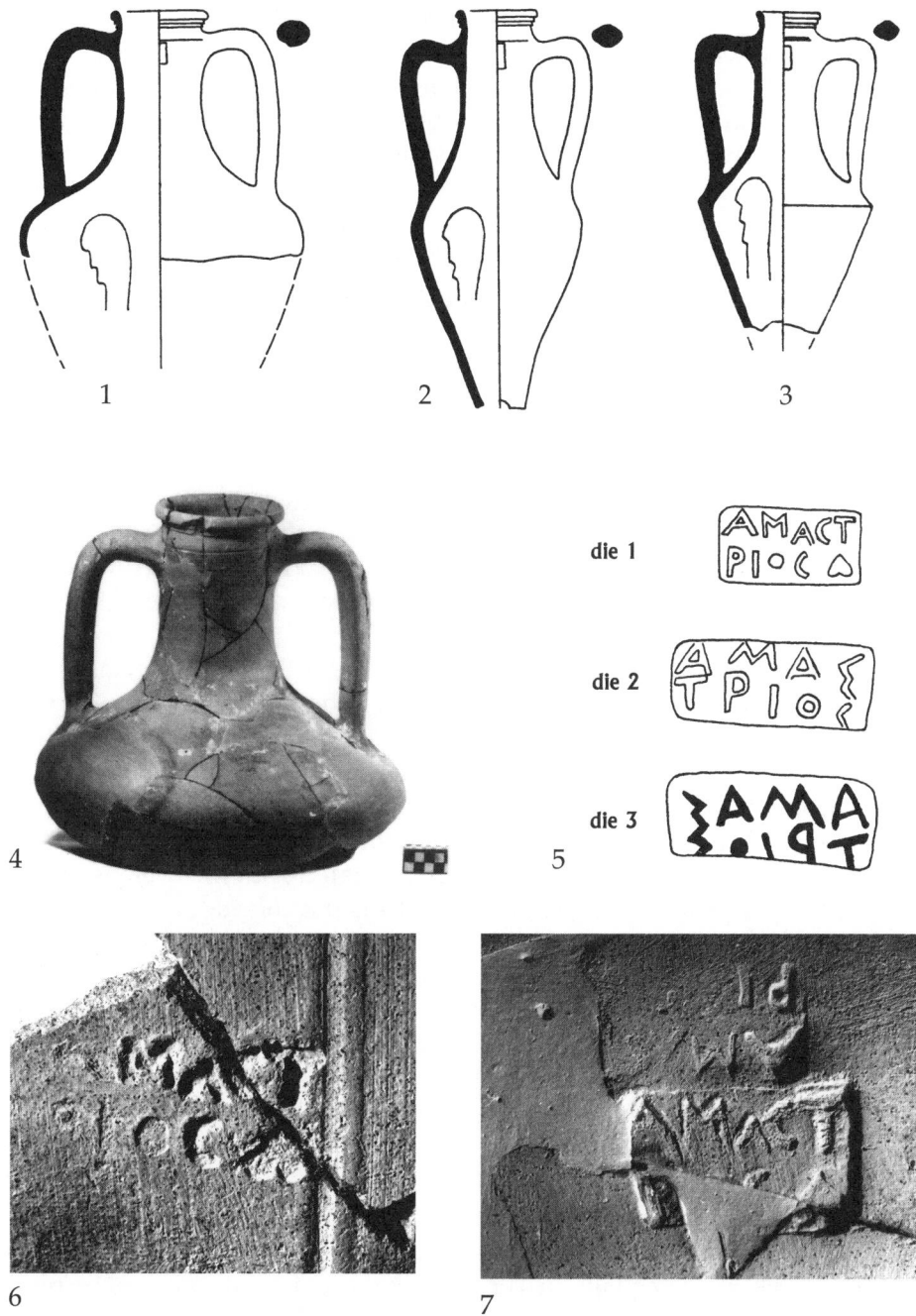

Fig. 1. Transport amphorae and corresponding stamps with the name of Amastris: 1 & 4) type 1; 2) type 2; 3) type 3; 5) stamp dies 1-3; 6-7) stamps of die 1 from the settlement of Panskoe I.

and proportions of their type 1, which is represented by a single specimen found at Panskoe I.[14] They suggest the containers from tumulus 76, grave 1, at the necropolis of Elizavetovskoe and the container from the Zelenskoj barrow on the Taman peninsula as the closest parallels. In this case, however, one may reliably judge only the upper bodies of this vessel. The shape of the foot of this type of amphorae, on which the reconstruction of the entire lower part is based, remains a topic of dispute.[15] The height of the upper body (H_1) is 30.0 cm; the diameter of the body is (D) – 38.0 cm. The volume of the amphorae, calculated on the basis of a graphical reconstruction, must thus amount to about 21-23 l.[16] However, the proportions of the upper part of a vessel in combination with a parameter such as capacity give no possibility of direct parallels. Resembling the Sinopean 'pithoid' amphorae of the first half of the 4th century BC (Monachov's type I A) as regards its body diameter and volume, to which also belong the aforementioned amphora from the necropolis of Elizavetovskoe, both types differ considerably from each other in the shape of their neck and handles, as well as in the index D/H_1 (1.27 *versus* 1.39). In this respect, the Sinopean jar from the Zelenskoj barrow constituting Monachov's type I C and datable by the stamp of Posideios, the son of Hephaistodoros, does not match either.

The Sinopean amphorae of Monachov's type II E demonstrate a similar body diameter and a slightly larger capacity, although their handles have a completely different shape and ratio D/H_1 (1.27 *versus* 1.46 on the average for the Sinopean amphorae[17]). The fractional jars of the type I E prove to be much closer in terms of both their D/H_1 (1.27 *versus* c. 1.2) and general appearance; their capacity, however, does not exceed 10 l. The broad neck with its inner rim of a diameter of 11 cm compared with the average of 7.5-8.5 cm for Sinopean amphorae of types I-III is the concluding point in the enumeration of the discrepancies in the main parameters. According to Monachov, type II E of the Sinopean amphorae is datable to the period from the third quarter to the beginning of the last quarter of the fourth century, while type I E covers a much wider period stretching from the second half of the fourth to the first third of the third century BC.[18]

Nevertheless, as we learn from the story of Athenaios (11.784), a new type of pottery may well have been encouraged by a number of models of various shapes and origins. Taking into account some degree of uncertainty as to the lower part of our jar, the Thasian amphora from the Hermitage collection[19] with its rounded rim and similarly shaped upper part (D 35 cm; D/H_1 - 1.23[20]) might equally be considered as a potential source of inspiration. The stamp of Dealkos preserved on one of its handles supply a date in the period of 325-310 BC according to M. Debidour,[21] or of about 300 BC as suggested by A. Avram.[22] The number of imitations evoked by Thasian amphorae (if indeed they were not manufactured by Thasian potters employed abroad) seems to be considerable, and both the Herakleian and Sinopean pottery industries certainly experienced their influence.[23]

Type 2 (Fig. 1.2). This type is represented by a single amphora excavated in the necropolis of Zaozernoe to the west of the city of Eupatoria. The toe and bottom are missing. Its dimensions are H_1 28.5 cm; D 23.2; d of rim 10 cm; d of mouth 8 cm. The capacity of the jar as estimated by Kac, Pavlenkov and Ščeglov is 5.6 l. As has already been noted by Ščeglov,[24] except for the slightly larger diameter of its rim, its biconical shape and main linear parameters match the so-called pseudo-Thasian type of the Herakleian amphorae (type III according to Brašinskij[25]).

The biconical Herakleian type (III), which apparently was first employed as early as the 370s and imitated the Thasian vessels of type I b, according to Bon,[26] continued to be employed for a long period of time, apparently ceasing, however, in the third century BC. Four such jars along with another five Herakleian amphorae of type II, as well as some from Sinope, have been found in tumulus 8 of the Five-Brothers' barrow group. According to the stamps of the Herakleian magistrates Andronikos, Lysitheos, Archippos and Peisistratos and stamp of the Sinopean official Chabrias, this deposit is dated to about 355-335 BC.[27] Two other deposits, pit 9 at the settlement near the village of Nikolaevka[28] and grave 2 in tumulus 9 near the village of Peski,[29] which are datable to the 330s[30] and 320-310 BC,[31]respectively, provide the chronological evidence for the late variety of the Herakleian type III amphorae.

Type 3 (Fig. 1.3). Similarly to type 2, type 3 comprises a single specimen originating from the necropolis of Zaozernoe. Its main dimensions are H_1 26.5 cm, D 23.5 cm, d of mouth 7.5 cm, and d of rim 9.7 cm. Being a one-fourth fraction of the same standard of capacity as type 1, it appears to be a very close replication of the Herakleian type IIA[32] according to Brašinskij's classification,[33] although the shape of its toe remains unknown. As may be judged from several narrowly dated deposits (complex II/1990 in the Beglickij necropolis,[34] grave 25 in the necropolis of Gorgippia,[35] dug-out 3/1969 in the settlement of Elizavetovskoe,[36] and grave 1 in tumulus 14 of the Five-Brothers barrow group[37]) the Herakleian type IIA was actively employed during the last quarter of the 4th century BC, but hardly continued into the following century.

The peculiar shape of the rounded rim with the two-stepped faceting below it, characteristic of all the three types, finds no parallels.

Stamps

All the stamps recorded until now were made by only four different dies. Two of the dies (dies 2 and 4 according to Kac, Pavlenkov and Ščeglov) are found only once, whereas dies 1 and 3 each have been recorded in eight instances. Dies 1 and 2 are engraved, while dies 3 and 4 are in relief (Figs. 1.5-7, 2.1). Certain differences are also observed according to whether their position is on the upper part of the vessel's neck or on top of its handle; those

Fig. 2. Amphora stamps: 1) with the name of Amastris (die 3); 2) Herakleian stamp of the eponym Karakydes; 3-4) Chersonesean stamps of Prytanis, son of Ariston.

impressed on the necks, with the only exception of one instance in which the legend cannot be read reliably,[38] are executed exclusively in the engraved form. In all cases the inscriptions contain two lines each, those in the relief stamps also being retrograde. Compared with dies 2 and 3, the stamps of die 1 have slightly differing spacing: AMACT | PIOC, caused by an ivy-leaf device at the end of line two (Fig. 1.6-7). The presence of the name devoid of an eponymous preposition (ἐπί) or indication of the magistracy causes our stamps to resemble typologically the stamps of the workshop owners.

Of special note is the palaeography of the stamps, in particular the peculiar lunate sigma found on die 1. Kruglikova and Saprykin regarded this feature as one of the indications that the stamps were of a later date than that proposed by their predecessors.[39] Regrettably, Kac, Pavlenkov and Ščeglov do not debate this problem, although such a palaeographic trait undoubtedly to some extent could serve as a chronological indicator. M. Debidour, who studied the palaeography of the Thasian stamps of the later type, came to the conclusion that the lunate sigma had not appeared earlier than 300 BC, and that it had not replaced the barred sigma used synchronously.[40] This observation, which is generally true with regard to the main trend in the characters' development, cannot be applied as rigidly to the turn of the centuries, as evidenced by, for instance, the stamps of the magistrate Poulyades, dated by Debidour to 310-300 BC.[41] In this respect the amphora stamps of

Herakleia are helpful as well, proving a slightly earlier transitional date. Thus, a biconical jar of type III with the stamp of Etymos showing the sigma of the lunate shape has been reported in the above-mentioned grave 9, tumulus 9, in the necropolis near the village of Peski. Based on the accompanying find of a Chersonesean amphora of type IB Monachov suggests c. 310 BC as the most probable date of the complex.[42] This agrees with a number of other deposits containing the stamps of Etymos, such as Well 10 (1984) in Gorgippia, complex XII in the Beglickij necropolis, Alexandropol burial mound, and an ash pit in Myrmekion, most likely closed in the late 4th century BC.[43]

The appearance of the lunate sigma earlier than the turn of the 4th and 3rd centuries BC is documented also by some stamps of Chersonesos. Of the sixteen known *astynomoi* of Kac's group 1B datable to 315-300 BC,[44] six (Apollonios,[45] Herakleios,[46] Herogeitos,[47] Heroxenos,[48] Xanthos[49] and Syriskos[50]) are represented by a series of stamps with the lunate sigma both in the middle of the word and in the final position. The stamps of Matris,[51] another *astynomos* of the same group, are recorded in combination with non-magistrate imprints ΠΑΣ, also with a sigma of the lunate shape. This list may be extended by the parallels among the graffiti; the palaeography of these, which like that of the stamps was considerably less conservative as compared with various lapidary inscriptions, demonstrates some fairly early examples of the cursive forms. Quite a number of examples are found among the *tabellae defixionum* of the second half of the 4th century BC from Olbia.[52] But perhaps the earliest appearance of the lunate sigma in the northern Black Sea region is recorded in a lead letter of the first half or the middle of the 4th century from Pantikapaion.[53]

Fabric

The fabric of the pottery in question is not uniform. Its visual characteristics, varying in colour from brown or light brown to reddish yellow, resemble to some extent (apart from the hue) the fabric of Sinopean jars or appear to be "visually identical with that of the Herakleian amphorae".[54] This similarity has been reinforced by studies of the samples in thin sections, which showed distinct similarities with the fabrics of Herakleia (petrographical groups I, II, III), Sinope (groups II, III, V) and Chersonesos (groups I, VI and VII).[55]

The petrographic analysis of the clay, as well as the typology of stamps and the amphora shapes, might suggest that they were produced in several *ergasteria* rather than in just one. Kac, Pavlenkov and Ščeglov arrived at the same conclusion, supposing two or three different workshops. This logical assumption clashes however with the fact that the vessels present three distinct petrographic groups (I, II, V), and that all of the three known types, as well as the different location of the stamps, prove to be united by stamps of one and the same die (die 1). These practical aspects seem to indicate that the potters were not licensed to stamp the newly made and yet unfired vessels.[56] This must have been a prerogative of the *keramarchos* (*ergasteriarchos*) or some other official. Therefore, the premise that the main function of the stamps was to guarantee the standard capacity of the vessels finds additional confirmation.[57]

Hence, we have to acknowledge that the general traits of the fabric and artificial tempers do not always satisfy (especially when small samplings are analysed) the expectations of modern scholars such as when the identification of the manufacturing place is concerned. As different petrographic studies show, these characteristics may have varied significantly not only from one *ergasterion* to another, but also within a single workshop. On the other hand, the clay composition of the products of different centres, which, however, were situated within the limits of a single mineralogical province, may be fairly similar.

Thus, according to the results of Selivanova and Ščeglov, eight stamps of Herakleia studied in thin sections constitute four distinct petrographic groups. Moreover, of the three stamps bearing the name of Herakleides (a workshop owner of the end of the 4th century BC), two proved to belong to the petrographic groups showing the most considerable variance (groups II and III). We may surmise that fabric properties reflect rather individual choices,[58] i.e., the methods of selection and processing employed by a particular potter (who in many instances may have been a foreigner[59]), methods which he had learned from his father.[60] Indeed, as the example of the stamps of Herakleides shows, the variances in fabric prove to be caused not by the natural peculiarities of the clay, but rather by the nature and percentage of the temper added. A similar situation is observed in the amphora production of Chersonesos. The clay of the samples investigated also showed great petrographical variation and constituted four clearly distinguishable groups. In a number of cases, similarly to the stamps of Amastris and Herakleia, the vessels of different fabric types are linked by stamps of one and the same magistrate.[61] I.K. Whitbread gives similar examples from the Aegean. Thus, four samples studied of the Koan amphorae with the stamp Ζώ πυρος belonged to three different fabric classes.[62]

Problem of attribution

Before drawing final conclusions from the above, let us consider once more the legend of the stamps with the name of Amastris. Despite the efforts of Kruglikova and Saprykin, it can hardly be doubted that we are dealing not with a city's name but rather with the personal name of the wife of the Herakleian tyrant. No references to the well-known amphora stamp legends like ΠΑΡΙΟΝ, ΘΑΣΙΟΝ, ΚΝΙΔΙΟΝ *et sim.* are conclusive here. Unlike these derivative forms (as a rule, nominative neuter adjective or, in a few cases, nominative masculine adjective[63]) or the city-ethnic in genitive plural (e.g.,

Fig. 3. Tile stamps of Bosporos.

ΘΑΣΙΩΝ, ΚΝΙΔΙΩΝ etc.) which agree completely with the numismatic evidence,[64] the city name in the form of a genitive singular appears neither on stamps nor on coins.

Actually, as stated above, the stamps with the name of Amastris are much more similar to the stamps of the workshop owners, in particular the series of the Bosporan tile stamps in which we find a number of names of representatives of the ruling dynasty of the Spartokids. In fact, the range of such examples should be much wider, including a considerable amount of the fabricants' stamps from various centres. The Bosporan tile production nonetheless enables us not only to identify the individuals whose names appear on the stamps, but also to judge their social status with a fair degree of certainty.

Considering that our stamps represent a personal name rather than a city-ethnic, the question arises whether it is justified to attribute them to the ceramic production of the city of Amastris, of which nothing is known either before or after Queen Amastris. Naturally, our ignorance to some extent is due to the insufficient archaeological knowledge of the city, and we can only hope for discoveries to be made in future. At the same time, assuming that they were produced in Amastris it would be natural to expect the legend ΒΑΣΙΛΙΣΣΗΣ ΑΜΑΣΤΡΙΟΣ or ΑΜΑΣΤΡΙΟΣ ΒΑΣΙΛΙΣΣΗΣ on the stamps, i.e.,

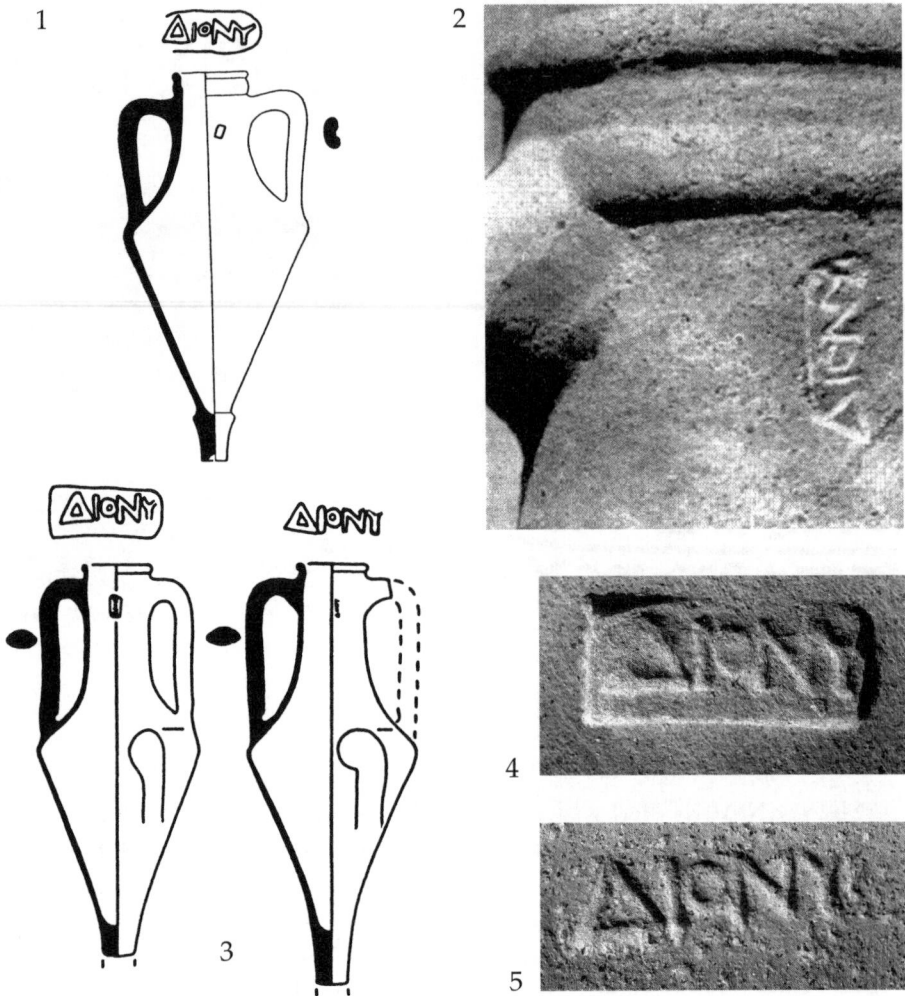

Fig. 4. Transport amphorae of Herakleia Pontike: 1-2) from Islam Geaferca, 3-5) from Panskoe I.

the form we find invariably on the silver[65] and copper coins[66] struck in the newly founded city. As regards the amphorae, we are apparently dealing with a private *ergasterion*, which functioned during the period preceding the acceptance of the royal title by Amastris. It is unlikely that having become the queen she could simultaneously act as a private person in the city ruled by her. This also seems to be true for the Bosporan tiles,[67] on which we find the names of representatives of the house of Spartokids either isolated (Σπαρτόκου, Παιρισάδου, Λεύκωνος, Γοργίππου), or accompanied by the title (βασιλέως Σπαρτόκου, ἄρχοντος ῾Υγιαίνοντος, or simply βασιλική) (Fig. 3).[68]

Theoretically, the acknowledgement of this fact would mean the possibility of ascribing the workshop of Amastris to any polis within the zone of Herakleian influence such as Tieion, or Sesamos before the *synoecism*, or indeed Herakleia itself. Nor can Kromna be excluded from the number of pretenders, since we still know nothing about the ceramic production of this city. Of all the enumerated cities only the coins of Kromna have a representation of an amphora,[69] although the flat-bottomed jar on the reverse of these copper specimens has nothing in common with any of the types of south-Pontic transport amphorae known to us.

Nevertheless, said the above-mentioned details about the shape of the vessels and the peculiarities of the stamps and fabric gives reasonable grounds to suppose that the origin of the group of pottery under consideration is in fact Herakleian. The peculiar shape of the rim of our vessels, which does not evoke a direct association with any products of Herakleia, might seem to contradict this. However, taking into account the already known examples of the "non-orthodox" Herakleian amphora rims imitating different ware from Thasos and Sinope, one should not consider this feature as a decisive argument. It cannot be ruled out that the main intent in changing the shape of the vessels was to make them more easily recognisable among other Herakleian jars,[70] due to the large volumes of manufacture within the city and the competition with other enterprises.

On the basis of this criterion, we would have to consider eighteen jars found in 1955 in Islam Geaferca in northern Dobrudja as foreign.[71] Most of these, being fairly close in shape to Brašinskij's type-II Herakleian amphorae, have a very distinctive broad cuff just below the rim, grooved handles and a peg toe which resembles that of the Knidian jars (Fig. 4.1). The characteristic fabric and well-known engraved stamps (ΔIONY, ΔOYΛOY, ΔI, NI) on the necks of eight of them (Fig. 4.2), however, leave little room for doubt that these were produced in one of the Herakleian workshops.[72] Moreover, similar to our die 1 stamp, which links a peculiar shaped jar with vessels of the typically Herakleian outward appearance and fabric, four stamps of Diony(sios) from Islam Geaferca prove to be of the same die as those on two "standardly" shaped Herakleian amphorae found at Panskoe I/U7[73] (Fig. 4.3-5).

Surprisingly enough, exactly these peculiarities of the stamps of Amastris (the presence of both engraved and relief stamps, and markings on different parts of the vessels), which were previously believed to have been just a spin-off of the organisation of their production on a new site, actually speak in favour of rather than against this new attribution. As the example of Herakleia shows, certain centres with old manufacturing traditions were not devoid of such phenomena. The third, concluding period of local stamping characterized by the return to the practice of marking the vessels with the fabricant's name yields examples of imprints applied both on the neck and the handles of amphorae, including those made in relief.[74] Chersonesos, despite the traditional notion concerning the relative homogeneity of its stamps, also offers numerous examples of this kind. Notwithstanding the prevailing tendency of relief stamping on the handles of jars, here we often encounter amphorae stamped on the neck[75] and in a few cases even on the toe.[76] Some magistrates are represented by both relief and engraved stamps. Especially indicative in this respect are the stamps of the *astynomos* Prytanis, son of Ariston, of which are known all the varieties except stamping on the toe (Fig. 2.3-4).

The characteristic device in the form of an ivy leaf recorded on one of the dies of Amastris (die 1) may perhaps be considered as an additional argument in favour of their Herakleian origin. Along with a grape and a club, a leaf of ivy is one of the most common emblems on the engraved stamps of Herakleia. Contrary to B.N. Grakov,[77] who considered them as marks of the workshop owners, I.B. Brašinskij correctly noted their fairly small number as compared with the many names of workshop owners and believed them to be "the substitute signs of some officials indicating their magisterial dignity/ (ἐπί)".[78] It seems, however, that neither of these interpretations can be regarded as satisfying. None of them explains the fact that we often find the officials' names neither with an eponymous preposition (ἐπί) nor with a device, and they do not explain those cases where the name of one and the same workshop owner accompanied by the same emblem is found in combination with different magistrates. Taking into account, however, that different fabricants appear with identical devices, we might assume that the latter were the symbols of the workshops themselves rather than of their owners, who may have been replaced after the expiration of the term of lease. It is quite probable that the leasing of public *ergasteria*[79] for each new term was conducted by means of competitive bidding similar to the leasing of quarries, mines and land plots,[80] without the security of being able to preserve these enterprises after the termination of the contract.[81] Such a hypothesis could explain the appearance of the same names accompanied by differing emblems. To a certain extent, the numismatic parallel with the lifetime and the posthumous issues of Alexander and Lysimachos may be helpful. Notwithstanding their uniformity and long-term emission in various parts of the vast empire, the emblems on their reverses have not infrequently been used to indicate the place of minting.[82]

It should be mentioned, however, that the recorded combinations of the fabricants' names with the names of magistrates and certain devices are not limited to the examples mentioned above. Quite a number of uniform imprints in the form of a grape and a legend running round the central emblem representing the same grape give us more than a dozen different names of fabricants in combination with the single name of Karakydes (Fig. 2.2). The invariable preposition ἐπί leaves no doubt as to the eponymous office of the latter (group III of the magistrates according to Kac[83]) and the appearance of all these stamps during one single year. It might seem that this fact confuses the matter hopelessly and proves the absence of any regularities in the appearance of emblems. However, everything would fall into place if one assumes that all these fabricants were joint owners. A particularly enlightening parallel is an agreement (συνθῆκαι) from the second half of the fourth century BC on the lease of an *ergasterion* at Peiraieus by a corporate body (μερῖται) consisting of eight persons.[84] Judging by the enormous number of stamps found at various ancient sites in the northern and western Black Sea regions, in its best years the amphora production in Herakleia must have reached an enormous scale.[6] Under such conditions, along with the appearance of new workshops it would be natural to expect the enlargement of the old ones, the lease of which might require joint capital.[86] Coming back to the devices, it should be noted, however, that the tradition of including them on the stamp did not always exist here, nor does it seem to have been followed very strictly.

Chronology

The possibility of attributing the stamps with the name of Amastris to a new source naturally raises the question of the rigid fixation of their upper date to 300 BC, which is the date of foundation of the city of Amastris. Their similarity to the Herakleian fabricants' stamps of the final period mentioned above allows us to consider the cessation of magisterial stamping in Herakleia and the transition to stamping with the fabricants' names as a kind of *terminus post quem*, also for the amphorae bearing the name of Amastris. This cessation, as supposed by Kac on the basis of a typology of the stamps and an analysis of closed deposits, occurred within the last quarter of the 4th century BC, most likely during its last decade.[87] A similar conclusion was drawn by P. Balabanov, who linked the abolition of the institution of eponyms with the division of power between Amastris and her sons, as well as with the internal conflicts which followed immediately upon the death of Dionysios in 305 BC.[88]

Although the interdependence of these events may not be ruled out, of greater significance seems to be the Dionysios's near contemporary acceptance of the title of king.[89] This took place not long before the death of the tyrant, in 306 or 305 BC, immediately after Antigonos Monophthalmos had done the same after his victory over Ptolemy's navy off Cyprus, thus claiming to be in possession of the empire of Alexander.[90] Apparently, this act of Dionysios, who thus put himself on a par with the Hellenistic monarchs, resulted in certain changes in the internal political system of Herakleia, particularly in the abolition of some of the former *polis* institutions.

It seems that we must date the transition of one of the largest *ergasteria* in the city into the ownership of Amastris precisely to this period just after the death of Dionysios. The slightly earlier date for the beginning of the manufacture, compared with that proposed by Sčeglov, agrees completely with the archaeological context of the finds. One of the main complexes which he relied on was the monumental building U6 at the settlement of Panskoe I, dated formerly to the period from about 300 to 275 or 270 BC, which is in complete accordance with the dates proposed for the amphorae. However, the recent comprehensive publication of the excavation results at Panskoe I/U6, including detailed analysis of all the groups of finds, showed the necessity to shift the upper chronological limits of the U6 building back to 320-310 BC. The cessation of the import of black-glazed pottery[91] and commonware as well as a significant decrease in amphora imports by the beginning of the third century BC are among the most important peculiarities of its ceramic assemblage. This was apparently caused by the crisis that struck the economy of the Chersonesean *polis*.[92] In view of this fact, it is more likely that the Herakleian amphorae from Amastris' workshops were brought to the settlement already at the very end of the fourth or the turn of the fourth and third centuries BC, rather than in the following years, when the decreased population of Panskoe met with difficulties in purchasing even the barest necessities.[93]

Owing to Photios' epitome of Memnon's writings we have an idea of the main events of Herakleian history during the period under discussion. At the time of the return of Amastris from Sardis in 300 BC, after a year spent there with Lysimachos, the oldest of her sons, Klearchos, had already come of age and had begun to rule the city on his own.[94] She probably moved to the *polis* founded by her and bearing her name in this same year. Hence, if the *ergasterion* of Amastris, as we suppose, really was situated in Herakleia, then the period of its existence cannot have been long, most likely limited to the period from 305 to 300 BC. This dating corresponds much better with the amount of known stamps and dies[95] than the fifteen years proposed by Sčeglov or the period of twenty to thirty years allotted to it by Kruglikova and Saprykin.

List of the stamps with the name of Amastris

Die 1. Engraved stamps on the amphora necks (apart from no. 6: amphora handle).
  a) Panskoe I/U6. 1972. Find list 3/25. St Petersburg, IHMC RAS. Publications: Sčeglov 1986, 367, fig. 1.7; Kac, Pavlenkov & Sčeglov 1989, 19, fig. 4.4, 24, no. 4 (inv. no. is mistaken); Monachov 1999a, 501, pl. 214.1; Kac, Monachov, Stolba & Sčeglov 2002, 124, no. Ae 115, pl. 60. (Fig. 1.6)
  b) Panskoe I/U6. 1972. Find list 3/73. St Petersburg, IHMC RAS. Publications: Sčeglov 1986, 367, fig. 1.7; Kac, Pavlenkov & Sčeglov 1989, 19, fig. 4.3, 24, no. 3 (inv. no. is mistaken); Kac, Monachov, Stolba & Sčeglov 2002, 124, no. Ae 116, pl. 60. (Fig. 1.7)

c) Čajka. 1964. Find list Č-64/103. The Eupatoria Museum. Publication: Kac, Pavlenkov & Ščeglov 1989, 24, no. 10.

d) Zaozernoe/necropolis. 1973. Find list ČN-73/86. The Eupatoria Museum. Publications: Kac, Pavlenkov & Ščeglov 1989, 19, fig. 4.14, 25, no. 14; Kruglikova & Saprykin 1991, 90, fig. 1.2.

e) Zaozernoe/necropolis. 1978. Find list ČN-78/6. The Eupatoria Museum. Publication: Kac, Pavlenkov & Ščeglov 1989, 25, no. 15.

f) Pantikapaion. Inv. no. Pan 1486. St Petersburg, State Hermitage Museum. Publications: Pridik 1917, no. 170; Kac, Pavlenkov & Ščeglov 1989, 25 no. 17.

g) Elizavetovskoe. 1986. Find list EG-86/XX-23. Rostov-on-the-Don Regional Museum. Publications: Kac, Pavlenkov & Ščeglov 1989, 26, no. 22.

h) Elizavetovskoe. 2000. Find list EG-2000/XXXVI-60. Rostov-on-the-Don Regional Museum? Unpublished.

* The stamp of die 1 illustrated by Kruglikova & Saprykin 1991, 90, fig. 1.3 as originating from Panskoe I does not belong to the finds from this settlement.

Die 2. Engraved stamp on an amphora handle.
a) Kara-Tobe. 1980. No inv. no. The Eupatoria Museum. Publication: Kac, Pavlenkov & Ščeglov 1989, 19, fig. 4.16, 25, no. 16; Kruglikova & Saprykin 1991, 90, fig. 1.4.

Die 3. Relief stamps on amphora handles.
a) Olbia. 1951. Find list O-51/1048. Kiev, Institute of archaeology. Publication: Kac, Pavlenkov & Ščeglov 1989, 24, no. 1.

b) Olbia. 1970. Find list O-70/3362. St Petersburg, IHMC RAS. Publication: Kac, Pavlenkov & Ščeglov 1989, 24, no. 2.

c) Čajka. 1964. Find list Č-64/317. The Eupatoria Museum. Publication: Kac, Pavlenkov & Ščeglov 1989, 24-25, no. 11.

d) Pantikapaion. Inv. no. B 5392. St Petersburg, The State Hermitage Museum. Publications: Pridik 1917, no. 169; Kac, Pavlenkov & Ščeglov 1989, 19, fig. 4.18, 25, no. 18.

e) Pantikapaion. Year of the find and present location unknown. Publications: Kac, Pavlenkov & Ščeglov 1989, 25, no. 19.

f) Gorgippia. Year? The Krasnodar Museum? Publications: Kac, Pavlenkov & Ščeglov 1989, 25-26, nos. 20-20a.

g) Elizavetovskoe. 1927. Inv. no. TE 1927.45. St Petersburg, The State Hermitage Museum. Publications: Zeest 1951, 120; Brašinskij 1980, 201, no. 781, pl. 34; Kac, Pavlenkov & Ščeglov 1989, 19, fig. 4.21, 26, no. 21; Kruglikova & Saprykin 1991, 90, fig. 1.5.

h) Herakleian Peninsula, farmhouse 57. 1988. The Chersonesos Museum? Publications: Kac, Pavlenkov & Ščeglov 1989, 26, no. 24; Kruglikova & Saprykin 1991, 90, fig. 1.1. (Fig. 2.1)

Die 4? Relief stamp on an amphora neck.
a) Majak, farmhouse 1. 1976. Find list ČM-76/66. The Eupatoria Museum. Publications: Kolesnikov 1985, 78, 91, no. 163; Kac, Pavlenkov & Ščeglov 1989, 19, fig. 4.7, 24, no. 7; Kruglikova & Saprykin 1991, 90, fig. 1.6.

Die unknown. Relief stamp on an amphora handle.
a) Kallatis. 1999. Unpublished.

Notes

1. Pridik 1917, 109, nos. 169-170.
2. For the single find of 1927 from Elizavetovskoe, see Zeest 1951, 120; Brašinskij 1980, 46, 201, no. 781.
3. Ščeglov 1986, 365-373.
4. Kac, Pavlenkov and Ščeglov 1989, 15-28.
5. An unpublished find of a stamp with the letters in relief from a salvage excavation in 1999 (conducted by A. Avram, M. Ionescu and N. Alexandru) in the area of the Roman wall of Kallatis. The stamp comes from a mixed layer that does not allow its dating on the basis of the context. This information is kindly provided (by letter) by Alexandru Avram.
6. In addition to the two stamps on handles published earlier by Kac, Pavlenkov and Ščeglov, the excavations in Elizavetovskoe in the year 2000 yielded one engraved stamp on the amphora neck (find list XXXVI/60). The stamp is of the same die as the specimens found in Panskoe I/U6. I am much indebted to V.I. Kac for information concerning this find.
7. Zeest 1951a, 120.
8. Ščeglov 1986, 372. However, E.M. Pridik (1917), who placed two stamps of the Hermitage collection among *incerti*, already regarded it as a personal name.
9. Ščeglov 1986, 371; Kac, Pavlenkov & Ščeglov 1989, 20.
10. Ščeglov 1986, 372; Kac, Pavlenkov & Ščeglov 1989, 21.
11. Memnon, *FGrH* 3B, 434F5.2.
12. Kruglikova & Saprykin 1991, 89-95. This stamp found in 1988 is also listed in the catalogue of Kac, Pavlenkov & Ščeglov (1989, 26, no. 24).
13. Kruglikova & Saprykin 1991, 93.
14. Kac, Pavlenkov & Ščeglov 1989, 16.
15. As demonstrated by the examination of the materials kept at the Institute of the History of Material Culture, Russian Academy of Sciences (IHMC RAS) in St Petersburg, the visual characteristics (colour, texture and discernible tempers) of the fabric of the base and upper body of the amphora (combined into one in the graphic reconstruction) actually proved to be non-identical, i.e., these parts may well belong to different vessels.
16. Ščeglov 1986, 366, 367, fig. 1.1; Kac, Pavlenkov & Ščeglov 1989, 16, fig. 1.3, 24, catalogue no. 3; Kac, Monachov, Stolba & Ščeglov 2002, 111, Ad 77, pls. 47, 53.
17. Calculated on the basis of S.Ju. Monachov's data (1992, 203, table 13).
18. Monachov 1992, 171, 176.
19. Zeest 1960, pl. 9.21b; Garlan 1987, 80, fig. 3.c.
20. Calculated according to a drawing by Zeest 1960, pl. 9.
21. Debidour 1986, 331.
22. Avram 1996, 74.
23. Zeest 1951b, 108; Brašinskij 1961, 178; 1984, 83, 114; Monachov 1992, 181. The production place (or places) of amphorae of the so-called "Thasian circle" remains unidentified. See Monachov 1999b, 48-50.
24. Ščeglov 1986, 369; Kac, Pavlenkov & Ščeglov 1989, 17.
25. See Brašinskij 1961, 178-181, figs. 2.1, 3.1; Brašinskij 1980, 24, pls. 4.114, 10.114; Brašinskij 1984, 83, pls. 15.5, 16.4. Cf. Zeest 1960, 158, pl. 22.46. On the chronology of the pseudo-Thasian amphorae, see Brašinskij 1961, 184; 1980, 24; 1984, 139; Monachov 1999a, 358-362, 428-430.
26. Bon and Bon 1957, 17-18, figs. 3.3-5, 6.2-3.
27. Kac 1997, 216; Monachov 1999a, 358-362. Cf. Brašinskij 1961, 184-185; 1980, 206: "second half of the fourth century BC."

28. Meljukova 1975, 24-25, 204, fig. 7.1-6.
29. Grebennikov 1987, 156-158, fig. 6.1-3.
30. Monachov 1999a, 371.
31. Monachov 1999a, 428-430.
32. Cf. Kac, Pavlenkov & Ščeglov 1989, 17.
33. Brašinskij 1980, 25, 213, pl. 5.119; Brašinskij 1984, 83-85, 224, pl. 15.6.
34. Monachov 1999a, 438-440, pl. 190.
35. Monachov 1999a, 444-446, pl. 193.
36. Monachov 1999a, 448-452, pl. 195.
37. Monachov 1999a, 452-454, pl. 196.
38. Kac, Pavlenkov & Ščeglov 1989, 18 f., figs. 3-4.7, 24, no. 7.
39. Kruglikova & Saprykin 1991, 92. Cf. Zeest 1951, 120: "If the stamp from Elisavetovskoe and that no. 169 from Kerch (reference to Pridik's catalogue – V.S.) based on epigraphical data (the four barred sigma – V.S.) could be assigned to the 3rd century BC, then the stamp no. 170 with lunate sigma has to be dated to the period not earlier than late 3rd – beginning of the 2nd century BC".
40. Debidour 1979, 287, n. 61, 302-303; 1986, 315-316. Cf. Vinogradov 1972, 12; Garlan 1979, 247.
41. Debidour 1986, 331. Cf., however, Avram (1996, 60), who places this official in the 270s BC.
42. Monachov 1999a, 430.
43. Monachov 1999a, 435-438.
44. Kac 1994, 76.
45. Kac 1994, 89, pl. 10, dies 1-20, 9 to 12.
46. Kac 1994, 94 f., pls. 19-20, dies 1-47-48, 11 to 21.
47. Kac 1994, 96, pl. 21, dies 1-52, 4 and 1-52, 5.
48. Kac 1994, 98, pl. 26, dies 1-58, 4 to 7.
49. Kac 1994, 106, pl. 37, die 1-88, 8.
50. Kac 1994, 112, pl. 44, dies 1-109, 5 to 9.
51. Kac 1994, 103, 125, pl. 56, die 2A-33, 1.
52. Vinogradov 1994, 105, no. 1, fig. 1 (late 4th century BC) = *SEG* XLIV, 669 = Dubois 1996, 106; Tochtas'ev 2000, 296-299, no. 1, fig. 1.1 (second half of the 4th century BC), 308-311, no. 3, fig. 2.1, 311-315, no. 4, fig. 2.2 (both: the middle to the second half of the 4th century BC). Cf. Stolba 2002, 234, H 32: ΔAMOC, graffito on the large black-glazed plate datable to the period 325-300 BC. For a discussion of the date of the plate, see Hannestad, Stolba & Blinkenberg Hastrup 2002, 142, B 147.
53. Saprykin & Kulikov 1999, 202, fig. 1.
54. Kac, Pavlenkov & Ščeglov 1989, 17. Cf. Zeest (1951, 120) speaking about the stamp from Elizavetovskoe (die 3): "the fabric is highly reminiscent of that of the Herakleian amphorae".
55. Ščeglov & Selivanova 1992, 45, table 1.
56. The group of Sinopean stamps in which we find the proper names specified as κεραμεύς implies, however, that a different practice might also have existed. On the so-called potter's stamps, see, e.g. Škorpil 1914, 131-135; Achmerov 1951, 77-84; Cechmistrenko 1960, 59-77.
57. See Dumont 1872, 42-43; Grace 1949, 178; Achmerov 1951, 84; Brašinskij 1965, 17-18; Grace & Savvatianou-Petropoulakou 1970, 292-293; Cechmistrenko 1971, 16 with n. 6; Jefremow 1995, 12, 16. Cf., however, El'nickij 1969, 94-95; Debidour 1979, 305; Garlan 1988, 28.

58. Cf. Whitbread 1995, 247.
59. There is no doubt that the skilled potters, shipwrights and metallurgists, to say nothing of sculptors, bronze-casters and architects, could find themselves employed outside their home cities. See MacDonald 1981, 159-168; Monachov 1989, 75-76; Whitbread 1995, 75-76, as well as Tochtas'ev 1997, 386-389, who points out the non-Doric form of several names on the amphora stamps of Herakleia. Cf. Ephesian citizenship decree for Athenian potters Kittos and Bakchios (Keil 1913, 232, I e; Preuner 1920, 69-72; IEph 1420): Κίττωι καὶ Βακχίωι παισὶ Βακχίο Ἀθηναίοις, ἐπειδὴ ἐπαγγέλονται τῆι πόλει τὸγ κέραμ[ον] | τὸμ μέλανα ἐργάσεσθαι καὶ τῆι θεῶι τὴν ὑδρίαν, λαμβάνοντες τὸ τεταγμέν[ον] | ἐν τῶι νόμωι, ἔδοξε τῆι βουλῆι καὶ τῶι δήμωι, Πλάτων εἶπεν, εἶναι αὀτοὺς | πολίτας παραμένοντας ἐν τῆι πόλει καὶ ἐπιτελοῦντας ἃ ἐπαγγέλλοντα[ι] | τῆι βουλῆι· ἔλαχον φυλὴν Ἐφεσεῖς χιλιαστὺ[ν Σαλαμίνιο]ι· | ταῦτα δὲ εἶναι καὶ ἐκγόνοις. It seems more likely that μέλας κέραμος is related to the black-glazed pottery rather then "Dachziegel für die städtische Bauten", as suggested by Preuner (1920, 70). On the movement of skilled labour in general, see Burford 1972, 66-67.
60. On the family traditions in the Greek pottery industry and in the development of the craft, see Burford 1972, 82-87.
61. In particular, the visually examined stamps of the astynomos Xanthos (group 1B according to Kac) from the excavation of building U6 at Panskoe I demonstrate variance in both the composition of the visually discernible temper and the texture and colour of the paste.
62. Whitbread 1995, 97-98.
63. E.g. ΘΑΣΙΟΣ (i.e. ἀμφορεύς, κάδος et sim.). Cf. discussion by Garlan 1999, 17-20.
64. Cf., e.g., ΘΑΣΙΟΝ (SNG Lockett 225-231)/ ΘΑΣΙΩΝ (SNG Lockett 232, 234-237), ΑΚΡΑΓΑΝΤΙΝΟΝ (SNG Morcom 520)/ ΑΚΡΑΓΑΝΤΙΝΩΝ (SNG Morcom 537), ΣΥΡΑΚΟΣΙΟΝ (SNG Lockett 870-912, 975)/ ΣΥΡΑΚΟΣΙΩΝ (SNG Lockett 971, 974, 976-980). An exceptional case is the nominative singular ΟΛΒΙΗ on the cast coins of Olbia (SNG BM 391-393).
65. SNG BM 1297-1299; SNG Stancomb 728.
66. SNG BM 1300-1301; SNG Stancomb 729-730.
67. Cf. Kruglikova & Saprykin 1991, 91.
68. Gajdukevič 1935; 1947; 1971, 158-160; Šelov 1954. For examples of the royal tile factories outside the Bosporos, see Gajdukevič 1947, 27, n. 1.
69. SNG BM 1344-1349; SNG Stancomb 744-745.
70. Cf. Athen. 11.784 on the selection of a new shape for Mendean wine jars.
71. Bujor 1961, 85-92; 1962, 475-487; Monachov 1999, 454-457.
72. Brašinskij 1965, 19-20; Monachov 1999, 454-457.
73. Monachov 1999, 455.
74. Štaerman 1951, 35-38; Brašinskij 1965, 15-16; Kac 1997, 215.
75. Achmerov 1949, 103; Kolesnikov 1985, 76, 79, table 1, 80, table 2; Michlin 1979, 142-143; Kac 1994, 82: Agasikles (300-285 BC), 85: Athanodoros, son of Nikeas (285-272 BC), 86: Alexandros (315-300 BC), 88: Apollonidas II (300-285 BC), 98: Herokrates, son of Neumenios (285-272 BC), 105: Neumenios, son of Philistios (285-272 BC), 109: Prytanis, son of Aristonos (285-272 BC), 114: Philippos (300-285 BC), 115: Phormion, son of Apollas (285-272 BC).
76. Michlin 1979, 143, fig. 1; Kac 1994, 86: Alexandros (315-300 BC).
77. Grakov 1926, 177.
78. Brašinskij 1965, 25. See also Kruglikova & Saprykin 1991, 91.

79. On the renting of workshops, see *IG* II², 2496 (second half of the fourth century BC). The lease records of the Delian *hieropoioi* testify the renting of "a potter's establishment" called Kerameion. See Kent 1948, 254, with n. 25; Reger 1994, 193.

80. Arist. *Ath*. 47.2,4; Behrend 1970, 109; Osborne 1988, 290. Cf. also Walbank 1983, 218 with n. 80; Reger 1994, 195-197. On the mine leases, see Crosby 1950, 189-312.

81. In this respect the significant fabric differences in the Herakleian stamps of the above-mentioned Herakleidas issued during the magistracy of Silanos and Pausanias (see Ščeglov & Selivanova 1992, 41) might indicate that he possessed two different workshops successively.

82. Mørkholm 1991, 31, 141, pls. 31.459-460 (Lampsakos), 464-465 (Sardis), 466-470 (Chios), 32.471-472 (Rhodos), 473 (Samos), 474 (Miletos), 478 (Korinthos). However, there is no doubt that various symbols were used by city magistrates and royal officials as well. Cf. discussion by Bellinger 1963, 24-26.

83. Kac 1997. See also his article in this volume.

84. *IG* II², 2496; Behrend 1970, 90-91, no. 35; Osborne 1988, 284.

85. V.I. Kac (in this volume) refers to more than 1200 dies analyzed in his study. The simultaneous employment of twenty to thirty pottery workshops as he suggests seems, though, to be an overestimation.

86. It is noteworthy that as long ago as 1926, B.N. Grakov (1926, 192-193) arrived at nearly the same conclusion when he considered the stamps with two names in the nominative singular as the marks of "double firms". Unfortunately, this thought has not been further developed, and in the introduction to the manuscript of *IOSPE* III, Grakov renounced his previous point of view. Cf. also Brašinskij 1961, 183; 1965, 16-17; Vasilenko 1970, 217-220.

87. Kac 1997, 216. See also his contribution in this volume.

88. Balabanov 1985, 21.

89. Memnon, *FGrH* 3B, 434F4.6.

90. Diod. 20.53.1-4; Plut. *Demetr*. 18.1-2; Iust. 15.2.10-13; Burstein 1976, 77; Bittner 1998, 42.

91. Hannestad, Stolba & Blinkenberg Hastrup 2002, 128.

92. Stolba (forthcoming).

93. Taking into account the similar shape of type 2 of these vessels and those of Herakleia of type IIA, as well as the practically identical visual characteristics of the fabric, it is possible that amphora Ad 78 from building U6 (Kac, Monachov, Stolba & Ščeglov 2002, 111, pls. 47, 53), assigned to Herakleia in the publication, also came from the same workshop.

94. Memnon, *FGrH* 3B, 434F5.1; Burstein 1976, 83; Bittner 1998, 45.

95. So, according to Kac's computations (1997, 216-217), the first fifteen years of pottery production in Herakleia (c. 415-400 BC) resulted in 123 various dies. That would give an average about eight dies per year. The same interval between 385 and 360 BC reveals 310 dies, i.e., about twenty-one dies per year, and, towards the end of the century this activity seemingly decreases to an average of about six dies per year for the remaining period. Taking into account the fluctuating intensity of production, which was highly dependent on the demand and crop yield, these figures seem to show that in our case we are dealing with a single, briefly used workshop rather than with production of the entire city.

Bibliography

Achmerov, R.B. 1949. Ob astinomnych klejmach ellinističeskogo Chersonesa, *VDI* 4, 99-123.

Achmerov, R.B. 1951. O klejmach keramičeskich masterov ellinističeskogo Chersonesa, *VDI* 3, 77-84.

Avram, A. 1996. *Histria*. Vol. 8. *Les timbres amphoriques*. 1. *Thasos*. Bucarest-Paris.

Balabanov, P. 1985. Analiz i datirovanie amfornych pečatej Geraklei Pontiki, *Thracia Pontica* 2, 12-28.

Behrend, D. 1970. *Attische Pachturkunden. Ein Beitrag zur Beschreibung der μίσθωσις nach den griechischen Inschriften* (Vestigia, 12). München.

Bellinger, A.R. 1963. *Essays on the coinage of Alexander the Great* (ANS Numismatic Studies, 11). New York.

Bittner, A. 1998. *Gesellschaft und Wirtschaft in Herakleia Pontike: eine Polis zwischen Tyrannis und Selbstverwaltung* (Asia Minor Studien, 30). Bonn.

Bon, A.-M. & A. Bon 1957. *Les timbres amphoriques de Thasos* (Études Thasiennes, 4). Paris.

Brašinskij, I.B. 1961. Amfory iz raskopok Elizavetovskogo mogil'nika v 1959 g., *SovA* 3, 178-186.

Brašinskij, I.B. 1965. Keramičeskie klejma Geraklei Pontijskoj, *NumEpigr* 5, 10-27.

Brašinskij, I.B. 1980. *Grečeskij keramičeskij import na Nižnem Donu v V – III vv. do n.e.* Leningrad.

Brašinskij, I.B. 1984. *Metody issledovanija antičnoj torgovli (na primere Severnogo Pričernomor'ja)*. Leningrad.

Bujor, E. 1961. Depozitul de amfore de la Islam Geaferca, *StCercIstorV* 12, 85-92.

Bujor, E. 1962. The amphorae deposit of Islam Geaferca, *Dacia* 6, 475-487.

Burford, A. 1972. *Craftsmen in Greek and Roman Society*. London.

Burstein, S.M. 1976. *Outpost of Hellenism: The Emergence of Heraclea on the Black Sea* (University of California Publications: Classical Studies, 14). Berkeley-Los Angeles-London.

Cechmistrenko, V.I. 1960. Sinopskie keramičeskie klejma s imenami gončarnych masterov, *SovA* 3, 59-77.

Crosby, M. 1950. The Leases of the Laureion mines, *Hesperia* 19, 189-312.

Debidour, M. 1979. Réflexions sur les timbres amphoriques thasiens, in: *Thasiaca* (BCH Suppl., 5). Athènes-Paris, 269-314.

Debidour, M. 1986. En classant les timbres thasiens, in: Empereur & Garlan (eds.) 1986, 311-334.

Dumont, A. *Inscriptions céramiques de la Grèce*. Paris.

El'nickij, L.A. 1969. Iz istorii drevnegrečeskoj vinotorgovli i keramičeskogo proizvodstva, *VDI* 3, 88-105.

Empereur, J.-Y. & Y. Garlan (eds.) 1986. *Recherches sur les amphores grecques* (BCH Suppl., 13). Paris.

Gajdukevič, V.F. 1935. Stroitel'nye keramičeskie materialy Bospora. Bosporskie čerepicy, *IGAIMK* 104, 298-315.

Gajdukevič, V.F. 1947. Nekotorye novye dannye o bosporskich čerepičnych ergasterijach vremeni Spartokidov, *KSIA* 17, 22-27.

Gajdukevič, V.F. 1971. *Das Bosporanische Reich*. Berlin 1971.

Garlan, Y. 1979. Koukos: données nouvelles pour une nouvelle interprétation des timbres amphoriques thasiens, in: *Thasiaca* (BCH Suppl., 5). Athènes-Paris, 213-268.

Garlan, Y. 1987. Prolégomènes à un nouveau corpus des timbres amphoriques thasiens, in: Lévêque & Morel (eds.) 1987, 73-86.

Garlan, Y. 1988. *Vin et amphores de Thasos*. Paris.

Grakov, B.N. 1926. Englifičeskie klejma na gorlach nekotorych ellinističeskich amfor, *TrudyGIM* 1, 165-206.

Grebennikov, Ju.S. 1987. Kurgany skifskoj znati v Poingul'e, in: *Drevnejšie skotovody stepej Juga Ukrainy*. Kiev, 148-158.

Hannestad, L., V.F. Stolba & H. Blinkenberg Hastrup 2002. Black-glazed, red-figure, and grey ware pottery, in: Hannestad, Stolba & Ščeglov (eds.) 2002, 127-149.

Hannestad, L., V.F. Stolba & A.N. Ščeglov (eds.) 2002. *Panskoye I*. Vol. 1. *The Monumental Building U6*. Aarhus.

Jefremow, N. 1995. *Die Amphorenstempel des hellenistischen Knidos*. München.

Kac, V.I. 1997. Chronologija klejm Geraklei Pontijskoj (sostojanie i perspektivy izučenija), in: *Nikonij i antičnyj mir Severnogo Pričernomor'ja*. Odessa, 212-217.

Kac, V.I., S.Yu. Monachov, V.F. Stolba & A.N. Ščeglov 2002. Tiles and Ceramic Containers, in: Hannestad, Stolba & Ščeglov (eds.) 2002, 101-126.

Kac, V.I., V.I. Pavlenkov & A.N. Ščeglov 1989. The Amastrian stamped pottery, *ArcheologiaWarsz* 40, 15-28.

Keil, J. 1913. Ephesische Bürgerrechts- und Proxeniedekrete aus dem vierten und dritten Jahrhundert v. Chr., *ÖJh* 16, 231-244.

Kent, J.H. 1948. The Temple Estates of Delos, Rhenia, and Mykonos, *Hesperia* 17, 243-338.

Kolesnikov, A.B. 1985. Keramičeskie klejma iz raskopok usadeb u Evpatorijskogo majaka, *VDI* 2, 67-93.

Kruglikova, I.T. & S.Ju. Saprykin 1991. Chersones i Amastrija po dannym amfornych klejm, *KSIA* 204, 89-95.

Lévêque, P. & J.-P. Morel (eds.) 1987. *Céramiques hellénistiques et romaines* II. Paris.

MacDonald, B.R. 1981. The Emigration of Potters from Athens in the Late Fifth Century BC and its Effect on the Attic Pottery Industry, *AJA* 85, 159-168.

Michlin, B.Ju. 1979. K izučeniju chersonesskich keramičeskich klejm, *VDI* 2, 139-159.

Monachov, S.Ju. 1992. Dinamika form i standartov sinopskich amfor, in: *Grečeskie amfory*. Saratov, 163-204.

Monachov, S.Ju. 1999a. *Grečeskie amfory v Pričernomor'e. Kompleksy keramičeskoj tary VII – II vekov do n.e.* Saratov.

Monachov, S.Ju. 1999b. *Torgovye svjazi v Severnom Pričernomor'e (po materialam grečeskoj keramičeskoj tary VII – II vv. do n.e.).* Saratov.

Mørkholm, O. 1991. *Early Hellenistic coinage: from the accession of Alexander to the Peace of Apamea (336-188 BC).* Cambridge.

Osborne, R. 1988. Social and Economic Implications of the Leasing of Land and Property in Classical and Hellenistic Greece, *Chiron* 18, 279-323.

Preuner, E. 1920. Archäologisch-epigraphisches, *JdI* 35, 59-82.

Pridik, E.M. 1917. *Inventarnyj katalog klejm na amfornych ručkach i gorlyškach i čerepicach Ermitažnogo sobranija.* Petrograd.

Reger, G. 1994. *Regionalism and Change in the Economy of Independent Delos, 314-167 BC* (Hellenistic Culture and Society, 14). Berkeley.

Saprykin, S.Ju. & A.V. Kulikov 1999. Novye epigrafičeskie nachodki v Pantikapee, *Drevnejšie gosudarstva Vostočnoj Evropy 1996-1997 gg.* Moskva, 201-208.

Stolba, V.F. 2002. Graffiti and dipinti, in: Hannestad, Stolba & Ščeglov (eds.) 2002, 228-244.

Stolba, V.F. (forthcoming). The Oath of Chersonesos (IOSPE I², 401) and Chersonesean Economy in the Early Hellenistic period, in: J.K. Davis, Z.G. Archibald & V. Gabrielsen (eds.) *Hellenistic Economies* 2: *Making, Moving, and Managing.* London.

Ščeglov, A.N. 1986. Les amphores timbrées d'Amastris, in: Empereur & Garlan (eds.) 1986, 365-373.

Šelov, D.B. 1954. K istorii keramičeskogo proizvodstva na Bospore, *SovA* 21, 119-130.

Škorpil, V.V. 1914. Nazvanija gončarnych masterov v keramičeskich nadpisjach, *IAK* 51, 131-135.

Štaerman, E.M. 1951. Keramičeskie klejma iz Tiry, *KSIIMK* 36, 31-49.

Tochtas'ev, S.R. 1997. K izdaniju kataloga keramičeskich klejm Chersonesa Tavričeskogo. Rev.: V. I. Kac. Keramičeskie klejma Chersonesa Tavričeskogo. Saratov 1994, *Hyperboreus* 3.2, 362-404.

Tochtas'ev, S.R. 2000. Novye tabellae defixionum iz Ol'vii, *Hyperboreus* 6.2, 296-316.

Vasilenko, B.A. 1970. Zametki o geraklejskich klejmach, *SovA* 3, 217-224.

Vinogradov, Ju.G. 1972. Keramičeskie klejma ostrova Fasos, *NumEpigr* 10, 3-63.

Vinogradov, Ju.G. 1994. New inscriptions on lead from Olbia, *Ancient Civilizations from Scythia to Siberia* 1.1, 103-111.

Walbank, M.B. 1983. Leases of Sacred Property in Attica, *Hesperia* 52, 100-135, 177-199, 200-206, 207-231.

Whitbread, I.K. *Greek Transport Amphorae. A Petrographical and Archaeological Study*. Exeter.

Zeest, I.B. 1951a. Keramičeskaja tara Elisavetovskogo gorodišča i ego kurgannogo nekropolja, *MatIsslA* 19, 119-124.

Zeest, I.B. 1951b. Novye dannye o torgovych svjazjach Bospora s Južnym Pričernomor'em, *VDI* 2, 106-116.

Zeest, I.B. 1960. *Keramičeskaja tara Bospora* (MatIsslA, 83). Moskva.

Abbreviations

IAK	Izvestija imperatorskoj Archeologičeskoj Komissii.
IGAIMK	Izvestija Gosudarstvennoj Akademii istorii material'noj kul'tury.
KSIIMK	Kratkie soobščenija instituta istorii material'noj kul'tury.
TrudyGIM	Trudy Gosudarstvennogo Istoričeskogo Muzeja.

The Formation of a Russian Science of Classical Antiquities of Southern Russia in the 18th and early 19th century[1]

Irina V. Tunkina

"Those who believe science begins with them do not understand science"
(M.P. Pogodin, 1869)

It is my firm belief, that studies of the history of science are possible only on the basis of a wide and detailed analysis of its authentic facts: this is inconceivable without proper consideration of the archival heritage of our predecessors. Without an examination and a critical analysis of various archive material, it is altogether impossible to write the history of any science at the level which scholarship has reached at the beginning of the third millennium. Most Russian archaeologists have paid little attention to, or have even completely disregarded, the history of their science, as demonstrated by the fact that no monograph about the foundation and activities of the central state body of pre-revolutionary Russian archaeology – the Archaeological Commission (1859-1919) has yet been published. There are still many gaps in our knowledge of the scientific heritage of Russian Classical studies. Quite a number of scholars whose field of study was the northern Black Sea region in Antiquity have simply been forgotten by modern archaeologists and thus deleted from the historical memory. Working from an investigation of the extensive archive materials, scientific literature and social-political periodicals of the 18th to the middle of the 19th centuries, I will attempt to present a general account of the establishment of the Russian school of Greek and Roman archaeology, epigraphy and numismatics of the northern Black Sea.[2]

The first stage of acquaintance with antiquities from the northern Black Sea region

The early period (1725-1802) was in fact concerned exclusively with the activities of the St Petersburg Academy of Sciences (founded in 1724) and those of the travellers with inquiring minds so characteristic of the Age of Enlightenment. This period can be subdivided into two chronological phases, the division between them being the year 1774 when Russia gained access to the Black Sea coast. At the time of the final reforms of Peter the Great, the social and cultural basis emerged which was necessary for the development (under rigid state control) of the basic research and the public institutions associated with it – the Academy of Sciences, the universities and the museums. The evolution of European science, based on the data of scientific fact and the consolidation of the inductive methods of cognition, was also reflected in Russia in the incipient science of antiquities, a field which had attracted the attention of academic scholars and well-educated officials, mostly foreigners in Russian service. In Russia in the 18th century, the humanities had not yet been differentiated into separate disciplines. Scholars of that time were true encyclopaedists applying their knowledge freely in a wide variety of fields. With the exception of a few scholars from the St Petersburg Academy of Sciences, no circle of specialists making a professional study of the material remains of the Greek and Roman periods had yet been formed. The scholars limited themselves to investigations of the literary tradition, the small number of ancient coins known at the time and a few other *Antiquitäten*, which had been assembled in various state and private collections in the capital.

The Classicism and Neo-Classicism of the 18th century, had established Antiquity as the normative ideal of science and the arts, and given rise to a group of antiquarians, brought up in the traditions of worshipping "antiquities", among the milieu of Russian educated society. It is during this period that the creation of the funds for the study of antiquities was started in Russia. Different cabinets of curiosities reflected the expansion of Russian science in the 18th century, accumulating along with specimens of natural history various objects of ethnography, epigraphy, numismatics, and archaeology. Private collections and the first museums (the *Kunstkammer* founded by Peter the Great in 1714, and the Hermitage founded by Catherine II in 1764) acquired antiquities – chance finds and artefacts from robbers' excavations of Sarmatian and Scythian barrows in the Don and Azov Sea areas. The most outstanding of these was the early Scythian Mel'gunov's hoard discovered in 1763 by General A.P. Mel'gunov during the excavation of the Litoj Kurgan and investigated by Academician G.F. Mueller (1705-1783).[3]

After the northern Black Sea region became part of Russia, Russian science during the period of encyclopaedism found a new object for study in the form of remains from the Greek and Roman periods. It became possible for the educated class of Russian society to familiarise itself with ancient sites not only in the Mediterranean but also in Southern Russia. The end of the 18th century saw the beginning of a virtual pilgrimage to Tauris and this became especially fashionable after the visit of Catherine II to the Novorossijskij Kraj (1787). The adoration of Antiquity is also reflected in the renaming of quite a number of Turkish and Tartar towns and fortresses in the Greek fashion. On maps of the newly acquired territories names like

Cherson (1778), Olbiopol (1781), Eupatoria, Leukopol, Sevastopol, Simferopol, Phanagoria, Theodosia (now Feodosia, 1784), Ovidiopol (1792), and Odessa (1795) appear. Simultaneously with the arrangement of the system of administration of the vast but sparsely populated steppe region, various large-scale interdisciplinary natural-science and geographical studies of these territories began.

Much of the land description consisted of topographical surveys of different archaeological sites in the context of the natural and anthropogenic landscape including the recording of different natural features as well as ancient architecture on the same basic maps. The name of the Prince of Tauris, G.A. Potemkin (1733-1791), is associated with the order to carry out surveys in the Crimea of all "sights and old buildings" (1777), a description of the lands of Novorossia (New Russia) and the Azov Province with drawings of "all the most important places" (1782), composing a natural-science description of Tauris and a "review of the Ekaterinoslav region" (1783), and to describe "roads and localities of the Crimean Peninsula with historical comments" each illustrated by "plans and facades" (1784). At the same time, the activities of General Land-Surveying (1766-1843) and mapping of the Tavričeskaja Oblast (Tauric Province) were conducted by military topographers from the General Staff. The latter were ordered to make descriptions of all towns and fortresses (1784), including Chersonesos and Kerch. It was during the same period that maps were drawn with tentative locations of the ancient cities known from written sources and a plan of the ruins of Chersonesos with registration of the urban system of defence and foundations of Christian churches visible on the surface was made. In December 1786, Potemkin ordered the Tauric governor V.V. Kachovskij to organise searches for ancient coins. Thus, the first information on antiquities in the Crimea was collected on the initiative of the military and civilian administration of Novorossijskij Kraj.

During the years of the famous "scientific travels" to Siberia by the Petersburg Academy of Sciences in the 18th century, the interdisciplinary programme of research objectives was developed. This was later successfully employed in the Black Sea area with the aim of investigating the material culture in general based on the understanding of the significance of antiquities as objective sources of information about the past. The scholar-encyclopaedists from the Academy of Sciences carried out precise and detailed descriptions of the finds, they learned to identify various tools and animal bones, and even attempted to classify chronologically different types of artefacts. Special attention was focused on the technique of investigation – the necessity of total registration of all finds (regardless of their "intelligibility" to the researcher or general "importance" to the science of the time), drawing the objects discovered, mapping the country, compiling dictionaries of local terms, the drawing of ethnographic parallels, and comparative analy-

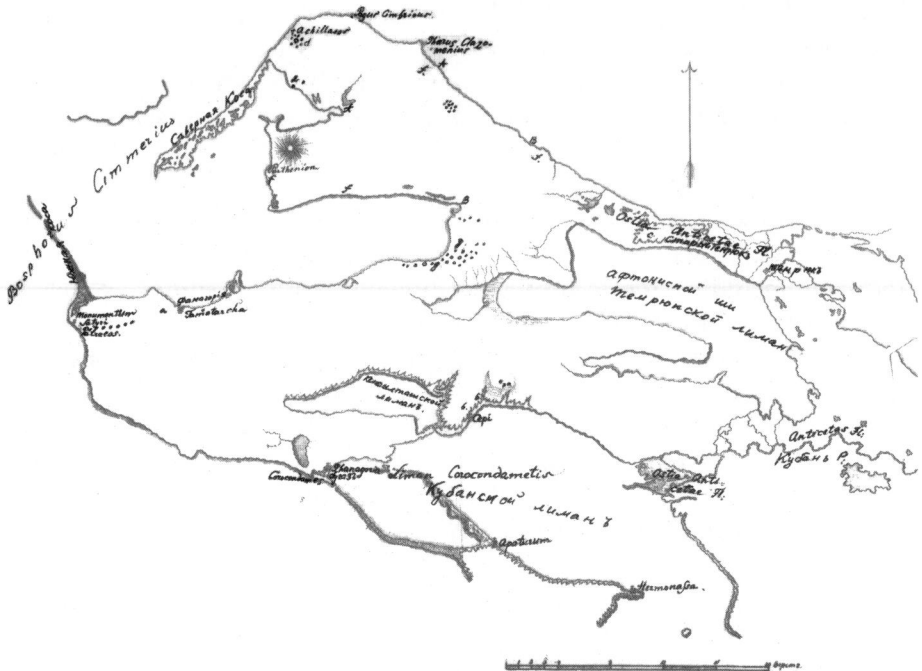

Fig. 1. Friedrich Marschall von Bieberstein. Archaeological map of the Taman Peninsula with location of ancient centres mentioned by Strabon. 1796. St Petersburg Branch of the Archives of the Russian Academy of Sciences (PFA RAS), category 1, inventory 110, file 9, sheet 15.

sis of various written and archaeological sources. A detailed account of the academic program was represented in the instructions of G.F. Mueller to Adjunct J.E. Fischer (1740). In the opinion of G.V. Vernadskij, this document is "the basic memorial of the methods of Russian historical studies" of that period. The interdisciplinary approach used by those scholars, which is reflected in descriptions and cartographic material of the time, yielded results which have not lost significance even today. This technique was most fully realised in the work of the predominantly nature science oriented expeditions of J.A. Gueldenstaedt (1773-1775), V.F. Zuev (1781-1782), K.L. Hablitz (1783-1796) and P.S. Pallas (1793-1794), who succeeded in locating and making detailed descriptions of the ruins of different fortifications, towns, settlements, systems of land-tenure and necropoleis which had not yet been excavated.

A wholly forgotten scholar of antiquities from Bosporos is the naturalist Baron F. Marschall von Bieberstein (1768-1826), who left an unsigned article about the epigraphic evidence from the European and Asiatic Bosporos and an unpublished treatise about monumental structures visible on the surface

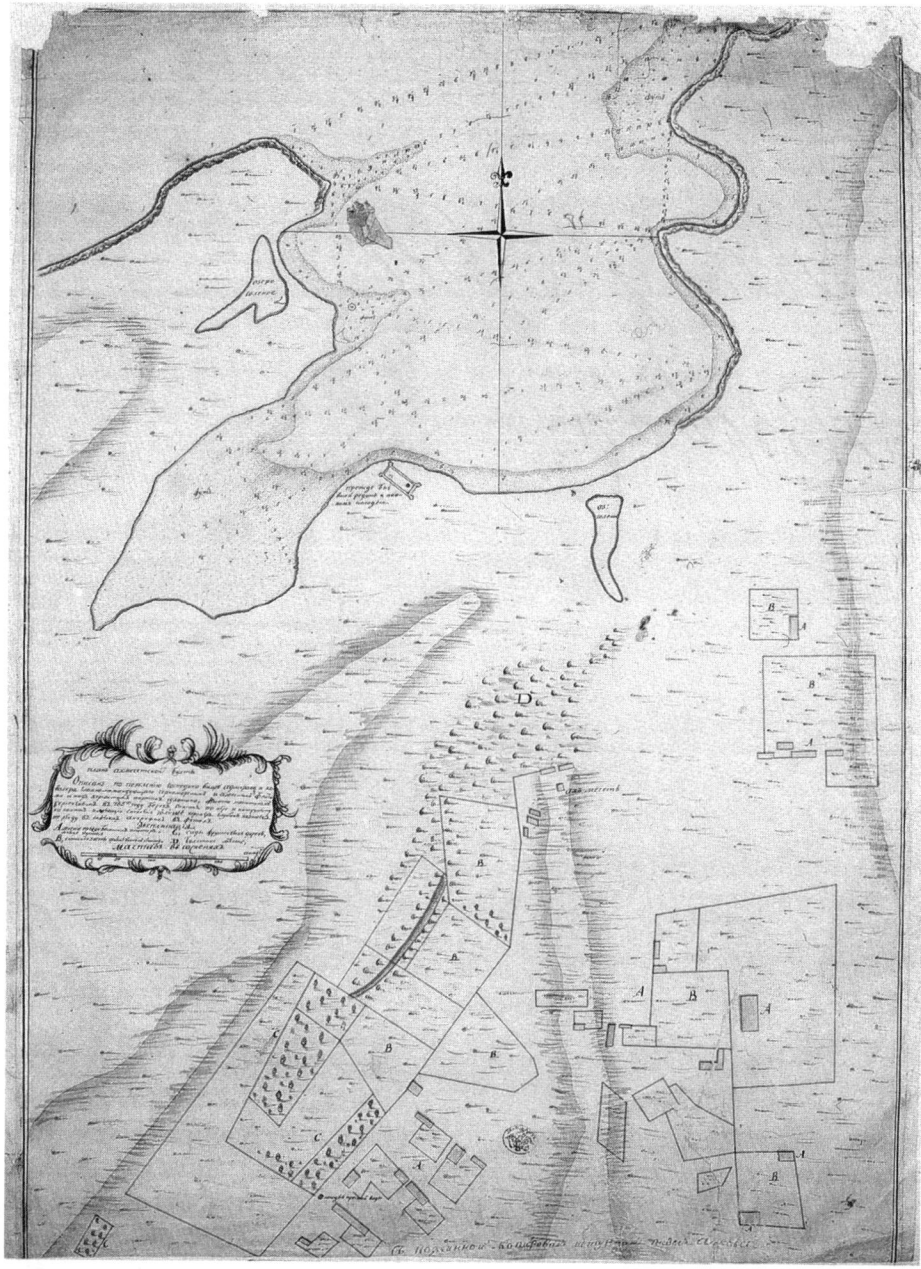

Fig. 2. Plan of Akmechet Bay ... by Captain of the Fleet Bersenev. Copied by Navigator P. Alekseev. End of the 18th century. Russian State Military-Historical Archives (RGVIA), manuscript group 846, inventory 11, file 23565, sheet 1.

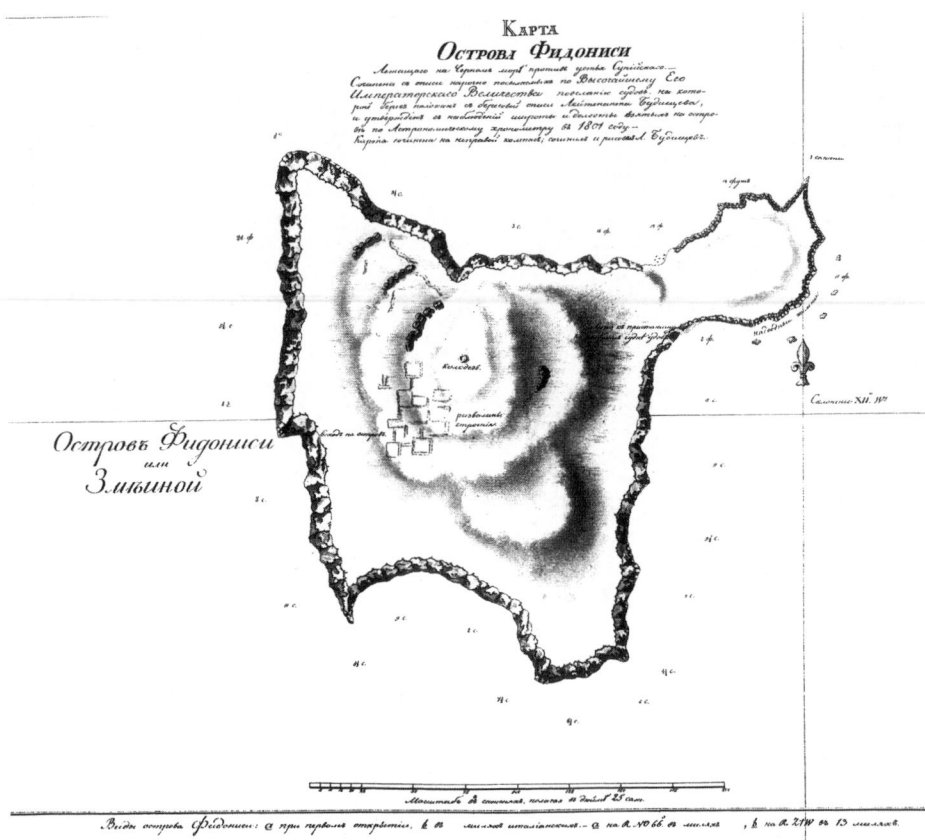

Fig. 3. Map of the Island of Phidonisi … Composed from the description … of Lieutenant Budiščev … in 1801. Composed and drawn by Lieutenant Budiščev (Scale: 27 sazhens to one English inch, 1:2100). Scientific Research Division of Manuscripts of the Library of the Russian Academy of Sciences (NIOR BAN), manuscript group 35, additional inventory 2, no. 331, sheet 1.

in the Eastern Crimea and Taman (1796), illustrated with the first archaeological map (drawn by him personally) of the Taman Peninsula with tentative location of ancient cities according to Strabon's information.[4] Similar
work by K.L. Hablitz (1752-1821) and P.S. Pallas (1741-1811) has recorded
traces of a uniquely preserved ancient cultural landscape on the Herakleian
Peninsula in the Crimea. Hablitz ensured that topographical surveys of the
Herakleian Peninsula were carried out with registration of the network of
ancient roads visible on the surface and of various ancient structures. These
surveys are now a document of great importance for studies of the agriculture of the Tauric Chersonesos during the Classical period. In the Russian
State War-Historical Archives, I found the original of this document, which
had previously been thought lost: "Plan of the ruins of ancient Cherson.

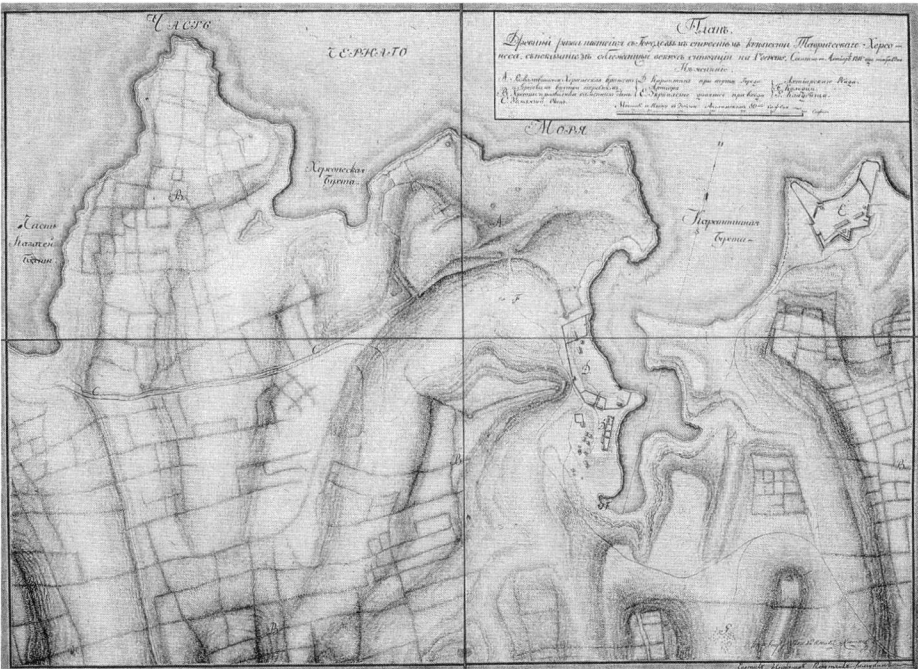

*Fig. 4. Plan of the ruined ancient fortress of Tauric Chersonesos and an urban build-
ing, shown together with the surrounding area to within 1 verst. Composed in
Akhtiar, 1st November, 1811. A – The ruined Chersonesean fortress with an urban
building inside; B – The ridges and ruins of stone walls; C – Earthen trench; D –
The quarantine of the port of the town of Akhtiar; E – The Tenth Fort at the entrance
to the Akhtiar Roadstead; F – Wells; G – Cemetery. Scale of the plan – 50 sazhens to
one English inch (1:4200). Drawn by Engineer-Lieutenant Ivan Simučin, certified
by Engineer-Colonel Čaponov. Russian State Military-Historical Archives
(RGVIA), manuscript group 349, inventory 37, file 3574, sheet 1.*

With indication of former straight streets marked with earth-coloured lines
and living blocks marked in red. Composed in 1786. Drawn by Topographer
of the Second Class Pepelev"; it was presented to Empress Catherine II (in
the right upper part of the plan is the signature of Hablitz). This plan was
drawn with high precision to a scale of 1:21000, and the total area surveyed
exceeded 100 km². This is the first map to indicate the remains of the ancient
land-division system (cadastre) in the *chora* of Tauric Chersonesos. The map
is an excellent example of the scientific documentation of "the brilliant age
of Catherine". We can discern here not only the hand of a very skilled topographer but also a reflection of the "ecosystematic" approach to landscape by
the initiator of the surveys – Hablitz. An engraving made after Hablitz's
plan, on which the surveys were erroneously attributed by A. Bertier de la
Garde (1842-1920) to A. Strukov, was republished by V.D. Blavatskij[5] and has

since taken its rightful, important place in the world literature of Classical studies. The plan has been used by many different scholars as an indispensable source for the reconstruction of the total number of land-plots demarcated on the basis of the rectangular grid on the Herakleian Peninsula in the Crimea.[6]

The descriptions and plans produced at the end of the 18th century are of a high source value as the only documents about sites which, having been partly disturbed or completely destroyed, may now only be discovered by chance or by means of aerial photographs. Students of Antiquity only returned to the "ecosystematic" approach, albeit at a new scientific level, in the second half of the 20th century within the frame of what is now one of the most rapidly developing fields concerned with the spatial organisation of Greek the *poleis*. The works of the encyclopaedists from the Academy of Sciences proved to be actually the first interdisciplinary regional studies and yielded results which are, at present, a primary source of the highest value.

However, in the 18th century archaeological methods were at a rudimentary level. Excavations in the northern Black Sea region were sporadic, and discoveries were made primarily during construction of fortification works. The primary "excavators" continued to be the armed forces: A.P. Mel'gunov (the Litoj Barrow, 1763), Van der Weide (the necropolis of Phanagoria, not later than 1793), F. de Wollant (Ovidiopol, 1795), et al. Only a few of the field works were documented – the officers, enthusiastic about antiquities, sent reports to the capital and articles about their finds to scientific societies in Europe. The search for antiquities pursued merely antiquarian objectives, and it was indeed the officers themselves who became the first collectors of *Antiquitäten* (V.M. Dolgorukov-Krymskij, P. van Suchtelen, F. de Wollant, L. de Waxel, et al.).

Thus, the initial stage included the acquaintance of Russian society with problems of the ancient world and with authentic antiquities, which became available for study after the northern Black Sea region became part of the Russian Empire. In the 18th century, scientific results were obtained and interpreted not only within the scientific community of the Academy of Sciences and the universities in Moscow and St Petersburg, but also outside that community. During the Age of Enlightenment, archaeology developed, in fact, from the "geographical practice" as a constituent element of land-description. Concerned with land-description (and within its context with archaeological, cartographical and topographical investigations), though from widely differing motives, were naturalists, naval officers, military engineers, statesmen, diplomats, land-planners, missionaries, and colonists. The most significant achievement of this phase was the development of the "ecosystematic" method of studies of ancient immovable objects within the context of the anthropogenic and natural landscape. At the same time, the science of antiquities was also regarded as part of museum and antiquarian research undertaken to serve as "illustration" for the narratives of ancient authors, and, according to the aesthetics of J.J. Winckelmann, it was also expert technical examination of art criticism.

The second stage of the formation of a Russian science of the antiquities in the northern Black Sea region

The period from 1803 to 1838 is characterised by the process whereby the study of Classical Antiquity came to recognise and define itself as a distinct discipline. During these years, two centres of ancient studies were established in Russia – in St Petersburg and Novorossia (Odessa and Kerch). In the northern capital, the Academy of Sciences lost its monopoly of studies of the ancient world. Various experts in the branch of ancient studies had appeared in the Academy of Arts, the Public Library, the Hermitage, and the University. In 1803, in the Academy of Sciences new regulations were accepted by which history was included in the circle of disciplines studied. The academic studies of the ancient world, represented particularly by certain purely armchair scientists, focused not on the archaeological evidence, but on various written, numismatic and epigraphic sources. The study of medieval traditions in the history of ancient Rus resulted in several unpublished works by the Academician J.Ph. Krug (1764-1844) about the island of Phidonisi (Leuke of the Classical tradition), which was renowned for its Sanctuary of Achilles. Academician Fr. Graefe (1780-1851), who was professor at St Petersburg University and the curator of the coins in the *Münz-Kabinett* and the Hermitage, is also known for his epigraphic studies. The first prominent scholar to enter the Academy of Sciences was H.K.E. Koehler (1765-1838), the curator of the Hermitage. In 1804 and 1821 Koehler made two archaeological expeditions across the Novorossijskij Kraj. He carried out excavations on the Majak Peninsula near Sevastopol (1804) and in Olbia (1821). Following this scholar's report, a decree of the Ministry of Internal Affairs, approved by Tsar Alexander I, was issued forbidding travellers to collect antiquities on the state lands of Tauris (1805). Koehler's journey of 1804 led to a remarkable discovery – the monument to the Bosporan Queen Komosarye, whose name was not known from the ancient literary tradition. From the inscription on its pedestal (*CIRB* 1015), the system of titles of the Bosporan kings became known for the first time. To this monument Koehler devoted a special treatise (1805) which laid the foundations for the study of the antiquities of the Bosporan Kingdom.[7] What one might call the "pearl" of Olbian epigraphy – the decree in honour of Protogenes (*IOSPE* I², 32)[8] – was first published in 1822 , another of Koehler's achievements.

Having returned from his expedition of 1821, H.K.E. Koehler argued that enormous damage to science was caused by robbers' excavations conducted without permission of the authorities. The Academician proposed to forbid any excavations until some means were found to conduct them "with

Fig. 5-6. 5) Portrait of the Curator of the Hermitage, Academician H.K.E. Koehler. Engraving by A.G. Afanas'ev after F. Krüger's drawing. 6) Portrait of J. de Blaramberg. Engraving by Kriguberi (1837) after M. Blaramberg's drawing. Odessa Regional Museum.

advantage to science". In Koehler's opinion, the excavations of barrows in the Crimea were to be entrusted to two officers who would undertake such work near Sevastopol, and then transfer their activities to the vicinity of Kerch and to the Taman Peninsula, in order to ensure that all the antiquities found, without exception, would be sent to the Ministry of the People's Enlightenment, under the jurisdiction of which the Academy of Sciences had been since 1802. This proposal was in no way fortuitous, since it was the army rather than the scientists who were the first excavators at archaeological sites in southern Russia. The field work was of a merely antiquarian character, being intended to satisfy the curiosity of the army and those officials who joined the rush to unearth monumental Greek architecture and spectacular antiquities – golden adornments, Greek sculpture, painted pottery, gems, coins, etc. In the course of such searches, a number of fine or valuable objects were torn out of their archaeological context, while most of the archaeological material failed to receive the attention it deserved. Most of the discoveries were made by chance; the finds were seldom transferred to museums, but were mostly distributed among various collectors, and thus as a rule lost for scientific research. Among such activities we should mention excavations at various ancient necropoleis: barrows near the village of Taman by Colonel Ja.L. Parok'ja (1817-1818), two barrows near Kerch by the

Fig. 7. Portrait of Duke A.E.S. Richelieu's aide-de-camp, Captain of Lifeguards of the Izmajlovskij Regiment I.A. Stempkovski. Lithograph after E. Buchardy's portrait (Paris). Between 1816 and 1818.

Commander of the Rowing Transport Flotilla N.Ju. Patignoti (1820-1821),[9] barrows in the neighbourhood of Anapa by Lieutenant-colonel Grinfel'd (1837), etc. The main task of the *Planter* (gardener) of the Black Sea Fleet, K. Kruze at the town-site of the the Chersonesos-Korsun was to bring to light the architecture of ancient buildings. By excavating the fills without making any records, Kruze unearthed the remains of three Byzantine churches and carried out excavations on the islet of St Climent near Sevastopol (1827, 1833). The excavations of the sanctuaries of Achilles conducted by hydrographers of the Black Sea Fleet, Lieutenant-commander N.D. Kritskij (1823, the island of Phidonisi; 1824, Tendra Spit) and Midshipman K.M. Navrockij (1824, Tendra Spit) also belong to this group. The sanctuary on the Tendra was an earthen hill, which was excavated to its full extent, though not all the way down to the bedrock. Having encountered marble statues and inscriptions, the naval detachment proceeded to sift the excavated soil through a sieve in order not to miss coins and graffiti. This site, which had not only been considered lost, but whose very existence had been doubted by a number of scholars, is now again becoming a subject of study owing to the survival of drawings and lists of coins.[10]

In his work based on the results of the archaeological expedition of 1821, Academician H.K.E. Koehler published a considerable volume of previously unknown evidence. A number of his works are devoted to an analysis of the literary tradition concerning the northern littoral of the Pontos and to different problems of the historical topography of the Black Sea area. Koehler, like the majority of the professional scientists-antiquarians of his time, interpreted the objectives of the science of antiquities within the conventions of aesthetics as laid down by J.J. Winckelmann. The St Petersburg Academician published mostly the new epigraphic and numismatic material, along with a few sculptures and in this his merits cannot be doubted. A professor at Moscow University P.M. Leont'ev[11] said of Koehler that, he "laid the foundation for the study of antiquities found in the south of Russia and raised this study to a high level of strict, scientific clarity". Nevertheless, as is clear from Koehler's published works, and the unpublished diary of his journey to Novorossia in 1821, the Academician was very poorly conversant with the building remains of Classical Antiquity, and quite often he was not capable (in contrast to the naturalists K. Hablitz and P.S. Pallas, who had described the same locations thirty years before Koehler, though they were not especially concerned with antiquities) of correctly evaluating and interpreting the particular archaeological situation of the immovable objects visible on the surface. Koehler manifestly neglected the cognitive possibilities of the archaeological evidence and underestimated its value. Thus, he spoke extremely sceptically of the ruins he examined in Pantikapaion: "Except for two or three ruined architectural memorials nothing has remained of this city".[12] This verdict was pronounced by the metropolitan antiquarian in the first quarter of the 19th century when most of the town-sites in the European Bosporos had not yet been treated as stone quarries, and the ground plans of different fortifications and separate buildings were easily discernible on the surface. In contrast, an Odessa antiquarian I.A. Stempkovskij, during the same years urged scholars to turn their attention without delay to the "most important site on the European coast of the Straits" – the capital of the Bosporan Kingdom – Pantikapaion (Kerch), and moreover not only to the barrows surrounding it but also to the city itself, especially its citadel, and to draw a detailed plan, as well as to record graphically the remains of other town-sites and ramparts in the Eastern Crimea.[13]

A "counterbalance" to the St Petersburg academic science was established by informal societies of antiquarians – various circles of laymen, which were arising spontaneously in various provinces across the country. Metropolitan historical and archaeological circles (that of A.I. Musin-Puškin, N.P. Rumjancev, A.N. Olenin, et al.) and literary and historical societies such as the Society of Russian History and Antiquities attached to Moscow University, the Free Society of Amateurs of Russian Letters, etc., had, as one of their activities, the history of Russia and a broadly conceived science concerning antiquities including epigraphy, numismatics, and archaeology. The informal social scientific organisations brought together professional historians and various amateur antiquarians, patrons of arts, collectors, servicemen, and representatives of the aristocracy and the local upper bureaucratic strata. Apparently, at the initial stage of the development of the science, the predominance of *dilettanti* in such groups was inevitable due to the

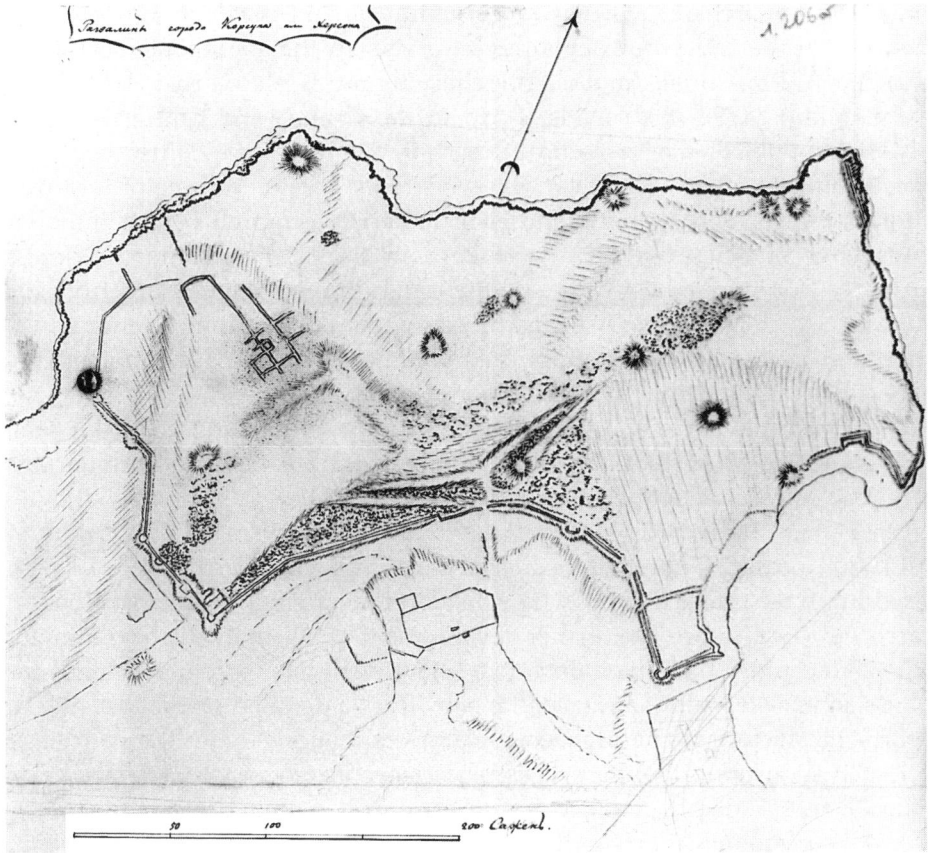

Fig. 8. Ruins of the town of Korsun' or Chersonesos. Copy by I.P. Koeppen from 1819. St Petersburg Branch of the Archives of the Russian Academy of Sciences (PFA RAS), manuscript group 30, inventory 1, file 475, sheet 206 (verso).

absence of a body of really scientific knowledge and principles, which was as yet unformed. Among those interested in the history and antiquities of Southern Russia were I.M. Murav'ev-Apostol, E.A. Bolchovitinov, V.V. Kapnist, S.V. Kapnist, N.I. Gnedič, A.S. Griboedov, P.P. Svin'in, K.N. Batjuškov, J.G.M. von Strandman, and A.A. Pisarev.

Among the most prominent scholars concerned with the antiquities of Southern Russia was the Russian German P. Koeppen (1793-1864), who lived alternately in St Petersburg and the Crimea. Results of his first trips to Novorossia have been reflected in the manuscript of his unpublished monograph about Olbia and two pamplets published in Vienna.[14] His "Krymskij Sbornik" (Crimean Collection, 1837) comprising descriptions of different historical sites and records of toponyms of Tauris is rightly considered one of the principal works in this field.[15] Preserved among Koeppen's documents in the archives are diaries of his travels and materials for scientific works on the archaeology of Southern Russia, which have still not been used to their full potential. Another traveller, the Swiss naturalist F. Dubois de Montpéreux (1798-1850) made a trip to the Crimea and Caucasus (1832-1834) and published a six-volume description of his journey illustrated with a magnificent atlas.[16] However, a considerably greater volume of information is represented by his manuscript materials acquired by the Imperial Academy of Sciences (1903) and kept in the St Petersburg Academic Archives. Of the highest value are the rough drawings and plans from his diaries, which remain undistorted by subsequent lithography or engravings and only partly used in the published volumes and atlas. These documents are still awaiting detailed investigation.

An informal circle of antiquarians also arose in the Novorossijskij Kraj, having brought together among its numbers various amateur antiquarians from Odessa (I.A. Stempkovskij, J. de Blaramberg, A.F. Panagiodor-Nikovul, A.Ja. Fabr, E. Taitbout de Marygny, A.F. Spada, A.I. Lëvšin, V.G. Tepljakov, et al.) and Kerch (P. Dubrux, R. Scassi, A. Digbi, A.B. Ašik, D.V. Karejša). These two informal colleges should be considered as a single Southern Russian archaeological centre, the further development of which by the beginning of the 20th century had given birth to a scientific milieu extremely fecund for Russian science. Antiquarians of the New Russia devoted several decades to particular historical and archaeological investigations under the patronage of such sponsors of Southern Russian science as Governor-Generals A. de Richelieu, L.A. de Langeron, M.S. Voroncov, the Commanders in Chief of the Black Sea Fleet and Ports J. de Traversay and A. Greig. The leading role in the Novorossiysk circle was played by persons superior to the average amateurs (the latter word being devoid here of any disparaging tinge) by their level of intellectual and scientific development. Such were the Corresponding Member of the Paris Académie des Inscriptions et Belles Lettres, J. Stempkovskij (1788-1832); Corresponding Member of the Berlin-Brandenburg Academy of Sciences J. de Blaramberg (1772-1831), and the initiator of Kerch field archaeology P. Dubrux (1770-1835). The amateurs commenced the investigation of town-sites and excavations of barrows: having a scientific perspective, they understood the necessity of properly documenting their excavations and the importance of topographical recording of the sites. The Polish archaeologist, Count J. de Potocki, then Dubrux, and later Ašik (1801-1854) developed the technique of the complete excavation of barrows down to the bedrock. Antiquarians from Southern Russia established active contacts with western researchers, adopting their methods of scientific source criticism (A. Boeckh, D. Raoul-Rochette, F. Dubois de Montpéreux, et al.), and published the first scientific works open for discussion, which received a broad reaction both in scientific studies and in Russian periodicals, as well as a certain resonance abroad.

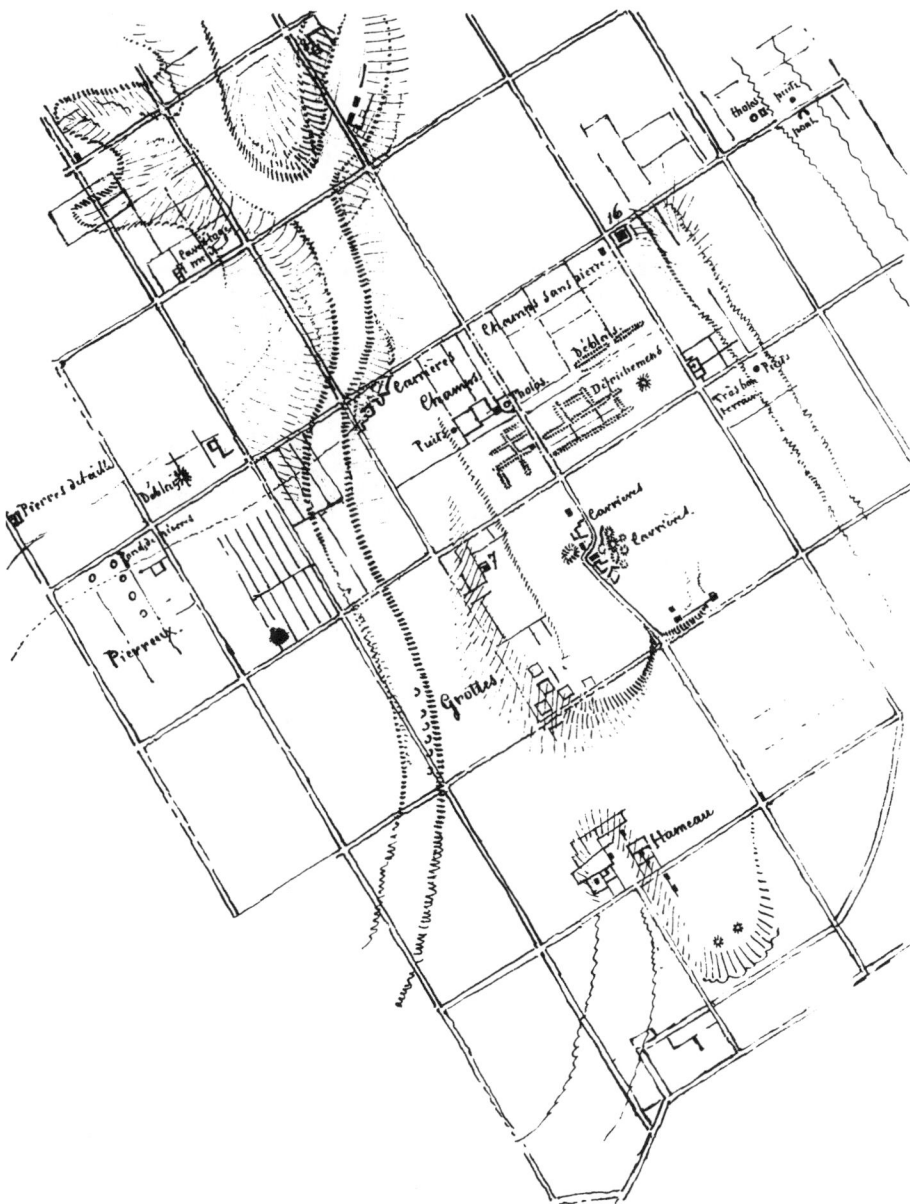

Fig. 9. F. Dubois de Montpéreux's travel diary with a plan of ancient land plots and indication of farmhouses on the Herakleian Peninsula in the Crimea. St Petersburg Branch of the Archives of the Russian Academy of Sciences (PFA RAS), manuscript group 86, inventory 1, file 24, sheet 176.

№ I

voyez l'explica
tion, page 8

87

NB:
Cet astre   est figuré au bas
                        du poteau

№ 3

85

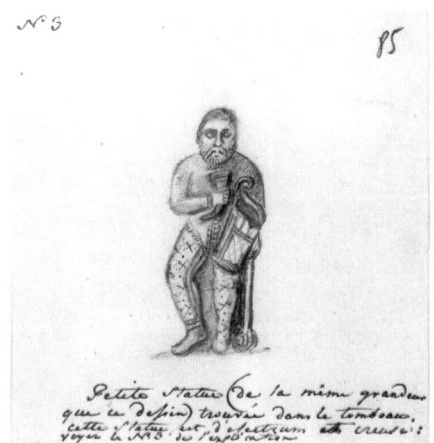

Petite Statue de la même grandeur
que ce dessin trouvée dans le tombeau,
cette statue est d'argent et creusée:
voyez le №3 de l'explication

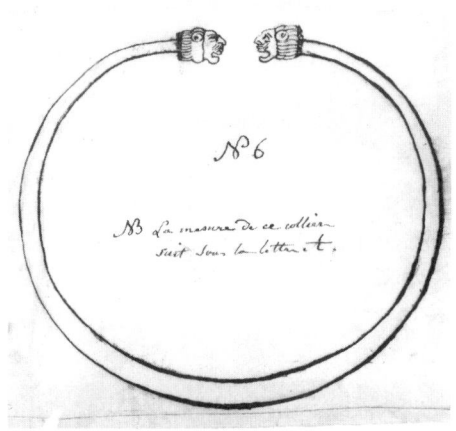

№ 6

NB La mesure de ce collier
suit sous la lettre t.

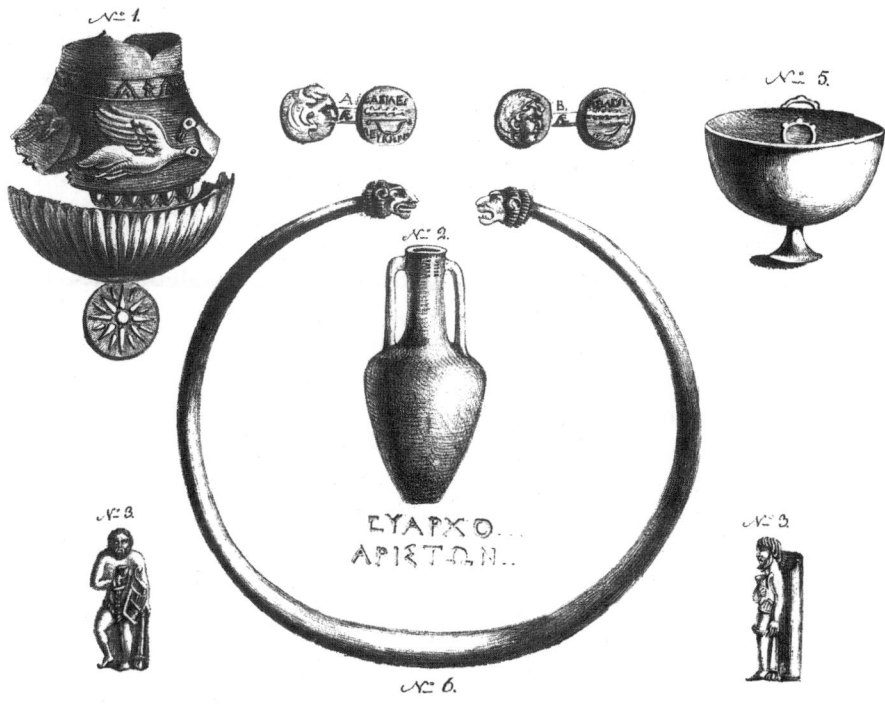

*Fig. 10-13. Finds from a kurgan excavated by N.Ju. Patignoti near Kerch (1821).
10-12) Left. Drawings by J. de Blaramberg. No. 1: round-bottomed vessel in two
fragments of silver, incrusted with gold, with swimming geese catching fish. No.
3: electron figurine of a standing Scythian with a* gorytos *at his belt and a* rhyton
*in his hand. No. 6: large silver torque weighing 480 g and 48.2 cm in diameter,
decorated with lion heads at each end. The Manuscript Archives of the Institute of
the History of Material Culture RAS (RA IIMK), manuscript group 7, inventory
1, file 11, sheets 85, 87, 90. First publication. 13) Above. Lithograph in I.P.
Blaramberg's article* "Aperçu, ou notice explicative de quelques objets d'antiquité découverts en Tauride dans un tumulus près du site de l'ancienne
Panticapée" *(Scientific Research Division of Manuscripts of the Library of the
Russian Academy of Sciences (NIOR BAN), F229).*

It is characteristic, that it was precisely among the milieu of provincial
rather than metropolitan antiquarians, that the first research programme in
the Russian science of Classical Antiquity in the northern Black Sea region
was developed, as formulated by J. Stempkovskij in his note to M. de
Voroncov: "Note sur les recherches d'antiquités qu'il y aurait à faire dans la
Russie Méridionale" (1823).[17] In this paper, the strategic aims and tactical
objectives of the development of the science are set out for the first time.

These include composing corpora of the narrative tradition, exhaustive corpora of epigraphic, numismatic and archaeological evidence, total records and study of all ancient sites, in particular of town-sites, and carrying out excavations for scientific purposes, taking measures towards preservation, restoration and protection of antiquities, drawing plans of the architectural remains. It was the author's belief that antiquarians should be brought together in a scientific society with a common programme of field and theoretical studies, and that they should promote the establishment of a network of specialised archaeological museums. According to Stempkovskij, all antiquities without exception had to be subjected to scientific studies, irrespective of their material and artistic value: "We must gather carefully and store each fragment of ancient manuscripts, inscriptions on stones, each medal, and each fragment of statues or bas-reliefs: the most insignificant thing can sometimes explain some ancient tradition and disperse the darkness obscuring it".

In the first third of the 19th century the Russian government and the local military and civil authorities took a number of measures for the protection of antiquities (1805, 1822, 1824, 1826, 1827, 1836, 1837, etc.). Objects of the Greek and Roman period, acquired with considerable difficulty in the course of wartime activities and marine and land travels started to accumulate in state and private museum collections in Southern Russia. The realisation of the significance of *Antiquitäten* not only as works of ancient art but also as historical evidence led to the foundation of the first public archaeological collections: the Chamber of Rarities of the Black Sea Depot of Maps in Nikolaev (1803); the Cabinet of Curiosities and the *Münz-Kabinett* of the Kharkov University (1805), and the Theodosian (Feodosian) Museum of Antiquities (1811). While at the beginning of that century, museums were created whose displays presented a wide range of exhibits, towards the end of the first quarter of the 19th century two specialised archaeological collections had been formed in those regions where numerous finds of antiquities had been made. These were: the Odessa Municipal Museum of Antiquities (1825) and the Kerch Museum of Antiquities (1826), which were headed by the Odessa antiquarian J. de Blaramberg. Blaramberg had built up a remarkable collection of Greek and Egyptian antiquities some of which later became part of the collections of the Odessa Museum.

The beginning of large-scale excavations at ancient necropoleis in the Novorossijskij Kraj was connected with the discovery of an extremely rich vault in the Kul'-Oba Kurgan near Kerch (1830). This event is rightly called the turning-point in the history of Russian archaeology, since from that time the Government began to consider the lands of Southern Russia as a source from which to supplement the Hermitage collection with works of ancient art of high artistic and material value, and to regularly allot considerable funds for excavations in the Crimea and on the Taman Peninsula. The event had significant consequences for the fate of Russian Classical archaeology, which from that time was oriented towards first and foremost Bosporan archaeology. According to the directive issued by the Minister of the Imperial Court, P.M. Volkonskij, H.K.E. Koehler and the President of the Academy of Arts, A.N. Olenin were to examine and investigate the objects delivered to the Hermitage from the northern Black Sea region. The carrying out of systematic excavations at the expense of the government, which commenced in March 1831, was entrusted to an official of the Chancellery of the Kerch-Yenikale City-Governor, D. Karejša (1808-1878) and to an official of the Asiatic Department of the Ministry of Foreign Affairs A. Ašik (1801-1854), who since 1833 had occupied the post of Director of the Kerch Museum following the death of J. de Blaramberg.

During the second phase, local antiquarians in the northern Black Sea region developed empirical field methods of excavation in settlement and cemetery sites. From the simple collecting of antiquities and digging into the cultural layer in search for works of art of the ancient times, they progressed to excavations with scientific purposes and realised the necessity of keeping a field record. The importance of recording features of the construction of ancient buildings and topographical location was recognised. They either drew personally or directed the drawing of the first plans of ancient town-sites of Bosporos and carried out the measurement of sepulchral vaults and catacombs. Comparing various information of ancient authors about the northern Black Sea region with the data of epigraphic and numismatic evidence, actually found within a layer at a site, yielded the first reference points for chronological identifications in the archaeology of Classical Antiquity. Having taken notice of the evolution of the standards of different artefacts in time, the antiquarians attempted to develop on the basis of the correlation of separate objects, in particular coins and inscriptions, a chronology and an ethnic and typological classification of different burial groups in Bosporos. The antiquarian approach to various ancient works of arts became a precursor of a whole scientific direction, which continues to develop even today at the point where the history of art and archaeology meet. It gave impulse to the first initiatives in the branch of iconographic and stylistic classification, as well as to the study of the development of the shapes of artefacts, in particular of ancient pottery.

The French emigrant P. Dubrux instituted a new practice for excavating barrows, which included excavation down to the bedrock, the keeping of progress reports, the drawing of scale plans and the writing of detailed descriptions of the objects unearthed. Of the utmost value for present-day science are the plans and descriptions of various ruins in Eastern Crimea, produced by Dubrux in the 1820-1830s with the assistance of Kerch-Yenikale City-Governor J. Stempkovskij at the request of the Grand Duke Michail Pavlovič.[18] Dubrux initiated surveys of the archaeological remains in Eastern

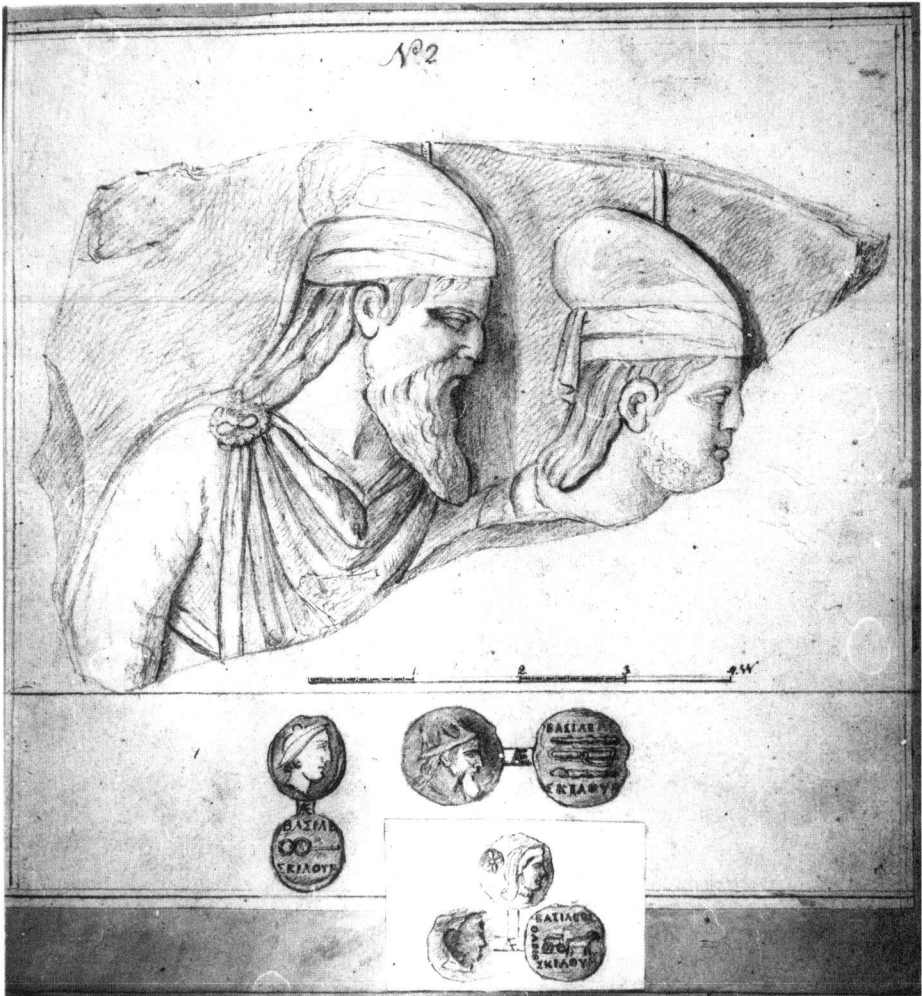

Fig. 14. Relief of Skilouros and Palakos from Scythian Neapolis (1827) and Olbian coins of Skilouros. Drawing by Michail Blaramberg. Institute of Manuscripts of the V.I. Vernadskij Library of the National Academy of Sciences of Ukraine (IR NBU), V, 1048, sheet 4.

Crimea with a clearly defined scientific goal: to gather detailed information about various immovable memorials of the ancient period on the European coast of the Kimmerian Bosporos. By means of a plane-table with a compass for measuring angles and a rope for measuring distances, Dubrux would perfect his plans, returning occasionally 20-30 times to the same locations, which in some cases were situated up to 60 km from Kerch. He devoted 14 years of his life to these extremely painstaking investigations, by which he erected for himself an eternal monument in the history of world archaeolo-

gy. Dubrux took notice of the ruins of cities and settlements and large barrows and their relation to the surrounding landscape, i.e. he studied simultaneously the adjacent territory according to the traditions of land description of the 18th century. The sites examined by him were described, measured and plotted on plans and maps. The graphical record was carried out
by Dubrux first in rough drafts in black and white, then on fully coloured
plans and drawings precisely measured and verified, which several generations of scholars of Antiquity have tried unsuccessfully to find in various
archives. In 2000 I found in the State Archives of the Russian Federation the
most complete manuscript of the key work of Dubrux containing a description of the ruins in Eastern Crimea illustrated with coloured plans and a
map, which had previously been thought lost. In Kiev, a draft manuscript of
the same work was found, and in the Archives of the State Hermitage, the
author's corrections and supplements to it and some more exact plans
turned up. As was proved by V. Schilts, a number of Dubrux's manuscripts
are preserved in the Archives of the Institut du France in Paris.[19] Two years
ago, preparations were commenced for a publication in French and in
Russian, with commentary, of all the texts of Dubrux from the 1810-1830s
based on the manuscripts preserved in the archives in Moscow, Kiev, St
Petersburg and Paris. With the help of Dubrux's descriptions and plans,
modern researchers will be able to better understand and reconstruct the
vanished objects and to identify the features of the construction and ground
plan of the town-sites of the European Bosporos, which for a very long time
have been quarried for stone to be used in the construction of new buildings.
The objectives put forward by Dubrux and Stempkovskij as early as the
beginning of the 19th century in the sphere of archaeological and topographical investigation of ancient towns and settlements on the Kerch
Peninsula, have only become pressing for Russian science since the middle
of the 20th century.

     The research tasks and technique of field works of D.V. Karejša and A.B.
Ašik, who were entrusted with field investigations in the name, and at the
request of, the authorities, developed under the influence of a certain regi-
men: the authorities in St Petersburg demanded the delivery to that city of
ever greater numbers of golden objects and other works of superb ancient
craftsmanship, choosing to neglect the various "poor" finds, which were
accumulating in the Kerch Museum. Judging by the surviving field reports,
the main attention was focused on the excavations of cemeteries which, from
the modern viewpoint, were carried out in a manner resembling treasure
hunting. There was a practice of selective excavation of single barrows or
clusters of mounds at the necropoleis of ancient towns in the Crimea and on
the Taman Peninsula. The excavations were conducted at different places
simultaneously, and not infrequently the individual excavations were left
incomplete. The originals of the reports of the excavations were sent to St

Petersburg where they were examined by metropolitan experts – H.K.E. Koehler, A.N. Olenin, and later by the curators of the Hermitage: F.A. Gille, B.K. von Koehne, E. von Muralt, L.E. Stephani. Regrettably, the development of methods of investigation of archaeological remains had not been reflected in any regulations on how to carry out excavations. The necessity for such regulations was noted by Olenin as early as 1833. Reports by Ašik and Karejša were often illustrated with drawings of finds, but very seldom with plans, drafts and sections of the sepulchral structures. A.B. Ašik, who at the beginning of his archaeological practice believed it unnecessary to follow the advice of Dubrux, came to the same conclusion as his predecessor only two years later, namely that barrows must be excavated not by trenches but rather removed completely down to the bedrock, and that it was indispensable to record the positions of the grave goods during excavation of the burials in order to be able to date them and identify the characteristic details of the burial rite.

A.B. Ašik and D.V. Karejša are often believed to have been odious figures – ignorant officials and career bureaucrats who thought exclusively about distinctions and rewards for their finds and who by their excavations damaged rather than benefited the science. In my opinion, such exclusively negative evaluation of their activities is in many respects unfair and one-sided – one should not condemn them out of hand since they worked within the limits of their abilities, powers and knowledge, and strictly adhered to the demands of the St Petersburg authorities, in the solution of archaeological problems which were interpreted by them according to the viewpoints of their time. Ašik and Karejša were accused of abusing the trust of the Government by selling antiquities abroad for the purposes of personal enrichment. Still, up to the middle of the 1840s their mode of living disproves such assertions. Notwithstanding a number of improper acts towards the end of their archaeological activities, which have been registered in documents (the affair of the discovery of two statues in Kerch linked with the resignation of Ašik in 1852; accusations that Karejša embezzled public funds in the last years of his archaeological excavations), many of the accusations are unfounded. These charges are disproved by certain documents preserved in the archives, in particular by the illustrated reports of Ašik and Karejša themselves which in the 1840s were received for examination by the Director of the 1st Department of the Hermitage F.A. Gille. In 1848 he and Karejša, examined the reports concerning the excavations of the years 1830-1847 checking them against the objects, which had actually been delivered. "I am convinced", Gille wrote, "that his manner of speaking, always simple and exact, is based on the things which he himself saw or found in the earth, and for that reason his reports about searches for Kerch's antiquities are in my opinion quite trustworthy documents". In 1843-1844 Gille visited the majority of the European museums with ancient collections,

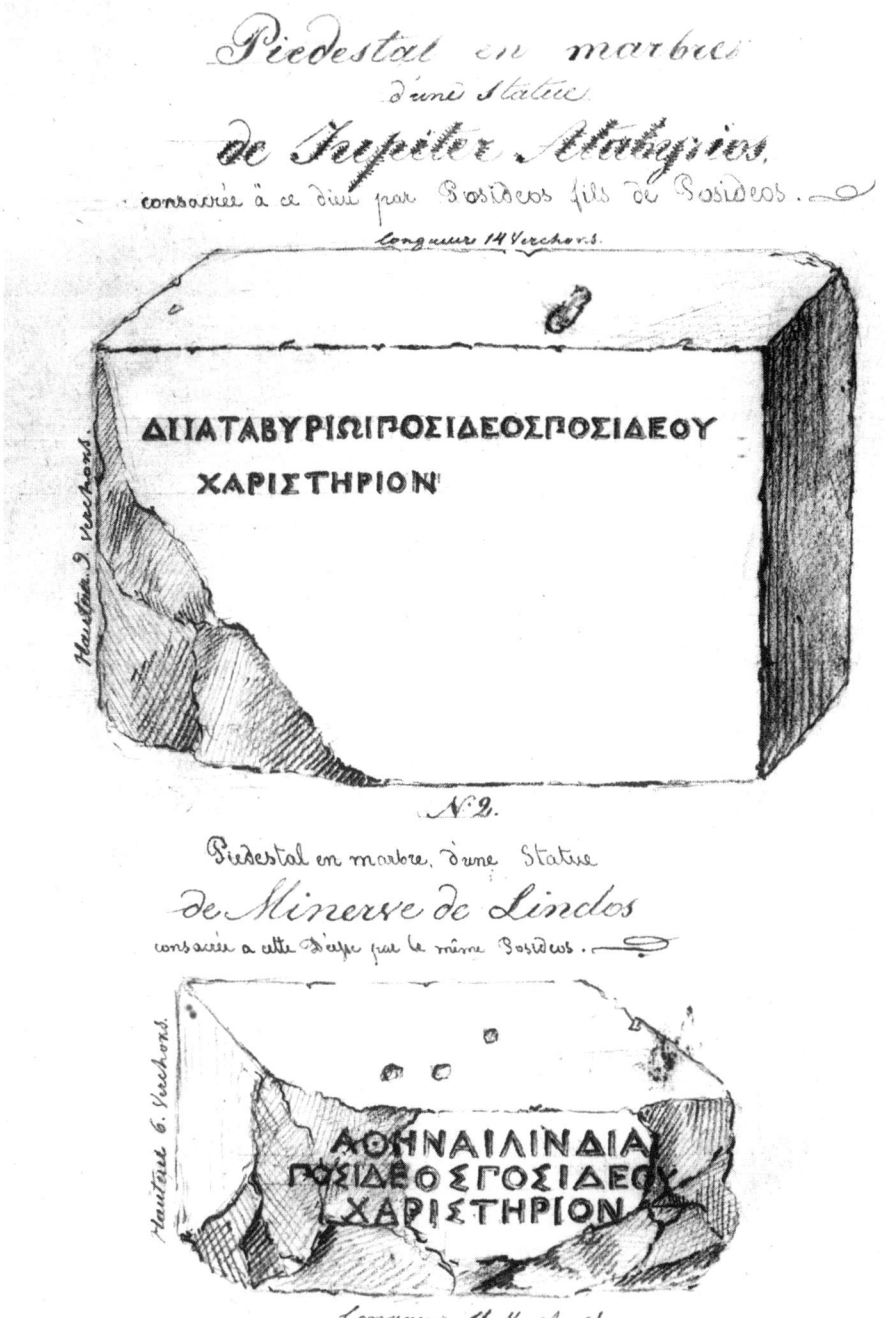

Fig. 15. Inscriptions with dedications to Zeus Atabyrios (IOSPE I², 670) and Athena Lindia (IOSPE I², 671), found in 1827 in Scythian Neapolis. Drawing by J. de Blaramberg. Institute of Manuscripts of the V.I. Vernadskij Library of the National Academy of Sciences of Ukraine (IR NBU), V, 1048, sheet 6.

and in none of them did he find "any gold objects, which ... could have belonged to the Kul'-Oba or any other barrows in the neighbourhood of Kerch". The legend about a "shop" of antiquities from which the finds would have been delivered to the Hermitage is made up, since, in addition to the attentions of various St Petersburg officials, the field works were continuously monitored by the Kerch-Yenikale City-Governor and the administration of the Novorossijskaja Province, through the mediation of which the financing of these works was carried out. The repeated inventories of grave goods, in particular the black-glazed pottery and the vases in the "Kerch style", cast doubt on many of the above mentioned accusations. In the long run, the scholars from the Hermitage had not issued any instructions on excavations in Southern Russia, therefore the methodological level of Ašik's and Karejša's works must be considered to remain above criticism. The disregard of the "official tomb robbers" documenting the locations of the investigated sites caused many first-rate burials, in particular a number of vaults with wall-painting from the Greek period, to be lost. However, we can reproach Ašik and Karejša's successors – M. de Blaramberg, K.R. Begičev and A.E. Ljucenko for the same lack of precision. The reports dealing with the excavations in Kerch during the 1850s published in the *Zapiski Odesskogo obščestva istorii i drevnostej* (Memoirs of the Odessa Society of History and Antiquities), give no indication of the location of the excavations, although they contain day to day progress records.

The accusation that the field works of the first half of the 19th century were scientifically useless due to the imperfection of their methods is in my opinion unfounded since many of these works are properly documented. From the modern viewpoint it is senseless to discuss the "correctness" of such excavations since after a lapse of 150 years any field investigations look poor in terms of methods. The truth that "everything is historical" is something of a commonplace – techniques of field archaeology investigations are constantly being improved, and the methods of fieldwork practised by many archaeologists now already seem to be anachronisms. All the surviving manuscript field reports (and the illustrations attached to them) of the first half of the 19th century, without exception, enable modern researchers to make a retrospective reconstruction of a number of archaeological complexes of basic importance. From the number of the excavation reports we are able to estimate the intensity and range of the works carried out in the European and Asiatic Bosporos in the 1830-1840s. Notwithstanding the fact that no daily diaries were kept of these excavations, the reports were submitted by Ašik and Karejša almost every month or every half year. Only by the end of the 1840s did these reports become more infrequent, provoking reproaches from the St Petersburg authorities.

While initially, the antiquarians focused their attention on excavations at necropoleis in the Eastern Crimea – those of Pantikapaion, Nymphaion, and

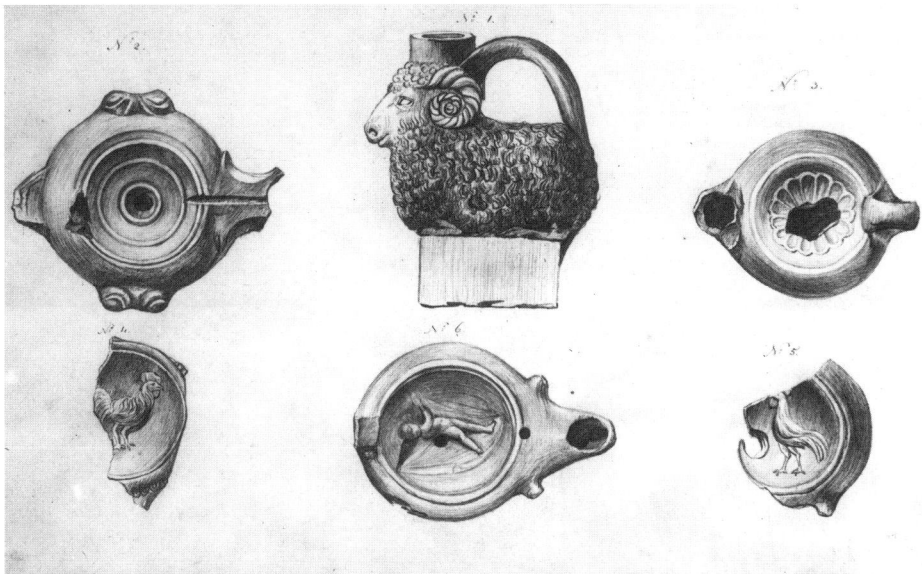

Fig. 16. Figured vessel (lekythos) *in the form of a ram, lamps and fragments of the disks of terracotta lamps, found in Olbia. Collection of J. de Blaramberg. The lekythos was recently published as a "figured vessel in the form of a ram" in* Ancient Greek Sites on the Northwest Coast of the Black Sea. Kiev 2001, p. 99. *Drawing by V. Blaramberg for the article* "Mélanges archéologiques, contenants monuments antiques découverts dans la nouvelle Russie". I Cahier. Pl. I. *Russian Section of the Archives of the St Petersburg Institute of History of the Russian Academy of Sciences (RSA SPbII RAS), manuscript group 36, inventory 1, file 779. Not earlier than 1822 g. First publication.*

Myrmekion – later, the Taman Peninsula also fell into the sphere of their interests. There, the main objects of excavations became the large barrows, most of which proved to have been robbed already.

As early as the beginning of the 19th century the first articles appeared in Russian literary and social-political periodicals attempting a definition of archaeology as a science, to mark the priorities and aims of the studies of the antiquarians, define the place and objectives of the science within the structure of other disciplines, and to identify the actual essence within the concept of "archaeology". During this period, the term "archaeology" was firmly introduced into the Russian vocabulary under the influence of Western-European literature. Archaeology was interpreted broadly as the science concerned with material objects associated with human activities, including both written documents (manuscripts, epigraphic evidence, coins) and works of ancient art, architecture and everyday life. Initially the only things which were regarded as legitimate objects of archaeological study were artis-

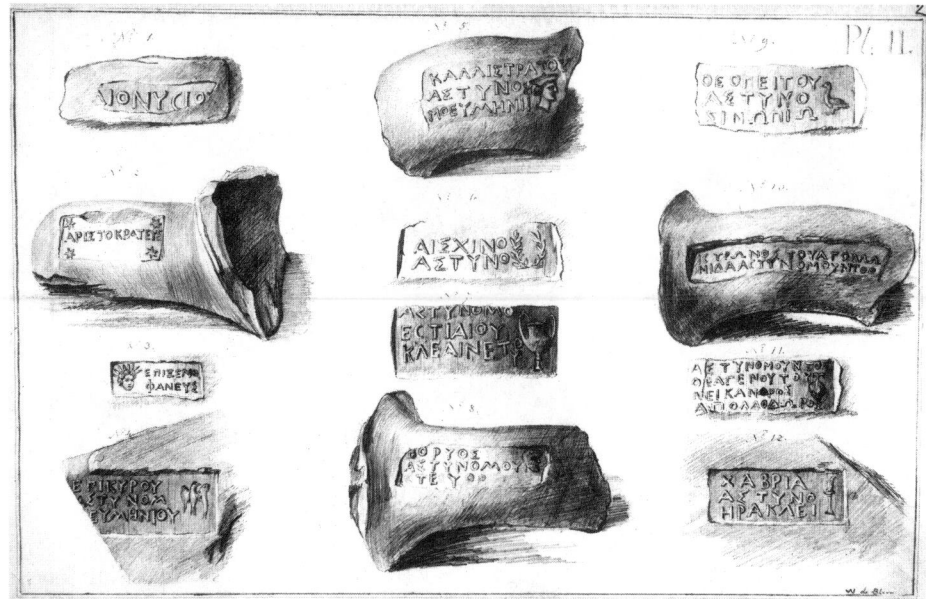

Fig. 17. Stamps of astynomoi *on amphora handles and tiles found in Olbia, from J. de Blaramberg's collection. Drawing by V. Blaramberg for the article "*Mélanges archéologiques, contenants monuments antiques découverts dans la nouvelle Russie.*" I Cahier. Pl. II, no. 1-12 Russian Section of the Archives of the St Petersburg Institute of History of the Russian Academy of Sciences (RSA SPbII RAS), manuscript group 36, inventory 1, file 779. Not earlier than 1822.*

tic artefacts of the highly advanced civilisations of ancient Egypt, Greece and Italy, their aesthetic-contemplative perception having been raised to the absolute. Most contemporary antiquarians were not devoid of Neo-Classicistic prejudices. Since 1809 the courses at Moscow University in "Archaeology and the History of the Fine Arts" and "Greek and Roman Antiquities" were taught by lecturers who were Germans by birth or Russian scientists who had studied at German universities (J. Buhle, M.T. Kačenovskij, J. Geim, M.G. Gavrilov, N.I. Nadeždin). The course in archaeology devised by A.N. Olenin and taught to students of the Academy of Arts included the study of the evidence of the political, military, and religious history, and presented "ideas about the customs, rites ... and the degree of enlightenment" of ancient peoples. It embraced a number of chronological periods and thematic issues: the "Primeval" and "Mythological" ages, and "antiquities proper, as represented in traditions and works of art of ancient peoples".

As regards the theoretical practice, the characteristic feature of the overwhelming majority of studies of the first half of the 19th century is the aesthetic approach to the description and interpretation of antiquities. It can be traced in the works of H.K.E. Koehler, A.N. Olenin, J. de Blaramberg, A. Ašik, et al. It is characteristic that Olenin considered the finds from the Kul'-Oba Kurgan in terms of the canons of Classical art. Describing a plate in the form of the figure of a recumbent horse executed in the traditions of the Scythian Animal Style, he explained what, in his opinion, was the incorrect treatment of the horns and hooves by "the lack of skill of the sculptor". The orientation towards art history also had some positive influence in the sense of bringing about an improvement in the methods of graphic presentation of the finds in publications. In the case of the unavailability of the authentic artefacts it was recommended that they be studied in the form of "casts and drawings". The services of professional architects and draughtsmen began to be enlisted for the drawing of plans and pictures of different antiquities. Olenin was inexorable in his demands for maximum information and quality of archaeological publications. They were to be provided with clear precise drawings of the antiquities without missing the slightest detail. He invented a method for making facsimile images for reading inscriptions and formulated strict rules for the execution of archaeological drawings. In the first third of the 19th century, before the advent of photography, the technique proposed by Olenin gave an opportunity to researchers and the general public to examine the archaeological evidence which had previously been inaccessible.

According to documents discovered in the archives, A.N. Olenin proposed in 1835 to found a Pan-Russian state body to supervise the archaeological and ethnographic investigations throughout the country. According to his plan, the Archaeological Commission, the Curatorial Committee of the Central Administrative Board for Searching for Antiquities in Russia was to be created with the aim of, "correct ... carrying out of archaeological research, and, which is of particular importance in the study of history, the accurate observation of the morals and customs of the various peoples who have inhabited Russia; also systematic and careful working methods in the course of the unearthing of antiquities and for resolving diverse misunderstandings encountered in the sphere of archaeology". As regards the actual geographical territory, however, he proposed to limit the activities of this board to the southern regions of the country. According to Olenin's project, this curatorial body was to become first and foremost a scientific institution bringing together the best scholars of the Academy of Sciences. Among the main tasks of the Commission was the surveying of antiquities in the Crimea, Caucasus and the lands adjacent to them, the systematisation and description of the sites and their publication, the devising of directions "for correct researches ... as regards the archaeological and historical aspects", the concentration of all financial means assigned for the excavations, supervision of the work of those locally engaged in such activities, and the submission of field reports. The researchers were to be assisted by an artist who would draw both the antiquities and any plans required and a stucco worker for casting copies of the finds. Olenin's project being two decades ahead of its time found no approval among the governmental circles of the period.

The cooperation of professional scholars from the St Petersburg Academy of Sciences and various amateurs and collectors of antiquities had a beneficial influence on the development of the study of antiquities in the 18th century, but this proved to be rather short-lived and from the beginning of the second quarter of the 19th century it gave way to jealous scientific rivalry. It was then that two scientific centres – in St Petersburg and in Novorossia – came into existence and into mutual competition. A characteristic example was the negative attitude of A.N. Olenin and H.K.E. Koehler towards the activities of P. Dubrux, who by his enthusiasm, scientific precision, scrupulousness and his innate power of observation compensated for his lack of general education and readily identifiable specialist knowledge in the field of studies of the ancient world. A modern specialist may be bewildered by the comments of the metropolitan antiquarians on the well-known manuscript by the initiator of the Kerch field archaeology presenting descriptions of town-sites and barrows in the European Bosporos. What seems to be in stark contrast, and hardly fortuitous is the regard of Olenin for the excavations of cemeteries carried out by Ašik and Karejša and the spectacular finds from kurgans of the European Bosporos. Yet at the same time there is his complete indifference to the activities of Dubrux who was occupied mainly with the investigation of the archaeological remains of settlements.

The history of the contacts of scholars from St Petersburg represented by H.K.E. Koehler with J. Stempkovskij, J. de Blaramberg, and P. Koeppen may be conveniently divided into two periods separated by 1822-1823 when the three amateurs published in Paris and Vienna the first works of a scientific character under their own names. Koeppen published a work about Black Sea antiquities, and a year later he presented to A. Boeckh his copies of the inscriptions from the Black Sea region. Koehler, however, was in no mood to forgive the amateurs for their intrusion into the field of scientific knowledge, which he regarded as his exclusive preserve: his severe criticism[20] exposed the inevitable errors in the writings of his opponents. We must add to this his disregard for the various investigations undertaken by the provincials and his compulsion to claim the right to – and the credit for – the first publication of evidence previously unknown. In some cases, the Academician did not even recognise the artefacts in their true form: many of his historical constructions were based on sources forcibly interpreted for the sake of certain personal presumptions. To a large extent it was owing to Koehler, that good relations between the representatives of academic science and provincial antiquarians failed to develop.

Fig. 18. Terracotta figurine of "Juno or Isis" (probably, Demeter) found in Olbia, from J. de Blaramberg's collection. Cf. recent publications: Greek and Cypriote Antiquities in the Archaeological Museum of Odessa. *Nicosia 2001, p. 50, no. 68: Female figurine. Olbia. Acquired in 1839 [error!]. 4th century BC. Height 26 cm. Inventory no. 22186. On the back of the pedestal is the inscription ΔIONYCIOY. Drawing for the article* "Mélanges archéologiques, contenants monuments antiques découverts dans la nouvelle Russie". *I Cahier. Pl. III. RSA SPbII RAS, manuscript group 36, inventory 1, file 779. Not earlier than 1822. First publication.*

As early as 1824, J. Stempkovskij publicly supported his associates in trying to prove the importance and significance of international contacts for the nation's science. Nevertheless, after a series of harsh reviews by H.K.E. Koehler, the publishing activities of provincial antiquarians faded out. Most of their studies from the 1820s and the beginning of 1830s have remained

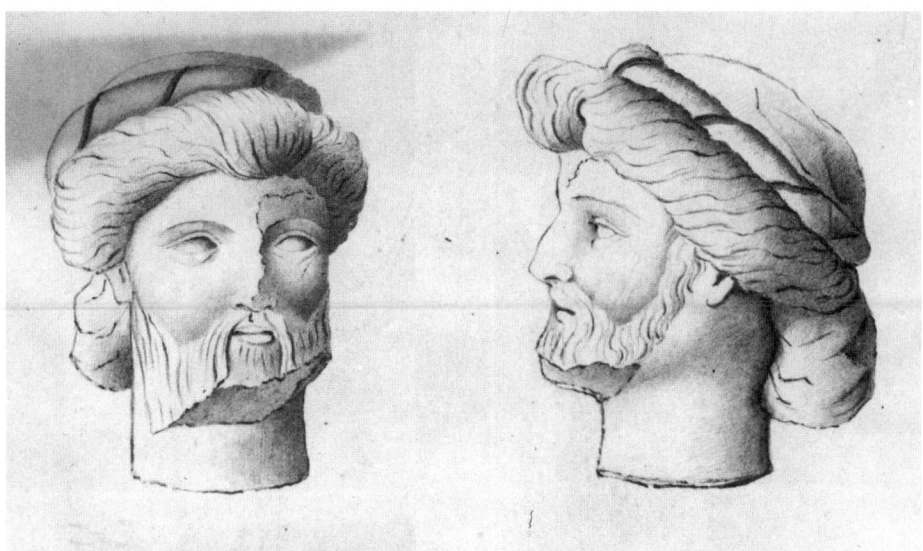

*Fig. 19. Male terracotta head found in Olbia. Drawing by Ippolit Blaramberg for the article "*Mélanges archéologiques, contenants monuments antiques décou-verts dans la nouvelle Russie*". I Cahier. Pl. IV. RSA SPbII RAS, manuscript group 36, inventory 1, file 779. Not earlier than 1822. First publication.*

unpublished, though their appearance would have enriched science greatly. Among these we may mention the work of P. Koeppen *Olbia, an ancient city on the Bug River*, the monograph of J. Stempkovskij on the history of Bosporos, based on a critical analysis of all the known literary, numismatic, epigraphic, and archaeological sources (the manuscript was submitted by the author to the Paris Académie des Inscriptions), and an entire series of J. de Blaramberg's articles on various archaeological issues. Koeppen, accused of unscientific archaeological practices, abandoned archaeological studies and turned to statistics and to the ethnography and geography of Russia, though till his last days he remained interested in antiquities. As a result, the Odessa Archaeological Circle lost its ties with the St Petersburg Academy of Science and its members preferred to send their studies to Paris, Vienna and Berlin where scholars proved to be more welcoming to representatives of Russian provincial science. Koehler, in contrast to his colleague from the Academy of Sciences orientalist Academician Ch.M. Fraehn, failed to give archaeology firm roots in Russian soil. He had no disciples and left no school. His chair at the St Petersburg Academy of Sciences remained vacant until 1850 when it was occupied by another German, Academician L.E. Stephani.

In the evaluation of the activities of the provincials from Odessa and Kerch, a kind of stereotype has been established. As a rule, their amateurish, dilettantish character (an insufficient level of research experience and knowledge of Classical languages, carelessness in carrying out the excavations, etc.) has been emphasised rather than the services rendered by amateurs to archaeology as pioneers in a number of its branches. However, from the standpoint of modern Classical studies the assiduous investigations of those amateurs on location (the materials from their excavations, descriptions and plans of various architectural remains of the Greek period) are of much greater significance than the works of the Academician H.K.E. Koehler, which were equal to the standards of his time, but are now of purely historiographic interest. The well-known postulate of the history of science that at the initial stages of the development of science dilettantism plays a role of no small importance, but its effectiveness drops at the level of an advanced, articulated science, is wholly justified in the analysis of the situation which had developed in the Russian science of antiquities in the first third of the 19th century.

In the second stage in the development of the study of the northern Black Sea region in Antiquity, the crystallisation from the complex of other disciplines took place, various local scientific centres in St Petersburg and in Novorossia were founded, the first museums were established in Southern Russia, and excavations with scientific purposes were commenced. It was in the first third of the 19th century that a conscious scientific interest in the ancient sites of the northern Black Sea region emerged. The pioneers of Classical archaeology succeeded in planting in Russian soil the interest in Classical Antiquity, developed the technique of conducting investigations and defined for the future the priority which should be assumed by fieldwork and theoretical studies.

The third stage of the formation of a Russian science of the antiquities of Southern Russia

The period from 1839 to 1859 saw Classical Studies finally adopt the form of an organised structure. This development was characterised by a new generation of scholars, who understood the importance of combining their efforts in the collection, study and protection of antiquities. P. Koeppen, who by that time had become a full member of the Academy of Sciences, tried to draw attention to the scandalous state of affairs in the study of the ancient necropoleis. He called for archaeological investigation of the kurgans in the Novorossijskij Kraj in order to identify their ethnic and historical context and proposed to assemble a collection of "grave goods" and to publish drawings of the antiquities in the museums. In 1843 Koeppen submitted a note memorandum to the Academy of Sciences proposing the taking of urgent measures for the protection of archaeological monuments, in particular "stone images standing over graves (kurgans)". Like the scientists of the Age of Enlightenment, Koeppen considered kurgans as objects of tomb architecture representing an integral part of the natural landscape, which was being destroyed by modern man. The attempts of the Academician K.E. von Baer in the middle of the century to amalgamate the humanities with the natural sciences elicited no response at that time among Russian historians. Von Baer attempted to promote the anthropological approach to studies of culture and ethnos independently of the corresponding historical context, and to introduce in Russia the "three period system" (1836) expounded by him in the preface to the Russian translation of the book by J.J. Worsaae, *Northern Antiquities from the Royal Museum in Copenhagen* (1861). The majority of specialists rejected Baer's hypotheses in the branch of the historical geography of the Black Sea area during the Greek and Roman periods.

In 1850 the academic Chair of Greek and Roman Antiquities passed to the curator of the Department of Classical Antiquities of the Hermitage L.E. Stephani. The main museum of the capital, the Hermitage opened to the general public in 1852 and became the richest archaeological museum in the Russian Empire. To a large extent this was due to the handing over of collections from elsewhere, in particular from different museums of the Academy of Sciences and provincial museums of antiquities in Novorossia. The Hermitage was being especially enriched with objects found during excavations in Olbia, on the Taman Peninsula, in the Eastern Crimea, Chersonesos and the Lower Don region. The studies were carried out in the museum by F.A. Gille, B. von Koehne, and E.G. von Muralt, who became active assistants of the St Petersburg Archaeological-Numismatic Society founded in 1846 (since 1851 and also according to the statute of 1866, called the Imperial Russian Archaeological Society). From the moment of its inauguration, the Society assumed the character of an aristocratic circle under the patronage of the Imperial Court comprising collectors and amateur antiquarians, a few scholars from the Academy of Sciences, assistants at the Hermitage and the Public Library – mostly foreigners in Russian service (J. Reichel, P. Sabatier and others). The reorganisation of the Society in 1851 resulted in many foreign specialists resigning and in a decline in the scientific level of the studies of Classical Antiquity, because the main attention of the Society's assistants was now focused on the investigation of Slavonic-Russian and Oriental antiquities.

Among the Members of the Society of Russian History and Antiquities (MOIDR) attached to the Moscow University, V.V. Passek and G.I. Spasskij became interested in ancient sites in Southern Russia. However, the main circle of interests of the MOIDR had not changed, and the study of Classical antiquities took second place to Russian and Slavonic ones. In 1843 the Temporary Commission for the Interpretation of Ancient Literature was founded in Kiev in the office of the Governor General of Kiev in co-operation with the chair of the local St Vladimir University. Members of the commission were occupied with archaeological investigations not only of

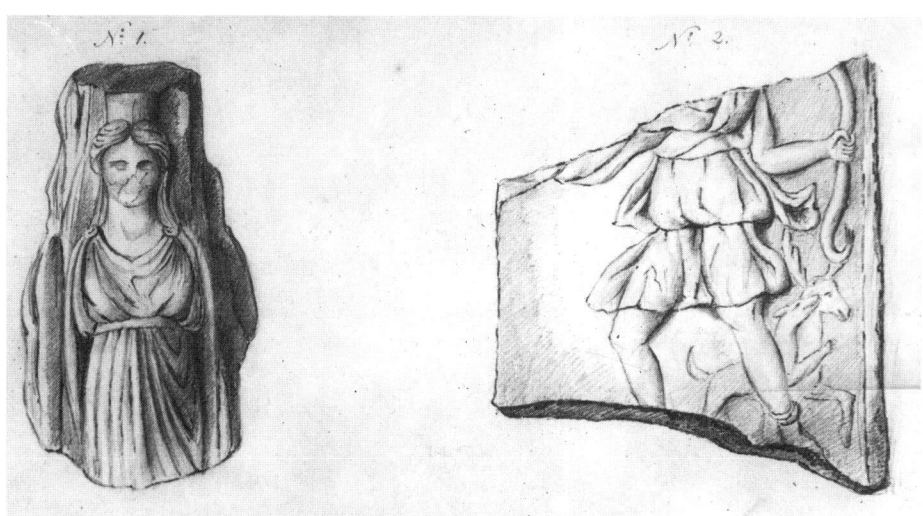

Fig. 20. Marble fragment with representation of triple-bodied Hekate and a relief representing Artemis as Huntress, found in Olbia. J. de Blaramberg's collection. Drawing by Vladimir Blaramberg for the article "Mélanges archéologiques, contenants monuments antiques découverts dans la nouvelle Russie". I Cahier. Pl. V. RSA SPbII RAS, manuscript group 36, inventory 1, file 779. Not earlier than 1822. First publication.

Slavonic-Russian antiquities of the ancient capital of Rus but also with the excavation of barrows in the South-Western Krai including various Scythian kurgans.

In 1839, the Odessa Society of History and Antiquities (OOID, in existence until 1922) was founded under the patronage of the Governor-General of Novorossia M.S. Voroncov. This contributed considerably to the study of antiquities in Southern Russia. Among its active members were A. Stourza, D.M Knjaževič, A.Ja. Fabr, M.M. Kir'jakov, N.N. Murzakewicz, N.I. Nadeždin, V.V. Grigor'ev, E. Taitbout de Marygny, Z.S. Chercheulidzev, A.B. Ašik, D.V. Karejša, A.F. Panagiodor-Nikovul, M.G. Paleolog, Ph. Brunn and P. Becker. In 1840, OOID secured five thousand roubles a year as a "grant" from the Exchequer as well as the right to carry out archaeological excavations throughout the entire territory of Southern Russia – both on state lands with the permission of the local authorities, and on private lands by consent of the owners. The programme of activities of the Odessa Society comprised the propagation of the historical and archaeological knowledge about Southern Russia by the collection, documentation and storage of antiquities from Novorossia, as well as the conducting of critical studies of the literary tradition concerning the northern Black Sea area. In addition to the archaeological investigations, the Society was also engaged with purely historical,

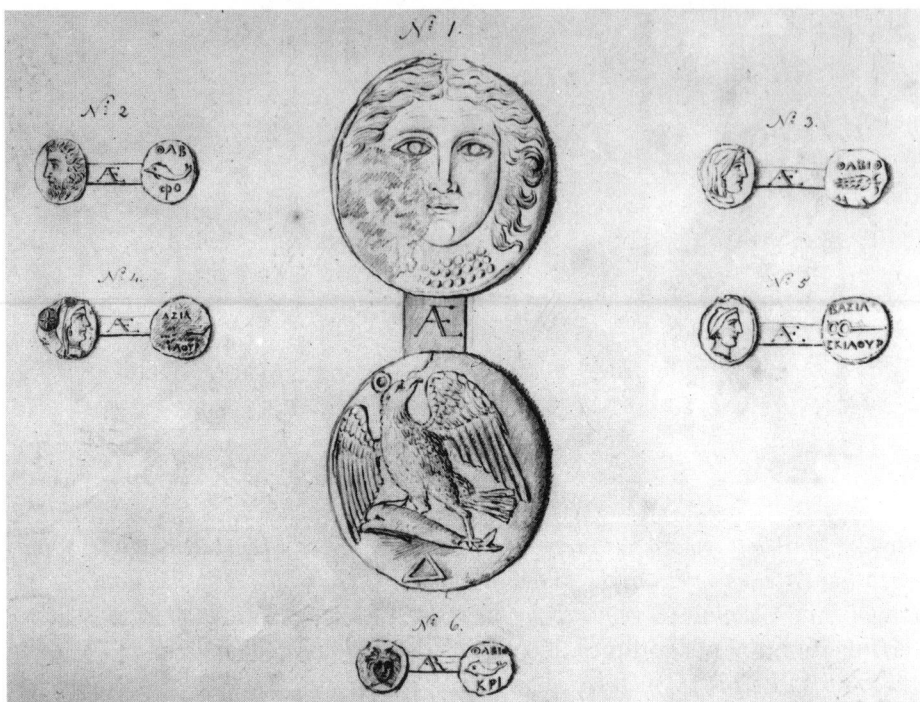

Fig. 21. Olbian "medals" and coins of the Scythian King Skilouros, struck and found in Olbia. J. de Blaramberg's collection. Drawing by Ippolit Blaramberg for the article "Mélanges archéologiques, contenants monuments antiques décou-verts dans la nouvelle Russie". I Cahier. Pl. VII. RSA SPbII RAS, manuscript group 36, inventory 1, file 779. Not earlier than 1822. First publication.

geographical, ethnographical, and statistical research. The Odessa Society carried out extensive work for the protection of the ancient sites in Novorossia. It undertook to co-ordinate the activities of all Southern Russian museums, which were becoming increasingly specialised, and the archaeological collections were incorporated into larger museum collections. The OOID became a worthy successor to the Odessa Archaeological Circle. For 50 years, a large scientific centre of ancient studies, as well as a first-rate collection of antiquities, had been built up thanks to the efforts of several generations of researchers in Odessa.

Various historical and archaeological societies became examples of a kind of methodological centre, which initiated work on questions about Classical antiquities in Southern Russia. Notwithstanding the absence of a permanent organisation and salaried personnel, these societies developed their own scientific programmes and succeeded in organising investigations of Black Sea antiquities, publishing various scientific works in their own periodicals or as separate monographs about antiquities of Bosporos, Chersonesos, Olbia, and the northern Black Sea area in general. The societies organised a number of scientific expeditions, started assembling collections of antiquities, founded their own museums and libraries, practised a broad exchange of scientific literature and "duplicate" antiquities with various institutions elsewhere, and established academic contacts with their scientific colleagues in Russia and abroad.

Although the Odessa Society of History and Antiquities had the right to conduct excavations throughout all of Southern Russia, the lack of money limited its field activities. In order to secure funds for excavations, the society tried to enlist new full and corresponding members who not infrequently conducted excavations at their own expense. The society carried out excavations in Theodosia (1852-1853, E. de Villeneuve, I. Karamurza, I.K. Ajvazovskij), Kerch (1843-1844, M.A. Kologrivov, M. de Blaramberg), and elsewhere. Notwithstanding the approval granted in the first of the national science regulations for conducting excavations *Regulations for excavating kurgans* (1843) and *Instructions on how uncovered antiquities should be treated* (1851), major clauses of the latter found no application in practice. Thus the information published by the Society's Secretary N.N. Murzakewicz (1806-1883) in the *Zapiski OOID* about his own excavations on the island of Leuke (Phidonisi, 1841) and in Olbia (1846), could on no account, even by the standards of the time, be considered as having any validity as field reports. Worthy of attention is the insistent striving of Murzakewicz to obtain some "duplicates" of the objects with which mostly collections of the Hermitage and Kerch Museum were supplemented. The idea that the original context of the objects might, in this way, be lost, never occurred to the antiquarians, and such practice was generally accepted at the time.

The methods of field studies developed in the 1810s-1820s by P. Dubrux, had by the beginning of the 1830s been forgotten and the scientific level of excavations dropped. The excavations of ancient settlements were not able to yield as great a number of spectacular finds as those of the barrows. In the 1830s-1850s the principal direction of investigations was deflected from the tasks formulated by J.A. Stempkovskij, and the harmony in studies of all groups of sites, which was advocated in the first quarter of the 19th century failed to develop. Nevertheless, the material from the excavations of those years plays an important role in present-day studies since the researchers of the 19th century collected large numbers of objects from kurgans, objects which are now preserved in various museums of Russia and Ukraine. From 1831, excavation with trenches both at settlements and cemeteries were the rule in Russian Classical archaeology until the turn of the 19th and 20th centuries. Now it is common to talk about the methods employed during that period as barbarian, but it has to be kept in mind that they were developed on an empirical basis, and the pioneers of those excavations had no teachers or instructors. Not until the first quarter of the 20th century did Russian science come to realise the necessity of systematic excavations of ancient townsites and cemeteries.

The necessity for a better organisation of archaeological activities and an expansion of the material resources in order to increase the number of scholars investigating the material remains of the past was also understood in governmental circles. Towards the end of the 1840s, the preconditions had been created in the country for the organisation of an archaeological service financed by the state. In 1850 the Commission for the Investigation of Antiquities under the direction of Count L.A. Perovskij was founded and initially attached to the Ministry of Home Affairs (from 1852 within the structure of the Ministry of Principalities). In 1856, the Stroganov Commission was founded and attached to the Ministry of the Imperial Court. Later in 1859, it was transformed into the Imperial Archaeological Commission (IAK). Perovskij (1792-1856) succeeded in creating a staff (11 assistants), whose brief was the study of antiquities and who also devised a programme of the systematic archaeological investigation of Southern Russia including the Scythian barrows in the Dnjeper region. Large-scale archaeological excavations were also undertaken at different sites in the northern Black Sea area: by A.S. Uvarov in Olbia, Scythian Neapolis and Chersonesos, and by P.M. Leont'ev in the region of the Lower Don (1853). Jointly with the members of OOID E. de Villeneuve, I.K. Ajvazovskij and I. Karamurza, Prince A.A. Sibirskij carried out excavations in Feodosia (1852-1853, 1856), and later at the necropolis of Gorgippia (1852, 1859). The document summarising the results of all the archaeological studies in Russia was to be a composite perennial report submitted to the Tsar (regrettably published only once, for 1853), which would comprise excerpts from different reports of excavations and, in addition, the information on the antiquities bought from the local population or acquired during the excavations. By means of administrative measures, Perovskij attempted to systematise excavations and strictly regulate their technique. Archaeologists were ordered to keep daily records of the works, draw plans and pictures of the finds, and compose detailed field reports. In the course of long-term field investigations of ancient sites near Kerch, many rules and techniques of excavation had been developed which were also used in other regions of the northern Black Sea littoral.

The Imperial Archaeological Commission (founded in 1859), which brought together specialists of the permanent staff (the chairman and three members) and a number of honorary and corresponding members throughout the entire country, became the national centre for the co-ordination of archaeological investigations. Its tasks included organisation and conducting of excavations throughout the entire territory of Russia, gathering information about different sites, and "scientific treatment and evaluation" of the

Fig. 22. Marble tombstone with a bas-relief representing a family standing on the threshold of a temple, from Olbia. J. de Blaramberg's collection, later in the collection of the Odessa Archaeological Museum. Drawing for the article "Mélanges archéologiques, contenants monuments antiques découverts dans la nouvelle Russie". III Cahier. Pl. II. RSA SPbII RAS, manuscript group 36, inventory 1, file 77. First publication.

artefacts found. According to the regulations of 1859, the Commission was granted the right to control all "other endeavours" of excavations. All the antiquities procured by private persons were, as far as possible, to be submitted, via the local authorities, to examination by the Commission. Subordinate to the Commission were the Kerch Museum of Antiquities and the Commission of Archaeological Research in Rome. The IAK also supervised the protection, registration, and systematisation of antiquities, as well as theoretical studies and publication of different materials. All the finds

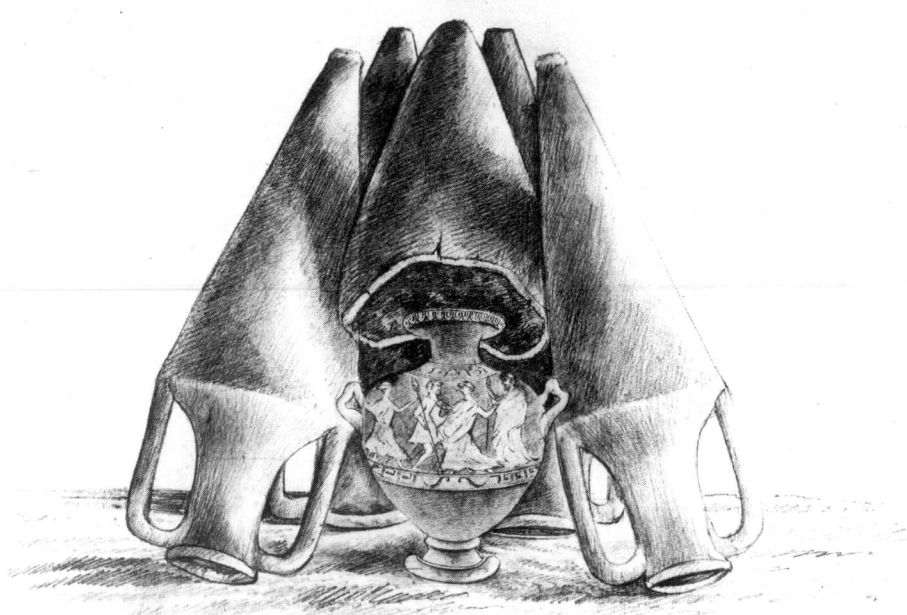

Fig. 23. Amphorae (a total of 13 examples found) installed in the form of a pyramid, and half an amphora, all covering a red-figured hydria *with ashes and calcined human bones from a cremation. According to P.P. Svin'in, a Greek letter was drawn on the middle part of each amphora, so that when all of the amphorae were placed together the letters constituted an inscription, which has not, however, been copied. They were found in the centre of a kurgan excavated by P. Dubrux near Kerch in 1817. The* hydria *came into the collection of Countess S. Potockaja or Princess Z.A. Volkonskaja (?); one of the amphorae was sent to Duke A.E. de Richelieu (Paris), the other antiquities came into P. Dubrux's collection (Kerch), and, possibly, into that of J. de Blaramberg (Odessa). Drawing for the article* "Mélanges archéologiques, contenants monuments antiques découverts dans la nouvelle Russie". III Cahier. Pl. III. RSA SPbII RAS, manuscript group 36, inventory 1, file 781. Not earlier than 1822.

from state and public land were to be transferred to the Archaeological Commission from which they were distributed to the Hermitage or to other museum collections.

The systematisation of all the knowledge accumulated in the course of excavations since the end of the 18th century became a vivid indicator of the third stage of the formation of Classical archaeology. The remarkable discoveries in the Eastern Crimea and on the Taman Peninsula stimulated the publication of quite a number of monographs on the history and archaeology of the Bosporan Kingdom. In contrast to the previous stage, when inscriptions and coins were almost the only items to be published, the work by Ašik on a painted tomb in Pantikapaion[21] encouraged the publication of other archaeological finds, in particular various ancient works of art. In the periodicals of the Ministry of Home Affairs and the Ministry of People's Enlightenment, the *Zapiski* of the Odessa Society, and various socio-political and literary periodicals, detailed information started to be appear on the excavations in the Novorossijskij Kraj. A.B. Ašik embarked on the scientific interpretation of the results of his excavations in Kerch and on the Taman Peninsula: these he then summarised in his three-volume book *The Bosporan Kingdom.*[22] Despite certain flaws in his writings, his successors should appreciate Ašik for his efforts in the sphere of popularisation of antiquities of the Black Sea region, and for his quite understandable efforts to shorten the time lapse between each archaeological discovery and its introduction into scientific knowledge. We must remember that books by the Kerch antiquarian are still used by scientists as the primary source of the information about many sites excavated at that time. A contemporary of Ašik, Professor of the Moscow University P.M. Leont'ev appealed for a degree of indulgence in the evaluation of the works of the Kerch archaeologist: "We are grateful for what we receive and do not expect merits which are impossible in the given case; we are thankful for the information rendered: the more so as we know how much greater are the services in the work done without the necessary preconditions in comparison with the knowledge acquired without any special efforts, merely by a regular Classical education".[23]

An epochal event in the history of Russian Classical studies was the appearance of the three-volume work *Antiquités du Bosphore Cimmérien conservées au musée impérial de l'Ermitage* (1854). The text of the book was produced by F.A. Gille (1801-1864) and L.E. Stephani (1816-1887) on the basis of excerpts from manuscripts of P. Dubrux, field reports by A.B. Ašik, D.V. Karejša, M. de Blaramberg, and K.R. Begičev, as well as their own examination of the artefacts in the Hermitage. The magnificent atlas included plates with lithographs executed after pencil and water-colour drawings of the finds. In the captions to the plates by Stephani, the artefacts are classified neither by the types of the objects nor by the archaeological context in which they were found (as this was quite impossible to determine from the reports of the Kerch archaeologists), but rather by the material of which the grave goods were made (gold, silver, bronze, clay, etc.). According to M.I. Rostovcev the studies of Stephani were predominantly of an antiquarian character with a bias towards various mythological and religious speculations.[24] In the analysis of the finds, a traditional art historical interpretation of the artefacts was the main objective. This residue of antiquarianism, encountered mostly among museum assistants, has not been completely overcome even today, nor is it exclusive to Russia. Classical archaeology in

Western Europe and America of the 20th century has not infrequently been considered part of art history. It is characteristic that Stephani paid little interest to "barbarian" (Scythian and Sarmatian) antiquities, which he treated from the viewpoint of Greek art. The Academician's attention was mainly focused on the works of the Classical period at the expense of the Archaic, Hellenistic and Roman objects. Nevertheless, it was the works of Stephani which were to be the basis for the scientific classification, dating and interpretation of the masterpieces of Greek art found in the northern Black Sea area. The works of the St Petersburg scholar were on an equal level with those of his Western European colleagues.

Thus, the third stage of the formation of Classical archaeology in Russia (1839-1859) is characterised by the establishment of state and public academic institutions of the science of Classical archaeology as part of national Classical studies. The museums became more specialised, systematic excavations at the ancient sites of the Black Sea region were carried out and a series of the first monographs about the antiquities of Southern Russia appeared. By the middle of the 19th century Classical archaeology was organised in the form of a number of archaeological societies and a special state commission. This organisational framework functioned along with different metropolitan and provincial museums practically without any changes until 1919.

Creation of corpora of the literary tradition about the northern Black Sea region

The chaotic state of Russian studies of Classical Antiquity in the middle of the 19th century exerted a significant influence upon the subsequent development of the science. For the Novorossian archaeological centre the main task was from the beginning the study of the Classical antiquities themselves. In St Petersburg, on the other hand, the series of important archaeological discoveries in Southern Russia caused a shift from a primarily philological approach to the study of Antiquity to a greater focus on the material evidence.

The first steps in the study of the literary tradition about the Black Sea area were taken by the members the Academy of Sciences in the 18th century, who were interested in early Russian history, which was closely linked to Byzantium. They turned to the works of ancient and Byzantine writers who wrote about the ancient history of the peoples of Eastern Europe. Academics who followed this line included G.S. Bayer, Ch.G. Crusius, V.N. Tatiščev, G.F. Mueller, J.E. Fischer, J.F. Hackmann, M.V. Lomonosov, and A.L. Schloezer. In the 1770s J.G. Stritter published in Latin a four-volume corpus of reference by Byzantine and other authors to the peoples who inhabited the territory of Russia in Antiquity.[25] The first attempts at writing a coherent history of the northern Black Sea area in Antiquity in the context of the Universal History belong to the hierarchs of the Roman-Catholic Church A.S. Naruszewicz

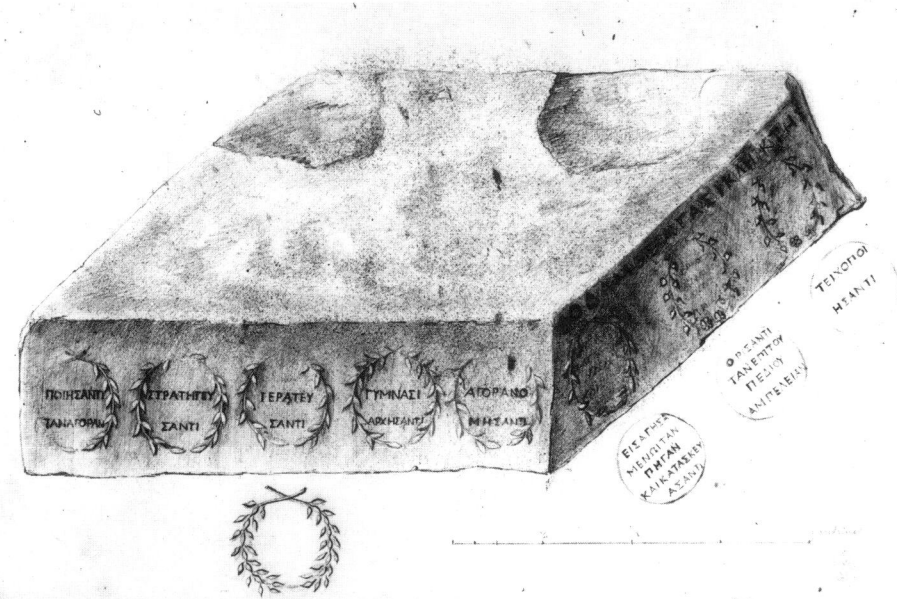

Fig. 24. The pedestal of a statue of Agasikles with an inscription in Doric dialect (IOSPE I², 418), found in 1794 in Tauric Chersonesos. Originally from the collection of Admiral R. Wilson, then transferred to the Chamber of Rarities of the Black Sea Depot of Maps in Nikolaev, since 1840 preserved in the Museum of the Odessa Society of History and Antiquities. J. de Blaramberg presented his annotations to the inscription in the article Paléographie, Journal d'Odessa. *1829, 2/14 novembre, 381-382. Drawing for the article* "Mélanges archéologiques, contenants monuments antiques découverts dans la nouvelle Russie". *III Cahier. Pl. V. RSA SPbII RAS, manuscript group 36, inventory 1, file 781. Not earlier than 1822. First publication.*

(1733-1796) and S. Siestrencewicz de Bohusz (1731-1826). The widely known book by the latter on the history of the Crimea presented an uncritical summary of the ancient literary sources of different periods about Tauris.[26] Antiquarians of the 18th century made attempts to identify particular sites and discernible traces of the ancient period with various towns and settlements mentioned in the literary tradition. The Polish historian Count J.O. Potocki (1761-1815), along with the publication of various inscriptions and coins known at the time, embarked on the study of separate bodies of documentary evidence about the northern Black Sea area.[27] He issued the first historical atlas of Eastern Europe, including the northern Black Sea coasts, devised on the basis of the data of ancient and medieval authors.[28]

Antiquarians of the first half of the 19th century realised the importance of gathering and comparing all available ancient literary evidence about the

Fig. 25. A circular fragment of a votive patera *(?) with a* gorgoneion *and an inscription, white marble (IOSPE I², 281), from Olbia. J. de Blaramberg's collection, then in the Museum of the Odessa Society of History and Antiquities. Drawing for the article* "Mélanges archéologiques, contenants monuments antiques découverts dans la nouvelle Russie". *III Cahier. Pl. VII. RSA SPbII RAS, manuscript group 36, inventory 1, file 781. Not earlier than 1822. First publication.*

northern Black Sea area. As early as 1823, J. Stempkovskij proposed to publish such a comprehensive corpus and the idea was taken up by the Odessa Society of History and Antiquities in 1840-1845. A teacher of Greek in the grammar school attached to the Richelieu Lyceum and member of OOID, M.G. Paleolog, proceeded to "extract those passages from ancient Hellenic poets and prose writers which are related to the history, geography or topography of the Novorossijskij Kraj. From this information, the Society intends to publish excerpts – similar to the well-known J.G. Stritter's *Memoriae populorum* – concerned predominantly with the southern part of Russia". R. Minzloff raised the question at the General Meeting of the Russian Archaeological Society in 1853 about the necessity for the publication of a *Collection of quotations from Classical writers about the countries now situated within the limits of the Russian Empire, especially about the northern and eastern coasts of the Black Sea* in the original languages and provided with a translation in Russian accompanied by explanatory notes and biographical information about the writers themselves. The Society resolved to publish the excerpts in its proceedings and "to compose gradually collections from these isolated reprints". However, at the time, national historical philological science had no means at its disposal for carrying out a critical analysis of such an enormous amount of documentary evidence. Therefore it proved to be unable to fulfil the task set. Only later with the appearance of the two-volume work by the Academician V. Latyšev (1893-1906) was a summary of Greek and Roman verse and prose with a translation into Russian realized.[29] Latyšev's two corpora of excerpts from works by Byzantine authors about the territory of Russia, and of excerpts from ancient and Byzantine authors about Central and Eastern Asia and the Caucasus ready for print in 1916-1920 remained unpublished but survived as manuscript.[30]

Epigraphy

The first collectors, copyists and publishers of lapidary inscriptions from the northern Black Sea region were naturalists, travellers and amateur antiquarians. Due to their deficient knowledge of the Classical languages and the poorly advanced state of epigraphy at the time, they often produced incorrect copies of the inscriptions. Copies of dozens of newly found, often badly damaged inscriptions are preserved among different manuscripts from the 18th to the first half of the 19th centuries. Being often well preserved and showing more exactly the shape of the letters later distorted during the publication of lithographs and engravings they are helpful for the reconstruction of the texts. The manuscripts not infrequently contain more precise information about the place and date of the discovery of the inscriptions. A number of them have now been lost, and familiarity with archive records is therefore an indispensable precondition for any republication of the corpora of ancient and medieval inscriptions from the northern Black Sea littoral.

The prioritising in Russia of the studies and publication of epigraphic evidence according to strictly scientific, critical methods must be credited to H.K.E. Koehler, who used simultaneously the methods of philological and historical interpretation. His severe, though often quite justified comments on the errors of other researchers contributed to the refinement of the epigraphic material: Koehler never left untouched any inscription unsuccessfully interpreted or inaccurately read by others. Articles by the Academician about the ancient Black Sea area abound in critical attacks on the epigraphic studies of D. Raoul Rochette, P. Koeppen, J. Stempkovskij, and J. de Blaramberg.[31] Koehler's caustic reviews and remarks to some extent promoted the rise in the scientific level of publications of epigraphic materials. Southern Russian amateur antiquarians published various inscriptions not only on the basis of the copies made by themselves but also of those received from other persons with no knowledge of Classical languages. Nevertheless we should note certain merits in the works of the *dilettanti* – in their drawings they attempted to reproduce with the greatest precision all the peculiarities of the copied lapidary material tolerating no arbitrary reconstructions of the inscriptions with damaged or poorly readable texts, while philologists not infrequently sinned against the truth in such cases.

Realising the limited extent of their own knowledge of ancient epigraphy, the Odessa antiquarians regularly corresponded with professional scholars in the West, rendering for publication the materials gathered by them to A. Boeckh and D. Raoul Rochette. Through his work, Boeckh promoted the creation of a professional community of epigraphists, not only in Russia but throughout the whole of Europe. Working with his *Corpus inscriptionum Graecarum* published in 1843 and comprising the Black Sea material, scholars learned the techniques of critical interpretation and scientific publishing of epigraphic sources. The development of Latin epigraphy in Russia was, however, impeded by the scantiness of the material available.

Russian Classical studies of the first half of the 19th century were as yet unprepared to undertake such a fundamental work as a corpus of the Black Sea inscriptions. Even so, as early as 1823, J. Stempkovskij advocated the necessity for the creation of a comprehensive corpus of all the "palaeographic" (i.e. epigraphic) evidence from the northern Black Sea coasts. Such a proposition was also supported by the Odessa Society of History and Antiquities. In 1846 its members resolved to publish at the expense of OOID a "complete collection" of the Greek and Latin inscriptions which had been discovered in Southern Russia, "having classified the latter … chronologically". The copying of the inscriptions was undertaken by the secretary of OOID N. Murzakewicz. Among the valuable documents of the Society are those discovered by the author, which prove to be materials prepared for this unrealised edition, in particular the copies of a dozen ancient and medieval inscriptions lost and unpublished till now, as well as a number of albums with drawings of the finds (including some lapidary inscriptions) exhibited in the Odessa City Museum of Antiquities and the museum of OOID.

Scholars from St Petersburg were also engaged in epigraphic studies. Publications of newly discovered inscriptions appeared in publications from the Hermitage, the Academy of Sciences, and the Russian Archaeological Society (Fr. Graefe, E.G. von Muralt, L.E. Stephani, A.S. Uvarov, P.M. Leont'ev, et al.), and special instructions on copying epigraphic documents were issued. In the second half of the 19th century, the question of preparing a corpus of Greek and Latin inscriptions from the northern Black Sea area was raised again. It was discussed at the meetings of the Russian Archaeological Society and at a number of Pan-Russian archaeological congresses held by the Moscow Archaeological Society. The initiator of one corpus project was the orientalist A.Ja. Garkavi, who in 1876 submitted a corresponding memorandum to the Russian Archaeological Society. The preparation of this work was entrusted to V. Latyšev. It was thus only in the second half of the century, when the national epigraphic school had already been created, that Russian science succeeded in initiating the publication of comprehensive corpora of Classical Greek and Latin as well as Byzantine inscriptions from the northern Black Sea coasts. Their publication marked a qualitative leap in the development of Russian Classical studies.[32]

Ceramic epigraphy

L.E. Stephani and P. Becker, who from the middle of the 19th century published large collections of ceramic stamps mostly from ancient settlements of the northern Black Sea region, are traditionally regarded as the founders of this science. In Western Europe, works of a similar character appeared only in the 1860s-1890s. However, some documents by Koehler, J. de Blaramberg and P. Koeppen allow us to push back the birth of this branch of Classical studies to the beginning of the 19th century. Amphora and tile stamps initially came into the hands of philologists, such as Koehler who influenced the way the study was prioritised. The main problems these scholars tried to resolve were the attribution of the stamps and their purpose. Koehler and Koeppen became pioneers in recognising the stamps with an emblem in the form of a pomegranate flower, as belonging to vessels produced on Rhodos. Undoubtedly, their observations had served as the starting point for B. von Koehne and L. Stephani, who proceeded in the middle of the century with the work of the identification of Rhodian stamps. Owing to Blaramberg, who transferred his copies of inscriptions to A. Boeckh, the latter correctly attributed one particular stamp to Chersonesos.

Not limiting himself to mere description of, and commentary on, stamps, J. de Blaramberg was to offer an attribution for the so-called *astynomos* stamps. Having noticed a considerable concentration of such stamps in Olbia and the presence of the emblem typical for Olbian coins (an eagle on a dolphin) on some of them, Blaramberg proposed a local provenience. He came to the conclusion that such finds indicated a developed ceramic production in Olbia. Moreover, as the antiquarian supposed, "the verifying of the quality of manufactured articles was imposed upon ... the *astynomoi*", who, with that purpose in mind, stamped amphorae and tiles. This is the first time that the question of the purpose of stamping various ceramic articles was put forward. Blaramberg's idea about the Olbian origins of the stamps underwent further development in the middle of the century in the works of P. Becker. The fallacy of the localisation became finally evident only in the 1920s.

J. de Blaramberg attempted to push back the limits of the philological analysis of stamps and drew attention to their potential use as a valuable historical source. He also realised the necessity of developing a chronology of stamps by means of their correlation with different evidence of other kinds – epigraphic and numismatic. Having identified precisely the dates when offices were held by the functionaries whose names are found in the stamps

*Fig. 26. Red-figured and black-glazed pottery from Olbia, J. de Blaramberg's collection. Drawing for the article "*Mélanges archéologiques, contenants monuments antiques découverts dans la nouvelle Russie*". IV Cahier. Pl. I. RSA SPbII RAS, manuscript group 36, inventory 1, file 782. Not earlier than 1825.*

we will be able to date reliably the construction of the buildings roofed with stamped tiles, the manufacture of amphorae, etc. In this context, Blaramberg, quite justifiably, used stamps, giving them parity with lapidary evidence and coins during his compilation of the *Onomastic List of Citizens of Olbia* which remained unpublished. And although the assumptions on which Blaramberg based his attribution of the *astynomos* stamps were erroneous, and many of his conclusions now seem to be unfounded, or often simply naive, the merits of this scholar in the work not only of gathering but also of interpreting the stamped ceramic material are undoubted.[33]

Interest in the inscriptions made on ceramic containers and tiles increased with the beginning of systematic excavations at different ancient sites in the northern Black Sea region. In the 1840s-1850s, various stamps, both classified and unclassified according to their provenance, were published by A.B. Ašik, N. Murzakewicz, P. Sabatier, L. Stephani, P.M. Leont'ev, B.V. von Koehne, and Uvarov. Stamps discovered were traditionally published in archaeological excavation reports, however the quality of the representations was usually rather poor. Most frequently, the stamp inscriptions were printed in majuscules, only occasionally followed by minuscules. Exact drawings of the imprints, which allow verification of the proposed reading,

Fig. 27. Fragmentary relief pottery, lamps, terracotta figurines, and glass and lead objects from Olbia, J. de Blaramberg's collection. Drawing by V. Blaramberg for the article "Mélanges archéologiques, contenants monuments antiques découverts dans la nouvelle Russie". *IV Cahier. Pl. II. RSA SPbII RAS, manuscript group 36, inventory 1, file 782. 1825. First publication.*

are extremely rare. As an exception, one might mention the plate with excellent copies of stamps from Olbia presented in the atlas appended to the treatise of A.S. Uvarov about antiquities of Novorossia. Thus the origin of ceramic epigraphy may be justly dated to the beginning of the 19th century.

Numismatics

During the period of the 18th to the middle of the 19th centuries, ancient coins were accumulated in various public and private Russian collections. This process acquired an intensive character with the beginning of regular excavations in the northern Black Sea region. I have succeeded in reconstructing the composition of a number of isolated finds and coin hoards, the information about which had previously been unavailable to specialists. This work includes the quantitative composition and the geographical and chronological range of the coins found during the excavations of the Sanctuary of Achilles on Tendra Spit (1824), in Scythian Neapolis (1827) and on the Majak Peninsula in the Crimea (1844), and research into the more precise circumstances of the discovery of the Pulencov hoard in the village of Taman (1845).[34]

In the first half of the 19th century Russian scholars started publishing considerable volumes of sources unknown to their West-European colleagues in an attempt to interpret and systematise the new numismatic material. The results were not long in appearing: from the 1840s-1850s, according to D.B. Šelov, who is quite justified in this assertion, "Russian science undoubtedly had won the first place in the studies of Bosporan antiquities in general and Bosporan numismatics in particular".[35] The accumulation of the new material necessitated the working out of principles of systematisation and methods of studying the numismatic evidence. Throughout the first half to the middle of the 19th century the geographical and chronological frames of the studies had widened considerably owing to the rapid growth in the fund of sources. In the 18th and the beginning of the 19th centuries the publications of coins were in many respects of an illustrative character in the treatment of the political history of the ancient Black Sea area. With time, however, the attention of researchers was drawn to the attribution of the coins (their type, legend, countermarks), the study of their typology and chronology, and the issuing of catalogues of the numismatic collections.

The chief authority in the field of ancient numismatics, H.K.E. Koehler studied coins from all regions of the northern Black Sea area, but Bosporos always had for him the highest priority.[36] Some of the Bosporan coins were persistently attributed by Koehler sometimes to Parthian, sometimes to Seleucid dynasties, bewildering his scientific opponents. The curator of the Hermitage also studied the issues of Theodosia and the coins, which he recognised as minted by the cities of "Hermision" and "Herakleion". J. Stempkovskij made his first priority the identification of the examples of the coinage of Rhadamsades son of Thothorses (he erroneously read the name of the king as "Rhadameadis"),[37] Gepaipyris,[38] Pharsanzes[39] and the development of the chronology of the Bosporan coins from the period of the Roman Empire.[40] Establishing the chronology of certain reigns in Bosporos, the correct names of the rulers not mentioned in the literary sources, identification of coin series and their dates were all matters which were subject to animated discussion among scholars of the first half of the 19th century. Almost any find of a coin that revealed a new king's name was commented on by each scholar in his own way, and the specimen might often be attributed to different rulers, the gap between the reigns of which sometimes amounted to 200 years. The variations in dating and attribution by the numismatists of the time are readily explainable by the novelty of the object of their studies, the fragmentary state of the evidence of literary and epigraphic sources, and the relatively small quantity (as compared with the present-day collections) of the material known to the science of that period. Of the 52,000 coins known at the time only 230 from the northern Black Sea region were included in the well-known corpus of the French numismatist

T.E. Mionnet.[41] Towards the middle of the century, the names of 15 kings and one queen of Bosporos which are not mentioned in the literary sources became known on the basis of coins alone, and nine new names of kings were provided by inscriptions found in the Crimea and on the Taman Peninsula.

An enormous role in the development of numismatics was played by the scientific societies – the Odessa Society of History and Antiquities (OOID) and the Russian Archaeological Society (RAO). In the Memoirs of OOID, N. Murzakewicz published catalogues of his own collection and of that in the Odessa Museum of Antiquities[42] as well as a number of articles on different aspects of Greek numismatics. G.I. Spasskij in his treatise on antiquities of the Kimmerian Bosporos made Count S.G. Stroganov's coin collection known, and his book became the first guide to Bosporan numismatics.[43] P. Sabatier on the basis of various inscriptions and coins proposed his own chronology of 33 Bosporan dynasts for a period of 448 years from "Mithridates VII to Rheskouporis VII".[44] He examined 492 coins, of which 352 were preserved in Russian collections. An "excellent" (as characterised by M. Rostovcev) catalogue of coins of Prince A. Sibirskij unfortunately has remained uncompleted. In the first part of the first volume, the author considered in detail the autonomous and regal coinage of the 6th century BC to the 1st century AD within the context of the political and religious history of Bosporos.[45]

In comparison to Bosporos, the studies of the coinage of Olbia presented a more difficult task. Prior to the publication of 225 Olbian coins from J. de Blaramberg's collection,[46] only one gold coin of Olbia had been known, and the silver coins were also considered as extremely rare. Credit must be given to J. Stempkovskij and Blaramberg for the publication of two types of coins of the Scythian King Skilouros struck in Olbia. A.S. Uvarov (1851) made an attempt at linking the antiquarian-numismatic analysis of coins with the revelation of peculiarities of the monetary circulation in the *polis* of Olbia within the context of its history, which that author divides into three periods: the Greek, the Scytho-Greek, and the Roman. The numismatics of Tauric Chersonesos had received hardly any study. H.K.E. Koehler published an explanatory catalogue of 93 coins (1823) distributed according to issues. On the basis of numismatic data, B. von Koehne made an attempt at the reconstruction of the more than millennial history of Chersonesos from its foundation until the reign of Basil II in the early 11th century.[47] The author classified all the coin types (204 specimens) known at the time according to three periods (Greek, Roman, and Byzantine), studied the weight-system, and identified the coins of Smyrna and Thracian Chersonesos erroneously attributed to Tauric Chersonesos.

In the first third of the 19th century the only specialist in Russia who was able to summarise all the numismatic materials from the northern Black Sea littoral was Academician H.K.E. Koehler, who first introduced many previously unknown coin types. In terms of the precision and meticulousness of his descriptions, the critical strictness in the selection of material and the soberness in his comments, Koehler's studies had been considered exemplary for many years. However, the Academician wrote no treatise, limiting himself to a mere series of articles and, as P.M. Leont'ev wrote, "not having had time to leave behind him any such an expansive writing which could have taken its place among the best works of the greatest scientists of the present. There is no doubt that he could have done it, since in his learning he surpassed the majority, or perhaps even all of the archaeologists of our time. His fame is great as it is, but most of his fame belongs to him rather for what he could have done than for what he actually achieved".[48] The first attempt at a wider study was made by the representative of the next generation of scholars B. von Koehne in his two-volume description of the museum of Prince V.V. Kočubej,[49] which was a kind of a corpus of coins (610 in total) of the Greek colonies of the northern and eastern Black Sea regions. This book became the first catalogue in Russian of coins from Olbia, Kerkinitis, Tauric Chersonesos, Bosporos (Pantikapaion, Phanagoria, Gorgippia, Nymphaion, Theodosia), Kolchis, and Dioskourias.

Almost thirty years later an imperfect catalogue of ancient coins from the northern Black Sea region (1884) by P.O. Buračkov was published,[50] and a further twenty years later corrections to it were made by A. Bertier de la Garde (1907).[51] Thanks to the efforts of many generations of scholars and collectors, towards the 1910s the way had been paved for the creation of a composite illustrated corpus of coins of the Black Sea area *Corpus numorum Russiae meridionalis* undertaken by M. Rostovcev and O.F. Retovskij, which, because of the revolution in 1917 has remained unpublished.[52] Modern scholars have chosen to make detailed studies of the coinage of separate Greek cities and to resolve particular problems in the numismatics of the northern Black Sea region. Thus the task of publishing, on a level with the modern scientific standards, a complete corpus of ancient coins of the northern Black Sea region, which had already been proposed by J. Stempkovskij, and which a century later A.N. Zograf called "an indispensable duty ... of a numismatist concerned with the Classical period",[53] remains urgent even today.

Historical geography and archaeological topography of the northern Black Sea region in the Graeco-Roman period

One of the poorly developed directions of historical archaeological studies is the source-study of the thematic archaeological maps and plans of the 18th and 19th centuries, including the examination of previously unknown material in various archives. There are numerous works dedicated to the history of national cartography and special (thematic) mapping, but they include no

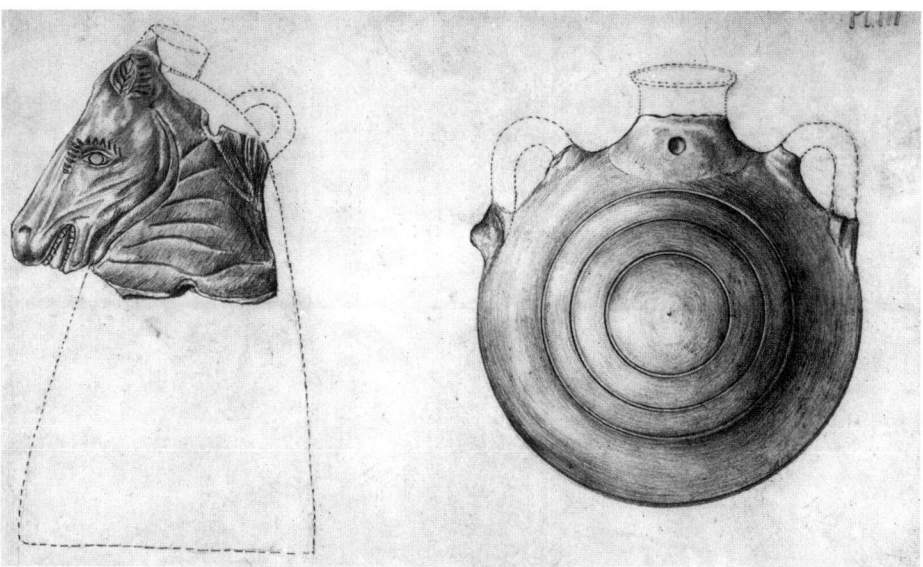

Fig. 28. Fragments of a figured vessel in the form of horse's bust and of a flat two-handled flask (askos?) *from Olbia.* Lekythos *in the form of horse's bust – Count Severin Osipovič Potockij's gift to the Odessa City's Museum of Antiquities. Cf.:* Odessa Archaeological Museum of the Academy of Sciences of USSR. [Album]. Kiev 1983, p. 51, 1, 72, no. 87; Greek and Cypriote Antiquities in the Archaeological Museum of Odessa. *Nicosia 2001, 46, no. 56: Plastic vessel. Olbia. 3rd-2nd centuries BC. Height 20.6 cm. Two-part mould. Inventory no. 22167. Vase in the shape of a horse's head. Product of Pergamon;* Ancient Greek Sites on the Northwest Coast of the Black Sea. *Kiev 2001, p. 28. Drawing for the article* "Mélanges archéologiques, contenants monuments antiques découverts dans la nouvelle Russie". IV Cahier. Pl. III. RSA SPbII RAS, *manuscript group 36, inventory 1, file 782. 1825 g. First publication.*

study of the history of the archaeological cartography, which indeed deserves a monograph. The rapid progress of Russian cartography and the improvements in hydrographic researches predetermined a high information level in the cartographic material from the end of the 18th to the middle of the 19th centuries used by specialists concerned with Antiquity. Sailing courses, field map-boards, and descriptions of coasts made in the course of topographical and hydrographical surveys, annual reporting charts, and summarised reports and maps constitute a highly important complex of documents for the study of the archaeological topography of the northern Black Sea region. Many of the maps of that time include archaeological details marking the ruins of different sites and kurgan chains. These documents are the primary source for the identification of cultural landscape

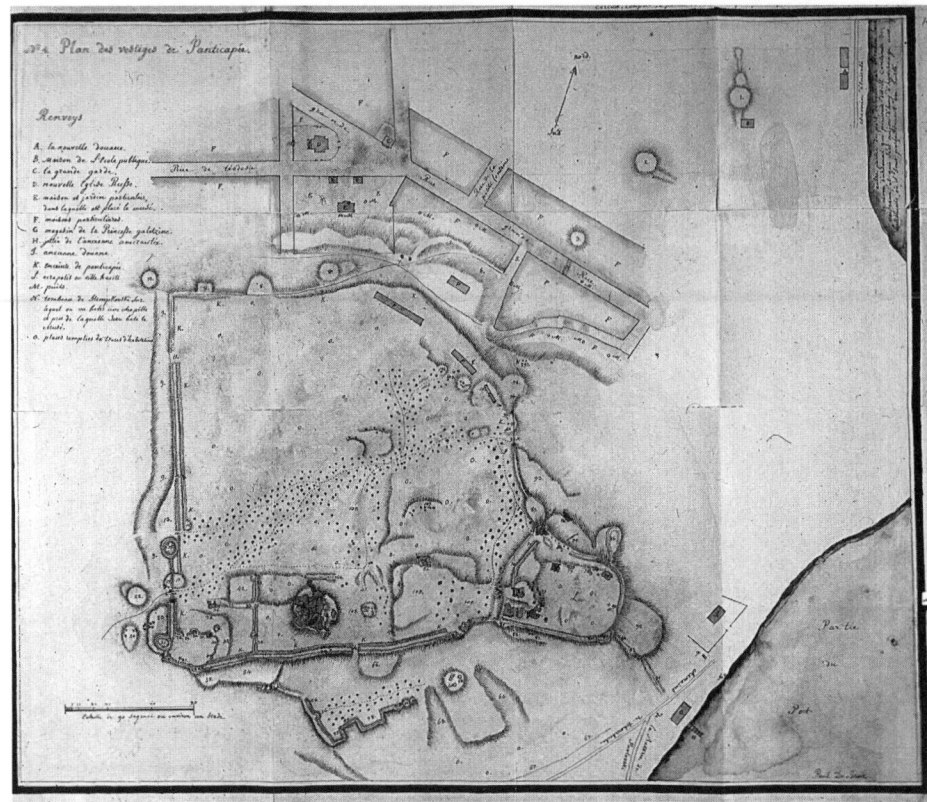

Fig. 29. P. Dubrux. Plan of the ruins of Pantikapaion. Not later than 1833. State Archives of the Russian Federation (GARF), manuscript group 666, inventory 1, file 534, sheet 126.

zones and for creating archaeological maps of particular regions, historical atlases, dictionaries of geographical nomenclature, etc. The task of investigating the spatial organisation of different territories in Antiquity, systems of settlement, and the ancient cultural landscape of the northern Black Sea area was already initiated by M. Rostovcev.[54]

The solution to the main problems of historical geography, first and foremost the location of individual Greek cities and settlements attested by literary sources on the coasts and in the Scythian interior, had been a subject of priority in Russian Classical studies until the middle of the 19th century. This demanded a comparison to be made between the isolated data of the narrative tradition with the archaeological realities. Indispensable preconditions for such an investigation are not only a good knowledge of the geographical location, but also the precise registration of the architectural and archaeological remains so that special archaeological maps can be drawn.

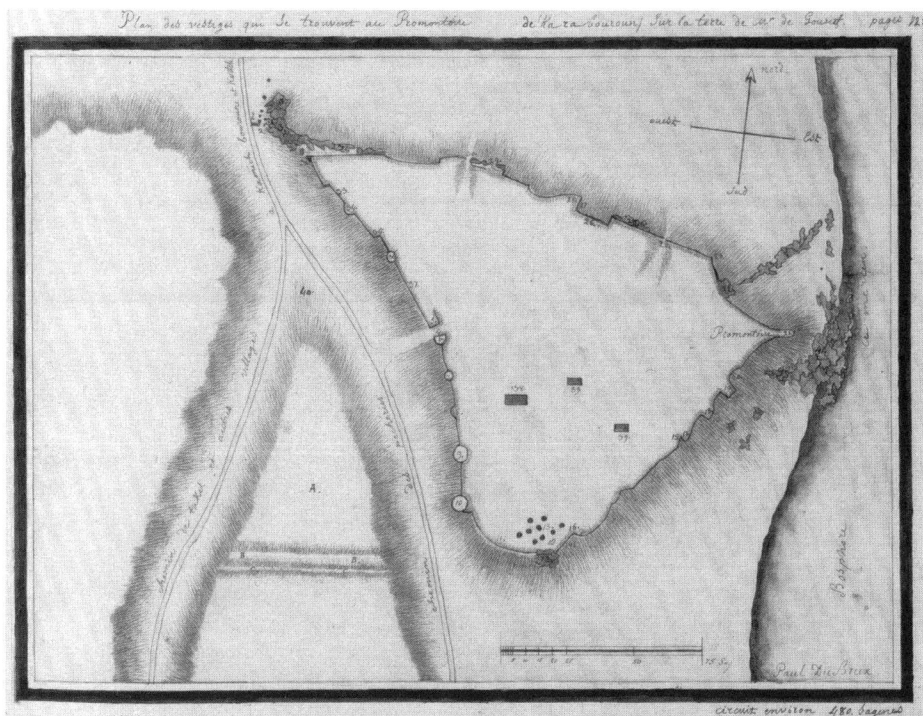

*Fig. 30. P. Dubrux. Plan of the ruins found on Cape Kara-Burun on the land of Mr.
Gur'ev near Kerch (the town-site of the ancient Nymphaion). Not later than 1833.
State Archives of the Russian Federation (GARF), manuscript group 666, inventory
1, file 534, sheet 129.*

Today's successors should give credit to the Russian administrators, military
topographers, travellers, scientists, officials and unassuming amateur antiquarians of the late 18th to the first half of the 19th centuries, who have done
much for the study of the historical geography and archaeological topography of the northern Black Sea littoral.

The contradictions in the ancient literary tradition and the absence of
"correct" maps of the northern Black Sea region in the beginning and middle of the 18th century led to the fact that various armchair scholars and
travellers made mutually exclusive assumptions about the location of even
fairly large centres. However, the finds of coins and inscriptions bearing the
names of Olbia, Chersonesos and Pantikapaion among the ruins of these
cities had already by the turn of the 18th to the 19th centuries left no doubts
as to their identification with the archaeological remains. It proved more difficult to locate the many smaller towns, *emporia*, and sanctuaries mentioned
in historical documents. The reconnaissance of such sites and the topographical registration of the ruins were started by Southern Russian anti-

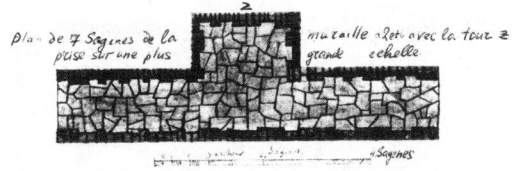

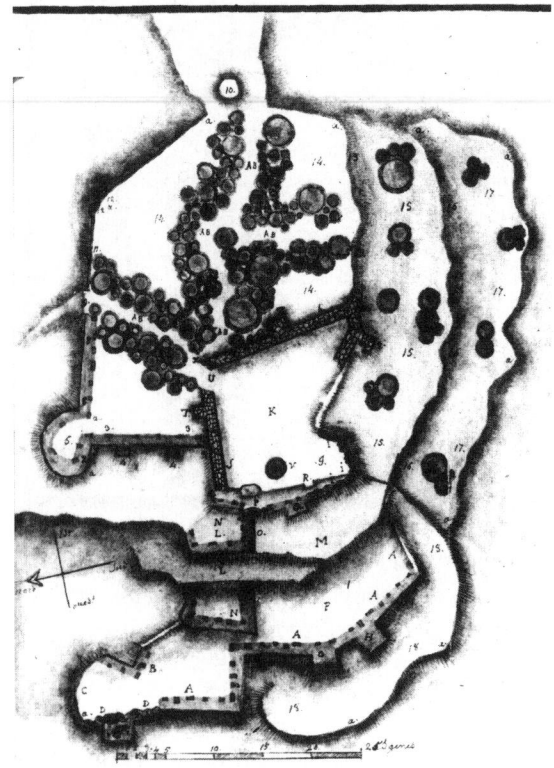

Fig. 31. The final plan of the settlement-site of Kuurdak (Andreevka Severnaja?), composed by P. Dubrux not later than 1834. Archives of the State Hermitage (AGE), manuscript group 1, inventory 1-1831, file 19, sheet 339.

quarians who by their publications initiated heated discussions in subsequent historiography. Many of their studies have not lost their significance even today having resulted in the identification of a number of centres, which had not previously been located. The results of these works became a realistic commentary on the writings of the ancient geographers, and were not slow to influence the publication of the sources, in particular the K.O. Mueller editions of Ptolemaios and the *periploi*. By the middle of the 19th century such large Greek centres as Tyras (Akkerman, now the city of Belgorod on the Dniester), Olbia (now the village of Parutino), the Tauric Chersonesos (on the coast of Karantinnaja Bay in Sevastopol), Pantikapaion (Kerch), Myrmekion (Novyj Karantin in Kerch), Gorgippia (modern Anapa), Tanais (village of Nedvigovka), and others were reliably located. Finally it became obvious that without systematic archaeological explorations, it was impossible to resolve disputes over the historical geography.

Regrettably, the questions of historical geography and archaeological topography had only rarely been raised in Russian scientific literature of the second half of the 19th century. These studies were delayed in the 1850s-1870s by the fact that the principal efforts were concentrated on excavations first of the necropoleis of Greek cities and then of large kurgans in the territory of Scythia. Scholars only returned to regional investigations in the 20th century. The turning away from the problems already posed in the articles of J. Stempkovskij, P. Dubrux and J. de Blaramberg was called by the Academician M. Rostovcev "one of the greatest sins of Russian science".[55]

Conclusion

The outstanding archaeological discoveries in Southern Russia from the end of the 18th to the middle of the 19th century gave a strong impulse to the national development of Classical studies. It was during this period that the organisational formation of Russian studies of Antiquity came about in the form of a system of state institutions and public scientific organisations which did not undergo any serious changes until the early 1920s; the strategic goals of the development of the science were defined and its main structure was established: archaeology, epigraphy and numismatics. The science of Classical antiquities did not emerge in Russia until the 18th century, considerably later than in Europe; nevertheless it succeeded in taking root and undergoing the same stages of scientific development and "growing pains" of the period of antiquarianism with increased rapidity – a period which lasted in fact for only one and a half centuries – the time from the Age of Peter the Great until the abolition of serfdom (1861). During these one and a half centuries, a systematic and continuous cultural tradition in Classical studies was established in Russia, having contributed essentially to the world science by the discovery of a unique, remarkable and peculiar material culture of the ancient zone of contact between the Greek colonies of the northern Black Sea littoral and the neighbouring world of nomads. Having begun as an activity for amateurs, Russian Classical science became a kind of "ground" for ideas which contributes to the discipline's structure, and developed the apparatus that gave birth to training of the first professionals brought together from various specialised scientific centres.

Towards the middle of the 19th century, scholars had realised that archaeological data should take priority over armchair interpretation of isolated and contradictory written sources concerning the northern coasts of the Pontos: "it is not with a book, with an ancient author in our hands, that we must study these countries, but by excavations at the already identified sites we will confirm or disprove our assumptions", A.S. Uvarov wrote.[56] Antiquarians of that period understood that excavations, uncovering not only archaeological, but also epigraphic and numismatic material, served to expand the source base of the historical science. They came to the conclusion that archaeological evidence increased the informative capacity of other kinds of data, serving as a criterion for the reliability of the ancient literary tradition, supplementing the information and making possible reciprocal cross-dating together with epigraphic and numismatic evidence. It is not surprising that during that period archaeological knowledge proved to be poorly differentiated from the historical kind. Archaeological data including inscriptions and coins served chiefly to supplement and to illustrate the political history of the ancient states of the region.

The documents found in the course of the present study (including various maps, plans, drawings, and representations of antiquities) reflect the state of the material at the moment of its initial registration and are of a considerable value for modern Classical studies. This evidence clearly demonstrates how important it is to use archives in the investigation of the objects known for a long time, because many of the most significant (from the viewpoint of modern science) discoveries were made at the dawn of Russian Classical studies. Of great value are various copies, drawings and lists of epigraphic and numismatic finds. These are documents of primary importance and they demand a comparison with the published corpora of inscriptions and coins – publications of some inscriptions do not correspond with their actual state of preservation and provide incorrect information about their provenience; the lists and drawings of coins found in different archives enable us to identify more precisely the chronology of particular contexts, and they yield new evidence about the geographical and chronological links of the Black Sea littoral with other regions of the ancient Greek world. Notwithstanding the loss of many archaeological, epigraphic and numismatic monuments, it is possible for us to retrieve new information from the archives – it answers questions unresolved till now and at the same time poses new ones, opening further prospects for a retrospective reconstruction of the evidence revealed in the past centuries.

By the end of the 19th and the beginning of the 20th centuries, with the development of the national school of history and philology, the science of Classical antiquities of the northern Black Sea region had become a considerable part of the finally "Russified" national Classical studies which had synthesised in full the achievements of Russian and West-European Classical philology, ancient history, archaeology, epigraphy, numismatics, and the history of art. Through the efforts of several generations of scholars, Russian Classical studies achieved an unprecedented peak – "the golden age of Russian Classical studies" – in the late 19th to the early 20th centuries. Whilst our knowledge about the scholars of the "golden age" (V. Latyšev, M. Rostovcev, B. Farmakovskij et al.) is fairly complete, the activities of those who had prepared this flowering of the scientific thought had until recently remained in the dark.

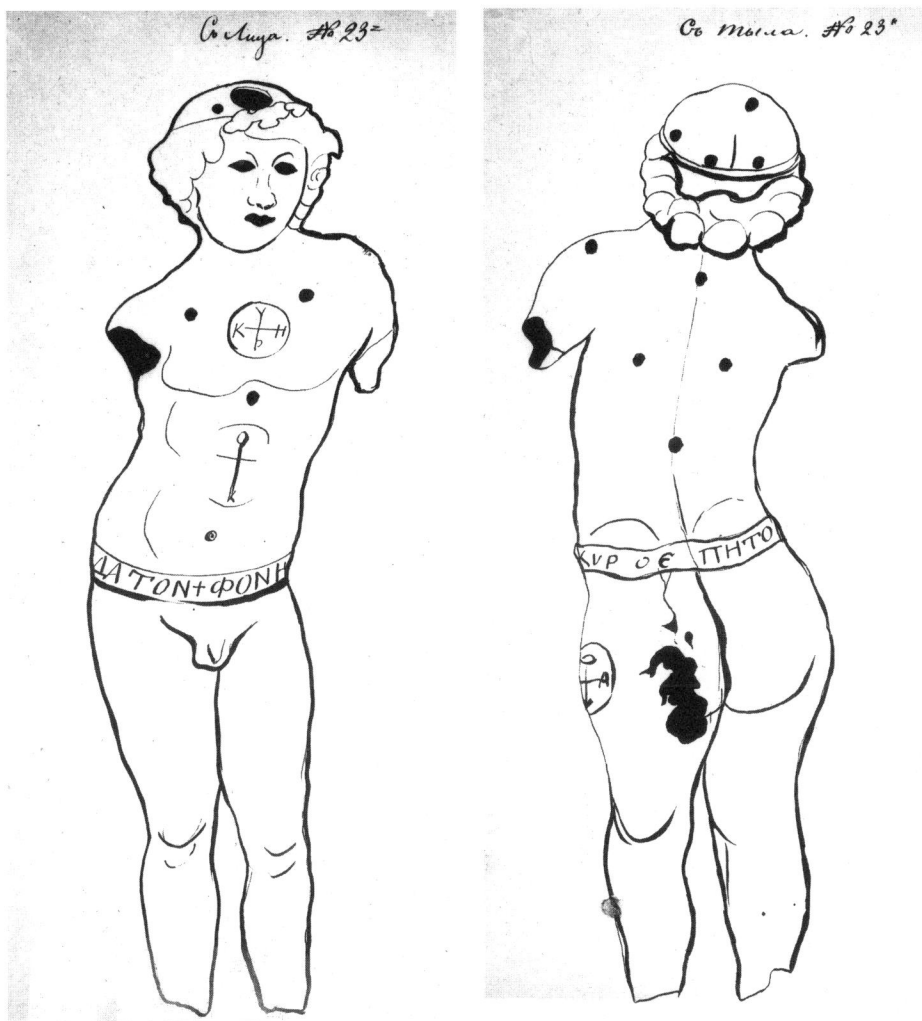

Fig. 32. Classical bronze figurine of Dionysos with a Greek inscription of the Byzantine period and Christian monograms. Height 0.5 arshins (c. 36 cm). The statuette was found in the area eroded by the waters of the Manych River at the Knjažij Kurgan near the village of Manyčskaja on the left bank of the Don above Aksai. A description of the figurine was published by L.E. Stephani: Otčet Imperatorskoj Archeologičeskoj komissii za 1867 g. p. 41 ff. Atlas. Plate 1, no. 4. *The inscriptions were published in: Latyšev 1896, 121-122, no. 116. A drawing of 1850 for* "Zapiski o mestnostjach v Vojske Donskom i veščestvennostjach tam otkryvaemych, zasluživajuščich vnimanija antikvariev i istorikov. S prisovokupleniem predanij" *by the Don student of local lore and history A.A. Martynov (1777-1865). Institute of Manuscript of the V.I. Vernadskij National Library of Ukraine of the National Academy of Sciences of Ukraine (IR NBU), V, 632, sheets 243-244. First publication.*

Irina V. Tunkina

At the beginning of the 20th century the Academician M.I. Rostovcev took advantage of the ideas proposed by J.A. Stempkovskij in the first research programme of the Russian science of Classical antiquities of the northern Black Sea region (1823). The studies of antiquarians of the first third of the 19th century, who succeeded in correctly understanding the chief tasks of the scientific investigation of ancient sites of the Black Sea area won high praise in a number of Rostovcev's works. As a matter of fact, the programme of Stempkovskij-Rostovcev is still valid. Its principal task – the creation of composite fundamental corpora of all kinds of evidence: literary, epigraphic, numismatic, and archaeological (*Corpus nummorum Russiae meridionalis, Corpus tumulorum Russiae meridionalis*, etc.)[57] remains, however, only half complete almost two centuries later. The tragedy of Russian science is in fact that its progress was forcibly interrupted by the historical cataclysms of the 20th century.

Notes

1. The study has been carried out with financial support of the Russian Foundation for Basic Research, project 03-06-80074.
2. The author's summary of Tunkina 2002.
3. Tunkina 1998, 12-26.
4. Tunkina 2002, 48-52, 564-570.
5. Blavatskij 1953, 38, fig. 13.
6. Ščeglov & Tunkina 1996, 27-29.
7. Koehler 1805.
8. Koehler 1822.
9. Blaramberg 1822b.
10. Tunkina 2002, 452-472, 627-630, 643-644.
11. Leont'ev 1851, 72.
12. Koehler 1826, 771.
13. Stempkovskij 1827b, 65-70.
14. Koeppen 1823a; 1823b.
15. Koeppen 1837.
16. Dubois de Montpéreux 1839-1843a; 1843b.
17. Stempkovskij 1827b, 40-72.
18. Dubrux 1858.
19. Cavignet, Ramos & Schiltz 2000.
20. Koehler 1823a; 1823b.
21. Ašik 1845.
22. Ašik 1848-1849.
23. Leont'ev 1851, 96.
24. Rostovcev 1993, 31-32.
25. Stritter 1771-1779.
26. Siestrencewicz de Bohusz 1800.
23. Potocki 1796a; Potocki 1796b; 1802; 1805a.
28. Potocki 1805b.
29. Latyschew 1893-1906.
30. Tunkina 1999, 273-287.
31. Koehler 1823a; 1823b.

32. Latyschev 1885-1916; 1896.
33. Tunkina 2002, 348-354.
34. Tunkina 2002, 464-470, 517-519, 543-544, 579-582.
35. Šelov 1956, 6.
36. Koehler 1850; 1853.
37. Stempkovsky 1822.
38. Stempkovsky 1827a.
39. Stempkovsky 1829.
40. Tunkina 2002, 367-369.
41. Mionnet 1807, 2, 366 ff.; 1829.
42. Murzakewicz 1835; 1841.
43. Spasskij 1846.
44. Sabatier 1849.
45. Sibirsky 1859.
46. Blaramberg 1822a.
47. Koehne 1848.
48. Leont'ev 1851, 84.
49. Koehne 1856.
50. Buračkov 1884.
51. Bertier de la Garde 1907.
52. Tunkina 1997, 90; 2002, 372, n. 328.
53. Zograf 1951, 21.
54. Rostovcev 1993, 30.
55. Rostovcev 1925, 258.
56. Uvarov 1856, 139.
57. Rostovcev 1993, 28-32.

Bibliography

Ašik, A.B. 1845. *Kerčenskie drevnosti: O pantikapejskoj katakombe, ukrašennoj freskami*. Odessa.

Ašik, A.B. 1848-1849. *Vosporskoe carstvo s ego paleografičeskimi i nadgrobnymi pamjatnikami, raspisnymi vazami, planami, kartami i vidami 1-3*. Odessa.

Bertier de la Garde, A.L. *Popravki obščego kataloga monet P.O. Buračkova*. Moskva.

Blaramberg, J. 1822a. *Choix des médailles antiques d'Olbiopolis ou Olbia faisant partie du cabinet de Blaramberg à Odessa*. Paris.

Blaramberg, J. 1822b. *Notices sur quelques objects d'antiquité, découverts en Tauride dans un Tumulus, près du site de l'ancienne Panticapée*. Paris.

Blavatskij, V.D. 1953. *Zemledelie v antičnych gosudarstvach Severnogo Pričernomor'ja*. Moskva.

Buračkov, P.O. 1884. *Obščij katalog monet, prinadležaščich ellinskim kolonijam, suščestvovavšim v drevnosti na severnom beregu Černogo morja, v predelach nynešnej Južnoj Rossii 1*. Odessa.

Cavignet, J.P., E. Ramos & V. Schiltz, 2000. Paul Du Brux, Koul-Oba et les Scythes: presence de Paul Du Brux dans les archives françaises, *Journal des savants* 2, 323-374.

Dubois de Montpéreux, F. 1839-1843a. *Voyage autour de Caucase, chez les*

Tcherkesses et les Abkases, en Colchide, en Géorgie, en Arménie, en Crimée 1-6. Paris.

Dubois de Montpéreux, F. 1843b. *Voyage au Caucase, chez les Tcherkesses et les Abkases, en Colchide, en Géorgie, en Arménie et en Crimée. Atlas.* Neuchatel-Paris.

Dubrux, P. 1858. Opisanie razvalin i sledov drevnich gorodov i ukreplenij, nekogda suščestvovavšich na evropejskom beregu Bospora Kimmerijskogo, ot vchoda v proliv bliz Enikal'skogo majaka do gory Opuk vključitel'no, pri Černom more, *Zapiski Odesskogo obščestva istorii i drevnostej* 4.1, 3-84.

Koehler, H.K.E. 1805. *Dissertation sur le monument de la reine Comosarye.* St-Pétersbourg.

Koehler, H.K.E. 1822. *Zwei Aufschriften der Stadt Olbia.* St Petersburg.

Koehler, H.K.E. 1823a. Remarques sur un ouvrage intitulé: Antiquités grecques du Bosphore Cimmérien, in: H.K.E. Koehler, *Serapis* vol. I. St Petersburg, 232-234.

Koehler, H.K.E. 1823b. Beurtheilung einer Schrift: Alterthuemer am Nordgestade des Pontus, in: H.K.E. Koehler, *Serapis* vol. II. St Petersburg, 5-44.

Koehler, H.K.E. 1826. Mémoire sur les îles et la course consacrées à Achille dans le Pont-Euxin, *Mémoires de l'Académie Impériale des Sciences de St.Pétersbourg*, 6ᵉ sér., 10, 531-820.

Koehler, H.K.E. 1850, 1853. *Gesammelte Schriften* 1-2, 6. St Petersburg.

Koehne, B.K. 1848. *Beitraege zur Geschichte und Archaeologie von Chersonesos in Taurien.* St Petersburg.

Koehne, B.K. 1856-1857. *Description de la musée de feu du prince Basile Kotchubey et recherches sur l'histoire des colonies grecques en Russie* 1-2. St-Pétersbourg.

Koeppen, P. 1823a. *Alterthuemer am Nordgestade des Pontus.* Wien.

Koeppen, P. 1823b. *Olbisches Psephisma zu Ehren des Protogenes.* Wien.

Koeppen, P. 1837. *Krymskij sbornik: O drevnostjach Južnogo berega Kryma i gor Tavričeskich.* St Peterburg.

Latyschev, B. 1885-1916. *Inscriptiones antiquae orae septentrionalis Ponti Euxini graecae et latinae* I-II, IV, I². Petropoli.

Latyschew, B. 1893-1906. *Scythica et Caucasica e veteribus scriptoribus Graecis et Latinis collegit et cum versione Rossica.* Petropoli.

Latyšev, V. 1896. *Sbornik grečeskich nadpisej christianskich vremen iz Južnoj Rossii.* St Peterburg.

Leont'ev, P.M. 1851. Obzor issledovanij o klassičeskich drevnostjach severnogo berega Černogo morja, in: *Propilei: Sbornik statej po klassičeskoj drevnosti, izdavaemyj P. Leont'evym* 1.2. Moskva, 67-101.

Mionnet, T.E. 1807, 1829. *Description de médailles antiques, grecques et romaines* 2. *Médailles grecques*, Suppl. 4. Paris.

Murzakewicz, N. 1835. *Descriptio nummorum veterum Graecorum atque Romanorum, qui inveniantur in museo N.M., ordine geographico et chronologico desposita tabulisque lithographicis ornate.* Odessae.

Murzakewicz, N. 1841. *Descriptio musei publici Odessani 1.* Odessae.

Potocki, J. 1796a. *Mémoire sur un Nouveau Péryple du Pont Euxin, ainsi que sur la plus ancienne histoire des peoples du Tavrées, du Caucase et de la Scythie.* Vienne.

Potocki, J. 1796b. *Fragments historiques et géographiques sur la Scythie, la Sarmatie et les Slaves.* Brunswick.

Potocki, J. 1802. *Histoire primitive des peuples de la Russie, avec une exposition complète de toutes les notions, locales, nationales et traditionnelles, necessaires à l'intelligence du quatrième livre d'Hérodote.* St-Pétersbourg.

Potocki, J. 1805a. *Histoire ancienne des provinces de l'Empire de Russie.* St-Pétersbourg.

Potocki, J. 1805b. *Atlas archéologique de la Russie Européenne.* St-Pétersbourg.

Rostovcev, M. 1925. *Skifija i Bospor: Kritičeskoe obozrenie pamjatnikov literaturnych i archeologičeskich.* Petrograd.

Rostovcev, M. 1993. Klassičeskie i skifskie drevnosti severnogo poberež'ja Černogo morja, *Peterburgskij archeologičeskij vestnik* 5, 25-38.

Sabatier, J. 1849. *Souvenirs de Kertsch et chronologie du royaume de Bosphore.* St-Pétersbourg.

Siestrencewicz de Bohusz, S. 1800. *Histoire du Royaume de la Chersonèse Taurique. Histoire de la Tauride* 1-2. Brunswick.

Ščeglov, A.N. & I.V. Tunkina 1996. Iz istorii izučenija antičnogo kul'turnogo landšafta v Krymu (konec 18-pervaja polovina 20 v.), in: *Tradicii rossijskoj archeologii.* St Peterburg, 27-29.

Šelov, D.B. 1956. *Monetnoe delo Bospora 6-2 vv. do n.e.* Moskva.

Sibirsky, A.A. 1859. *Catalogue des médailles du Bosphore-Cimmérien, précédé d'études sur l'histoire et les antiquités de ce pays* 1 (1-re partie). St-Pétersbourg.

Spasskij, G. 1846. *Der Kimmerische Bosporus mit seinen Alterthuemern und Denkwuerdigkeiten.* Moskau.

Stempkovsky, J. 1822. Notice sur les médailles de Rhadaméadis, roi inconnu du Bospore-Cimmérien, découvertes en Tauride en 1820, in: *Antiquités grecques du Bosphore-Cimmérien publiées et expliquées par M. Raoul-Rochette.* Paris, 218-235.

Stempkovsky, J. 1827a. *Médaille de Mithridate III, roi du Bosphore-Cimmérien et de la reine Gépaepiris.* Odessa.

Stempkovskij I. 1827b. Mysli otnositel'no izyskanija drevnostej v Novorossijskom krae, *Otečestvennye zapiski* 29, 81, 40-72.

Stempkovsky, J. 1829. Médaille de Pharéanzès, ancient roi du Bosphore-Cimmérien, *Journal d'Odessa*, 18/20 sept., N 75, 328.

Stritter, J.G. 1771-1779. *Memoriae populorum, olim ad Danubium, Pontum*

Euxinum, Paludem Maeotidem, Caucasum, Mare Caspium et inde magis ad septentriones incolentium et scriptoribus historiae Byzantinae erutae et digestae. Petropoli.

Tunkina, I.V. 1997. M.I. Rostovcev i Rossijskaja Akademija nauk, *Skifskij roman.* Moskva, 84-123.

Tunkina, I.V. 1998. Pervyj issledovatel' skifskich kurganov: K biografii A.P. Mel'gunova (1722-1788), *Očerki istorii otečestvennoj archeologii* 2. Moskva, 12-26.

Tunkina, I.V. 1999. V.V. Latyšev: Žizn' i učenye trudy (po materialam rukopisnogo nasledija), in: *Rukopisnoe nasledie russkich vizantinistov v archivach Sankt-Peterburga.* St Peterburg, 172-288.

Tunkina, I.V. 2002. *Russkaja nauka o klassičeskich drevnostjach juga Rossii (XVIII-seredina XIX v.).* St Peterburg.

Uvarov, A.S. 1853-1856. *Issledovanija o drevnostjach Južnoj Rossii i beregov Černogo morja* 1-2. St Peterburg.

Zograf, A.N. 1951. *Antičnye monety* (MatIsslA, 16). Moskva-Leningrad.

The Statue Bases of Claudius
A Reassessment of *The Portraiture of Claudius* by Meriwether Stuart[1]

Jakob Munk Højte

Meriwether Stuart observed in 1938 in the introduction to his study on the portraits of Claudius: "Problems have arisen in the study of the extant portraits whose solution eludes the evidence they furnish. For supplementary evidence the long neglected record of non-extant portraits must be searched". His study contained, apart from a traditional catalogue of portraits in marble and bronze, a collection and discussion of all the different types of evidence relevant to the subject: literary sources, coins, papyri, and as a novelty the first systematic compilation of inscriptions pertaining to statue bases and other types of monuments designed to carry sculptural representations of Claudius.[2] The epigraphic material, being close to three times as numerous as the preserved portraits, was by far the largest body of evidence and the one to yield the most interesting information. They offered for the first time answers to questions about geographical distribution, chronological distribution and occasions and motives for erecting imperial statues, which hitherto had been left largely to guesswork.

Although the results of Stuart's investigation of the epigraphic material were remarkable, this approach has never received the attention it deserves among scholars of Roman imperial portraiture. The following year, Stuart published a *corpus* of statue bases of the Julio-Claudian emperors,[3] and a few years later a study along similar lines concerning the relatives of Augustus appeared.[4] More recently studies of the portraits of Sabina, the Late Roman emperors, Julia Domna, Caligula and Hadrian have included epigraphic material.[5] However, Stuart's work remains the most thorough and consistent attempt at using this type of evidence to address issues related to the erection of imperial statues.

In the intervening 65 years, the study of imperial portraits has advanced immensely and has become a highly specialized field with increasingly more sophisticated typologies and dating schemes based on details in the reproduction of the hair. The first comprehensive treatment of the portraits of Claudius since Stuart still awaits publication,[6] but Stuart's catalogue has long been outdated both with regard to the number of entries and to the method of identifying and categorizing the portraits. Similarly, much new

*Fig. 1. Marble portrait of
Claudius in Ny Carlsberg
Glyptotek, Copenhagen, inv.
no. 1423.*

epigraphic evidence has been published.[7] Stuart enumerated 104 inscriptions from statue bases; today they number 156, an increase of 50%. This
increase necessitates a reassessment of Stuart's results, and as will be shown,
the currently available evidence on central points leads to different conclusions.

Geographical distribution

The geographical distribution of the statue bases in Stuart's study showed
that the distribution of imperial portraits was much wider than could be
assessed from the extant portraits, which for the most part derive from Italy.
Bernoulli's groundbreaking study from 1886[8] had almost exclusively dealt
with portraits found in Italy, and Rome in particular. Even though several
portraits had been found outside the Italian peninsula in the fifty years
between Bernoulli and Stuart, three quarters of the portraits in Stuart's catalogue originited in Italy. The distribution of the statue bases was exactly the
opposite, with three quarters originating in the provinces. As a consequence,
production centres outside Rome and Italy with a substantial capacity must

Region	Number of bases	% of total
Italia with Sicilia and Sardinia	39	25.0
Northern frontier provinces	8	5.1
Spain and Gaul	21	13.5
Western North Africa	11	7.1
Greece with Cyrene	31	19.9
Asia Minor	45	28.8
Eastern provinces and Egypt	1	0.6

Fig. 2. The geographical distribution of the statue bases of Claudius.

have existed to supply the local demand for imperial portraits. Today even more portraits from the provinces are known but they still constitute a minority.[9] At least three factors have contributed to the overrepresentation of Italian material among the extant imperial portraits. First of all, marble, being more durable than bronze, was always more favoured for honorary statues in the Latin West than in the Greek East. Secondly, imperial portraits in private contexts are known primarily in Italy, and marble busts which because of their high durability constitute a considerable portion of the preserved portraits seem to have been the favoured medium for private display.[10] Finally, in Italy there has been a strong tradition for collecting ancient sculpture which goes back at least to the 15th century, whereas marble sculpture in many other parts of the Roman empire until well into the 19th century was likely to end up in the limekilns.

The new material has not significantly changed the list of provinces with statue bases of Claudius.[11] The provinces of Alpes Maritimae, Cilicia, Sardinia et Corsica and Tarraconensis have each been included with one inscription.[12] However, the inscriptions from Alpes Maritimae and Tarraconensis had already been noted by Stuart, who listed them as doubtful.

The relative importance of each region has remained largely unchanged since Stuart's study even though the rate of publication of epigraphic material has not been the same everywhere. The material from Asia Minor, which was poorly published at the time Stuart wrote, has in some areas received more attention in recent years, but this has not resulted in a significantly larger percentage of statue bases. It is still, however, the area with the most statue bases, with Italy second and Greece third. These constitute the three major centres. There are almost an equal number of bases east and west of the traditional linguistic dividing line through the Adriatic, but 57% of the inscriptions are in Latin, since sixteen inscriptions in Latin have been found in the eastern half of the empire, and only one in Greek in the western half. Bilingual inscriptions have been found in Ephesos and Sagalassos.[13]

Fig. 3. Statue base for Claudius in the Agora of Athens with cuttings typical for a bronze statue on the top.

A few curiosities concerning the geographical distribution are worth pointing out. In Cyprus an abundance of Julio-Claudian, particularly Tiberian, statue bases have been found, but so far none for Claudius.[14] In Gaul, the Julio-Claudian emperors apparently enjoyed great popularity if we are to judge from the number of statues dedicated. Claudius, a native of Lugdunum, is no exception. Together with Tiberius, statue bases for Claudius are the most frequently encountered of all emperors. After the reign of Claudius, there is a large gap in the series of imperial statue bases in Gaul. In Narbonensis, for example, only one base is known from the hundred years following the base for the Divus Claudius in Arles,[15] and in Belgica a base for Claudius is the last for an emperor in that province until the third century AD. The same tendency can be observed for the preserved portraits, although not quite to the same extent.[16]

Stuart did not discuss how the non-extant portraits relate to the extant ones, or to what extent the documentary sources are representative of what was originally set up. It seems that he took for granted that the evidence of the documentary sources was applicable to the portraits as well.[17] Survival of epigraphic evidence, however, requires the presence of a stone suitable for cutting inscriptions, just as the survival of portraits requires the presence of and preference for marble over bronze. In areas where stone suitable for cutting inscriptions was not quarried locally, built-up bases covered with bronze sheets were a good alternative to imported stone, and these naturally have as little chance of surviving as the accompanying bronze statues. This is the case in many regions of the northern part of the empire, where most of the relatively few known bronze bases have been found,[18] including one for Claudius in Augustomagus in Lugdunensis,[19] where our knowledge of imperial statue bases is meager. The use of bronze plaques for inscriptions was however not restricted to areas without stone suitable for inscriptions, as shown by the finds of bronze plaques for statue bases for Claudius in Herculaneum and in Rome.[20]

Even if the epigraphic material does not tell the complete story of the distribution of imperial portraits in antiquity, its evidence is certainly much more reliable than that offered by the portraits themselves. The relative importance of each region as a market for imperial statues therefore deserves to be taken into account in any discussion of how the production and distribution was organized. The portraits of provincial manufacture, which are often treated parenthetically in studies of imperial portraiture, may have in fact been the norm rather than the exception.

Chronology

The statue bases can, contrary to the portraits, often be dated very precisely because of the titles, offices and epithets frequently found in the imperial name in the dedicatory inscription. 56% of all the inscriptions including pre-accession and posthumous statue bases contain internal criteria for dating. Among the bases set up during the reign of Claudius 52.4% can be dated more precisely. 42% of the inscriptions can be dated to specific years, mostly on the basis of the tribunician count, and another 10.4% can be dated within a limited period within the reign. These are for the most part dateable because the bases have been found together with ones for family members which supply a shorter date range. There is a very clear linguistic difference in the percentage of dateable bases. 75% of the Latin inscriptions and only 30% of the Greek are dateable, since the Greeks generally were not interested in the Roman cursus, preferring traditional epithets like σωτήρ and ευεργέτης instead.

Stuart's interest in the documentary sources concerning the erection of portraits of Claudius was twofold: 1) to establish the chronological distribution of the dedications throughout the reign independently of the preserved portraits themselves in order to obtain an objective criteria for dating the portraits, and 2) to investigate which occasions caused the erection of portrait statues and what motives the dedicator had. Stuart's primary source was the epigraphic evidence but the literary and papyrological testimony was included in the discussion of the chronology as well. Consequently one document, the London Papyrus 1912, which mentions eight or more statues of Claudius set up in Alexandria in AD 41 or 42, had a considerable impact on the conclusions drawn from the chronological distribution of the docu-

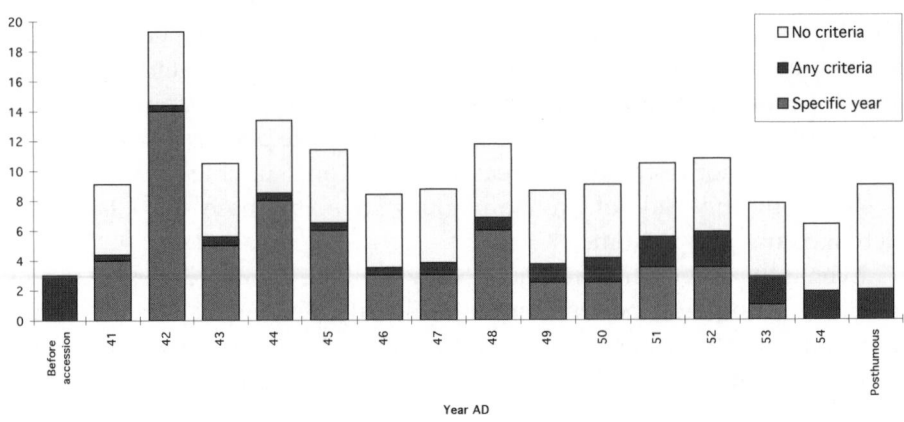

Fig. 4. The chronological distribution of the statue bases of Claudius.[21]

mentary evidence. Stuart calculated that 46.5% of the dateable evidence belonged to the period AD 41-43 and "the significance of this percentage for the extant portraits seems obvious. Approximately half of them should date from the first three years of Claudius reign. And most of the types of Claudius's portraits should go back to this period".[22] This is stretching the evidence. The present *corpus* of epigraphic material from the statue bases has an overrepresentation for the period AD 41-43 much lower at 28% of the material. With an even distribution throughout the reign, it ought to be 20%, since Claudius ruled for approximately fifteen years. Thus, there is no reason to suppose, as Stuart did, that half the portraits of Claudius should be dated within the period AD 41-43.

Regarding the question of the number of portraits of the young Claudius, no new pre-accession statue bases have come to light. This contradicts the situation for the portraits since many new specimens supposedly have been identified.[23] Although the provenience of the so-called "arch at Pavia" still remains a mystery,[24] its inscription at any rate constitutes our only evidence for portrait statues of Claudius during the reign of Augustus. In a senatorial decree of AD 19 concerning the posthumous honours for Germanicus, preserved in the Tabula Siarensis, one of the honours is an arch to be erected in the Circus Flaminius.[25] The document describes the inscription on the front and the statue group on the attic with statues of Germanicus in a triumphal chariot; Drusus, his father; Tiberius, his brother; Antonia, his mother; Agrippina, his wife; Livia [Livilla], his sister, and, just before Germanicus's children are mentioned (here only referred to as his sons and daughters), his brother Claudius. Although he was the emperor's nephew and for a long period the closest adult male relative, this is the only evidence of statues of Claudius during the reign of Tiberius. From the reign of Caligula, we know of two bases: one in Pola and one in Alexandria Troas.[26] Considering that the average ratio between extant bases and portraits of approximately two to one,[27] we should expect very few pre-accession portraits of Claudius to exist. Even if we allow for a different distribution pattern for portraits of members of the imperial family, since the reason for setting up statues of them may have been somewhat different, portrait statues of Claudius could by no means have been common before his sudden and unexpected elevation to power in AD 41.[28] The reasons for erecting a statue of a young or (during the reign of Caligula) middle-aged prince must have been related to his role in the dynastic policies or in anticipation or appreciation of benefactions. On both counts Claudius seems to fall behind other male members of the Julio-Claudian dynasty, whose statue bases are encountered much more frequently.[29]

The number of posthumous dedications, on the other hand, has risen considerably to nine and they now account for 5.8% of the total.[30] This brings the evidence for statues of Divus Claudius in accordance with the number of statue bases for the following *Divi*, for whom between ten and thirteen are known.[31]

The extant portraits and the non-extant portraits, represented by the statue bases, constitute two separate excerpts of what was originally set up – the portraits being of marble and deriving predominantly from Italy, whereas the bases have a much wider distribution and often carried images of bronze. Only in two instances do the two excerpts overlap: the bronze statue and base from Herculaneum and the high relief with inscription from the *sebasteion* in Aphrodisias [32] Despite this, the chronological distribution of the bases within the reign most likely applies to the portraits as well. This is rendered probable by the fact that the length of the reign is not a factor in determining the ratio between extant portraits and bases, which for most emperors during the first two centuries AD amounts to approximately two bases for each portrait. If there was a difference in the chronology of the two excerpts – for example a certain form of portraits being produced primarily in the beginning of the reign, we would expect a difference between Nerva who only reigned one year and four months and Antoninus Pius who reigned nearly twenty-three years. Since this is not the case, the chronological distribution of the two excerpts must have been approximately the same. Thus, the evidence of the statue bases can be employed to determine the chronological distribution of the portraits of Claudius.[33]

Occasions for erecting statues of Claudius

In his analysis of the occasions for setting up statues of Claudius, Stuart took for granted that there was a close connection between events related to the emperor and the dedication of statues. In many instances, however, this assumption easily leads to an overinterpretation of the evidence. A statue set up in AD 48/9, for example, could have been inspired by the downfall of Messalina and the marriage to Agrippina, but not necessarily, as is evidently the case with the statue found in Herculaneum set up that year *ex testamento*.[34]

Stuart noted that there were very few portrait statues of Claudius in existence before AD 41 and, probably as a consequence of this, that "Claudius's accession gave a strong impulse to the erection of his portraits."[35] However, it was not the first year of his reign that produced large quantities of statues; it was the second. On these grounds, Stuart concluded that the administration was unconcerned about the speedy or widespread distribution of the imperial portrait, a phenomenon noticeable to all the Julio-Claudian emperors. The administration's active involvement should allegedly only have begun with the rapid succession of emperors in AD 69 without the legitimacy of a Julio-Claudian ancestry.[36] The theory rests primarily on Tacitus's references to statues of Galba and Vitellius within a very short period of their accession[37] and on third century and later sources.[38] Tested against a large body of epigraphic material it proves incorrect. For Vespasian, Domitian and Trajan the accession of the new emperor did not give impetus to a rapid and wide distribution of imperial portraits.

Stuart pointed out the fact that most of the dedications in the first two years of his reign were made by communities rather than by individuals, and considered this as a confirmation of the belief that showing loyalty to the emperor by erecting his image immediately upon accession was a highly motivating factor for communities.[39] Stuart enumerated thirteen public dedications and only three by private individuals in the first two years of the reign, but the figures need revision. In the present *corpus* the statue bases of AD 41-42 were dedicated by nine communities, one corporation, and five private individuals with one more private individual and four corporations in AD 43,[40] and the argument concerning the composition of the dedicators is thus not as strong as believed by Stuart, although there is still an overrepresentation of public dedications among the early bases.

The peak in AD 42 is significant, but there could be an explanation other than the wish or even duty of communities to pay their respects to the new emperor by erecting his image.[41] After Caligula was overthrown there must have been a substantial number of monuments and statues of Caligula available for reworking at a favourably low expense, and furthermore in the cities there must have been a number of public places in every city which looked conspicuously empty after the removal of Caligula's statues. The reason why the dedications took place in AD 42 rather than 41 could be that city magistrates awaited instructions from the new administration in Rome as to how they should treat the images of the previous emperor. The removal and reuse of portraits and inscriptions had many precedents, but none had the same judicial and religious implications as those of the imperial image.[42] While the evidence for re-use of inscriptions for Caligula is limited to the arch in Thugga,[43] perhaps because new bases were relatively inexpensive, there are several examples of portraits of Caligula remodelled into the likeness of Claudius[44] and in most instances a mere swapping of heads was necessary to bring portrait statues into current fashion.

Some fifty years later, following the murder of Domitian, the chronological distribution of the statue bases of Nerva show some of the same tendencies as for Claudius: few dedications the first year and then a very large number the following.[45] It is of course impossible to say how things would have developed had Nerva not died after having reigned for only sixteen months, but judging from the number of dedications to Trajan in the first years of his reign, the high figure for Nerva would not have lasted long.[46] During the first years of Vespasian's reign, however, there are relatively few dedications of statues even if the bases for Vespasian, Titus and Domitian are added up, although there must have been an abundance of statues of several different emperors ready for re-use. Perhaps communities and individuals had become very cautious; Vespasian was after all the fifth emperor in just over one year.

In most studies of imperial portraits military success figures among the most important occasions for erecting statues, and Claudius, who had no prior military experience and owed his position to the intervention of the praetorian guard during the uncertainty following the murder of Caligula, relied heavily on military support, as seen in several reverse types on the coinage[47] and in the unsurpassed 27 imperatorial acclamations. Direct reference to military engagements, however, can only be found in two inscriptions belonging to arches set up in Rome and Kyzikos.[48] Among the other inscriptions that probably belong to arches of Claudius,[49] the one set up in Rome may have been associated with the British campaign. It is one of four dedications made in AD 43 by corporations, some of which undoubtedly profited from the military operations in Britain by acting as suppliers for the army.[50] Furthermore, the two arches in Verona set up in AD 44 may have been inspired by the triumph in AD 43. Possibly Claudius even visited the city on his way back to Rome.[51] In fact, four out of five dateable arches were set up in AD 43/4 and 51/2, the years of the most important victories in Britain. There is a slight increase in the number of dedications in these particular years (Fig. 4), which to a large extent can be explained by these arches. The number of ordinary statue bases, however, does not rise significantly. That the inscriptions referring to military activities belong to arches is hardly surprising. Honorific arches and city gates dedicated to the emperor were more closely connected to victories and imperial visits than ordinary statue bases.[52]

The importance of military exploits during Claudius's reign does not seem to have encouraged military personnel to erect statues either. None of the bases were dedicated by military units, but these are admittedly rare among the dedicators under the Julio-Claudian emperors.[53] Three bases were set up by officers and of these only [...]glitus Barbatus could still be on active duty. Both C. Norbanus Quadratus and [...]essus Seneca's dedications were testamentary and C. Norbanus Quadratus had left his military career for civic office.[54]

Important occasions for erecting statues connected to Claudius's private life occurred in AD 41 with the birth of Britannicus, an heir to the throne, and with the events following the downfall of Messalina in AD 48: the marriage to Agrippina[55] and the betrothal of Octavia to Nero in AD 49 and finally the adoption of Nero in AD 50. The birth of Britannicus within weeks of Claudius's accession was overshadowed by this event, and the one statue group associated with the birth of Britannicus cannot have been set up before AD 43.[56] Infants sometimes appear in Julio-Claudian family groups, but with the possible exception of the statue group on Thasos of Julia and Livia holding her granddaughter Julia[57] nothing suggests that childbirth was an occasion for erecting dynastic statue groups.[58] London Papyrus 1912 refers to groups of statues to be set up in AD 42 consisting of Claudius and his family, but none of Claudius's children are mentioned by name.

Stuart observed that the period after the downfall of Messalina was "marked by the impetus given the erection of Claudius's portraits by his marriage with Agrippina", but the six inscriptions referred to as results of the new alliance in fact all antedate the marriage which took place early in AD 49.[59] The adoption of Nero in AD 50 neither aroused enthusiasm for erecting statues of Claudius, as the year has the least bases of any apart from AD 54, which Claudius did not live throughout (Fig. 4). Stuart proposed that this was a result of Claudius's alleged modesty in private affairs,[60] but per- haps imperial statues generally were not meant to commemorate such occa- sions.

Strack's identification of a new portrait type on coins of Trajan, suppos- edly in connection with his *decennalia*,[61] has had a great influence on the study of the portraits in the round, and anniversary types have been pro- posed not just for Trajan, the "*Dezennalienbildnis*", but for several other emperors who reigned more than ten years. The *decennalia* has so far not been suggested as the reason for the third portrait type of Claudius, the "Typus Turin", whose similarity to the portraits of the young Nero could indicate that they were conceived together on the occasion of the adoption.[62] The *decennalia* has, however, been seen as an obvious occasion for showing loyalty towards the emperor by erecting his portrait. So far no consensus has been reached about the exact moment and duration of an emperor's *decen- nalia*. One suggestion is that it occurred sometime between the *dies imperii*

nine years after the accession and the end of the tenth year.[63] For Claudius
this corresponds approximately to the year AD 50 in which only one base
can be dated with certainty,[64] and in this case the anniversary can thus not
have been a cause for erecting statues of Claudius. The other possibility, that
the *decennalia* started only after the completion of the tenth year,[65] brings the
celebration into the year AD 51 to which three inscriptions can be dated with
certainty. However, one of these, the arch spanning the *Via Lata*,[66] celebrates
Claudius's Britannic victory rather than the *decennalia*. Further research
must show whether anniversaries can be documented as occasions for erecting statues of other emperors.

Apart from the large number of dedications in the early part of the reign
clearly inspired by the accession of the new emperor, there is remarkably little evidence pointing towards a close relation between events related to the
emperor and the dedication of his portrait statues. One possible explanation
for the rather uniform number of statue bases throughout the reign could be
that the occasions were related not to the emperor whose statue was set up,
but rather to the dedicator of the statue.

Dedicators

Even though the inscriptions seldom state the motives for erecting the imperial statue directly, the cause can sometimes be inferred from the identity of
the dedicator. Of the 156 inscriptions from statue bases for Claudius, thirty-
eight are in a state of preservation that does not allow us to determine
whether a dedicator was named or not. Of the remaining 118 only sixteen
(14%) specify no dedicator, and it is certainly a possibility that the identities
of the dedicators of these monuments were obvious in their original context,
either because the location dictated it or because the dedicator was mentioned in a separate inscription associated with the statue base. The dedicators of the remaining 102 inscriptions are divided almost evenly between
public and private.

Communities or their executive bodies are mentioned in fifty inscriptions
or 42%. It is not always clear whether public funds actually paid for the statue, or whether an executive body simply authorized the use of public space
for the dedication. The well-known expression *l(ocus) d(atus) d(ecreto) d(ecurionum)* leaves no doubt as to the private nature of the monument, but the
shorter, more common *d(ecreto) d(ecurionum)* is more elusive. Generally it
indicates a public dedication, but there are examples of statues paid for by
individuals.[67] Four of the seven inscriptions for Claudius set up by decree of
the decuriones specify that public funds were used, while the remaining
three contain no further information.[68] Similarly, in Greek inscriptions, cities
decide to set up statues (twenty-eight examples), but may leave it to one or
more ἐπιμεληταῖto carry out the work.[69] Due to the brevity of the inscriptions
the function of the ἐπιμελητής is often not entirely clear. Did they, for exam-

ple, sometimes take the initiative themselves or were they appointed, and were they expected to pay for the dedication out of their own pocket or were public funds supplied? Normally the ἐπιμεληταί were office holders, which could indicate that office holders were obliged to display munificence, as is well documented in North Africa. An inscription from Tralles is particularly illustrative in this respect.[70] The city dedicated the statue, but the inscription informs us that it was paid for by Tiberius Claudius Diogenes at the time he was *gymnasiarchos*. Clearly he intended the monument to glorify his own achievement as well.

Only four inscriptions from public dedications offer precise information as to the motive for setting up the statue of Claudius. Two belong to the above-mentioned arches commemorating Claudius's Britannic victories. The other two were set up by the city of Volubilis because Claudius had granted Roman citizenship to its inhabitants. The first could have been set up to commemorate this event, while the other was a posthumous dedication.[71] Sometimes epithets like saviour and benefactor allude to imperial benevolence, but the exact nature of the gifts, if indeed there were any, almost always elude us.[72] Exceptions are the unusual epithet νεὸς κτίστης in the inscription from Samos, which probably refers to reconstructions paid for by the emperor after the earthquake of AD 47,[73] and σωτὴρ καὶ εὐεργέτης in an inscription from Kos.[74] Claudius seems to have had good relations with Kos also prior to the grant of *immunitas* in AD 53,[75] and the Koans dedicated more statues of Claudius than of any other emperor.[76] The use of the epithets εὐεργέτης and σωτήρ in inscriptions found in Koroneia and Patara is more curious, since the background for the dedications was far from favorable.[77] The dedication of the statue in Koroneia by the league of Achaeans, Phoceans, Euboeans, and Boeotians occurred shortly after Claudius had returned the province of Achaea to the senate in AD 44,[78] an event not likely to have been of benefit to the provincials, and the one in Patara was set up only two years after Claudius had deprived the cities of Lykia their freedom and put the province under the administration of a *pro praetor* because of internal strife.[79] However, as London Papyrus 1912 clearly illustrates, honorary statues could be used to mitigate the anger of a displeased emperor.

Corporations were responsible for seven statue bases (6%) and individuals for forty-five (38%). Among these the most obvious explanation for the time and occasion for the dedication is offered by the four dedications made *ex testamento*.[80] Two of them were gifts from soldiers, while the other two inscriptions offer no information about the deceased.

The profession or the public office of the dedicator can give a clue as to the motive for erecting the emperor's portrait. Two points are worth noting in this connection: 1) the dedications seem to take place while the dedicator is holding office, and 2) the most active group consists of priests, particularly priests in the imperial cult, who had a personal interest in promoting the imperial worship.

A curiosity among the statue bases of Claudius is the numerous dedicators, mostly Greeks, who because of their name Tiberius Claudius seem to have received Roman citizenship from Claudius.[81] Newly enfranchised citizens figure among the dedicators of statues of other emperors but never in such numbers. This is probably to be explained by Claudius's generosity in granting citizenship, and we can expect that at least some of these statues were set up as a result of the newly acquired status of the dedicator.

One last monument worth mentioning is the *sebasteion* in Aphrodisias.[82] On the two porticoes flanking the processional way from the *propylon* to the temple, reliefs were placed between the columns in the two upper stories. On the northern portico personifications of conquered peoples and cosmic figures are depicted, on the southern portico mythological scenes and members of the Julio-Claudian family. Two reliefs show Claudius vanquishing Britannia and Claudius clasping hands with Agrippina. Beneath the reliefs on a panel the names of the depicted are written in the nominative case as a caption for the scene. Although the monument falls outside the definition of a statue base and the portraits are not in the round, I have decided to include the relief with the associated inscription in the catalogue.[83] The original dedicators of the southern portico and the temple were two brothers, Diogenes and Attalos, and the latter's wife Attalis, but repairs after an earthquake including the reliefs showing Claudius and his family were carried out by Diogenes' son Tiberios Claudios Diogenes, who had received citizenship from Claudius as the inscription on the architrave on the south portico informs us.[84]

The fact that at least 86% of all the inscriptions specify who donated the statue gives some idea of the importance attached to such monuments by their dedicators. Erecting a statue was a costly affair, and great care was taken to ensure that the publicity such a display afforded was used to its full potential. Although specific references to the occasions for erecting the statues are rare, there are several indications that in many instances the events leading to the dedication related to the dedicator rather than to Claudius.

Conclusion

When Stuart wrote his treatise on the portraits of Claudius, he could only suspect that the chronological distribution of the documentary sources had any bearing on the preserved portraits. With the availability of comparative studies today and evidence of the constant ratio between statue bases and portraits, we can say with great certainty that the chronology of the statue bases applies to the portraits as well. The available data belonging primarily to late first and second century AD emperors point to a ratio of about two statue bases for each preserved portrait.[85] The ratio for Caligula seems to be an exception to the rule. According to Boschung there are fewer statue bases than preserved portraits of Caligula.[86] Likewise, the evidence for Augustus

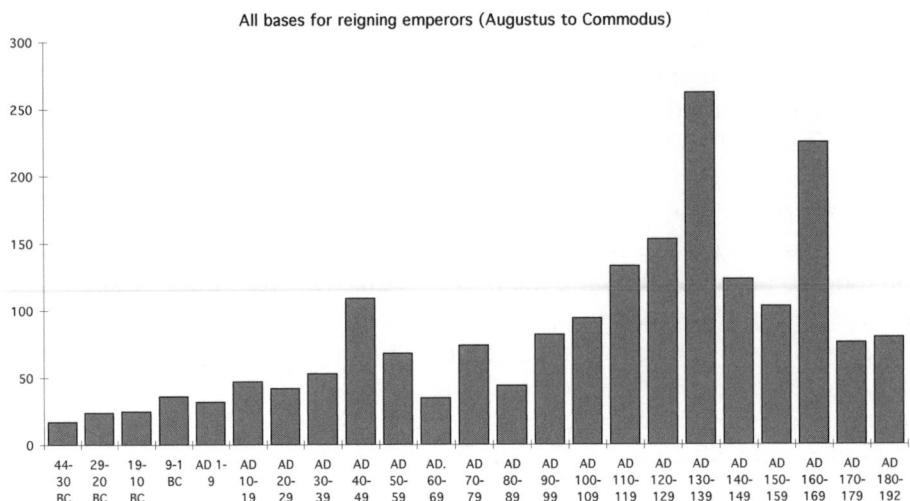

Fig. 5. The chronological distribution of all statue bases for reigning emperors from Augustus to Commodus.[90]

indicates a fairly low ratio,[87] but the historical background for both these emperors – Augustus's extraordinary position as founder of the principate and Caligula's fall from power and the subsequent removal of monuments commemorating him – could very well have distorted the figures. It is interesting, therefore, that the ratio for Claudius corresponds closely to the evidence for the Flavian emperors and the emperors of the second century AD, with ratios close to 2:1 According to A.-K. Massner there are in the vicinity of eighty-five portraits identifiable as Claudius,[88] which together with the 156 statue bases gives a ratio of approximately 1.8:1.[89]

We learn from the chronological distribution of the statue bases that portrait statues of Claudius were erected continuously throughout the reign. The accession of the new emperor gave some impetus to the erection of his portraits (28% of the bases date to the first three years of his reign), but other occasions traditionally believed to offer motives – military exploits, anniversaries and family-related events – seem to have been of minor importance. On the other hand, a number of inscriptions indicate that the occasions instead were closely related to the dedicator of the statue, whether a city or a private individual.

The frequency at which statues of Claudius were erected is remarkably high compared to other first century AD emperors. 10.3 statue bases of Claudius are preserved for each year of the reign, a level that, apart from the short reign of Nerva, was not reached again until the reign of Hadrian. Naturally, the figures for his immediate predecessor and successor – Caligula and Nero – are unreliable due to the removal of monuments after their deaths, but the frequency for Caligula at least seems to have been fairly high. From Tiberius, with 5.4 statue bases per year, to Claudius the frequency almost doubled. Since the geographical area in which the statues were set up remained largely unchanged, it is within the same cities that increased pressure or perhaps rather enthusiasm for erecting portraits of the emperor was felt.

The frequency of imperial statue bases during the first two centuries of the principate (Fig. 5) recalls that of the general evolution of the epigraphic habit of the Roman Empire as presented by MacMullen.[91] In this case, however, it concerns not only the epigraphic habit but even more so the sculptural habit, since the inscriptions were after all only of secondary importance to the imperial statues. On the otherwise gently rising curve of the frequencies from the reign of Augustus and into the second century AD, the reign of Claudius stands out as a particularly active period. Perhaps a combination of the stability of the period and the favourable economic situation created an ideal climate for individuals and communities to show munificence and loyalty towards Rome and the emperor by erecting his statue – a climate that was dramatically changed in the late 60s only to return under the adopted emperors.

Notes

1. Stuart 1938.
2. For definition and identification of statue bases see, Stuart 1938, 13-14.
3. Stuart 1939, 601-617.
4. Hanson & Johnson 1946, 389-400.
5. Carandini 1969; Stichel 1982; Fejfer 1985; Boschung 1989; Evers 1994.
6. A.-K. Massner, who is currently working on *Die Bildnisse des Claudius. Das römische Herrscherbild* I 5, has kindly supplied me with information about the number and format of the portraits included in her catalogue.
7. Menichetti (1983-84, 188-192) made a cursory survey of the inscriptions published after 1938 and briefly discussed the chronology of the bases. However, his revised list is far from complete, and a number of the included inscriptions do not belong to statue bases of Claudius.
8. Bernoulli 1886, 327-355.
9. Updated figures will hopefully appear soon in Massner (forthcoming). Until then the most important recent studies are: Balty 1963, 97-134; Fittschen 1973, 55-58, no. 17; Jucker 1981, 236-316; Massner 1982, 135-139, 159-160; Menichetti 1983-1984, 182-226.
10. For display in private contexts, see Neudecker 1988.
11. See the revised catalogue at the end of this article.
12. *CIL* XII, 5; *SEG* XX, 69; *CIL* X, 7515; *CIL* II, 3105.
13. Ephesos: *SEG* XXXIX, 1178. Sagalassos: *CIL* III, 6871.
14. Augustus: *SEG* XX, 241. Tiberius: *IGRR* III, 933, 941-943; *CIL* III, 12140; *JHS* 9 (1888) 260, no. 14; Pouilloux et al. 1987, nos. 132-133. Caligula: *SEG* XXX, 1633. Nero: *IGRR* III, 971; Pouilloux et al. 1987, no. 134, 136.
15. *CIL* XII, 666. The following is a base for Hadrian (*CIL* XII, 1797) presently placed next to the church in St. Jean-de-Muzols.

16.   Apart from the imperial portraits from the Chiragan Villa, whose original con-
      text is unknown – they could have been secondary imports in the late antique
      period – the portraits of emperors in Gaul in the hundred years after Claudius
      are Domitian (re-cut from Nero) in Vaison-la-Romaine; Trajan in Avignon,
      Musée Calvet; Hadrian in Vaison-la-Romaine; Hadrian in Nevers, Musée
      Lapidaire no. 84; Antoninus Pius in Toulouse, Musée Saint-Raymond (from
      Béziers) and Antoninus Pius in Bourges Mus. There exist no fewer than ten
      portraits of Augustus alone! (Boschung 1993, 206).
17.   Stuart 1938, XIV, 41.
18.   Driehaus 1969, 424-436; Boon 1980, 98-101. In Vienne, Mus. Beaux-Arts, there is
      a fine example of a bronze statue of a *privatus* found along with a dedicatory
      inscription on a bronze plaque (France-Lanord 1960, 93-104).
19.   Piganiol 1959, 450-457 (with photo of the inscription); Wuilleumier 1984, 147-
      148, no. 357.
20.   Herculaneum: *CIL* X, 1416. Rome: *CIL* VI, 40307. The inscription on the last-
      mentioned marble plaque was originally engraved on bronze plaques, as
      shown by the presence of the duplicate inscription *CIL* VI, 40334.
21.   The inscriptions are divided into three categories. 1) inscriptions dateable to
      specific years. 2) inscriptions dateable within a limited period within the reign.
      These are distributed evenly within the date range. 3) inscriptions which can-
      not be dated more precisely within the reign or in the case of posthumous
      inscriptions any time after AD 54. These are evenly distributed throughout the
      reign as well. This "conservative" method tends to flatten the curve while dis-
      tributing them according to the distribution of the dateable inscriptions, will
      accentuate the differences. It is difficult to determine which is the more correct
      method to use. Since two thirds of the undated inscriptions are Greek, the date-
      able Greek inscriptions should perhaps accordingly weigh more. These have a
      distinct chronological distribution with more bases towards the end of the
      reign. The eighteen dateable Greek bases are, however, too limited a sample to
      be statistically significant.
22.   Stuart 1938, 40-41.
23.   Balty 1963, 97-134.
24.   *CIL* V, 6416. Rose 1990, 163-168. For a rejection of Rose's theory, see *CIL* VI, p.
      4301.
25.   *Tab. Siar.* I, 1-21. Gonzales 1984, 58-59. Tacitus (*Ann.* 2.83) mentions the arch and
      the content of the inscription but not the statue group.
26.   *CIL* V, 24; *CIL* III, 381.
27.   See below and Højte 1999, 228-229.
28.   For Tacitus's personal reflections on the prospects of Claudius becoming
      emperor, see Tac. *Ann.* 3.18.
29.   See Stuart (1938, 42) for statue bases for Britannicus; Stuart (1939, 601-617) for
      Tiberius, Caligula, and Nero, and Hanson & Johnson (1946, 389-400) for Gaius
      and Lucius Caesar. The numbers found in the cited works are naturally as out-
      dated as Stuart's figure for the statue bases of Claudius. Forty pre-accession
      bases for Tiberius are known to me, eight for Caligula and ten for Nero. The fig-
      ures derive from a catalogue under preparation of all the statue bases for the
      emperors between Augustus and Commodus.
30.   The posthumous bases are Ephesos: *SEG* XXXIX, 1178; Regium Lepidum: *AE*
      1996, 668; Savaria: *AE* 1944, 131; Volubilis: Euzennat & Marion 1982, 235-236,
      no. 370; Carthago: *CIL* VIII, 1015; Panormus: *CIL* X, 7281; Arelate: *CIL* XII, 641;
      Larissa: *IG* IX, 2, 605 & 606.

31. Vespasian: 12; Titus: 13; Nerva: 13; Trajan: 10.
32. Herculaneum: Napoli, Museo Nazionale inv. no. 5593 and *CIL* X, 1416. Aphrodisias: Smith 1987, 115-117 (plates XIV; XV, 3). Stuart (1938, 46-47) furthermore combined the semi-nude statue from Lanuvium with the base *CIL* XIV, 2097, but the attribution is unfounded.
33. Højte 1999, 228-229.
34. Stuart 1938, 27, 41.
35. Stuart 1939, 608.
36. Pekáry 1985, 23-25.
37. Tac. *Hist.* 3.7 and 3.13.
38. For a discussion of the evidence, see Swift 1923, 297-300; Pekáry 1985, 24-25. Pekáry draws attention to an inscription mentioning festivities on the day the portrait of the new emperor was brought to Oinoanda by a magistrate (Holleaux and Paris 1886, 226-229, no. 8 = *IGRR* III, 481). The complete lack of evidence for the first and second century AD, however, makes it unlikely that such centralized distribution took place, perhaps with the exception of portraits to be set up in military camps.
39. Stuart 1938, 52-53.
40. AD 41: Veii: *CIL* XI, 3790 (private); Thugga: *CIL* VIII, 26519 (private); Athens: *IG* II², 3268 (public); Athens: *IG* II², 3269 (unknown). AD 42: Rome: *CIL* VI, 40307 (corporation); Lanuvium: *CIL* XIV, 2097 (public); Sestium: *CIL* XI, 5998 (public); Veleia: *CIL* XI, 1169 (public); Augusta Taurinorum: *CIL* V, 7150 (unknown); Burdigala: *CIL* XIII, 590 (private); Hippo Regia: *AE* 1935, 32 (public); Henchir Zian: *CIL* VIII, 1102 (private); Athens: *IG* II², 3271 (public); Athens: *IG* II², 3272 (public); Korinthos: Kent 1966, 40, no. 74 (private); Delphi: *Syll.*³ 801 B (public); Olbasa: *CIL* III, 6889 (public); Sagalassos: *CIL* III, 6871 (unknown). AD 43: Rome: *CIL* VI, 915 (corporation); Moguntiacum: *CIL* XIII, 6797 (corporation); Mediomatrici: *CIL* XIII, 4565 (corporation); Epora: *CIL* II², 7, 142 (private); Serobriga: *CIL* II, 3106 (unknown); Ephesos: *IGSK* 17, 1, 3019 (corporation). AD 41-43: Lepcis Magna: *AE* 1987, 989 (private). In Stuart's collection a number of bases with either uncertain dates or unknown dedicators were included among the public dedications of AD 41/2.
41. Alföldy 1984, 56: "Die Verehrung des Herrschers mit Statuen war für die Gemeinde eine ständige Verpflichtung politischer und zugleich religiöser Natur, ohne daß sie hierfür jeweils einen konkreten Anlaß benötigt hätten. Die Hauptsache war offensichtlich, daß jede Gemeinde jedem Herscher – wohl je früher nach seinem Regierungsantritt, desto besser – mit einer Ehrenstatue huldigte."
42. The after life of imperial images was a precarious matter. The example of the unfortunate Granius Marcellus, *praetor* of Bithynia, is well known (Tac. *Ann.* 1.74), and the letter from Marcus Aurelius and Lucius Verus to Ulpius Eurykles regarding the old imperial portraits in precious metal stored in the *synedrion* of the *gerousia* in Ephesos (*IGSK* 11, 1, 25) illustrates the caution exercised by local magistrates.
43. *CIL* VIII, 26519.
44. Jucker 1981, 254-281. A.-K. Massner has kindly informed me that approximately one out of eight portraits in her catalogue are reworked from Caligula.
45. AD 96: *CIL* XIV, 4341; *CIL* III, 216. AD 97: *CIL* II, 956; *CIL* III, 3006; 8703; 12041; 12103; 12238; VI, 950; 951; XII, 104; *AE* 1940, 186; *AE* 1993, 471; *AE* 1993, 474; Kern 1900, 125-126, nos. 168-169. To these should be added a substantial part of the seventeen statue bases that cannot be dated more accurately within the reign.

46. AD 98: *CIL* III, 3942; 12682; *AE* 1949, 42; *SEG* XXXXI, 1109. AD 98-99: *CIL* III, 14147, 2; *IG* VII, 2236. AD 99: *CIL* IX, 728; XIII, 7285; Gsell 1922, 120, no. 1243. According to Bergmann (1997, 141) all the portraits of the two earliest portrait types of Trajan are reworked from Domitian.

47. Mattingly 1965, clii-clix; Kaenel 1986, 280. Reverse types associated with military exploits: *Constantiae Augusti, De Germanis, Ob cives servatos, Imper(ator) recept(us) - praetor(ianus) recept(us in fidem), Paci Augustae, De Britannis, Victoria Augustae.*

48. *CIL* VI, 40416: [q]uod reges Brit[annorum] XI d[iebus sine] I ulla iactur[a devicerit et regna eorum] I gentesque b[arbaras trans oceanum sitas] I primus in dici[onem populi Romani redegerit]. The reconstruction is not beyond dispute. *CIL* III, 7061: Vind(?) lib(?) de vi[ctori regum xi] britanniae. Reconstruction based on the previous inscription, which is far from certain. The identification of the monument in Kyzikos as an arch rests on the restoration of ar[...] in l. 5 as *arcum*. On the arch, together with Claudius, were statues of Divus Augustus and Tiberius. This inclusion can be interpreted as an attempt to make up for the actions which caused the citizens of Kyzikos to be deprived of their freedom first by Augustus in 20 BC and then again in AD 25 by Tiberius.

49. Rome: *CIL* VI, 915. Verona: *AE* 1992, 739 a-c. Verona: *AE* 1992, 740 a-c. Lepcis Magna: *AE* 1987, 989. Thibaris: *CIL* VIII, 26177 a. Thugga: *CIL* VIII, 26519. Perge: *IGSK* 54, 33 (this inscription is no longer associated with the arch at Perge, for which a newly excavated Domitianic inscription has been identified. It does, however, belong to a monument carrying a statue of Claudius, possibly an arch).

50. Stuart 1938, 53-54. The base in Vicus Marosallensis seems to have been voted before Claudius came to Britannia – if the titles of Claudius are correct – but not dedicated until 23 September, the birthday of Augustus, the following year.

51. Halfmann 1986, 172-173.

52. Imperial visits around the empire, for example, were more often commemorated by erecting an arch or a gate than by setting up a statue, see Højte 2000, 221-236 and Halfmann 1986, 129-133.

53. Prior to the reign of Claudius, I only know of *CIL* III, 2908 for Tiberius in Iader and *CIL* III, 14147, 1 for Caligula in Syene.

54. *CIL* V, 6969; *IGSK* 53, 15; *CIL* X, 1416.

55. The wedding was arranged late in AD 48 (Tac. *Ann.* 12.1-9) but did not take place until AD 49.

56. Aezanoi: *IGRR* IV, 559. Britannicus received that name in AD 43.

57. *IGRR* I, 835.

58. For a discussion of the groups, see Rose 1987, 76.

59. Stuart 1938, 41 and n. 208.

60. Suet. *Claud.* 12.

61. Strack 1931, 29.

62. Fittschen & Zanker 1985, 17.

63. Mattingly 1966, lxxvi.

64. *AE* 1989, 138. The inscription almost certainly mentions a statue of silver weighing 300 pounds.

65. Rachet 1980, 200-242; La Roux 1999, 55-65.

66. *CIL* VI, 920.

67. Vespasian: *CIL* VIII, 20857; Antoninus Pius: *CIL* VIII, 23599; Marcus Aurelius: *CIL* VIII, 17864.

68. *CIL* XI, 1169; *CIL* XI, 5999; *AE* 1924, 66; *AE* 1979, 174; *AE* 1992, 740 a-c; *AE* 1996, 668; Kent 1966, 40-41, no. 71.
69. *IG* II², 3268; *IG* II², 3271; *AE* 1888, 39.
70. *IGSK* 36, 1, 37. Ὁ δῆμος καθιέρωσεν ἀναθέντος ἐκ τῶν ἰδίων Τιβερίου Κλαυδίου Ἀρτεμιδώρου υἱοῦ Κυρείνα Διογένους ἐν τῶι τῆς γυμνασιαρχίας χρόνωι.
71. *AE* 1924, 66 = Euzennat and Marion 1982, 233-235, no. 369 & 235-236, no. 370.
72. For examples at Athens and Kalymna, see Stuart 1938, 60, n. 337 and 61-63. Inscriptions employing epithets unknown to Stuart have been found at Hydai, Laertes, Patara, Skepsis, Sidyma and Tymnos (see catalogue).
73. *IGRR* IV, 1711; Stuart 1938, 48-49.
74. *IGRR* IV, 1099.
75. Tac. *Ann.* 12.61.
76. During the first two centuries of Roman rule, fifteen imperial statue bases are known. Four belong to statues of Claudius: *IGRR* IV, 1099; *IGRR* IV, 1103; Segre 1993, 237, no. EV 243; Segre 1993, 248, no. EV 248.
77. *IG* VII, 2878; *SEG* XXXXIV, 1205.
78. Dio Cass. 60.24.1; Suet. *Claud.* 25.
79. Suet. *Claud.* 25.
80. *CIL* X, 1416; *CIL* XII, 641; *IGSK* 12, 259 b; *IGSK* 53, 15.
81. Tiberii Claudii as dedicators: *IGRR* IV, 559; *IG* IV², 1, 601-602; *SEG* XXXI, 918; *IGSK* 2, 512; *IGSK* 12, 259b; *IGSK* 36, 1, 37; *IGRR* III, 579; *CIL* XIII, 3200. Eight of the nine inscriptions are in Greek, and these comprise almost half of the private dedications in the Greek east.
82. Erim 1982, 277-281; Smith 1987, 88-138.
83. *SEG* XXXI, 918 = Reynolds 1981, 323, no. 8.
84. Reynolds 1981, 317, no. 1.
85. Højte 1999, 229. Vespasian, Titus, and Domitian 1.8:1. Nerva, Trajan, and Antoninus Pius 2.6:1. Hadrian 2.4:1. Lucius Verus and Marcus Aurelius 1.4:1. Note that the ratios are dependant on the date of the last catalogue of the portraits. Up-dated lists of the portraits in existence result in lower ratios.
86. Boschung 1989, 80-83. Smith (1981, 209-211) remarks on the curiosity of this ratio.
87. Boschung (1993) lists 211 portraits of Augustus in the round including miniature heads. He has also collected part of the epigraphic material (1993, 98-103). There is probably a total of approximately 200 statue bases.
88. Massner (forthcoming).
89. Using the number of statue bases and portraits listed in Stuart's catalogues the ratio would be 2.7:1.
90. Based on a catalogue of all imperial statue bases from Augustus to Commodus in preparation by the author. The peak in the 130s is for the most part caused by the extraordinary number of statue bases for Hadrian found in Athens, particularly in the vicinity of the Olympieion, where multitudes of statues were dedicated at the inauguration of the temple in AD 131-132. In the 160s Marcus Aurelius and Lucius Verus reigned simultaneously, which seems to have doubled the number of dedications. *Damnatio memoriae* has affected the values for the 30s (Caligula), the 50s and 60s (Nero), the 80s and 90s (Domitian), and the 180s (Commodus).
91. MacMullen 1982, 233-246; pl. 1 and pl. 5.

Revisions to Stuart's catalogue of statue bases of Claudius

Inscriptions from statue bases in Stuart's catalogue:

Roma: *CIL* VI, 915; *CIL* VI, 31283; *CIL* VI, 40412=*CIL* VI, 31205; *CIL* VI, 40416=*CIL* VI, 920. **Regio I**: Herculaneum: *CIL* X, 1416. Lanuvium: *CIL* XIV, 2097. **Regio IV**: Napoli: *IG* XIV, 728. Trebula Mutuesca: *CIL* IX, 6361. **Regio V**: Urbs Salvia: *CIL* IX, 5532. **Regio VI**: Forum Sempronii: *CIL* XI, 6114. Sestinum: *CIL* XI, 5999. **Regio VII**: Luna: *CIL* XI, 6954. Unknown: *CIL* XI, 7793. Veii: *CIL* XI, 3790-3792. **Regio VIII**: Veleia: *CIL* XI, 1169. **Regio X**: Acelum: *CIL* V, 2088. Brixia: *CIL* V, 4309. Pola: *CIL* V, 24-25. Verona: *CIL* V, 3326. **Regio XI**: Augusta Taurinorum: *CIL* V, 6969. Mediolanum: *CIL* V, 5804. Ticinum: *CIL* VI, p. 4301. **Sicilia**: Panormus: *CIL* X, 7281. **Germania Superior**: Mogontiacum: *CIL* XIII, 6797. **Belgica**: Vicus Marosallensis: *CIL* XIII, 4565. **Lugdunensis**: Eburovices: *CIL* XIII, 3200. **Aquitania**: Ager Vellavorum: *CIL* XIII, 1610. Burdigala: *CIL* XIII, 590. Mediolanum Santonum: *CIL* XIII, 1037-1038. **Narbonensis**: Arelate: *CIL* XII, 641. **Baetica**: Cartima: *CIL* II, 1953. Epora: *CIL* II², 7, 142=*CIL* II, 2198. Ipagrum: *CIL* II², 5, 593=*CIL* II, 1518; *CIL* II², 5, 583=*CIL* II, 1519. Castro del Riò: *CIL* II², 5, 394=*CIL* II, 1569. Regina: *CIL* II², 5, 5978=*CIL* II, 1027. **Mauretania Tingitana**: Volubilis: *AE* 1924, 66. **Africa Proconsularis**: Ghardimaou: *CIL* VIII, 14727. Hippo Regius: *AE* 1935, 32. Thugga: *CIL* VIII, 26517 & 26519. Henchir Zian: *CIL* VIII, 11002. **Pannonia Superior**: Unknown: *CIL* III, 4591. **Dalmatia**: Salona: *CIL* III, 1977. **Thracia**: Mesembria: *AE* 1928, 150. **Macedonia**: Lamia: *IG* IX, 2, 81. Larissa: *IG* IX, 2, 605-606. **Achaea**: Athens: *IG* II², 3268-3274. Delphi, *Syll.*³ 801 A-C. Epidauros: *IG* IV², 1, 601-602. Koroneia: *IG* VII, 2878. Megara: *IG* VII, 67. Minoa: *IG* XII, 7, 265. Rhamnous: *IG* II², 3275. Thebae: *IG* VII, 2493. Thera: *IG* XII, 3, 473 & 1395. **Asia**: Aezanoi: *IGRR* IV, 558-559. Alexandria Troas: *CIL* III, 381 & *CIL* III 6060. Antimachia: *IGRR* IV, 1103. Aphrodisias: *CIG* 2739. Kyzikos: *CIL* III, 7061. Ephesos: *IGSK* 17, 1, 3019=*AE* 1924, 69. Eresos: *IG* XII, 2, 541. Golis: *IGRR* IV, 551. Halasarna *IGRR* IV, 1099. Kalymnos: *IGRR* IV, 1023. Klazomenai *IGSK* 2, 512=*IGRR* IV, 1550. Kys: *BCH* 11 (1887) 306-308, no. 11. Magnesia Hermi: *TAM* V, 2, 1359=*BCH* 1 (1877) 83, no. 12. Pergamon *IGRR* IV, 321. Samos: *AE* 1912, 215. Sardis: *IGRR* IV, 1502. Tralles: *IGSK* 36, 1, 37=*CIG* 2922. **Lycia et Pamphylia**: Arneia: *TAM* II, 760=*IGRR* III, 328. Perge *IGSK* 54, 33=*IGRR* III, 788. Sagalassos *CIL* III, 6871. Sidyma: *TAM* II, 1, 184=*IGRR* III, 579. Galatia: Jali-jük: *CIL* III, 288. Olbasa: *CIL* III, 6889.

Inscriptions from statue bases in Stuart's catalogue which do not belong to portrait statues of Claudius:

Regio VII: Caere: *CIL* XI, 3593 (statue of the emperor's genius). **Lusitania**: Emerita Augusta: *CIL* II, 476 (statue of Tiberius). **Pontus et Bithynia**: Amastris: *CIL* III, 6983 (not a dedication of a statue). **Asia**: Lindos: *IG* XII, 1, 805 (statue of Nero). Mylasa: *IGSK* 34, 33=*CIG* 2697 (personification of Claudius pietas). **Aegyptus**: Tentyra: *IGRR* I, 1165 (inscription under a relief depicting Claudius in Egyptian style).

Inscriptions listed by Stuart as doubtful, which I think ought to be included:

Regio I: Ostia: *NSc* (1909) 128, no. 2 (AD 41-54). **Regio XI**: Augusta Taurinorum: *CIL* V, 7150 (AD 42). **Narbonensis**: Nemausus: *CIL* XII, 3160 (AD 41-54). **Alpes Maritimae**: Vintium: *CIL* XII, 5 (AD 41-54). **Tarraconensis**: Segobriga: *CIL* II, 3105 (AD 43). **Africa Proconsularis**: Carthago: *CIL* VIII, 1015 (AD 54-?). **Dalmatia**: Iader: *CIL* III, 2942 (AD 41-54). **Macedonia**: Thessalonika: *AE* 1888, 39 (AD 44). **Asia**: Apollonia: *MAMA* IV, 56, no. 144 (AD 41-54).

Inscriptions included in Stuart, How Were Imperial Portraits Distributed Throughout the Empire?:

Achaea: Athens: *IG* II², 3276 (AD 41-54).

Inscriptions published before 1938 not mentioned by Stuart:

Regio VIII: Caere: *CIL* XI, 3599 (AD 41-54). **Sardinia**: Sulcis: *CIL* X, 7515 (AD 48). **Germania Superior**: Noviodunum: *CIL* XIII, 11468 (AD 41-54). **Narbonensis**: Arelate: *CIL* XII, 666 (AD 41-54). **Africa Proconsularis**: Thibari: *CIL* VIII, 26177a (AD 41-54). **Dalmatia**: Novae: *CIL* III, 13880 (AD 51-52). **Asia**: Ephesos: *IGSK* 12, 259b (AD 41-54). Eresos: *IG* XII, 2, 542 (AD 41-54). Tralles: *IGSK* 36, 1, 38 (AD 41-54). Tymnos: *IGSK* 38, 206 (AD 41-54). **Lycia et Pamphylia**: Attaleia: Lanckoronski 1890, 153, no. 1 (AD 41-54).

Inscriptions published after 1938:

Roma: *CIL* VI, 40307 (AD 42); *CIL* VI, 40414-40415 (AD 45). **Regio I**: Herculaneum: *AE* 1979, 174 (AD 46). Minturnae: *AE* 1989, 138 (AD 50). Puteoli *AE* 1995, 309 (AD 45). **Regio V**: Montegiorgio: *AE* 1985, 341 (AD 41-54). **Regio VIII**: Regium Lepidum: *AE* 1996, 668 (AD 54-?). Regium Lepidum: *AE* 1996, 669 (AD 41-54). **Regio X**: Verona: *AE* 1992, 739 a-c (AD 44). **Lugdunensis**: Augustomagus: *AE* 1960, 149 (AD 48). **Lusitania**: Ammaia: *AE* 1969/70, 238 (AD 44). Emerita Augusta: Vives 1971, no. 1063 (AD 41-54). **Baetica**: Iliturgi: *CIL* II², 7, 30 (AD 44). **Mauretania Tingitana**: Volubilis: Euzennat & Marion 1982, 235-236, no. 370 (AD 54-?). **Africa Proconsularis**: Lepcis Magna: *AE* 1987, 989 (AD 41-43). Lepcis Magna: *AE* 1948, 15 (AD 45). **Pannonia Superior**: Savaria: *AE* 1944, 131 (AD 54-?). **Macedonia**: Beroia: *SEG* XXVII, 263 (AD 41-54). Dyrrachion: *AE* 1966, 390 (AD 44). **Achaea**: Korinthos: Kent 1966, 40, no. 74 (AD 42). Korinthos: Kent 1966, 40-1, no. 77 (AD 47-54). Epidauros: *AE* 1980, 855 (AD 49-54). Lykosoura: *IG* V, 2, 532 (AD 41-54). Thebae: *AE* 1974, 599 (AD 41-54). **Pontus et Bithynia**: Herakleia: *IGSK* 47, 40 (AD 41-54). **Asia**: Aphrodisias: *SEG* XXXI, 918 (AD 50-54). Ephesos: *IGSK* 12, 259a (AD 48). Ephesos: *SEG* XXXIX, 1178 (AD 54-68). Hydai: *IGSK* 38, 256 (AD 41-54). Kos: Segre 1993, 237, no. EV 243 (AD 51). Kos: Segre 1993, 248, no. EV 248 (AD 49-54). Skepsis: *AE* 1973, 508 (AD 41-54). **Lycia et Pamphylia**: Patara: *SEG* XXXXIV, 1205 (AD 45). Seleukia Sidera: *AE* 1999, 1642 (41-54 AD). Side: *IGSK* 43, 31 (AD 41-54). Sidyma: *SEG* XXXVII, 1221 (AD 41-54). **Galatia**: Olbasa: *AE* 1998, 1393 (50 AD). Cilicia: Laertes: *SEG* XX, 69 (AD 41-54). **Aegyptus**: Thebae: *AE* 1982, 913 (AD 41-54).

Bibliography

Alföldy, G. 1984. *Römische Statuen in Venetia et Histria. Epigraphische Quellen.* Heidelberg.

Balty, J.-Ch. 1963. Note d'iconographie julio-claudienne, *MonPiot* 53, 97-134.

Bergmann, M. 1997. Zu den Porträts des Trajan und Hadrian, in: Caballos & León (eds.) 1997, 139-148.

Bernoulli, J.J. 1886. *Römische Ikonographie*, Zweiter Teil, I. *Das julisch-claudische Kaiserhaus.* Berlin.

Boon, G.C. 1980. Bronze-mounted Statue-bases at Carmarthen and Silchester, *AntJ* 60, 98-101.

Boschung, D. 1989. *Die Bildnisse des Caligula. Das römische Herrscherbild* I 4. Berlin.

Boschung, D. 1993. *Die Bildnisse des Augustus. Das römische Herrscherbild* I 2. Berlin.

Caballos, A. & P. León (eds.) 1997. *Italica MMCC*. Sevilla.

Carandini, A. 1969. *Vibia Sabina. Funzione politica, iconografia e il problema del classicismo adrianeo*. Firenze.

Driehaus, J. 1969. Bronzeverkleidungen römischer Statuenbasen aus Weißenthurm Landkreis Koblenz, *BJb* 169, 424-436.

Erim, K.T. 1982. A New Relief Showing Claudius and Britannia from Aphrodisias, *Britannia* 13, 277-281.

Euzennat, M. & J. Marion. 1982. *Inscriptiones antiques du Maroc* 2. *Inscriptiones latines*. Paris.

Evers, C. 1994. *Les portraits d'Hadrien. Typologie et ateliers*. Bruxelles.

Fejfer, J. 1985. The Portraits of the Severan Empress Julia Domna. A New Approach, *AnalRom* 14, 129-138.

Fittschen, K. 1973. *Katalog der antiken Skulpturen in Schloss Erbach*. Berlin.

Fittschen, K. & P. Zanker 1985. *Katalog der römischen Porträts in der Kapitolinischen Museen und den anderen kommunalen Sammlungen der Stadt Rom*. Band 1. Mainz am Rhein.

France-Lanord, A. 1960. La statue de bronze reconstituée, dite de Pacatianus, au Musée de Vienne, *MonPiot* 51, 93-104.

Gonzáles, J. 1984. Tabula Siarensis, Fortunales Siarenses et Municipia Civium Romanorum, *ZPE* 55, 55-100.

Gsell, S. 1922. *Inscriptions latines de l'Algérie* I. Paris.

Halfmann, H. 1986. *Itinera Principum. Geschichte und Typologie der Kaiserreisen im Römischen Reich*. Stuttgart.

Hanson, C. & F.P. Johnson 1946. On Certain Portrait Inscriptions, *AJA* 50, 389-400.

Holleaux, H. & P. Paris 1886. Inscription d'Oenoanda, *BCH* 10, 216-235.

Højte, J.M. 1999. The Epigraphic Evidence Concerning Portrait Statues of Hadrian's Heir L. Aelius Caesar, *ZPE* 127, 217-238.

Højte, J.M. 2000. Imperial Visits as Occasion for the Erection of Portrait Statues?, *ZPE* 133, 221-236.

Jucker, H. 1981. Iulisch-claudische Kaiser- und Prinzenporträts als "Palimpseste", *JdI* 96, 236-316.

Kaenel, H.-M. von. 1986. *Münzprägung und Münzbild des Claudius*. Berlin.

Kent, J.H. 1966. *Corinth* VIII, 3. *The Inscriptions 1926-1950*. Princeton.

Kern, O. 1900. *Inschriften vom Magnesia am Mäander*. Berlin.

Lanckoronski, K. 1890. *Städte Pamphyliens und Pisidiens*. Wien.

Le Roux, P. 1999. Sur les puissances tribuniciennes de Trajan, in: Schallmayer (ed.) 1999, 55-65.

MacMullen, R. 1982. The Epigraphic Habit in the Roman Empire, *AJPh* 103, 233-246.

Massner, A.-K. 1982. *Bildnisangleichung. Untersuchungen zur Entstehungs- und Wirkungsgeschichte der Augustusporträts (43 v.Chr.-68 n.Chr.). Das römische Herrscherbild* IV 1. Berlin.

Massner, A.-K. 1994. Zum Stilwandel in Kaiserporträt claudischer Zeit, in: Strocka (ed.) 1994, 159-173.

Massner, A.-K. (forthcoming). *Die Bildnisse des Claudius. Das römische Herrscherbild* I 5. Berlin.

Mattingly, H. 1929. *A Catalogue of the Roman Coins in the British Museum* I. *Augustus to Vitellius*. Reprint with alterations 1965. London.

Mattingly, H. 1936. *A Catalogue of the Roman Coins in the British Museum* III. *Nerva to Hadrian*. Reprint with alterations 1966. London.

Menichetti, M. 1983-84. Il ritratto di Claudio, *AnnPerugia* 21, 182-226.

Neudecker, R. 1988. *Die Skulpturenausstattung römischer Villen in Italien*. Mainz am Rhein.

Pekáry, T. 1985. *Das römische Kaiserbildnis in Staat, Kult und Gesellschaft. Das römische Herrscherbild* III 5. Berlin.

Piganiol, A. 1959. Une inscription romaine inédite de Senlis sur un socle de bronze, *CRAI* 1959, 450-457.

Pouilloux, J., P. Roesch & J. Marcillet-Jaubert 1987. *Salamine de Chypre* XIII. Paris.

Rachet, M. 1980. Decennalia et vicennalia sous la dynastie des Antonins, *REA* 82, 200-242.

Reynolds, J. 1981. New Evidence for the Imperial Cult at Aphrodisias, *ZPE* 43, 317-327.

Rose, C.B. 1997. *Dynastic Commemoration and Imperial Portraiture in the Julio-Claudian Period*. Cambridge.

Rose, C.B. 1990. The Supposed Augustan Arch at Pavia (Ticinum) and the Einsiedln 326 Manuscript, *JRA* 3, 163-168.

Schallmayer, E. (ed.) 1999. *Traian in Germanien. Traian im Reich*. Bad Homburg.

Segre, M. 1993. *Iscrizioni di Cos*. Rome.

Smith, R.R.R. 1981. Review of Die Bildnisse des Caligula. Das römische Herrscherbild I 4, by D. Boschung, *JRS* 75, 209-211.

Smith, R.R.R. 1987. The Imperial Reliefs from the Sebasteion at Aphrodisias, *JRS* 77, 88-138.

Stichel, R.H.W. 1982. *Die römische Kaiserstatue am Ausgang der Antike. Untersuchungen zum plastischen Kaiserporträts seit Valentinian I. (365-374 n.Chr.)*. Rome.

Strack, P.L. 1931. *Untersuchungen zur römischen Reichsprägung des 2. Jahrhunderts I. Reichsprägung zur Zeit des Traian*. Stuttgart.

Strocka, V.M. (ed.) 1994. *Die Regierungszeit des Kaisers Claudius (41-54 n.Chr.) Umbruch oder Episode?* Mainz am Rhein.

Stuart, M. 1938. *The Portraiture of Claudius. Preliminary Studies*. Ph.D. diss., Columbia University.

388   *Jakob Munk Højte*

Stuart, M. 1939. How Were Imperial Portraits Distributed throughout the
     Empire?, *AJA* 43, 601-617.
Swift, E.H. 1923. Imagines in Imperial Portraiture, *AJA* 27, 286-301.
Vives, J. 1971. *Inscriptiones latinas de la España Romana*. Barcelona.
Wuilleumier, P. 1984. *Inscriptions latines des Trois Gaules*. Paris.

Abbreviations

CIG	A. Boeckh, *Corpus Inscriptionum Graecarum*. Berlin 1828-1877.
IGRR	R. Cagnat, *Inscriptiones Graecae ad Res romanas pertinentes*. Paris 1906-1927.
IGSK	*Inschriften griechischer Städte aus Kleinasien*. Bonn 1972-.
MAMA	*Monumenta Asiae Minoris Antiqua*. Manchester 1928-.
Syll.[3]	W. Dittenberger, *Sylloge Inscriptionum Graecarum* I-IV. Leipzig 1915-1924. 3rd ed.
TAM	*Tituli Asiae Minoris*. Wien 1901-1989.

Index Locorum*

*Please note that the statue bases of Claudius included in the catalogue on the pages 384-385 are not listed in the index.

Contributors

Alexandru Avram
Université du Maine
Faculté des Lettres
Avenue Olivier Messiaen
F-72085 Le Mans Cedex 9
France
E-mail: Alexandru.Avram@univ-
lemans.fr

Pia Guldager Bilde
Danish National Research Foun-
dation's Centre for Black Sea Studies
University of Aarhus
Ndr. Ringgade 1
DK-8000 Århus C
Denmark
E-mail: klapg@hum.au.dk

David Braund
University of Exeter
Queen's Building
The Queen's Drive
Exeter UK EX 4 4QH
United Kingdom
E-mail: D.C.Braund@exeter.ac.uk

Jaroslav V. Domanskij
Dept. of Archaeology of Eastern
Europe and Sibiria
The State Hermitage Museum
Dvortzovaya nab., 34
190000 St Petersburg
Russia
E-mail: oaves@hermitage.ru

Pierre Dupont
Laboratoire de Céramologie
Université de Lyon II
7, Rue Raulin

F-69007 Lyon
France
E-mail: pierre.dupont@mom.fr

Nadežda A. Gavriljuk
Institute of Archaeology, Ukranian
National Academy of Sciences
Geroev Stalingrada av. 12
04211 Kiev
Ukraine
E-mail: gavr@iananu.kiev.ua

George Hinge
Danish National Research Foun-
dation's Centre for Black Sea Studies
University of Aarhus
Ndr. Ringgade 1
DK-8000 Århus C
Denmark
E-mail: klagh@hum.au.dk

Jakob Munk Højte
Danish National Research Foun-
dation's Centre for Black Sea Studies
University of Aarhus
Ndr. Ringgade 1
DK-8000 Århus C
Denmark
E-mail: klajh@hum.au.dk

Vladimir I. Kac
Dept. of the Ancient World History
The Faculty of History, Auditorium 41
Saratov State University
4 Uchebny corpus
ul. Universitetskaya 59
410027 Saratov
Russia

Valentina V. Krapivina
Institute of Archaeology, Ukranian
National Academy of Sciences
Geroev Stalingrada av. 12
04211 Kiev
Ukraine
E-mail: krapivin@svitonline.com

Evelina A. Kravčenko
Institute of Archaeology, Ukranian
National Academy of Sciences
Geroev Stalingrada av. 12
04211 Kiev
Ukraine
E-mail: evelina_75@hotmail.com

Sergej D. Kryžickij
Institute of Archaeology, Ukranian
National Academy of Sciences
Geroev Stalingrada av. 12
04211 Kiev
Ukraine
E-mail: sdk@svitonline.com

Konstantin K. Marčenko
Dept. of Classical Archaeology
Institute of the History of Material
Culture RAS
Dvortzovaya nab., 18
191186 St Petersburg
Russia

Evgenij A. Molev
University of Nizhny Novgorod
Highway of Kazan, h. 3, f. 300
Nizhny Novgorod 603163
Russia
E-mail: ist@unn.ru

Sergej Ju. Monachov
Dept. of the Ancient World History
The Faculty of History, Auditorium 41
Saratov State University
4 Uchebny corpus

ul. Universitetskaya 59
410027 Saratov
Russia
E-mail: berdnov@info.sgu.ru

Galina M. Nikolaenko
The National Preserve of
Tauric Chersonesos
Drevnyaya Street, 1
Sevastopol 99045
Ukraine
E-mail: gnik@chers.stel.sebastopol.ua

Anna S. Rusjaeva
Institute of Archaeology, Ukranian
National Academy of Sciences
Geroev Stalingrada av. 12
04211 Kiev
Ukraine

Sergej Ju. Saprykin
"Vestnik Drevney Istorii"
Institute of the Universal History RAS
Leninsky prospekt, 32A
117997 Moscow
Russia
E-mail: vdi@igh.ras.ru

Vladimir F. Stolba
Danish National Research Foun-
dation's Centre for Black Sea Studies
University of Aarhus
Ndr. Ringgade 1
DK-8000 Århus C
Denmark
E-mail: klavs@hum.au.dk

Irina I. Tunkina
St Petersburg Branch of the Archives
of the Russian Academy of Sciences
Universitetskaya naberezhnaya, 1a
199034 St Petersburg
Russia
E-mail: tunkina@bk.ru

Marina Ju. Vachtina
Dept. of Classical Archaeology
Institute of the History of Material
Culture RAS
Dvortzovaya nab., 18
191186 St Petersburg
Russia
E-mail: Marina@MV7818.spb.edu

Jurij A. Vinogradov
Dept. of Classical Archaeology
Institute of the History of Material
Culture RAS
Dvortzovaya nab., 18
191186 St Petersburg
Russia
E-mail: vincat@rednet.ru

Vitalij M. Zubar′
Institute of Archaeology, Ukranian
National Academy of Sciences
Geroev Stalingrada av. 12
04211 Kiev
Ukraine
E-mail: zubar@i.com.ua